Stage Lighting

FUNDAMENTALS AND APPLICATIONS

RICHARD DUNHAM

University of Georgia

Routledge
Taylor & Francis Group

LONDON AND NEW YORK

First published 2011 by Pearson Education, Inc.

Published 2016 by Routledge
2 Park Square, Milton Park, Abingdon, Oxon OX14 4RN
711 Third Avenue, New York, NY 10017, USA

Routledge is an imprint of the Taylor & Francis Group, an informa business

ISBN : 9780205461004 (pbk)

Cover Designer: Ilze Lemesis/T—9

Library of Congress Cataloging-in-Publication Data

Dunham, Richard.
    Stage lighting : fundamentals and applications / Richard Dunham.
        p. cm.
    Includes bibliographical references and index.
    ISBN 978-0-205-46100-4 (alk. paper)
1. Stage lighting.   I. Title.
    PN2091.E4D87 2010
    792.02'5—dc22

                                                                    2010008074

Contents

11 Basics of General Illumination 189

12 Plotting the Design 212

13 Moving into the Venue 240

PART FIVE   **LIGHT: ONLINE
APPLICATION CHAPTERS**

19 The Music Scene (Revues, Clubs, and Concert Lighting)

20 The Spectacle Performance

21 Trade Shows, Industrials, and Corporate Events

22 Film and Video Basics

Preface

ighting design forms one of the most influential design specializations existing in today's society. Light gives us the primary means by which we sense our environment. It also plays a fundamental role in our perception of the world and has a profound effect on how we observe it. Light can hide or reveal an object and its features, modify the perceived shape of an object, suggest motion, distort or enhance an object's colors or texture, and can be used to create or alter moods. These are only a few of the many ways that light can manipulate our perception of the world.

This book has been written for the beginning to intermediate level student. While a certain amount of technology must be understood before moving on to concepts involving design, the majority of this book is focused on the design process and a variety of lighting applications. Although the book will be used primarily in theatrical lighting classes, it will also be useful to those in the electrical engineering and architectural or interior design fields. It speaks to a broader audience—one that addresses the fundamentals of lighting regardless of lighting discipline and encourages crossover between the many lighting specialties.

I believe that the future of lighting design lies in a designer's ability to understand and deliver designs in light—period. Whether designing an opera or a building, the basic principles of lighting hold true despite the differences in equipment and specific design applications that exist between the disciplines. Many theatrical designers already move naturally among any number of genres of entertainment, and while most were trained predominantly in theatrical design, there is immense potential for designing in non-traditional areas of entertainment and architectural lighting. Likewise, designers with an electrical engineering background are also bringing more theatrical elements into their designs as well. All one needs to succeed can be found in a positive attitude in making the shift, becoming familiar with the equipment and practices of the specialty, looking for opportunities to observe and learn a new discipline, and being able to modify techniques to suit the new avenue of design. Regardless of individual preferences, more and more lighting designers are finding themselves crossing back and forth among a variety of lighting areas in order to maintain a successful career.

The premise of this book lies in providing a link between many of these lighting disciplines. While there is a solid introduction to theatrical lighting design, it is my hope that you can use this book as a reference that focuses on lighting design and the design methodology that connects these many related fields rather than simply focusing on the equipment and technological emphasis that are characteristic of many lighting books. The topic of crossover to this degree has not really been attempted in a lighting text before. A fairly detailed discussion of the design process spans several chapters and also forms a critical element of this book. While the book outlines a fairly specific process, it should not be thought of as the only process. It is simply a place for the beginner to receive fairly detailed instructions that can then be tweaked as a designer's skills and process evolve. In keeping with the more universal applications of lighting, a variety of specific lighting disciplines are introduced by the text. Chapters 16 and 17 provide a brief introduction to these disciplines, while the online chapters go into considerable detail and further exploration of these specializations. The online chapters focus on essential design issues and equipment differences that are unique to working in a number of different areas of lighting design. Questions relating to special considerations, luminaires, control and equipment needs, and design concerns that are characteristic of a particular lighting specialty are also raised in these chapters. Having said this, the online chapters only provide an introduction to an area, and further information on each specialty can be obtained through the references that are listed at the end of each chapter. In many cases, entire books are dedicated to these disciplines. While technology cannot be avoided, it's been my goal to present the technical material as it becomes relevant and best pertains to the design needs of a "total" lighting designer. Because equipment is constantly in a state of evolution, we have chosen to dedicate many of our figures to illustrations that present design concepts rather than the traditional photographs of lighting equipment and production shots. Instead, in order to remain current, we are providing an appendix with a listing of lighting equipment manufacturers along with a link to their Web sites where up to date product information is always available.

Finally, the most important element of this book is to simply demonstrate the profound effect that light and a lighting designer can have on our lives. My hope is that I can not only provide the spark of inspiration that will allow a reader to have a deeper appreciation of the art and tools of lighting but also equip them with enough information to use these tools to develop effective art while painting with light.

ACKNOWLEDGMENTS

As with anything of this magnitude, there are many people who have provided help in producing this project. You don't have to work very long in this business to discover that many professionals in our line of work are truly giving and are willing to share their knowledge and experiences freely. This extends from the designers who have worked on common projects with me, to fellow educators, to the Tony Award nominees and winners who form the mainstay of Broadway lighting design. Our equipment manufactures and professional organizations are also truly interested in sharing their expertise and knowledge with us as well. It is impossible to mention every one of them here, but there are a number of individuals that deserve a special mention and thank you. First, my editors and the rest of the staff at Allyn and Bacon who put up with the many cuts and revisions since we first embarked on this journey nearly 5 years ago: Molly Tailor, my initial editor, who first convinced me to write the book; Jeanne Zalesky (senior editor), Megan Lentz (associate editor), Anne Ricigliano (project manager), and Carrie Fox (project editor) whose patience had to be tried as I was off doing shows, USITT business, recruiting, or anything else that could possibly keep me from sitting behind a computer and completing this project. I am most appreciative of their helpful suggestions as we have gone through the process of producing this book. I also want to thank all of the designers and manufacturers who shared materials with me or who were kind enough to be interviewed and let me feature them in the sidebars. These are among some of the busiest people in the business and I appreciate their willingness to share their knowledge with the next generation of lighting designers. Also the many students that I have had the pleasure of teaching and, in some cases, even learning from, over the 20 plus years that I have been involved in lighting education. Nobody is an expert in all areas, and the breadth of this book makes this an even more relevant issue. To that point I enlisted several colleagues and friends who graciously read and offered comments and corrections on several of the chapters representing various specialty areas of the lighting industry. Many, but not all, of these individuals are featured in the sidebars, but to make sure that none are missed I want to publicly acknowledge and thank the following individuals for their support and comments: Marilyn Lowey, Jim Moody and Jeff Ravitz (Concert and Spectacle Lighting), Bill Klages, Jim Moody, and Jeff Ravitz (Film and Television Lighting), Bob Shook and Bill Warfel (Display, Landscape, and Architectural Lighting), Tom Ruzika (Themed Design), and finally Mike Hussey and John Kundert-Gibbs (Virtual Lighting). These folks are all at the top of their respective areas of specialty. I also want to thank those colleagues who reviewed portions of the manuscript as we went through the writing process. I'm appreciative of the comments and suggestions that came from these individuals, who include: Darrell Anderson, University of Dayton; Robert Bowen, University of North Carolina, Asheville; Don Childs, Sam Houston State University; Clayton Kenneth Cole, University of Notre Dame; Joseph Flauto, University of Evansville; D. Andrew Gibbs, University of Arkansas; William Kenyon, Penn State; David R. Krajec, Cardinal Stritch University; Jonet Leighton, Antelope Valley College; Tom Marhenke, University of Central Arkansas; Michael McNamara, University of Arizona; Kathy A. Perkins, University of Illinois, Krannert Center; Douglas B. Rankin, Monmouth College; Howard L. Reynolds, Marshall University; Vickie J. Scott, University of California, Santa Barbara; Boyd H. Wolz, University of Louisiana, Monroe; and Kenton Yeager, University of Tennessee. It's difficult to be a sole writer on a project as large as this, and the book is much improved through all of the comments and input that I received from all of these individuals. Finally, a special thanks to my family (Joelle, Chelsea, and Richy) and our many friends and extended family who dealt with the fact that I always had "the book" somewhere in my list of priorities over the last several years. Their patience and support have been remarkable.

Rich Dunham

ABOUT THE AUTHOR

Richard E. Dunham, LC, IESNA (Associate Professor and Head of Design at The University of Georgia) has been involved in lighting design for over thirty years. He has numerous design credits in both academic and professional lighting and scenic design. Several lighting credits include designing for: Brunswick Music Theatre (Maine State Music Theatre), Music Theatre North, The Springer Opera House, Atlanta Lyric Theatre, and many New York metropolitan and Off/Off-Off Broadway productions with companies like Broadhollow Theatres, The Circle Repertory Lab, and Jean Cocteau Repertory Theatres. He has served on the Board of Directors of USITT and has been active in the leadership of the lighting commission of USITT for many years—most notably as Lighting Co-Commissioner from 1998–2006. He is a frequent presenter and has authored articles for Theatre Design and Technology, edited the second edition of Practical Projects for Teaching Lighting Design: A Compendium and has won two Herbert D. Greggs Honor Awards for his articles. He also coordinated the latest revision of the RP-2 Recommended Practice for Lighting Design Graphics (2006). He is also involved in architectural lighting and holds the LC certification granted by the NCQLP (National Council for Qualifications for the Lighting Profession) and is a member of IESNA (Illuminating Engineering Society of North America)and an Associate Member of IALD (International Association of Lighting Designers).

1 The Nature of Light

Before you can learn to design with light it is important to gain a basic understanding of the nature of light. Unlike other areas of design; light isn't tangible. It appears to be mysterious, can cause unpredictable results, has an impact on everything it touches, and is controlled in ways that require at least some understanding of optics and electricity—topics that easily intimidate many people. Light itself is our medium, and we can usually only convey our design ideas through indirect methods such as with pencils, paints, draftings, or computer simulations. This is very different when compared to other artistic disciplines where the mediums are very tangible. You can't easily draw or render light like you would with a scene or costume design or a sketch of a building, where a viewer can easily gain an understanding of the structure and color schemes that are created by an artist. The effects of light are in many cases a mystery until the lights are turned on and a subject is illuminated. Because of this, it is important to develop an understanding of the actual medium of light. What is it? How does it behave? How might we control it? What is its effect on other objects? With experience, more of the answers to these questions can be predicted by a designer, but even then, you can't be completely sure of your design choices until you see them actually revealed in light.

In this chapter I examine the physical properties of light, its makeup, and how it moves through space. I also examine the human eye and how it behaves as a receptor/sensor of light as well as provide you with several methods that we use to describe light. Finally, I examine how light functions within our daily lives. These fundamental principles hold true not only in lighting dramas and other entertainment programs, but also for lighting buildings and natural settings where the sun and other light sources can be observed.

WHAT IS LIGHT?

Quite simply, light is a form of energy. Specifically, it is a form of radiant energy that is associated with a given portion of the **electromagnetic spectrum.** Radiant energy is a form of energy given off by radiant bodies (heat/light sources) such as stars or our sun which moves away from its origin at a constant speed. Light is but one form of radiant energy and has a constant speed of 186,000 miles/second. Most of us know this as the "speed of light."

The Electromagnetic Spectrum

The electromagnetic spectrum represents all forms of radiant energy. Some researchers identify the electromagnetic spectrum with a particle-based theory while others refer to a wave-theory approach. Regardless of which theory one observes, the general principles are the same. In each case, the energy is thought to pulsate outward from a source at the speed of light in oscillations that create a wavelike effect that forms patterns that may be measured. In fact, the variables that we generally use to describe radiant energy are based on wave theory. Most commonly we make distinctions between different forms of radiant

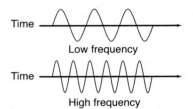

λ = wavelength over one cycle
I = intensity/amplitude over one cycle

a. Relationship of intensity (I),
   wavelength (λ), and cycle

Low frequency

High frequency

b. Frequency (*f*) and wavelength (λ)
   are inversely proportional

FIGURE 1.1 Wave
Relationships

energy through measurements of either **frequency** (*f*) or **wavelength** (λ). These variables are inversely proportional to one another; as frequency increases, the wavelength gets shorter, or as frequency decreases, the wavelength will get longer. The strength or amplitude of the waves is commonly called the **intensity (I).** In visible light we often refer to this as the brightness of the light. Figure 1.1 illustrates the relationship between intensity, frequency, and wavelength.

We commonly choose frequency or wavelength to distinguish between different forms of electromagnetic energy. In lighting, we generally use wavelength to make a distinction between different types of light. The range of measured wavelengths produced by radiant sources is extreme. At one end of the electromagnetic spectrum we find electrical waves with wavelengths measured in miles. The 60-cycle electrical currents that are used in our homes may have a wavelength of over 3,000 miles. Many other forms of electromagnetic radiation (ER) are associated with wavelengths so small that a special unit, the **angstrom (Å),** has been introduced to measure them. One angstrom is equal to 1/254,000,000 of an inch. At the opposite end of the electromagnetic spectrum from electricity are cosmic rays, which may have a wavelength as small as 1/10,000 of an angstrom. The electromagnetic spectrum is a collection of different types of radiant energy that can be specified through their varied wavelengths.

The Visible Spectrum

What concerns us as lighting designers is a very limited range of wavelengths contained within the electromagnetic spectrum which we commonly refer to as the **visible spectrum.** This is a collection of wavelengths that can be sensed by the human eye. Those energy forms that lie outside of our perception with wavelengths that are longer than we can sense include: infrared, radar, television and radio waves (with increasingly longer wavelengths), and those with progressively shorter wavelengths that also lie outside the realm of our visibility (ultraviolet, x-ray, gamma and cosmic rays). Figure 1.2 illustrates the relationship

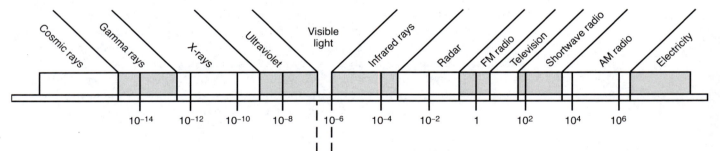

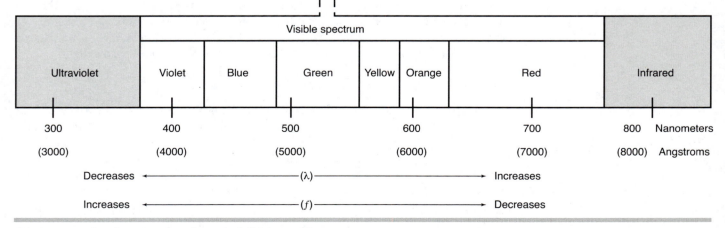

FIGURE 1.2 The Electromagnetic and Visible Spectrums

between wavelength and the individual classifications of energy that make up the electro-magnetic spectrum.

The visible spectrum can be further broken down into smaller components repre-senting individual colors—each color representing a specific wavelength of radiant energy. We have all witnessed the rainbow effect produced through the refraction and separation of these individual colors by a prism or the natural effects of a storm cloud or water spray. Every color represents light of a different wavelength or frequency. The range of wave-lengths generally found within the visible spectrum includes approximately 400 (violet) to 700 (red) nanometers. A nanometer is one-billionth of a meter. A second manner of ex-pressing wavelength has already been introduced through the measurement known as an angstrom (Å). An angstrom is one-tenth of a nanometer. In this case the visible spectrum would be expressed as having wavelengths in the range of 4000–7000 Å.

ILLUMINANCE AND LUMINANCE—FIVE METRICS

In addition to examining the characteristic wavelength or color of the energy we also at-tempt to describe light through its **intensity.** Intensity can generally be thought of as the strength or amplitude of the energy associated with light. More commonly we think of this as brightness. However, while at times one must consider the absolute intensity of the light or the actual amount of energy represented by it, we are more often concerned with the brightness perceived by a viewer. To quantify the manner in which we describe the intensity of light, the **Illuminating Engineering Society of North America (IESNA)** has established five metrics or measurements for describing intensity (Figure 1.3).

Luminous Flux

The first, **luminous flux,** relates to a measure of the actual flow of energy from a light source. The most common unit being the lumen. However, we do not generally observe light itself, but rather, we see the effect of light on other surfaces. Also, light moves away from its source in all directions . . . meaning that in most cases much of the lumen out-put created by a light source is wasted. Think of the poor efficiency of a bare bulb that hangs in an attic or garage ceiling. What we, as designers, are more concerned about is how this light responds to being reflected off surfaces and how we can then process this information into a significant image.

Illuminance

As light radiates away from its source with a given luminance flux it can only proceed through a straight path until it comes into contact with an object. At that point it may ei-ther be **reflected** or **absorbed** to some degree by any object that lies in its path. In some cases, the light may also be **refracted** if it should pass through the material. Most objects have a surface area that is capable of reflecting or absorbing the light that strikes it. **Illuminance** is the second metric given by IESNA and relates to the density of the light that has the potential of striking an object's surface and being reflected back to an observer. It can be thought of as a measurement of concentration. Two typical measure-ments of illuminance include the lux (1 lumen per square meter) or the footcandle (1 lu-men per square foot). A light meter will typically measure illuminance, and most specifications in architectural projects will be based on recommend levels of illumi-nance for a given task (job) or environment. While the effect of illuminance can be seen . . . illuminance itself cannot be seen.

Luminous Intensity

The third metric specified by IESNA relates to the ability of a light source to produce in-tensity in a given direction. This is referred to as **luminous intensity** and is generally measured in candelas. Simply put, no light source produces light of equal luminance flux

a. **Luminous flux:** (lumens)
The flow of light

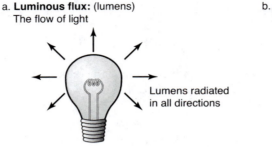

Lumens radiated
in all directions

Power (watts) is converted
to light (lumens)

b. **Illuminance:** (footcandle or lux)
The density of light striking a surface

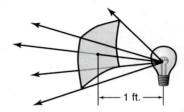

├— 1 ft. —┤

A density of lumens over a square area
• Lux = 1 lumen/meter²
• Footcandle = 1 lumen/foot²

c. **Luminous intensity:** (candela or candlepower)
The intensity of light in a given direction

Intensity will vary at different positions around lamp
(i.e., stronger intensity at sides, less at top,
and virtually none below base)

d. **Luminance:** (candelas/foot² or candelas/meter²)
The intensity of a source or surface in a given
direction over the area of the source seen
by an observer

Observer sees

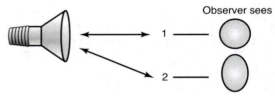

1
2

(1) PAR lamp viewed straight on (higher luminance)
(2) Same lamp viewed from off-center (lower luminance)

e. **Luminous exitance:** (lumens/foot² or lumens/meter²)
The intensity of a source or reflective surface
in all directions—the total luminous flux being
reflected or transmitted

FIGURE 1.3 *Five Measurements for Describing Light* *General Note:* Illuminance relates to intensity of light (luminous flux) being emitted or reflected from a source or surface—you *cannot* see illuminance. Luminance *can* be seen and is a product of light being conducted over a given surface area (source or surface).

or intensity in all directions. Luminous intensity forms a manner of measuring this unequal distribution pattern around a light source. If we go back to our example of the bare bulb it can easily be recognized that the area above and below the bulb (where the socket and base are located) will be deficient in the amount of light produced as compared with those areas located to the sides of the lamp.

INVERSE SQUARE LAW   The importance of these three metrics comes about through their interrelationships. When brought together, they create a relationship that can be expressed through a formula known as the **Inverse Square Law.**

$$E = I/D^2$$

where:

E = Illuminance I = Luminous Intensity D = Distance

The law simply states that the illuminance of a light source is inversely proportional to the square of the distance from the source. Practically speaking, this means that the light's intensity

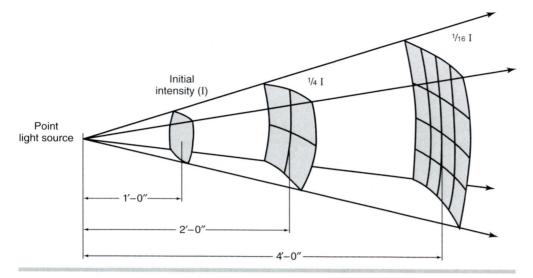

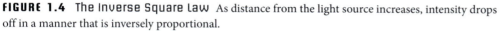

FIGURE 1.4 The Inverse Square Law As distance from the light source increases, intensity drops off in a manner that is inversely proportional.

drops off much more quickly per unit area as the distance from the light source is progressively increased. A quick examination of this principle can be demonstrated through playing a flashlight on a wall and noting the apparent brightness of the light while varying the distance that the light is held from the wall. Figure 1.4 illustrates the effect of distance on illuminance.

Luminance

There are two more metrics that allow engineers and designers to describe light. Unlike those already mentioned, the final two metrics can be directly observed by a viewer. The first, **luminance,** relates to the intensity divided by the surface area of the source as observed by the viewer. This is a directional function, and its value will be dependent on the viewing angle of the viewer to the source. The viewer would actually observe the light source but the source may or may not be in a direct path of observation from the viewer. An example of this impact can be seen when viewing a theatrical light source dead on versus from a position somewhere to the side. In this case, the surface area of the source would appear as a circle from dead on, while from the side, the same source would appear oblong and distorted while also presenting a smaller surface area to the viewer. Therefore, even with no change in illumination there would still be a lower luminance associated with viewing the source from the side position.

Luminous Exitance

The final metric for quantifying intensity is **luminous exitance.** This, too, relates to light reflecting or leaving a surface, but is not direction dependent like luminance. In this metric we relate the amount of luminous flux to a given reflectance or transmission value for the material of the source or object being considered. Hence, in a situation where two objects are exposed to the same luminous flux, one colored black while the other is white; the object with the white coloring would have a higher associated level of reflectance and therefore higher luminous exitance than the black object.

THE EYE AND SEEING

Our observation of the world around us is based solely on the manner in which we sense our environment. We can't directly observe anything without the aid of various senses. If you think back to a basic biology class you will probably remember that the normal human body is equipped with five sensory devices. We have come to refer to these as our senses, and they include: sound, touch, smell, taste, and sight. Each sense consists of a series of sensory organs that convert physical phenomena into nervous impulses that our brains process in a way that helps us to observe the world around us. Our skin allows us to feel the world around us, our ears allow us to hear, and our eyes allow us to see.

The visible spectrum exists within the electromagnetic spectrum where it does because it represents the range of wavelengths at which the human eye can sense light. If we were sensitive to light relating to a different range of wavelengths our visible spectrum would shift to a different portion of the electromagnetic spectrum. An infrared camera, such as the ones used in defense or security systems, is sensitive to a different portion of the spectrum than the human eye. Hence, in a situation such as a dark night where we cannot see the movements of people like prowlers or soldiers, the camera is able to "see" for us.

Physiology of the Eye

In order to understand the eye, we often make a comparison between the way it is created and the manner in which a camera is constructed. Figure 1.5 illustrates the principle components of the eye. The primary structure of the eye is known as the **sclera,** which is

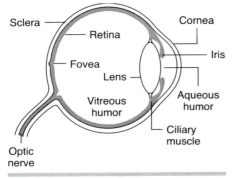

FIGURE 1.5 Physiology of the Eye

most recognizable as the white portion of the eye that surrounds all of the other components and extends all the way to the back of the eye. The eye is essentially an assembly of three primary groups of components. Each of these is responsible for a step that is required in the task of seeing. These are also directly comparable to parts of the optical system found in any camera. The first group controls the amount of light that enters the eye. Basic components of this group include the **cornea,** which is the clear outer layer of the eye; a layer of fluid directly behind the cornea (*anterior chamber*); the **iris,** which is the area of the eye that has color; and the black dot at the center of the eye that we call the **pupil.** Finally, a crystalline lens is located directly behind the iris, and a second area of fluid is found between the lens and the back surface of the eye (**vitreous humor**). The cornea and anterior chamber function much like a lens—focusing the light on the back surface of the eye where the optical sensors are located. The pupil can be modified in size by a set of muscles in the iris that control the amount of light entering the eye. The more light that the eye is exposed to results in an ever decreasing size in the pupil. The crystalline lens is controlled by a second set of muscles (**ciliary muscles**) which modify the shape and thickness of the eye to enable it to focus on different objects and distances.

The second primary element of the eye is the **retina.** The retina is the interior wall at the back of the eye. This is the portion of the eye where the optical sensors are located and where the eye attempts to focus its images. A special portion of the retina known as the **fovea** is located near the center of the retina. This area has a much higher concentration of photosensitive cells and is responsible for the majority of our ability to distinguish colors and detail in our viewing. A second area of the retina is the **optic disk,** which forms the location where the nerve endings of the photoreceptors are bundled together to form the **optic nerve.** The optic nerve will then carry the impulses to the brain where they will be processed into an image.

The third and final group of primary eye components includes the actual photoreceptors. These are specialized cells that convert light exposure to a neural impulse that is sent to the brain. A typical eye contains approximately 128 million photoreceptors. There are two types of photoreceptors found in the human eye and each has a different function. The first, the **rods,** are sensitive to light across a wide range of wavelengths and luminous levels. This results in the rods being predominantly responsible for our sight both at low levels of illumination and for distinguishing our peripheral vision. This is often referred to as **scotopic vision.** The second type of receptors, *cones,* are responsible for both our color and detail vision within light levels associated with typical interior and exterior illuminances. This type of vision is known as **photopic vision.** Only cones are found in the fovea while both cones and rods are found throughout the remainder of the retina.

These produce results that equate rods and scotopic vision with night vision and cones and photopic vision with day vision.

The structure of the eye and its various photoreceptors will ultimately determine an individual's sight. The need to wear corrective lenses is just one effect of having an abnormality of the eye. In this case, the lens doesn't focus the light properly on the retina. This may also change throughout one's lifetime as the lens slowly ages and becomes more rigid and less pliable. Some of us are light sensitive and find a bright sunny day to be a painful sensation, while others have problems seeing objects in the dark. The causes of these problems are often related to a physical impairment of the eye. In addition to any problems with the eye itself, there are also a number of physical and psychological effects that can have an additional impact on one's vision. Some of these can improve your sight, while others can create problems. More importantly, these effects generally relate to your perception of light and vision, not necessarily to the actual amount of light sensed by your eyes. In any case, a lighting designer must be aware of these effects in order to create designs that will compensate for any of them. Chapter 2 discusses several of the most important issues related to lighting and perception.

THE CONTROLLABLE QUALITIES OF LIGHT

It is important at this point to introduce the reader to a vocabulary that enables us to define and describe light. One of the most difficult tasks for a lighting designer is in describing the lighting that they envision for a project. Light is our medium and it cannot be illustrated effectively through an indirect means such as a model or rendering. A scenic designer or architect can illustrate to a reasonable degree of success a final design and color palette for a project through the use of markers, pencils, or paints. Likewise, in addition to renderings, a costumer can present swatches or scraps of fabric to indicate the materials from which a costume will be created. This isn't so with a lighting design, where light itself is our medium and where nobody can get a true sense of the outcome of a design until the actual lights (**luminaires**) are placed, colored, and balanced through setting specific brightness levels for each light. Because of this, several descriptive qualities have been defined to help us communicate with one another about light. These are generally not thought of in terms of quantitative elements but are used instead to help us set up a comparison between various lights and lighting effects. While absolutes may come into the discussion, most of these qualities are used solely within a descriptive or comparative basis. These qualities are also universal and can be translated to any field of lighting, whether working in traditional drama or lighting an office tower, a garden, or the latest Rolling Stones tour. While there may be slight variations in terminology between lighting disciplines, most designers have come to refer to four primary qualities for describing light. Any light, no mater how produced, filtered, or modified can be described through these four attributes. The variation of any one of these qualities will make a distinction between any given example of light. These qualities include: **intensity, distribution, color,** and **movement.** As a whole, these are essentially the same qualities that Stanley McCandless described in 1932 when he first wrote *A Method of Lighting the Stage*.

Intensity

The most easily described quality of light is **intensity** and relates to the brightness of the light. While it might be described very specifically and can be evaluated through measurements such as the candela or footcandle, it is more often described through a comparative basis. "This light is brighter than that light," "this light is approximately half the intensity of another light," or "that light is as bright as the moon" are examples of this type of comparison. The human eye can perceive light at an extreme range of intensities. In World War II soldiers learned that a German scout plane nicknamed Bed Check Charlie could see the tip of a lit cigarette from several miles away. If spotted, soldiers could anticipate a visit from a bomber sometime later that night. On the other hand, intensity can be so bright that it becomes harmful to our senses and could even cause damage to our eyes. Examples of this would include looking directly into the sun or being exposed to the bright light that accompanies a welder as he strikes an arc. In most theatrical venues we are generally concerned only with the relative appearance of the light and whether there is enough visibility to see what has to be seen at any given moment on the stage. In video and film lighting, the intensity isn't as flexible, and there is a minimum threshold of intensity that a **director of photography** must provide to maintain a proper exposure for a setting. We have all rushed to the one-hour photo store in anticipation of viewing the photographs that we took of last Friday night's party to find that the results only produced some shadowy silhouettes that we think we recognize as our friends. Architectural lighting designers speak of a minimum amount of illumination for a given task or job. These tasks actually require a minimum number of footcandles of illumination. The lighting levels required for a personal home are much lower than those needed at a rest home where elderly residents often have trouble seeing. A meeting room would require higher intensity levels than a restaurant seating area . . . although neither would require nearly the illumination levels required for an assembly line producing high-tech products. Regardless of whether describing a specific level of illumination (i.e., footcandles) or simply describing intensity on a comparative basis, intensity becomes one of the most important ways of helping us distinguish between different types of light and lighting.

Distribution

The second controllable quality of light is known as **distribution.** McCandless described this as form. Most lighting designers actually relate distribution to two specific properties of light. These properties include angle (or direction) and quality. **Angle** refers to the direction from which the light is coming. Where are you hanging the light source? How does it play upon the subject? Where are the highlights? Where do the shadows fall? A light coming from behind the subject presents a completely different image and associated mood than a light coming from in front of the subject. A couple walking hand-in-hand into a sunset presents a much more dramatic image than if the sun were directly overhead. Dracula would most likely not appear so scary if we chose to light him in any other way than through a silhouette. The angle of the light helps to define or reveal the form of an object. Directly from the front it tends to flatten a subject and will cause the subject to appear two-dimensional, while from the side it tends to sculpt and etch the subject away from its background. **Backlight** tends to push objects forward, while **downlight** tends to squash the subject. A light from below generally appears unnatural and can be used to create effects that clue audiences into peculiarities within a production. Architects can also make use of these principles to make a room appear larger or smaller. **Quality** refers to the texture and characteristic features of the light. Some lighting may be harsh and crisp—representing strong parallel rays—while other lighting will reflect a soft diffuse quality. A clear sunny day in summer versus the cold gray light associated with a December afternoon form comparisons of these types of lighting conditions. Is the light even in distribution, or are there patterns? A typical classroom lighting scheme of today will most likely result in a soft, even wash of light over the entire room by some form of fluorescent fixtures. In comparison, a warehouse set in 1930 would probably be lit with single-bulb fixtures with simple shades that would produce cones of light throughout the structure. A walk on a sunny day through an open field exposes you to a very different kind of light than the textured light that you would expect once you move into a wooded area where the trees create patches of light and shadow along the path that you follow. Lighting designers can even create their own textured light by inserting patterns known as **gobos** into the fixtures that illuminate a space. While gobos were first utilized in entertainment designs, they have now become elements of architectural and display lighting as well.

Color

The third controllable quality of light is **color.** Color is considered by many to be the most dynamic of the controllable qualities of light. Light will have an associated color that is determined through the specific collection of wavelengths present within its makeup. Hence, you might have a lavender light, a red light, or a blue light—each one distinguished from the others by those wavelengths of light found within its composition. However, color is actually a perception based on how specific wavelengths of the light stimulate the photosensors in our eyes. Light, more importantly, has a major impact on the color of any objects that it falls on, and the resultant color is a factor of both the object's actual color and that of the light that strikes that object. All objects selectively absorb or reflect various wavelengths of light—which becomes the means by which we determine the color of any object. The use of a light containing some or all of the wavelengths of light that are naturally reflected by an object will generally result in enhancing that object's color, while the use of a colored light with limited or no common wavelengths with that of an object will result in a distortion and graying of the object's color. Color is produced either through the spectral makeup of the light source itself, through the removal of specific wavelengths of the light through filtering, or by the selective absorption of a light's wavelengths by a surface. While it is generally agreed that color is the easiest quality of light to observe, it is also commonly acknowledged that due to the unpredictability of its results, it is perhaps the hardest quality to master and control.

Movement

The final quality of light is **movement.** Movement refers to changes in the light from moment to moment. This might be represented in a number of different ways. First, one might observe the actual movement of the light source. This is quite common and can be illustrated through watching a candle or flashlight being carried across a room, when you actually see the source move from one location to another. A second form of movement involves the movement of the light without actually observing the light source directly. Two examples of this include watching the effect of a follow spot on a rock musician and the use of a progression of lamps to light an actor as they move from one position on the stage to another. In the first example, you see the effect of the light following the musician, but you can't see the actual spotlight because it is located somewhere behind you at the rear of the auditorium. In the second example, lights slowly come up along the path that an actor walks such that the individual lights precede the arrival of the actor to specific locations on the stage. For even more effect, the individual lights could also slowly dim down once the actor moves beyond their positions to other locations along the path. The last element of movement relates simply to changes within the lighting over time. For all practical purposes this would come about through any changes in any of the other three controllable qualities of light. Lights suddenly getting brighter or dimmer, shifting to another color, or slowly moving to a different angle all form examples of this kind of movement. The movement may be nearly instantaneous, such as in flipping a light switch on or off, or could involve long transitions like sunset sequences that are so subtle that a viewer isn't aware of the lighting changes being made from one moment to another. Movement can also be thought of as a transition in lighting. While there are occasions where the lighting for an environment may be static, most of us consider transitions in lighting to be just as important as the actual images that a designer creates for a given project.

In summary, all lighting conditions reflect the manipulation of these four qualities. Whether you light a building, a museum display, an opera, or any other form of entertainment, each moment that a viewer observes can be associated with a given combination of intensity, color, and distribution in the lighting. Movement can most often be directly related to the transitions between different "moments" (also called "looks," "states," or "**cues**"). Each of these terms relates to names that a designer may use to refer to a static view of the lighting. Movement provides the fluid, dynamic quality required in a lighting

Ken Billington

Ken Billington is one of the most successful Broadway lighting designers, working the Broadway scene since the mid-1970's. After graduating from high school, he went directly to New York City where he studied at The Lester Polakov Studio and Forum of Stage Design. In his early years he apprenticed with both Peggy Clark and Tharon Musser. In fact, he often claims that he went to "Musser U" and credits her with his first big break. Billington has designed numerous Broadway and Off-Broadway shows and operas for companies like the New York City, Chicago Lyric, and Houston Grand Operas. He is often associated with lighting large musicals and spectaculars, with design credits that include Disney's *High School Musical, Sweeney Todd, White Christmas,* and *Footloose*. He has regularly designed the Radio City Music Hall Christmas and Easter shows and has lit personalities like Ann-Margret, Shirley MacLaine, Carol Channing, and Liberace. He has also won a number of design award nominations and a Tony Award for productions like the revival of *Chicago*. He has gone on to light other projects such as *Fantasmic* at Disneyland, ice shows like *Stars on Ice* and *Barney* (the purple dinosaur), and restaurants. He was also honored as the United States Institute for Theatre Technology (USITT) Distinguished Lighting Designer in 1996.

Billington had always liked lighting ever since the fourth grade. In fact, from that point on all he wanted to do was lighting. It wasn't until he was in junior high school that he realized that there were lighting designers and that it was a proper design discipline. Ken usually says that he's a "Broadway lighting designer," but he also designs for Off-Broadway, touring productions, opera, spectaculars, theme parks, television, and architecture. "It is hard to say how much time is spent on each since, as a freelance designer, you have no idea where the jobs will come from each year. I have done as many as five Broadway shows in a year and only one the following year, but that year might include six shows that tryout and hope to come to New York." Billington learned how to design for the stage from the

lighting classes at the Polakov Studio and by being an assistant. He also claims that, "By using what I know about stage lighting it was through good common sense that I learned how to work in other areas of lighting design——the basics of lighting (angle, color, intensity, and having a concept) are necessary in all forms of lighting. The way of execution is different and there is a different language in the way you talk to a contractor from a stage electrician, but the final look of the space is still the same——it's designed lighting."

Billington has been active in the lighting profession for many years and believes that lighting is a collaborative process which requires a designer to have good personal relationships with their colleagues. Things that continue to attract him to the profession include his work as a creative member of a design team. In fact, creativity is what he likes most about the profession. "I can't paint or draw a picture . . . but I can paint with light. It is the same for any artist, why do you do this? It is also thrilling to sit in a theatre and see what you have created on paper start to come to life." What he likes least is sitting in a dark theatre from eight in the morning to midnight. In order to remain current he reads the lighting trade magazines, attends lighting conventions, and will make himself available to sales people that come to his studio, or talk to the company reps directly. He also adds that one of the best ways to remain abreast is simply going out and seeing what your colleagues are doing and seeing for yourself what the current trends are. When quizzed on what he considers Rule #1 he states, "Concept! No matter what the project or whether it is big or small—if there is no concept, you will usually get yourself and the production into trouble." Ken closes with the following advice. "The best way to learn is to do lighting no matter what the project. You might do a great job or an OK job but remember that even if you really screw up the worst that will happen is that you'll get fired—— they don't take you out back and shoot you. No matter what the project learn from it—look at what worked and what did not work and file it away and remember it for the future."

Photo credit: Photo courtesy Ken Billington

design—a quality that many of us argue is equally important to the combination of fixtures, colors, and intensities that one sees at any given time. If mounted correctly, the lighting can greatly enhance a production or project. If done incorrectly, it can quickly become an interruption or distraction for the viewers or audience.

FUNCTIONS OF LIGHTING

There are numerous functions associated with lighting. Light is used to reveal. Many of the functions of lighting relate specifically to the manner in which light is used to reveal an object(s) or setting. While most lighting designers and illuminating engineers agree in principle with many of the named lighting functions discussed in the following paragraphs, sometimes designers may combine several of these functions into larger groups or may have a different term associated with a given function. In these cases, what is important is the performance of the function rather than the specific name used by a given individual. In reality, we combine and modify the controllable qualities of light to produce the varied functions that we find within lighting. As a rule, I discuss the functions of lighting from a more traditional theatrical or entertainment background first and will then go on to relate to several other functions that are more specific to other practices. Again, it is important to be aware that many of the functions are characteristic of all types of lighting design.

Visibility

Most designers would argue that the most important element of lighting is **visibility.** Many even refer to it as the primary function of lighting. After all, isn't this why we created artificial light in the first place? Visibility simply refers to the principle of using light to reveal or illuminate objects. In the early days of both theatrical and architectural lighting the job of the designer was nothing more than to create enough light so that the audience or occupants of a space could see. In many ways this philosophy of lighting was based on the premise that more was better. It was believed that the higher the quantity of footcandles or lumens placed on a stage or in a room, the better visibility you had. Since the 1950s or '60s, theatrical designing moved toward a concept that we call **selective visibility,** which simply relates to revealing to an audience only what needs to be seen. Hence, a less revealing image on stage might be more appropriate for the dramatic action than a fully illuminated stage. In selective visibility, areas of low intensity, shadows, silhouettes, and high contrast can become effective elements in a lighting designer's arsenal of tools. An image of Dracula appearing from the shadows is much more terrifying than seeing him come to his next victim in full light. Until recently, architectural lighting has been known for being largely dependent on the quantity rather than the quality of its lighting, and most recommended practices of the past carefully specified the minimum number of footcandles that were required for a given **task** or environment. As of the latest printing of the *IESNA Lighting Handbook,* which was printed in 2000, the recommended practices for many architectural lighting installations now follow guidelines that place an emphasis on not only the quantity but also the quality of light for a given specification. Finally, while it may appear obvious that the level of illumination plays a dominant role in the visibility of an object, it is not the only control that has an effect on whether you see something or not. The angle of the light also determines how much or little of an object is revealed to you. The color of the light might help an object either blend in or pop out from its background and will also enhance or gray the object's color. These are just a few of the many additional elements that can have an effect on visibility.

Establishing a Scene

Some functions of lighting are related specifically to the discipline that you are designing within, while others are consistent with almost any kind of lighting. For instance, in a theatrical production it would be critical for the lighting to help establish or communicate specific information about the play or environment that is being created. Time of day, season, and geographical location are all parts of this function. Many refer to this as **establishing a scene.** In short, the lighting, as well as all the other elements of the scene, must combine to create a single cohesive environment that creates a "true" world of the play. A play that requires a night scene must be lit in some fashion that would be suggestive of night. This could be a night with lights on or lights off, lights that would suggest a specific interior lighting (i.e., a chandelier versus a fireplace or table lamp), or even lights that are suggestive of a specific type of light source or historical period (electric versus gas or candlelight). All of these form specific design considerations that a lighting designer should consider as they light the given night scene. Establishing a scene is much more important for an entertainment lighting designer who is concerned with creating a world for a performance than an architectural lighting designer who is simply lighting a particular space. In reality though, even the architectural designer must create a design that deals in some manner with establishing a scene that is consistent with producing the proper response or ambience for a building or environment. An example would be in creating the appropriate lighting for a five-star restaurant versus an office suite. There is an appropriate and unique approach to lighting each of these projects.

Modeling

Another common function of lighting is in **modeling** or sculpting. Some designers refer to this as "revelation of form." This function relates to using light for enhancing the three-dimensional qualities of an object. We can best distinguish form through carefully observing the **highlights** and **shadows** of an object. Highlights represent the flashes of reflected light from areas that are directly illuminated by a light source, while shadows may be represented by either the area of an object that is not lit or the area of darkness or shadow that is cast by a lit object. Areas that are raised are prone to highlights, while recessed surfaces usually fall into shadow areas. However, this revelation of highlight and shadow is dependent on both the angle and number of lights that strike an object. As an object is lit from different directions more, or less, of its surface textures and associated form are revealed to the observer. As a rule, the best light for revealing an object's form or three-dimensional qualities is to its side. Angles that come from either behind or in front of an object tend to create more of a two-dimensional or profile-like image of the subject. The vertical angle of the light source(s) also has an effect on how the object is revealed to an observer. As an experiment, try shining a light on a piece of molding like a cornice from different angles. The light can change one's perception of which parts of the molding are inset or raised. In fact, when lit from straight front, the individual shapes might even be masked and may not reveal any depth at all.

Mood

Another function of lighting relates to creating **mood.** Mood refers to a given emotional response to the lighting by an observer. Lighting can be foreboding or inviting, carefree and light, energetic versus passive, or tragic and oppressive. In all of these and many more moods, the light provides an atmosphere or ambiance for the environment that is being lit. Other than visibility, mood is probably the function of lighting that has the next most important impression or effect on a viewer. Studies have shown that light can have a profound effect on individuals and their associated moods. In entertainment lighting, we often produce extreme ranges of mood for a given theatrical production or special event. These moods may also be changed many times throughout a two or three hour performance. Mood changes may occur quickly or may be so subtle that the audience isn't necessarily aware that the changes have even taken place. A well-lit production will have lighting that reflects the varied moods of a piece while also following the rhythm of the changes that occur throughout the script. In architectural lighting, more subtle choices are used to produce environments for more productive offices and more welcoming reception areas, and to provide calming effects for patients in medical facilities. Lighting has also been used to produce an impact on sales volumes and turnover rates in retail markets. As an example, consider the lighting associated with a fine restaurant like a favorite bistro versus any number of fast food restaurants. The soft, amber lighting associated with the bistro is very different from the harsh, bright, fluorescent lighting that is characteristic of the fast food restaurants where turnover is key to a successful business. In this case, the lighting helps create an environment that prevents patrons from becoming too comfortable in the fast food establishments.

Focus

Focus is a lighting function that relates to drawing attention to various elements within an environment. Architectural designers often refer to this as **accent lighting.** It is even common in many environments to have several different layers of attention or focus established for a stage or given space. The single most important focus is generally referred to as the **primary focus** of a scene or environment. While a given subject may be less prominent than the primary focus, it may well appear more prominent than the rest of the environment, which results in creating a **secondary focus** for a scene. One role of a lighting designer is to help point out where a viewer or audience member's attention should be directed at any given time. In a typical theatrical application the audience view is confined to the stage, while in a building an occupant has the potential to look wherever they wish. The signage at an airport should be lit to allow passengers to easily navigate between locations such as gates, ticket counters, and baggage claim areas. On a stage, what should the audience be watching at any given moment? Who in the band has the solo? Manners in which a lighting designer may control focus include many familiar tricks. One example comes from simply blacking out an entire stage except for those areas where the focus must be directed. Highlighting an actor delivering a monologue within a single spotlight or pulling lights down to a single light on a significant prop like an empty wheelchair form examples of this type of directed focus. In a more subtle manner a designer may simply boost or raise the intensity of the light around an area to which they want to direct your focus. Brightening the lights around furniture clusters such as tables or seating areas is a common practice for lighting relatively long conversations that take place at specific locations. Another example of this is when an entrance is pointed up by boosting the level of a **special** that is focused on the door from which an actor will enter. It is important to understand that we use relative brightness to help direct focus. While I have spoken of raising the intensity of light on a subject, an equally valid and at times even preferred technique involves lowering the intensity of the areas surrounding the point to which we want to draw focus.

An architectural lighting designer uses the same concepts to draw an occupant's attention to various details in a room or building. Directing track lighting onto wall hangings or photographs, placing more light around a hotel lobby's reservations desk, or creating focusable lighting for product displays in a department store all form examples of using light to direct focus. The eye is unique in that it will usually focus on the element within our vision that is different from the rest of the objects. Color can also be used by lighting designers to control focus. Placing a single white light on the lead singer while the rest of a band is bathed in magenta-colored light is an example of using color to establish focus. A designer does not necessarily have to make use of extreme color differences to make use of this principle. A night scene in which the entire stage is cast in blue light, with bluish lavender moonlight streaming through the French doors where Dracula is to appear can form just as effective of a use of contrast in color.

Composition

Composition is a function of lighting that relates to combining all of the elements of a stage or room together into a complete visual package. We see nothing until it is revealed to us through light, and one of the lighting designer's primary responsibilities lies not only in choosing what to reveal to us but also how it is revealed to us. While other collaborators give us the primary elements of a composition, such as the scenery and costumes, the actors or characters, and the furniture and building itself; the lighting designer can reveal these objects in an infinite number of ways. By comparison, the lighting designer often makes the largest single contribution in determining the overall composition of a stage or environment. The same objects or space can appear quite differently through making just a couple of simple alterations to the lighting of that event or environment. The lighting also determines how all of the individual objects and designs tie together as a whole and becomes a unifying element for most design projects.

Style

Style forms yet another function of lighting. It relates to creating visual traits that allow a characteristic overall visual quality to be connected to a given production. In reality, style is specifically determined through the collaboration and discussions of the entire production team. While we may discuss the style of any given production, we may also use style to compare and contrast the project to other productions or projects. An architect may refer to postmodernism, while a director might speak about absurdism. In each case, style is representative of various visual qualities that are characteristic of each school or movement. A scenic designer, director, costume designer, and lighting designer must share a common understanding of the style of a production in order to realize a successful unified project. Most importantly, once agreed upon, a production or project should remain consistent in the manner in which it approaches style throughout a project. A number of designers will discuss theme as an element of style. How is the play constructed? Does the playwright use a specific type of delivery? Are there social and visual themes within a production? A lighting design must help reinforce the visual quality associated with the remaining elements of a project. One manner in which style becomes most readily identified is through establishing the degree of realism in a production. How literal is the world that we are creating? Could this be a naturalistic environment? Are there any symbolic elements? Are there any recurring themes to be reinforced or emphasized? Are we simplifying our image so that it only contains those elements that are absolutely essential to the action? Is period realism and historical accuracy important to the piece? Should there be a limited color palette? How are the traditional elements of design (line, form, texture, etc.) characterized within a given project? All of these questions form examples of issues that will help a design team define a project's style.

Staging the Story

In the case of entertainment design we also need to consider the actual techniques of production as another function of lighting. A number of designers refer to this as "**staging the story.**" In principle, this simply means taking the script and finding a proper mechanism for presenting it to an audience. In a production making use of a single box setting, a design team may simply use the act curtain and a series of blackouts to make distinctions between various scenes. A very different approach would be required for a production containing 20 independent scenes in which each scene requires a different location. Do we need to observe the entire space, or can we break it up through using smaller locations such as platforms? Is a unit set part of the design solution? Can tightly confined specials be used to define the spaces required by the action of the play? What scenic mechanisms might we utilize to move from one scene to another? What theatrical conventions will be used throughout the production? Are there specific lighting techniques or equipment available that will help us present the play to an audience? How are transitions handled? Lighting transitions have become one of the most important means of enabling us to quickly shift the reality of a play from one location to another. The answers to these and other similar questions will help establish the style of both the production and its lighting.

Rhythm

A final function of light that relates primarily to entertainment lighting is **rhythm.** Rhythm in lighting relates essentially to movement and transitions and may be very subtle and unobserved or may become dramatic and very apparent to the audience. Rhythm can relate to transitions based simply on the logistical needs of making the production workable (staging the story) for an audience, or more importantly, rhythm can follow the dramatic tensions of a production. Do changes from one scene to another occur in a natural, fluid manner, or are they disruptive to the flow of the show? We've all witnessed those times where the lighting isn't quite in sync with the actors, scene changes, or other elements of a production. A second form of rhythm relates to the changes that occur as a result of various movement (blocking) patterns with the actors, changes in mood, focus, or any other requirements that make a dramatic comment on the play through the lighting. As tensions mount and are resolved, the lighting should underscore the associated emotional changes throughout a production. Often, the lighting will build as a scene moves towards its climax. A well-designed production will be dynamic and will have lighting that follows the rhythm of the rest of the show. In fact, it has been demonstrated that lighting that remains too static may actually have a negative impact on audience members. In contemporary practices even architectural lighting applications now make allowances for rhythm when lighting many projects. Not only is rhythm varied throughout the day in offices and other workplaces, but also, it can become a major design element for large exterior objects such as building facades and towers, landscape architecture, and even bridges. In these cases, the lighting of a structure may slowly change color through intervals of as little as 30 seconds to as long as a half-hour or even longer. Rhythm can also be observed in something as simple as the spacing intervals and patterns that are used when laying out a group of luminaires such as in the case of laying out an arrangement of ceiling fixtures.

FOR FURTHER READING

Illuminating Engineering Society of North America, *IESNA Lighting Education 100 (Fundamental Level)* (New York: Illuminating Engineering Society of North America, 1993).
Illuminating Engineering Society of North America, *IESNA Lighting Education 150 (Intermediate Level)* (New York: Illuminating Engineering Society of North America, 1993).
Illuminating Engineering Society of North America, *IESNA Lighting Handbook,* 9th ed., ed. Mark Rae, (New York: Illuminating Engineering Society of North America, 2000).
Illuminating Engineering Society of North America, *IESNA Lighting Ready Reference,* 4th ed. (New York: Illuminating Engineering Society of North America, 2003).
McCandless, Stanley, *A Method of Lighting the Stage,* 4th ed. (New York: Theatre Arts Books, 1958).
McCandless, Stanley, *A Syllabus of Stage Lighting* (New Haven, CT, 1941).

Light and Perception

2

The importance of light in the perception of our world cannot be overstated. Light, by its very nature, allows us to see and therefore perceive the environment around us. Because we observe the world through images that are created through the stimulation of our optic nerves and nerve impulses, we have to account for the fact that what we sense is actually an indirect means of observation. Therefore, images can be interpreted very differently from one person to another. This, to some degree, is due to our personal backgrounds, which add an interpretive element that is based on our past experiences. At other times, we may simply have different degrees of stimulation from one individual to another. For instance, we learn to define the color that we call red based on our experiences of what our parents taught us was the color red. After a time, we learned to associate the color red with a given experience of sight. However, if given a more complex color, such as an orange-red or an orange-orange-red, more people would have trouble distinguishing the point at which the orange-red shifts into becoming an orange-orange-red as we go through the process of adding more yellow to the color. In this case, we define the new color based on our personal experience, and one person's experience may be quite different from that of another's. The color hasn't changed . . . only our perception of that color. A second manner in which we might perceive different experiences in light comes from simply sensing the light in different ways from others. For example, some people are color blind. Their experience of the world is considerably different from those of us who have normal color vision. Other people are light sensitive and may find even moderate levels of brightness to be painful, while others have acute night vision. All of these factors relate to people sensing light in different ways. In most cases, our sense of sight actually undergoes changes throughout our lives. Children might have to wear contacts or glasses, people in their late forties to fifties may begin to need reading glasses, and the elderly often have difficulties with night vision. While some of these experiences are determined by the actual physical properties of light and our eyes, others are related to our psychological perceptions of light and the environment.

Possibly more important than the way that we are stimulated or experience light through our senses is the manner in which light is used to modify or reveal an object. In the last chapter I stated that without light there would be no vision. To be seen, an object must be capable of reflecting some degree of light. This is in addition to assuming that it can be sensed through a sensory device like an eye or camera. Without a surface to reflect upon, light will continue to expand outward unnoticed. We have all seen the effect of a car's headlights becoming observable in the mist of a foggy night. On a clear night it is often impossible to distinguish the edges of the beams that the fog so clearly defines. Through light, we can selectively reveal an object in any number of different ways. We can use varied degrees of brightness to allow differing degrees of visibility. The angle between the viewer and light source might be modified to create very different revelations of an object. The color of the light could also be changed to create a significantly different response in the way that the subject is seen by an observer. Everyone knows that a white T-shirt under red light will appear red even though we know that the color of the shirt remains white. All of these represent examples of light being used to modify a viewer's perception of an object.

In this chapter I examine many of the ways in which light can be used to shape a viewer's perception of the world around them. Several fundamental principles of visibility also form a significant focus of this chapter. What are several appropriate manners in which a lighting designer might reveal a subject to an audience? What are several aspects of control that we can use to create a given response in a viewer? Are there issues that may cause a negative impact on an observer's experience? How much does a designer have to reveal to an audience? Each of these questions and many like them relate to how our vision is impacted by light and its manipulation. An effective lighting designer will learn to take command of the immense range of possibilities that are both available and acceptable for completing the task of visibility. At the same time, they must also remain sensitive to the repercussions that might come from lighting an object or environment.

VISIBILITY

Visibility relates to allowing the eyes and mind to be stimulated to such a degree that we can make an observation. Visibility, however, is a relative term, and we need to examine it in terms of a specific context. In a most basic sense, it relates to the effect of providing enough visual information so that a viewer can establish a meaning from what you have presented them with. In a way, visibility becomes a means of communication. If done well, the message is received . . . if done poorly, the message becomes confused or is lost. Historically, there have been two basic approaches for creating visibility through light. The first is based on providing good uniform illumination over a widely dispersed area—where **quantity of light** is considered a major component of visibility. The second relates more to the quality of the visual experience and refers to visibility in terms of what needs or doesn't need to be seen by an observer—a concept that we refer to as **quality of light.** In other words, we simply increase visibility to a point where we reveal only enough of a subject to bring meaning to an audience. We are more selective in what we do or don't reveal to an audience. Most lighting designers refer to this as **selective visibility**—revealing only what is necessary to bring meaning to a viewer. Directors of the 1940s and '50s were frequently trained to believe that the audience had to see the actors' faces in order to hear them, a concept that by today's standards is severely limited. Today, shadows, distorted colors, and even low intensities have become common techniques for manipulating the lighting to express mood and style associations, which can actually produce a much more effective image than simply bringing visibility to an environment.

Illuminating engineers generally refer to the demand for successful vision as **visual acuity.** This essentially relates to being able to manipulate the visual stimulus and environment in such a way that a given visual task can be completed. Visual acuity is actually a function of factors such as the size of the object, distance between the object and viewer, surface reflectivity of the object, amount of illumination present, and sensitivity of the sensors. For example, small text has a more limiting effect on visual acuity than large text, while a reading lamp will help raise the visual acuity of a page. A general rule has been to associate more critical tasks with the need for more illumination. Hence, working in a classroom demands brighter conditions than eating in a restaurant. Surgery in a hospital operating room would require still higher levels of illumination. However, a number of consequences have also been associated with maintaining overly consistent levels of illumination within a given environment—especially when those levels are maintained at either relatively high or low intensity levels. A number of these effects are examined later in this chapter.

INTENSITY OR BRIGHTNESS

While visibility may be modified through any one of the controllable qualities of light, we often associate the most important element of visibility with the control of intensity or brightness. For now, we'll primarily examine the effects of intensity on vision. The other controllable qualities and their effects on vision will be addressed throughout later portions of the chapter and book. The eye is an amazing mechanism in that it can observe an incredible range of light intensities. While at one extreme we might observe light so bright that it could damage our eyes (such as in looking at the sun or a welder's arc) we can also observe light in as small of an increment as a candle flame or match strike from over 10 to 15 miles away. Additionally, we can perceive relatively small variations in intensity as we look across our field of vision. This extreme range of sensitivity is characteristic of the human eye and can not be found in equipment such as cameras or other optical sensors. A camera is usually not as susceptible to these variations and will only recognize the broader extremes of illumination levels within a given camera frame. When we work with cameras, we often refer to their **contrast ratio,** which refers to the range of intensities that exist between the brightest and darkest elements of a camera's view. The reason many of us shoot so many "bad" photographs when we take snapshots is due most commonly to the limited sensitivity and contrast ratios of the film and/or cameras that are characteristic of these home devices. Fortunately, technology continues to improve and produce cameras that are ever more sensitive to light and a wider range of contrast ratios. The personal digital-video camera that I currently own probably has better light sensitivity than many of the commercial cameras of just a few years ago.

Relative Intensity

In many cases, what is more important to a theatrical lighting designer is the perceived rather than the actual or absolute brightness of an object or light source. We have also learned that simply adding more light to an environment doesn't always produce better visibility. An object's perceived brightness is a function of several items . . . not just the amount of light focused onto it. Other factors include the distances between the source, object, and viewer; the reflectivity of the object; and the sensitivity of the optical device (eye or camera). In the early days of television and film lighting, the cameras weren't nearly as sensitive as they currently are, and directors of photography were much more concerned with creating minimum intensity thresholds so that the cameras could simply process the information necessary to create an image. The film speeds (ASA, American Standard Association) that you select on a single-lens reflex camera simply help you adjust the camera's light sensitivity to a given film. If you set the ASA setting incorrectly you will end up with photographs that are either over- or under-exposed. Even though cameras are vastly improved, it is still quite common for designers working in the video and film industries to use a light meter to ensure both even and minimal intensity levels for a shoot.

As a whole, we consider the brightness of a subject compared with that of both the surrounding environment and other objects—the relative intensities of these objects. What is important is that an object often receives focus if it is lit more brightly than the objects that surround it. On the other hand, our attention might also be drawn to the darkest part of a stage—like the upstage entrance tunnel of a cave in a production of *Swiss Family Robinson*. In both cases, the eye goes to the most different element of the scene and the relative intensities of the objects play a more significant role in determining the focus than the actual intensities. We also refer to **brightness perception** when we consider all of the variables that result in determining the overall brightness of a particular subject. The amount of light falling on the object, our optical sensitivity, and the degree of reflectivity are all factors in determining the perceived intensity of an object.

Psychological Responses

Finally, there is the element of psychological response to the intensity of light. Most importantly, this plays a role in the determination of the mood of the occupants in a lit environment. As a whole, well-lighted environments produce an emotional response in the occupants that is positive and healthy. Poorly lit rooms and corridors can produce gloomy environments which tend to have a negative impact on the inhabitants' moods. Studies have also indicated an actual association between the mood of people and the hours of sun exposure that they receive in a typical day. A condition known as **Seasonal Affective Disorder (SAD)** affects people during the winter who live in high latitudes where they aren't exposed to enough sunlight in a typical day. Elevated brightness has been associated with increases in an individual's heart and respiration rates, while studies have also shown that increased productivity and more friendly work environments have been created through modifications in the lighting intensities of a workplace. Finally, psychiatric hospitals and social service clinics make use of intensity to alter the behavior of their patients.

INTENSITY RELATED ISSUES

Some of the most common design problems in lighting design can be related to intensity issues. First, everyone's visual system is slightly different and people will often have varying responses to a given design. Some individuals are light sensitive while others may struggle with issues of depth perception. Some may have good night adaptation while others may have issues related to color blindness. Even with people who have what we would consider to be normal vision we often find large variations in the individual responses that people will have to the same visual stimuli. Due to this, we typically design for the individuals that will require the most stringent visual requirements. For example, our eyes degenerate over time, and our vision generally becomes more impaired as we get older; therefore, we should design the lighting for the oldest occupants who will be seeing a play or making use of a given room. Older patrons struggle more with dimly lit scenes than people in their twenties and thirties. Likewise, we also design lighting based on the most critical task to be performed in a room or building. An operating room requires brighter lighting than a stairway in an apartment building. In following this practice, we can fulfill the lighting needs for all the people using an environment since most individuals will be comfortable with the minimum intensity levels set by the most demanding needs of the occupants or tasks.

While individual reactions may be responsible for much of how we both respond and perceive light, there are many other factors that can also have a significant impact on our visibility and how we sense light. Many of these relate specifically to how our eyes function and compensate for varying conditions created within an environment. Some of these observations may be due to the physical properties of our visual systems, while others are related primarily to psychological responses to the brightness of a given object or environment. Many of these effects can have a negative impact on a visual experience and a designer must be both aware of and sensitive to these effects in order to produce the most effective designs for a client or production. Several visual effects that are specifically related to the intensity of a given light include: mood associations, afterimages, glare, color shifts, fatigue, and adaptation.

Mood Alteration

Intensity is a primary determinant in helping a lighting designer create mood. The contrasts that you observe in the brightness levels found in many buildings quickly demonstrate the association that intensity plays upon mood. Bright offices create productive atmospheres, while funeral homes are lit in soft warm tones in order to create a somber reflective mood. A fast food restaurant will be lit in a way that produces a less inviting environment than a formal sit-down restaurant. Low lighting levels can create mysterious foreboding moods while brightly lit scenes are associated with celebratory or comic moods. On stage, we have traditionally used higher intensities for comic plays, while tragedies have characteristically been lit with low intensities and shadows. As a comparison, think back to the lighting levels found in the recent *Batman* and *Pirates of the Caribbean* films. Each can be associated with a very different overall mood and lighting—even though both films had both comic and scary moments. The lighting and moods of the *Batman* films were generally darker and more sinister then those found in *Pirates of the Caribbean* films. On the other hand, the intensity of the lighting for each of these is very different than that for a much more upbeat film like *Caddyshack*. Mood is very dependent upon the intensity of the light that illuminates a given environment. As a reminder, intensity may also be used to draw focus to specific elements within a project or stage picture. Light can creep up on locations where the action will be shifting to, while brightness can also be used to draw customers to more interesting displays in a department store. In each case, brightness is used to not only create a mood, but to also draw focus for the designer.

Overstimulation

A common occurrence in theatrical design relates to over-stimulating various combinations of rods or cones within the eye. This may happen through exposing the eye to disproportionally high levels of light in a given color range or through simply leaving the environment unchanged for extended periods of time. In these cases, upon the removal of the stimulus or light, the eye is tricked and continues to provide sensory information that gives an appearance that the environment remains unchanged. We refer to these illusions as **afterimages.** An example of this phenomenon is the old trick of looking onto a neutral surface after staring at a colored box or single dot for a given amount of time. Once your view is shifted to the neutral surface, an afterimage of the box or dot is commonly observed to be floating on the neutral background. A variation of this effect may happen on stage during blackouts where a brightly lit scene is suddenly plunged into darkness. In most cases, a momentary glow or afterimage of the scene can be perceived several seconds into the blackout by many audience members.

Glare

Glare refers to the presence of distracting light within a viewer's field of vision. This may come about through a number of ways. The first is nothing more than the result of seeing an unusually high level of reflectance off of an object. The sometimes painful experience that you might have while looking at white beach sand or newly fallen snow on a bright sunny afternoon form examples of this type of glare. Another type of glare occurs when an observer is forced to look directly into a light source. Common examples of this include the oncoming headlights of an approaching car at night, or when a person might look directly into a spotlight or the sun. How often have you struggled with the glare of the sun while driving due west around sunset? As a rule, the farther that the source of glare is located from the subject, the less effect or distraction that it will present to the overall scene. As designers we usually try to avoid glare and choose lighting angles that place our light sources either out of the observer's view or within the peripheral vision of the observer. In theatrical lighting, a designer must be especially mindful of glare when working in thrust and arena theatres where audience members could easily look directly into the lenses of lighting fixtures that light the opposite side of the stage. On the other hand, there are times when glare may be considered a positive element of a scene. We often refer to this positive element of glare as **sparkle** or **glitter.** In the case of architectural lighting we may occasionally want to create a limited amount of glare simply to add visual interest and perhaps some focus to a scene or project. An example would be the lamps and crystals that form a chandelier. In this case, the chandelier may or may not be the primary light source of a room, but it certainly takes on a primary focus simply through the glitter that occurs from the reflections of its lamps and crystals.

Color Perception

The color of an object may be perceived as being different if viewed under light sources of different intensities and colors. Colors will generally appear more saturated if viewed under light of a lower intensity. Under increased levels of illumination red-colored objects tend to have colors that shift towards the shorter yellow wavelengths, while violet colored objects shift toward the blue wavelengths. Conversely, under lower intensities red objects will appear more red while violet objects will appear even more violet. Colors found near the center of the spectrum are less affected than those at the extreme ends of the spectrum. We also lose our ability to differentiate colors as the intensity of the light is lowered. When we see a wide variety of individual wavelengths of light as a full spectrum, we perceive the combination as white light . . . a condition that we see as normal. One of the most interesting concepts of color perception lies in the wide range of deviation in what our mind will accept as white light. In exterior settings white light tends to take on a cooler quality that has an overall blue tint, while interior light sources are most commonly associated with lamps that produce an overall warm amber-like tint. In each case, we still accept the associated light as being white. What I have discussed to this point has been limited to the effects of brightness on color. There are a number of additional effects related to color and perception that are due to the actual color of the light itself. These are expanded upon in Chapter 3.

Adaptation

While we may be able to see an immense range of brightnesses, the eye quickly narrows its response to a limited range of brightness perception. We refer to this as **adaptation.** Adaptation allows the eye to become more efficient and sensitive within a relatively narrow range of brightness. The eye tends to accept this as a normal brightness and at the same time tends to ignore anything with brightness levels that lie outside of this range. Unfortunately, being stimulated by the same intensity of light over a longer period of time can also have negative impacts on your vision. One of the most commonly experienced problems is **visual fatigue.** In this case, a viewer is subjected to an unchanging visual environment, and their eyes grow tired through the overuse of some of the optical sensors. Due to this, the viewer might experience effects like eyestrain, headaches, and blurriness that negatively impact his or her vision. We commonly correct for this while reading or doing detailed paperwork through simply glancing across the room and away from our work for a minute or so once we feel the effects of fatigue setting in. A common practice used in theatre to avoid this condition simply involves creating subtle shifts in the lighting over an extended period of time. Care must be taken when a dark scene follows a bright scene to ensure that the dark scene doesn't appear excessively dark. The effects of maintaining a bright scene generally require that the brightness be continually raised in order that the perceived brightness appears unchanged throughout the scene. Many times, the most effective lighting of bright scenes will occur immediately following dark scenes during which an audience's eyes have undergone adaptation based on the lower intensity of the dark scene. It takes much less light to give the appearance or perception of a brightly lit scene in these cases. Another effect of adaptation is often experienced when walking into a darkened room after returning from the outside during a bright, sunny day. In this case, most people find it nearly impossible to see anything until after their eyes have grown accustomed to the dark. The opposite effect commonly occurs as people get up in the middle of the night and turn on the lights in order to make their way to the bathroom or kitchen. In both cases, the experience not only limits one's vision but may also bring painful sensations to your eyes.

DEFINING FORM AND SHAPE

Light is the primary medium through which we can determine the form and shape of objects. It also helps us to determine the relative positions of objects from one to another. While we could use our sense of touch to feel our way around a collection of objects, it is much quicker to observe them and the surrounding environment through our sense of sight. As light strikes a surface it is reflected back toward the viewer, where it stimulates the eyes and creates a series of impulses that can then be interpreted by the mind. These visual clues not only allow us to identify an object but also allow us to judge spatial relationships between objects based on our prior experiences and memory. Light travels only in straight paths and can therefore have its direction easily determined through careful study of the shadows and highlights that it produces on objects. We see those areas where light strikes the surface as **highlights,** while those that are not lit are seen as shadow areas. In many ways, **shadows** are simply the absence of light, while highlights are restricted to those surfaces directly in the path of the light. We use highlights and shadows to help distinguish depth and form within objects. In a complete void, where there is no chance of scattered reflections, a single light source will produce characteristic highlights and shadows that allow us to determine an object's directional relationship with the light source. We often take these relationships between highlights and shadows for granted and have learned to analyze this information moment by moment based on our daily experiences. In order to demonstrate this principle you only need to play a flashlight on an object from a variety of positions to observe the changing relationships between the shadows and highlights and how these are readily linked to the angle from which the light is coming and the viewing angle of the observer. For instance, a basketball will appear as a circle or disk, not a sphere, if viewed from straight on and lit by light that strikes directly from a frontal orientation. This image will change considerably as the light is moved around the ball.

We must also consider the relationship of the viewer to the object or subject as well as the correlation that exists between the positions of the object and light source. One of the most obvious day-to-day illustrations of this phenomenon in the natural world is in the observation of the phases of the moon. In this case, at different times of the month we observe more or less of the reflected highlights and shadows of the moon's surface. At full moon, the sun is behind the earth and we observe an image of the moon that looks like a full circle because all of the surfaces that we see are exposed to the sun's light. However, at either quarter-moon phase, we see only half the moon's exposed surface (actually only a quarter of the total surface) because the earth is oriented in such a manner that we observe half of the moon in highlight while the other half is left in shadow—despite the fact that the sun still fully illuminates the same amount of the moon's surface. In most cases, things aren't as simple as in the moon phases example, and having a single light source is more often the exception than the rule. In addition to being under the influences of several light sources, there are additional impacts such as reflections that will further complicate the lighting of an environment.

FIGURE 2.1 Flat Front Light

The relative angle between an object and a light source can be used by a designer to either enhance or diminish the three-dimensional qualities of an object. Most designers relate this principle to the controllable quality of distribution. In fact, angle becomes a major determinant in how we perceive the form of an object. Figures 2.1–2.7 provide illustrations of how light plays on a subject from a variety of angles that are common to theatrical lighting. Light from the front tends to flatten a subject. This is due to the fact that from a **flat angle** (relatively straight-on) the entire surface appears to be equally well lit and there isn't a distinction or contrast between the shadow and highlight areas. This results in the object appearing mostly two- rather than three-dimensional. As the direction of the light rotates to the sides and back, the viewer will see a more modeled three-dimensional quality that designers commonly call **revealing form.** What has happened is that the light now reveals those surfaces and shadows that the eye uses to define depth. The effects of several principle lighting angles are summarized in the following paragraphs.

Front Light

Front light is popular because it reveals details of a subject. Most designers associate front light with visibility. It is utilized for tasks such as lighting an actor's face, making the lettering of a large piece of signage readable, or simply providing enough illumination for people to clearly see the walls and background of a setting. Front light is an overall naturalistic angle but can be distorted through either raising the angle until it becomes so steep that unnatural shadows form in areas like the eye sockets or lowering it to the point that it produces unnatural highlights from underneath the subject. As stated earlier, a significantly flat front light angle can cause a subject to appear two-dimensional.

Light from a **front diagonal** is considered to be one of the most naturalistic angles that a lighting designer can use. The reason for our attraction to this angle isn't so much in when a light is used as a single light source as in when it is combined with a second light. One of the most familiar lighting combinations places two different lights on opposing 45° diagonals so that the two fixtures mirror one another. Through this, the front of the subject is under a significant influence of two lights—producing one zone on the subject that is lit with an equal mixture of light from both sources while also creating two additional areas that are lit predominantly under the influence of one light or the other.

FIGURE 2.2 Low Front Light (Uplight)   **FIGURE 2.3** Front Diagonal (Approximately 45°)

FIGURE 2.4 Sidelight

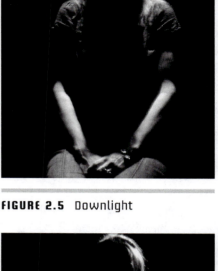

FIGURE 2.5 Downlight

FIGURE 2.6 Backlight

FIGURE 2.7 Back Diagonal Light

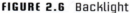

The front diagonal provides a good combination between the visibility desired by a front light and the modeling capabilities of a sidelight.

Sidelight

Sidelight may come from either side of the subject and helps to reveal the depth and form of an object. It can take on qualities that may appear either dramatic or naturalistic depending on how it might be colored or mixed with other combinations of light. Sidelight may also come from a variety of vertical angles. The steeper-angled high side is generally more naturalistic than light shining on a subject as a direct sidelight. An even further dramatic quality can be achieved through using low sidelight that may even be angle upward. In this case, the light reveals areas such as the undersides of a subject that would normally fall into shadow.

Downlight and Backlight

Several additional lighting angles are important because of their ability to bring drama to a setting as well as to create still other influences on the appearance of a subject. The

SIDEBAR 2.1 DESIGNER PROFILE

Marilyn Lowey

Marilyn Lowey's lighting specialties tend to be along the lines of spectacle performances and productions. However, her experience and impressive list of credits span a considerable breadth of the lighting industry. Areas that she frequently designs within include concerts, arena spectacles, ice shows, large revue shows and stadium projects, and theme park shows. She holds a BFA from Emerson College and an MFA from Carnegie Mellon University. She is the recipient of an Emmy Award as well as other awards and nominations for lighting projects that she has designed. Several notable concert credits include designing for Neil Diamond, Diana Ross, Liza Minnelli, Harry Connick, Jr., Whitney Houston, and Stevie Wonder. Her lighting of spectacle events and live theme park productions include: *Siegfried and Roy*, *Champions on Ice*, *Disney on Ice*, and a number of shows for Universal Studios at Orlando and LA (*Phantom of the Opera*, *Beetlejuice Rockin' Graveyard Revue*, *Universal Studio's Islands of Adventure Lost Continent Attractions*, *Star Trek—The Adventure*, and *The Flintstones Live*. Television credits include lighting specials for many of the above artists plus special events like the *Disney Hall Opening Gala*, *The Opening Ceremonies of the World Cup Cricket Games*, *Olympic & World Figure Skating*, *Nickelodeon Kids' Choice Awards* and the *MTV: New Year's Eve Show*. Her industrial clients include: Nissan, Sony, Anheuser-Busch, Buick, Calvin Klein, and both Epson and Apple Computers. Finally, she has also compiled a list of impressive architectural lighting credits, including: The Mandalay Bay Theatre and Arena (Las Vegas), The Bellagio Hotel Lobby Lounge, Golden Nugget Showroom, IBM Facilities, Disneyland Hotel, Lloyds Art Gallery, and several private residences.

Marilyn received solid training in her formal education but made it a point to also learn from other experiences as well. "I always worked every summer from my senior year in high school through grad school in summer stock . . . beginning as an apprentice and climbing up the ladder to the role of lighting designer." While at college, she also worked at a lighting shop in order to understand how gear was rented and what equipment was available outside of college. She came to work on the projects that she now designs through taking the opportunity to light as many different types of projects as she could. "I went after every project that I heard about and began lighting everything. After a period of time, I developed clients and continued working in the many avenues in which lighting was needed." By working in so many different areas she has also found that her work tends to remain more stable. "It's difficult to say what amount of my work comes from particular areas. What happens is that each discipline has its peak period while others are in slower times. Recessions hit the disciplines at different times and the work at any given time is reflected in that way." When discussing the differences between lighting for different types of projects, she first states that, "Lighting for me is learning how to see. Once I realized how to see, I could light any discipline easily . . . it's the givens and parameters that will change between the disciplines."

Her movement into lighting outside of theatrical design came through her employment by Imero Fiorentino Associates (IFA) in New York City. It was through this association that she was introduced to different aspects of the entertainment industry and where she received her initial break. Stig Edgren, a lighting designer at IFA during that time, had an abundance of work and gave her several projects, which began her career in this part of the entertainment industry. "One of the more significant differences between working in these areas of lighting is that there is more money for equipment . . . and the more expensive gear at that." On the other hand, she also speaks of the importance of working with other people in this part of the business and states, "The lighting is easy—the people will kill you!" On the other hand, "I love lighting all the areas of design that I presently work in. I felt that theatre was too slow for me and a bit self-indulgent for me at that period of my life. I was also more interested in the larger-scale work." On the downside, she hates having to work all the nights that this type of lighting often requires.

She closes by sharing, "The lighting business has changed since I selected it as my career and is now flooded with potential designers where everyone thinks that they can light a show. This in some ways has caused the quality of the lighting in some areas of the industry to be lower than we might like." Equipment is changing at an ever-increasing pace and she likes to talk to shops and manufacturers to learn what is new. She also receives calls from vendors about using new equipment as it becomes available for beta testing and will sometimes work this gear into the productions that she is working on. When asked what she considers to be the most essential principle of lighting for these events she shares that, "Art takes time no matter what discipline of lighting you are working within. Despite this, you had better be both fast and good in this type of work. Go the distance and do whatever it takes to make it perfect for yourself and the client."

Photo credit: Todd Kaplan

downlight creates one of the most dramatic angles available for lighting a subject. The dramatic quality is primarily due to the excessive shadows that are created from the overhead light source. Flashes of highlight on the very top of the subject are also characteristic of this angle. While it creates a strong sense of dimension or modeling, it also tends to produce shadows that aren't very naturalistic. A viewer will typically see the eye sockets of a subject develop into deep shadows (raccoon eyes) under strong downlights. A certain harshness or distortion is often characteristic of this lighting angle. Downlight may also give the perception of a shortening or squashing appearance in a subject. **Backlight** comes from behind the subject and can create a silhouette. It can also produce a rimming effect around the subject through casting an outline of highlight around its edges. It may also produce a halo-like appearance and has been known to cause performers' hair to glow. A look at concert videos where performers have afro-style hair treatments (popular in the 1970s) will clearly illustrate this effect. Backlight also has the ability to help separate a subject from its background and can seemingly push the subject forward towards the viewer. A **back diagonal** source simply forms an angle that is a combination of the back and sidelight angles.

Key and Fill

In practice, most objects are typically under the influence of several light sources—each with varying intensities and qualities that may make it more difficult to identify the specific source of each light. The fewer the number of light sources, the more stark the associated lighting will appear. From our perspective, we almost always see light sources coming from above. The sun is generally high in the sky, most rooms are lit from ceiling fixtures, and even the sky itself becomes a source of illumination through the effects of atmospheric scattering and diffusion. Because of this, we tend to view lighting from above as a natural condition. Light that isn't consistent with this is often thought to be more dramatic or may be directly linked to a low elevation light source like a fireplace, candle, or table lamp.

In a performance situation we usually prefer that stray light, or **spill,** be quickly absorbed once it passes beyond a subject. In theatre, we color most of our masking fabrics, walls, and floors black to absorb and prevent reflections of excess light. However, in architectural lighting, direct beams of light are often too harsh, and designers prefer to make reflections a major component of many designs. We usually refer to the light that is primarily responsible for lighting a scene as the **key light.** Many times this is in the form of a single source. In theatres, there is usually little ambient light, due to all the non-reflective surfaces, and a single key light often produces extreme contrasts between the highlight and shadow areas of a subject. On the other hand, a subject may also be under the influence of light as a result of diffusion or scattered reflections that add light to the areas of a subject that would normally be shadowed. We refer to this light as **fill light,** and it can be thought of as the ambient light that exists within an environment. Fill light is typically diffuse and often cannot be readily associated with a directional angle; it is simply present. In video and film design, fill light specifically relates to the light that is provided through additional fixtures, which softens the shadows and "fills in" those areas of a subject that would otherwise be cast into dark shadow. Figure 2.8 illustrates the effect of a combination of key and fill light on a subject.

FIGURE 2.8 Combination of Lighting Angles On a Subject Two opposing front diagonals (approximately 45° to each side and vertical)

FIGURE 2.9 Silhouette Lighting A tree silhouetted against a fence

Silhouettes and Grazing

Primarily in architectural applications, but also in most other areas of lighting design, we may also describe two other forms of light that relate to the direction in which they illuminate an object. The first, **silhouette lighting** (Figure 2.9), relates not to lighting the object itself but to lighting the background behind an object. Under this type of lighting the object is seen as a dark outline or silhouette against its background. The second, **grazing** (Figure 2.10), occurs when a light is played on a surface of an object at an extreme angle. This angle is commonly used to enrich or enhance the textures of a surface. Ceiling lights that are mounted relatively close to a wall can enhance the shadows formed by the downward direction of the light and make the unevenness of the rocks and cracks or mortar in a masonry wall much more interesting. Grazing techniques are a common practice for lighting building facades, where a designer wants to initiate interest in a section of wall. These techniques are also used in entertainment lighting.

FIGURE 2.10 Grazing Lighting The same stone wall lit from straight-on at left (a) and a grazing light at right (b)

Shape

Light may also have shape. This can best be described as the area or volume to which the light is confined or projected. In a spotlight, the shape of the light is generally in the form of a cone. The apex forms at the **luminaire,** while the light spreads outward away from it in a conical volume. A performer within a single spotlight forms an example of this type of illustration. Other styles of fixtures produce light in other shapes or distribution patterns. If the light from a spotlight is cast directly onto a wall you will observe a circle if the angle is dead on . . . but the shape becomes an ellipse if the angle is skewed. Light can be shaped to a rectangle as it enters a room through a doorway or window. This might be skewed if the position of the light is to the side or above the opening. Light may also be defined through a combination of several different fixtures that together define a particular shape in light. An example of this would be a roadway that is composed of hundreds of light fixtures, which together produce a path of illumination along an interstate or highway.

While what I have written of up to this point only relates to the overall shape of a light source, there can also be shape within the light. In the case of light passing through the slats of a louver door or Venetian blind, the resultant shape will be altered into slivers of light. An outdoor location will typically have textured light as a result of light passing through overhead trees and branches. A popular technique for initiating texture and pattern into a light is through using **gobos.** Gobos are simple patterns etched into pieces of metal or glass that are inserted into lighting fixtures to create shadow projections. Gobos may also be called **patterns, templates,** and **cookies.** While a single gobo might be used to project the image of a window with all its decorative mullions, a group of a half-dozen units with leaf-breakup patterns can be used to create a tree canopy over an entire stage. Gobos may be custom manufactured or purchased from catalogs that contain hundreds, even thousands of pre-designed patterns. Figure 2.11 illustrates the effect of a breakup gobo on a subject and the surrounding floor.

FIGURE 2.11 Light Shaped By Gobos

COMPOSITION

Since light is the primary means by which we sense an environment, it is through its revelation of composition that we can comprehend a space. Without light, our perception of an environment would be severely impaired. Whether lighting a stage, exhibit hall, or office, the entire environment is seen as a total composition. The architectural or scenic units, people and their clothing, as well as the furniture and building materials are all elements that must be revealed through the lighting. Light provides us with a means of indicating depth, modifying the colors and textures of the other elements, revealing form, and indicating areas of focus or interest within the composition of a stage or room. Elements that are more important will usually be treated through higher light intensities, while the degree of overall visibility can be established through setting threshold levels that illuminate the environment as a whole. At any given time, there will always be a complete composition for an environment, and much of the way that it is revealed to us is through the simple task of illumination.

While many environments incorporate a relatively constant lighting treatment, entertainment lighting generally makes use of ever-changing compositions and a very dynamic lighting style. Unlike a painting, which has a static composition, the stage is constantly evolving into new compositions. Where is the focus at this particular moment? How bright does the room absolutely have to be? Is there an area we wish to take an audience's attention away from? Can a certain color be enhanced at a particular time? All of these questions relate to how the composition and lighting might change from one moment to another. The idea of creating dynamic lighting was for many years limited to the entertainment field, but today architects and illuminating engineers also recognize the need for creating dynamic environments for their clients. Although generally subtle in comparison to theatrical venues . . . the lighting of buildings, trade shows, and exhibits can also employ active lighting elements for many projects.

MOVEMENT AND LIGHT

Movement relates to changes within the light and composition from moment to moment. As stated in Chapter 1, this may present itself in one of three manners. First, a light source might move in full view of the observer . . . as in the case of a lantern being carried around in the dark. Another variation of this type of movement comes from seeing a sequence of lights turned on and off in order to produce particular patterns. The most obvious form of this comes from lights associated with **chase** or **ropelights** and marquees. Other familiar examples are found in sales displays and restaurant or casino signage. The flashing beacons of emergency and maintenance vehicles also rely heavily on this principle. A second form of movement involves observations of the movement of the light without seeing the light source itself move. A followspot located at the rear of an auditorium forms an example of this type of movement. Another example of this type of movement is illustrated through the use of progressive specials that light the path of a moving actor. Finally, the most common form of lighting movement simply relates to changes taking place in the lighting over time. The changes might be so subtle that the observer isn't fully aware of them, which in some cases might only appear to operate on a subconscious level. Sunset sequences often display this type of subtlety. Other examples might include foreshadowing by slowly creeping the lights up around an actor for a monologue or slowly building the intensities of a scene to alter the mood for an impending sequence or action. In other cases, such as flipping a light switch to the on position, the movement might appear to be nearly instantaneous. While there are occasions where the lighting for an environment may be static, most of us consider the lighting transitions themselves to be just as important as the actual images or cues that a designer may have created.

Cues and Transitions

While there are applications in which light will remain static over a period of time, this is generally the exception rather than the rule in entertainment lighting. Static lighting is for the most part limited to architectural and display applications, although even these may incorporate dynamic properties for the design of a particular project. In most entertainment venues, lighting is expected to take on a dynamic role and the changes add to the drama and theatricality of an event. In entertainment lighting we refer to the individual moments as **cues.** A cue simply reflects a snapshot that forms a record of a specific combination of lighting and compositional qualities of an environment at a given time. You may also hear designers referring to cues as moments, states, or looks. In reality, the lights in a typical lighting design for most performance events are undergoing some form of change or transition throughout much of a performance.

The timing that occurs as one cue changes into another becomes a major component of a successful lighting design. These are called **transitions.** If done poorly, this can create potential distractions in a performance. Yet, if done well, they play a major factor in enhancing the effectiveness of an actor as they proceed toward the climax of a given scene. Cue timing is generally measured in seconds and is often referred to as a **count.** A five-count cue would take place over 5 seconds. With the computers that we now use for lighting control we can create subtle effects that may take minutes or even hours to complete. At the same time, we can create other sequences so complex that an observer may have to see the sequence run a number of times to fully comprehend the extent of a cue. Today's light boards are also capable of completing a number of operations simultaneously while giving separate timings to each of the components of a cueing sequence. In fact, it is quite common to have lights fading down at one rate while other lights fade up at a different rate. It's also possible to draw the focus to one performer, lower the lights around the rest of the set, and maintain a sunset sequence that all run on a series of completely different time intervals. Even with all this, you can run even more overlapping cues if you think that it might be necessary.

Lastly, you can cause an implied or perceived motion in objects simply through applying changes in other variables, such as the angle from which different lights strike an object. By switching back and forth between a front and backlight, an object will be perceived to swing forward and backward. The same object can be made to look as if it is swinging side to side if you alternate between lights that are oriented directly to the sides of the object. It can also appear to rise and sink if lit alternately between an up light and down light. In sidelighting, we can use light to seemingly either push or draw the performers across a stage. Ballet and other forms of dance lighting make common use of this phenomenon. What's important through all of this is that all of these effects are the result of our perception being led by the visual clues that are being provided by the lighting.

FOR FURTHER READING

Illuminating Engineering Society of North America, *IESNA Lighting Education 100 (Fundamental Level)* (New York: Illuminating Engineering Society of North America, 1993).

Illuminating Engineering Society of North America, *IESNA Lighting Education 150 (Intermediate Level)* (New York: Illuminating Engineering Society of North America, 1993).

Illuminating Engineering Society of North America, *IESNA Lighting Handbook*, 9th ed., ed. Mark Rae, (New York: Illuminating Engineering Society of North America, 2000).

Illuminating Engineering Society of North America, *IESNA Lighting Ready Reference*, 4th ed. (New York: Illuminating Engineering Society of North America, 2003).

Palmer, Richard H., *The Lighting Art: The Aesthetics of Stage Lighting Design*, 2nd ed. (Englewood Cliffs, NJ: Prentice-Hall, Inc., 1994).

Color and Its Effects 3

O f all the controllable qualities of light, color produces one of the greatest impacts on how we see an object and the surrounding environment. In fact, many say that color is the most difficult element for a young designer to control in a lighting design. Some of the reasons for this profound impact come from the fact that color has both physiological and psychological effects on how we view a scene or object. It has the ability to completely alter the observed color of a subject, change the perceived distance of objects, and can even cause objects to blend in or pop out from their backgrounds. More importantly, the color of light has been associated with the ability to affect our heart and breathing rates, influence our productivity, and to alter our moods. With light and color having such an impact on how we view the world, I have chosen to dedicate a whole chapter to color and its effects. The first portion of the chapter provides essential color theory, while later elements of the chapter address specific design considerations, techniques, and equipment that a designer may use to manipulate color.

WHAT IS COLOR?

Color is a perception. It simply refers to how we see an object and how we have come to associate specific visual responses with the naming of given colors. Color is therefore dependent on memory associations. As children our parents taught us what was red, blue, or any other color, and we have learned that these basic color names can be associated with a given visual response. We simply refer to these color names as **hues**—the generic description or name for a given color. As long as we aren't color blind these hues become a familiar way of communicating color information from one person to another. Basic hues such as red, orange, or purple are easily understood, while hues like fuchsia, ultramarine, or sepia may be harder to understand for people who are less familiar with describing hues. On the other hand, a color like sandy rose will most likely cause a problem in color understanding no matter who is discussing this particular hue.

In practice, the color that we actually see is a function of three factors, and a change in any one of these will result in our perceiving a different color. These factors are: the color of the light itself, the ability of the optical sensor such as an eye or camera to distinguish between different colors, and the color of the objects being observed. Each of these effects are described more specifically throughout this chapter, but for now, here is one familiar example that illustrates the effect of changing just one of these elements. I'm sure that you have worn a white T-shirt while you have either ridden an amusement-park ride or attended a club where there were a variety of different colored lights. It should come as no surprise that as you walked under the different colored lights you saw your shirt change to whatever color the light was at any given time. This is a basic example of the color of the light changing your perception of the color of the shirt. In reality, the shirt never changed color, just your perception of it. While this forms a drastically simple example of how colored light can alter the appearance of an object, the effect is always present, and we are constantly seeing less obvious shifts in an object's color due to the constant lighting changes that exist in our world.

THE VISIBLE SPECTRUM

In further examination of the electromagnetic spectrum that we discussed in Chapter 1, we are now going to consider only the narrow band of wavelengths that can be sensed or experienced by the photoreceptors in our eyes. This very narrow portion of the electromagnetic spectrum is known as the **visible spectrum** and simply forms a range of wavelengths to which our eyes are sensitive (Figure 1.2 in Chapter 1). Within the visible spectrum, the wavelengths can be further differentiated through the varying color responses that they elicit from our eyes. Most light sources like the sun or a lamp contain elements of all the individual wavelengths of the visible spectrum, with the combined result producing an overall color that is perceived as white light. In reality, this white light is actually a mixture of all the other colors or wavelengths. The visible spectrum can be observed through a prism that through refraction breaks a light source into its component wavelengths. The familiar rainbow of red, orange, yellow, green, blue, and violet is the product of each hue being separated from the others as an effect of their ever-decreasing wavelengths. Red is associated with the longest wavelengths while violet is associated with the shortest wavelengths.

As illustrated earlier, hue may not give enough information for communicating a color from one person to another. While I may describe the color of an object as red, what distinguishes the red of an apple from the red of an old book cover? The red of a rose verse the "rosy" red cheeks of cold? All of these carry a degree of vagueness in their descriptions and may mean different things from one person to another. Because of this, we have additional ways of describing color. **Saturation** relates to the purity of a color. The more saturated the color, the more specific and limited the range of wavelengths associated with it. A saturated color cannot have a diverse range of wavelengths—instead, saturated colors contain a very limited range of wavelengths of light. Saturation may also be referred to as **chroma.** We often describe the opposite effect of saturation as a **tint.** In tints, a color is combined with either white light or a mixture of other wavelengths to produce a softer, less saturated variation of the hue—a greater variety of wavelengths are present in the light. We also describe color through referencing its overall lightness or darkness based on a gray scale ranging from black to white. We describe this component of color as **value.**

Primary Colors

The eye contains a collection of photoreceptors called **cones** and **rods.** While the rods aid the eye in night vision, the cones provide the color reception for an individual. You can refer back to Chapter 1 if you wish to review the physical properties of the eye. The cones are separated into three specific types, each one sensitive to a different range of color frequencies or wavelengths of light—red, blue, and green. The cones simply detect and respond to varying levels of each of these three colors of light and help us sense and create an understanding from a given stimulus of light. These colors have become known as the **primary colors** of light because they are used in various combinations to produce every other color. A close examination of your computer monitor or television screen will also illustrate a composite use of these primaries to produce colored lighting effects.

CIE Chromaticity Chart

The relationships between the many varied colors of light can be related to one another through a chart called a **CIE Chromaticity Chart** (Figure 3.1). While this chart derives from illustrating the wavelengths of color radiation given off by various temperature

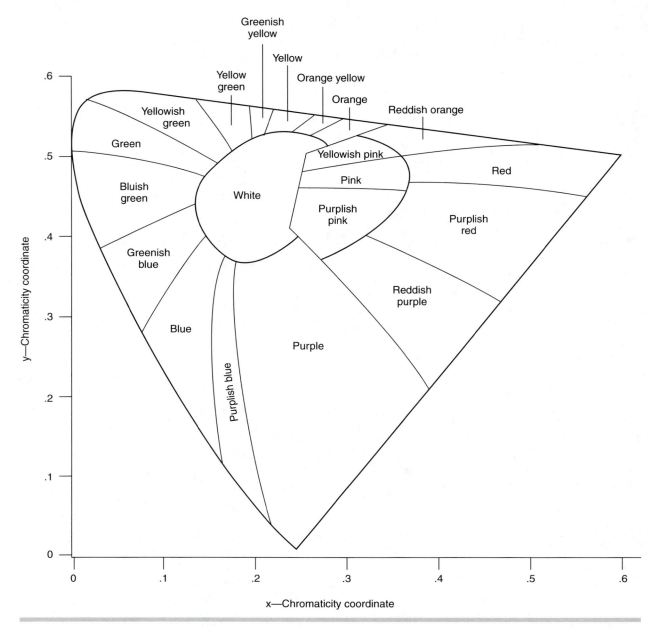

FIGURE 3.1 **CIE Chromaticity Chart** The most saturated hues are located along the outer edges of the diagram, with the primary colors (red, blue, and green) falling at the corners and the secondary colors (magenta, cyan, and amber) at approximately the midpoints between these. White light is found at the center with tints found between the white and the basic hue of the tint. *Credit:* Figure based on a variation of the 1976 C.I.E. Chromaticity Diagram by Photo Research, Inc.

levels of a black body radiation, the importance to us as lighting designers lies in its depiction of the relationships that exist between each of the three primary colors of light. Through using this chart, a fairly accurate prediction can be determined for a resultant color made by mixing various combinations of different colored lights. The resultant color of any combination of light sources can be predicted through locating the point that lies within the center of all the plotted positions for each of the individual colored sources. If only two sources are represented, the resultant color will lie at the midpoint of a line drawn between the points representing the two colors. If three sources are indicated, the resultant color will be found at the middle of the field of a triangle that is created by connecting the points that represent the three colors. Points associated with colors that fall towards the outside extremes of the chart are associated with colors that have higher saturations and can be seen as more pure, while colors plotted near the center of the chart are indicative of tints and white light that contain a wider selection of individual colors or wavelengths. Colors falling between the primary colors will be shifted more or less toward one of the two primaries, such as red-orange or red-violet, or could fall equally between the primaries, representing a given **secondary color** of the two initial colors.

As described earlier, white light is a combination of many different wavelengths of light. We are typically under the influence of light created by the sun, which we see as normal light. In reality, even though we perceive the light of the sun to be white, it is actually changing color throughout the day. In the early mornings the sun tends to have a yellow tint, at midday we often associate an overall cool or bluish color to the sunlight, and as sunset approaches, the color once again shifts toward more saturated hues of yellow, red, and orange. The light associated with the sun may also be influenced by the time of year and physical location of the observer. Regardless, we all tend to register each of these conditions as white light.

Color Temperature

Since sunlight is constantly undergoing color shifts, we need a way to describe the associated color that we perceive as white light. This is done through a referencing technique that we call **color temperature.** Color temperature compares the sum of all the individual wavelengths of a given light source with the color emitted from a black body radiation of a given temperature (measured in degrees Kelvin). All materials emit radiation or glow when heated, and as the temperature rises, the material glows from red to yellow, yellow to white, white to blue, etc. In this way, every color of radiant energy can be equated to a referenced temperature on the Kelvin scale, where absolute zero (where no molecular action occurs) equates to 0°. All light sources, the sun, the arc from a welder's flame, the light bulbs in our homes and businesses, and the light sources used on our stages can be described through their color temperatures. The general range of color temperatures to which we are typically exposed is from about 2,000–13,000° Kelvin. Light sources with low color temperatures (approximately 3,000°) will appear relatively warm and have an overall reddish tint, while sources with higher color temperatures (4,000–5,000° and higher) will appear cooler and have more white or blue color. Low color temperatures have an abundance of red or orange/yellow colored wavelengths while higher color temperatures are associated with an increased presence of blue and violet wavelengths. Several approximate color temperatures for everyday light sources include: candles (2,000°), 50-watt incandescent lamps (2,500°), stage and studio lamps (3,500°), cool fluorescent lamps (4,000°), arc sources (6,000°), and skylight (7,000° or even higher).

Color Rendering

While color temperature relates to the cumulative color of the light, many light sources produce light with very different spectral compositions despite having an overall appearance of white light. In other words, the actual wavelengths present in a white light source may vary considerably from one source to another. In fact, light sources may share the same color temperature while still having very different spectral compositions. In this case, while they may for all effective appearances appear the same, they will, in fact, produce very different responses to the materials that they illuminate. If a source contains a lot of red wavelengths within its composition, a subject with a fair amount of red in its color will be enhanced, while another source that contains predominantly blue wavelengths will tend to mask, or **gray,** the red color of the subject. On the other hand, the second source will enhance blue objects, while the original source will gray a blue object. The ability to reflect or absorb a variety of wavelengths is generally referred to as

color rendering. This principle is readily seen in the high-pressure sodium lighting that is characteristic of interstate highways. In this case, the illumination has a pinkish-yellow tint produced through the given color temperature of the roadway lamps. However, these lamps also have a very narrow spectral composition, which results in poor color rendering for many of the colors that we see. Many colors that we would normally see under daylight conditions become masked, and it is hard to determine the original color of objects like cars under the effects of the sodium lighting. In fact, many colors simply turn to varying shades of gray and black under these conditions. Make a note to observe the changes in color that you see in the objects in your car the next time that you travel on roadways that provide different types of illumination. This effect is even more drastic in low-pressure sodium lighting, which is found along some roadways and is identified by its dark yellow coloring (similar to bug lamps).

The natural color of any object is due to the fact that its surface selectively absorbs and reflects different wavelengths of light. A red sweater reflects primarily red light, while it tends to absorb other wavelengths or colors of light. A green shirt reflects green light, while a purple shirt will reflect some combination of blue and red light. An object appears best when it is illuminated with lighting that contains some of the wavelengths that it naturally reflects. In these situations it is said that the lighting **enhances** an object. The red object will look good not only under red light but also under white light because the white light contains red light as one of its components. A white light source that contains a diverse range of wavelengths will usually make most objects look relatively good. On the other hand, light that has a very narrow or limited spectral composition will make many objects appear dull and gray. In the extreme cases, white objects reflect all colors of light and will take on the color of any light that is shone on them, while black surfaces tend to absorb all wavelengths of light and will generally appear black no matter what color of light strikes them.

One of the problems in choosing light sources in architectural and display lighting relates to the diversity of the spectral composition of the light. Many light sources such as fluorescent lamps have an overall high concentration of blue light within their spectral composition. When these lamps are used to light sales displays such as the meat at your local grocery store the meat often doesn't look very attractive—most likely appearing dull and gray. The meat would look better if the light source contained an element of red light to help enhance the bright red color of the blood that the meat contains. By enhancing the color of the blood, the meat takes on a fresh, healthy appearance. If your products have a wide range of colors, the light source that you choose should have a wide distribution of colors in its spectral composition. We can address these issues through making a comparison of a property known as the **Color Rendering Index (CRI)** for each light source. Color rendering relates to how well a source can render or accurately depict an object's color. Sources with high CRIs will have more individual wavelengths present within their associated light and will enhance a larger range of individual colors. The maximum value that a source may have for its Color Rendering Index is 100. This is a point where color rendering is considered to be ideal and is generally associated with daylight or incandescent light sources. A typical fluorescent lamp will have a CRI rating of 40–50. If we go back to the example of the meat, we would find that a lamp with a CRI rating of 80 or 90 or better would make the meat look the best. Unfortunately, the expense of using lamps with higher CRI ratings also increases as the CRI gets higher, and at some point a designer must weigh the factors of appearance versus cost as part of the design solution.

ADDITIVE AND SUBTRACTIVE MIXING

There are two different methods by which color may be created. One is through **additive color mixing,** while the other is through **subtractive color mixing.** Colors are modified through either the addition or removal of specific wavelengths of light. Both of these principles produce variations in color through very different means and each has a different group of associated primary and secondary colors. Each system also has a unique color wheel that illustrates the relationships between the principle hues of each color system. In each color wheel the three primary colors are located equally distant around the perimeter of the circle while the **secondary colors** are placed at points equally distant between the primaries that mix the given secondary color. A **complementary color** is a color that lies directly across the color wheel from a color and forms a pair between the two colors.

Additive Mixing

Additive color mixing comes about when different wavelengths of light are combined or added together. The process can only occur by having two different colored light sources and their associated light illuminating a common surface. The overlapping light then combines or mixes to produce a third and different color. Earlier we identified the primary colors of light as red, blue, and green. All colors are determined through various combinations of these three colors. A mixture of red and blue light will produce a violet or magenta colored light, while a mixture of blue and green light will produce a turquoise or cyan colored light. A combination of all three colors with a bit more presence of red will produce a pink colored light. While we define the primary colors of light as red, blue and green as based on the cones, we can refer to the combination of equal mixtures of any two primary colors as secondary colors. These colors include: magenta (red and blue), cyan (blue and green) and amber (green and red). An equal mixture of all three primaries produces white light. The relationships between all of these colors are indicated through the Color Wheel of Light (additive mixing), which is illustrated in Figure 3.2. The Color Triangle (Figure 3.3) is a variation of the CIE Chromaticity Chart and color wheel that is commonly used as an aid to illustrating the relationships between the primary and secondary colors of light. It also helps to illustrate how complementary colors interact with one another. The primary colors are located at each of the corners of the triangle, while the secondary colors lie at the midpoint along each of the triangle's sides. These positions also correspond to the complementary relationships between each of the colors. White light is located in the center of the triangle. An unequal mixture or combination of the primary colors will produce **tertiary** or **intermediate colors.**

Subtractive Mixing

Subtractive color mixing comes about through a process where various wavelengths of light are removed by an object or material. All materials selectively absorb (or reflect) different wavelengths of light. An object appears to be a given color such as blue because it absorbs the wavelengths of all colors except blue—which it instead reflects. This is the basic color system that most of us have been instructed in since elementary school, and the primary colors include the familiar colors of red, blue, and yellow. These are often called the primary colors of pigment. Just as in the case of additive mixing, if you combine equal portions of any two primary colors you will produce a secondary color, which in this case will produce the colors of orange, violet, and green. Finally, if you combine an equal mixture of all three primaries you will create a muddy warm brown color that we often refer to as **neutral gray.** The Pigment Color Wheel is based on subtractive mixing and illustrates the relationships between each of these colors.

FILTERING LIGHT

As a whole, the light that we experience naturally throughout the day comes directly from its source unaffected, the exception being atmospheric conditions such as cloud cover or physical obstructions to the light such as branches or architectural structures. As we go outside sunlight falls directly upon us or we might read a book under the light of a table lamp. In both cases, the light leaves its source and is not altered in any way.

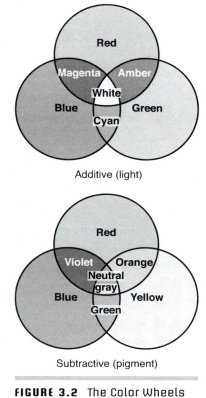

Additive (light)

Subtractive (pigment)

FIGURE 3.2 The Color Wheels

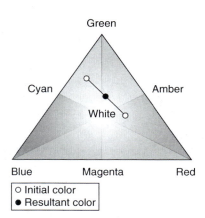

| ○ Initial color |
| ● Resultant color |

FIGURE 3.3 The Color Triangle
Resultant color of mixing two different colors can be determined by locating the approximate position of the initial colors on the triangle and drawing a line between them. If colors are balanced, the resultant color will be located midway along the line. If unbalanced, the color is found along the line based on the relative proportions of the two initial colors. Additional colors may also enter into consideration, in which case the central point of any field defined by the initial colors (e.g., a triangle for three colors) is identified with the resultant color.

However, many times we may want to change either the quality or color of the light to better suit our purposes. In fact, in the theatrical and entertainment worlds it is much more common to modify or change the color of the light than to keep the color the same as originally produced by a lamp. In architectural lighting, we more often want to alter the quality rather than color of the light. **Filtering** simply relates to placing an object in front of a light source that will selectively filter or remove various frequencies or wavelengths of light from the source. The remaining wavelengths will pass through the material and continue onward to interact with the environment. Some wavelengths are absorbed or removed, while others will be **transmitted** or permitted to pass through the material. Those that are absorbed are converted into heat. Through this technique, the color of a light source can be altered through selectively choosing which wavelengths of color pass through a filter and continue on to a target. Historically, many devices have been used to filter light, including colored glass, plastic, and even fluids like wines and oils.

Filtering also takes place when light strikes an object. We perceive an object's color through sensing those wavelengths that the object has selectively reflected back to us. All other wavelengths are once again absorbed and converted into heat. The reason we might wear a dark sweater in the winter is derived from the principle that most wavelengths of light are absorbed and converted into heat, warming the individual. On the other hand, a white T-shirt reflects nearly every wavelength of light and therefore undergoes little absorption, which keeps the wearer relatively cool. All materials go through a selective absorption or reflection of these visible wavelengths, which will ultimately determine the color that we perceive for a given object.

COLOR MEDIA

Color media is the name that we give to the materials that we use to either filter or modify the color of the light that is produced by a lighting fixture. The media may be made from a number of different materials such as glass or plastic—even fluids or silks have and are used for these purposes. The media is usually placed in some type of holder that is positioned at the front of a lighting instrument. Light from the fixture then passes through the color media, where it is altered and continues to travel towards its intended target. The most common type of color media, by far, is the colored plastic filters that we call **gel.** Light passes through the material where certain wavelengths of light are filtered out while others continue to pass through to the other side. Due to this filtering effect, many designers also refer to gel as **filters.** In fact, filters are a more accurate name for color media. Gel was originally made from a specific material (animal gelatin) that was tinted to produce a variety of different colored filters. As lighting fixtures improved and lamps of higher intensities were developed, gel could no longer stand up to the extreme temperatures that were produced by the newer lamps and would melt or burn out (pale or fade in its center where the heat and light were concentrated) resulting in inconsistent coloring of the light. Along with more efficient light sources engineers also developed filters in plastic media such as acetate and mylar that could survive the higher temperatures. Today, even though we rarely use actual gelatin media, we often refer to all these filters collectively as gel—regardless of the actual material.

Plastic Media

Plastic media is by far the most common form of filter in the entertainment lighting industry due to its overall low costs and ease of replacement. The media is purchased in 20" × 24" sheets or in rolls that allow the user to individually cut the media to any size as needed. The material that is used to manufacture these sheets may be acetate or mylar, plastics that were developed to withstand the higher temperatures of contemporary lighting fixtures. Some gel systems have the color applied to the surfaces of clear sheets of plastic like acetate, while others, such as mylar, have the color actually embedded in the plastic through the manufacturing process. By far the most important advantage of these filters is in the range of colors from which a designer may make their color selections. There are four primary filter manufacturers (Apollo, Gam, Lee, and Rosco) who each produce approximately one hundred different colored filters. Each company produces a booklet with samples of the colored filters called **swatch books** that contain every color filter that they manufacture in a given system (several produce three or four different color systems).

While plastic media is the most popular filtering material, it does have a drawback in that it will fade or burn out over time. The rate of burnout is related to issues such as the intensity of the light source (the brighter the light, the quicker a gel will burn out), the hanging position of the fixture (lights pointed upward will result in more heat passing through a filter than those where the light is pointed downward), and the color saturation of the filter (the more saturated the filter, the quicker it will experience burnout). In most theatrical venues burnout often isn't a problem, and gels can be used and reused over many different productions. If burnout becomes an issue through using very saturated colors or through being used over an extended period of time, such as at a theme park installation, the designer may either replace the gel as needed or consider more permanent and often more expensive filtering materials like glass.

With so many different colors available there have been issues in trying to name and reference each individual color. While each manufacturer has given a name to every one of its colored filters, the name assigned to any particular filter will often not give a clear indication of the actual color that the filter will create. It is also impossible to indicate all these names on the light plot and paperwork. Therefore, each manufacturer has also referenced each filter by a numbering system in addition to giving a specific name to each filter. Through this, filters or gels can be quickly indicated throughout a designer's plans by writing a simple two- or three-digit number. While designers in the past often chose to use a single manufacturer's gels on a given project, today's designers often use a variety of gel selections that represent color choices from several different manufacturers. In order to keep the color designations straight we often place a letter in front of the gel number that corresponds with the manufacturer of the specified filter (i.e., R-33 for Rosco #33 , L-120 for Lee #120, G-160 for Gam #160, and AP-7900 for Apollo #7900). It is important to note that each of these color systems is completely independent from one another and that while you may find the same name or even number in two or more of the different filter systems, these filters may, in fact, be quite different from one another. Even those that at first glance appear to look quite similar may upon further examination respond quite differently to light.

Glass Media

In the past, glass provided a very favorable form of color filter. However, due to problems such as color consistency (keeping colors consistent from one manufacturing run to another), limited color selection, breakage, and costs, glass has quickly been replaced by the gel products. However, if a filter is to be used over a long-term project such as an architectural installation or a themed environment where the filters will be subjected to years of service, glass once again becomes a viable alternative to gel.

Many of the glass filters of earlier times were in the form of **roundels** that are circular glass filters installed in many striplight fixtures. These fixtures contain a series of lamps mounted side-by-side in a single bank. The lamps are wired into circuits that allow every third or fourth lamp to be controlled together—independent from the other lamps that are also wired into their respective circuits. These fixtures are often used for color toning, and each circuit is typically equipped with a different set of colored filters. In many cases, these striplights were installed permanently in theatres, and color was created through using roundels to color each of the independent light sources. Due to expense, roundels were only made in a few colors (typically red, blue, green, amber, and

SIDEBAR 3.1 Spectral Analysis of Gel

To illustrate the response of light under the influence of a given gel, manufacturers provide a spectral analysis for each filter. This is presented as a graph on a sheet of paper that is mounted behind each filter in a swatch book. This analysis provides two essential types of information for a designer. The first, given in the form of a percentage, identifies the overall transmission of the filter. This tells you how much light passes through the gel and is available to illuminate your subject. In many cases, a filter will reduce the light by a significant amount. Pastel or lightly tinted colors frequently have transmission rates in the 70–80% range, while colors of even medium saturation quickly drop down to transmission rates in the 30–40% range. The transmission rates of heavily saturated colors like the deep blues often have transmissions of less than 10%, meaning that over 90% of the light is being absorbed and converted into heat!

Secondly, the graph displays the individual transmission values of specific wavelengths of light as affected by the given filter. The individual wavelengths of the visible spectrum are identified by wavelength (usually nanometers) and plotted along the horizontal axis while the individual transmission rates of each wavelength are plotted along the vertical axis. The importance of this graph lies in how each wavelength responds as different colors of the visible spectrum to that filter. Tints generally reflect an overall high transmission across many of the wavelengths (Figure 3.4a), while highly saturated colors (Figure 3.4b and c) generally have low transmission

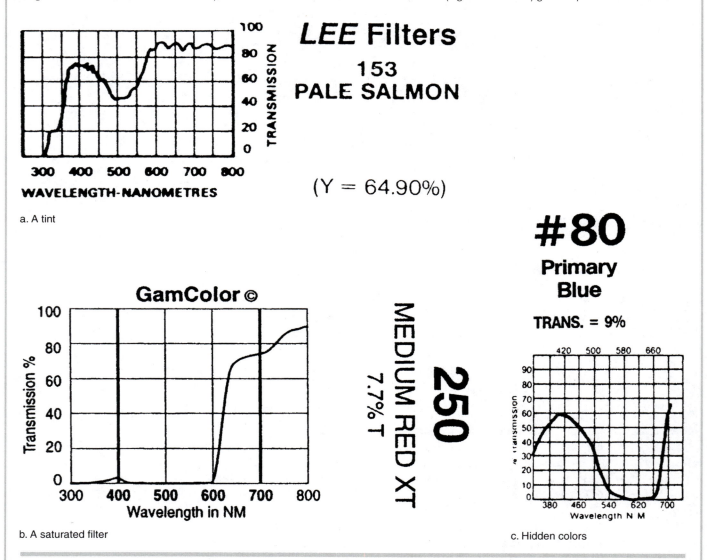

a. A tint

b. A saturated filter

c. Hidden colors

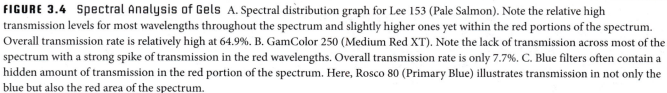

FIGURE 3.4 Spectral Analysis of Gels A. Spectral distribution graph for Lee 153 (Pale Salmon). Note the relative high transmission levels for most wavelengths throughout the spectrum and slightly higher ones yet within the red portions of the spectrum. Overall transmission rate is relatively high at 64.9%. B. GamColor 250 (Medium Red XT). Note the lack of transmission across most of the spectrum with a strong spike of transmission in the red wavelengths. Overall transmission rate is only 7.7%. C. Blue filters often contain a hidden amount of transmission in the red portion of the spectrum. Here, Rosco 80 (Primary Blue) illustrates transmission in not only the blue but also the red area of the spectrum.

rates across the spectrum while spiking in specific wavelengths. A saturated red filter will have its highest transmission values in the 700–800 nanometer range while a saturated blue will have its peak transmission in the 400–500 range.

A designer can make use of these graphs to help predict how a filter will affect the surface color of any objects that it strikes. If one wants to enhance an object with a green color, a filter should be chosen that has a fair to good amount of transmission in the green portion of the spectrum, high red transmission if the object is red, or high blue transmission if the object is blue. If a designer wants a wide range of colors to appear unaltered then they need to choose a filter that is more of a tint with a high degree of transmission across the entire spectrum. On the other hand, a designer can also use the transmission curves to predict what colors a given filter will have a negative impact upon. Any color that is found to correspond with a wavelength of an overall low transmission will generally be darkened or grayed. One of the strange effects of deep blue lighting is in that many blue filters also have a high degree of transmission in the red portion of the spectrum, resulting in many objects that contain any red dye taking on a reddish glow despite the overall blue color of the lighting. Costumes, paint, and even **maskings** such as legs and borders have surprised designers when they have not carefully planned their color selections. Even colors that appear to be strongly dominant in a given color may contain some hidden transmissions in other parts of the spectrum. If this effect is undesirable, then the designer needs to carefully choose a filter with very limited, if any, transmission in the particular portion of the spectrum where these problems have been encountered. These spectral distribution charts are also posted on the manufacturers' websites. Rosco even provides an indication of where the filter is located on the CIE Chromaticity Diagram.

It should be noted that as a general principle a designer should avoid placing or stacking several layers of gel in an instrument. While this practice may occasionally prove desirable, such as in the case of bringing two relatively unsaturated colors together to produce a new color, this practice typically causes problems. This is particularly true if the colors are saturated and unrelated to one another. If you think about how a filter works, it should become apparent why stacking gels usually doesn't work. For instance, if you were to try to combine a red and blue gel together to produce a purple colored light, you would find that the red filter would eliminate all the light except the red light and that the blue gel would filter out all except the blue light—including the red light transmitted by the red filter. The outcome of mixing these filters therefore results in effectively eliminating all of the light through absorption. This condition not only creates virtually no light transmission but also produces the added effect of a large heat conversion that will most likely result in melting

the gels together and causing them to burn out. Because of this, it is best to select a single gel for producing a color than to try to combine several gels in the same unit. Over time, especially with more saturated gels, the media will eventually break down and fade or **burn out.** Several methods of slowing down or preventing this include placing a **heat shield** or **color extender** on a fixture. Heat shields are a special variety of clear gel that are placed in a second slot of a fixture's color holder (between the lens and the gel). This creates a gap between the gel and the fixture that allows additional air to circulate and cool the gel while also filtering out some of the harmful ultraviolet heat. Not all lighting instruments have this feature to hold a second filter. A color extender looks like a top hat and works in much the same way but has internal slots that allow the gel to be placed further away from the lamp. Another technique involves running a pouncing wheel over the gel to create a number of small holes in the gel's surface to help dissipate the heat buildup.

One of the largest problems of traditional filters lies in the fact that only one filter can be used in a fixture at a given time. Until the last twenty or so years, the only way to remotely change the color of light coming from a given direction was to hang a second fixture containing a second color next to the first light. The color was then chosen through selecting which fixture was used at any given time. It also provided a way to use additive color mixing to produce a host of new colors through adjusting the intensity proportions between the two fixtures. This is commonly called **double-hanging.**

In recent years, manufacturers have created an accessory that holds a variety of filters that are taped together into some form of scroll. The scroll can then be rolled back and forth to specific positions that correspond to different colors. These devices, called **automated color changers** or **scrollers,** slide into the color attachment of a lighting instrument and allow a single fixture to have its color changed numerous times throughout a production. Scrollers can substantially reduce the number of fixtures required for a project. Earlier models of automated color changers often contained 10–20 different filters in a scroll or **gelstring,** while more recent models can contain 30 or more colors. In the last several years we have seen a new generation of scrollers that produce their colored light through the movement of two different scrolls that lie in front of one another. These later generation scrollers have an enormous range of color selection and allow the light to be mixed in various combinations through using the relative positions of the two scrolls. This effectively allows a designer to actually mix the color of light that they feel is appropriate for any given moment. The positioning of the scrolls in each type of scroller is done through simple electronic commands that come from a typical lighting control board. These accessories have become quite popular and can be found in both entertainment and architectural/display applications.

white). By using combinations of these colors, it is possible, through color mixing, to create almost any color that a designer might want. While roundels may be used in striplights even today, most designers now specify colors for striplights from gel choices. In addition to providing color filtering, the roundels may also provide some form of patterning or diffusion that modifies the softness and focus of the lamps.

A new line of glass filters has recently been introduced by manufactures that are inserted into the optical train of a lighting instrument rather then being placed at the front end of a fixture. These filters are being referred to as **variegated glass filters** and in general are used primarily to alter the physical quality of the light. While they may provide color filtering, the majority of their effect is in creating various diffusion patterns and textures in the light. The variegated glass may also be used in combination with traditional color filters to make further changes in the light. These filters are inserted into the area of the fixture known as the **gate,** which corresponds approximately with the focal point of the fixture, and are manufactured so that they will slip into the same pattern holders and slots as a gobo. Some manufacturers even refer to these filters as glass gobos. You may also use these products in combination with traditional steel gobos to produce more sophisticated patterns. Due to their placement within a fixture, color media other than glass will not hold up to the extreme temperatures of the gate.

While there are a number of pre-manufactured glass gobos that can be purchased through theatrical and architectural suppliers, a glass or steel gobo may also be custom designed for specific events. Custom gobos have been manufactured for topics including show titles, trade and product names, restaurant logos, and even team names and mascots. Additional effects can be produced through adding an accessory called a **gobo rotator** to a lighting fixture. This is a device that generates a rotational motion to any gobo that is placed within the accessory.

Dichroic Filters

A special version of glass filter is the **dichroic filter.** These filters work on the principle of reflecting unwanted wavelengths of light rather than absorbing them. A red dichroic filter will allow red light to pass through it while the majority of the remaining light is reflected backwards away from the filter. In this case, the reflected light will appear cyan (the complementary color to red). Dichroic filters need to be oriented correctly within the light path to work properly. An angle that isn't acute enough may result in scattered reflections of the light rather then allowing the desired wavelengths to pass through the filter. Advantages to dichroic filters lie in their color permanence and increased purity or saturation of a produced color. Dichroic filters can produce some of the most vivid strongly saturated colors that are available to a lighting designer. Because of this, it has become popular to include a selection of dichroic filters in the color wheel of many automated fixtures that are rigged for lighting spectacle events like concert and themed activities.

While expensive, the costs of dichroic filters continues to drop, and in applications where a filter may be used for many months or years, more designers are choosing to use dichroic filters for their projects. They are especially attractive for themed environments and architectural applications. Manufacturers like Rosco and Gam are producing a solid collection of colors in dichroic filters. The range of colors that are available is still quite limited when compared to traditional filters but continues to improve with every passing year. Dichroics may also be used in gobo designs where crushed pieces of dichroic glass are mounted on a slide to produce effects like water reflections or stained glass imagery.

Diffusion

Technically speaking, diffusion isn't an actual color medium. This is due to the fact that it primarily alters the quality rather than color of the light that passes through it. Many designers and manufacturers refer to **diffusion** media as **frost.** The materials of which diffusion media or frost are made are usually derived from plastics and are therefore manufactured by the same companies that make color media. In fact, manufacturers combine their diffusion and color filter media together into the same swatch books. As a rule, diffusion softens the beam of light that passes through it. Various degrees of diffusion can be created through a wide selection of frost materials. However, diffusion can not be used to sharpen or harshen a light, it can only produce a softening effect. Frost may be very light or quite heavy depending on the individual needs of a design. There are even frosts that can spread or diffuse the light differently in different orientations. Several uses of frost include softening the edges of lights that won't quite focus soft enough, to even out the spread and eliminate any shadows between two or more adjoining light sources, and to knockdown any hot spots between comparable lights. As a side effect, frosts can also cause a large amount of ambient or spill light.

Frost is often combined with color filters but should always be placed on the side of the color media that is away from the light source. Not doing so may cause excess heat to form and the two sheets could melt together. The effect will occur even more quickly if you try stacking several layers of frost together. In order to remedy problems like this, most gel manufactures have designed a limited selection of media that combine a color filter with a diffusion treatment in a single product. This color selection is for the most part restricted to primary colors and several other colors that are typically used to light cycs and drops. Finally, diffusion media can also be used to change fundamental qualities like the color temperature of any light passing through it. In the film and video industry it is imperative that light from different sources be modified to share common traits like color temperature. Many of these filters are known as **color correction** and are used for applications like converting fluorescent lighting to daylight or incandescent color temperatures, shifting daylight (crews actually gel over the windows of an on-location set) to tungsten color temperature so that the two light sources will be compatible with one another, or reducing the higher color temperatures of arc light to match incandescent light sources. This principle of correcting for color temperature is also common in architectural applications of lighting design.

CREATING COLOR THROUGH LIGHT

The color that we perceive for any object is actually the result of several variables. Most importantly we need to consider: the actual color of the object (those wavelengths of light that are reflected or absorbed), the color of the light (what wavelengths are present), and the color sensitivity of the viewing device (those wavelengths that an eye or camera respond to). Changes in any one of these can alter the perceived color quite significantly. We don't really have to consider the response of the eye since, for most practical purposes, we all have similar responses to color. However, this does become a factor when comparing color perception between devices like film and video cameras, where different cameras and films may respond to light quite differently from one another. The two primary questions that a lighting designer needs to answer in regard to color perception are: What does this object look like under different colored light sources, and what do all these different colored objects look like under this color of light?

Color Prediction

I have found that you can get a pretty good indication of the perceived color of an object through simply thinking of the light in terms of its primary and secondary color components. By thinking of what colored wavelengths are present in a light and how each is affected by filtering and reflection you can get a pretty good indication of how an object's color might be changed under the influence of a given color of light. Figure 3.5 illustrates this principle through showing different colored shirts illuminated by a magenta light source. In the first case (Figure 3.5a), the light leaving the lighting fixture contains white light with equal proportions of red, blue, and green light (the primaries). In order to create a magenta light a filter is placed in front of the light to filter out green light but allows the blue and red to continue on to the shirt. The shirt, being red, will absorb the blue light and reflect the red light, resulting in us seeing the shirt as red. This is

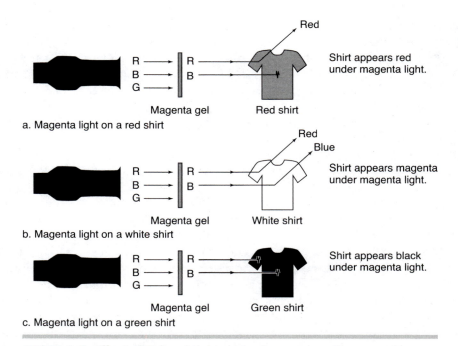

FIGURE 3.5   Effect of Colored Light a. The shirt appears red because red wavelengths of magenta light are reflected while the blue ones are absorbed. b. The shirt appears magenta because both red and blue wavelengths of magenta light are reflected. c. The shirt appears black because both red and blue wavelengths are absorbed.

an easily predictable result. The same is true if we don't change the magenta lighting and switch to a white shirt as indicated in Figure 3.5b. In this case the magenta lighting goes on to strike the white shirt, which reflects both the blue and red light, which results in the shirt appearing magenta in color. On the other hand, if we switch to a green shirt, the magenta light will strike the green shirt, but both the blue and red light will be absorbed. This results in the shirt reflecting no light, which gives it a dark or black appearance as illustrated in Figure 3.5c.

If you think of white light and objects as having all three wavelengths present or being capable of reflecting all three wavelengths, and black as both absorbing and lacking all three wavelengths, you can give some initial predictions as to how a colored light will theoretically affect the colors of any materials that you may be lighting. This same approach can be used to predict the resultant color from combining two or more filters with the same light source.

In Figure 3.6a the initial light from the source provides red, blue, and green wavelengths. Upon passing through the first filter (amber) the blue light is filtered away and the red and green continue towards the second filter. In passing through the second filter the red light is absorbed while the green light passes on toward its target. The second example (Figure 3.6b) illustrates profoundly why we shouldn't combine filters. In this example, the first gel (red) filters out each of the wavelengths except red while the green gel will proceed to absorb the remaining red light, which results in no light continuing beyond the two filters. Through experience and careful study of the spectral graphs that accompany the color samples

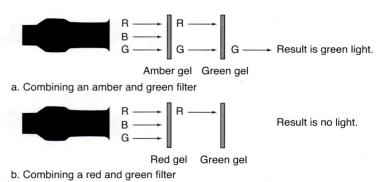

FIGURE 3.6   Combining Color Filters a. Light coming from the fixture contains red, blue, and green primaries. Upon passing through the amber gel, the blue is absorbed, while the red and green continue on to the green gel, where the red is absorbed. Only green light passes completely through both sets of filters. b. Again, the fixture provides red, blue, and green light, which is filtered to only red light once passing through the red gel. The red light continues on to the green gel, where it, too, is absorbed—resulting in all light being filtered out by the gels.

in a swatch book a designer can make educated guesses regarding the perceived color of various combinations of filters and colored objects. Despite these techniques for predicting the effects of different colored objects and light sources, there are still surprises that come about due to various combinations of fabrics, dyes, and filters. Because of this, there really is no substitute for experimenting with the actual materials and filters and trying various combinations through using mechanisms like **light labs** or **mockups.**

The effect of angle should also be considered when looking at the effect of colored light on an object. This is particularly noticeable if an object is lit by lights that are colored quite differently from one another (see Figure 3.7). If the two sources come from essentially the same direction the object will provide a common surface where the light from both sources will mix quite evenly, producing a third color through additive mixing of the two different sources. On the other hand, if the lights are positioned in such a manner that they are directly opposed to one another they will strike very few common surfaces and you will see that some surfaces of the object will be colored with the light of the first source, while others will be lit by the second source. In effect, the shadows of the first light source will be filled by the color of the second source, while the shadows of the second light source will be filled by the color of the first light source. Finally, if the lights are mounted as mirror images in such a manner that they are both slightly to the sides and front of the subject, the resultant colors will begin with different colors to each side of the subject that will slowly grade or blend into an equal mix of both colors on those surfaces that are under the influence of both light sources.

Red Shift/Amber Drift

A final effect that needs to be considered is the color of the light source itself. As stated earlier in this chapter, different light sources have different color temperatures. Most color systems for the stage (filtering systems) are based on a light source having a color temperature of around 3,200° K. This is fine when the lamp is operating at full capacity, but in most stage applications we like to dim the lights, which lowers the color temperature of the lamp. In reality, the light output of the lamp shifts to producing a much larger proportion of red and yellow wavelengths of light. We call this effect **red shift** or **amber drift.** The effect can have a dramatic impact on any colors and filters used with light sources that are run at lower intensity levels. Art directors in film and video need to be extremely conscious of color temperatures and have special lines of filters that are used to correct color temperatures for a variety of situations. In fact, film productions usually prefer to run lamps at full intensity so that they don't have to contend with the effects of red shift.

COMPLEMENTARY TINT SYSTEM

Over time, we have come to use several of the principles outlined throughout this chapter to produce fairly naturalistic lighting for a number of environments and stages. The basic theory is generally referred to as a **Complementary Tint Theory** and is often credited to a pioneer in the field of stage lighting named Stanley McCandless. We often simply call it the **McCandless System** or **McCandless Method** of stage lighting. While this system or variations of it were so widely adopted that theatres were even wired to accommodate its needs, McCandless himself suggested that this was only one way of producing effective lighting designs. In brief, McCandless felt that very naturalistic lighting could be produced if two lighting fixtures containing complementary colored tints were hung on opposing 45° angles from one another. The two lights are hung 45° to each front and side of the subject (splitting centerline) with a vertical angle of 45° for each light. Tinted pairs that form complementary colors with one another are then used to color the two spotlights. A pink light might be combined with another fixture that is gelled with a cyan tint, or an amber

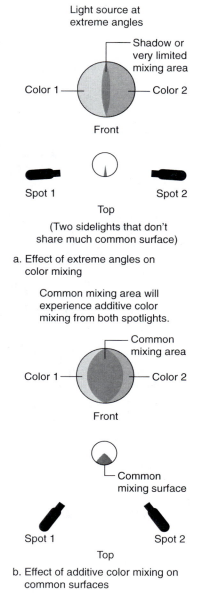

FIGURE 3.7 Angle and Color Mixing a. Spotlights 1 and 2 are positioned at opposing angles to the sphere or subject. The areas to each side indicate those areas that are under the influence of only one light, while the central area will most likely represent some form of shadow area where there is no or little light from either spotlight and therefore virtually no color mixing. b. Spotlights 1 and 2 are brought closer toward the front of the subject, which once again results in the two side areas being lit by only a single source, but this time much of the light overlaps in a common mixing area where additive mixing produces a third color that is derived from the two spotlight colors.

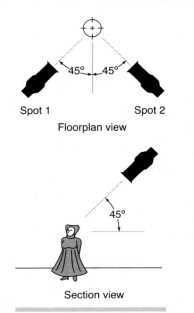

FIGURE 3.8 A McCandless Hang for Naturalistic Lighting Two lighting instruments are gelled in complementary tints that are hung at 45° to either side of a subject along with a 45° vertical angle.

colored spotlight might be combined with a pale lavender unit as a second example of a complementary pair. The pair of lights form a **key/fill** relationship on each side of a subject's face which aids in creating shadows and modeling while also mixing to a variation of white light on the central portion of the face. Figure 3.8 illustrates the mounting positions for a McCandless lighting system.

PSYCHOLOGICAL EFFECTS OF COLOR

Color can be an extremely effective tool in creating an overall mood or emotional effect for an environment. This is primarily due to the effectiveness that it can have in shaping moods and other psychological responses of a viewer. After intensity, color is the next most likely element of a lighting design to shape the mood that will be produced through a given lighting condition. One of the most distinguishing ways of characterizing light is by its sense of warmth. Light that has an overall abundance of red, yellow, and orange wavelengths is said to be **warm,** while light that is dominated by blue, green, and lavender is said to be **cool.** Warm and cool light each produce distinctive psychological responses in most observers. Most people tend to associate warm colors with conditions of higher energy, tension, and excitement, while cool colors tend to generate a response that coincides with a more peaceful, tranquil feeling. As a whole, there are fairly consistent emotional responses that can be observed in a viewer when we examine color associations and mood. For instance, red brings about arousal and draws our attention or focus. It also creates relatively strong responses and can be associated with emotions like passion, conflict, and anger. Yellow forms that area of the spectrum to which we are most sensitive and tends to be perceived overall as white light. Green tends to react poorly with skin tones and is associated with unnatural feelings. It also tends to provide an overall neutral response. Blue helps create the illusion of distance and is associated with tranquility and more peaceful emotions (particularly in tints or medium saturations). Finally, violet produces a more solemn or melancholy response.

We also tend to have more positive responses to colors that aren't as strongly saturated. Pink produces a more pleasant association than red. A golden color can be associated with light sources that are based on our daily experience (sunlight, candlelight, or a table lamp) and are seen as natural, while a light with a strong orange or red color is more unnatural and can take on a greater symbolic interpretation—many times in a negative frame of reference such as in the implication of hell or anger. A medium blue could be associated with romantic moonlight, while a deep blue might help create the mystery of a scene set near Count Dracula's crypt. Warm colors tend to attract our attention while cool colors tend to be submissive and draw a more neutral response from a viewer. We choose to paint emergency vehicles red because of the attention-gaining power of the red color. Understanding these properties allows a designer to use color to draw focus to particular elements of a scene. Another practical observation lies in the tendency of warm colors to advance or jump toward us while cool colors tend to recede into the background or distance. A look at a distant landscape horizon clearly illustrates this principle of distancing.

In the manufacturing and health care industries the overall color temperature of the light that illuminates a space is often used to modify the behavior of the occupants. Psychiatric hospitals incorporate lighting to create non-threatening environments for their patients, while the birthing rooms of traditional hospitals are often illuminated in warm incandescent lighting that suggests the warmth that you would find at home. Relief of anxiety, productivity, sense of contentment, and overall degree of comfort are all psychological feelings that have been shown to be correlated with the lighting of a given environment. Architects are working to create additional ways of incorporating daylight into building designs because it has been discovered that the number of hours of natural daylight exposure that we experience has an impact on our overall moods.

Color Contrast

It must also be understood that color can be relative. It is easy to compare a red colored light to a blue one to determine which of the two colors is warm or cool. However, a designer can make use of the relative warmth or coolness of any two colors to make a design statement. Is this blue cool in comparison to that blue? Is this pink warm compared to that pink? In fact, most colors will be warm when compared to some colors and cool when compared to others. We refer to these changes and relative comparisons of warmth and coolness as **color contrast.** What we acknowledge isn't so much the degree of color contrast (large or small) but that color contrast is simply present in a given scene. Designers can use this to their advantage in a number of ways. First, in a broad sense, color can be used to draw focus through simply placing a single object in a different colored light from everything else on stage. The eye has a natural tendency to be drawn to whatever is different in a given composition. A concert stage washed in red light with a single amber spotlight on the lead vocalist will bring attention to this performer. A room bathed in deep blue light with light-lavender moonlight streaming through the window will bring attention to the area lit by the window. Second, it is possible that a scene might work best in an overall single hue, but in order to make it more interesting and modeled some form of contrast will need to be initiated into the image. By using variations of a basic hue where small differences in relative warmth or coolness are found, a designer can go a long way toward creating a scene that has believable overall coloring without necessarily using a distinctly warm versus cool color scheme. In going back to the example of the moonlight streaming through the window, it can be seen that variations of several distinctly cool colors will most likely produce a much more effective scene than simply picking a warm and cool color.

Adaptation and Afterimages

A final effect of color relates to two generally negative principles called **color adaptation** and **afterimages.** These occur when the eye has been over-stimulated in some way. If the lighting remains unchanged for an extended period of time there is a possibility that color adaptation will become an issue. Fatigue may play upon the viewers' eyes or colors may appear to shift in hue and value. The effect is especially pronounced if there are strong color saturations in the lighting of a scene. For a night scene that is lit under predominantly blue lights, the blue cones of the eye will become desensitized and sluggish through color adaptation. If the scene is followed by a day scene that is lit under essentially white lighting, the day scene will often initially appear to be too gold or yellow in color. This is due to the fact that the red and green cones are fully sensitive while the blue ones aren't as reactive. For the second scene, the eye simply misses some of the blue light sensitivity that would normally balance the color to its normal white appearance. In time, the blue cones once again become fully functional and the gold quality will eventually fade away. Afterimages come about through a similar phenomenon where the eyes remain stimulated even though the source of the stimulation has been removed. In this case, the cones will overcompensate once the initial image is removed—causing an afterimage to appear on a neutral surface. These images often appear to be colored in the complementary tint of the original image. You can create an experience that produces an afterimage through simply staring at a colored object for a period of 30–60 seconds. After 1 minute shift your sight to a neutral piece of paper or white wall and you will experience the temporary sensation of seeing the second object in the complementary hue of the original object. A similar effect can occur on stage when a strongly saturated hue forms the dominant lighting color for a scene that is immediately followed by a blackout. In this case, an afterimage is quite commonly experienced by the audience in the initial moments of the blackout. A designer may even make use of this principle to add to the dramatic impact of the final image for a scene.

PRACTICAL USE OF COLOR

One of the fundamental concepts that a lighting designer must ultimately master is the use of color in a lighting design. This generally takes time and experience before you learn to feel comfortable with making appropriate color assignments. The primary reason for this lies in the dramatic impact that color can have on our perception of a scene. Young designers often choose colors that are either too pastel, which adds little interest or contrast to a design, or so saturated that they significantly distort a project. More importantly, a designer needs to play the middle of the road . . . knowing when pastels are appropriate versus when saturated hues might be required to successfully light a project. Color choices need to always be made within the context of the project. What worked in one situation may not be successful at all in a similar situation and every choice comes down to a consideration of whether the color is appropriate or not for a specific image. There are a wealth of filter choices available for a designer's color consideration—not only through the hundreds, if not thousands, of colors of gel that are available but also through the additional abilities of color mixing as well as using automated fixtures to mix still more colors. The one technique that a designer can use to best come to grips with the color selection for a project is in the act of experimenting. The use of a light lab or software simulations like WYSIWYG™, LD Assistant™ or Virtual Light Lab™ can greatly assist in this process. Even shining light through a sample from a swatch book to view the results of the filtered light on the skin, costume fabrics, and painted colors of a set rendering or paint elevation will give the designer some indication of how these materials will react under a specific filter. There are designers who like to peer through a filter to see its effect on sample materials but I prefer to shine sunlight or an incandescent drafting lamp through a filter to observe how the light reacts on my skin, paint elevations, and costume swatches. If using this method, try to be sure that the color temperature of the light source is compatible with that of the fixtures that you will be using in your design (i.e., don't use a florescent drafting lamp).

Although color considerations are discussed in later chapters of this book through several specific design applications, there are a couple of practical considerations that I have chosen to explore at this point in my discussion. First, as a general rule, a lighting designer is typically trying to enhance the colors of a subject as they light a scene or object. This requires that, to some degree, the colors that are present in the costumes, scenery, or any other portions of the stage must also be present within the light that is being used to light a scene. If these colors aren't present, or if there is a high presence of the complement of these colors, the lighting might actually produce a dulling or graying effect on these objects. A prevalent rule of lighting relates to the trend that the more lights and varied colors that you initiate on stage at any given time generally increases the amount of graying that is found within a scene. On the other hand, it is also possible to overcompensate for this effect and cause some colors to be so enhanced that they might "zing" or become neon-like in their appearance. This, too, is usually considered an undesirable effect of choosing the wrong colors. Sidebar 3.2 provides a list of several practical considerations that lighting designers tend to use as they consider color for a given project. While these observations may tend to be true in most situations, be forewarned that none of these statements are absolute and that in some cases it might even be appropriate to use a completely conflicting technique for a given production. Stick to the principle that all design decisions are relative and must be made within the context of the given project. Also remember that your color decisions commonly change from one moment to another and that a stage composition doesn't remain static.

SIDEBAR 3.2 Designer Considerations for Color and Light

1. Use colors that enhance the skin tones of the performers. For Caucasian performers these tend to be tints in the pink and lavender hues. Care must be taken when using amber gels because the green within the amber tends to emphasize the arteries that lie just below the skin's surface, which can produce an overall sullen or sickly color on the performer. Green light should generally be avoided because of both its unnatural color and, once again, the effect that it has on the arteries of performers. Dark complexions such as those found in African Americans and performers from areas of the world such as India are generally enhanced by lavender tints while colors with strong elements of red may give an unnatural glowing quality to the skin tones of these performers. The yellow tint of Asian performers will also react differently to color than any other ethnic subjects and this, too, must be considered when choosing gels for a production or event. In projects where there is a constant mixture of individuals reflecting a diverse range of ethnic backgrounds, the best choices of color will reflect various tints that have a wide range of colored light.

2. In addition to the obvious effect of colored light on the skin tones of various ethnic groups, a designer should also consider the social effects of color on a given design. Color often represents different meanings from one society to another. For instance, in Western tradition black is a color often reserved for mourning, while in Eastern society white is commonly associated with death. In our society, social implications of color include examples like white light being associated with purity while red light is often symbolically associated with anger, passion, or even demonic events.

3. Any natural colors found in the environment should be enhanced through choosing lighting colors that reflect a spectral composition that augments these natural colors. Fabrics, paints, and other colors that are characteristic of the individual design areas will look best if lit with similar colors. The principle is also true in architectural and display lighting where the product should be made to look its best through selection of colors that have an enhancing effect on the natural color of a subject. In some cases, especially in the areas of theatrical design and themed environments, materials may be painted or colored intentionally with different colors that can be purposefully modified through making changes in the color of the light that illuminates the material at any given time. Through this, some design elements may be quite visible under one lighting condition while becoming hidden under another.

4. Color can be used to mold/shape or to increase the dimensionality of an object through using progressively more saturated variations of a color in light sources that wrap around the subject from front to back. Colors from the front that are too saturated will distort an object.

5. Additive color mixing will have an increased effect as the angles between two separate light sources (with different colors) becomes less pronounced. In other words, there will be more surfaces that are commonly illuminated by both sources, resulting in a larger display of color mixing between the two colors on these surfaces.

6. In examining overall hues: warm colors tend to advance, while cool colors tend to recede, and warm colors generally have a better ability of attracting focus although it needs to be understood that all colors must be considered on a relative basis.

7. If creating motivational lighting, or light that is linked to an apparent light source, the color of the light needs to reflect the natural color properties of that source of illumination. For example; the light lavender of moonlight, the golden glow of a candle, the red glow of embers, or the warm amber of a late afternoon sun are all based on the color of each source of light.

8. Lighting color plays a dominant role in developing the mood and character for an environment or setting. Light airy moods are generally associated with warm colors, while somber moods tend to be associated with cool colors. The depiction of psychological energy can also be associated with color choices—warm colors are characteristic of more energetic feelings and tension while cool colors are more often associated with tranquility and more peaceful, reflective moments. The argument of using pink light for comedy comes out of these observations.

9. In many theatrical applications lighting forms the dominant manner of producing colored backgrounds for the stage. This is done through creating large washes of evenly colored light on large scenic surfaces like a **cyclorama (cyc)** or **skydrop.** In this case, filter colors are chosen that can either mix a large range of colors (i.e., the primary colors) or will work together to amplify a given range of color that is found in the scenic elements of these backgrounds.

Even after discussing several general principles for color selection, the importance of experimentation needs to be re-emphasized in the process of working with color. Color can be unpredictable and there can be no better way of gaining an understanding of the hidden properties of a gel than through trying it out on a sample of the materials that will actually be illuminated. Many fabrics with colors such as navy blue and black are dyed with chemicals that contain hidden colors that aren't immediately apparent under white lighting conditions. A second element to understand is the sense of relativity that exists in the color applications of lighting. Also, what was an appropriate color choice for one setting or project might be completely wrong in another situation. Most gel manufactures have developed a set of tables that suggest many applications for which a given color of gel might be appropriate for helping designers sort through some of the effects that many gels might produce. Finally, if worse comes to worse, gel is relatively cheap and can be changed fairly easily if you should decide that you have made the wrong choice. In fact, next to changing intensities, color is the most easily changed variable of the controllable qualities of light. The significance of color to the lighting's overall design forms a major impact on any project and through time and experience a designer will learn how to control color and make it an effective element of their design tools.

SIDEBAR 3.3 DESIGNER PROFILE

Mark Stanley

Mark Stanley is best known for his dance lighting. He has been associated with many of America's premier dance companies and continues to actively light for dance companies that include The New York City Ballet, Joffrey Ballet, San Francisco Ballet, and Boston Ballet, among others. His reputation has also led him to designing internationally for companies like the Royal Danish Ballet, Royal Ballet, London, the National Ballet of Canada, and the Stuttgart Ballet. While he has frequently designed for ballet, he has also designed for leading modern dance companies and choreographers like Susan Marshall, Pilobolus, Alvin Ailey Dance Theater, and David Gordon. He has also designed for opera and drama, with credits at venues that include the Paper Mill Playhouse, Kennedy Center, Radio City Music Hall, Long Warf Theatre and New York City Opera. He also heads the lighting program at Boston University.

Stanley began his lighting training through earning a BA in Theatre from The College of William and Mary. His MFA is in Lighting Design from the University of Wisconsin, where he studied under the legendary Gilbert Hemsley. His interest in lighting dance is best recounted through his own words. "Some of my earliest exposure to lighting design was in the dance world. Visiting companies like Nicholas Dance Theatre and Paul Taylor came to my undergrad school. It was something I connected with from the very beginning. During graduate school, and then through assisting Gilbert Hemsley, I was introduced to the world of opera and that became my primary area of focus early in my professional career. In 1986 I was offered the opportunity to work with the New York City Ballet and since that time dance has been a major component of my design work." Like many other lighting designers, Mark works in other areas of lighting as well and says that while the proportions of his work change from year to year, at this point, dance lighting accounts for about 80% of what he does, with the other 20% being made up of opera, special events, and an occasional play or musical. More importantly Mark claims that, "There are no traditional areas of lighting anymore. Careers are made up of everything from lighting theatre to car shows, from opera to corporate events and cruise ships. The fundamentals are the same, even though some of the techniques might change. But the crossover is important." To remain current, he suggests, "See as many productions and the work of other designers as possible. Read reviews. Explore ideas with other designers and try to work with as many new people as you can."

When asked about what additional training he had to do to cross over into dance lighting he replied, "Every area of lighting has techniques and approaches that are unique, but it is all built on the same fundamentals. For lighting dance, an understanding of its history, the breadth of the form, the process and discipline of the dancers, and the vocabulary of the choreographers are all important. Basically, it's exposure and immersion in the art form, and getting your head wrapped around the idea of lighting abstract images and ideas that aren't grounded in a text."

Mark claims to have had a lot of great mentors along the way—starting with a TD at the Arlington, VA Recreation Department back when he was only in the 7th grade. However, his big break came as a result of his association with Gilbert Hemsley. He shares that, "The single biggest influence on my career and me was Gilbert Hemsley—both as a teacher and professional designer whom I assisted. He not only opened doors, but opened my eyes and thinking in ways that were profound. His death was a great personal loss to me and to the theatre community. It was a tough way to get a break."

What Mark likes most about lighting dance is the challenge of creating lighting that moves through time and space in a graphic, abstract environment. "It's also great working with creating a complete idea from scratch with a choreographer rather than starting with an existing text or libretto." Lighting dance also often requires you to wear several hats. "Many times you need to have production management skills, scenic design skills, and technical direction skills. Frequently you are the only designer on the production team and you need to think of more than just the lighting. It also requires you to conceive of an entire environment for the world of the dance." Finally, dance lighting requires you to be focused on the critical components of the design. "By working in a non-text format, and generally in 30–40 minute periods of time, your design ideas must be concise and clear." What he likes least is that there is never enough time. "The dance world works on such tight budgets and schedules that there is often little time to explore. You need to come to the table prepared and focused and there is rarely a chance for trying something really new or working through an idea or design choice." He suggests the following as an essential rule for lighting in the dance discipline: "Choose a single quality of light as the basis for your ideas and build layers. Don't try to do too much. Don't forget that even though there isn't a text to a dance—there is still a beginning, middle, and end, and that you have to help connect them to one another in your design."

Photo credit: © Rosalie O'Connor Photography

FOR FURTHER READING

Bellman, Willard F., *Lighting the Stage: Art and Practice,* 3rd ed. (Louisville, KY: Broadway Press, Inc., 2001).

Illuminating Engineering Society of North America, *IESNA Lighting Education 100 (Fundamental Level)* (New York: Illuminating Engineering Society of North America, 1993).

Illuminating Engineering Society of North America, *IESNA Lighting Education 150 (Intermediate Level)* (New York: Illuminating Engineering Society of North America, 1993).

Illuminating Engineering Society of North America, *IESNA Lighting Ready Reference*, 4th ed. (New York: Illuminating Engineering Society of North America, 2003).

Illuminating Engineering Society of North America, *IESNA Lighting Handbook,* 9th ed., ed. Mark Rae (New York: Illuminating Engineering Society of North America, 2000).

Palmer, Richard H., *The Lighting Art: The Aesthetics of Stage Lighting Design*, 2nd ed. (Englewood Cliffs, NJ: Prentice-Hall, Inc., 1994).

Warfel, William B. and Walter R. Klappert, *Color Science for Lighting the Stage* (New Haven, CT: Yale University Press, 1981).

The Practitioners

4

Lighting design, just as with many other professions, is rarely completed by a single individual. In reality, there are a number of different specialists connected to a lighting department and overall project. In a typical entertainment situation, a director will be in charge of the overall vision of a production while design specialists are secured to design the specialty areas of scenic, costume, sound, and lighting design. A **lighting designer** designs the lighting. In the construction industry, a project is usually under the control of an architect or client, and specialists are brought in to design or specify each of a building's systems (HVAC or Heat Ventilation and Air Conditioning, mechanical engineers for materials and structural specifications, interior designers for finishes and furniture consultation, and **illuminating engineers** for the lighting).

We also make a distinction between the individuals who are charged with the design responsibilities or the artistic considerations of a project and those who actually execute the designs. Each professional can be identified through a prevalent set of job responsibilities along with, in many cases, the specific unions or trade guilds that collectively represent a particular position. While I may refer to general responsibilities that fall under the jurisdiction of a given job title, it needs to be understood that there are gray areas between the responsibilities of many of these positions. Frequently, a single individual may be charged with the responsibilities of two or more of these jobs for an organization. This is particularly true of small theatre companies and independent production agencies. The actual determination of an individual's duties lies within that person's job description for a particular organization. Responsibilities often vary from one venue to another, and tasks that a person may not have been responsible for at one firm could fall within their responsibilities for another organization—even though both positions may share the same job title. In most moderate- to large-scale operations, the unions are more involved and have worked to create consistency from venue to venue for individuals sharing a particular job classification.

This chapter examines the responsibilities typically associated with a variety of lighting professionals and how these positions fit into the overall chain of authority for an organization. The positions are organized primarily by the lighting industries with which they are associated (live performance, film, and architectural) and by whether the position is primarily artistic or trade oriented in its duties. At the end of the chapter I also provide a brief introduction to several of the professional societies, certifications, and unions that are representative of the lighting profession.

THEATRICAL AND LIVE PERFORMANCE PRODUCTION

Many of the career positions throughout the entertainment industry are based on positions that were originally associated with the theatre. This is due to the fact that theatrical production dates back further than other forms of entertainment lighting. In general, the theatre also tends to be more specific in delegating which duties belong to a given position. The crew that is responsible for all electrical requirements for a production is called the **electrics crew,** which traditionally covers the lighting and sound departments while also providing power to effects, lifts, hydraulic pumps, winches, and any other equipment that might be powered by electricity. Even though we use electricians on stage, these individuals are not licensed in the same manner that an electrician working on your home would be. In fact, other than experience, there is currently no regulatory action controlling the qualifications of stage employees. In 2006, a voluntary certification program that qualifies stage electricians through an independent test became available, but it's still too early to see what ramifications this program may have on the industry. As of 2009 there were around 175 individuals who had passed the electrician test and were holding active certifications. The strong unions that controlled theatrical production in large east-coast cities like Philadelphia, Baltimore, Boston, and especially New York probably played the most significant role in defining the responsibilities of each theatrical employee's position. On a practical side, this preserved job security, benefits, and wages for the unions' memberships. Later, these positions and their associated duties, were widely accepted across the entire industry, and we now use these classifications whether a production is associated with a union or not. There is also a distinction between those professionals who are associated with the crafts (execution) and those who are charged with the design or artistic aspects of a production. Both are represented by different unions, and it is considered improper for a member to accept any tasks that fall under the jurisdiction of another union. Lighting designers are members of the same union that other designers belong to, and the crews belong to the union represented by the craftsmen of the various theatrical trades. The designers' union is the **United Scenic Artists (USA),** which represents both designers and scenic painters, while the crews are unionized under the **International Alliance of Theatrical Stage Employees (IATSE).** It is often common to hear professionals referring to these unions as USA, USAA, IATSE, the IA, or even the local. A couple of years ago USA shifted its association with its parent organization and it too is now affiliated with IATSE.

Design Professionals

LIGHTING DESIGNER (LD)   The most significant member of the design team is the lighting designer. This individual is charged with the overall artistic contribution of the lighting for a production. A lighting designer works with the director and other designers to produce an artistic vision for the production. Typical tasks of a lighting designer can be broken down into two specific time frames for a production: the pre-production and production phases. Pre-production is associated with tasks that are done prior to the **load-in** of the show, while production generally relates to the time in which the show is being developed in the theatre. Pre-production responsibilities for a lighting designer often include: generating a script analysis, attending rehearsals and production meetings, developing a conceptual framework for the production, and producing the lighting plans and specifications for a production. The production phase occurs once the show moves into the theatre and includes: **hanging and circuiting** or positioning and wiring the lighting equipment, **focusing** (pointing and adjusting each light for optimum performance), **cueing** (establishing the looks and recording them so that they can be duplicated from performance to performance), and tweaking or refining the lighting throughout the final rehearsals and preview performances. Once the lighting designer and director are satisfied with the lighting (generally upon opening night) the designer is typically released and moves on to the next production.

Anything related to lighting a show is under the jurisdiction of a production's lighting designer. While an extremely small theatre may require a lighting designer to execute their own design, this is usually the exception, and a designer more often delegates the execution of the lighting to other professionals. This makes for a more efficient design process since most productions are on schedules that require many people to realize a design in a very limited amount of time. This also supports the union's need to provide jobs for its members. The truth of the matter is that even simple productions have become so complex that a designer has enough to worry about in just dealing with design-related issues. Because of this, it is best to have other lighting professionals working by your side to help make the lighting the best that it can be.

In addition to making design decisions, the lighting designer must also communicate the design to other members of the production team. This relates first to communicating artistic information to the rest of the design staff, and then once an artistic vision for a production has been agreed upon, the designer turns to making the design a reality through making selections in lighting equipment and accessories, hanging positions, and wiring specifications that are then communicated to the people who will physically prep and install the lighting. All of this information is communicated to the lighting crews through a scaled drafting called a **light plot.** The light plot communicates the information that a crew will require to execute a design prior to the designer actually coming to the theatre. Typical information presented in a light plot includes choice of type and number of lighting fixtures, hanging locations, color assignments, and control or wiring information. Many light plots develop into drafted plates that can be up to 36 inches wide or larger. This can make the plots difficult to store or use when consulting them during a load-in. In order to make the information more accessible, lighting designers also prepare forms that provide the same information in a table or schedule format. We refer to these schedules or tables as the **paperwork** for a project. Often, the paperwork contains even more information about the design than the plot itself. Chapter 12 presents a full discussion of the light plot and the many types of paperwork that are generated for a design project.

In large productions, a lighting designer may feel that a project is large enough that they cannot manage all of the design responsibilities on their own. Schedules may also be an issue because there could be very little time to actually mount the design in the theatre. Here, two or more individuals working on various aspects of a design could enable a designer to produce a better design. This divide and conquer approach allows a designer to be more productive. Most lighting designers will also have a number of projects at various stages of completion at any given time—often scattered across the country and resulting in the designer not being available to attend every meeting or discussion regarding a specific project. In these cases, a lighting designer often brings additional individuals to the project who are assigned specific responsibilities that the lighting designer delegates to them. The most common partner is the **assistant lighting designer** although an **associate lighting designer** may also be used on a project.

ASSOCIATE LIGHTING DESIGNER   An associate lighting designer operates at a level of authority just below the lighting designer. The responsibilities of an associate designer can vary considerably but are more along the lines of providing artistic input and decisions for the lighting designer and production. Being a second set of eyes for the designer forms a primary duty of an associate designer. Other duties might include supervising elements of the design during a designer's absence and being an overall source of input and feedback for the designer. An associate designer may occasionally be placed in charge of specific parts of a lighting design. Because of the importance of all these duties, this position is often assigned to an individual with whom the lighting designer is comfortable, trusts, and with whom the designer has had a long-standing professional relationship. Most associate designers have worked for a designer as an assistant on a number of projects that have spanned many years. These relationships often resemble some form of partnership that can range from an associate being assigned to a series of specific tasks or responsibilities to having a true design partnership where both designers function together in most if not all of the artistic decision making. One of the more famous Broadway lighting teams is that of Jules Fisher and Peggy Eisenhauer. This team has created some of the most successful musical theatre hits of all time. Eisenhauer began her association with Fisher as an assistant who through the years became entrusted with more and more design responsibilities. Over time, Fisher moved her into the role of an associate designer and in recent years it is difficult, if not impossible, to find a major musical credit

DESIGNER PROFILE

John Martin

John Martin's involvement in lighting spans a variety of credits in both theatrical events and themed venues. His recent work has been in architectural lighting design. At a young age he focused his creative interests in lighting and has been happy ever since. Martin's formal education includes a BA from University of California—Irvine and a MFA from the University of California—San Diego, the first generally in drama and the latter specifically in theatrical lighting design. Shortly after finishing graduate school he became involved in environmental themed projects. This experience led to his work in architectural lighting. Currently, he is a senior associate for Kaplan Gehring McCarroll lighting where he continues to design a variety of projects.

When Martin speaks of education he relates that, "I believe that theatre training programs share a good deal with what used to be called a 'liberal arts' education—learning to think and articulate through the lens of literature. It creates a new kind of businessperson that is capable of collaborating with others to bring vision to reality. Theatre taught me how to make things: start with the core idea in the script, overcome restraints of budget, time, and space, and culminate with an aesthetic response that goes beyond the collection of the individual parts."

A big break was joining a World Expo team (similar to a World's Fair) in South Korea. It was a short 7 weeks leading up to the opening. Next was a small park in Japan where he spent months on the construction site translating paper designs into the final realized product. During this time he received an NEA/TCG Young Designer's Fellowship. This exposed him to a whole new set of mentors and experiences by traveling throughout the United States, with stops in South America and the United Kingdom. Upon completing the grant, a friend invited him to interview for a position with Universal Studios' creative team. For over 3 years Martin worked on Orlando's Islands of Adventure park—including the exterior lighting for Port of Entry and Marvel's Super Hero Island. The park won a Thea Award from the Themed Entertainment Association.

Commenting on such a variety of work he advises young designers: "Networking, networking, networking. This is a business of people making things. Find the people that share your interests and develop with them. Be open to the possibilities that come up and seize them with the best energy possible." He chooses not to point to a single event or individual who helped him. Instead, he states that there were many generous people who helped him out along the way and that each project presented the introductions needed to branch out into different areas of the industry.

An important aspect of both themed and architectural lighting is the extended timeline of a project. While a theatrical production may take 1–3 months of involvement, a themed or architectural project will typically take 1–3 years to complete (or more). Because of this, projects may go through several different designers before they are finally realized. "Core ideas and presentation are very important in these designs—napkin sketches have their place in the design process but articulated narratives and color renderings are much more successful for getting the funding for a project." On the other hand, one of the frustrations of working in these areas is that, ". . . with the longer time frames of these jobs, the project may be completely designed and never get built—this makes putting one's gusto into the next job all the harder." He also notes that the contracting community is not typically sensitive to the lighting needs of a project. This is in stark contrast to a technical theatre staff.

Regardless of what he is lighting Martin's most important advice is to make something compelling and relevant. "No matter what project you light, two things are consistent—collaborating with a client and taking fixed resources and making them into something aesthetic." He also speaks of several important lifestyle choices that have influenced his career. "The earlier part of my career had a good deal of exciting travel. Once I had a family I sought out other options. Architectural designing fits well with my choice to spend time with my family. There is a normalcy to the job and there are many opportunities to collaborate. I work in a large office and cannot think of any other time in my past where there have been 20 lighting designers in one room that can go home to their own beds at night. The collegiate atmosphere is very fulfilling, sharing ideas with younger designers trained in architecture and interior design. His final recommendations are, "Develop a healthy passion. Lighting is my first love but so are compelling spaces and life partners. Community comes in many forms. We should always focus on the global good and play it forward."

that Fisher has designed in which Eisenhauer has had little or no involvement. They even shared the 1996 Tony and Drama Desk Awards for *Bring in 'da Noise, Bring in 'da Funk.* A production doesn't have to have an associate lighting designer since many of the tasks that they might complete can be completed by the designer themselves or by an assistant lighting designer. As a rule, only the largest productions will have an associate lighting designer, and they typically come through the specific request and negotiations of the lead designer.

ASSISTANT LIGHTING DESIGNER (ALD)   The last member of the lighting design staff is the assistant lighting designer (ALD). Like an associate lighting designer this individual also serves as a personal assistant to the lighting designer. However, while an assistant's duties may vary considerably from one situation to another, the primary task of an assistant lies in the organization and documentation of a design. They should have a background in design and are frequently charged with specific duties that come under the jurisdiction of the lighting designer. Assistants are hired to take care of the mundane yet important tasks that can take a designer's focus away from the actual lights and design that they are creating. Tasks like drafting the light plot and generating all of the paperwork are often assigned to an assistant lighting designer. Once a production moves into the theatre an assistant is often in charge of making sure that all the paperwork is kept up to date, recording the focus of the show, keeping work notes, and tracking (maintaining a record of all the levels and cue settings) for a production. In large productions, assistants may be asked to help coordinate the designer's efforts related to special interests like cueing, integration of moving lights, or coordination of the followspots. In many ways, the assistant becomes a second set of hands and can be asked to help a designer in almost any particular need—even to the point of making coffee runs, keeping the design table clear of trash, and being a sense of moral support for the designer. I know several assistants who were placed in charge of the candy and ashtrays (not permitted any longer) that were kept at the design table. Assistant designers must be liked by the lead designer . . . you spend too many hours a day cooped up in a dark theatre for this relationship to be anything but friendly and encouraging. A good assistant will also know not to offer any opinions until asked by the senior designer and should be thoughtful, tactful, and supportive when responding to any questions. Large productions may have several assistant lighting designers on their staffs. In these cases, each assistant will be charged with specific duties and will be identified as the 1st Assistant, 2nd Assistant, 3rd Assistant or even given a title such as Assistant to Mr. Smith. The order of the ranking typically relates to either the importance of the tasks that are assigned or the time that they have been associated with the primary designer. In small venues, especially in those that don't typically use assistants, a designer will have a lot more say in the hiring of a specific individual as their assistant. However, in situations where a designer can't convince a producer to hire an assistant, the designer themselves may actually employ the assistant . . . including being responsible for the assistant's pay! On the other hand, if a designer works on more demanding productions (especially shows under union jurisdiction), a producer usually hires and is often even required to provide assistants to the designer. In these situations a designer may or may not have negotiating power in the hiring of their assistants. If the show is under a union contract, the designer can be assured that the assistants will also be union members.

A second opportunity for associate and assistant designers occurs when a production is operating under a condition in which the show will have to be remounted or toured. It is rare that a designer will commit to, or be available for, the daily or weekly needs of moving a design around the country for an extended period of time. When this occurs, an assistant or associate designer is hired with the notion that they will learn the design well enough that they can maintain it and keep the personal aesthetic of the show as it plays different venues throughout the tour. Associate and assistant designers may also be affiliated with productions that are moved between different cities as part of the regional theatre movement. A final situation where assistant lighting designers might be utilized is found in resident companies that have a practice of jobbing in guest designers on a per-show basis. In this situation, an assistant lighting designer is a permanent member of the company's staff and will function as the lighting coordinator for the guest designers (usually high profile designers). The assistant then acts as a facilitator between the guest designer and the theatre organization. Typical duties of a resident lighting assistant may include: coordinating the schedule for the guest designer's residency; making sure that the designer is supplied with the proper plans, inventory, and lighting suppliers; budget issues; and communicating any unique issues related to the company and its facilities. They also often act as liaisons between several different designers who may book-end a project so that there are no complications in moving from one production to another. If the company is a repertory company the assistant lighting designer is the individual who will most commonly be responsible for bringing the production out of storage and remounting it. Again, the assistant is primarily responsible for documenting the show so that it can be remounted easily the next time that it is produced. Some of the operas contained in the repertory of the Metropolitan Opera in New York City were originally produced 30 or 40 years ago; yet, a detailed record has been created for each one so that they can be brought out of storage and included in future seasons.

Theatrical Crews

Designers may occasionally be required to participate or complete the actual hang and focus of a production but this is usually delegated to other professionals. As productions get larger, crew positions become more clearly defined, and designers are not permitted to help with responsibilities that are charged to the crews. This separation of duties first developed as a means of protecting crew employment but has created an added benefit in that it guarantees that crews have the necessary skills to competently complete their duties—allowing a designer to concentrate on designing a show rather than with the details related to executing a design. Even with the separation of duties, a designer must be familiar with the mechanics of mounting a production so that they are knowledgeable and sensitive to the needs of the crews who are executing their designs. While a designer can't usually physically participate in the crew activities, they, an assistant, or another representative of the designer should be on hand at every work call to deal with any issues that a crew will need to have answered.

MASTER ELECTRICIAN (ME)   The technician who plays the most important supervisory role in the lighting department is the **master electrician (ME).** Even though the specific duties of a master electrician may vary from production to production, this individual is charged with the overall task of making sure that the lighting is installed and operated in a safe, efficient manner. Depending on the type of production, the master electrician may be a permanent member of a facilities staff or a temporary employee who is contracted for the length of a production. A master electrician may also be associated with touring productions. Several tasks that typically fall within the responsibilities of a master electrician include: being the mediator between the designer and the electrics crew, ensuring that the proper lighting gear is acquired (purchasing or renting it or pulling it from an inventory and prepping it for a production), determining wiring configurations that meet the designers specifications (circuit layouts and planning), supervising the electrics crew and personnel, ensuring that the equipment is installed and wired according to safety practices, and supervising the electrical department (board operators, deck electricians, and followspot operators) during the run of the show.

In large operations a master electrician may delegate aspects of their responsibilities to other members of the electrics department; in a small venue the master electrician may take on additional tasks like becoming the board operator. Master electricians should be familiar with the *National Electrical Code (NEC)* and other safety practices to ensure that the lighting can be installed and operated in a way that is safe for the crews, performers, and audiences. A master electrician needs to be one of the more experienced crew members associated with a production and often trains less experienced members of a crew. In a union situation, the master electrician will often be the union steward for the theatre or touring personnel. A variation of the master electrician position is the **house electrician,** who typically has the same duties as a master electrician but is assigned to a specific theatre or performance space. This is simply a change in title, although professionals who have this title are often both members of a union facility and representatives of **road houses,** or theatres that cater to touring productions. These individuals provide key links between the master electrician of a touring production and the management of a touring facility. This person is also responsible for the maintenance of a facility's lighting equipment, hiring local crew members on an **overhire** (per show) basis, and will usually do the **tie-in** of the touring company's equipment. Both a master electrician and house electrician may have an assistant to help them perform their duties. A master electrician's second in command is the **assistant master electrician (AME),** while a house electrician's assistant holds the title of **assistant house electrician.**

ELECTRICIAN   The majority of the technicians working in the electrical department are simply called **electricians.** Although they may be assigned to any duties that have a connection to electricity, the majority of them are associated with the preparation and execution of the lighting for a production. Some will have duties within special areas like projection, followspot operation, special effects, and sound. Typical duties that are assigned to electricians include: hanging and circuiting lighting fixtures, cutting and placing the specified gel into the fixtures, and focusing the lights. Additional duties may include: wiring lamps and other prop/scenic units and running the light board or followspots for a production. A production will typically require a number of electricians to help with the initial put-in or installation of a show but will release many of them once the show moves into its performance run. This is simply due to the fact that most productions don't require many individuals to operate the lighting during the run of a show. At the end of the final performance, once again a number of electricians will be brought in to **strike** all the lighting gear. Once a production moves into technical/dress rehearsals and its performance run, the electricians that continue to work are usually identified by the specific function and equipment that they operate. A **board operator** works with the designer to program the light board and executes the cues as ordered by the stage manager during the performances. A **followspot operator** is assigned to run a followspot, and a **deck electrician** works backstage to help connect and disconnect temporary circuits, shift electrical equipment, and make new circuit assignments throughout a performance. While the design staff's jobs are finished upon opening a show, the electricians who complete tasks like these continue to be employed for as long as a show is running. They are also charged with maintaining a production throughout its run. Common tasks that they complete include fixing burned-out lamps, replacing faded gels, and touching up the focus of lights that have slipped—whether the performances extend for a single week or a number of years. In long running shows, electricians often rotate on and off productions as they deal with other projects and commitments.

PROGRAMMER   There is one more crew member that has been added to the list of electrical specialists over the last 10 or so years. This person, usually called a **programmer** or **moving light operator,** is responsible for the programming and operation of a specialized console that controls moving lights. This person is also often responsible for the maintenance of any moving lights that are part of a show. Changes in color, beam quality, gobo pattern, and most importantly movement are all under the control of this console. While a traditional console may be capable of controlling moving lights, when more than a couple of moving lights are used it is often easier to use a specialized console that is more adept at controlling all of the parameters associated with the automated lighting. It is common for large-scale productions with automated lights to actually use two different lighting consoles—one for the "conventionals" and one for the "movers." There are numerous people working in the lighting industry who are making a living solely as moving light operators or programmers.

FILM AND VIDEO

There are a number of similarities between the professionals who work in the film and video industries and many people float back and forth equally well between both areas of lighting. Additionally, these industries hire professionals that have production responsibilities that are quite similar to those that work in the theatrical industry. The two industries even have many of the same union affiliations as theatrical professionals. Designers are usually members of USA, while the crews are covered by IATSE. While many of the responsibilities and departments are quite similar, there are also different titles associated with many of these production personnel. Due to their similarities, I am keeping my discussion of the professionals in the film and video industries more abbreviated. In many cases, even though the titles may be different, the positions are quite parallel to those already discussed in theatrical applications. There are also several significant differences between theatrical and film production. Some unique differences between these are: the live versus recorded nature of the final product, the direct exposure to the eye versus the indirect means of transferring images through a camera and film or monitor, and the viewer being exposed to an entire environment or scene (with distractions) versus the confined and very selective focus of a camera. While an entire stage or performance venue must be dealt with for a live event, a film or video shoot only requires a designed environment within the frame of the camera.

Design Professionals

CINEMATOGRAPHER/DIRECTOR OF PHOTOGRAPHY (DP)   The most visible designer in video or film production is the Cinematographer or Director of Photography (DP). This person works extensively with the director and is responsible for creating the entire visual environment for a production. Although the director of photography is responsible for the lighting for a production, it is only one of the areas in which this individual has primary responsibilities. The director of photography also has responsibilities in choosing the location of a setting, determining the camera angles and range of an individual shot, and selecting the camera lenses and film speeds for a take. Having said this, storyboarding and lighting probably form two of this individual's most significant contributions to a film or video. **Storyboards** are simple drawings that are created to give an indication of the view and individual composition of each camera shot. This allows a director and cinematographer to discuss each shot prior to working with the cast and crews. While storyboards tend to be underutilized in theatrical production, they form a major type of communication in the film and video communities. Often a director of photography or cinematographer will have other design professionals or assistants working under them. Directors of photography may be certified members of a professional society called the **American Society of Cinematographers (ASC)** and are identified through the ASC abbreviation following their names in a production's credits.

LIGHTING DIRECTOR (LD)   Due to the size of many film and video projects it is common for a director of photography to bring another individual on board to supervise the lighting of a project. This lighting specialist is the **lighting director** and will have overall charge of the lighting for a film or video. This position is actually more commonly affiliated with video rather than film production. The video industry will almost always employ a lighting director, while cinematographers are more characteristic of the film industry. Just as in theatrical production, each of these professionals may have associates or assistants working under them. Several duties of a lighting director include: analyzing and researching the script; working with the director or director of photography to develop a lighting concept for a project; researching light sources and creating the plot (if needed), producing the associated paperwork for the shoot, and designing the specific cues/looks for each segment of the project. One special problem in video and film production relates to **continuity.** Continuity is paying attention to details in a way that ensures that everything remains consistent in terms of prop placement, scenic details, and costume treatments. For a lighting director, this means that each camera angle and **take** of a scene must be lit in exactly the same manner. Since film and video productions are usually shot out of sequence, special care must be taken to make sure that these details are dealt with consistently in each of the takes that are recorded for a given scene.

Production Crews

GAFFER   Production crews in the film and video industries have similar responsibilities to their counterparts in the theatrical world. In many cases, despite titles, the duties are the same, although there are additional professionals in film and video production that aren't typically found in most theatrical applications. The gaffer or **chief lighting technician** is the individual who is the most similar to a master electrician in theatrical production. There is a unique twist though in that the chief lighting technician actually translates the image of a DP into the actual instrument choices and placements of the lights and other related equipment for a shoot. This person works directly with the lighting director or director of photography to provide the specified lighting equipment, filters, and power for each shoot. They are also responsible for the direct supervision of the lighting staff for a project. If a gaffer has an assistant, this person is called the **best boy.** In recent years, it has become preferable to call the person in charge of this aspect of the lighting the chief lighting technician.

GRIPS   The actual crew members for film and video are most often called **grips** and are responsible for the movement and setup of any equipment required for a shoot. This position is equivalent to being called a stagehand in theatrical production. Typical duties include the setup and strike of all scenic or prop elements, lighting equipment, and any reflective or diffusion devices. They are also responsible for the installation and operation of camera gear like dollies and cranes—although a **camera operator** will be responsible for the operation of the camera itself. Some organizations like to make a distinction between those grips that are assigned to lighting responsibilities and the rest of the crew and refer to those with a lighting specialty as **gaffers.** In this case, rather than having the chief lighting technician credited as gaffer, this person will usually be given the title of **head gaffer.** With all of this confusion in titles, it can be seen why the title of chief lighting technician has become so popular. The head gaffer generally supervises the entire lighting department for a television or film production. As in theatrical production, light board operators and moving light operators/programmers may also be used.

Two additional lighting specialists are often added to a film or video team when there is a location shoot. When shooting on location, there is seldom enough power for the needs of the cameras, lighting equipment, and other gear that a shoot will require. Therefore, the production team needs to provide its own power by bringing a **generator** to a production site. These units may be as small as a portable unit that can be carried by a single crew member or large, trailer-mounted units that are as big as a semi-trailer. In major televised events like the broadcasting of network football games, producers often have several trailers of mobile production gear and semi-sized generators positioned just outside of an arena. The individual who operates and monitors these generators is the **generator,** or **genny, operator.** A second specialist associated with film and video production (**set wireman**) is an electrician who is responsible for the wiring and maintenance of all of the practical lighting fixtures. A **practical** is a lighting fixture like a table lamp or wall sconce that is mounted on a set and seen by an audience.

ARCHITECTURAL LIGHTING

The specialized field of lighting that relates to architectural installations is called **illumination engineering.** Projects that commonly fall under this umbrella include: building interiors and exteriors, display lighting like that found in museum and retail exhibits, roadway and bridge lighting, installations like monuments, themed designs like amusement parks and attractions, and garden or landscape lighting. Architectural lighting includes a number of different applications, but all share a common trait in that the installations are permanent. Unlike entertainment lighting where a production may go up in a few hours and then be struck immediately following a performance, or where long runs are measured in weeks or months, architectural practices demand that an installation be operational for years if not decades. The concept of permanent versus temporary dictates a very different approach to lighting these projects. Mistakes can be expensive, and design solutions need to be accurate the first time. A mistake in fixture type or placement in an architectural application could become a permanent problem or safety concern. Due to the issue of permanence, architectural lighting requires a more rigorous regulation of designers and installers to ensure that a project is designed and installed safely. While mood and style play a role in architectural lighting, the emphasis of these designs is usually on the functionality of a lighting application. Therefore, the activities that are planned for an environment determine the minimum amount of light to be specified so that the activity or **task** can be completed in an efficient, safe manner. The more critical the task, the higher the illumination level that is specified.

Lighting design professionals that work in architectural lighting generally have two different backgrounds. The first, **Illuminating Engineers,** are the more traditional of the two professionals. Many individuals who design the lighting for architectural projects come from the electrical engineering discipline and are identified as illuminating engineers. These professionals are often part of a design team of an architectural or engineering firm that designs large projects like office buildings, hotels, shopping malls, etc. In the past, it was common for these professionals to be part of a department of electrical engineers that specified all of the electrical systems for a project. Outlet specifications, communication systems, elevator control, power for heat and ventilation equipment as well as lighting form several of the building systems that these engineers are responsible for. Interior designers are another group of professionals who might design the lighting for a project as an additional part of their design services. Another professional, the **Lighting Designer (LD),** has come about more recently. In the last 20 years, architects and their clients have gravitated toward a more artistic rather then solely functional approach to lighting buildings. With this new interest, many architects turned to entertainment lighting designers working with illuminating engineers to produce more innovative lighting projects. The title of lighting designer came with this crossover and initially was reserved for designers who were providing a more aesthetic contribution to a design than simple illumination. Today, it has become a fairly common practice for even individuals with electrical engineering backgrounds to refer to themselves as lighting designers if they are charged with the responsibility of lighting architectural projects. Just as in entertainment lighting, an architectural lighting designer is responsible for the choice and location of luminaires, filter decisions, control assignments, and wiring specifications. They are also responsible for the focusing or **aiming** of the fixtures and cueing any dynamic elements of a design.

An architectural lighting designer should also have a keen awareness of several additional design parameters that entertainment designers rarely have to consider. Several of these include: an understanding of both the *National Electrical Code* and any building or other electric codes that are specific to a given municipality, knowledge in construction documents, familiarity with illumination engineering practices and calculation techniques, and an understanding of lighting economics and **green power.** Green power relates to using conservation practices to lower the energy demands of a project. There is a vast amount of regulation in architectural lighting as compared to virtually none in the entertainment industry. Not specifying enough footcandles of illumination for a stairwell or creating a design that consumes too much power could result in civil lawsuits or regulatory charges. If a lighting designer has not been trained as an electrical or illuminating engineer, the detailed specifications for items like conduit sizes, wire gages, number of wires in a conduit, and power specifications are handed off to an electrical engineer. There are a host of professionals who are charged with the installation of architectural lighting systems. It is beyond the scope of this book to provide a full discussion of their duties, but several specialists that execute these designs include **project managers, electrical contractors,** and **electricians.** A significant difference between these and entertainment lighting professionals is that nearly all of them must be licensed by a local or state authority.

UNIONS AND CERTIFICATIONS

Nearly every one of the professionals discussed earlier are represented by one of several unions. Whether an individual becomes a member of a union usually depends on whether membership becomes a requirement for obtaining gainful employment in a profession. If not, union membership is often seen as a professional credential, although it needs to be emphasized that there are both good and bad union and non-union professionals working in any profession. Often, an individual cannot be employed in certain markets (theatres or studios), without becoming a union member first. However, this is typical of only the largest, most prestigious markets. Broadway theatres, feature films, significant touring productions, television studios in major markets (cities), and many regional theatres form venues where an individual will most likely have to become a union member before being employed. Several of the reasons that unions became established relate primarily to providing the crews with access to employee benefits. Health and pension plans are major benefits available to union members that aren't often provided to non-union employees. There are also provisions for regulating wage and working conditions in the studios and theatres that are under union contracts. Even with so many areas covered by union jurisdiction, the majority of the professionals working in the industry are most likely not affiliated with a union. Finally, it can usually be assumed that individuals with a union affiliation have demonstrated a minimal standard of proficiency, experience, and professionalism. The majority of the union members that I have worked with over the years reflect some of the best professionalism and competence in the business.

A certification is very different from a union membership and has nothing to do with providing any tangible benefits like pay scales, pensions, or health plans for an individual. Instead, a certification provides recognition that the bearer has demonstrated a particular degree of competence in a discipline. Certifications are earned or awarded by independent agencies or professional organizations of a chosen field and are commonly identified through a series of initials that are placed behind an individual's name. Just recently the theatrical community began certification programs for stage electricians and riggers. The program for electricians (Entertainment Electrician) is coordinated by the **Entertainment Technician Certification Program (ETCP).** The certification is based on the satisfactory completion of a standardized test. Those who complete their certification must be recertified every 5 years by participating in a series of educational activities or through retaking the test. It is thought that the certification practice will have a significant impact on the industry over the next several years. In the area of film, certification is earned through the **American Society of Cinematographers (ASC).** This is conferred upon directors of photography who are members of the organization. A member is identified by the ASC that is seen after the name of the director of photography on most feature films. Most lighting certifications are found in architectural practices and are either earned through an exam or are conferred by professional societies. The **LC** (Lighting Certified) certification by the **National Council on Qualifications for the Lighting Profession (NCQLP)** is such a certification.

Most entertainment design professionals, lighting designers included, are covered by the **United Scenic Artists (USA).** This union has three primary offices located in different regions of the country. New York is the primary office (Local 829) and represents the east coast, while the midwest is under the jurisdiction of Chicago and the west coast is overseen by Los Angeles. While the United Scenic Artists still remains an independent identity, the union has formed a partnership with the stagehands' union to form a more solid future for its membership in regard to health care plans and pensions. Membership is earned primarily through exam or by professional experience. There is also an apprenticeship program. While the majority of the membership is concerned with theatrical designing, the union also covers a significant number of individuals, studios, and projects in the video and film industries as well. The west coast office is quite heavily affiliated with these industries.

The **International Alliance of Theatrical Stage Employees (IATSE)** is the stage-hands' union and has a much larger membership than the design union. The union covers professionals who work in all forms of entertainment technology. Members may build, install, or form the run crew in scenery or electrics in a variety of different venues. Prop, wardrobe, and other crew areas are also covered by this union. Examples where IATSE is well represented include employment in theatres, touring productions, film and television studios, nightclubs and variety shows, arenas and convention centers, concert productions, and trade or industrial productions. Rather than three regional offices, most medium to large cities will have a local organization associated with the union that we commonly call a **local.** Membership requirements can vary considerably between different locals and can range from being a member of the right family to gaining experience through an overhire program or becoming involved in a full apprenticeship or initiation program.

In the broadcasting industry, many directors of photography and lighting directors along with other television employees and engineers like cameramen and other technicians belong to **The National Association of Broadcast Employees and Technicians (NABET)** union. While this union has members and locals scattered throughout the country its primary membership is associated with major network studios like ABC, NBC, and CBS in large cities or television markets. This union is affiliated with a larger constituency representing the Communications Workers of America (CWA).

PROFESSIONAL ORGANIZATIONS AND SOCIETIES

Professional societies and organizations provide a variety of resources for their members and profession. In the lighting industry there are numerous professional societies with which an individual might become affiliated. Some organizations are national or international, while others operate at the regional and local levels. Some are rather generic, while others relate to very specific niches of the lighting industry. In addition to providing resources for its members, these organizations also bring public awareness to that portion of the lighting industry. Member benefits may include training seminars, publications, networking with other professionals, exposure to potential clients, and introductions to new technologies and lighting applications. Most organizations also recognize exceptional projects and award individuals for various design achievements. An extremely important service that these organizations provide is coordinating industry standards and self-regulation from within the lighting profession. Most of these societies also produce or co-produce at least one major trade show or conference each year and publish regularly produced trade magazines and newsletters.

The most prevalent theatrical society that is aimed towards technicians and designers is the **United States Institute for Theatre Technology (USITT).** This organization represents designers and technicians from across all areas of stagecraft, and while most of its members are based in theatrical production, many are involved in a variety of entertainment areas. While the institute caters to all theatre professionals, there are also discipline-related groups called commissions like the Lighting Commission that deal with specific areas of design and technology. There is also an international association affiliated with USITT—**Organisation Internationale des Scénographes, Techniciens et Architectes de Théâtre (OISTAT).**

One of the largest organizations for individuals connected with video lighting is the **National Association of Broadcasters (NAB),** while a specialty society of the film and video industries that was formed to represent lighting directors and gaffers is the **American Society of Lighting Designers (ASLD).** There are a number of additional organizations that represent special interest groups of the lighting industry. These organizations cater to the specific needs of theatrical dealers, manufacturers, and even to the special needs of venues like theme parks and nightclubs.

Architectural lighting is represented by several major trade organizations, the two most prominent being the **Illuminating Engineering Society of North America (IESNA**

or IES) and the **International Association of Lighting Designers (IALD).** The IES is particularly important because it represents all aspects of the lighting industry, including designers and specifiers, manufacturers, distributors, and even researchers. The IES is comprised of a number of working groups that make a major contribution to the industry through reviewing and maintaining the *Lighting Handbook* and *Recommended Practices* that the IES publishes. These publications form the industry's specification standards for virtually any conceivable lighting application.

FOR FURTHER READING

Geraghty, Katie (Certification Director), *ETCP Candidate Handbook (Entertainment Electrician)* (New York: Entertainment Services and Technology Association , 2006).

Moody, James L., *The Business of Theatrical Design*, (New York: Allworth Press, 2002).

Watson, Lee, *Lighting Design Handbook,* (New York: McGraw-Hill, Inc., 1990).

5 Electricity

Developing a basic understanding of electricity is essential to the success of any lighting designer. While the actual pulling of cable, wiring, and installation are often delegated to the electrics crews, a designer still needs to have an understanding of topics like basic electrical theory, power distribution, electrical safety, and fundamental electrical calculations. This knowledge is essential for making the specifications that are required to complete a lighting project. This holds true whether the application is for a temporary installation such as for a stage or touring production or for a permanent installation like a building, garden, or exhibit.

Due to electricity's potential for causing injuries and even death, it is imperative that proper safety procedures be taken throughout both the installation and operation of any lighting design. A designer is responsible for the safety of not only the crews, but also the performers and audience as well. In the case of permanent installations, the safety requirements become even more stringent for protecting a building's occupants. These installations are guided by a number of safety codes as well as the requirement that all designs must be certified and installed by licensed professionals. While regulations may vary somewhat from municipality to municipality, the basis of most electrical standards and safety are found in the *National Electric Code (NEC)*. All lighting specifiers and designers should have an understanding of those portions of the NEC that are directly applicable to their niche of the industry. In today's practices, where many theatrical designers are being used as consultants on architectural projects, it is common for a designer to make design recommendations that are given to licensed electrical engineers who work out the detailed specifications of a project. In architectural practices, the codes are strictly enforced and the designs and installations are always inspected by municipal authorities at various stages of a project's completion. In either case, it is important for a designer to apply safe practices throughout their designs because they could be held liable for any decisions that fall outside the codes and common practices.

This chapter is not meant to present a complete guide to electricity, and the reader should refer to the books listed in the Further Reading portion of this chapter for more in-depth explorations of electricity. More importantly, this chapter should be used as a means of introducing those elements of electrical theory that are most applicable to a lighting designer's needs. The chapter begins with an introduction to general electrical theory and the means by which we measure it and relate these elements to one another. The second portion of the chapter presents information related to how power is created and distributed, while the following segment goes on to describe basic electrical equipment. A final segment explores some issues that are specific to architectural applications that we generally don't have to consider in entertainment projects at this time, but which might have to be considered someday in the future. Issues like power densities, efficiency, and lighting economics form topics contained in this final segment of the chapter.

BASICS OF ELECTRICITY

Most theories of electricity relate to the concept of creating an electrical flow of electrons from one place to another. This flow begins at the atomic level of an object and can result in a relative electron flow through both small and great distances. The following sections address many of the issues relating to the fundamental qualities and nature of electricity.

Atomic Theory

In basic atomic theory most scientists recognize the concept of **particle theory,** in which all substances are made up of small particles called **atoms.** These, in turn, are made up of even smaller particles that are associated with given charges. **Protons** carrying a positive charge are found in the central cluster (**nucleus**) of the atom along with the neutrally charged particles called **neutrons.** Orbiting this cluster are additional particles called **electrons** that carry negative charges. The most basic form of any material is called an **element** and can be identified through a specific atomic structure as defined by the number of protons that are contained in each atom. Most atoms contain an overall neutral charge, which is reflected through their containing the same number of protons and electrons. The familiar model of the solar system, with the sun at its center and a number of orbiting planets, forms a good model for the basic concept of an atom. As atoms become more complex, the number of protons and electrons increases, and the electrons shift to positions or energy shells that are farther away from the nucleus and contain progressively more and more electrons. Each energy shell becomes progressively more stable as additional electrons continue to fill its empty orbital or shell positions. Any material with a completely filled outer shell represents the most stable materials found in nature. If an energy shell only has one or two electrons in its outermost shell it can become unstable, and these electrons might be dislodged or shared between adjoining atoms that have a similar structure.

Electrical Potential

How electrons are instigated into forming an electron flow may come about through a number of different means, but what is characteristic to all is the fact that an excess of electrons or charge is introduced between two different points or locations. This gathering of electrons or electrical charge is known as **electrical potential.** All forces in nature work to reach a neutral level of energy, or what scientists often call a state of equilibrium, in which all forces are in balance. An example of this principle would be that given enough time, all mountains would erode as valleys would fill in to create flat planes. If a ball is released from the top of one of two adjoining hills, it will roll and come to rest at some point in the lowest area between the higher elevations. Electrical charges also strive to reach a state of equilibrium through a basic principle in which electrons always try to create a neutrally charged environment. This becomes the driving force in creating electrical flow. How might an excess electrical charge be created? It could be a gathering of electrons on particular storm clouds, as in the case of lightning, or a battery might provide the electrical potential through a chemical reaction, or a physical device like a generator might be used to convert one form of energy (gas) into an electrical potential.

A second requirement for electrical flow is that a path must be established between those points where an excess of electrical potential exists and the point of neutrality. If a path doesn't exist, there will be no electrical flow unless the potential difference becomes so great that the electricity actually jumps from one place to another. Lightning forms an example where electricity literally jumps from cloud to cloud or from a cloud to the ground. More commonly, we create the electrical pathways by initiating materials like wires into the system. If a wire breaks at any point in an electrical system, the electricity will fail to complete its journey and the task of turning on lights, operating a motor, or heating a toaster cannot be achieved. While some scientists believe that electrical flow actually represents a shifting of electrons from atom to atom along these paths; most believe that the electrons nudge one another, which still displaces the energy without actually shifting electrons from one atom to another. This is similar to the chain reaction that might occur when a person near the back of a line shoves the person directly in front of them, who then falls into the person in front of them, which continues to act on additional people progressively down the line. The waveforms that are created through this progressive movement of electrons are quite long and form a particular type of **electromagnetic radiation** or energy.

GROUNDING

Electricity, like any other form of energy, constantly strives to reach the lowest energy level possible. For all practical purposes this is the natural surface of the earth, which corresponds to a zero voltage potential. More commonly we refer to this as the earth or absolute **ground,** and all electricity strives to flow to it. One of the most common accidents connected with electricity results from an accidental path being provided for an electrical flow from one place to another. This may happen between areas of high and low potential or the actual earth ground itself. A short circuit, an electrical shock, or even a lightning strike are all results of instances where electricity was presented with a pathway to a lower electrical potential. All electricity attempts to flow towards the ground, and when you grab a live wire, the shock that you receive is simply due to your body becoming the pathway that the electricity uses to flow to the ground. The result of this happening in buildings can produce heat and sparks that might culminate in a fire.

In order to protect ourselves, electrical codes now insist that we provide a special safety path or wire that forms a path of least resistance for any electrical potential that may be let loose within an electrical device. If for some reason a device becomes electrically unstable, this path provides for the safe conduction of electricity away from the device and user which in turn helps to prevent shocks and fires from occurring. This emergency path is called the **ground** and will always connect an electrical device to an actual earth ground in some way. The grounding device with which you are most likely familiar is the third prong that is common to most wall outlets and appliances that have appeared over the last 40 or 50 years. The third pin is connected to a wire that extends from the device back through all the branch circuits to the main circuit box of a building. At the circuit box, the wire is joined with all the other grounding wires of the building, which are ultimately connected to a heavier wire that leads to a stake or rod that is driven into the actual ground outside of the building. Most wires associated with a grounding function can be quickly identified by the practice of color coding these wires green or by leaving the wire bare and uninsulated. Some wires will be identified by bearing green insulation while others will be black and have green tape applied near their ends. Grounding hardware such as screws are also often colored green as a means of identifying the ground. These pathways form a means of providing a safe electrical service to the occupants of a building, and at this time, virtually every electrical project imaginable must provide grounding in order to comply with current electrical codes and regulations. Even in theatrical practices, where codes have been lax, most equipment is now provided with grounding features, and stage electricians need to make every effort possible to provide grounding for every situation.

FUNDAMENTAL CIRCUITS

Electricity does not occur unless there is an energy flow. A stored potential is of no use unless we can set the electrons into motion to create work. In order for the flow to occur we must provide three elements: first, an area where an excess charge or potential is stored or created; second, an area of lower potential that the excess energy will seek; and finally, a device or material that connects the two areas by creating a pathway for the electrical flow. Most importantly, since electricity attempts to create a stable or neutral condition, the pathway must also form a return path back to the source. An electrical device requires both a connection that supplies the excess electrical flow and a second one that forms a return path back to the source. Through all of this, a complete circle is created for the electron flow, and together, we refer to this as a basic electrical **circuit.** If you remove any one of these elements you interrupt the flow of the electrons and there will be no electricity. The mechanism with which we are most familiar for conducting electrical flow is the **wire,** and if a wire becomes broken at any point—there will be no electrical flow.

Conductors and Insulators

Wires are made of metals which are generally very good **conductors** of electricity because they readily allow electrons to flow through them. Virtually all materials will conduct electricity if you apply enough power to them, even the human body—the results may not be pleasant but the fact remains that you can still get an electrical flow to pass through nearly any material. One of my most vivid memories as a teenager includes a demonstration where a youth leader had 20 of us stand in a circle where we were instructed to tightly hold each others' hands. At one point the leader broke into the circle and gave the teen on each side of him a single lead from a 12-volt car battery. One lead was conveniently equipped with a switch, and the two teens holding the leads from the battery were instructed not to touch one another. As one might imagine, when the leader pressed the switch we all felt the effects of electricity passing through our bodies until someone had the good sense to let go. A human chain became the wire for our leader's circuit, and when that one person let go, the human wire failed along with the electrical force that was traveling through us. *Do not* try this demonstration—with what we now know about shocks and heart rhythms, and how we are now mindful of anything that could possibly be construed as abusive behavior, you would be setting yourself up for a lawsuit. What's important is what the demonstration taught me about electrical flow through my experience from many years ago.

Just like all materials demonstrate some form of conductivity, they also display some form of **resistance** to electrical flow. In this case, there are characteristics of the material's composition that form a barrier to electrical flow. If a material has an overall high resistance to electrical flow we refer to it as an **insulator.** We cover wires with insulation to prevent accidental contact between the individual conductors and any other objects. The reason some materials are better insulators than others lies in their atomic structures causing them to be more resistant to electron movement. As a rule, metals form the best conductors. Gold and silver provide the least amount of resistance and are used in high quality wiring components like those found in critical applications like the space program and high-end audio/video industries. These metals are too expensive for most general purposes so other metals like copper and aluminum have become the most popular conductors for common wiring practices. Popular insulators that have been used in the electrical market include: rubber, nylon, porcelain, Bakelite, and asbestos. Asbestos is no longer used due to its potential for causing cancer, although it can still be found on occasion in older equipment that was manufactured prior to the 1980s. If you run into any equipment with asbestos you should take extreme care to protect yourself and others from inhaling the fibers and dust that are associated with this material. In all practicality, these units should be either retrofitted or retired.

Series Circuits

While I have already described a fundamental circuit, most circuits are more complex than this. We use a circuit to identify how components are connected to one another, while also tracing the electrical path from the source through the circuit and back again. There are essentially only two variations of a basic electrical circuit regardless of how complex the individual wiring or number and type of devices that it might contain. These are the series and parallel circuits. A **series circuit** simply connects the leads of each device together in a daisy-chain fashion that stretches between the leads of a power source. Figure 5.1 illustrates a series circuit containing seven lamps. All lamps in a series circuit share the power equally, and there are several side effects that might be considered undesirable in this type of circuit. First, if a single lamp burns out, the pathway for the electricity is interrupted for all the lamps and they all go out. Second, assuming that all the lamps are the same, as more lamps are added to the circuit, the lamps will glow equally bright but become progressively dimmer as the additional lamps are introduced to the circuit. A common example of a series circuit is found in the miniature lights that we use dur-

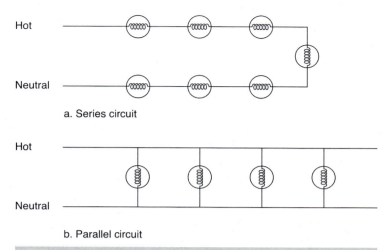

Hot

Neutral

a. Series circuit

Hot

Neutral

b. Parallel circuit

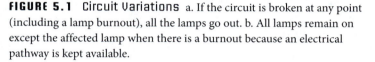

FIGURE 5.1 Circuit Variations a. If the circuit is broken at any point (including a lamp burnout), all the lamps go out. b. All lamps remain on except the affected lamp when there is a burnout because an electrical pathway is kept available.

ing the holidays. These can cause all sorts of frustration when through a single lamp's failure a whole string becomes inoperable. While these strings are designed to plug into a wall outlet of 120 volts, each individual lamp is only rated for 1 to 3 volts. If you were to shorten the length of the string from the manufactured 100 lamps to 50 you would probably discover that the lamps would glow about twice as bright as normal . . . until they burned out from the excessive voltage. They might even burst from the initial surge of power.

It is extremely important to ensure that an electrical device is connected to a power source that matches its designed voltage requirements—especially considering the fact that different areas of the world use different operating voltages. An appliance that is designed to work on the 120-volt United States standard will be damaged or destroyed if connected to the 240-volt service that is typical throughout much of Europe. While most equipment is rated for a single voltage, some gear, such as many of the moving lights used on world tours, are equipped with switches that permit the voltage to be matched to an electrical service.

Parallel Circuits

The second type of circuit is the **parallel circuit,** also illustrated in Figure 5.1. The parallel circuit differs from a series circuit in that each device is wired directly to the power source, providing several advantages for the user. First, since each device has a direct pathway to the power source, the power flow can continue independently of any other device in a circuit. If any one of the lamps were to go out or be removed from a parallel circuit the remaining lamps would continue to burn unaffected. A second advantage is that each device has full access to the power supply so that the lamps fully glow regardless of the number of lamps in the circuit at any given time. The parallel circuit forms the primary type of circuit that we use in most lighting applications. A typical application of the parallel circuit is found in wiring multiple lighting fixtures. All of the lights burn equally bright, and as one light burns out the remaining fixtures remain lit at the same brightness that they've always had. In practice, many circuits make use of both parallel and series elements. While all of the light fixtures in the last example may have been wired in parallel, they are typically under the control of a single switch. The switch is located at a place in the circuit that allows the power to be cut off from all the fixtures, therefore becoming a series element in this circuit. Note how the switch should also be located along the segment of the wiring that provides power to the

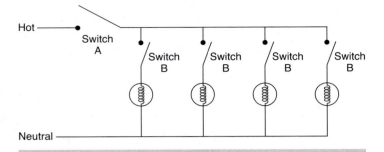

FIGURE 5.2   The Effect of Switch Location on Combination Circuits Switch A (wired in series) will control all of the lamps, while any switch labeled B (wired in parallel) will only control the lamp that is wired to that part of the branch circuit as long as switch A is also closed. Fuses and circuit breakers are frequently placed in the location of switch A.

circuit as opposed to being along the return path. While it would still work (you've still interrupted the power flow), for obvious reasons, it is safer to place switching devices near the source of the power. If an electrician wanted to control one group of lights in the above circuit separately, they would only have to add a switch to that portion of the circuit. We refer to these circuits as **combination circuits.** Figure 5.2 illustrates a combination circuit, in which all the lamps are under the influence of a single switch A while they are also individually controlled using the B switches. Protective electrical devices like fuses and circuit breakers should also be located near the power source and are wired as series components in most electrical circuits.

UNITS OF MEASUREMENT AND ESSENTIAL FORMULAS

A system of measurements has been devised as a way of both quantifying and making comparisons between circuits or for describing specific characteristics of a circuit itself. These may be measured through a variety of meters and can be related to one another through several different formulas. The following paragraphs describe several of these components and then relate them to one another through two different formulas.

Units of Measure

VOLTAGE (E)   The first measurement that we use to describe electricity relates to a measurement of the potential difference that exists between two different points. This is known as **voltage (E)** and is measured through a unit known as a volt. We may also refer to voltage as electromotive force (EMF). It is nothing more than a measurement of the energy difference between electrons at one location and electrons at another. Typical voltages with which we are quite familiar are the 12-volt systems in our cars, the 1.5-volt batteries that are common to handheld devices like flashlights and personal CD players, and the 120-volt systems that power most of our households.

AMPERAGE (A)   The second measurement of electrical flow relates to the rate of electrons flowing through a point at any given time. This is called **amperage (A),** and its unit of measurement is the ampere. Most wiring devices and appliances carry product warnings that relate to their electrical capacity. This is simply a statement that specifies either how much amperage a device may draw or the maximum amperage that the device may safely conduct. If a user exceeds these specifications, problems such as heated wires, fires, and short circuits can develop. The practice of plugging too many appliances into a household extension cord forms a common example of this type of safety violation. The basic rule is to never exceed the amperage specifications of a device.

RESISTANCE (R)   I spoke earlier of the principle that all materials have an ability to conduct or resist electrical flow. While some materials such as metals have a low resistance and become conductors, others resist electrical flow and are known as insulators. The basic measurement of electrical **resistance (R)** is measured in ohms (Ω) or kilo-ohms (1000 ohms). A large-diameter wire will conduct more electrons per unit time than a smaller diameter wire in much the same way an interstate with four lanes will carry a larger volume of cars than a two-lane highway. Just as in traffic, if you suddenly try to reduce the size of a wire or number of lanes, you create problems as more traffic tries to get through a point than intended for a given location.

POWER (P)   While I have provided several manners in which we can describe an electrical circuit, I haven't talked about the concept of how the electromotive force can be used to perform a task for us. How does this electromotive force accomplish the task? How can we determine if this manner is more efficient than another? How does energy change from electrical potential to performing a practical task? This is what physicists would refer to as work. The most common manner of determining how an electrical force is performing work or consuming power is through a measurement known as the **watt.** The watt is simply a measurement of the rate of doing work and can be thought of in terms of how much power a task might be consuming. Many appliances are rated in watts, which simply gives a reference to how much energy the device translates from electricity to some other form of energy. The most common everyday example of this is in the varying wattages of light bulbs. The higher the wattage, the more light that a lamp will produce, but with a side effect of the higher wattage lamps also consuming more power.

Power Formula and Ohm's Law

In order to relate each of these components of electricity to one another we have several essential laws or formulas that correlate each measurement to the others. The most common law is known as the **Power Formula** and relates the Power (P) or wattage to the voltage (E) and amperage (A). If you can determine two of the three variables you can easily calculate the final unknown. Many designers and electricians also use a variation of this formula, which they refer to as the **West Virginia Formula,** due to the way in which its units are expressed in regard to one another. Both formulas follow:

Power Formula	**West Virginia**
Power = Amperage × Voltage	Wattage = Voltage × Amperage
P = I × E	W = V × A

A second popular formula for an electrician to become familiar with relates the resistance of a circuit to the remaining measurements. This relationship is represented by **Ohm's Law** and is indicated below. By using various combinations of these two formulas, all of the components of an electrical circuit can be related to one another.

Ohm's Law

$$I = E/R$$

$$\text{Amperage} = \text{Voltage/Resistance}$$

$$A = V/R$$

The most practical use of these formulas comes in making load determinations for any circuits that are used in a lighting application. As stated earlier, a primary safety consideration in an electrical circuit is to not overload or exceed the rated capacity of any electrical device. If a wire is rated for 100 amps then you cannot safely extend this to incorporate a load of 110 amps. If a lighting fixture's safety label says not to exceed a 60-watt lamp then placing a 75-watt lamp within the fixture could present a fire hazard. The simplest use of this determination is to simply add up the wattages of all the lamps or devices contained in a circuit and to make sure that the total combined wattage does not exceed the rated wattage of the circuit. A circuit containing three 20-watt lamps and four 100-watt lamps has a total load of 460 watts [(3 × 20) + (4 × 100)]. If a circuit is rated for 2,400 watts and you were asked how many 500-watt lamps it could safely support you would simply divide 2,400 by 500 to determine the number of lamps. In this case, the result is 4.8 lamps, or four lamps. You should always round the number of lamps downward since rounding up will always create an overloaded condition.

SIDEBAR 5.1 Determination of Lamp Load

A final common application of these formulas is to make load determinations for circuits that are usually specified in amps (even though most fixture specifications are expressed in watts). This is perhaps the most common application of these formulas in lighting practices. For example: assume that you want to determine how many 575-watt fixtures that you can place on a single 20-amp circuit. In this case: Standard voltage in the United States is 120 volts, therefore: V = 120 volts and A = 20 amps. Using the West Virginia formula we can determine that:

$$W = V \times A \text{ or } 120 \text{ volts} \times 20 \text{ amps} = 2,400 \text{ watts}$$

We can then determine the number of lamps (x) by:

$$x \text{ lamps} = 2,400 \text{ watts}/575 \text{watts}/\text{lamp}$$
$$= 2,400/575 \text{ lamps}$$
$$= 4.17 \text{ lamps Rounded down to: 4 lamps}$$

Therefore: The 20 amp circuit can safely hold four 575 watt lamps.

DIRECT CURRENT VERSUS ALTERNATING CURRENT

Electrical power may be produced in a variety of manners. It can be created by rubbing surfaces together (static electric), sun activity (photo electric), chemical reactions (batteries), or by moving wires through magnetic fields (electromagnetism). Each of these and other types of electrical power production can be measured using the components that were discussed in the last several paragraphs.

Direct Current (DC)

We usually make reference to our power through two different forms of voltage. In the first type, the voltage remains constant through time, and we call it **direct current (DC).** A device such as a battery produces electricity where the voltage remains steady and relatively constant . . . although over time the voltage will gradually drop as a battery's life weakens. DC power is produced by relatively inefficient methods and can not be transported over great distances due to voltage drops and wire resistance, which has led to it becoming a very limited power source in contemporary society. It is also much easier to convert AC to DC power through electronic components like diodes than to convert DC power to AC power. The benefit of DC power lies in its portability for personal devices that can make use of batteries. However, battery life is always a factor—even when considering rechargeable batteries. Its fascinating to note the interest that hybrid and electric cars are creating in the auto industry as batteries get smaller and more efficient and as gas prices increase while the ranges of these newer cars becomes greater.

AC Power Generation

The most important means of electrical power creation is through **generators** and **electromagnetism.** A generator is nothing more than a device that allows mechanical motion to be transferred into electrical potential or power. Whether a power plant is nuclear-, hydro-electric-, or steam-based doesn't really matter. What is common to each is that a force is created by elements like water or steam that pass through a turbine, which translates the spinning motion to a generator, which converts the force into electrical power. A generator actually functions in much the same way as an AC motor with the exception that the motor translates the electrical impulses back into mechanical motion and energy.

Generators operate on the principle that you can produce a current in a wire by moving that wire through a magnetic field. The orientation of the wire within the magnetic field becomes an important element in determining both the direction and magnitude of any current that is created or **induced** in the wire. The basic action simply results from the tendency of electrons to be attracted or repelled by the two poles of a magnetic field. In a basic generator we take a wire and form it into a coil which is then rotated around a central axis (armature) that extends through the associated magnetic field. If the armature is rotated to an orientation that coincides with the coil being closest to the poles of the magnetic field, the electrons will be attracted to one end of the coil while being repelled by the opposite side of the coil. If the coil is rotated through half a revolution the electrons would be acted on by the magnetic force in the same manner, but since the coil is now reversed, the relative charges now accumulate in the opposite manner as found in the earlier position. In this way the electrons have moved the same amount but in the opposite direction from the first point. As the armature is rotated it is discovered that the movement of the electrons shifts from a maximum potential in one direction to a maximum potential in the opposite direction at these two points within the spin or cycle. As the armature continues to complete a full rotation we are once again brought back to the same position as when we began and a maximum flow of electrons shift to the initial direction. Furthermore, at the points that coincide with a quarter turn, the electrons come to a point where they are under an equal influence from both poles of the magnetic field, which results in a condition where there is no net movement of electrons from one side of the coil to the other. Between these points, electrons will slowly either increase or decrease their flow and collection to one of the two sides of the coil, depending on the relative position of the coil in the magnetic field.

ALTERNATING CURRENT (AC)   A single revolution of a generator will produce a variety of voltages that begin with a maximum in one direction that gradually decrease to zero at the 90° orientation, then once again build to a maximum potential in the opposite direction at the 180° point of rotation, then decrease back to zero at the 270° interval, and finally increase once again to a maximum as the rotation comes to a complete revolution of 360°. A single rotation or revolution of a generator is typically called a **cycle,** and the type of electricity that is produced in this manner is commonly known as **alternating current (AC)** because of both the varying directions and voltage associated with it. In order to make power generation more efficient we increase the size of the coils to include miles of wire and spin the armature through many revolutions per second. In the United States the standard for power generation is 60 cycles per second, meaning that the armature and associated voltages are undergoing the above changes and revolutions 60 times every second. Figure 5.3 illustrates these changing voltages at various orientations in an armature's revolution.

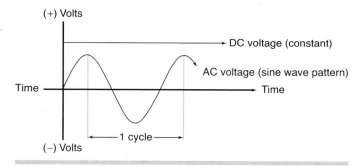
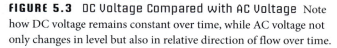

FIGURE 5.3 DC Voltage Compared with AC Voltage Note how DC voltage remains constant over time, while AC voltage not only changes in level but also in relative direction of flow over time.

PHASES   In AC wiring, the wire that runs from the power source is called the **hot wire** because it is providing the energy for the circuit, while the wire that provides the return path is termed the **neutral.** In order for power production to become more efficient we generally wind three identical yet separate coils on an armature of a generator so that in a single revolution we can provide three times the power production of a single coiled generator. All three coils will be oriented slightly differently on the armature so that each produces its maximum and minimum associated voltages at points in the revolution that are slightly skewed from one another. Each of these separate power sources or hot wires are known as a **phase,** and together they form a type of electrical service that we typically call **three-phase power (3ϕ).** Each phase lags slightly behind the other phases, as illustrated in Figure 5.4.

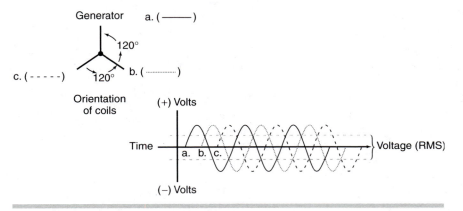

FIGURE 5.4 Three-phase Power Generation A three-phase generator places three separate coils and power taps on the same armature of a generator—each oriented 120° from one another. By using the offset orientation, each of the three generated currents/voltages produced through a cycle will be at a different point in the rotation at any given time and therefore at a different voltage as well. The result is that three separate voltages can be drawn from a single generator and a resultant overall higher average voltage (208 Voltage RMS) is produced.

Transformers

In the early days of commercial power, electricity was provided through DC services which could not travel over long distances because of its relatively low voltage. It was too difficult to raise the voltage to a point where it could be easily transported from one location to another. However, it was also discovered that with sufficient voltage increases, electricity could be distributed over long distances with little effort. This set the stage for the emergence of AC power for electrical transmission because its voltage could be easily regulated due to its electromagnetic nature. In short time, the standard for distributing commercial power quickly shifted to alternating current. The importance of alternating power lies in the fact that it contains rapidly moving electrons that can be used to modify the voltage of a current through simply making use of electromagnetic principles. The devices that we use to regulate AC voltage are called **transformers** and we use them to either increase or decrease the voltage of a given circuit.

Transformers work in much the same manner and principles of electromagnetism as a generator does. In the case of a transformer, two or more coils are wrapped around a ferrous or iron metal core. The iron core is critical because of its ability to take on magnetism. The two coils are electrically insulated from one another and lead to separate circuits. If AC power is provided to one of the coils, the pulsating energy of the moving electrons can create a reaction that produces a pulsating magnetic field that corresponds to the strength or voltage of the AC power. This pulsating magnetic field then influences the second coil in such a way that an electrical current and corresponding voltage are produced in it as well. This is considered an **induced current.** More importantly, the strengths of the two currents are proportional to one another and are directly related to the relative number of turnings that are found in each coil. The coil that is associated with the supply of electrical power is called the **primary coil,** while the coil associated with the induced current is the **secondary coil.** If a primary coil has fewer windings than the secondary coil the voltage will be increased, or stepped up, and we call the transformer a **step-up transformer.** Conversely, a **step-down transformer** has more windings on the primary coil than the secondary, and the voltage is reduced or stepped down. In the United States, we make use of a number of transformers to help distribute power from a power plant to a customer. While most of our appliances are designed for 120-volt operation, the voltage of the power that is provided to us actually changes several times as it makes its way to our homes and businesses from a power-generation plant. In other countries many appliances are designed to operate on a 240-volt standard. While our generators in the United States create power based on a 60 cycles/second standard, other countries have other standards like the popular 50 cycles/second power that is common in South America and Europe.

POWER DISTRIBUTION

The whole networked system of wiring that delivers power from a generating plant to a customer is usually referred to as the **power grid.** In the United States, we have grown so accustomed to the flawless performance of our power grid that we tend to take its operation for granted. When we experienced the widespread blackout of the entire northeast during the summer of 2003 it caused major disruptions in our activities for the day or two before normal conditions were once again restored. I personally experienced this blackout, and modern tools like traffic lights, gas pumps, and refrigeration were just a few of the necessities that failed while we were out of power.

At a typical power plant in the United States the initial voltage of the power produced at a generator is on the order of several thousand volts (actual voltages here and across the power grid frequently vary from utility to utility). Immediately outside of most power stations you will find a large metal structure that we call a **transmission substation,** which is composed of heavy metal cables, insulators, and mast-like structures. A principle component of these structures are step-up transformers, which will boost the voltage up to a point where it can be easily transmitted or conducted over long distances—this voltage can be as high as 155,000 to 765,000 volts. The electricity is then fed to **transmission lines** that are used to carry the power across the countryside and over long distances. The transmission towers that carry this power are generally found in more remote locations and contain three separate wires. Each wire corresponding to the three different power phases that are created by the generators. Often we refer to each of these hot wires or phases as **legs.** It should be obvious that these lines are very dangerous and that you should stay clear of these structures. We also generally consider them to be unsafe in populated areas. Because of this, these lines will terminate at a second substation just outside of a populated area where the voltage is stepped down by transformers to voltages that are still high but not as threatening to a neighborhood. At this point **subtransmission lines** may distribute the power to smaller distribution stations that send power to a couple of central locations before stepping the power down even more before going into specific neighborhoods. Most of these voltages are typically under 10,000 volts, with the most common being on the order of 7,200 volts. Additional equipment at these substations will help regulate the voltage and might also allow the power to be split up or distributed to several different locations. These lines will then lead to additional substations where the voltage is once again stepped down to something on the order of 500–750 volts. These lines can be observed through the typical utility poles or power lines that you normally see along a roadway or street. These, too, carry three wires that represent each phase of the power. Many urban and contemporary communities bury these cables as opposed to distributing the power through overhead wires. Finally, the voltage is once again stepped down to the 120- or 240-volt standard that we use in our households by a final transformer. These transformers are identified as the cylinder-shaped devices that are mounted on utility poles or, in the case of underground wiring, the green metal vaults that are sprinkled throughout a neighborhood. Each transformer will generally service two or three buildings and will have several wires leading from it to each property. A residential or small commercial service will provide two of the three phases of power to an individual building, while other buildings will be provided with two phases from other combinations of the three phase power. A device that breaks either one or two phases off of a three-phase service is called a **tap.** A commercial property that has more demanding power needs will often be provided with all three phases of power and might also have increased service voltages. Transformers within the building can then be used to regulate the power and step it down as required. You can often see many of these transformers near the service entrances of schools and commercial buildings.

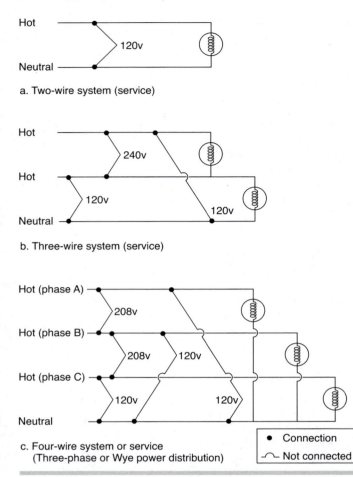

a. Two-wire system (service)

b. Three-wire system (service)

c. Four-wire system or service
(Three-phase or Wye power distribution)

• Connection
⌐ Not connected

FIGURE 5.5 Electrical Service Configurations a. This form of power distribution provides a single hot wire to a customer and was characteristic of residential distribution prior to around 1950. b. This power distribution provides two separate hot power sources along with a neutral and is the most popular form of distribution for current residential customers. c. This form of distribution contains three hot wires and a neutral (Three-phase or Wye Power Distribution) and is characteristic of the power that is provided for commercial and industrial installations. Ground is added as an additional element of each circuit but is independent from the actual distribution system.

Electrical Services

Electrical power can be provided to a customer in one of several configurations. The actual configuration or **service** is dependent on the number of wires that are brought into a building at the **service entrance.** The electric meter is provided at the service entrance and is the point at which the responsibility for the electricity and electrical equipment shifts from the utility company to a customer. An electrical service is also specified by the maximum capacity that it can handle and is typically expressed in amps. In homes of the 1940s and '50s it was common to have an electrical service of only 75–100 amps. The service for the home that I built only a few years ago has a 200-amp service, illustrating how contemporary homes demand much more power. Services that are provided in a theatre or commercial building typically run on the order of 400–800 amps and can actually run considerably higher. In each power configuration, the electrical distribution is based primarily on the number of legs of power brought into the building, regardless of service capacity. Several typical service arrangements are: 150 amp single-phase, 200 amp single-phase, 100 amp three-phase, and 400 amp three-phase. The service may also be expressed according to voltage as in: 120/240-volt, single-phase, three-wire; 120/208-volt, three-phase, four-wire; or 277/480-volt, three-phase, four-wire.

As a shorthand method of indicating phase, we may also use the Greek letter ϕ to indicate power phases. This might be used to indicate specific legs of power (e.g., Aϕ, Bϕ, or Cϕ) or it could be expanded to describe the particular service (i.e., 120/240-volt (3ϕ)). It is important to note that the voltage may change across different legs of power and that it will also vary to some degree from one service type to another. Figure 5.5 illustrates these configurations and associated voltages. It should be understood that in order to provide a safe circuit that an independent grounding system and wire should also be contained in each of these service arrangements. The service can often be identified by the number and type of wires leading into a building from a transformer. Any insulated wires are usually the hot wires, while the neutral is often the metal cable that is used to support the hot cables. The neutral also commonly terminates at or near the transformer, where it is often run to an earth ground. In this manner, a consideration in many installations is the link between the grounding system and the neutral. At one point in time it was a common practice to actually share connections between the neutral and ground systems in some wiring installations. This is no longer considered safe, and current codes discourage it because it defeats the purpose of an isolated ground. If installed properly, there should be no voltage between the neutral and the ground of any building.

TWO-WIRE SYSTEM (SERVICE)   A two-wire system provides a single hot wire or leg and a neutral to a customer. This system was popular in homes built before the 1960s but due to the increased power needs of air-conditioning, water heaters, heat pumps, and other large appliances it is no longer considered sufficient for most homes. The voltage between both of these wires is around 120 volts, although I have personally seen it drop to as low as 95–98 volts. The utility is responsible for maintaining a consistent voltage between the two wires, and if the voltage drops too much it may cause problems in the operation of sensitive electronic equipment. **Surges** or **spikes,** sudden increases in voltage, can also cause problems that could create safety hazards or damage equipment.

THREE-WIRE SYSTEM (SERVICE)   A three-wire system provides two hot wires or legs and a common neutral. The electrical potential between either one of the hots and the neutral will be 120 volts, while the voltage between the two hots will be 240 volts. This is due to the fact that even though each phase only represents a 120-volt potential they are oriented in opposition with one another, resulting in the total potential difference between the two hots becoming 240 volts. This forms the most popular service available for today's residential power services. Small appliances and lights typically operate on the 120-volt power while large appliances like ovens, water heaters, or air-conditioners will use the 240-volt power.

WYE OR FOUR-WIRE SYSTEM (SERVICE)   In most commercial operations there is a need for more efficient power. The most popular power configuration for providing these needs is known as the wye or four-wire system. In this configuration a utility provides three different hot wires and a common neutral. These three phases are the same phases associated with the power produced by the generators at the power plant, and each leg's alternating voltage lags slightly behind each of the others. Large motors are typically connected to all three legs of the power supply in order to create more efficient work or motion. The efficiency of this arrangement results in an overall higher average voltage over a given cycle when comparing voltages across any two hot wires, despite the fact that the net voltage is still balanced. This voltage is called the **RMS voltage (V_{RMS})** or **Root Mean Square Voltage.** The voltage that can be observed between any single phase and the neutral is 120 volts, while the voltage between any two hots, due to this shifted orientation, will be on the order of 208 volts.

In order to produce a truly safe condition, electrical engineers design circuits so that the neutral carries no net potential as electricity flows back to its power source. In systems where more than one leg of power is provided we try to orient the phases in such a way that the sum of the voltage of all the phases equals a net of zero potential on the neutral. In the case of services with two hot wires, the phases are oriented in direct opposition with one another, while the skewed orientation of a three-phase system accomplishes the same task. We also strive to **balance** an electrical system so that the demands of the entire service are evenly distributed on each of the legs to ensure that the neutral will not carry any excess current. It must be understood that in any AC distribution system an electrical device should always be connected between the hot and neutral wires of a circuit. Bringing two hots in direct contact with one another, the neutral, or ground will result in creating a **short circuit,** which commonly results in shocks, sparks, and a possible fire. A short circuit can be thought of as an accidental flow of electricity. If you've ever cut through a power cord you have most likely witnessed the effects of a short circuit.

ELECTRICAL HARDWARE

As stated earlier, every device has a natural ability to either conduct or resist electrical flow. This innate ability results in every material or object having some natural capacity for conducting electricity. If we exceed this level there will be consequences such as heat buildup or sparks due to the natural resistance of the material. All electrical components are rated by a capacity, in amps, that specifies how much electricity they can safely conduct. This rating is usually stamped or labeled on the product in some way. Switches, outlets, and lamp fixtures are but a few of the devices that will have their capacities indicated somewhere on their bodies.

Wire

The most common conductor is wire, which can be made of a solid piece of metal (**solid core**) or smaller strands of metal that are woven together much like a fibrous rope (**stranded**). Solid core wire conducts electricity better than stranded wire but is not as flexible and can easily break if flexed too often. Because of this, solid core wire is used in permanent installations, while stranded wires are used in situations where the wires are moved around like in theatre or film production. While metal forms the conductive path, we have to take measures to prevent unwanted power from flowing from it, and cover each conductor with a highly resistant material called **insulation.** In any circuit, every wire has a unique purpose, and we color-code the insulation as a means of quickly identifying a wire's purpose. The most important electrical coding includes: red or black for hot wires, white for a neutral wire, and green for a ground wire. If a third phase is contained in a service, the last leg will often be color-coded blue. The color code is also modified for connecting hardware such as screws and clamps, where brass or brown forms a hot connection, silver is used for neutral connections, and green is once again used for identifying ground connections. Nearly all switches, lighting hardware, and receptacles use these coding practices.

The capacity of a wire for conducting electricity is related to its thickness or diameter. The thicker the wire, the more electron flow that can occur and the greater capacity that a wire will have. This is similar to a larger diameter pipe being associated with a larger volume of water flow. We size wire according to its diameter or **gauge.** The smaller the diameter of the wire; the larger the number of the gauge. A #10 gauge wire is larger then an #18 gauge wire. Each gauge also is specified with a maximum capacity rating that increases as the gauge number goes down. The #12 and #14 gauge wires are the most common gauges found in entertainment and architectural practices. These are rated for loads of 20 and 15 amps respectively. In areas where we have a significant power flow we use large gauge wires called **feeders** that deliver high-capacity power (i.e., 100 or more amps) to a panel or device. These typically have diameters that are approximately the size of a finger and are called 0, 00, or 000—each one getting progressively larger. While we are predominantly concerned with wire, on some large-capacity applications we actually use metal bars called **bus bars** rather than wires to move the electricity from one location to another. This is quite common in large-capacity dimmer racks and distribution panels.

Cables

It is rare that we have a need to run single wires in most lighting applications. More commonly, we combine several insulated wires together to form a **cable.** The most common cable contains three wires and is used to carry a hot, neutral, and ground wire. Each wire typically has its own insulation that is then molded together into a single sheath or jacket along with the other wires and insulators. While the ends of a cable may be wired directly to a device, it is more common to include **connectors** that allow the connecting and disconnecting of the cables to occur with relative ease. Just like wire, connectors are also rated for specific capacities. There are two types of connectors, **male** and **female.** A male connector should always be placed on the device or wire that will be receiving the power, while the female should always be reserved for the location or tap that will provide the power source. Household plugs form an example of connectors. Several of the most common connectors include the Edison plug (standard household), the pin connector, and the twist-lock connector. A photograph of these plugs is found in Figure 5.6. In each case, the connector provides specific contacts associated with the hot, neutral, and ground wires for each blade of the connector. In the twist-lock and Edison connectors, the ground wires are mounted to the blades that are shaped quite differently from the other two (often with a green mounting screw), while in the pin connector the ground is mounted on the center pin. The neutral for a twist-lock or Edison connector is associated with the larger of the two remaining blades (these will also frequently have silver screws), while the pin connector's neutral is reserved for the outside pin that is mounted closest to the ground. The final blade or pin in both cases is reserved for the hot connection and is often the smallest or most distant pin from the others.

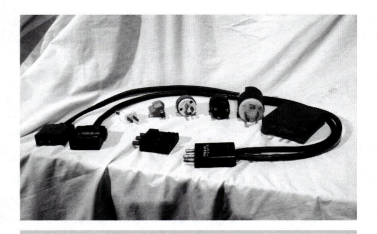

FIGURE 5.6   Common Electrical Connectors From left to right, beginning with back row: Polar Edison male, Ground lift, grounded Edison male, grounded Edison female, male twist-lock (30 amp), and a three-fer block. In the front row is a 20-amp male three-pin connector (opened), while all the connectors are surrounded by a two-fer.

In entertainment lighting we make constant changes in the wiring from show to show, and using permanent wiring practices would be both tedious and strenuous on the equipment. Because of this, a number of pre-wired cables and connectors are used that allow us to quickly connect and disconnect electrical devices. A **jumper** or **cable** is the term often given to a cable that contains three conductors and a male and female connector. These come in a variety of lengths from 3 feet to 200 feet and function in the same manner that an extension cord might work. Lengths of these cables are normally measured in 5- or 10-foot intervals like 5, 10, 15, 25, and 50 feet. An **adapter** is a short length of cable that has different types of connectors on each end and allows a cable to be adapted from one system of connectors to another (as in twist-lock to pin connector or pin connector to Edison). Most cables are designed for use on a single circuit and contain a single hot, neutral, and ground wire. No cable or adapter should ever be created using either male or female connectors on both ends.

While we might occasionally wire a device directly to its power source, it's more common to combine several devices together by wiring them to a single circuit. In architectural installations, objects may be permanently wired together, as in the case of wiring several ceiling lights together or connecting all the convenience outlets of a room to a common circuit. However, in entertainment lighting the need for both speed and constant modification has brought several specialty devices that allow two or more cables to be plugged together into a common circuit. These devices typically join two or more female plugs to a single male connector. Most electricians refer to these specialized accessories as **two-fers** (two females) or **three-fers** (three females). Occasionally electricians have the need to service many circuits through a given cable. In this case there are two options. The first uses cables that are manufactured with a number of independent conductors whose ends terminate in a given number of male and female connectors that correspond to the number of circuits contained in the cable. These are called a **multi-cable** or **multi** which will often contain six or more independent circuits. An alternative to using a multi is to create a **bundle,** which combines individual cables that run along common areas like an electric by tying the individual cables together so that they effectively become a single entity. Bundles are frequently used to provide pre-wired electrics for touring productions.

Circuit Protection

A second major group of electrical components are used as circuit-protection devices and include **fuses** and **circuit breakers.** These are designed to be the weakest link in a circuit and are meant to trip or blow if the circuit should become exposed to a short circuit or is overloaded. Every fuse or circuit breaker is rated by a capacity that specifies the actual power requirements or **load** of all the devices that may be assigned to a given circuit. A breaker or fuse is designed to stop the power flow by causing a physical break in the wiring if its capacity is exceeded by the current in the circuit. The protection device should be wired in series on the hot wire of a circuit as close to the power source as possible. This ensures that as many of the components as possible are protected from any overload conditions. A typical distribution panel contains a central power source along with a number of fuses or circuit breakers that are wired to numerous branch circuits.

Most circuit protection devices react to either a heat build up or significant change in the electromagnetic activity of a circuit. They may trip in an immediate catatonic sense due to a sudden overload like a short circuit or could simply fail due to excessive heating through having too many devices drawing power from a source at a particular time. Many electricians refer to this second condition as a **slow blow,** characterized by a condition in which everything appears to be working fine but that over time causes a breaker to trip for no apparent reason. Slow blows are most often due to conditions such as excessive resistance being created in a circuit through extra-long jumpers, cables being undersized, loose connections, or a slight overload in the capacity assignment or load of a circuit. While **circuit breakers** may be reset, **fuses** need to be replaced once they blow. Figure 5.7

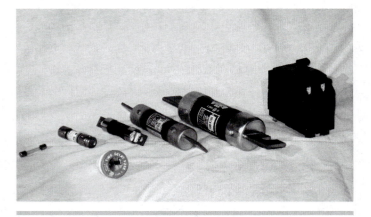

FIGURE 5.7 Several Circuit Protection Devices A sampling of electrical fuses. A buss, cartridge, and knife-blade fuses along with a plug fuse. A 50-amp single-phase circuit breaker is shown at the extreme right.

illustrates several fairly common circuit-protection devices. Fuses come in a variety of sizes and shapes, and while many small-capacity fuses are of a plug or screw-type style, larger-capacity fuses are of a cartridge style with either ferrule or knife-blade conductors. Ferrule fuses will generally be used in applications under 100 amps while knife-blade fuses are common for capacities of 100, 150, 200, 400, and 800 amps or more. Circuit breakers are also manufactured in a variety of sizes that cover the entire range of load capacities. Some respond to thermal monitoring, while most use magnetic detection as a means of protecting a circuit. Several of the advantages of using circuit breakers include their ability to be reset and their faster detection and reaction to an overload condition. The magnetic breakers can also be reset more quickly than the thermal ones because there is no need to wait for the breaker to cool down. Another variation of circuit protection is the **Ground Fault Circuit Interrupter (GFCI),** which detects any flow of electricity between the neutral and the earth ground. If it should detect a flow, it will trip in much the same manner as a circuit breaker. These devices are typically installed in areas where there is a good chance of a person coming in contact with a live wire and equipment or materials that may be associated with moisture or an earth ground. By code, these devices are often required in wet environments such as kitchens, bathrooms, and exterior locations. In the Cirque du Soleil production of *O* at the Bellagio Casino in Las Vegas the entire production takes place in and around a large pool, and specially designed dimmers that incorporate GFCI protection were developed and installed throughout the facility that houses this production.

Switches

A **switch** is nothing more then a device that is used to control the flow of power through an electrical circuit. A switch is wired in series along the hot wire of the circuit and just like a fuse or circuit breaker, it should be located somewhere in the circuit ahead of all of the devices that it is controlling. The common wall switch used in electrical lighting is the most common switch available and when closed completes the circuit, allowing power to flow throughout the circuit. If moved to the open position, it puts a break in the line which interrupts the flow of power. Most switches that we are familiar with are considered **light duty** and are only rated for 15 or 20 amps, while many of the switches found in commercial and entertainment applications are considered heavy duty and may carry up to several hundred amps. There are a number of different kinds of switches available to a lighting designer. Some provide power to a single load, others are assignable to multiple loads. A **three-way switch** allows a single circuit to be controlled through several switches placed at different locations. Finally, there are specialized switches that may be activated by a timer, photosensitivity, or even through motion detection. In each case the switch becomes the mechanism by which power is made available to a circuit.

Dimmers

A **dimmer** is a control device that is used for adjusting the intensity of any lights that are contained in a circuit. In most cases, a dimmer varies the voltage to control the brightness of the lamps. In theatrical applications we use dimmers to help control the mood and focus of the lighting. We also use them to make adjustments in the balance of a stage as well as for making adjustments in intensity throughout a performance. These devices are also popular in restaurants and residences as well as for other architectural applications where a more artistic quality and mood are desired for an environment. Dimmers also provide a sound means of achieving energy management by allowing a space to be sufficiently lit without using the lamps or luminaires at their full power. Additionally, lamp life can be increased significantly by as little as a 20% drop in voltage or intensity—something that most individuals can't distinguish. Dimmers are examined in more detail in Chapter 8 (Control Fundamentals).

COMPANY SWITCHES AND DISTRIBUTION PANELS

Once an electrical service enters a facility the electricity splits off into a number of different directions as it is conducted through a series of devices and wires that distribute the power throughout a building. Figure 5.8 compares the electrical distribution patterns of a stage lighting system with that of a commercial lighting application.

Commercial Distribution

In a typical commercial application a building is first serviced with a transformer or vault that allows electricity to be stepped down to voltages that are in line with the equipment needs of that business. The electricity then flows through a series of **secondary service conductors** to the **main switchboard** where it is separated into additional cable runs (**main feeders**) that connect to **distribution panels** located throughout the building (e.g., wings or floors) which further separate the power into **branch circuits** that lead to specific electrical equipment such as lights and outlets throughout the area that is serviced by a given panel. Each branch circuit will have its own breaker or fuse, and each distribution panel will be under the control of a main breaker that is specified for the total load of all of the branch circuits contained within that box. At times this breaker is located in the distribution box, but more commonly the main breaker for each distribution panel is located on or near the main switchboard for the facility. It actually isn't uncommon for a main breaker to be found in both locations.

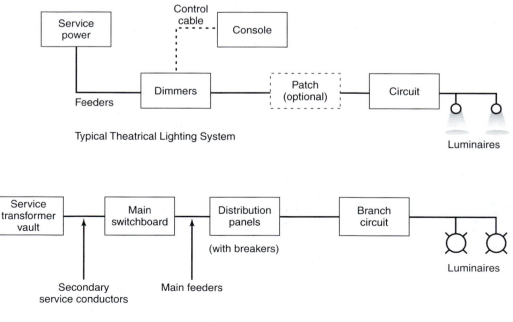

FIGURE 5.8 Electrical Distribution for Theatrical and Commercial Power Systems

Theatrical Distribution

A theatrical lighting system is a specific variation of a commercial lighting application. In most cases, a performance facility is wired in the same manner as any other commercial building with the exception that the theatrical lighting systems will be powered from separate distribution panels. In the case of a permanent installation, the lighting system is wired directly to a distribution panel that has been specifically designated for the lighting system. However, in many productions such as in touring, it is common to package an individualized system based on the specific needs pertaining to that tour. In this case, the touring company provides the entire lighting system, which is simply connected or tied into a theatre's power supply. Broadway theatres typically operate in this manner. A **company switch** or **road-tap** is a specialized distribution panel or **disconnect box** that is used to make these connections. Most company switches are located somewhere backstage and provide the majority of the power that a touring system will connect to. Traditional locations for company switches are in the wings of a theatre, along an upstage wall, or below the stage in the trap room. It is becoming a common practice to place company switches above the wings on a catwalk as a means of getting the lighting gear and cable out of the way, with the added benefit of also reducing the length of cable runs that will have to be run from the electrics to the dimmers. These disconnect boxes typically provide 200–800 amps of three-phase service to a stage, and extreme care must be taken when wiring a company's feeders to the connections contained within these panels. Disconnect boxes typically don't contain any branch circuits and simply provide the hardware that will allow for the connection of the feeders that will lead to the touring equipment. Fuses for each leg of power and a main switch or a single heavy duty breaker are the only other features contained in many of these boxes. Some touring facilities make things even easier and have special **camlock** fittings on these boxes that will allow the touring company's feeders to be plugged directly into the box. Many road houses provide several company switches that are located throughout a backstage area. The photograph in Figure 5.9 shows a typical company switch with the front panel opened. The wiring of a company switch is a dangerous job and should be reserved only for an experienced electrician. In many municipalities only a licensed electrician may perform this service.

In a typical theatrical lighting system we want to control a number of lights independently of one another and must therefore provide numerous dimmers so the lights can be individually controlled. We also run a number of individual circuits to many locations throughout a theatre to provide permanent wiring for many of the most popular hanging positions of a theatre. Some of these locations may include anywhere from 30 to 50 or more individual circuits—each allowing additional lights to be added to the design through a process that is as simple as plugging the light's connector into a pre-existing receptacle. We refer to each of these pathways as a **circuit**. Contemporary theatres often wire each circuit to its own dimmer (**Dimmer per Circuit or DPC**) but many theatres can't afford this practice and instead make use of a relatively high number of circuits that are then assigned or connected to a limited number of dimmers. In these cases, theatres make use of another specialized piece of electrical hardware called a **patchbay** or **patch panel** that allow the circuits to be assigned to individual dimmers through some form of quick-connection device.

FIGURE 5.9 A Typical Company Switch/Disconnect
Two road house disconnects (two 400-amp services). The 400-amp box on the left is open to reveal its fuses and cam-lock connections. Note lock-out procedures with locks on power switches and cover panels.

SIDEBAR 5.2 **Electrical Safety**

Safety not only for yourself, but also for the other occupants of a facility, is extremely important when working with electricity. An accident can occur without warning and the consequences can be extreme—even fatal. When an electrician is entrusted with wiring an electrical device there are several general rules that should be followed:

1. If you have any question about what you are doing—stop—and get somebody who knows how to safely complete the electrical connections.

2. Always make sure that the box or circuit is **dead** (off) before working on it; then check it with a meter to make sure that its actually off.

3. Only strip enough insulation off a wire to allow a good solid connection between the wire and any electrical hardware . . . there should never be an excess of exposed conductor in any connection.

4. Always check to make sure that every connection is secure and tight and that there are no loose strands of wire extending beyond your connections. Wires secured by screws should be wrapped clockwise around a screw before being tightened down.

5. Never cross any wires or make a connection directly between phases, a hot leg and the ground, or a hot leg and the neutral. This produces a short circuit. Always observe proper color codes when making any connection.

6. Secure the ground first, then the neutral, and finally the hot legs as you install the power, and reverse this procedure when you strike the power.

7. Always check your wiring, test your connections, and, especially in those cases where there is a substantial amount of power involved, verify your wiring with a meter before adding power to the circuit.

FOR FURTHER READING

Bellman, Willard F., *Lighting the Stage: Art and Practice,* 3rd ed. (Louisville, KY: Broadway Press, 2001).

Cadena, Richard, *Electricity for the Entertainment Electrician and Technician* (Boston, MA: Focal Press, 2009).

Illuminating Engineering Society of North America, *IESNA Lighting Education 100 (Fundamental Level)* (New York: Illuminating Engineering Society of North America, 1993).

Illuminating Engineering Society of North America, *IESNA Lighting Education 150 (Intermediate Level)* (New York: Illuminating Engineering Society of North America, 1993).

Illuminating Engineering Society of North America, *IESNA Lighting Handbook,* 9th ed., ed. Mark Rae (New York: Illuminating Engineering Society of North America, 2000).

Illuminating Engineering Society of North America. *IESNA Lighting Ready Reference* 4th ed. (New York: Illuminating Engineering Society of North America, 2006).

Lindsey, Jack L., *Applied Illumination Engineering,* 2nd ed. (Lilburn, GA: The Fairmount Press, Inc., 1997).

National Fire Protection Agency, *The National Electrical Code: 2005* (Quincy, MA: National Fire Protection Association, Inc., 2004).

Lamps and Other Light Sources

6

A light source is nothing more than an object or device that produces light. When we discuss **lamps,** lighting designers are usually referring to a device that produces some manner of artificial light. There are a number of different light sources that have been used throughout history. A torch or campfire, candles or lanterns, arcs or electrical sparks, and finally the common incandescent lamp all form examples of light sources that have been used throughout recorded time. What is most important about light sources is the particular quantity and quality of light that a given source can create. While there are a number of natural ways of creating light, such as in the atomic reactions of the sun, the discharge of a spark, a chemical reaction, or the burning of a material to produce a flame, there are essentially only three ways in which we commercially produce light in today's society. These techniques involve light production through **incandescence,** an **arc,** or a **gaseous discharge.**

Incandescence is by far the most common form of light production and is represented by the common light bulb. In incandescence a metal material is heated to the point that it glows and gives off electromagnetic radiation. Because of the significance of this light source, a large portion of the chapter is devoted to a discussion of incandescent lights. While incandescent sources are the most popular way of creating light, they also have several significant drawbacks like their overall inefficiency, high heat production, and relatively limited potential for creating high-intensity light. In fact, there are movements that are creating legislation to "ban the bulb" as communities struggle with the concept of switching to more efficient light sources like compact fluorescents.

Due to the inefficiencies of the incandescent lamp, alternative methods of light production have been developed. An arc source creates a very bright light in comparison to incandescent sources and is nothing more than an electrical spark jumping between two electrodes. A gaseous discharge source places an arc in an atmosphere of a specific mixture of gases that glow. Two special versions of sources that are popular in architectural applications include the **fluorescent lamp** and the **high-intensity discharge** or **HID lamp.** Both are discussed later in this chapter. In some applications, these alternative sources have become even more popular than incandescent lamps. For instance, in commercial architectural applications, the fluorescent lamp has taken on a very significant role in illumination. Due to issues related to energy management and quality of light, there are distinct differences between the sources that we use for architectural and theatrical applications. Many of these considerations are also examined throughout this chapter. Two good references relating to the historical development of light sources include Brian Bowers' *Lengthening the Day: A History of Lighting Technology* and Maureen Dillon's *Artificial Sunshine: A Social History of Domestic Lighting.* Finally, Frederick Penzel's *Theatre Lighting Before Electricity* provides an especially good history of theatrical lighting.

LUMENS AND LAMP LIFE

One common practice for comparing light sources relates to the actual amount of light or **lumen output** that is produced by a lamp. This is simply determined by the amount of work that the lamp completes as it converts electrical energy into light. The most common way of measuring this is by rating a lamp according to its wattage. However, it should be noted that although lumen output generally corresponds to wattage, the principle doesn't always hold true; some lamps are more efficient than others. As a rule though, it can be said that lamps of a higher wattage usually appear brighter and generally produce more light than lamps of comparatively lower wattages. We also consider how long a lamp will last before burning out as another criteria before selecting a lamp for a given task. We measure this in **lamp life.** Simply put, lamp life is a means of determining the average number of hours that a lamp will burn before failing. It is based on trials in which a number of lamps are tested until either they actually fail or their light output drops to below 80%. Obviously, if you are specifying exterior spotlights for a church steeple, where the lamps are going to be hard to replace, it would be more practical to use lamps with higher lamp lives. Another general rule relates to the fact that lower wattage lamps tend to have longer lives than those with higher wattages. Therefore, it can also be concluded that, in general, brighter lamps tend to have shorter lamp lives. Some special-duty stage and studio lamps have a lamp life of as few as 50 hours while most theatrical lamps can average several hundred hours. Household lamps on the other hand will be rated for up to a 1,000 hours, while fluorescent lamps typically have lamp lives that can extend to approximately 10,000 hours. Some extended-service lamps, such as the familiar mercury street or utility lamp, can have lamp lives up to 24,000 hours or more. In addition to lamp life, it is also important to consider how quickly the light output from a lamp drops off over time. This relates to the efficiency of the lamp and is called **lumen maintenance.** Some lamps or light bulbs progressively cloud or darken over time, which can have a serious impact on the amount of light actually being produced by the lamp. As time progresses, this effect on lumen output becomes greater and greater. Other lamps stay essentially clear throughout their lives and maintain a more consistent light output as they age.

Lamps are designed for a specific operating voltage. In incandescent lighting the actual light production is directly proportional to the amount of resistance and voltage that are applied to a lamp. If a lamp is subjected to a higher voltage than for which it was designed, it will glow brighter but will also burn out much quicker. If the voltage is high enough it might fail instantaneously or even explode. On the other hand, a lamp that is often dimmed or that only runs at 80% intensity will have its lamp life increased significantly. In theatrical applications, where lamps are seldom run continuously or at full intensity, lamp life can often be extended two or three times beyond the lamp life ratings that are specified by the manufacturers.

LAMPS AND COLOR

Regardless of light source, we also make reference to the **color temperature** of a lamp as a way of comparing its overall spectral composition with that of other light sources. As you may recall, color temperature is based on a color reference to a particular Kelvin temperature. However, in addition to the overall color temperature, a designer might also have to consider the specific spectral composition of a light source to predict its effect on different objects. Light sources that emit a wide distribution of wavelengths tend to enhance objects across a wider range of colors. This ability is referenced in a comparative manner by assigning numbers that represent a lamp's **color rendering index (CRI).** As a light source's CRI increases, its ability to render a wider selection of colors also increases. Comparisons of a light source's CRI and its individual spectral responses to various wavelengths of light can be used along with color temperature to identify the best light source for a given project.

INCANDESCENT LAMPS

Incandescent lamps still form the most common means of producing light in the world today. The original lamps produced by Edison and others worked on the principle of incandescence, and while we have gone on to create thousands of variations on the basic design, the overall principle of its operation has not changed much from his original concept. Incandescent lamps remain popular due to the ease and low cost with which they can be manufactured. Additionally, they are not only functional but can also be created in a variety of shapes and sizes for any number of decorative applications. On the other hand, they are inefficient as energy sources and much of the energy that they consume to produce light is actually wasted as heat.

The basic principle in which an incandescent lamp works is by heating a highly resistant material or wire (**filament**) with electricity to the point that it begins to radiate or glow with visible energy. This process is known as **incandescence.** Due to the high resistance of the wire, the filament first will glow red and then glow progressively brighter as the voltage is increased until it gives off white light. The primary components of a lamp are illustrated in Figure 6.1. We usually refer to the whole assembly as a **lamp** rather than a light bulb. The **bulb** is the actual glass envelope of a lamp. If a filament were to be exposed to the natural air while energized with electricity it would oxidize rapidly and burn out. The bulb forms an atmosphere that prevents this natural reaction from occurring so quickly by providing either a vacuum or other gas-filled environment that is oxygen-deprived. The filament, often made of tungsten, is the resistant wire that is heated by the electric current. It is often wrapped into a tight coil as a means of compacting the surface area upon which the light is actually produced. The smaller and more compact the coil can be made, the more effective the lamp will become. The filament must be located at a specific location within a bulb to maximize the efficiency of the lamp, and a set of **support wires** is used to hold the filament in this proper position and orientation. A set of **lead-in wires** is then used to provide electrical connections to each side of the filament. Finally, a **base** provides the electrical connections between the lamp and the **luminaire** as well as the physical mounting of the lamp in a way that ensures its proper position and orientation in a lighting instrument.

Each of the lamp components can be modified in a number of ways to produce a variety of qualities and orientations of light that would be characteristic of a particular style of lamp. Ultimately, there is no single combination of components that make for the most efficient light source, but rather, every combination relates to a lighting solution that is more pertinent for one situation or circumstance over another. Hence, there are literally thousands of individual lamp types, each with a different combination of filament, base, size, bulb, etc. Even if all the components of a lamp's construction are kept the same, variations in wattage, color temperature, efficiency, and overall lumen output can also be made from one lamp to another. The following pages only address a few of the key variations that may occur in the primary lamp components.

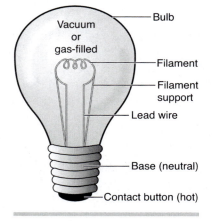

FIGURE 6.1 Components of an Incandescent Lamp

Filaments

The filament is the most important element of a lamp because it is the component that actually produces the light. One of the objectives of lamp manufacturing is to make the filament and resulting lamp as small as possible. Optical devices like lenses and reflectors work best when light is concentrated at an infinitely small point. A light source that can concentrate a majority of its light at this point will make the associated lens or reflector all the more efficient and powerful. This principle is generally referred to as creating a **point light source.** Today's lamps are much smaller than lamps from 30 or 40 years ago because of this trend. The importance of this principle will become even more apparent through the optics discussion that you will find in the next chapter.

Filaments have been made more efficient by coiling the tungsten wire into a tight **coil (C)** as opposed to simply stringing it between its support wires—**straight (S).** This provides a more concentrated light source by producing a greater amount of filament surface area at a given point or location. More recent lamps have effectively made use of a **coiled-coil (CC)** filament design that takes an already coiled wire and then coils this, too, into a secondary coil. As a lamp manufacturer varies the specific shape and orientation of the filament, the associated light is produced in different orientations. This allows the lumen output of the lamp to be increased in one direction or another. Figure 6.2 illustrates many of the more popular filament configurations that have been used in lamp designs over the years. A couple designs of special significance include: the **C-7** or **corona** filament which is typical of many everyday or general purpose (bare bulb) lamps that produce light in a spherical pattern extending outward in nearly all directions, the **C-5** or **barrel** filament that produces light in a torus or donut-shaped pattern that extends around the filament, the **C-13** or **monoplane** that produces light primarily in two opposing directions, the **C-13D** or **biplane** which further concentrates the filament in a set of two offset planes that result in even more light being produced in two directions, and the CC or coiled coil that produces very concentrated light in a comparatively small space that expands outward in most directions. Finally, the **C-8** filament was used as the basis of a new lamp developed in the early 1990s as part of a more efficient light source used as a foundation in the revolutionary design of the **enhanced ellipsoidal reflector spotlight** (The Source Four by ETC). This filament orients four coiled filament elements in a tight vertical box-like arrangement that produces a concentrated light source in most directions. A couple of specialty lamps make use of multiple filaments within a single bulb. An example of this is the three-way lamps commonly found in many table or floor lamps and a variety of studio lamps used in video or film settings where multiple brightness settings are created through applying power to one or more filaments of a lamp at any given time.

Bulbs

The most dominant part of many lamps is the actual glass enclosure or bulb that encases the filament and its associated support and lead wires. The bulb forms the atmosphere for a filament. It is important that this environment prevents the natural oxidation of the filament, and gases such as nitrogen and argon are typically added to the bulb as a means of slowing down this process. A bulb's shape and size may be fully functional or could be based on a decorative element. We may also characterize a bulb based on its finish or color. In stage and studio applications designers prefer to have **clear** finishes, which ensures that there is very little change in the quality of the native light. Although lighting designers will later modify the light through placing it on a dimmer, adding colored filters to it, or placing a diffuser in front of it; they initially want the light to be as pure as possible. However, in architectural practices, clear lamps may become a distraction and can lead to glare. In these cases, lamps with alternative finishes are often used. The most popular finish for lamps in these applications are the **frosted** finishes that modify the bulbs in a way that softens and diffuses the light of a lamp. A limited number of colored lamps (red, white, blue, yellow, and green) are also created by manufacturers for decorative applications like carnival and amusement marquees, advertising signage, and Christmas lights. Incandescent lamps with light pastel tints have also been introduced to the consumer market by lighting manufactures such as Philips and General Electric to create more personal lighting throughout a home or office. Finally, a number of specialized lamps like those found in candelabra and chandelier fixtures are also shaped and finished in highly decorative manners.

For most lighting designers an important element of lamp designation relates to the overall shape and size of the bulb itself. We usually refer to a bulb type by a combination of a letter or two and a number. The letters are given first and refer to the bulb's shape,

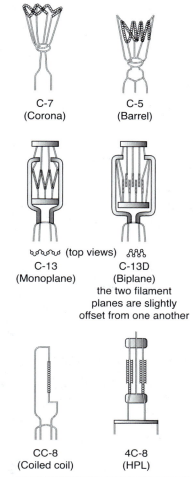

FIGURE 6.2 Common Filament Styles

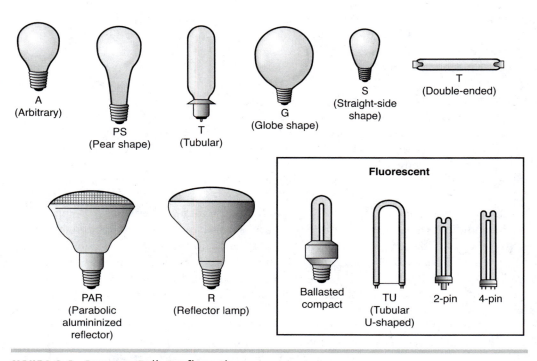

FIGURE 6.3 Common Bulb Configurations

while the number relates to the size of the bulb. The size is expressed in units that are equivalent to ⅛" intervals of the diameter of the bulb at its widest point. In other words, if a bulb is 2 inches in diameter it would be associated with the number 16. A lamp with a diameter of 1-¼" would be assigned a value of 10. More importantly, the shape of the bulb and filament type will determine the distribution pattern associated with a particular lamp. Figure 6.3 provides an illustration of a number of popular bulb shapes. The shape that most people are familiar with is the **arbitrary (A)** shape, which is typically used in most household fixtures. The **globe (G)** lamp is often used in today's bathroom vanity or mirror applications. Each of these lamps attempts to disperse the light in a fairly even pattern away from the source. On the other hand the **tube (T)** lamp is often used to disperse light in a more cylindrical or linear fashion, while the **Parabolic Aluminized Reflector (PAR)** and **Reflector (R)** lamps act as spotlights and direct the light primarily in a single direction. A lamp can be readily identified with simple combinations such as: T-12, meaning a tube-shaped lamp that is 1-½" in diameter, or a G-25, which indicates a globe-shaped lamp that is 3-⅛" in diameter.

The R and PAR lamps are special types of lamps in that they not only include the elements of a lamp but also add several optical features that allow them to further enhance their light in a more efficient directional or spotlight-like manner. The R lamp contains a reflector and diffuse lens that allows the light to be concentrated in a pool with a soft edge that spreads gently away from the lamp, while the PAR lamp contains a pre-defined lens (as well as reflector) that allows the light to be more concentrated and focused as it leaves the lamp. Both units are unique in that they are in a sense complete lighting fixtures within a single lamp. Each lamp is manufactured with a unique set of optical properties which cannot be modified. However, there are a number of different optical configurations available through the manufacture of different lamps. While most of these lamps provide a circular or conical distribution pattern there are also variations that have an oval pattern. When designating PAR lamps from one another many designers and manufacturers use abbreviations that designate the approximate beam or distribution pattern of the lamp. Popular lamps include the Medium Flood (MFL), Wide Flood (WFL), Narrow Spot (NSP), and Very Narrow Spot (VNSP).

Bases

The last of the primary components of a lamp is the base. The base provides the means by which a lamp is mounted within a luminaire as well as the manner by which the lamp might be oriented. It also forms the electrical contacts that will ultimately connect the lamp's filament to a source of power. Most lamps have their bases at one end while some T lamps may have bases mounted at each end of their tubular-shaped bulbs. Just as there are different bulb sizes, there are also different base sizes. The smallest bases are primarily associated with decorative lamps and are called **miniature** or **candelabra** bases. Miniature bases are approximately ⅜" in diameter, while candelabra bases are around ½" to ⅝" in diameter. The most common base size is the **medium base,** which is 1" in diameter. For large lamps, a 1-½" base called a **mogul base** may be used. There are numerous styles of bases and a variety of ways

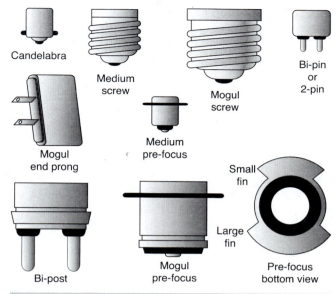

FIGURE 6.4 Common Lamp Bases

for mounting a lamp to a socket and associated lighting fixture. Figure 6.4 illustrates several of the more common base styles that are used in stage, studio, and architectural applications. In many cases, the bases are designed to ensure that a lamp will be properly oriented as it is put into a lighting instrument. This is extremely important for those lamps that make use of filaments that create a directional light source. A **screw base** like the ones typically found in residential lamps does not require precise orientation, and its threads simply need to hold the lamp in place while providing the electrical connections for the lamp. On the other hand, spotlights that require a very directional light output will make use of lamps with bases such as the **bayonet, pre-focus, bi-pin or 2-pin,** or **bi-post** configuration. Through using bases like these, a lamp can be placed in a fixture with confidence that the filament will be set in its proper orientation and that the majority of the light will be directed either to the reflector or through the front lens of the fixture.

TUNGSTEN HALOGEN OR QUARTZ LAMPS

The **tungsten halogen lamp** or **TH lamp** is a specialized version of an incandescent lamp. These lamps first appeared in the 1970s and began a trend toward creating smaller light sources for stage and studio applications. The lamps are also popular in many flood-lighting applications in the field of architectural lighting. Tungsten halogen lamps substitute a halogen gas for the traditional gases that are enclosed in a bulb and have paved the way for the manufacturing of much smaller lamps by refining the atmospheric requirements and thickening the glass for the bulbs of these lamps. In a traditional lamp, the filament slowly breaks down as molecules of tungsten slowly drift away from the filament, becoming weaker and weaker. In most cases, the filament material is redeposited on the coolest portion of a lamp (the bulb) resulting in the black, cloudy deposits that appear on the surface of many older lamps. Tungsten-halogen lamps, on the other hand, make use of the **tungsten-halogen process,** in which the tungsten particles are redeposited on the hottest portion of the lamp, which once again coincides with the filament. These lamps therefore create a recycling effect that increases the lamp's life while also preventing the tungsten buildup on the bulb that has such a negative impact on the performance of traditional incandescent lamps. Due to this process, TH lamps maintain a more consistent light output throughout their life while also benefitting from an overall increased lamp

Light Center Length (LCL)

When making comparisons between lamps it is quite possible to have a lamp that will physically mount in a socket of a luminaire and will operate while still being completely inappropriate for that fixture. This most commonly relates to the problem of locating the filaments of the lamps at different heights in a luminaire. In fixture design, a lamp is chosen based on its ability to locate the filament along the primary optical path of any lenses and reflectors that are used in that fixture. If a lamp's filament is placed too high or low, the efficiency of the fixture is compromised. This was a particular problem in the 1970s and '80s when newer lamp styles were introduced as replacements or **retrofits** for fixtures that dated back to earlier times. In fact, many retrofit lamps are still in common use today. As a means of specifying these filament placements a critical measurement called the **light center length (LCL)** has been added to lamp specifications. The LCL is simply a measurement from the center of the lamp's filament to a specified location on the lamp's base. This base location will vary depending on the type of base but remains consistent between all bases of a given style. For instance, the LCL for a pre-focus base is taken from the fins at the top of the base to the center of the filament, while the LCL for a screw base is taken from the center of the filament to the contact button at the bottom of the base. If you replace a lamp with any type of lamp other than a direct substitution of the one that you are removing, you need to make sure that the two lamps share a common LCL. Several retrofit lamps are shown in the top row of Figure 6.5.

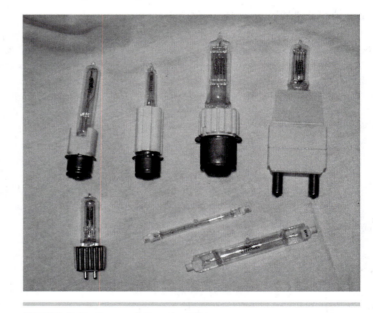

FIGURE 6.5 Several Popular TH lamps

life. The primary issue that ultimately results in the failure of this lamp is that the tungsten particles cannot be redeposited evenly over the filament, so eventually a weakness will develop that results in the filament breaking and the lamp failing. Stage and studio lamps of this style have become so popular that **retrofit** versions of TH lamps have been created for nearly every earlier lamp configuration, while most new luminaires are designed around the smaller TH lamps. Even most headlamps in today's cars use TH lamp technology. While not technically correct, some individuals may also refer to TH lamps as **quartz lamps.**

The increased operating temperatures of TH lamps require several additional precautions on the part of a lighting designer or electrician, the most significant being that these lamps should not be handled with bare hands or fingers. If you handle the lamps, the deposits that are made by the oil contained on your fingertips will actually become etched into the quartz glass once the lamp is powered up. This etching will often cause a weakness to develop in the bulb, and the lamp will eventually melt through and burn out. Occasionally, a lamp may even fail from this in an explosive manner. If you should accidentally touch a quartz lamp, take care to wipe your finger marks from the bulb with alcohol before applying any power to the lamp. Quartz lamps are also fragile when hot and will not take sudden shocks or bumps that might occur if an electrician should be careless as they handle a lit fixture.

ARC LIGHT SOURCES

An arc source quite literally produces an **arc** of electricity or spark that jumps between two differently charged contacts or electrodes. Light sources of this type are created in much the same manner as a welder produces an arc to fuse metal together. The spark that is created by the electricity flowing across the gap between the two electrodes actually becomes the light source. The light source is extremely bright and can damage your eyes if you are exposed to it without any eye protection. In addition to being one of the brightest light sources available, it also produces light that has a much higher color temperature than standard incandescent lighting. It is easily distinguished from other light sources not only by its brightness but also by its characteristic bluish-white tint. Many arc sources have color temperatures in the 6,000° K range as compared to 3,000°–3,600° K range of incandescent lamps. Due to the visible contrast between arc and traditional lamps, arc sources are often used in fixtures such as followspots and moving lights, where the light needs to cut through or be noticeable in comparison to other more traditional sources that are lighting a stage.

Limelight

In the early days of theatrical spotlighting a special spotlight was created called a **limelight.** This fixture simply contained a block of lime that was heated with a gas flame to a point where it created a bright source of light for the stage. The flame required constant monitoring, and operators were used not only to manage the flame but also to shift the spotlight to accommodate the movements of the principle performers. These fixtures formed what may have been considered some of the earliest appearances of followspots. The limelight produced an overall quality of light that was very pleasant for the actors and allowed a director to add some focus to a performer without adding distortion to a scene. The limelight was so popular that when electricity appeared it didn't take long for its basic principle of operation to be adapted so that electricity became the means of producing the flaming light source.

Carbon-Arc

Some of the most common arc lighting fixtures of the last 50 or 60 years combined two pencil-shaped electrodes or rods (a positive and negative) that were made of carbon material with an outer sheathing of copper for producing their light. These were often called **carbon-arc spotlights.** The electrodes were oriented in an end-to-end configuration so that the two tips were separated by a gap of approximately ½" while the location of this gap was set to coincide with the focal point of any reflectors and lenses that were contained within a fixture. In order to begin the electrical flow and resulting spark, the electrodes are briefly brought together and then gently separated. This is what we commonly call **striking** an arc. By maintaining the proper distance between the two rods, the flame or arc stays lit between the electrodes. While the arc remains lit the rods slowly burn down and an operator or mechanical device must continually feed the rods together as a means of making up for the material that has been burned away. This process of maintaining the arc is called **trimming.** A typical set of carbon rods was expendable and would only last for about 30–45 minutes before they would have to replaced. Additionally, an operator would have to ensure that the position of the arc remained at the focal point of the fixture and that the gap between the electrodes didn't become too close or far apart. If the rods get too close together they can cause excessive amounts of material to be burned and splattered over the optical components of the fixture, or the flame might be extinguished through actually fusing the rods together. If the gap becomes too wide, the arc simply fizzles out. While arc lamps cannot be dimmed electrically, operators learned to gently pull the rods farther apart to cause the light output of the lamp to drop by about 10–20 percent. This became known as **backing off the rods** or running the fixture at **ballet dim.** Most arc sources require that the power be converted to a DC voltage before being administered to the electrodes through the use of a special power supply or **ballast.** Despite these issues, the carbon arc remained one of the most popular arc sources for film projectors and followspots for many years in the entertainment industry.

SHORT-ARC AND HIGH INTENSITY DISCHARGE (HID) LAMPS

A significant side effect of carbon-arc sources is the carbon monoxide that is given off as a byproduct of the illumination process. Over the years, many operators have become victims of carbon monoxide poisoning due to the poor ventilation that was once common to many projection rooms and spotlight booths. Additionally, the constant need for monitoring and maintaining the rods and flame made the operation of carbon-arc fixtures relatively difficult. As technology became more advanced, engineers developed other ways of producing arc sources without actually having to burn materials like carbon.

Short-Arc Lamps

Modern arc sources commonly used in followspots, projectors, and other high intensity fixtures of today more commonly make use of a **short-arc lamp** (Figure 6.6). This is a specialized lamp that is made of extremely heavy glass with permanent electrodes that are built right into the lamp. The lamp is filled with a variety of different gases that are kept under high pressure. Most importantly, these sources produce the same high-quality arc that is characteristic of the earlier fixtures without the need for constant rod adjustments and side effect of producing carbon monoxide. These lamps last much longer than carbon rods and often have lamp lives that extend to 100 hours or more. On the other hand, the lamps are usually quite expensive and require a warm-up period that can take 3 to 5 minutes from first striking the arc to having the lamp come up to full power. On initial power-up these lamps have a low-intensity and very bluish-purple color until they complete the warm-up process. This warm-up period exists even if the arc has just been used or been powered down. A number of concert encores have been screwed up because spot operators using these short-arc sources have powered down too soon when a band has come out to do a second or third encore. Another issue that plagued earlier versions of these sources, such as the xenon arc lamp, was that the lamp was under such considerably high pressure that they would occasionally explode. Heavy duty lamp housings were added to these fixtures as a means of protecting operators from this. Several more recent versions of short-arc lamps make use of other gases and materials that work under less threatening pressures. The most common short arcs used in today's applications include the HMI (hydrargyrum medium-arc iodide or halogen metal iodide) and HTI (tubular metal halide) metal halide lamps which produce a very

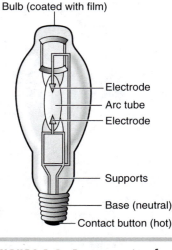

Bulb (coated with film)

— Electrode
— Arc tube
— Electrode

— Supports

— Base (neutral)
— Contact button (hot)

FIGURE 6.6 Components of a High-Intensity Discharge (HID or Short-Arc) Lamp

intense light source comparatively for the number of watts that they consume. They also have a relatively high color temperature that is in the range of 6,000° K. Metal halide lamps are commonly found in commercial movie projectors, today's followspots, and many moving or automated lighting fixtures.

High-Intensity Discharge (HID) Lamps

Short-arc lamps are special variations of a broader class of light sources called **high-intensity discharge** or **HID lamps.** We tend to use the name short-arc more commonly with stage and studio lamps, while architectural practices refer to these light sources as HID lamps. Initially, fixtures containing these sources were used to light large open spaces. HID lamps have become quite popular in large architectural applications such as warehouses, arenas, and manufacturing plants. Fixtures employing this technology produce a bright, widely distributed wash of light that is much more efficient than incandescent or fluorescent light sources. In general, the mounting height of these lamps is also relatively high in comparison to more traditional light sources. Lighting fixtures typically used in gymnasiums and large warehouse stores like Home Depot or Bed, Bath, and Beyond form common examples of facilities using HID light sources. Probably the most common application of HID lighting is found in roadway and parking lot lighting. With increasing energy costs, the basic design has been modified to produce small HID fixtures that are used in display lighting, such as those found in many recently renovated supermarkets and retail stores. Several of the most popular HID sources used today include the familiar bluish-green **mercury lamp,** the pinkish-amber light of **high-pressure sodium lamps,** and the crisp, white light of **metal halide lamps.** The mercury lamp is most commonly seen along highways and exterior building applications. Many of the security lamps that are installed on the properties of personal residences use mercury light sources. The roadway lighting typically associated with interstates and urban areas, on the other hand, uses primarily high-pressure sodium light sources. Their orange tint makes them easily identifiable. Metal halide lamps are more expensive to operate but produce a more diverse spectrum of light and are commonly found in retail spaces. Metal halide and mercury lamps are quite similar—both use mercury as an interior gas for the arc's conduction—but metal halide lamps differ through the introduction of additional materials (metal halides) into the gas as a means of improving the lumen output and color rendering of the lamps. Sodium lamps make use of a sodium vapor. The high-pressure sodium lamp has become the most popular source for roadway lighting due to its great energy efficiency and has the pinkish-orange tint. There are also **low-pressure sodium lamps** marked by their strong yellow color (similar to a bug light) that are very energy efficient but have only limited applications due to their extremely narrow spectral composition . All of the HID lamps require a ballast and cannot be ignited instantly. In fact, most HID lamps can take 10 or more minutes to come up to full lumen output. Just as with stage and studio short-arc lamps, these lamps glow dimly when first ignited and then slowly build to full brightness over a warm-up period. If the lamp is extinguished, it will take a period of 5 or more minutes from the re-strike until the source once again comes up to full power.

In stage and studio applications the HID lamps are typically limited to being used in followspots, moving lights, and several high-intensity fixtures like large studio **luminaires.** You may also see many of these sources used in fixtures that are used as sky trackers or search lights for bringing attention to malls, car dealerships, sports attractions, and other special events. In film, these light sources are often used on location shoots to fill in shadows on large interior or exterior settings. Several of the most popular HID lamps in use today are specific variations of the metal halide lamp and include the **HMI (halogen metal iodide)** that has color temperatures that make it comparable to daylight, the **CSI (compact source iodide),** the **CID (compact iodide daylight),** and **xenon** lamp. Each lamp has a specific mixture of components and is associated with a different overall color temperature, spectral composition, and lumen output.

GASEOUS DISCHARGE LAMPS

The most common form of gaseous discharge lamp is the **fluorescent lamp** (Figure 6.7). For many years, due to both its ability to produce uniform washes and its comparable power efficiency, architectural practices have used fluorescent rather than incandescent lamps as a primary light source. In fact, the need for power conservation toward the end of the 1990s has resulted in a trend in which even more fluorescent fixtures are becoming attractive alternatives to the incandescent sources traditionally used in many residential and hospitality applications. The **compact fluorescent lamp (CFL)** is an adaptation of these lamps that is becoming more and more popular as an alternative source for many residential lamps. Modifications of these lamps are appearing in all areas of fixture design and include table and floor lamps as well as downlights and wall washer designs. It is hard to enter a hotel these days where compact fluorescent lamps can't be found in nearly any area or lighting application within these facilities. There's even a new trend to replace the once-efficient HID lighting installations of factories and warehouse stores with even more energy efficient fluorescent lighting sources.

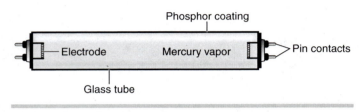

FIGURE 6.7 Components of a Gaseous Discharge (Fluorescent) Lamp

Fluorescent Lamps

The **fluorescent lamp** works on the principle of energizing a field of low-pressure gas between two electrodes or cathodes. However, unlike an arc source whose actual light production comes from the arc, this arc is of a relative low intensity and instead energizes another material that begins to glow or create light. In the case of fluorescent lighting, the gas for the electron flow has traditionally been mercury, and the material that glows is phosphorous. The electron flow through the excited gas causes radiation to be emitted primarily in the ultraviolet rather than visible portion of the spectrum. The energy is then used to excite the powdered phosphorous material to a point where it will fluoresce or give off light. A similar effect can be noted on a moonlit night as the glowing waves of plankton spread away from a boat's wake or across the breakers that form along a beach. While fluorescent sources don't usually create strong enough intensities to be considered for theatrical applications, they are often the source of choice for many commercial operations where distances between a fixture and task are relatively close, there are extended hours of operation, and there are other concerns about energy conservation. In addition to relatively low light output, another disadvantage of fluorescent tubes relates to the negative impact that cold temperatures can have upon their operation. The fluorescent tubes that are commonly found in gas stations can often be seen to pulsate and sputter when exposed to winter temperatures. Dimming is another issue that will be discussed later.

A fluorescent lamp cannot be turned on through simply applying power to a lamp, and in most cases, fluorescent lamps require that cathodes be used to stimulate their electrical arcs. There are both cold and hot cathode systems, but due to energy efficiency, most fluorescent lamps make use of hot cathode or rapid-start technology. In the majority of cases, a transformer-like device called a **ballast** is wired in series with a fluorescent lamp to regulate the current and voltage of the lamp while also providing the initial burst of voltage that is needed to start the ignition process. A starter element may also be required with some fluorescent lamps. HID lamps also make use of a ballast. Ballasts are specified or matched to a given lamp and are not interchangeable between different wattages of fluorescent lamps. It should also be noted that the power load of a circuit containing fluorescent lamps must not only include the wattage of the lamps but also any ballasts that are in a circuit. However, the power requirements for a fluorescent lamp are much smaller than for a comparable incandescent lamp that would be used for producing the same amount of light. A typical installation consists of a single ballast being shared between two lamps, although there are also fixtures that make use of a single lamp and associated ballast. In addition to their overall energy efficiency, fluorescent lamps also have lamp lives that are as high as 10,000–20,000 hours, which is up to 20 times longer than comparable incandescent lamps. In areas where it is difficult to change lamps, the fluorescent source becomes a popular design choice.

The most popular form of fluorescent lamps are in the shape of tubes that vary in lengths of up to eight feet. The thickness or diameter of the tube is also considered; with the most popular lamps being variations of the T-12, T-8 and T-5 lamps. These numbers relate to a tubular construction with a diameter expressed in ⅛" intervals. The T-8 lamp therefore is 1 inch in diameter. The T-12 was the primary workhorse of fluorescent lighting for many years, while the T-8 is becoming the most popular current configuration. There's also a lot of interest in further development of the T-5 lamp that is already popular in applications like compact florescent lamps. The lamps also don't necessarily have to be in the straight tube shape of traditional fluorescent fixtures. U-shaped and circular-shaped lamps are also popular. In fact, many compact fluorescent lamp designs shape the lamp into a coil. On the whole, most fluorescent lamps have a strong spectral response in the green area of the spectrum and are therefore not the most flattering form of illumination. Through varying the mixtures of the gases and fluorescent materials, manufacturers have been able to create a range of fluorescent lamps with a variety of different light qualities and color rendering indexes. The most popular versions include "cool white" and "warm white," which relate to the spectral composition of the light produced by each lamp. The "cool white" lamp produces a bluer light, while the "warm white" lamp has better spectral responses in the warm portions of the spectrum. Additional variations of these lamps include the "daylight," "cool deluxe," and "warm deluxe" lamps that in each case makes use of phosphors that have a better response to a wider selection of lighting wavelengths. On the other hand, most incandescent lamps have a CRI of nearly 100, while most fluorescent lamps have CRIs on the order of 50–90. There are specialty fluorescent lamps used in areas such as televison production, display, and advertising work that can achieve much better color rendering, but their associated prices also increase significantly as better CRIs are obtained.

LOW-VOLTAGE LAMPS

In the last fifty years there hasn't been a strong demand for low-voltage lighting in the area of general illumination. As a rule, low-voltage sources were more commonly associated with applications in which power supply became an issue (e.g., portable devices such as in transportation—cars, planes, utility equipment, etc.) or in a situation where a specific lighting effect was required. For a number of years, the most common use of low-voltage lighting in entertainment applications was in the use of **aircraft landing lights (ACL)** for concerts. These are very narrow-beamed PAR lamps that have been adapted from their designated use in airplanes. However, in the last 20 or so years we have seen a significant appearance of low-voltage lighting systems migrating into the entertainment and architectural fields of lighting. In general, low-voltage lamps operate on a relatively low DC voltage, the most common voltage being 12 volts although 24-volt sources are also in use. The advantage of low-voltage systems lies in their ability to make a smaller lamp and filament—thus becoming a more efficient lamp through a closer approximation to a point light source. On stage these sources have typically been confined to mini-strip units where numerous lamps are wired together into alternating circuits that provide for the creation of several even washes of light. The individual lamps that are utilized in these fixtures are **MR (miniature reflector) lamps.** Much like their larger R and PAR lamp cousins these lamps come in a variety of sizes and pre-engineered beam patterns. Several common configurations of the MR lamp include the MR-11, MR-13, and MR-16 lamps. In architectural applications these lamps are popular low-voltage sources for decorative display and track lighting. They are also a dominant source for landscape lighting fixtures.

A significant difference between low-voltage light sources and traditional lamps is that the voltage which is provided to the lamps must be reduced to a comparatively small percentage of the standard 120-volt line voltage that we typically use to control our lighting fixtures. If a low-voltage lamp were to be plugged directly into a standard wall outlet it would quickly blow out due to the excessive voltage. Low-voltage lamps require that a transformer be incorporated into the circuit as a means of reducing the line voltage to a point that is within the safe operating range of a lamp. While a single source fixture may have its own transformer, there are other applications where a transformer may be used to power several different fixtures or lamps. In stage and studio applications this would be true of many fixtures that use multiple low-voltage light sources like the brute or ministrip fixtures, while in low-voltage landscape lighting a single transformer is often used for powering 20 or more fixtures.

ANSI CODES

As a means of referencing any given lamp with a specific combination of components we make use of a three-letter code as a shorthand manner of identifying each type of lamp. This code has been devised by the **American National Standards Institute** and is known as the **ANSI** code. This code is consistent between manufacturers and becomes an easy manner to quickly identify a particular lamp type. Although some properties will ultimately vary to some degree due to quality and individual manufacturing techniques, the primary characteristics of each type of lamp will remain the same between different manufacturers. While there are similarities between lamps that share similar codes, the codes themselves do not provide a clear indication of individual components for a given lamp. Even though essential properties such as base, bulb, and filament styles and sizes are dictated by an assigned ANSI code, each of the major lamp manufacturers provide catalogues that allow a designer to further compare specifications like color temperature and lumen output of a given lamp from one manufacturer to another.

LEDs

Light-emitting diodes (LEDs) are a relative new form of light source. We all recognize them primarily from their initial use as indicator lights for electronic devices. Beginning in the '70s virtually all power indicators in this equipment made use of a red LED to inform the observer that the power for a device was on. As time went on we saw variations in LEDs that produced yellow, green, and even blue light for monitoring electronic devices. We saw them appear in CB radios to indicate transmission strength, while the audio industry used them to monitor signal strength in sound gear like mixers and amplifiers. In the last 5 to 10 years LED intensities have developed to the point that they are now being used in various capacities as a light source and are starting to make significant contributions to several specialty areas of lighting despite the fact that their potential as an actual source of light is still rather limited.

LEDs are a solid-state device that produce light through a process where electricity is applied to a crystal or diode material. Diodes only allow electricity to flow in a single direction, and the result creates light in a very limited range of wavelengths. By varying the construction and material of a diode, different colored light outputs can be achieved. The excitement in the lighting community in regard to these devices lies more in the potential that they offer than in what they are now contributing to the industry as a light source. The devices are extremely small—about the size of a pencil eraser in most cases—which means that they come much closer to creating the point light source that we desire than the larger lamps of traditional incandescent sources. Their size also allows for many more of them to be mounted in a given area, and they are extremely efficient and waste very little energy through byproducts like heat. Other advantages of LEDs include their extreme durability and ruggedness, their ability to produce light in a very narrow range of wavelengths, and the low amount of power that they require as well as their ability to respond quickly to voltage changes like pulsating. There is an additional and possibly even more significant advantage in that these devices have lifespans that are significantly longer than any traditional light source. In fact, LEDs can often be associated with lasting through the entire life of most electronic devices; meaning that equipment will most likely become inoperable before the LEDs within a device will fail. While a traditional halogen lamp will have a lamp life in the hundreds of hours, LEDs have life spans in the neighborhood of fifty thousand hours or more.

With all of these advantages, we must then ask the obvious question of why haven't LEDs been used in more applications than we see currently. The answer lies predominantly in a single factor: intensity. For all their advantages LEDs have not been capable of producing a great amount of light or lumen output. However, this is constantly changing as the technology becomes more sophisticated. As LEDs have become brighter, they have found their way into an increasing number of applications, and this trend should continue into the future. While we have not reached the point that LEDs are capable of producing a good white light source that is bright enough to be used to illuminate a room in the same way as a traditional fixture, LEDs are continually getting brighter and are being used in a growing number of areas of lighting design. Several popular uses of LEDs in today's society include: traffic lights, various chase and effects lighting equipment, video walls, decorative architectural applications like along stair and platform edges or cove lighting, and a number of display and exhibit lighting applications. As a source, LEDs may be viewed directly (e.g., a video wall where a composite image is produced through a matrix of LEDs) or indirectly, where the emitted light is cast onto another surface. A very popular use of LEDs is in their being mounted in clusters that contain at least one LED of each of the three primary colors (red, blue, and green) as well as possibly additional LEDs of other colors like yellow or cyan. Several variations of this technology have been incorporated into fixtures that mimic both striplights and PAR-64 luminaire designs. The voltage of each LED is regulated to control the intensity of light being created by each LED color or circuit. The overall mixture results in producing colored light through additive color mixing. Many of these fixtures produce a high color temperature version of white light when using LEDs of only the three primary colors. By creating an even more sophisticated array of multi-colored LEDs, a fixture can be created that has the potential for producing almost any conceivable color of light, and the unnatural white of the three-colored fixtures can be improved upon significantly. Wash fixtures that make use of this principle have become extremely popular in the museum, retail, and display industries. Some smaller stages are also making successful use of this technology. Figure 6.8 illustrates an LED wash luminaire. The development of multi-colored LED wash luminaires has become a driving force in the lighting industry, and although these fixtures began with a fairly low capability for producing illumination, they continue to improve yearly. Another concern has been in the ability of these units to maintain consistent color output between units, especially if they have been purchased over a period of time where LEDs may have come from different sources or manufacturing runs. As the ability to generate more footcandles improves, these fixtures are migrating into ever larger

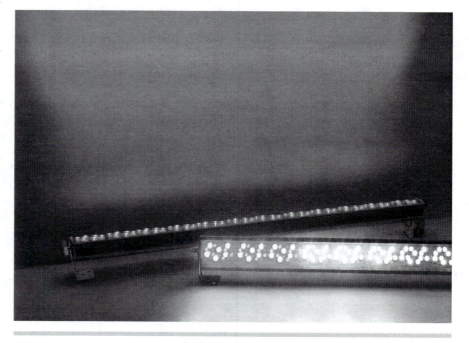

FIGURE 6.8 An LED Wash Luminaire ColorBlaze Striplight *Photo credit:* Philips Solid-State Lighting Solutions, Inc.

applications despite the fact that their relative light output is still low in comparison to traditional luminaires. On the other hand, manufacturers have already introduced fixtures with enough brightness to be used effectively for stage luminaires, although the costs often remain beyond the means of many production organizations. Each year brings brighter and brighter LED fixtures into the market while the costs of this technology at the same time becomes more affordable. It is only a matter of time until LEDs become a practical source of illumination for the entertainment industry. They are even appearing as sources in automated lighting heads. The evolution of the white LED and its comparatively low intensity is the main obstacle to this technology being incorporated into traditional fixture designs at the present time. However, there are a number of people who feel that innovators are on the cusp of developing a white LED with enough brightness for these, too, to become viable sources for more traditional luminaire designs. Many feel that LEDs form the next major innovation in the lighting industry and that they represent the future of lighting.

LASERS

Lasers are a special form of light. While they may combine several different wavelengths, they still represent a fairly narrow range, if not single wavelength, of light. More importantly, although most light is emitted as a scattered form of energy, a laser produces its light in a very narrowly defined direction. This degree of directionality makes it an ideal source for defining lines, which is precisely why we use it in line referencing applications in trades like the surveying or construction industries. Additionally, a laser emits light in a synchronized manner. Rather than creating a random or continuous emission of light, a laser emits its energy in such a way that corresponding wavelengths and the waveform of each individual wave correspond or are in step with one another. In this manner there is a cumulative effect that produces a higher overall amplitude for the light and associated energy of a laser. This cumulative effect is responsible for the energy of lasers and is called **stepping.** The principle is quite similar to that of AC power creation, with the exception being that with a laser we are trying to maximize, rather than neutralize, the strength of the combined wavelengths. For all practical appearances a laser will only appear as a bright dot of light on any objects that it happens to be played upon. However, if the air is charged with particles like dust, the laser becomes clearly visible as a line of light. This is the effect that originally made lasers so popular. Lasers are often played on theatrical fog and haze for many productions. In outdoor environments, clouds and even smoke from fireworks are used as projection surfaces for laser effects.

Even up to now lasers have not played a great role in the area of lighting for illumination. This is in part due to the extreme concentrated effect of these light beams. However, this intense concentration of energy is precisely what makes them so attractive to industries that use laser technology for various cutting or precision measurement applications. Engineers often refer to lasers as being "coherent forms of light." The medical and manufacturing communities have been using lasers effectively for medical or machining procedures for a number of years, using them to cut and shape metal, take bearings for surveying, remove damaged tissue in surgery, and create straight reference lines for hanging pictures or ensuring that a course of masonry remains level. Several years ago I even had a cavity treated with the use of a dental laser. Despite all the beneficial uses of lasers, the lighting industry to this point has only come to use them as a means of creating effects or for spotting purposes. On the small scale, these effects can be on the order of a single point of light that is comparable to the popular laser pointers that are used in class or business presentations, while grander schemes include displays during pop concerts and aerial displays where the laser effects can be seen for miles around. Just outside of Atlanta, Georgia, is the Stone Mountain Park, which houses one of the largest aerial laser shows in the world. This 30- to 40-minute production is performed nightly over the summer and contains numerous laser effects and fireworks that have been choreographed to popular music. The closing show that occurs nightly at Epcot Center in Disney World (*IllumiNations*) also incorporates a number of laser effects that are projected throughout the lagoon portion of the theme park. This presentation culminates in a grand finale of fireworks and a laser image of a rotating globe that is projected onto the signature sphere that houses the *Spaceship Earth* ride.

Laser devices should always be considered dangerous due to the extreme concentration of energy that is associated with these light sources. Even relatively small laser pointers bear warnings that speak of the potential damage that a laser can bring to a person's eyesight. Commercial lasers always require that some form of protective measures be taken to guard against accidental exposure to both the operator and other individuals. In entertainment applications there are specific guidelines that operators must follow in order to protect not only the audience but the performers as well. In many circumstances a laser may not even be used unless the operator is licensed. Some practical considerations of laser operation include ensuring that the laser paths are far enough off the ground that nobody can look directly into a laser beam or that a laser reflection won't be directed onto an unsuspecting victim. A popular concert effect at one time involved directing laser beams several feet above the heads of an audience, which worked fine until audience members got the brilliant idea of standing on each other's shoulders to "touch the light."

There are several notable laser effects that are used in the entertainment industry. The first, a **scanner,** makes use of the principle of rapidly moving the beam of a laser from place to place. The eye cannot distinguish this rapid movement and does not see the laser as the single point of light that it actually is. Instead, through perception, we connect the points and see the image as a series of lines that lie along the path of the laser. In this manner, we use the laser and scanning to actually trace or draw basic images. A similar effect can be seen at raves or club gatherings where glow-activated tubes and balls are placed on a string and twirled around. If spun fast enough the path of the tube will appear as a circle rather than as a single object moving in the path of a circle. The second type of laser display creates **interference patterns.** These images are less predictable and are more organic in nature. In this case, the laser is distorted by passing it through an irregular piece of material such as glass or plastic so that the individual waves become either scattered or knocked out of phase with one another. This produces colored patterns of light that are capable of being transported over long distances. In either case, a laser can bring very dramatic effects to a production.

FOR FURTHER READING

Bowers, Brian, *Lengthening the Day: A History of Lighting Technology* (Oxford, UK: Oxford University Press, 1998).

Dillon, Maureen, *Artificial Sunshine: A Social History of Domestic Lighting* (London, UK: National Trust Enterprises, Ltd., 2002).

Elenbaas, W., *Light Sources* (New York: Crane, Russak and Company, Inc., 1972).

Friedel, Robert and Paul Israel, (*Edison's Electric Light: Biography of an Invention* (New Brunswick, NJ: Rutgers University Press, 1986).

Gerlach, Robert, "LEDs To Light the Theatre," *Theatre Design and Technology (TD &T)*, 39 (4):11-22.

Gordon, Gary, *Interior Lighting for Designers,* 4th ed. (Hoboken, NJ: John Wiley and Sons, Inc., 2003).

Illuminating Engineering Society of North America, *IESNA Lighting Handbook,* 9th ed., ed. Mark Rae (New York: Illuminating Engineering Society of North America, 2000).

Illuminating Engineering Society of North America, *IESNA Lighting Ready Reference,* 4th ed. (New York: Illuminating Engineering Society of North America, 2003).

Lindsey, Jack L., *Applied Illumination Engineering,* 2nd ed. (Liburn, GA: The Fairmont Press, Inc., 1997).

Millerson, Gerald, *Lighting for Television and Film* 3rd ed. (Woburn, MA: Focal Press, 2000).

Penzel, Frederick, *Theatre Lighting Before Electricity* (Middletown, CT: Wesleyan University Press, 1978).

Rhiner, James L., *A Complete Guide to the Language of Lighting* (Elk Grove Village, IL: Halo Lighting Division, McGraw-Edison Company, 1983).

luminaire fundamentals 7

hen we refer to **luminaires** we are discussing the actual lighting fixtures. We also refer to luminaires as **lighting units, instruments,** and **lamps.** While all of these names are technically correct, you may find one used more commonly throughout different regions of the world or in various specialty areas of lighting. For instance, luminaires with a permanent mounting like those used in architectural practices are frequently called **fixtures.** In entertainment lighting we often prefer to use "lighting instruments" or "units."

In the purest sense, luminaires are the devices that we use to both produce and control light. A luminaire can be as simple as a ceiling or table lamp, as large as the rotating light of a lighthouse, or as sophisticated as the moving lights that you see in concerts. By definition, luminaires contain several specific elements that provide critical functions in producing light. First, the luminaire must contain a light source. This is often nothing more than a **lamp.** Once the light is produced, we add mechanisms to make the light more controllable and efficient. Most luminaires contain a **reflector** that allows the light to be gathered or directed in a particular direction. Many also use **lenses** as an additional way of focusing the light into a more controlled beam. Finally, a luminaire has a **housing** or **body** that holds the optical assembly together while also providing electrical connections and mounting accessories for the fixture. All luminaires represent a specific combination of lenses, reflectors, and light sources that ultimately determine the unique quality of light that is associated with a given fixture.

Since luminaires create the light, many lighting designers believe that their consideration forms the single most important factor in the design process. In this chapter I discuss the components of a luminaire based on the functions that each provides to a unit, offer an introduction to **photometrics,** and examine several of the principle luminaires associated with entertainment lighting. I also examine the means by which we control or manipulate light. What makes one luminaire different from another one? What is the quality of light associated with a particular luminaire? What type of optical control might a luminaire provide? In entertainment lighting there are only a few basic lighting instruments that a designer needs to become familiar with, while there are thousands of designs in architectural practices. Because of this, a designer must also be able to interpret graphs and tables to understand the unique qualities of a particular unit.

BASIC PRINCIPLES OF OPTICS

The primary reason that there is such a diverse collection of luminaires (most notably in architectural lighting) is due to the fact that each luminaire design provides a unique combination of light source and optical control. In this segment I examine the primary components that are used to control light once it has been produced by a light source.

Reflection and refraction form the basis of this discussion, which then expands to illustrate how these principles are used in the design of different luminaires.

Reflection

Reflection is a physical principle by which light is bounced or reflected from a surface. The basic principle of reflection is governed by the **Law of Reflection** (Figure 7.1), which states that the angle of incidence is equal to the angle of reflection (when considering an angle that is normal or perpendicular to the surface of the object). In essence, this simply means that when light bounces off a surface, it does so at an angle that is complementary (or equal) to the angle at which it first struck the surface. Materials that have shiny mirrored surfaces create reflections that follow the Law of Reflection quite specifically, and we call these reflections **specular reflections.** Other materials don't provide as good a surface for reflection and create either a **spread reflection,** where most of the light is reflected off the surface in the same general direction, or a **diffuse reflection,** where the light is scattered in numerous directions. A crumpled piece of aluminum foil can create spread reflections, while most objects that have an uneven surface or are made of un-mirrored materials characteristically produce diffuse reflections. In reality, most surfaces are associated with diffuse reflections.

As you may recall from Chapter 6, most light sources produce light in many, if not nearly all, directions. This isn't efficient since we usually want to direct light to a specific location. Sources that create light in many directions waste energy because only a small amount of their total light will fall where we actually want it. A **reflector** uses the principles of reflection to gather or redirect this otherwise unutilized light so that it can help support the primary lighting task. Some reflectors have matte finishes (with their surfaces dulled or painted white to diffuse the light) while others have polished mirror-like materials that create specular reflections that redirect the most light possible.

A fundamental element of reflector design lies in the principle that the shape of a reflector determines the behavior of the light that it reflects. Every reflector is designed around an optical point known as the focal point. The **focal point** is a point along the optical path of a lens or reflector that coincides with the location from which light rays will either be directed from or toward when using a reflector or lens. This point is infinitely small and in reality only exists in theory. However, if a light source (i.e., the lamp) is located at the focal point of a reflector, the light that leaves the lamp in the direction of the reflector will be reflected or redirected in a way that is dictated by the shape of the reflector. There are several notable reflector shapes, and each produces a characteristic directional effect on any light that strikes it (see Figure 7.2). In each case, it is important to understand that focal points are infinitely small, and while only a small amount of the total light will follow the path exactly, in reality, a source that is centered around the focal point will for the most part follow the suggested reflection pattern. Smaller sources permit a larger portion of a lamp's total output to be concentrated around the focal point of a reflector which allows a greater percentage of the light to be harvested by the reflector. This principle once again demonstrates the importance of developing **point light sources** for more efficient luminaire designs.

SPHERICAL REFLECTOR   A spherical reflector reflects light that initiates at the focal point, but would otherwise exit through the back of the fixture, back through that same focal point through the front of the luminaire. In this manner, light that would normally be wasted by exiting through the back of the fixture can be redirected through the front of the fixture. Spherical reflectors are usually created with a polished, mirrored surface that helps to maximize the light output in a frontal direction.

PARABOLIC REFLECTOR   A parabolic reflector is similar to a spherical reflector with the exception that it is flattened to some degree. Because of its flattened (or parabolic) shape, any light that strikes it after leaving a source at its focal point is reflected in parallel rays.

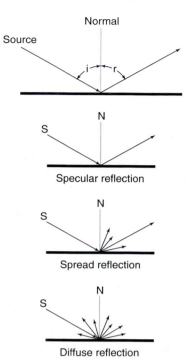

FIGURE 7.1 The Law of Reflection and Three Variations on Reflection The angle of incidence (i) is equal to the angle of reflection (r). Light is reflected from a surface at an angle to the normal (perpendicular) that is the same as the light that strikes the surface. Also note comparisons between specular, spread, and diffuse reflections.

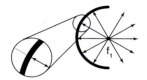

a. Spherical reflector:
Light is reflected back through the focal point (f₁) at the same angle as it strikes the reflector.

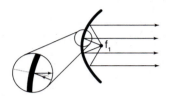

b. Parabolic reflector:
Light is reflected into parallel rays.

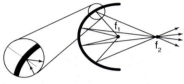

c. Ellipsoidal reflector:
Light is reflected back through a second or conjugate focal point (f₂).

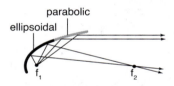

d. Compound reflector:
This reflector combines the principles of several types of reflectors. Illustrated is a combination of parabolic and ellipsoidal reflector shapes. Wash units with double-ended T-lamps often make use of this combination of reflectors.

FIGURE 7.2 Four Popular Optical Reflectors Each reflector illustrates the path of light waves associated with placing the source at the primary focal point (f₁).

ELLIPSOIDAL REFLECTOR An ellipsoidal reflector differs from the other reflectors in that its shape is based on an ellipse and its special trait of having two focal points. The focal point closest to the reflector is called the **primary focal point** and is the point at which we locate a light source. The second focal point is the **secondary** or **conjugate focal point** and is the location to which all of the reflected light will be directed. A unique property of this reflector is that any light or images that pass beyond the conjugate focal point are reversed. An ellipsoidal reflector forms one of the most efficient means of concentrating light at a given location and is the basis of many spotlight designs.

COMPOUND REFLECTORS A compound reflector is shaped with more than one principle shape along its surface. In this manner they more efficiently direct light in a primary direction. Variations of such a reflector shape are common for many lighting fixtures that use tubular lamps to wash a large area. The quartz floodlamps that are used in security or cyc lighting often make use of this type of reflector.

All reflectors work best when matched to a proper light source. In luminaire designs it is important that the lamp be oriented so that its light is directed primarily to either the front of the fixture or to the reflector at the back of the instrument. If the filament of the lamp is not oriented with the focal point of a reflector, the light will not be reflected in an optimal manner. Much of the light will become scattered and will be converted to heat within the body of the fixture. An electrician should always confirm that the proper lamp is selected for a luminaire and that the lamp is properly mounted for maximum efficiency with the reflector. Properties such as a lamp's light center length (**LCL**) should form part of this consideration. There are a number of lamps with bases that are designed to assure this proper orientation. Most luminaires are also equipped with controls that allow technicians to adjust the relationship between the reflector and lamp for maximum light output. This is referred to as lamp **alignment.** If the filament and focal point of the reflector are not oriented properly the light output of the fixture will be diminished.

Finally, since the focal point of a reflector relates to an infinitely small point, it is impossible to have a lamp with a filament small enough to follow the ideal ray patterns for any of the reflectors illustrated earlier. We can only approach these as technology improves and light sources become smaller. In the meantime, many manufacturers have developed a variation of a mirrored reflector that creates a series of prismatic faces over the entire surface of a reflector. This creates a limited amount of scattering but more importantly produces an effect that results in more light behaving in a way that would be dictated by the shape of a given reflector. These are called **flatted reflectors** and are quite common in a number of luminaires that use ellipsoidal reflectors. In an even more recent innovation, manufacturers have created reflectors that permit heat and low-energy electromagnetic radiation to pass through the back of the reflector while visible light is reflected. These are **dichroic** or **cold mirror reflectors** which create nice crisp beams and tend to produce a cooler operating temperature for luminaires, reducing heat damage to gel, gobos, shutters, and other devices that may be placed in a fixture.

Transmission

Transmission relates to the principle by which light moves through materials. While most theatrical designers prefer to use light in its purest form, there are occasions when a lighting designer may want to soften a light. Just as with reflection, there are different forms of transmission (direct, spread, and diffuse). In many luminaires a piece of glass, plastic, or other material called a **diffuser** is placed over its front to scatter and soften the light while preventing a view of the light source. The prismatic lenses of fluorescent ceiling fixtures are examples of common diffuser panels. Other examples include frosted glass and opal ceiling panels—skylights are often made of diffuser material. In entertainment lighting (especially in the film industry) we use a variety of diffusion materials that range from gel-like media to silk fabrics that are commonly called **frost** or **diffusion media.** They are made by many of the gel manufacturers.

Refraction

One of the most important principles of optics that affects the design and function of luminaires is associated with the effects of refraction. **Refraction** simply relates to light being bent by moving through materials of different densities. In earlier discussions I presented the fact that light has a specific speed (186,000 miles/sec). This speed is only true of light moving in a vacuum, and in reality, light travels through different materials with varying degrees of success and at different speeds. This effect is called the **optical density** of a material. Through measurements, scientists have been able to express the relative speed of light moving through **translucent** materials as a proportional ratio compared to the speed of light in a vacuum. This is called its **index of refraction,** which all materials that transmit light will have. Air, water, oils, plastics, and different types of glass all have different indexes of refraction.

More importantly, refraction or the bending of the light occurs at the surfaces where light passes from one material into another. As the light enters the new material it will be slowed down or sped up depending on whether the material that it is passing into is more or less dense than the material that it is traveling from. The degree of bending is dependant on the relative densities and thickness of the two different materials. A common effect of refraction is the apparent offsetting that can be observed in objects such as a stick placed in a pool or a straw in a glass of water. The effect of this physical principle is governed by **Snell's Law,** which has commonly been simplified into a basic principle known as the **Law of Refraction** (Figure 7.3). The law of refraction simply states that as light passes into a more dense material; at the surface boundary between the two materials the light will be bent toward a normal angle with the surface, while light passing from a more dense material into one of less density will be bent away from the normal angle with the surface. Refraction is responsible for separating natural light into the various component light rays of different wavelengths. Natural phenomena displaying this behavior include the formation of rainbows, prismatic effects within the spray of a water hose, and the use of prisms. The effect is due to the slightly varying speeds of the different colored light wavelengths along with the differences between the optical densities of various materials. At times, this can produce unwanted side effects in luminaires, such as a rainbow effect produced along the edge of a beam of light. The effect is more typical of luminaires containing inferior lenses, and we refer to this as **chromatic aberration** or the resulting prismatic effects as **color fringes.**

Refraction is a major consideration in optics due to the fact that it determines one of the primary means by which we control light within a luminaire. We do this by making use of the principles of refraction to create specialty devices called **lenses.** By varying the thickness and shape of the front and back surfaces of a lens any light passing through the lens can be redirected. The curvature of a lens can be thought of as a plane of "infinite prisms" where varying degrees of refraction occur along the curvature of the lens's surface. Lenses are created in a variety of shapes and sizes to control the distribution of any light that passes through them. Like reflectors, a distinguishing characteristic of all lenses is their **focal length.** This is a measurement taken from a given point of a lens (its optical center) to its **focal point.** The focal point is the point at which parallel light rays entering the lens will converge or be focused upon. As a rule, thick lenses provide more refractive power and have relatively short focal lengths, while thin lenses provide less refraction and have longer focal lengths. Larger diameter lenses also capture more light (making them more efficient) and tend to have longer focal lengths. Lenses are named by the shape of their front and back surfaces. A **plano** surface is flat like a plane, while **concave lenses** dip inward and **convex lenses** flex outward.

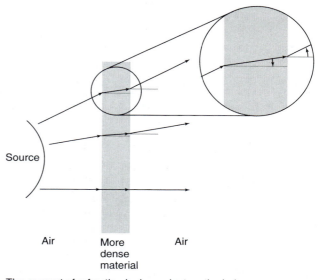

The amount of refraction is dependent on the index of refraction and the thickness of the materials.

FIGURE 7.3 Law of Refraction As light passes through a medium it is bent or refracted at the surface boundaries that exist between different materials or mediums. If the light is moving from a less dense to a more dense material it is bent toward the normal angle with the surface. If the light is moving into a less dense material it is bent away from the normal angle. The effect results in the light and objects appearing parallel and offset.

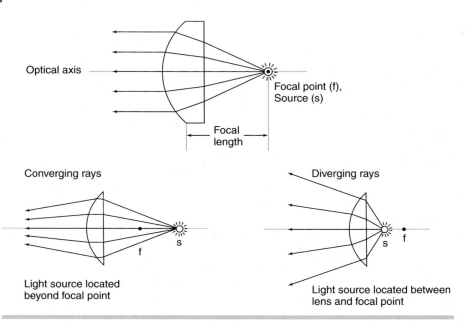

FIGURE 7.4 A Plano-Convex Lens with its Optical Relationships and the Effects of Light-Source Placement Parallel rays of light are created by placing a light source at the focal point of the lens.

The most popular lenses used in the lighting industry are variations of a **plano-convex lens** design. In this case, the lens will have one flat side while the other side has a convex-shape. In principle, if a light source or lamp is located at the focal point of a lens the resultant light should form into essentially parallel rays. If the light source is placed between the lens and focal point the resulting light will undergo **divergence** and will spread outward while if the light source is moved outside of the focal point the lens will produce **converging rays** that will cross over one another. Figure 7.4 illustrates these three conditions. Lenses are not identified in any way that reflects their focal lengths, and while they may appear to be the same, they can actually be quite different from one another. One way of differentiating between lenses lies in a measurement of their diameter, while a second relates to estimating their focal length. While the diameter is easily measured, lenses can appear the same while having very different focal lengths. To identify the focal length, we can hold a lens above a surface upon which we focus an image of a distant light source. This is the same principle as using a magnifying glass to scorch a piece of paper with the sun. By moving the lens back and forth until the image comes into sharp focus you identify the point where the distance between the surface and the lens is equal to the focal length of the lens. While there is only one point or plane (the focal point) where a lens will form a perfect image of an object or truly parallel rays, there is actually a range of distance on either side of the focal point where objects will remain in relatively good focus. This is commonly called **depth of field** and will vary according to the construction of a luminaire and its lenses. In lenses designed for cameras, this range is affected by the f-stop setting, which regulates how much light enters a lens. Smaller f-stop settings (with higher numbers) allow for a larger depth of field, while larger f-stop settings (with smaller numbers) provide a relatively narrow depth of field.

Lenses are prone to both crack and shatter from heat buildup because they are traditionally made of glass, which makes them heavy while also having poor coefficients of expansion (when placed under the extreme heat of stage lamps). Several variations of plano-convex lenses have been developed that approach the optical qualities of a single plano-convex lens without the shortcomings of the traditionally thick lenses. In the first variation, two separate plano-convex lenses are placed in line with one another (plano sides facing outward) as a means of replacing a single, thicker lens. This is a common arrangement for many spotlight designs that are still used today. In other designs, high quality plastics are used rather than glass. Other variations include removal of some of the glass from either side of a lens, which reduces the thickness of a lens while still approximating the overall shape and properties of the lens. The **Fresnel lens** (easily spotted by its concentric rings and dimpled or frosted back surface) is a variation of the plano-convex lens that has portions of the convex surface removed. The dimpled texture adds a diffusing effect that softens any images that the rings on the other surface might cause. A less popular version that removes elements of the plano surface while leaving the convex surface intact is the **step lens.** The step lens was popular in the 1950s and '60s but produced a series of concentric rings in the beam of many spotlights that used them. Figure 7.5 illustrates each of these different lenses.

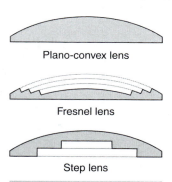

Plano-convex lens

Fresnel lens

Step lens

FIGURE 7.5 Popular Spotlight Lenses

AN ESSENTIAL LUMINAIRE

In order to create a luminaire a designer only needs to produce a given combination of light source, reflector, and lens along with an enclosure to mount the components in proper relationship with one another. Light created at the focal point of the reflector by the light source is gathered and redirected along the optical path in a way that provides a maximum concentration of light near the focal point of a lens (if the fixture has a lens). This light is then directed into essentially parallel rays that radiate away from the fixture. In reality, the production of perfectly parallel light rays is not possible, and the light produced by most luminaires approaches a conical pattern. The enclosure of a lighting instrument forms the actual body of a luminaire and not only provides a method for mounting the reflector and other optical components but also provides a way to hang a fixture in the theatre along with any accessories that might be added to its design. This enclosure is often called the **body** or **hood** of the luminaire. The body also provides electrical connections for the light source. We broadly distinguish between **spotlights** and **floodlights** as the two primary groups of luminaire design. A floodlight tends to have a soft, diffuse light with undefined edges and usually washes a large area evenly. A spotlight is more focused and defined than a floodlight. It will have well-defined edges and a fairly tight distribution pattern. As a rule, spotlights contain lenses and floodlights do not. Because of their sharp beams, many spotlights contain devices that enable a designer to actually shape the beam of light.

PHOTOMETRICS

While most lenses may be identified through their diameter and focal length this information is not all that helpful to most lighting designers. What is more important for a lighting designer is the overall distribution pattern that a lens or luminaire will produce. Due to this, it has become common for lighting designers to identify lenses by their distribution angles rather than by focal length. In fact, even if we know the focal length of a lens, we must still translate this information into an angle or beam pattern when plotting a design. Every luminaire creates a specific pattern of light that radiates away from the instrument in a variety of intensities in different directions. Most luminaires cast light outwards in a conical shape, while others create more complex patterns like an elliptical beam. **Photometrics** is the study of light intensity and distribution. More importantly, we use photometrics for making fixture selections as well as for plotting the coverage of the lighting instruments. When determining distribution patterns, light is measured around the principle optical path or axis of the fixture as it radiates away from the luminaire. Presently, most manufacturers of entertainment luminaires present their photometric data based on the distribution patterns of beam and field angles, while architectural manufacturers use a more comprehensive study of **candlepower distribution curves.** The architectural method provides much more information and is determined from actual intensity measurements at various angles around a luminaire. The **Illuminating Engineering Society of North America (IESNA)** has created a standard by which

SIDEBAR 7.1 Luminaire Maintenance

In order to maintain maximum light output from a luminaire several maintenance procedures should be performed on a regular basis. Dust and grime accumulate on the lens and reflector of luminaires and can create a significant effect on the light output of a unit within a very short period of time. A typical schedule for many theatrical companies is to clean and perform routine maintenance on their lighting instruments annually. Other organizations modify their maintenance schedules based on how dusty an environment that the units must perform within, degree of use, etc. Unfortunately, there are a number of lighting installations, especially in the architectural arena, where luminaire maintenance is ignored—resulting in energy efficiency losses as well as compromised lighting levels.

Basic luminaire maintenance is quite simple and involves not much more than cleaning the optical components and making adjustments in a luminaires alignment. The body can be cleared of dust through blowing compressed air into the fixture. For cleaning reflectors, most manufacturers recommend that a soft cloth be used to wipe the reflector(s) clean. A mild solution of vinegar and water may also be used to clean a reflector. Lenses can be cleaned with a mild solution of soap and water or a high-quality glass cleaner. Care must be taken to thoroughly rinse the lenses to avoid any streaking and soap film or build-up. An electrician should also check all the electrical and mechanical components of the luminaire for both safety and ease of operation. Any questionable connections, knobs and bolts, or other features should be repaired or replaced at this time. Once all of this has been done, the unit is aligned in order to produce the best beam of light possible.

manufacturers report this data. The result has been the representation of this data in a format that allows easy comparisons to be made between luminaires. Through the efforts of **The Entertainment Services and Technology Association (ESTA),** there is now a movement to adopt the IESNA standard for reporting photometric data for entertainment luminaires as well.

Beam Angle and Field Angle

The most common way of expressing distribution patterns for theatrical lighting fixtures relates to the concepts of beam and field angles. This is due to the fact that most distribution patterns for theatrical luminaires are quite directional, with light radiating away from a lighting instrument as a cone. By contrast, many architectural luminaires distribute light as a wash over a wide area in many directions. If projected onto a flat surface from straight on, the field of light produced by most luminaires is a circle. Beam angle and field angle are simply measurements of the relative intensity of the light as you move toward the outer regions of its pool and away from its optical axis. In older luminaire designs the highest intensity concentrations were typically found at the center of this pool, and there was a significant drop in intensity as one measured the brightness from the center of the pool toward its edges. By definition, **beam angle** relates to the angle that represents that area of the beam where the intensity has fallen off by no more then 50% of the initial intensity. The **field angle** represents a larger portion of the pool and represents an angle where the intensity drops off to 10% of the initial intensity. The beam angle is contained within the larger field angle of a luminaire. Both beam and field angles are illustrated in Figure 7.6.

Most lighting fixtures contain mechanisms that allow an electrician to manipulate the beam in ways that adjust the evenness of the distribution pattern while also maximizing the amount of light that leaves a luminaire. These adjustments in a beam are called **alignment** and may be set through the manipulation of several screws (traditional) or a knob or joystick-like device on the back of more recently designed fixtures. These adjustments may be used to create a concentrated hot spot near the center of a

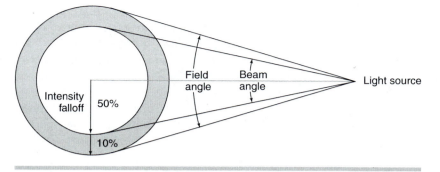

FIGURE 7.6 **Beam and Field Angles** Beam angle represents the most intense portion of the light—where intensity falloff drops to 50%—while the field angle is inclusive of the beam angle and is defined by an intensity of at least 10% of initial light output.

beam (**peaked field**) or to create an even coverage over the entire beam of light (**flat field**) where for all practical purposes the field and beam angles become nearly the same. Many of the newer enhanced spotlights that have come into popular use since the early 1990s have relatively flat fields when compared to earlier luminaires and are often called **flat field luminaires.**

Photometric Data and Cut Sheets

There are numerous luminaire designs that have been developed throughout the years. Each one creates a unique pattern and quality of light as a result of the specific combination of the individual components that are used in a fixture's physical construction. While luminaire designs may vary considerably from one field of lighting to another, there are a limited number of principle luminaire styles that are found in each area of lighting design. Each of these groups include luminaires that can vary considerably in beam pattern, size, and power. Furthermore, the actual light output will commonly be different between manufacturers of similarly named fixtures. This may be due to the use of superior components, slightly varying optical controls, or better efficiency in one design over another. It therefore becomes important for a lighting designer to not only understand the difference between different types of fixtures but to also be able to make comparisons between fixtures of essentially the same design. Because of this, luminaires should be matched (if at all possible) by both type and manufacturer when completing similar tasks in a particular lighting application. Otherwise variations might be observed in the light from one luminaire to another. The best way that we have of understanding the specific optics and light output of a fixture is through the use of comparative graphs that report specific photometric data regarding each luminaire. Manufacturers will make this information available through **cut sheets.** While the actual display of information will often vary from one company to another, these sheets typically provide a photograph or sketch of the luminaire, physical data like the weight and dimensions of the luminaire, lamp information, and most importantly photometric data relating to the instrument's specific beam pattern and distribution levels. Fixtures that have an adjustable beam angle (spot or flood settings or zoom features) often have additional photometric graphs that represent the extreme ranges of the fixture.

The IESNA has developed a specific means of representing photometric data so that comparisons can easily be made between a wide variety of luminaires. Nearly every architectural manufacturing firm has adopted this format for representing photometric data in their cut sheets. The most common element of these tables include a graphical representation of the light output (intensity) of the luminaire at various angles to either side of a fixture's centerline. These graphs are **candlepower** or **candela distribution**

Candlepower Distribution

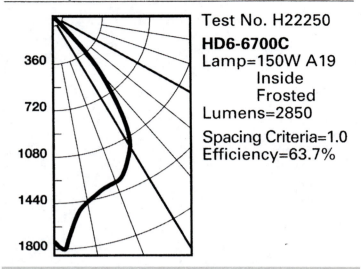

Test No. H22250

HD6-6700C

Lamp=150W A19
Inside
Frosted
Lumens=2850

Spacing Criteria=1.0
Efficiency=63.7%

FIGURE 7.7 An Architectural Photometric (Candela Distribution) Chart This luminaire data is for Eaton's Portfolio recessed downlight fixture (Model HD6-6700). Note the pattern of intensity over distribution angles.

Credit: Distribution chart by Eaton.

curves (Figure 7.7). Zero degrees represents a point directly below the luminaire, while ninety degrees represents points on the horizon directly to either side of the fixture. The plotted line represents the intensity (distribution pattern) of the luminaire's light in each direction between these extremes. In some cases, light may be measured above the horizontal position which is indicated by distribution curves that continue above the ninety degree positions. Other important data such as spacing considerations, overall efficiency, physical dimensions, lamp and ballast data, and other forms of photometric data are also found on a typical cut sheet. While the entertainment industry has not yet adopted the IESNA standard for reporting photometric data, the information is still readily available and a fairly common method of representing the data has been in use for many years (although often changing slightly between manufacturers). Figure 7.8 illustrates a common manner of displaying photometric data for entertainment luminaires. In the future, the IESNA format will most likely also be adopted for entertainment luminaires.

Even though terminology may vary, the basic principles of measurement are essentially the same between architectural and entertainment lighting systems. In theatrical measurements we speak of **throw distance** as the line of sight distance between a luminaire and its target. This is roughly equivalent to the **mounting height** of an architectural fixture because architectural fixtures are typically mounted in a straight-down orientation, while theatrical fixtures are normally angled toward a subject. In theatrical-based graphics, the throw distance is plotted along the central axis of the fixture, while the beam angle and field angle bisect this axis and extend outward from the luminaire toward its target. Most importantly, a series of numbers are displayed along the axis of theatrical photometric charts that indicate both the size of the light pool as well as the intensity of the light at corresponding distances from the light source. The intensity is usually expressed in either candelas or footcandles. Some manufacturers provide additional information such as multiplying factors that allow a designer to determine a pool size for a luminaire at any distance by simply multiplying a throw distance by the multiplying factor. Since individual cut sheets and photometric tables may vary considerably from one theatrical manufacturer to another Robert C. Mumm has compiled a reference handbook called the *Photometrics Handbook* that presents luminaire data in a standard format for nearly every theatrical luminaire that has ever been manufactured. This reference is an essential tool for anyone working in the entertainment lighting industry. Figure 7.8 illustrates a theatrical luminaire's photometric data in Mumm's standardized format. The same information is also available through software packages like John McKernon's *Beamwright,* which not only provides the photometric data but also allows you to determine the effect on pool size and intensity falloff while manipulating the hanging position of the unit. *Beamwright* can even recommend a list of luminaires for an application by allowing a designer to establish a set of parameters like pool size and hanging position (trim and distance from target) prior to making a fixture selection.

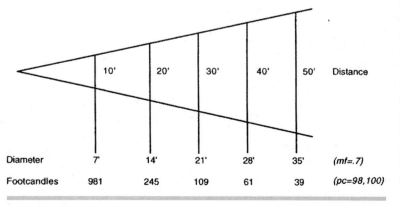

	10'	20'	30'	40'	50'	Distance
Diameter	7'	14'	21'	28'	35'	(mf=.7)
Footcandles	981	245	109	61	39	(pc=98,100)

FIGURE 7.8
A photometrics diagram by Robert Mumm for an Altman "Shakespeare" S6-40 luminaire as published in *Photometrics Handbook,* second edition, Broadway Press, 1997.

CHOOSING LUMINAIRES

Luminaire choices or specifications form one of the most critical tasks that a lighting designer must accomplish when designing the lighting for any production or environment. A lighting designer learns how to match the quality and distribution of the desired light with the specific characteristics of a given luminaire. Once the quality of light and style of fixture have been determined, the designer considers more specific variations of that fixture based on issues like desired intensity levels, distribution patterns, and the throw distances required for an application. While there are luminaires like moving lights or units with zoom features that allow some modification in the light qualities associated with a particular fixture, most lighting instruments can only produce a single quality of light with only minor adjustments in their beam. Therefore, luminaires are chosen for the unique contributions that they make to a design.

Several considerations that a designer will face when making specific luminaire choices include: the desired quality of light (harsh, diffuse, textured, edge definition, etc.), the type of light source (source characteristics, intensity, and color temperature), control desired within the fixture (beam shaping and focus modification), throw distances, and finally any physical restrictions that may effect how and where a luminaire may be mounted. While entertainment luminaires are typically mounted with ease from a pipe with a clamp device, architectural fixtures are more commonly mounted in ceilings and walls where ceiling clearance (both within and outside of the ceiling) and other mounting obstructions such as duct work and conduit runs may exist. Additionally, a designer must also avoid obstructions in the path of the actual light that moves away from a luminaire. Typical obstructions that entertainment designers must be on the lookout for include scenic elements and maskings like borders and legs. Theatrical designers must deal with a series of pre-existing conditions that require them to be adaptive throughout their design. Luminaire selections must also take into consideration the mounting or hanging positions that exist in a theatre as well as the inventory of luminaires that are available to a designer. In situations where luminaires are rented from a production house, transportation costs and rental budgets place further controls on a designer's choice and placement of luminaires. Even on a Broadway stage, considerations like these have a large impact on a design.

ENTERTAINMENT LUMINAIRES

Unlike architectural luminaires which are mounted permanently, entertainment luminaires are mounted on a temporary basis (one production to another)—in many cases being hung and struck in a period of only a few days or weeks. In touring, the luminaires may be hung for only a few hours. Entertainment luminaires therefore contain a number of mounting features and readily accessible controls that allow the fixture to be easily manipulated from one project to another. Many controls are easily changed through a couple of hand or wrench adjustments. They are also simply clamped to pipes or **battens** that are hung throughout a venue. The most popular clamp is the **C-clamp,** which not only secures the fixture to a pipe but also allows the unit's orientation to be pivoted from side to side **(pan).** The C-clamp is typically attached to a U-shaped piece of metal called a **yoke** that actually holds the body of the luminaire. By loosening or tightening the bolts or handles that mount the luminaire to the yoke, the fixture may also be adjusted upward or downward **(tilt).** To make hanging and focusing the units easier, the C-clamp should be mounted as close to a straight down orientation as possible or in another position that places it perpendicular to this orientation. Two variations on mounting a fixture include: **yoking out,** or spinning the C-clamp around the pipe so that it is mounted somewhere between straight down and 90°, and a **rooster mount,** in which the unit is spun up so that it is mounted directly above the pipe. The former is used to shoot around obstructions such as adjoining luminaires, while the latter is used to stretch some additional height out of a mounting position. In entertainment venues a lighting instrument should always have a **safety cable** mounted to the body of the luminaire so that it can be further secured to the position from which it is hung.

Spotlights

As discussed earlier, spotlights produce a more controllable light than other luminaires. The overall quality of light produced by spotlights is relatively intense and even throughout their beams. This is due to the inclusion of a lens in most spotlights. Spotlights will usually have well-defined beam edges and often contain optical devices that also allow the light to be shaped or altered in some way. Because of this, they are also the most common luminaires used in entertainment lighting.

FRESNEL SPOTLIGHTS   The **Fresnel spotlight** (Figure 7.9) is named for the inventor of the Fresnel lens, Augustine-Jean Fresnel. The essential elements of this spotlight include a lamp, spherical reflector, and Fresnel lens. The light from Fresnel spotlights is moderately harsh and even throughout the beam of light that they produce. While you can determine roughly where the pool of light from a Fresnel begins and ends, its actual edges aren't clearly defined. Several Fresnels are often used together to create washes that cover adjoining areas since their beam edges can be easily blended between different spotlights.

For the most part, a Fresnel spotlight is simply pointed in the direction in which a designer wishes the light to be focused. While there isn't much optical control, these luminaires do contain an assembly that allows the reflector and lamp to move together along the optic axis of the fixture. This allows the light to be modified through its relationship to the focal point of the stationary Fresnel lens. If the lamp is moved closer to the lens, the light undergoes divergence and is spread out—what we call a **flood focus**—while if the assembly is moved toward the back of the fixture (beyond the focal point of the lens) the light converges though a central point—what we call a **spot focus.** Some Fresnels may use a crank device to change the spot/ flood setting.

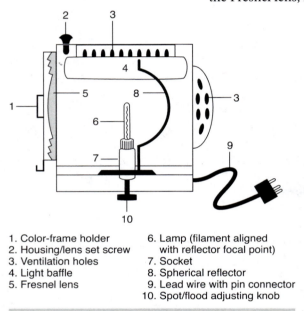

1. Color-frame holder
2. Housing/lens set screw
3. Ventilation holes
4. Light baffle
5. Fresnel lens
6. Lamp (filament aligned with reflector focal point)
7. Socket
8. Spherical reflector
9. Lead wire with pin connector
10. Spot/flood adjusting knob

FIGURE 7.9 The Fresnel Spotlight

Fresnels come in a variety of different wattages and sizes. The manner in which we identify these variations is based primarily on the diameter of a unit's lens. As the diameter of the lens increases, Fresnels have progressively smaller field angles and are therefore utilized for increasingly longer throw distances. The 6- and 8-inch variations form the most common fixtures found in many theatrical applications, while 12-inch versions may be used on large stages. Six-inch Fresnels are common in small venues like community theatres and black box facilities where there are relatively low hanging positions and small throw distances. On the other hand, Fresnel spotlights may have lenses as large as 36 inches or more. If you enjoy going to the beach, you may be familiar with a variation of the Fresnel spotlight that is used in lighthouse designs. As a rule, the wattage of the fixtures increases with larger diameter lenses. The smallest version of the Fresnel is the 3-inch **inky** that can be mounted in confined spaces like a cove or balcony trim. While most Fresnels use incandescent TH light sources, many of the larger versions used in video and film have arc sources. In the video and film industry it is common to refer to Fresnels by their wattage (1K's, 2 K's, 5 and 10 K's, etc.).

PLANO-CONVEX SPOTLIGHTS   The **plano-convex** or **P-C spotlight** is quite similar to a Fresnel spotlight in the way in which its optics are created. This luminaire represents one of the earliest forms of theatrical spotlights and consists of nothing more then a spherical reflector, light source, and single plano-convex lens. These spotlights have sometimes been called **box-spots,** since many of the units were housed in a box-shaped enclosure. They could also be outfitted with a Fresnel lens. Although variations of this spotlight are still in common use throughout Europe and other parts of the world, it has been virtually eliminated in North America by the **ellipsoidal reflector spotlight (ERS).** The P-C spot can be adjusted in much the same manner as a Fresnel to produce pools of light with a variety of different sizes. The range of field angles that a P-C spotlight will be able to achieve is fairly extensive, with typical ranges on the order of 10-60 degrees. Like the ellipsoidal reflector spotlight this luminaire produces a crisp beam of well-defined light.

ELLIPSOIDAL REFLECTOR SPOTLIGHTS (ERS)   The **Ellipsoidal Reflector Spotlight,** or **ERS** as it is often called, forms the most extensively used spotlight in the world today. The optics of this luminaire are superior to most other spotlights and produce a crisp, evenly distributed pool of light. Most noteworthy is its ability to create a very sharp, well-defined beam edge along with its capacity to actually shape the light. The beam shaping is accomplished through the use of various accessories that are placed in the optic path of the luminaire. While a crisp edge may be given to the pool of an ERS, it can also be softened or fuzzed so that the light from two or more of the fixtures can blend easily from one unit into another. Since they produce little **spill,** they are often used in hanging positions such as the **front of house (FOH)** where control of the light is particularly important. When these luminaires were first introduced to the theatrical community many companies produced their own version of the luminaire and marketed their fixtures by unique brand names like Klieglight (Kliegel Brothers) or Lekolight by Strand-Century, which was simply shortened to **Leko.** The Leko (named for its developers, Joseph Levy and Edward Kook) became such a popular fixture that many people began to refer to all ERS spotlights as Lekos.

There are essentially three variations to the basic design of an ellipsoidal reflector spotlight. The earliest version, the **radial ERS,** made use of lamps which burned in a base up configuration that resulted in their lamp housings being located on the top of the unit, while later models placed the lamp directly on the back of the instrument where the lamp was inserted into the very center of the reflector. These later fixtures are known as **axial ERSs** and produce a much more efficient light. The axial fixtures appeared in the mid 1970s, and both types of ERSs can be found in many theatre inventories even today. Century Strand Lighting manufactured a very popular model of radial ERS spotlight in the 1960s and '70s that was known for its characteristic blue-gray bodies, while Altman Stage Lighting produced an axial ERS (the 360Q) that continues to be a staple of many theatres and rental houses. Figure 7.10 illustrates these two variations in ERS design. The third version of the ellipsoidal reflector spotlight was introduced as the Source Four® by ETC

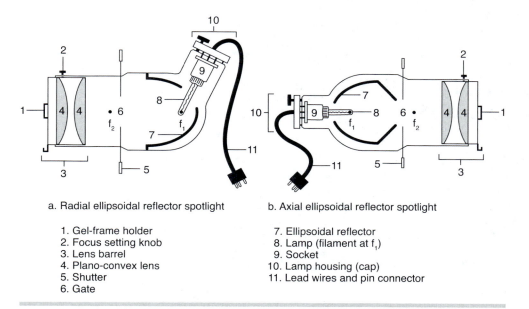

a. Radial ellipsoidal reflector spotlight

b. Axial ellipsoidal reflector spotlight

1. Gel-frame holder
2. Focus setting knob
3. Lens barrel
4. Plano-convex lens
5. Shutter
6. Gate

7. Ellipsoidal reflector
8. Lamp (filament at f_1)
9. Socket
10. Lamp housing (cap)
11. Lead wires and pin connector

FIGURE 7.10 Cross-Sections of Ellipsoidal Reflector Spotlights

in the early 1990s and has come to be known as the **enhanced ERS** design. The enhanced ERS produces far superior light when compared to the traditional designs and is rapidly becoming the luminaire of choice for most designers. Another variation of the ellipsoidal reflector spotlights are **profile spotlights,** which are popular throughout Europe and other regions of the world.

The primary optical elements of an ellipsoidal spotlight include the lamp, a single or double set of plano-convex lenses, and the ellipsoidal reflector for which the luminaire is named. In ellipsoidal reflector spotlights the lamp and reflector are mounted in a fairly permanent manner, while the lens or lenses (mounted in the **lens barrel**) move back and forth to control the focus of the light. The lamp housing holds the electrical connections along with a special socket that keeps the fixture's lamp in proper orientation with the reflector. A set of four screws or joystick-like device on the top or back of the lamp housing allows electricians to position the lamp within the reflector. This is known as **lamp alignment.** Figure 7.10 provides cross-sectional views of the optical components of two of the popular ERS spotlight designs. Light that leaves the lamp (located at the primary focal point of the reflector) is reflected by the reflector and passes through a secondary (conjugate) focal point that is located near the center of the fixture. This area is also known as the **gate** and forms the place where the light is most concentrated. A number of optical controls are introduced to the luminaire at the gate for shaping the emerging light.

The most important controls in ellipsoidal reflector spotlights are four **shutters** (top, bottom, left, and right) which are metal plates that can be inserted into the path of the light to flatten or shape an edge of a spotlight's pool. Shutters may also be rotated so that diagonal cuts can be made across the light. Since the conjugate focal point is actually located a bit closer to the lens than the gate, light actually crosses over or is inverted as it passes through the lens system and continues on to its target. This results in all optical devices, such as the shutters, working in a manner that is opposite of the light actually observed on the stage. To shutter in the top of a light an electrician would use the bottom shutter, while they would have to use the right shutter to close in the left side of the light. While this may sound confusing electricians quickly become skilled in manipulating the shutters as required by a designer. Most ERSs also have a secondary slot at the gate that allow patterned images created from slides fashioned from thin plates of metal or glass called **gobos** or **templates** (Figure 7.11) to be inserted into a spotlight. While a designer may choose to design their own gobos, thousands of designs are commercially available through a number of manufacturers. Additional accessories may also be used to add movement to the patterned light. In addition to shutters and gobos, a designer may also place an **iris** within the gate of an ERS spotlight. An iris allows the light to be shuttered in a circular manner that permits an operator to change the diameter of the pool of light. Followspots typically have an iris.

Ellipsoidal reflector spotlights come in a wide variety of styles and sizes. A general rule states that the beam angle decreases as focal length increases. Most have fixed focal lengths, while others have zoom capabilities where the beam and field angles can be varied. These zoom or variable-focus spotlights have an extra lens. There is a slight tradeoff in comparing the

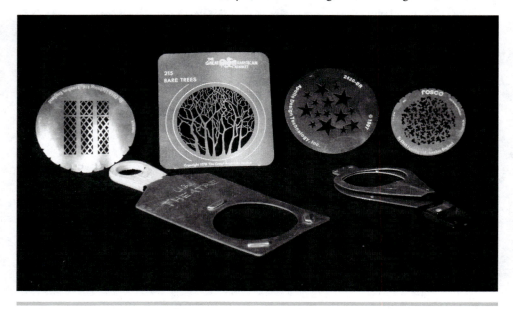

FIGURE 7.11 Sample Gobo Patterns with Template Holders Patterns are from left to right: Rosco Lattice, Great American Bare Trees, Apollo Stars, and a Rosco Medium Leaf Breakup Pattern. Pattern Holders are shown in the front row.

light produced from a zoom fixture with the more efficient light of a comparable unit that is equipped with a fixed focal length lens system. For this reason, the most common ERS designs in use today are still of a fixed focal length. As a compromise, some companies developed ERSs with lenses that could be swapped out and positioned in different orders to produce different beam spreads for a luminaire. Unfortunately, changing the lenses was time consuming, and in theatres where there were inexperienced electricians, the units were frequently assembled incorrectly, having a detrimental effect on the unit's light output.

There are two popular manners of distinguishing between ellipsoidal reflector spotlights of various sizes and focal lengths. Ultimately, each can be associated with different beam spreads. Most traditional ERSs are distinguished from one another by using a nomenclature that relates to both the lens diameter and focal length. The first number states the diameter of the lens, while the second relates to the focal length (e.g., 6 × 9). Both are measured in inches. In this example, the luminaire has a 6-inch lens diameter and a focal length of 9 inches. Several of the more popular units include the: 4½ × 6½, 6 × 9, 6 × 12, and 6 × 16. However, this method of specification doesn't provide any information regarding beam size, and designers have to commit luminaire field and beam angles to memory or look them up in materials like cut sheets. Due to this, some manufacturers created lines of ellipsoidal reflector spotlights that are specified according to their field angles (e.g., 20°, 30°, and 40°). A special group of ERS spotlights are based on a 3½-inch diameter lens (3½ × 6, 3½ × 8, and 3½ × 10), which many designers fondly nicknamed **pinspots** (not technically correct). Earlier versions of ERSs made heavy use of larger diameter lenses (8-, 10-, and even 12-inch fixtures) that produced narrower beam angles as the fixture and lens sizes got bigger. To allow more fixtures to be placed along a hanging position, designers now frequently choose to use 6-inch diameter luminaires with ever-increasing focal lengths (e.g., the 6 × 16 and 6 × 22) for longer throws instead of the units with larger lens diameters.

Matching a luminaire with an associated throw distance and beam diameter forms a critical aspect of any lighting design. Luminaires with narrow beam angles are usually better for longer throws, while wide-angled luminaires are better for small venues and short throws. Although a fixture with a large field angle will quickly open up and spread across a larger portion of a stage, its intensity also drops significantly due to the inverse square law. This can be compared to adding a packet of KoolAid™ to the recommended amount of water. Yes, you can add more water to produce twice as much drink, but it will be diluted and not be as satisfying. Also, if significant shuttering needs to be applied to a fixture, it is better to select another luminaire with a smaller field angle so that more light can be directed to the target rather than being blocked by the shutters and converted into heat. Due to the need for traveling longer distances, it is also common for narrower beamed spotlights to be equipped with lamps of higher wattages.

Finally, a number of companies have introduced ellipsoidal reflector spotlight designs with variable beam and field angles or a zoom capability (Figure 7.12). These designs allow the pool of light to be easily changed within a range of beam and field angles. In most cases, this is done through the movement of an additional lens that is housed in the luminaire. A typical range of field angles associated with zoom spotlights is 25–50°, although it is common to have zoom spotlights with ranges that are narrower (15–30°) or (30–50°). One popular version of these spotlights has a box-shaped silhouette called a **shoebox design.**

ENHANCED ERS   In 1992 Electronic Theatre Controls (ETC) introduced a new variety of ellipsoidal reflector spotlight that has revolutionized luminaire designs in the theatrical community. This new ERS, based on a new lamp design, was called the **Source Four® Spotlight** and produced a far superior light

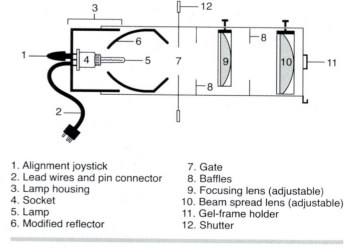

1. Alignment joystick	7. Gate
2. Lead wires and pin connector	8. Baffles
3. Lamp housing	9. Focusing lens (adjustable)
4. Socket	10. Beam spread lens (adjustable)
5. Lamp	11. Gel-frame holder
6. Modified reflector	12. Shutter

FIGURE 7.12 Sectional View of a Zoom Ellipsoidal Reflector Spotlight (ERS)

FIGURE 7.13 Enhanced ERS Design (Fixed Focal Length) *Photo credit:* Electronic Theatre Controls, Inc.

when compared to traditional ERSs. Other manufacturers have developed their own versions of this design, and we collectively refer to these units as **enhanced ellipsoidal reflector spotlights** (Figure 7.13). In addition to ETC's Source Four, Strand Lighting offers the SL Coolbeam Spotlights, while Altman provides the Shakespeare series of luminaires. One of the most significant improvements involved the newly conceived 575-watt HPL lamp whose filament design along with the unit's enhanced optics can produce about the same number of footcandles as a traditional 1,000-watt ERS. Other significant improvements include a dichroic reflector that allows heat to escape through the rear of the fixture, which reduces the temperature at the gate and prevents heat damage and warping of the shutters (also adding to gobo and gel life), improved shutters that produce sharper edges, and a body that allows the shutter plane to be rotated for better control of the shutters. The units also have enlarged gobo slots that allow for the insertion of modular accessories at the gate (e.g., multiple or composite gobos and effects equipment like gobo rotators). These fixtures are especially good at producing sharp shutter cuts and crisp gobo patterns. The luminaires have a slightly smaller profile than traditional fixtures and also have slightly smaller lens diameters. Many enhanced ERS luminaires can be upgraded to a 750-watt lamp for even more punch.

Enhanced ERS luminaires produce a crisp, intense beam that can be focused to an extremely sharp edge. They are essentially a flat field fixture with smooth and even light across the entire beam. These qualities may at times make softening their edges a bit more difficult during focusing. In fact, a number of designers actually add diffusion media or frost to nearly every enhanced ERS in their designs to further soften the edges of a unit's beam. On the whole, they mix fairly well with traditional fixtures although their increased intensity and slightly cooler color temperature can cause them to punch through the light of traditional fixtures. Like traditional ERS luminaires the enhanced ERS comes in a variety of sizes and beam spreads. These, too, may be have fixed focal length or zoom lenses. Common sizes include the 50°, 36°, 26°, and 19° varieties. Larger versions include the 5°, 10°, and 14°. The enhanced ERS designs have become widely accepted for not only their superior lighting capabilities but also their efficient use of energy. In fact, many of these enhanced fixtures have been embraced as a luminaire for some architectural applications. Recently, ETC developed even better optics for these fixtures and is now offering an optional lens tube called the **Enhanced Definition Lens Tube (EDLT)** that produces even sharper beam edges and gobo images.

One final form of ERS that has been gaining popularity in recent years is the Selecon Pacific enhanced luminaires. These have unique designs when compared with other enhanced ERS fixtures. They, too, cut down significantly on heat buildup but are designed around the principle of placing the lamp in an orientation that inserts the lamp through the base of the instrument (like the radial designs but with the lamp on the bottom). These also come in a variety of beam spreads and zoom designs.

BEAM PROJECTORS **Beam projectors** produce a very intense harsh beam of nearly parallel rays of light. This is due to the parabolic reflector that is used in its design. The beam projector is unique in that it is the only spotlight that does not contain a lens. In this luminaire (Figure 7.14), a small spherical reflector is also placed directly in front of the lamp as a means of maximizing the parallel rays coming from the unit. Light that would normally scatter from the front of the fixture strikes this reflector and is redirected back to the parabolic reflector, where it is redirected again toward the front of the unit as parallel rays of light. An undesirable effect of this reflector is a noticeable dark spot at the center of the luminaire's beam. Because of their strong directionality, we typically use beam projectors where strong light sources are needed. Backlighting doors and windows, indications of sunlight, and specials like "God lights," or even short-throw followspots are effectively created by beam projectors. At one time, it was common to use banks of beam projectors in backlighting dance productions.

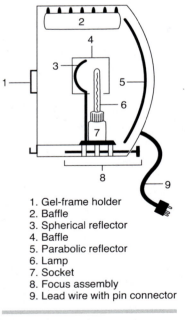

1. Gel-frame holder
2. Baffle
3. Spherical reflector
4. Baffle
5. Parabolic reflector
6. Lamp
7. Socket
8. Focus assembly
9. Lead wire with pin connector

FIGURE 7.14 The Beam Projector

Beam projectors come in a variety of sizes based on the diameter of the fixture. The 10-inch and 12-inch varieties are the most popular ones associated with theatrical applications. Fourteen and eighteen-inch versions are also available, and the film industry may make use of beam projectors with even larger diameters. Some beam projectors use an arc or DC lamp to reduce the filament size and produce a smaller point light source that creates an even more powerful luminaire. Despite their unique quality, beam projectors are not as popular as they once were due to the invention of PAR lamps, which produce light that is nearly identical without the central shadow.

PAR LUMINAIRES   The **PAR fixture** formed a critical development in which a fixture that was durable and easily hung and focused was produced for the quick turnarounds required of concert lighting. The light produced by a PAR is harsh and crisp with relatively soft edges that allow adjoining units to be easily blended from one light to another. Since the beam quality is essentially the same as a beam projector, it has pretty much replaced beam projectors for producing this particular quality of light. The central element of the PAR fixture is a parabolic aluminized reflector (PAR) lamp. The lamp contains a parabolic reflector, a filament and light source, and a lens that focuses the light to a given beam pattern—forming a self-contained luminaire within the actual lamp. The fixture is no more than a cylindrical housing that has a socket for the electrical connections and a spring ring for securing the lamp and a series of troughs or clips for securing gel to the front of the unit. Due to their simplicity many designers refer to these luminaires as **PAR Cans** (Figure 7.15). PAR Cans are unique in that they have no provision for altering the light and are simply pointed to where the light needs to be focused. As a means of controlling distribution, a designer specifies a lamp with a specific beam pattern. Lamp options are named according to the amount of spread that the lamp will produce and include: Very Narrow Spot (VNSP), Narrow Spot (NSP), Medium Flood (MFL), and Wide Flood (WFL). While some lamps produce a circular beam, most PAR lamps create an elongated or elliptical pattern. Electricians are often asked to turn or twist the lamp within the fixture to orient the axis of the lamp's filament **(spinning the bottle).**

PAR units come in a variety of sizes, each based on the lamp used in a specific luminaire. Popular sizes include PAR-38, PAR-56, and PAR-64 designs. PAR-64s often use 500- and 1,000-watt lamps. PAR-38s and 56s have lower wattages. Smaller versions like the MR-11 and MR-16 are used in applications where there is limited space and are often called **birdies.** Low-voltage versions of the MR-11 and MR-16 units are often found in landscape and display applications. The PAR-64, through developers like Chip Munk and Bill McManus, has become the most popular unit associated with the concert industry. Full assemblages of PAR-64 fixtures are often rigged (along with their circuiting) into modules of six fixtures that are hung together on short pipes called **PAR-bars** which are then mounted in larger frames that can stretch across an entire stage **(trusses).** Each is easily assembled and struck with no need to hang, circuit, or color the individual units from one show to another. Many trusses simply bolt together after rolling off the trucks. The **aircraft landing light (ACL)** is another version of PAR that runs on a 24-volt DC current and produces an extremely narrow beam of light. These units were adapted from actual landing lights and are also popular in the concert industry.

Electronic Theatre Controls (ETC) also designed an improved version of the PAR fixture around the same lamp that they used in their Source Four ERS design. This was called the **Source Four® PAR** and opened the way for the production of **enhanced PAR** fixtures. This luminaire also produces a superior light when compared to traditional PAR-64 fixtures. A special feature of the Source Four® PAR is its four interchangeable lenses that are used to change the beam spread without having to change a fixture's lamp. Each lens produces a pattern that is roughly equivalent to the traditional PAR lamps. Also, in order to "spin the bottle," an electrician only has to turn a ring located at the front of the unit. Finally, ETC has developed yet another luminaire that combines the light output of a PAR with the adjustable beam of a Fresnel. This luminaire, appropriately named a **PARNel®** is also designed around the 575-watt HPL lamp, but an

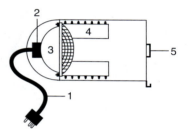

1. Lead wires with pin connector
2. Socket
3. PAR lamp
4. Light baffle
5. Gel-frame holder

FIGURE 7.15 Sectional View of a PAR (Parabolic Aluminized Reflector)

electrician can vary its beam spread from a spot to flood setting through twisting a knob at the front of the unit. Unlike Source Four® PARs' elliptical beams, the PARNel® has a circular-shaped beam.

Followspots

Followspots are special variations of ellipsoidal reflector spotlights. The optics are essentially the same as the zoom spotlights with the exception that followspots are larger, have additional controls for manipulating the light, and use more powerful light sources. Followspots (Figure 7.16) are used to punch through the light of conventional fixtures to establish focus on whatever lies in their beam. Anyone who has seen a concert, ice show, or musical has seen these luminaires used to follow the performers around the stage.

A followspot gets its intense brightness from a high-wattage lamp or other intense light source like an arc or short-arc. When followspots use an incandescent lamp they may be assigned to a dimmer, but a separate non-dim circuit must be provided for the unit's fan or damage could occur to the unit's lamp, gel, or lenses. With arc sources, the lamp must be dimmed by a mechanical dimmer called a **douser.** If a followspot uses an arc source, it will also require a ballast or transformer for striking and regulating the lamp's voltage. While many followspots used to be powered by carbon arc sources, these have for all practical purposes been replaced with newer short-arc lamps like xenon, HMI, and HTI lamps. A primary consideration of these short-arcs is the initial warm-up time that it takes for them to come up to full power—often nearly 5 minutes! One of the principle controls of a followspot is an **iris** so that the diameter of the beam can be easily modified by the light's operator. Another control, the **damper,** provides a set of

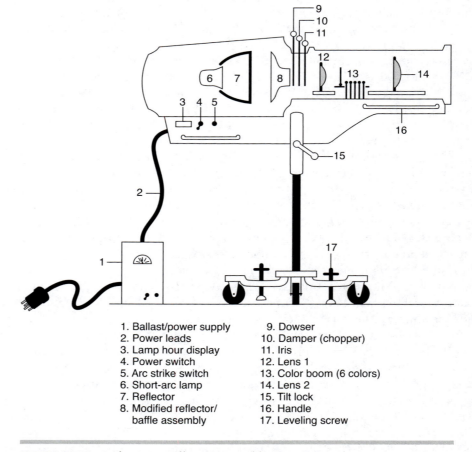

1. Ballast/power supply	9. Dowser
2. Power leads	10. Damper (chopper)
3. Lamp hour display	11. Iris
4. Power switch	12. Lens 1
5. Arc strike switch	13. Color boom (6 colors)
6. Short-arc lamp	14. Lens 2
7. Reflector	15. Tilt lock
8. Modified reflector/	16. Handle
baffle assembly	17. Leveling screw

FIGURE 7.16 A Short-Arc Followspot and its Components

SIDEBAR 7.2 Followspot Pickup Techniques

One of the problems of followspots is ensuring that an operator's spotting or **pickups** are accurate. There aren't many things more distracting than spots coming up somewhere other than on their intended targets. An experienced operator will achieve this quickly and accurately, but a number of systems have been developed for novices who need help in hitting the mark for their pickups. One of the more simplistic solutions involves mounting a scope-like mechanism to the spotlight that allows the operator to use a laser-like device to line up on their targets. More primitive variations of this include taping pencils or nails to the fixture as a means of creating a sighting tool. A second method involves placing a saturated color(s) from the color boom into the light while irising the fixture down as far as possible. The dowser is then opened so that the operator can sight the spot on the target in a subtle manner that won't be noticed by the audience. When it's time for the actual pickup the color is dropped to the intended pickup color and the iris is opened to the desired size. A final technique involves drilling a hole in the housing of the followspot that allows a pin-point of light to play on a nearby wall. A piece of paper is mounted to the wall, and as pickups are identified during rehearsals the associated points are marked and labeled on the adjacent wall. At performance time an operator simply lines up the dot of light with the pre-labeled marks for the pickups before opening the dowser (performers must hit their marks when using this system).

---

shutters that allow an operator to quickly cut the light across its top and bottom edges. Other controls found in most followspots include easily adjustable pan and tilt controls, a **boomerang** or **color boom** to quickly change the spotlight's color, and a zoom and focus assembly (called a **trombone**) that allows the unit's beam angle and focus to be modified easily. A typical color boom provides up to six different frames of color.

SHORT-THROW   Short-throw followspots are designed with beam angles that are sized for small venues. The throw distances that these followspots are optimally designed for are usually in the range of 25 to 50 feet. These units are miniature versions of their full-size cousins (long-throw followspots) and can be as small as 30 inches in length and often weigh in at less than 100 pounds. Short-throw followspots and their operators can even be mounted in the overhead trusses of concerts. They are often used in hotel lounges, churches, and many night- and dance-club venues. Designers may even use ERSs with iris kits as alternatives for these followspots.

LONG-THROW   Long-throw followspots are used in venues like large auditoriums, arenas, and sports stadiums. They have more narrow beam angles, contain more powerful light sources, and are usually much larger than the short-throw spotlights. Many of these followspots are over 6 feet long and can weigh several hundred pounds. Today, nearly all these spots use short-arc sources that require a ballast. The ballasts are a separate box-shaped unit that is placed on the ground near the followspot. Power is fed to the ballast, where it is converted and then directed to the lamp via a second cable. Long-throw followspots are designed for distances of up to 500 feet. Strong International produces several long-throw followspot models called the Trouper and Super Trouper that have been very popular for use in concert and arena productions. The long-throw followspot is an essential element of many large scale events and spectacle productions.

Floodlights

While spotlights contain lenses, are controllable, and produce well-defined intense sources of light, floodlights are designed to cover a broad area evenly, don't have lenses, and have soft edges that allow them to be easily blended with other units. This makes them popular choices for **wash** luminaires. There are essentially two types of floodlights in popular use. The first makes use of a single lamp and reflector, while the second

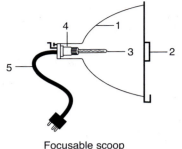

Focusable scoop

1. Ellipsoidal reflector (matte finish)
2. Gel-frame holder
3. Lamp
4. Socket
5. Lead wire with pin connector

FIGURE 7.17 Sectional View of a Scoop or Ellipsoidal Reflector Floodlight (ERF)

uses multiple lamps or chambers and gels. This second type, allows a luminaire to mix colors through circuits that are controlled and colored independently from one another.

ELLIPSOIDAL REFLECTOR FLOODLIGHT (SCOOP)   The **ellipsoidal reflector floodlight (ERF)**, or **scoop** (Figure 7.17) as it is more commonly known, is the simplest floodlight in common use today. These fixtures create a wide distribution pattern that spreads soft, diffuse light evenly over a large area. The edges are very soft so that they can be blended with other fixtures quite easily. The reflector is of the ellipsoidal reflector style, but the soft diffuse quality comes from a matte, rather than polished, reflector surface. In some cases the reflector is made of untreated spun metal, while in others the reflector is painted with a flat white paint. Scoops are relatively large, and many theatres stock sizes that are 10, 14, 16, or even 18 inches in diameter. Lamp wattages can be as small as 250 watts for the 10-inch variety to up to 1.5–2kW for the larger 18-inch versions. The 14-inch scoop is fairly standard and is typically lamped to 750 or 1000 watts. While most scoops are nothing more than a lamp placed in an ellipsoidal reflector with a mechanism for holding gel, there are also several focusable versions that will allow the scoop to be altered between a spot and flood focus.

Due to their wide beam distribution and uniform coverage, scoops are often used to light large expanses of scenery like drops and cycloramas. A bank of scoops is hung downstage of the scenic element with a spacing interval that allows the units to blend with one another while evenly washing the associated scenery. Additional circuits of scoops can be placed between the first set of scoops for each additional color that the designer wants to use in a design. A popular version of this wash lighting has been used for lighting cycs and includes alternating three different circuits of scoops in each of the primary colors (red, blue, and green). By using various combinations of these three colors a designer can theoretically create any color on the cyc's neutral surface.

STRIPLIGHTS   Striplights are a unique luminaire in that they are one of the few fixtures that make use of multiple lamps. These units get their name from their elongated trough of individual lamps that are arranged in a side-by-side fashion, forming a strip of lights. Each lamp is set apart from its adjoining lamps by a baffle that allows its chamber to be colored and wired separately from the others. A typical striplight contains three of four circuits with every third or fourth lamp wired to a common circuit. These luminaires produce an even wash of light along a linear axis that is parallel to the length of the unit.

Striplights are often used for washing scenic elements like drops and cycloramas as well as for toning a stage from overhead. It is common to run a series of striplights in an end-to-end configuration that is parallel to the scenery that the units are illuminating. Most striplights are wired with a set of male connectors for each circuit on one end and a set of female connectors on the opposite end that facilitate this end-to-end configuration. When placed the correct distance from the scenery, the lamps sharing a common circuit or color will blend evenly from one lamp to another. If placed too close, scallops appear between each of the individual lamps. Due to the close proximity that these fixtures might share with scenic elements a designer often adds **frost** to the luminaires to keep these scallops from appearing. While each lamp may be gelled with any color, several especially popular colors are created through using glass filters called **roundels.** These are offered in only four or five colors (the primaries, a canary yellow, and white), and in situations where color is not often changed, the more expensive roundels are a popular alternative to using gel. Unfortunately, roundels also have a limited color selection and are expensive, fragile, and hard to match from one manufacturing run to another.

Striplights come in a variety of sizes and shapes. One of the most popular versions is a 6-foot unit containing twelve lamps and three circuits. Another popular variety is the 8-foot/sixteen-lamp version, which has four circuits. Lamps may vary in size from the small low-voltage MR-16 lamps (Figure 7.18) to units containing banks of PAR-64 lamps. Many other luminaires use R and PAR lamps or double-ended tube lamps in their designs. A fairly recent innovation even makes use of the Source Four PAR design (Source Four® MultiPAR). Striplights are often hung above the stage along battens with

FIGURE 7.18 Low-Voltage MR-16 Mini-Striplight (Altman 3 Circuit/30 Lamp Econo Strip)

specialized hardware called **hanging irons**—one on each end of every fixture. They may also be mounted on the stage floor using **trunions,** which allow the luminaires to sit on the floor and point upward while washing a drop from below. We refer to this as a **groundrow.** Some stages even have a trough in an upstage position so that a groundrow can be hidden from an audience's view. Other stages will have a trough of footlights placed along the front edge of the stage to form another wash variation using these units.

Before spotlights became the dominant luminaire for creating general illumination, stages were often equipped with several overhead banks of permanently wired striplights that stretched across the entire width of the stage. These banks were called **borderlights** because they ran along the border maskings. Most general purpose auditoriums and high school stages built in the 1950s–'70s had borderlights specified as part of their basic lighting package. Regardless of whether a designer uses borderlights or individual striplights, each can be used to provide general illumination and color toning of the entire stage. Dance companies have even used striplights vertically as a source of sidelight by simply mounting the units on booms. In the mid-1980s, manufacturers introduced a **mini-striplight** that was based on a low-voltage MR-16 lamp design. The low voltage (typically 12 volts) allowed for a more efficient lamp that took up much less space. Each fixture has a transformer associated with the three circuits, and the lamps are often wired in pairs where every two adjoining lamps operate together as a single unit. The new striplights are only about half the width and height of traditional striplights, which allows them to be placed much closer to their targets while avoiding the unwanted scallops. Just as with PAR lamps, the distribution patterns of many of these units are altered through the selection of different lamps.

CYC LUMINAIRES Lighting manufacturers have developed another luminaire as an alternative to using scoops and striplights for lighting cycloramas and backdrops and while there are brands associated with these fixtures, most of us have come to know them as **cyc lights** or **far cycs** (Figure 7.19). These units are usually developed around double-ended TH lamps that are placed within a specially designed asymmetrical reflector. The lamps are generally rated at 500 or 1,000 watts with each lamp/reflector unit forming an independent circuit (1,500- and 2,000-watt versions also exist). The reflector typically has a pebble finish that creates a spread reflection and a shape that wraps around the back of the lamp that is flattened out across the lower portions of the reflector. This produces an intense wash of light that is dispersed over a wide area. Due to the uneven shape of the reflector, the luminaire produces a sharper upper edge and a smooth graded wash over the lower part of its coverage. A single unit can cover the entire height of many cycs or drops. In addition to this large vertical coverage, these units also have a wide horizontal coverage that will often allow as few as four to six units to cover the entire width of a stage.

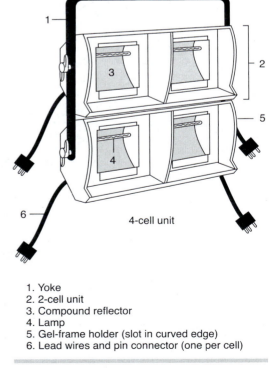

4-cell unit

1. Yoke
2. 2-cell unit
3. Compound reflector
4. Lamp
5. Gel-frame holder (slot in curved edge)
6. Lead wires and pin connector (one per cell)

FIGURE 7.19 A Cyc Luminaire (Far Cyc)

Just as with striplights, far cycs are also used as a multi-colored wash luminaire. This is done by combining several individual lamp/reflector assemblies into a larger fixture—each individual assembly being referred to as a **cell.** Cells are bolted together and then hung from a common yoke/C-clamp assembly even though they are wired independently. Each cell is equipped with its own color frame. Typical far cycs contain three or four cells and are often gelled in different colors. The actual arrangement of cells can vary from a series of side-by-side cells to an orientation where four cells are mounted in a two-above-two arrangement. Because of their greater intensities and smooth coverage, far cycs are now the preferred luminaire for lighting large flat pieces of scenery. However, their large size and need of being mounted farther away from their target can make them hard to use in some situations. For instance, due to their size, striplights are more commonly used in groundrow positions.

Optical Accessories

These accessories are devices that allow for the additional manipulation or control of light coming from a luminaire. I've already mentioned a number of internal accessories when I discussed ellipsoidal reflector spotlights. Iris kits and gobos form the most common accessories that are used with ERS and enhanced ERS luminaires. Images can even be printed on high-temperature acetate which is then inserted into the gate of an ERS spotlight (enhanced ERS designs). A **gobo rotator** is an accessory that allows gobos to be spun in a circular motion. Some hold two gobos that can be spun in different directions and speeds.

External accessories (see Figure 7.20) are placed in front of a luminaire to modify the fixture's light as it leaves the lighting instrument. In most cases, these accessories simply slip into the gel-frame holder of a luminaire. The first device is a **gel frame** or **color frame.** It is nothing more than a thin square of sheet metal that has a large hole in its center whose size is proportional to the diameter of the luminaire. Gel is cut and inserted into the color frame, which is then held in place by slots located at the front of a fixture. Gel frames come in a number of sizes that are based on the size and shape of their associated fixtures. Another accessory that is commonly slipped into a gel-frame holder is a **doughnut.** This is a thin sheet of metal or foil that is similar to a color frame, except that the hole in the center is relatively small in comparison to a luminaire's lens diameter. Doughnuts are used to sharpen gobo patterns that are difficult to focus through using the luminaire's focus adjustments alone. The simplest accessory is a black foil that is simply bent around the face of a luminaire to control **spill** (e.g., GAM's Blackwrap™).

FIGURE 7.20 Popular Luminaire Accessories Front row (left to right): a template or gobo holder and a gel frame. Back row (left to right): a top hat, an eye lash or half-hat, an egg crate or baffle, and a 4-way barn door.

Two of the most popular accessories for theatrical luminaires are **barn doors** and **top hats.** Barn doors provide folding panels that can be tilted to block unwanted light that may be coming from a fixture. They are also used to reduce glare from luminaires that are hung in positions where audience members might glance into a light. These accessories slip into the gel frame holder of a luminaire and can usually be rotated to orient the panels. There are **four-way** (top, bottom, and two sides) and **two-way** (two opposite sides) barn doors. Barn doors are commonly used with Fresnels and PAR luminaires. Top hats, on the other hand, provide no means for modifying a light and are simply tubes that are soldered to a gel frame that prevent the light from opening up or spreading too quickly. Like barn doors, top hats are used to control spill, glare, and ambient light that may be coming from a fixture. They are frequently used to eliminate glare from backlights or in arena setups where the lens of a fixture is within view of an audience. A variation of top hat design that provides only half a cylinder is called a **half hat** or **eyelash** and is used to control spill in only one direction. As a way of preventing glare, particularly with Source Four® PARS, **egg crate** accessories are also available that help shield viewers from the direct glare of a fixture's lamp. These are especially helpful in small theatres. Another accessory that may be used with large capacity Fresnels or other luminaires that make use of arc sources is a **douser.** This is a mechanical device that uses a set of panels or blinds to produce a mechanical dimming effect on a luminaire.

Hanging Accessories

In addition to the luminaires themselves, there are a number of accessories that might be used to hang the lighting instruments. Some of these provide additional methods for mounting fixtures, while others form safety devices that can protect the crew, performers, and audiences. Most entertainment professionals tend to collectively call all of this hardware **irons.** The most popular mounting device for entertainment luminaires is the **C-clamp** (of which there are several models). Some irons combine a C-clamp with other hardware to produce alternate ways of hanging theatrical luminaires.

Sometimes luminaires must be mounted on pipes that are oriented vertically. These vertical positions are called **booms,** although some refer to these pipes as **trees.** Booms are secured to the floor by a flange or through a heavy metal base called a **boom base.** Booms frequently become top heavy and are often tied off to the grid from above. A **ring top** is a piece of hardware consisting of a metal loop that is screwed to the top of a boom pipe, which creates a method for attaching the rope that is then tied off to the grid. If an electrician uses a traditional C-clamp to hang a luminaire on a boom it is much more difficult to adjust the pan and tilt of the unit during focus. An iron called a **sidearm** provides a way of hanging lights so that the pan and tilt adjustments can be oriented normally. A typical sidearm consists of a pipe about ¾" in diameter that is mounted to a C-clamp. The C-clamp secures the sidearm to the boom pipe, while a second piece of hardware called a T slides over the smaller pipe and secures the yoke bolt of a luminaire. The T also has set bolts that allow its position to be locked anywhere along the length of the pipe. Typical sidearm sizes include: 1-foot, 18-inch, 2-foot, and 3-foot lengths. While many sidearms only have one T, a designer may specify two or even three luminaires and associated Ts for a sidearm. While not required, it is preferable to use sidearms to hang luminaires in vertical positions.

Every luminaire and associated piece of hardware that is hung from above should be secured with a **safety cable** as a precaution to falling equipment. The only exception should be in those areas where a protective mesh or other device is provided for catching falling objects. C-clamps fail and handles that lock the tilt of a unit can slip, causing a light to dump its contents like a barn door to the ground below. While most safety cables simply slip around the yoke of the luminaire and are clipped around the pipe that forms the hanging position, the best precaution requires that the safety cable actually be secured to the body of the luminaire. Heavy accessories like color scrollers and barn doors should also be safety cabled by running an additional safety cable to a luminaire's yoke.

PRACTICALS

One last area of lighting relates to luminaires and accessories that may be required to produce a visual effect. A **practical** is nothing more than a lighting fixture that must actually appear to work on a stage or set. Popular examples include desk or table lamps, wall brackets, floor lamps, and ceiling lights. Such fixtures do not give off enough light to actually light a scene and are typically supplemented by stage lights that give the illusion that the practicals are lighting a scene. These lights should be placed on a dimmer so that the console has control of the fixture and so that the relative brightness of the units can be kept in balance with the rest of the scene. These lights also tend to cause glare and usually need to be run at intensities of 25% or lower.

FOR FURTHER READING

Illuminating Engineering Society of North America, *IESNA Lighting Handbook*, 9th ed., ed. Mark Rae (New York: Illuminating Engineering Society of North America, 2000).

Mumm, Robert C., *Photometrics Handbook,* 2nd ed. (Louisville, KY: Broadway Press, 1997).

Pilbrow, Richard, *Stage Lighting Design: The Art, The Craft, The Life* (New York: Quite Specific Media Group, Ltd., 1997).

8 Control Fundamentals

When we discuss lighting control, we usually refer to manners of controlling the brightness or intensity of the luminaires. This often relates to two aspects of luminaire control. First, it determines which fixtures are wired together so that they function collectively as a unit, and second, it determines the actual intensity or brightness of a unit(s). This can be done by using different wattages or powers of lamps or by using devices that regulate the power, which are called **dimmers.** Efficiency and luminaire placement also play a role in luminaire control but will not be considered here. In some cases, lighting intensities can be modified with electrical hardware as simple as the dimmer used for a dining room chandelier. While this forms a very simple control system, entertainment lighting systems are usually quite complex and can contain hundreds if not thousands of dimmers and luminaires. In reality though, many of the principles of dimming remain the same no matter how complex a control system becomes.

This chapter presents an overview of a number of principles relating to brightness or intensity control. The first segments of the chapter provide materials related to control through circuiting and dimmers. Principles of dimmer operation and several specific types of dimmers are introduced in these discussions. Later portions of the chapter provide an introduction to both manual and memory-control systems, in which the dimmers are controlled through some form of light board or console. Following this discussion of control systems, two additional sections present more specific information relating to control protocols and several relatively new developments in dimming technology.

BRIGHTNESS CONTROL AND DIMMING

We most often refer to brightness or intensity control as **dimming,** and while the name naturally implies dimming a lighting fixture to lower intensities, it in fact may also mean that the brightness of the fixture might be raised as well. Dimming, relates to any change in intensity (up or down), and we refer to either **dimming up** or **dimming down** based on whether the intensity is being raised or lowered. In most cases, dimming is achieved through introducing a specialized device called a **dimmer** to a circuit. As a general principle, dimmers are used to regulate the amount of electricity (voltage) that is available for any lamp(s) contained in the dimmed circuit. In this way, a lamp will glow to approximately half its potential intensity if only half of the required voltage is available for its use. If the dimmer provides full voltage, the lamp will glow to full brightness. The dimmer is placed in a circuit in the same manner as a switch and alters the voltage that is made available to all of the lamps that are wired in that circuit. While most dimmers vary the voltage, some will dim the lighting through other methods, such as adding resistance to a circuit. Like fuses or switches, a dimmer should be placed on the hot wire and located at a point in the circuit that is ahead of the lamp(s) that it controls. There are a number of different principles upon which a dimmer may be constructed but only those that are used in today's lighting systems are examined in this chapter.

A second means of controlling intensity is through varying the amount of light that is being produced in an environment. The simple choice of a particular luminaire or lamp can produce an incredible range of lighting intensities. Lamp wattage alone can make the difference in whether you can clearly see a stage or are forced to strain your eyes to decipher the materials that may be in front of you. The distance that separates the light source from the task also plays a role in the intensity that is observed in an environment. Rooms with higher ceilings require higher wattage or more efficient luminaires than rooms with lower ceilings to produce the same amount of footcandles on a desktop. Another popular method of controlling intensity is simply by selectively turning on and off various elements of a lamp, luminaire, or circuit. In the simplest case, a lamp will be provided with two separate filaments of different capacities. In order to provide one level of brightness, power is provided to one of the filaments. To provide a second level of brightness, power is provided to the other filament, and for maximum brightness, power is provide to both filaments. This is the basic principle in which a three-way table lamp operates. On a larger scale this principle is applied to luminaires that contain multiple lamps, in which one or more lamps may be powered at any given time. Bathroom vanities and makeup mirrors often contain lamps wired in several circuits that can provide a limited amount of intensity control. In office buildings, the familiar ceiling fixtures that contain four fluorescent lamps were frequently modified during the energy shortages of the 1980s and '90s so that only two of the lamps were used during normal conditions while the other two were placed on a separate switch and turned on only when needed. Finally, a room's lighting can be broken down into several different circuits as opposed to having all of the lights controlled by a single switch. In commercial buildings, this allows the occupants to turn on the lights only in those areas of the room that they are using—once again saving power and lamp life.

CIRCUITING

Circuiting forms the pathway by which electricity is distributed to the individual luminaires (see Figure 8.1). A circuit may provide power to a single fixture or to a number of lighting units. Regardless of the number of fixtures that are contained in a circuit, they all respond to any electrical change as a group. For more specific information regarding electrical distribution refer back to Chapter 5 (Electricity).

In the simplest form of electrical distribution, power is provided directly to the dimmers through a **distribution box,** or **company switch,** and **feeder cables**. The lights

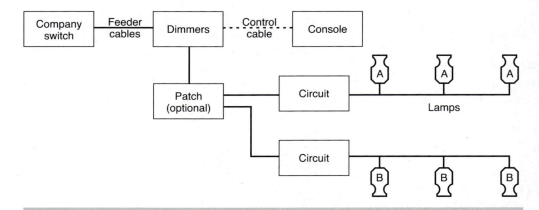

FIGURE 8.1   Common Theatrical Electrical Distribution Circuits may be plugged directly into the dimmers or may actually be the same as the dimmer in a dimmer/circuit system (DPC). The Patchbay is optional and usually found only in older systems that have a limited number of dimmers.

are wired directly from their hanging positions all the way back to the dimmers through a series of cables that are often called **jumpers.** This type of wiring is called **spidering** and is often used in road houses or rental facilities where maximum flexibility is required for the lighting installations. Some electricians may also refer to this as creating **home runs.** Most Broadway theatres are equipped in this manner, and all lighting equipment—luminaires, cables, and even the dimmers—are rented from a rental house or shop. Cable is only run where required, any batten can be converted to an electric, and producers need only rent the exact amount and type of gear that is required for a given production.

In cases where many circuits are run to a single position (like an electric) a number of individual cables are simply tied together to form a single larger unit known as a **bundle.** A second version of cabling makes use of **multi-cables (multi)** where a number of electrically insulated circuits are combined into a sheathing and run together as a single cable. These cables terminate in individual male and female connectors that are placed at the ends of each circuit. A multi may also have fittings that allow specialized adapters to be added where the wires are split into their individual circuits and connectors. The male end of the cable will often interface with a special connector in a circuit box, while a female fitting with the individual circuits and connectors is typically added to the other end of the cable and is called a **break-out.** If the male end separates into individual circuit connectors, it is called a **break-in.** One popular style of multi-cable that is used quite extensively in entertainment applications are **Socapex Cables** (a brand name that has become fairly universal), which carry six individual circuits in one of its most popular configurations. Multi-cables, despite being expensive, reduce the overall weight and volume of cable that is required for a hang. They also make for much more efficient cabling by the electricians. Bundles or multi-cables are often used for circuiting hanging positions like electrics or booms and are typically stored in hampers or cable boxes as they are transported from one theatre to another. In many touring operations, bundles and spidering are used for wiring the **overheads** (lights above the stage) while different provisions are made for circuiting locations like the **front of house (FOH)** positions. Most contemporary theatres provide a combination of pre-wired electrics along with other circuiting features that can facilitate cabling throughout a facility. Some venues even have **transfer circuits** or **panels** so that permanent circuits from locations like the front of house can be plugged directly into a touring company's dimmers or console.

In permanently wired facilities, many circuits are pre-wired to popular hanging positions within the theatre. These circuits are often provided through permanently wired raceways such as along an electric where individual circuits are located roughly every 12 to 18 inches apart. In some facilities the spacings are greater due to the costs involved in their installation. In most theatres it is common to have pre-wired circuits provided in the front of house catwalks, along several overhead battens at various depths throughout the stage, and to **floor** and **wall pockets** (circuit boxes containing four to six circuits each) located in the wings and upstage areas as well as along front of house positions like the **balcony rail** or **box booms.** Additional circuits are often provided through **drop-boxes** that are lowered from the grid to locations such as booms and additional battens. Through this, much of the cabling required for spidering is eliminated, and luminaires can often be plugged directly into a nearby circuit outlet without any additional cable. Some raceway circuits use **pigtails** (a 12–18-inch cable with a female connector), while others provide female outlets that are face-mounted directly to the raceway. Each circuit is usually labeled independently and is wired permanently to a central distribution center for the theatre.

In the last 20 years the costs of dimming equipment, like most electronic gear, has dropped significantly, and it has now become popular to provide individual dimmers for every circuit in a theatre—a **dimmer-per-circuit (DPC)** system. However, there are a number of older theatres that predate DPC systems or where the costs of such a system is prohibitive. In these situations, each circuit is run to a panel called a **patch panel** or **patchbay** which allows the circuits to be temporarily connected or assigned to a limited number of dimmers. While a theatre utilizing a DPC system often has **low-capacity**

FIGURE 8.2 Interconnection Patch Panel

dimmers (dimmers with wattages of 1.2 or 2.4 kW), theatres with patch systems frequently make use of dimmers with a variety of load ratings—many being of higher capacities such as 3.6, 4.8, and 6.0 kW or even higher. The two most popular versions of patch panels are the **interconnection panel/patchbay** (Figure 8.2) and the **slide patch** system.

The interconnection patch system is very similar to the telephone switchboard that operators used in the early days of telephone service. A single cable and plug is provided for each circuit, while each dimmer contains outlets for plugging four to six circuits. To make a **patch** or dimmer assignment the plug of a given circuit is simply inserted into an outlet of a specific dimmer. The second system, the slide patch, contains a small handle that is wired to a circuit and slid over a row of electrical contacts that are in turn wired to each dimmer. By sliding the handle over the desired dimmer's contact and pressing the handle downward into position, a connection is created between that circuit and the assigned dimmer. Overload protection is also usually provided to each circuit through a circuit breaker that is located on the patch panel.

MASTERING

Most early dimming systems mounted individual dimmers into metal assemblies or frames that held six to twelve individual dimmers. Even today, many systems are based on some combination of twelve dimmers. **Mastering** relates to the way that dimmers are operated or controlled together. In the early days, electricians could only run the systems manually with some clever manipulation of the handles that were assigned to each dimmer. As additional dimmers were added, more electricians were required and complex mechanisms were developed for mastering the dimmers. As control became even more complex, designers demanded larger systems that eventually grew to the point where they could no longer be controlled mechanically. Through **electronic control,** today's dimming systems can have hundreds of dimmers and control channels—all controlled by a single computer or operator.

Mechanical Mastering

Mechanical mastering is more of a control form of the past, although it can still be found in facilities where the lighting installations date back to the 1950s–'70s. In **mechanical mastering** a physical device is used to mechanically link the control handles of the individual dimmers of a lighting system. In most early dimming systems the operator manipulated controls at the actual dimmer to raise and lower the intensities of the lights. Electricians pulled leavers up and down, rotated circular coils, or flipped switches on or off to control these lights. This was called **manual dimming.** By far the largest disadvantage of these types of systems was the fact that every cue had to be performed live. It wasn't possible to prepare cues ahead of an execution point, and it should come as no surprise that manual dimming was rapidly discarded as the industry developed the ability to pre-set cues once electronic dimming became readily available.

The most popular form of mechanical mastering is done through **interlocking handles** and involves mounting the dimmers in banks that allow their control handles to be aligned in a row. Each individual handle has a twisting device that allows a spring-loaded pin to be inserted or withdrawn from a hole drilled into a shaft that is mounted to a larger submaster arm. For independent control, the handle is twisted so that the pin is withdrawn from the pipe; for mastering, the handle is twisted so that the pin is inserted into the hole. Any handle with its pin engaged in the shaft will be under the control of the larger handled **submaster** and will operate in tandem with all the other handles that are locked into a given shaft. A submaster often controlled six individual dimmers. Submaster handles are also mounted to common shafts using the interlocking technology, which allows them to be placed under the control of an even larger single handle known as a **grand master.** By using this technique, a single operator has a reasonable chance of achieving full-stage blackouts and dim ups.

Electrical Mastering

In electrical mastering, as in mechanical mastering, individual dimmers are grouped into larger banks that are controlled by submasters, which in turn are controlled by a grand master. The difference with **electrical mastering** lies in the fact that rather than a mechanical connection being created between the different dimmers, the individual dimmers are wired together and assigned to dimmers of a larger capacity. For instance, six 1,000-watt dimmers could be assigned to a single 6,000-watt dimmer that would operate as a submaster. Additional submasters, each with an associated six dimmers, would finally be wired to a single grand master that had a large enough capacity to hold the load of all the submasters together. In this example, two banks of six 1,000-watt dimmers would require two 6,000-watt submasters and a single 12,000-watt grand master. Many dimming systems making use of **rotary dimmers** (dimmers operated by a knob) will use this form of mastering. Most cueing performed by this type of dimming also has to be executed live, although there is some ability to preset the levels of the individual dimmers prior to powering up the grand master or a given submaster. Manual cues requiring the movement of more than two dimmers is difficult due to the rotary design.

Electronic Mastering

Electronic dimming and mastering has become the standard for control systems over the last 30 or so years. As electronics have become smaller, control boards have gotten more compact, become more sophisticated, and grown to incorporate the individual control of hundreds, if not thousands, of dimmers. **Electronic mastering** is actually a low-voltage variation of electrical mastering that became possible through the development of electronic dimming and solid state electronics. In essence, these variations contain two systems—a high-voltage segment where the actual dimmers and circuits are contained, and a low-voltage control segment in a remote location away from the actual dimmers. In an electronic lighting system an electrician uses a control board like a computer to operate the system, which in turn is connected to the high-voltage components via a **control cable.** A major improvement offered through electronic mastering is the ability to place the control board away from the actual dimmers, allowing board operators to be placed in the wings or rear of a theatre where they can actually see the effect that they are having on the lights that they are controlling.

The importance of electronic dimming lies primarily in the many ways in which the control voltages of individual dimmers can be manipulated to produce ever more sophisticated dimming operations. The low-voltage provides a means of combining control signals from individual dimmers so that many dimmers might be controlled as a single unit with no consideration for the actual loads of the dimmers. It is important to note that the rated capacity of the dimmers still must not be overloaded and that we are discussing only the signal and control voltages of the dimmers. Individual dimmers are frequently assigned to specific controllers known as **channels.** A channel is the actual identity of control that a console recognizes as a basic element for assigning specific control voltages. Channels are typically assigned an intensity level that falls between 0–10 or 0–100%. Today, even if only using a moderate number of dimmers, a designer often assigns each dimmer to a control channel as a means of both arranging the console into a control system that is logical for that designer and providing a means of combining dimmers that operate together under a single unit of control. The concept of assigning dimmers to channels is known as creating a **soft patch**—one of the most common examples being the control of cyc lighting that requires several dimmers to power a single color wash over the entire length of a cyc. Since all of the assignments are done electronically, the actual loads of the dimmers do not factor into the mastering assignment at the control board, and all of the dimmers that are assigned to that color may be assigned or patched to a single channel. In fact, every dimmer in a facility could technically be assigned to a single control channel if that were the desired effect.

More importantly, an electronic control system provides a number of features that give designers a variety of tools for creating more complex cue operations. Probably the most important quality of an electronic control system lies in the ability of an operator to preset cues. While one cue is live on stage, future cues are set up on a second set of controls **(controllers)** prior to the execution of the cue. Both sets of controllers are duplicate copies of one another. When it comes time to execute a cue, the operator simply uses a lever or **fader** to shift between the two sets of controllers or presets. Consoles may contain only one or two presets (additional sets of controllers) or can have provisions for storing hundreds of cues (as with computer boards). The terms controller, fader, and channel are often used interchangeably, although there actually are subtle distinctions between each of them. While the channel forms the ultimate form of control assignment, a controller relates to a piece of hardware that in most cases comes in the form of a slide control that provides command of any lights, dimmers, or effects that are assigned to it. Controllers generally provide a range of intensity control from 0–10 or 0–100%, while a fader is used for moving or fading from one assignable item to another. An example is in fading between two different cues on a console. The amount and types of special features on any board is directly proportional to the board's expense. The more expensive the console, the more individual channels it can control and the more sophisticated effect and playback features it will have.

PRINCIPLES OF ELECTRONIC DIMMING

The event that provided the most significant impetus for our current dimming systems was the development of the **SCR (Silicon Controlled Rectifier).** In many ways this was directly attributed to the drive of producing solid-state devices and the need to provide miniaturization for electronic components like tubes. Since the theatrical industry is relatively small, with little money for extensive product development or research, much of this technology came through borrowing or modifying equipment that had been developed by other industries.

Most electronic lighting systems place the control board in a booth at the rear of the house. The dimmers, on the other hand, are typically located backstage, which allows the high voltage cables associated with the power that feeds the dimmers and stage circuits to be located close to the hanging positions—near the **company switch** and hopefully out of the way of the operator, crews, and performers. Traditionally, the **racks** or cabinets containing the dimmers are located in the wings, traproom, or along the upstage wall of a theatre. In many permanent installations, the racks are located in a room that may not even adjoin the stage but is only in the vicinity of the stage. In recent years, especially in road houses where spidering is commonly practiced, dimmers and their associated disconnects can be placed on a catwalk in the wings somewhere above the stage. This helps reduce the hazzards of all the extra spidered cable that is typically piled on the floor in front of the dimmer racks. More importantly, it frees up space on the deck for scenery storage and movements of the cast and crew.

Gating

In electronic dimming a low-voltage control signal is created at the light board, which in turn is used to regulate the high-voltage power supply that provides power to any circuit and luminaires under control of a given dimmer. SCRs are a specialized form of electronic hardware that function as a switch that can turn on and off very rapidly. This actually happens once every AC cycle (60 times every second for a 60-cycle service). To further complicate things, SCRs are similar to diodes in that they only permit electricity to flow through them in a single direction, which results in two SCRs being required for any AC-powered dimmer (one for each side of the AC curve). SCRs are actually silicon rectifiers under the control of a low-voltage signal and are in many ways quite similar to transistors. By applying a low-voltage signal to an SCR it can be instructed when to turn on and off during an AC cycle. In doing so, they effectively sample the voltage at a given point in the AC cycle and then provide that voltage to the circuit from that initiation point onward through the remaining part of the cycle. It is said that the SCR **fires** when it is instructed to turn on or sample the voltage. Once the voltage is reduced to zero as the wave passes through its zero point and begins to shift direction, the SCR shuts off until it is instructed to come on again during the next cycle. If the SCR fires at any point after the voltage reaches its maximum potential (at half cycle where full voltage is supplied, e.g., 120 volts) the voltage provided to the circuit will be something less than 120 volts depending on the exact point at which the SCR was fired. This process of dimming through firing an SCR is called **gating.** Since a typical AC current goes through 60 cycles every second, SCRs must be capable of switching on and off or firing at this extreme rate of speed. Figure 8.3 illustrates several examples of how gating controls an SCR dimmer. Another electronic component, a **triac,** has also been used in electronic dimmer designs and functions in a way that is quite similar to SCRs.

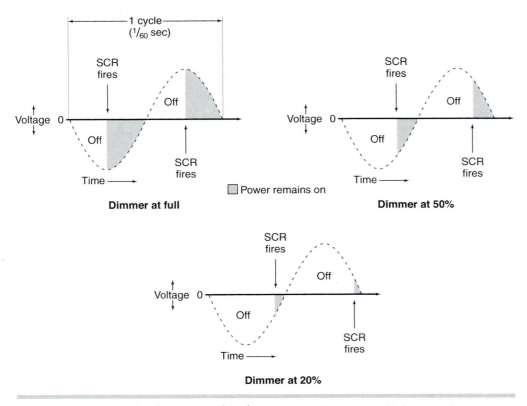

FIGURE 8.3 Electronic Dimmers and Gating Two SCRs fire (once each) during each half cyc (60 times/sec).

FIGURE 8.4 A 48-Dimmer Touring Rack by Leprecon Lighting *Photo credit:* Leprecon Lighting

Due to the rapid on/off switching, many early electronic dimmers created various forms of noise in lighting systems. The most noticeable being a buzzing or "singing" quality that could be observed in the lighting fixtures caused by a vibration of the lamps' filaments. Audio cables located in close proximity to lighting cables not only pick up on this interference but also often amplify it into a noticeable hum in the sound system, which might even change pitch as lighting levels are adjusted. Even contemporary dimmers have the potential for creating this problem if a dimmer gets out of adjustment or if sound technicians place their cables too close to any lighting cables. The fix for this generally comes through introducing large coils called **chokes** to the dimmers that filter the unwanted electronic noise.

Most dimmers are manufactured in a modular design format that combines two dimmers and all their components in a single unit. A typical dimmer module is relatively small and contains the SCRs, chokes, circuit breaker, **heat sinks** (a metal fin-like assembly for mounting and cooling the SCRs), and an electronic interface that forms the link between the low- and high-voltage portions of the dimmer. Most dimmer modules house the components of two separate dimmers. These modules are then mounted in rack systems that allow the modules to be easily inserted and exchanged or replaced as needed. In today's applications, we often use **high-density racks** with numerous dimmers due to the negligible space required by today's modules. Where a rack once held 36 to 48 dimmers, a comparable amount of space using today's racks can hold close to 200 dimmers. Several of the more sophisticated racks and dimmers can monitor individual dimmer voltages and profiles, sense burnouts and overloads, store backup cue information, and can even monitor rack conditions like temperature for overheating conditions. Figure 8.4 illustrates a high-density touring rack.

Both triacs and SCRs are quite susceptible to damage and can blow before a circuit breaker reacts to a heavy overload or short-circuit condition. Also, while it's natural to understand that a blown SCR can result in no current being provided to a circuit, they can also blow in the closed position, which results in the circuit remaining at a constant full intensity **(continuous fire).** Another word of caution relates to the fact that even if a console has a channel turned off, there is still current in the circuit that could be potentially dangerous to an electrician. This current is a **warming current** and is used to pre-heat the lamps so that a sudden surge of a dimmer coming to full intensity won't over-stress the filaments. While the actual amount of shock will most likely not be fatal, the surprise may be enough to cause an electrician to fall from a ladder. For this reason, care must be taken to unplug any items that are being worked on when dealing with a problem circuit.

SIDEBAR 8.1 Dimmer Curves and Trimming

One problem of electronic dimmers occurs when a dimmer does not react smoothly as the control voltage is regulated from its off through full up settings. The relationship between how smoothly a dimmer controls its load as it progresses from off to full is often regarded as a **dimming curve.** A properly adjusted dimmer will be synchronized with the control voltage so that it not only goes fully up and down but will also progress smoothly and proportionally as the voltage is regulated across the full range of dimmer settings. A dimmer that never quite goes out or appears not to move and then rapidly shifts to full intensity, or appears to stay full long after being lowered, must be adjusted. We use the term **ghosting** to refer to a dimmer that does not go completely out. The process by which we make adjustments to the dimming curve is called **trimming** a dimmer. In most cases, a dimmer has two trim settings, one for low trim and one for high trim, with each typically being adjusted as simply as through an adjustment with a screwdriver. An electrician simply adjusts the trim screws so that the dimmer goes completely out while the controller is set in the off position and at full when the controller is brought to full.

New Trends in Electronic Dimming (Sine Wave Dimming)

In the last several years a new type of electronic dimming has been perfected by the leading lighting manufacturers. This new technology makes use of a variation of the SCR called an **Insulated Gate Bipolar Transistor (IGBT)** as one of the principle components of its design. This device has the capability to sample an AC current several hundred times throughout each half-cycle of a dimming cycle, unlike the single sampling that occurs with traditional SCRs. The sheer frequency of the sampling allows the pattern of the sampled voltages to much more closely reflect the true pattern of a sine wave than the choppy samplings associated with traditional electronic dimmers (Figure 8.5). Along with this ability to more closely match the sine wave comes several other unique advantages for the newer IGBT, or **sine wave dimmers.** First, these dimmers effectively eliminate the harmonic distortion that is often associated with electronic dimmers. The hum or interference that lighting systems can introduce to audio, video, and other electronic systems can be drastically reduced with this technology. Another side effect of traditional electronic dimming that can be essentially eliminated is **filament** or **lamp sing.** Since this new technology virtually eliminates lamp sing, the dimmers no longer need choke coils, which ultimately reduces both the cost and weight of the dimmer modules. Other important benefits of these dimmers include the ability to produce an effective dimming curve regardless of how small a load is assigned to a dimmer (good for low-wattage practicals and LED loads that create sensitivity problems for traditional dimmers) and the ability to place many types of non-traditional loads on the newer dimmers, including motors and ballasted units like HMI and fluorescent lamps. Two other benefits relate to the fact that these dimmers can use electrical power more efficiently and they react to load changes so quickly that they can sense and react to overloads like short-circuits more quickly than conventional dimmers. Three of the more popular concerns discussed regarding these dimmers tend to revolve around the issues of higher initial costs (due to the more sophisticated components), the need for maintaining better cooling and air circulation at the racks (because of the increased amount of heat produced by these dimmers), and possible reliability issues (there are many more components and therefore more to go wrong with these dimmers). Despite these initial concerns, many believe that IGBT or sine wave dimming represents the next major advance in dimming technology.

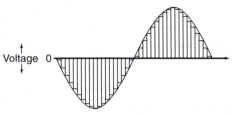

FIGURE 8.5 Sine Wave Dimming Note the increased sampling method (gating) that more closely follows the overall AC analog cycle.

CONTROL PROTOCOLS

A control protocol is nothing more than the language in which an electronic lighting controller communicates with the dimmers. The light board is connected to the dimmers via a control cable constructed of a series of small-gauge wires that conduct the low-voltage signal between the console and dimmers. There are several different protocols, but in each case the voltage is relatively small. Also, most electronic dimmers have been designed around one of two basic control variations. The first, **analog control,** places a continuous signal voltage between the controller and the dimmers while the second, **digital control,** sends packets or bursts of information to the dimmers.

Analog Control

The only control format available for early electronic dimming systems was analog control. In these systems, the console or light board created an actual low-voltage signal that was proportional to the desired voltage that would be made available to the actual circuit and its associated luminaires. In most cases, this voltage was on the order of 0–12 volts, although some systems had control voltages of as high as 24 volts. The larger the control voltage, the higher the voltage at the dimmer. In analog dimming, a physical wire must be connected between each individual controller and dimmer throughout the entire system. In addition to a control wire for each dimmer there also are additional wires that form common connections between the dimmers. Every control wire was quite small (approximately #22 gauge) and was contained in a control cable with a number of other control wires that ran the entire distance between the console and dimmers. The cables terminated with low-voltage connectors called **Cinch-Jones Connectors** that were designed to control from 6 to 36 dimmers at a time. Control cables could vary from five to hundreds of feet in length.

One of the largest problems of analog control relates to the need of an actual physical connection between the console and each of the dimmers. If a control cable became disconnected or the Cinch-Jones Connectors wiggled loose, luminaires would often flicker or go completely out as the control signal was interrupted and no longer available to the dimmers. In permanent installations, this wasn't so much of a problem, but in touring situations many of us cursed the connections between our control cables and dimmer packs. Maintaining good electrical connections was often difficult because the control cables had a tendency to become dislodged as larger circuit cables were plugged into other outlets within the dimmers. In many dimmer packs the cables used to plug the circuits, feeders, and control cables all came together into a very tight space, which created a snake pit of cable that frequently caused a host of problems in trying to troubleshoot or make power connections to and from the dimmers. The control cables were also very fragile, developing breaks from being bent excessively, breaking solder joints at the connectors, or being crushed due to too much weight or pinching. Many control cables were destroyed by having a forklift or heavy road case roll over them. A final problem in analog dimming relates to the fact that many manufacturers used different control voltages in their dimmer and console designs. This meant that a console might only be capable of communicating with dimmers that had been designed by the manufacturer of the light board. While some dimmers and consoles were compatible between manufacturers, the majority of the companies had their own protocol, which prevented designers from selectively matching their favorite console to a particular set of dimmers. More importantly, it also meant that in many renovation projects, both the dimmers and light board had to be replaced at the same time using the same manufacturer's equipment.

Digital Control

As dimmers got smaller and electronic control became more sophisticated, designers began to specify more and more dimmers for their productions. This also meant that each dimmer required a physical connection to the console and more of the famed control cables that everyone was having so much trouble with. Much of the driving force behind the use of more dimmers was the acceptance of computer-based control systems that made it easy to control a countless number of dimmers. In the past, the number and talents of the lighting operators dictated how many dimmers were used for a production. Productions that were lit by 24 dimmers in 1970 are now frequently lit with 100 or more dimmers. It is rare for a Broadway production mounted today to use fewer than several hundred dimmers. With productions using an ever-increasing number of dimmers, it became apparent that there was a limit to the number of dimmers that could reasonably be controlled by the analog control systems.

In order to accommodate the needs of the increased number of dimmers, manufacturers developed a new control protocol that was based on sending bursts of information to the dimmers. This form of dimming is based on **digital control.** A digital console can control several hundred dimmers through a cable no thicker than a standard microphone cable containing only three to five conductors. Rather than requiring a constant control voltage, as with analog dimming, this protocol sends bursts of information to the dimmers only when a change is required in the levels, and the cable remains inactive except for when a lighting change actually occurs. A digital controller packages information regarding the location or dimmer number (**addressing**) and level setting for each dimmer under its control. One of the most significant advantages to this protocol is that many more dimmers can be controlled through a single control cable. Today a single control cable can provide instructions for up to 512 individual channels or dimmers. Also, if there is an interruption in control signal by an event like the control cable becoming disconnected or the console being shut off, the dimmers remain in the same state in which they were last addressed or instructed. In an analog system this would result in plunging the stage into darkness. Digital control also allows for more specific control of the electronic dimmers, causing the digital intensity scales to be shifted from a 0–10 to a 0–100% scale.

Just as with analog dimmers each manufacturer initially created their own digital protocols, and it was rare that a designer could get a console from one manufacturer to communicate with the dimmers of another manufacturer. The process was further complicated during many renovation projects when facilities managers wanted to upgrade to a digital console while leaving the original analog dimmers in place. In these cases, where digital and analog systems were actually mixed, a **digital-to-analog converter** was required to act as an interface for translating the digital outputs of the control cable into analog signals that could be sent to the dimmers. Some refer to these converters as **multiplexers.** A **Jones Box** was often used as a means of connecting all the individual control cables of the analog dimmers to an interface with the converter. Several protocols that came out of these early digital systems included Strand Century's AMX (Analog Multiplex Data Transmission) control and Colortran's CMX control. AMX is more properly regarded as AMX192 because a single control cable could be used to communicate with 192 analog dimmers housed in two of Strand's dimmer racks (96 dimmers/rack). Other companies such as Lighting Methods, Inc. (LMI) used still other control protocols. It didn't take long for manufacturers to discover that they could significantly increase the sales of their new digital consoles by creating a universal control standard which allowed any manufacturer's console to communicate with any dimmers.

DMX512   **DMX512 (Digital Data Transmission Standard for Dimmers and Controllers)** is a digital protocol that has been specifically dictated through the standards committee of USITT (United States Institute for Theatre Technology). The standard developed primarily out of a 1986 conference session where industry leaders and manufacturers got together and worked out a common control protocol. Simply put, a manufacturer who uses DMX512 agrees to abide by a predetermined set of guidelines regarding the protocol that they use in the manufacturing of their dimmers and control consoles. This includes technical specifications as to what type of information must be carried on each conductor of a control cable, how addressing and level information are packaged or sent, and specific wiring and connector specifications. The current DMX512 standard makes use of a five-conductor cable with 5-pin XLR style connectors. Although only three wires are critical for conducting control signals in the majority of today's dimming applications (pins 1, 2 and 3), the other conductors are reserved for future uses. If a manufacturer is fully compliant, their consoles and dimmers should work perfectly well with any other DMX512-compliant device. With the creation of this universal protocol it is now possible for designers to mix and match consoles, dimmers, and any other DMX-controlled equipment in nearly any manner that they wish. The 512 notation relates to the fact that a single control cable has the capability of addressing 512 individual dimmers—what we call a **universe.** In some cases, manufacturers have opted to wire their gear using control cables with only three conductor plugs and cables. While this saves money and allows the gear to be controlled with readily available microphone cables, it departs from the five-pin standard for data-compliant cable and will most likely cause problems when later control standards requiring the use of all five conductors become popular.

At the time that the DMX512 protocol was developed everyone agreed that 512 dimmers represented a more-than-adequate configuration for dimmer control. However, lighting designs expanded, and we began using DMX512 to control not only more dimmers but also all sorts of other equipment. Moving lights, pyro devices, foggers/hazers, scrollers, and strobes forming several of the more common devices that can now be placed under DMX control. As equipment manufacturers developed more advanced gear they also started to place more stringent demands and additional functions on top of the standard DMX512 control. In some cases, automated lighting companies even created variations of the DMX standard that actually placed voltages on the rarely used pins 4 and 5 of the control cables, once again resulting in some manufacturers' equipment not being compatible with other gear. This practice even resulted in causing damage to unmatched equipment from different manufacturers. Since DMX512 became the standard for controlling equipment that wasn't even produced when it was first developed, the standard was once again updated and revised to accommodate the more stringent needs of the newer gear. This resulted in a new version of the standard known as **DMX512A** which was formally accepted in 2004. We have also outgrown the 512 channel limitations and now provide duplicate control systems of two, three, or even more universes of DMX control in many lighting systems, each universe containing an additional 512 channels. As we further tax our systems, new standards are already under development so that the ever-growing amount of data can be communicated between each element of a lighting installation. More recent means of managing all of this control data have been developed through two new standards that are addressing the more demanding needs of our newer equipment. These are presented in more detail in Chapter 9 and include both the **ACN (Architecture for Control Networks or Advanced Control Network)** and **RDM (Remote Device Management)** standards.

ETHERNET   A relatively new technology for control and dimming is borrowed from the world of computer communications. Nearly everyone should be familiar with ethernet and the high-speed, fast-access communication that is commonly employed for computer networks that can connect computers to one another and the Internet. Lighting manufacturers now use this technoloy to move control information throughout a facility. While many of the components still utilize standard DMX512 protocol, various elements of the control circuitry are replaced by high-speed computer networking cable and interfaces. This not only provides for faster communication between the console and the networked devices but more importantly allows signals from multiple universes and individual DMX control signals to be conducted over a single ethernet cable. A number of termination points called **nodes** are generally located throughout a facility and become the points where the ethernet signal is converted to individual DMX universes and a standard DMX512 connection. A lighting console might control both the stage and architectural dimming for a performance space or possibly the entire physical plant. Ethernet systems have become extremely popular in architectural applications where a number of rooms, wings, or even floors can be monitored or operated through some form of central lighting control. Another advantage of the networks is in their ability to support two-way communication between the console and the dimmers or other equipment. Rack temperatures can be monitored, lamp burnouts can be detected, and modifications in dimming curves might be observed or controlled by these systems. In each case, a window containing an alert is displayed on the monitor of the control console. Examples of this technology include ETC's ETCLink and Strand's ShowNet systems. As networks become a more integral part of our lighting systems the industry will once again be required to define more specific standards so that everyone's components will be compatible with one another. With the advancement of more sophisticated gear requiring two-way monitoring (e.g., moving lights), the need to link several consoles together for online backup systems, and the fact that many lighting consoles are now being used to control additional devices (such as video and MIDI), we will see even more extensive uses of networking in future lighting systems.

LIGHTING CONTROL CONSOLES

Lighting control consoles, often called the **front end** of a dimming system, have become exceedingly complex over the last 50 years. In the early days, control changes could only be made live, and the operators had to physically move levers, dials, or switches to make changes in the levels of the dimmers. Due to the development of electronic dimming our consoles soon went through a host of changes that evolved into the complex consoles and control systems that we use today. This section provides overviews of several of the more important control systems that have been used since the appearance of electronic dimming.

Preset Control

Preset control provided the first truly practical manner in which designers could have one cue on stage while being able to set up future cues ahead of time on an additional set of controllers. These boards (Figure 8.6) provided a set of duplicate controllers (**a preset**) for each of the dimmers or controllers that were contained in the lighting system. A second portion of the board, often called the control section, provided master controls and some form of fader that would allow operators to shift (**crossfade**) between the presets. In this manner cue operation became much simpler since an operator could now set a number of individual controllers to their pre-assigned levels ahead of time without the stress of trying to manipulate each controller to their proper levels while the cue was actually being executed. The consoles were typically built to provide control in multiples of six channels or dimmers (popular varieties included 12, 18, 24, and 36 dimmers). Larger versions such as a 48-channel board were also available. As always, designers wanted more, and these boards soon grew in number of presets and control features. While the 2-scene board was the simplest, many boards were designed around three, five or even more presets. In these cases, an additional set of buttons allowed the fader to be reassigned to different presets between cues. Some of these controls are outlined in Sidebar 8.2, which provides a list and explanation of several of the more common features of many electronic consoles. These are general features, and individual names may vary from one console or manufacturer to another.

Preset boards were used quite heavily in the early days of rock and roll lighting. Many of these were equipped with special features that allowed a designer more control and even the ability to flash the lights in accompaniment to the musicians. While a number of these features developed out of the needs of the concert industry, many also found their way to consoles that were used for more traditional forms of theatrical entertainment as well. Sidebar 8.3 provides a summary of a number of these features.

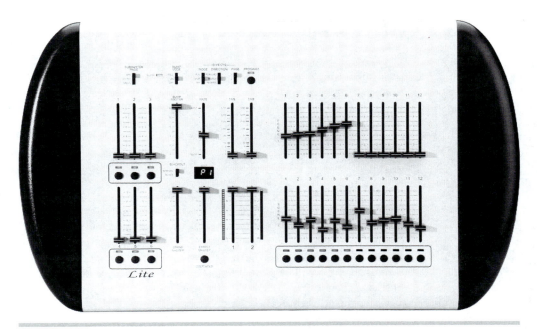

FIGURE 8.6 A 2-scene Preset Lighting Board (Lite Control Console by Electronics Diversified, Inc.) *Photo credit:* Eaton

SIDEBAR 8.2   Common Control Functions of Preset Consoles

Controller	The actual slide switch that permits individual levels to be set for a channel or dimmer. Controllers for preset systems generally range from 0 (off) to 10 (full).
Crossfader	A specialized fader that allows a board to shift or fade between two or more presets. In one position one preset will be active or live, while in the opposite position a second preset will become live and the first one will be faded out.
Splitfader	A variation of crossfader that accomplishes the same task but through the inclusion of a second fader (wired in opposition to the first) that allows a board to fade between presets at varying rates and proportions (e.g., preset A goes out to a four count while preset B goes up in a ten count).
Autofader	A variation of crossfader or spitfader that has a timing device. Times for each part of the crossfade are preset and run at the assigned times once cues are initiated.
Submaster	A controller to which individual controllers or channels may be assigned as a group. This might allow a designer to bring up all the blue lights on a single submaster while still having individual control of the dimmers that have blue lights assigned to them (e.g., the blues on the first, second, and third electrics).
Independent Master	A special form of master controller that allows those channels assigned to it to function independently of any other mastering assignments on the board. Use of the independent master would allow all the lights except for a select few to be dimmed up or down as a group, and any master controls would have no effect on the associated dimmers (e.g., leaving a set of specials on a podium at an awards show).
Grand Master	A single controller that can effectively lower the intensity settings of every other controller or channel on the board, regardless of their individual level assignments. The grand master can be used to proportionally lower the intensity of an entire cue.
Blackout Button	Generally a push-button switch that allows the entire board to instantly drop every channel to a zero intensity.

SIDEBAR 8.3 • Rock and Roll Console Features

Bump/Flash Buttons	Most controllers and submasters were provided with an additional push-button switch that could instantly bump the level up to full regardless of the actual controller setting.
Applause Button	A button that is similar to a blackout button but which instead bumps the intensities of all the lights to full rather than out.
Pin Matrix	A manner of using a pinned grid system to electronically assign control channels to a specific submaster that also usually featured a bump/flash button. The pinning system was quite similar to those found in the game of Battleship®.
Effects Module	A pre-programmed effect such as a chase sequence that could be assigned to specific control channels. Operators could usually vary the speed and intensity levels of these effects.
Soft Patch	A means by which specific dimmers, accessories, and other lighting hardware are assigned to controllers on a lighting console. Individual dimmers that shared a common purpose could be assigned to the same controller using a board's soft patching features.
Proportional Patch	Allows channels to be locked into a maximum setting that is lower than 100%. An example might be running work light dimmers at only 80%.

Memory Control

When we discuss **memory control** we refer to lighting consoles that actually store cues in some type of memory. Computer consoles form the most notable example of memory control. The first memory boards were variations of the preset board that could store cues in a temporary memory. Some lighting designers refer to these boards as **smart preset boards.** Levels of the individual controllers were set on a given preset and then a record/store button was pushed, which created a snapshot of the individual settings. These settings were then stored in the board's memory until the cue was actually executed. Once a cue had been stored the operator was free to move the preset's controllers to set up an additional cue. While this represented a huge improvement from the basic two-scene boards, these boards typically only held four cues at a time. As cues were executed they were dropped from the board's memory and new cues would be entered into the preset memory in their place. Despite what now appears to be an awkward manner of recording cues, these boards allowed operators to work farther ahead and were a welcomed improvement at the time. These boards can still be encountered as backup boards in many theatre and studio operations.

At the same time that the first memory boards were being introduced the world was being overrun by the computer revolution. With computers becoming more popular for every imaginable application, it didn't take the lighting manufacturers long to see the potential for using modified computers for lighting control. Broadway lighting designer Tharon Musser is given credit for bringing the first computer lighting to Broadway and laying the groundwork for the acceptance of the computer console for the entertainment industry. Through Musser's sensational lighting of *A Chorus Line* Electronic Diversified's LS-8 computer was introduced to Broadway. Computer lighting happened so quickly that many manufacturers skipped the smart preset boards and instead opted to leap right into developing computer-controlled lighting consoles (full memory boards). However, in the early days, computer lighting experienced many problems, some from untrained operators, some from equipment that wasn't perfected, and many from the memory or storage devices themselves. In most cases, both the cues and level settings reside on a storage device or hard drive that is a basic component of a computer console. As many of us have learned the hard way, productions need to be backed up frequently, and if you become careless you can lose your entire show and hours of work nearly instantly through a simple combination of incorrect instructions. With the initial lack of memory reliability, it was quite common to keep two, three, or even more backup copies of a show's cue data. Even now, backups should be a regular practice for anyone using a computer console.

One of the biggest problems that the first computer consoles had was that when a computer crashed there was often little hope of returning a show to normal operation if the console went completely down. With systems that preceded computers, problems were usually confined to specific dimmers, one segment of the control board, or a given dimmer pack, and the show could continue by using those dimmers that were still in operation. In cases where designers feared complete crashes of a lighting console a smart board was often specified as a backup board. Today's computers are extremely reliable when it comes to both storing and backing up a production's cueing data, and most problems tend to be associated with operator error. In extreme cases, when it is critical for the lighting to remain on track, two consoles with duplicate programming are run in tandem during a performance. The precision of computer lighting not only provides an accurate means of replaying complex cues with vast amounts of control data, but also allows for smooth transitions by pre-programing the cue executions. As far as most designers are concerned the increased number of channels that computer boards can support is secondary to the manipulation of the cue data. In reality, because of their ability to control transitions, it's actually fairly common to see computer systems controlling lighting systems with 24 dimmers or fewer despite the fact that a preset system could still be used successfully in these situations.

Due to the level of complexity that we now associate with the programming of a production we rarely refer to these computers as light boards anymore. Most people in the industry prefer to call these specialized computers **lighting consoles** or **desks.** A key distinction between lighting consoles is in whether they are **tracking** or **non-tracking** as a basic form of operation. Non-tracking consoles essentially record data in the form of a specific intensity level for every channel in each cue. This creates an immense amount of data. Tracking consoles, on the other hand, only record any differences that are made between one cue and another. If a group of channels is never brought up in a series of cues no data will be recorded for these channels. This manner of recording data makes more efficient use of a console's memory. Since tracking consoles only record the changes that occur from one cue to another they can also provide for several particularly useful secondary benefits. First, and most importantly, if a series of cues must be modified, the designer only needs to make a change in the first cue of the sequence and all the subsequent cues will be updated automatically. The modifications will continue to track to the point where the original channel levels change once again. This is particularly helpful for fixing an entire scene such as when an area of the stage is too dark, a special has been added, or a background color must be modified. On the downside, tracking can cause problems or unpredictable results when cues are not run in order or when a cue is inserted between cues where tracking information is contained. One of the most common mistakes is having a change track through large segments of a show (i.e., changes tracking through several scenes). This can become a particular nuisance when programming moving lights where additional parameters like pan and tilt positions can quickly become altered accidently by a programmer. Most tracking consoles offer the option of recording a lighting change in either a track or single cue (cue-only) mode, and designers will frequently alternate between both modes while programming a show.

Computer lighting (Figure 8.7) has created several changes in the manner that designers make reference to their consoles and cueing information. The most significant change probably lies in the manner in which we make reference to individual channels. A **channel** now simply becomes a reference of control. Where in the past it was always synonymous with a dimmer, today, channels don't necessarily have to be assigned to a dimmer

and can be assigned to lighting accessories like scrollers and gobo rotators or any number of **attributes** that are associated with an automated light. Other practical changes have resulted in the practice of channel levels being referenced from a percentage scale (0–100%) rather than the former scale of 0–10. Rather than physical controllers, much of the level setting with a computer console is entered through a series of keyboard instructions that are displayed on a monitor. The consoles are also typically operated through recalling pre-recorded cues simply by the push of a button. Even despite this automation, provisions are always made so that an operator can override the computer and take manual control of a cue or controller. While not necessary, computer consoles are also often equipped with a few additional controllers that may be used as submasters, individual channel controllers, or even to store full presets. Through this, cueing can also be improvised or done **on the fly.** With the shift to computer desks and increased complexity of these systems it has become appropriate to call individuals who run the lighting console **programmers** rather than light board operators.

FIGURE 8.7   Strand Lighting's Light Palette (Classic Model)—A Later Generation Console   *Photo credit: Phillips Strand Lighting*

SIDEBAR 8.4 Additional Controls in Computer Consoles

Stage Mode	A console or monitor mode that illustrates the channels and their associated levels for the actual intensity settings that are live on stage.
Blind/Preview	A console or monitor mode that illustrates channels and their associated levels for any previous or upcoming cue. This allows a designer to work on both past and upcoming cues while another cue is live on stage.
Tracking Mode	A mode by which level changes made in one cue are copied, or tracked, through future cues, at least until those channels undergo another level assignment. Tracking allows a designer to make a change such as adding a table lamp to an entire act without having to type the information into every cue.
Cue Only Mode	A mode by which any changes made in a cue are performed and recorded on that cue only and will not have any impact on any future cues.
Time/Count	A pre-programmed timing element (in seconds) for a cue that aids in providing smooth transitions between sequential cues.
Rate	Relates to modifying timing sequences in a cue. While a cue is generally given a count (a predetermined transition speed) these may have to be slightly modified due to changes in a given performance. Rate settings allow operators to speed up or slow down a given cue sequence.
Wheel	A mechanical device that allows an operator to manually adjust any channels or rates that are placed under its control. The wheel is often used to manually set channel levels during a cue writing session.
Autofader	When cues are played back they are assigned by the computer to a fader where they run automatically (operators still generally initiate the cue and can take control of it at any time). Most computers have several autofaders and can run eight or more cues simultaneously.
Effects	An elaborate set of menus that allow a designer to create sequencing effects through being able to fully program selected channels into a sequence, set up transition speeds between steps, and create lighting patterns. A chase pattern is a common effect.
Pages	A utility that allows controllers to be assigned to several different functions. In this manner controllers may be reassigned to multiple tasks throughout a production. For instance, controllers might be assigned to various dimmer channels for page 1 and then in page 2 could be reassigned to scroller control.

To this day, most computer lighting consoles are **dedicated controllers,** meaning that they are designed specifically for the operation of lighting gear, with no other function. Over the years though, several control systems have appeared with specialized lighting software that can transform common personal computers into practical lighting consoles. In the late 1970s and early '80s the MicroStar (MAC) and ProStar (DOS) lighting systems were popular, while today we have systems like Sun Lite's Control System and Rosco's Horizon software, which work in a Windows environment. These, and similar packages, can even be run on a laptop computer. When using this type of control system a hardware interface must be purchased that allows the computer to convert its output to DMX instructions. In fact, many companies give the software away so that designers can use the full-blown program to pre-cue or edit their designs **off-line.** Manufacturers also offer hardware like Rosco's Wing Panel, which provides an interface of manual controllers for the computer system. Unfortunately, Rosco has discontinued the Horizon product line, although other DMX software packages like Chaovet's ShowXpress continue to be popular alternatives to traditional lighting consoles. Rosco still supports Horizon and, designers will frequently come upon it in smaller theatre companies and some architectural applications. ShowXpress provides a control interface not only for programming the lighting, but also the control of any DMX device—including multimedia applications. It also contains a 3D visualization module that provides a computer simulation of a show's programming as well as tools that aid in the programming of moving lights.

Automated Control Consoles

From the late 1970s through '80s luminaires were developed with a series of parameters that could be controlled remotely. The new generation of fixtures are often called **automated lights** or **automated luminaires.** Other popular names include: **intelligent lights, wiggle lights,** and **moving lights.** Even though there is debate as to the acceptance of the term moving lights, many continue to use this term when referring to automated fixtures. Intelligent fixtures simply have multiple control features, or attributes, that allow elements of the luminaire to be changed by a series of commands. Attributes commonly controlled in these fixtures include pan, tilt, intensity, and color changing. In the early days of intelligent lighting a dedicated or specialized console was required to operate the automated luminaires and was used in addition to the standard console that controlled the traditional luminaires and dimmers—what we often call the **conventionals.** Concert tours that first used automated lighting saw companies develop specialized consoles like the Vari*Lite (who first introduced intelligent fixtures) Artisan Board, which was used for the control of just their own fixtures. Now, through the DMX512 standard, most automated fixtures can be operated with a traditional console even though these boards weren't designed to deal with the additional control elements that are demanded by these luminaires. Programming becomes tedious and the memories of the conventional consoles can become overtaxed with the increased amount of data generated by these fixtures. Automated lighting consoles form a group of more specialized consoles that have been designed to respond to the increased demands of automated lighting. They are also equipped with a number of special features that allow them to have more convenient control of the intelligent lights. There are automated luminaires that require 40 or more individual channels of control.

What sets automated control consoles (Figure 8.8) apart from other lighting consoles generally relates to the increased number of channels that such consoles can control, the variety of display and assignment modes that a console can produce, and the presence of additional control devices that help create more designer-friendly operation of the automated fixtures and their attributes. The number of control channels that many of these consoles might be outfitted with is typically in the thousands. Another feature often includes the addition of several specialty knobs or rotary devices, called **encoders** that are particularly helpful for programming intelligent fixtures. Touch screens are also popular with these consoles. Finally, control attributes may be assigned to encoders, groups, and submasters, which can be reassigned through multiple page assignments that provide an easy way of giving operators access to all the data they will need for programming a show. We often refer to these control assignments as **palettes,** and common manners of organizing them might be by colors, focus points, gobo assignments, and beam shaping qualities. Two of the most popular automated lighting desks in current use include the Whole Hog console by High End Systems and the GrandMA by ACT Lighting, Inc. The recent introduction of consoles like the Eos by ETC moves in a slightly different direction through being designed to control both conventionals and automated lighting with equal ease.

FIGURE 8.8 An Automated Lighting Console (Eos by ETC). Eos is a later generation console that is designed to work equally well with both automated and conventional lighting units *Photo credit:* Electronic Theatre Controls, Inc.

Show Control

Show control relates to linking two or more consoles or other remotely controlled devices together in a master/slave relationship. One console controls other consoles, which in turn execute their pre-programmed cues and associated effects. Through this, multiple effects can be coordinated so that they can be executed consistently from one show to another. Several applications where show control is commonly used include linking traditional and automated lighting consoles together, triggering specialized equipment like video projectors, video walls, and fog machines from a lighting console, and coordinating the firing of pyro devices. In a number of entertainment events like musical reviews or theme-park rides the timing and soundtracks for an event and its associated cues remain the same for every performance. In these situations, the lighting console (as well as all the devices that it controls) might be triggered by instructions that are associated with specific cue placements in a soundtrack. This is commonly done with a **timecode** that places signals at specific points in a soundtrack that trigger the light cues or other effects at a specific time. When played back, a signal is sent to the console that triggers the cue, which in turn executes a previously programmed set of instructions. In effect, the instruction simply tells the console to execute a cue from a **cue stack** much like an operator would execute a cue by hitting the "go" button. Some of the more common programming codes used to control this type of automation include **MIDI Show Control (MSC), MIDI Time Control (MTC),** and **SMPTE (Society of Motion Picture and Television Engineers).** MIDI Show Control simply connects devices together so that one can control another while the two timecode protocols are embedded in a soundtrack or run from a console's internal clock and are used to automate a console and its associated cues. The SMPTE code initially came from the film industry and was used to sync the sound and images of a movie together. Just as with having to set addresses properly for DMX-controlled devices, these consoles must also be set up with addressing information so that the slave units can communicate with the master console or timecode signal.

STATE OF THE ART CONTROL

Modern lighting control has gone through a number of changes since the appearance of electronic dimming. The availability of smaller, more efficient dimmers coupled with the means of controlling more and more data has resulted in the continual growth of contemporary lighting systems. In a way, we have created a cycle that encourages increasingly more complex systems each year. While most recent improvements in lighting control have evolved around providing better control of larger numbers of dimmers and attributes there have also been several other innovations that allow us to bring additional control to our luminaires.

Dimmer-per-Circuit

With the drop in electronic component prices and the continued miniaturization of dimming modules it has now become cost effective to simply provide every circuit of a lighting installation with its own dimmer. These are known as **dimmer-per-circuit (DPC)** systems. The practice has become especially popular in areas like educational facilities where the majority of the circuits are permanently run to different locations throughout the theatre. The need for long runs of cable is virtually eliminated, and luminaires can frequently be plugged into nearby circuits with no need for any additional cable at all. Issues of maintaining cables and connectors, failed connections, and messy installations are minimized by dimmer-per-circuit systems. A further benefit of these systems is that there is less need for ganging luminaires into common circuits, which results in less demand for high-capacity dimmers. Many dimmers in DPC systems only have capacities of 1.2 or 2.4 kW. It is also a common practice for dimmers and circuits in DPC systems to share the same numeral designation.

Multiplexing (Dimmer Doubling™)

As the need for more dimmers continues to be a concern for lighting designers, many facilities have reached a point where they are locked into their current dimmer configuration, which cannot be expanded any further. The costs of renovation, limited space for racks, or inadequate sources of power form some of the more common factors that might prevent a facility from upgrading their lighting system with additional dimmers. A fairly new development, called **multiplexing,** allows designers to add additional control to a lighting system through adding specialized hardware to an existing dimmer that supports multiplexing, which effectively converts the original dimmer into two separate dimmers. Electronic Theatre Controls (ETC) has developed a system called Dimmer Doubling™ in which a specialized two-fer is circuited in combination with an ETC Sensor® dimmer that allows the original dimmer to be split into two different outputs. These dimmers must be in a rack controlled by a special control module that essentially creates a dimmer A and dimmer B from a single dimmer. The multiplexing two-fer contains a mechanism for splitting the two signals and can be located at any point along the circuitry of the assigned dimmer. The basic concept of Dimmer Doubling™ comes from assigning each load to voltages on either side of the 120-volt output of the associated dimmer. One circuit's voltage is associated with one side of the dimmer's AC output, while the other's voltage comes from the opposite side of the power supply. In reality, this output is around 77 volts (due to phase control) for each side of the dimmer rather than the 120 volts that is associated with a normal dimmer's output voltage.

There are two catches to using multiplexing. First, is the need to use special lamps that are rated for 77 volts. The lamps are pinned in a unique manner that prevents them from being plugged into a socket rated for a standard 120-volt circuit. The luminaires and specialized two-fers are also equipped with special plugs and cabling that prevent accidental plugging of the wrong lamps into a circuit or dimmer. The second catch relates to the numbering and patching of the multiplexed channels. More sophisticated consoles that provide alphanumeric input can support the multiplexing by simply inputting the dimmer number and then an A or B for either side of the multiplexed signal, while boards that do not have this feature must assign the first dimmer by using the actual dimmer number and then adding 256 to this for the second dimmer (i.e., the dimmer numbers associated with a multiplexed dimmer 5 would be designated by dimmer 5 and 261 (5 + 256)). This will work for up to 256 multiplexed dimmers, which will complete a single universe of 512 channels. After dimmer 256, the new multiplexed channels are assigned to a second universe. The 77-volt lamps provide full intensity for the multiplexed fixtures and blend seamlessly with lamps of normal voltages. Total lamp loads, however, can still not exceed the rating of a dimmer.

Distributed Dimming

Another innovation is distributed dimming. **Distributed dimming** makes use of solid-state electronics for shortening circuit runs by placing the actual dimmers in locations that are typically occupied by circuits. In this case, a circuit box or raceway much like any standard circuiting hardware is mounted in a position relatively close to where the luminaires are hung. The housing not only contains the dimmer outlets but also the electronics of the dimmers themselves. A distributed dimming strip or box needs only a cable supplying power to the dimmers and a control cable in order to provide a complete dimming system contained within a single housing. Typical distributed dimming units are manufactured with four to six dimmers of 600- or 1,200-watt capacities. The only setting that many of these units require is a series of wheels or dip switches that allow the unit to be assigned to specific DMX addresses or channel numbers.

Distributed dimming has actually been around for quite a while, with the most popular application being in the portable lighting systems that many small bands or lounge acts carry with them. We've all seen them—two booms with four PAR heads each that are operated through a control system of two dimmer modules (one to each boom) and a simple controller. Smaller club set ups can contain as few as four 600 w dimmers per module and can be plugged directly into a standard 20-amp convenience outlet. While there have been previous attempts at distributed dimming for larger stages, these dimmers have only recently received more thorough attention for these larger applications. Two popular systems that make use of distributed dimming principles include the SCRimmer Stik by Electronics Diversified (with four 600-watt dimmers) that makes use of the older SCR technology and the recently introduced IPS (Intelligent Power System) dimmers by Rosco Laboratories. The IPS system makes use of a newer technique that combines micro-processors with the same IGBT technology associated with sine wave dimming. Since the noise of the dimmer and weight of the chokes are eliminated in these designs, these dimmers can be manufactured into smaller housings that allow them to be placed near the luminaires. Although a number of these systems were designed around a modular box design, many newer models have linear designs that resemble a traditional raceway that contains multiple dimmers that are simply attached to a batten and are then supplied with a control cable and power feed. These dimmers often have relatively low load capacities of 1.2 kW (as compared to traditional dimmers) but in some cases can be upgraded to 2.4 kW.

Wireless Dimming

A new revolution in control technology is **wireless dimming,** of which there are two slightly different variations. The first simply transmits DMX data between two locations. These systems make use of special radio frequencies that transmit control data from the console to a receiver that is located at the dimmers or other DMX-controlled devices. This eliminates some of the control cables that are required between devices. Rather than running separate receivers for every device, a transmitter located at the console will typically send signals to a receiver that is then connected to some form of splitter device where individual DMX runs are then split out and run to other locations or to specific lighting equipment. Outdoor concert venues frequently use this technology in order to transmit control signals between a console and the onstage control and data lines. Large exterior architectural installations can also use wireless control for the more distant luminaires of an installation. In reality, the wireless solution is much better than trying to create DMX cable runs between luminaires that are located in hard to reach places like adjoining rooftops. These devices can also be used to eliminate the more complicated cable runs that would be associated with theatrical applications like controlling color scrollers mounted on the balcony rail or other FOH positions.

One concern of wireless dimming relates to radio interference from neighboring networks that use similar wireless technology. If your venue is in a populated area, the chances of running into shared-frequency problems are much greater and could determine how successful this technology is for you. On the other hand, it only takes one person sharing your frequency to cause all sorts of havoc with your control system. In locations where many theatres are found in a relatively small area, precautions must be taken to help ensure that the frequencies used in one theatre are different from those being used by other theatres in the immediate area. Also, the frequencies currently assigned to wireless dimming are in close proximity to the wireless frequencies that are assigned to the computer networks that our personal laptops and home networks are using, which once again can lead to interference problems. It is best if there is a clear line of sight between the transmitter and receiver and that the distances between the transmitter and receivers are kept to less than 300 or 400 feet, even though the actual distances can vary considerably depending not only on what other wireless networks are in an area but also issues like the overall electrical and radio activity of an area, the weather, and how much metal is in a venue. Each transmitter is usually capable of distributing the data for 512 DMX channels or a single universe.

A second variation of wireless dimming provides control of low-voltage battery packs (12-volt DC) that allow all of the cables of a networked device to be done away with. Costumes, props, and even modular scenic devices may now contain a dimmer, DMX receiver, effect devices, and a power supply, all of which can ultimately be controlled wirelessly by a lighting console. Much like wireless microphones, a separate pair of receivers/transmitters and an assigned frequency are required for every control module/device that is addressed by a wireless system. Some battery systems are outfitted with several channels, while others only provide a single channel of control. One manufacturer (City Theatrical) offers a system that can provide power and control for up to four dimmers/channels, each with a capacity of 150 watts. If a larger load is required, the dimmers/channels can be ganged together so that a single 500-watt load might be carried. Even though this technology is quite new and there are skeptics, many designers and electricians are already finding numerous applications for this technology.

Another variety of wireless control that is being experimented with in theatrical applications involves transmitting DMX data over the normal electrical lines that already exist in a facility. In this way a DMX signal is carried by the same wires and circuits that provide power to each lighting device, effectively eliminating the need for control cables altogether. These carrier technologies have been used in architectural lighting control and data transmission systems on a regular basis in recent years. Problems that still need to be ironed out include dealing with the electrical noise or interference that is present on a normal electrical line (i.e., the large motors from equipment like air-conditioning systems), the effect of power surges, and any interference that the control signal might create with the other electrical systems of a building.

FOR FURTHER READING

Bellman, Willard F., *Lighting the Stage: Art and Practice*, 1st–3rd ed. (Louisville, KY: Broadway Press, 2001).

Cadena, Richard, *Automated Lighting: The Art and Science of Moving Light in Theatre, Live Performance, Broadcast, and Entertainment* (Burlington, MA: Focal Press, 2006).

Huntington, John, *Control Systems for Live Entertainment*, 1st–3rd ed. (Newton, MA: Butterworth-Heinemann/Focal Press, 2007).

Illuminating Engineering Society of North America, *IESNA Lighting Handbook*, 9th ed., ed. Mark Rae (New York: Illuminating Engineering Society of North America, 2000).

Mobsby, Nick, *Practical Dimming* (Cambridge, UK: Entertainment Technology Press, 2006).

Mobsby, Nick, *Practical DMX* (Cambridge, UK: Entertainment Technology Press, 2006).

Penzel, Frederick, *Theatre Lighting Before Electricity* (Middletown, CT: Wesleyan University Press, 1978).

Sandström, Ulf, *Stage Lighting Controls* (Oxford, UK: Focal Press, 1997).

Simpson, Robert S., *Lighting Control: Technology and Applications* (Burlington, MA: Focal Press, 2003).

9 Advanced Equipment and Personal Computers in Lighting

After the appearance of electricity, theatrical lighting quickly evolved and rapidly became exponentially more complex through the benefits of technology. When lighting manufacturers provided us with piano boards, we brought on more boards and operators; as they delivered presetting and electronic control, we discovered the need to use more dimmers and wanted a more rapid yet accurate means of setting cues; when the manufacturers gave us computer control, we wanted even more lighting fixtures and dimmers, and this time additional luminaire functions, including moving lights, were developed and added to our rigs. Now, we've come to the point that it's almost impossible to keep track of all the data associated with a lighting design. What may be even more amazing is that despite all the increased numbers in fixtures and data, we still set our cues in roughly the same amount of time that we have been using for the last 20 or 30 years, becoming more efficient in order to maintain the sophistication that a lighting design now requires. While some of the technology introduced in this chapter relates to creating specific effects, much of it has been developed simply to provide lighting designers with more alternatives. Other materials in the chapter relate to additional equipment and the means of controlling it, while much of the chapter introduces technologies that allow luminaires to take on more than a single purpose. Creating multiple colors, textures, and positions for a light form just a few of these possibilities. This flexibility traditionally resulted in additional units being hung for each new feature and was the reason lighting inventories during the 1970s to '90s increased so drastically. At some point, a limit was reached in the number of fixtures that could be physically mounted in a lighting position, and automated luminaires (moving lights) became an alternative to conventional fixtures.

A significant amount of lighting innovation can be credited to the concert industry. It was here that the special needs of touring forced developers to look at alternatives to hanging hundreds of conventional luminaires for a show. It also was one of the few areas of the industry where research and development (R&D) money was available. More traditional forms of entertainment had to wait until the price of the technology became more affordable. It's now quite common to see automated gear on Broadway stages as well as other venues like road houses and nightclubs, regional theatres, and in spectacle productions like arena programs and ice shows. Many university theatres can also afford this gear and use it to introduce their students to the new technologies. Despite this, automated lighting is still unaffordable for many organizations. The majority of the theatres that use this technology rely most heavily on conventional fixtures while making selective use of the advanced equipment. This restricted use isn't solely attributed to the high costs of the equipment but also to the steep learning curve associated with its use. There are also issues related to the higher color temperature lamps and effects qualities of many of these fixtures, which can bring attention to the units and make them difficult to blend with conventional fixtures.

This has made them less desirable for theatrical applications in the past, though ironically the same qualities made them attractive to the concert industry. There are now variations of this gear with smaller fans and incandescent sources that make them easier to use in theatrical applications.

PRIMARY CONTROL OF ADVANCED GEAR

Most advanced gear was developed to produce some form of special effect. Some of the equipment isn't that sophisticated and includes devices like **color wheels, flicker devices, and animation disks** that produce a shadow or color effect that is simply loaded into the color frame holder of an instrument. Many were nothing more than a disk with patterned holes that was rotated in front of a fixture's beam by a low-speed motor. There are also special effects projectors like GAM's **scene machines** that produce similar, but more advanced, moving effects. For the most part, all these effects had a single AC motor that was simply plugged into a non-dim circuit. The effect would be turned on just prior to its use, allowing the motion to already be established as the fixture was dimmed up. In an attempt to control the effect's speed, many of these effects include a potentiometer that provides a way of presetting the speed of the rotation. Unfortunately, the speed is usually changed only by going to the instrument and changing the potentiometer's setting. Because of this, many designers plugged these motors into a dimmer so that the speed could be varied. This wasn't the best practice, and designers had to take care that this didn't damage the motor or dimmer. Many other effects like fog or hazing machines, strobes, and pyro devices also had controllers that operated independently of the lighting system.

DMX Control

With the advent of digital control and the acceptance of DMX512 as a standard protocol it became evident that lighting consoles could be used to control many more elements of a show than just dimmers. As new equipment evolved, manufacturers capitalized on the DMX512 format and it wasn't long before lighting consoles were used to control virtually any type of stage equipment. Foggers and hazers can be instructed to begin and end on cue, while strobe lights can be triggered while making adjustments in their speed and intensity. Even complex pyro sequences are now being fired through DMX signals and lighting consoles. Power for the majority of these units is provided through a non-dim circuit that powers any motors and lamps that are used by the units, and a separate control cable provides the instructional information required for linking the device to the console.

In simple dimmer operations a designer assigns or **patches** a dimmer to a specific control channel that then becomes the ultimate form of control for that dimmer. The board operator then uses that channel whenever they wish to make modifications to the level of that dimmer. In the day of analog dimming this was always a **one-to-one** assignment (dimmer 1 was assigned to channel 1, dimmer 2 to channel 2, 3 to 3 , etc.) and a designer had to think about how they arranged their dimmers so that operators could run the board efficiently. Load or capacity of the dimmers also played a role in the assignments since dimmers of the same capacity were grouped together in the dimmer packs. If dimmer assignments weren't done properly, the operation of the board could become more complex, making the execution of some cues impossible. Designers also tried to make these assignments in a logical board layout that kept dimmers with similar functions near one another (i.e., grouping all of the dimmers controlling a given color or area). As the number of dimmers increased, a limit was reached in the number of faders that the electricians could control. Digital control brought about the concept of **soft-patching,** in which dimmers could be assigned to any controller or channel regardless of the load of the dimmers. This gave designers the ability to assign the dimmers based on the best organizational means of arranging a light board. While dimmers may still be assigned to a one-to-one patch, it is now far more common to use soft-patching to create a logical board arrangement for the dimmers. This is especially true where dimmer-per-circuit systems are in use.

In basic principle, a DMX channel produces a control signal that sends bursts or packets of digital information that identify both the particular channel and its intensity to a DMX-controlled device. In DMX512, the system is capable of controlling up to 512 different channels. This is based on the principle of computers storing information in the form of **binary numbers,** which are the product of a base-two numbering system that is used to represent whether circuits are turned on or off. In DMX control, one binary number represents a specific channel, while a second number represents its intensity. While the control system is based on 512 channels, the actual levels are only represented through a numbering range of 0–256. This is because 256 is the highest number that can be represented with eight digits of binary code. Why eight digits? Because most microprocessors at the time that the code was written used 8-bit processors. The levels are then equated to an intensity range of between 0 and 100% based on a binary number between 0 and 256. While this explains the individual levels, a console also needs to identify the particular dimmer with which the intensity level is associated. To do this, a designer must also assign each piece of gear like the individual dimmer packs or racks to a particular group of channels. This is usually done by turning a series of **addressing switches** on or off at the dimmers or other DMX controlled device. The process of assigning the beginning channel to a DMX-controlled device is called **addressing.** The first channel of any multi-channeled device is the one that is actually assigned and is called the **starting address.** Virtually all DMX equipment has only one set of addressing switches and a single starting address regardless of the number of **attributes** that a unit may have.

While a dimmer has only one function (intensity), most specialty equipment has several control functions, each requiring a separate channel assignment—an example being strobe units that typically require three elements of control (intensity, duration, and speed). More advanced gear, like **media servers,** may require several hundred channels. When making addressing assignments, each dimmer in a dimmer pack is automatically assigned a progressively increasing number until all of the dimmers have been assigned a channel. At that point, a new starting address is assigned to the second and any additional packs that are included in the control system (a six-pack would assign the next set of dimmers beginning with channel 7, while a 48 dimmer rack would start the next set of dimmers at 49). This same process holds true of all other DMX-controlled equipment with multiple attributes. Although a designer cannot rearrange the specific order of the attributes associated with a particular unit (unless reassigning them in the console), they do assign the beginning channel, which coincides with the first attribute associated with a device. By assigning the strobe unit mentioned above to channel 30, what I have actually done is set its first attribute (intensity) to channel 30, while the duration and speed attributes are assigned to channels 31 and 32. While soft-patch assignments are easily made at the console through a keyboard, the equipment addressing must also be assigned at the device and needs to be matched to the channel assignment. If either one is not set correctly the equipment will not communicate with the console. The actual addressing is done through one of several mechanisms that are located on the fixture. This might include an independent LED display and keypad, a set of three numbered wheels (one wheel representing each digit up to 999), or a series of dip switches (miniature slide switches) that are set in various combinations to represent the address.

All DMX addresses are in binary code that is simply coded into the system based on the on/off positions of a set of eight switches that represent the address in a binary format. Zero is represented by all of the switches being in the off position while 1 is indicated by the last switch being set to the on position. Each switch actually represents a digit of the binary code (from left to right; 128/64/32/16/8/4/2/1) As the numbers increase, each progressive number is represented by turning on the next available open switch and resetting any switches previously assigned to an on position back to zero (off). In this way, there is a constant rollover of switches as higher numbers are assigned to progressively higher addresses. Continuing with the example, 2 is indicated by a rollover in which the second switch is turned on while the first resets to 0, 3 once again fills the first position and is represented by both switches being on, while 4 causes another rollover where the third switch is turned on and the two previous switches reset to zero. Every number can be represented by a combination of switches that are set to particular on/off positions. While the sensitivity for most level assignments are adequately represented through the standard range of 0–256 (with the exception of moving lights), even the early days of DMX control saw the need for addressing more than 256 channels, and provisions were made for adding one more switch and digit of addressing information. This led to the 512 (256×2) channels that have become the industry standard. While you can determine which switches to set on and off for a particular address through following the rollover illustration or by using division techniques (Sidebar 9.1), most of us rely on tables that cross-reference the DMX channels with the appropriate settings of the addressing switches.

Most DMX devices provide not only switches for addressing a fixture but also a second set of switches for making alterations to a unit's personality. A **personality** simply sets specific qualities to a unit. Unlike addressing switches, these switch functions can vary considerably from one piece of equipment to another. Several features that are seen regularly in the personality settings include setting the fixture's lamp to a power-saving mode, reversing the normal direction of a unit's pan and tilt controls (used when a unit is mounted in a reversed condition), running a diagnostic/self-testing mode, setting attributes to high- or low-resolution modes, and placing the unit in a stand-alone mode (i.e., rather than using DMX, the unit uses an audio sensor to trigger its responses). As lighting equipment has become more sophisticated, DMX512 has struggled to deal with the ever-increasing amount of data generated by this gear, and as one set of 512 channels becomes completely assigned, additional groups or **universes** are added to the system (each with another 512 channels). Many of today's consoles are manufactured with three or more universes and have the capacity to be expanded even further. A lot of the gear can even provide **bi-directional** data or feed back to the console and operator.

Over the years designers have required more control of an increasing number of dimmers and DMX gear, and console manufacturers have developed a number of features that aid operators in effectively controlling the many attributes and their related channels. The most popular technique for doing this has been through creating ways to group a console's channels into common elements. There are several different levels of this type of control. The first technique is arranging the board into groups of channels where dimmers with common functions are assigned next to one another. A second technique involves assigning channels to **groups** that share similar qualities. For instance, all of the warm area light might be assigned to a single group or **submaster,** while all the cool area light would be assigned to another group. In more complex consoles that provide a **page** feature, many of the submasters and **encoders** may be reassigned by simply pushing a button. Another variation of this layering is found on the more advanced consoles **(palettes)** that are popular in the concert scene. Palettes are nothing more than a group of pre-determined settings or presets that have been stored in a console. These can speed up the programming of a show considerably because a programmer only has to pull up a series of palettes to set the basic elements of a new cue instead of programming each channel individually. Predetermined settings for color, focus and position assignments, moving effects, and gobo combinations form several of the more popular palette settings that many programmers create before writing the actual cues for a production. Most automated lighting consoles provide a means of creating and storing numerous palettes that are then used for writing the majority of the show. A fairly common example of when palettes can streamline the cueing process is when a designer wishes to shift all of the moving lights to a given performer. Such a moment exists just before each sequence

---

SIDEBAR 9.3   Several Programming Tips for Working with Automated Lighting Gear

1. Take advantage of a console's tracking functions when programming automated lighting equipment. This conserves storage and memory demands on the console.

2. Use **block cues** or **hard blackouts** to record all channels to a level of zero at critical breaks in a program. This prevents tracking information from continuing past these points. For example, place these at the beginning and end of each song for a concert or at the end of a scene in a play or musical. By doing so, cues can be edited through tracking instructions that track through all the cues up to the block cue but not into future songs or scenes. In productions like concerts, where the order of the show may change from one performance to another, this becomes especially important since all of the attributes of a light must start with the same initial settings for the beginning of a musical number.

3. Create a number of palettes before you begin the actual cueing of a show. Many programmers have a library of palettes that they store on disks or flash drives and simply load them into a console as part of their initial setup process. Create **focus palettes** for principle performers and stage positions that are frequently used, **color palettes** that provide a variety of colors in a range of tints/saturations, a selection of gobo/texture breakup palettes, and a selection of effects that are tailored to the types of productions that you work on. Develop a manner of organizing these palettes so that you can access them quickly.

4. Use focus palettes whenever possible for defining focus positions for moving lights. This is especially important for productions that tour and where focus positions will shift as the spacing of a stage or the height of the trusses or other hanging positions are adjusted from one venue to another. By doing this, an entire show can be quickly updated by simply redefining the focus points.

5. Use **mark** or **move cues** to preset scrollers, focus points, and other attributes ahead of the time when the effect is actually executed. This prevents the distraction of "live moves" where scrollers scroll through a series of colors or moving lights sweep to a new position as they come up. Many of us create specific numbering systems that clearly identify a mark cue. I personally try to use either a .2 or .7 assignment for many of my mark cues. You should also label the mark and block cues if the console has the ability to label cues on your display.

6. Don't use moving effects just because you have them available. Carefully consider if the effect will add to the performance. If the answer is yes, then go about working the effect into the show. If not, it may be better not to use it. In theatre, subtle cueing is often more effective than pulling out the stops and creating a distraction. Designers and programmers often speak of **flash and trash,** which relates to using lighting predominantly for effect. The only problem with this is that after a while many of these designs seem to come down to just flashing and moving the lights around with no real connection to the event.

of questions are asked in the television show, *Who Wants to Be a Millionaire,* when all of the moving lights sweep from the perimeter of the stage to the center podium where the host and contestant are seated. Two different position or focus palettes would be used to define the central and perimeter positions of each light, while color palettes would be used to assign different colors to not only the sweep itself but also for both before and after the effect.

SOPHISTICATED CONTROL OF ADVANCED GEAR

As lighting has become more sophisticated, additional demands have been placed on consoles in terms of the number of channels and universes that they must support. By the year 2000, the DMX512 standard had been extended to the point that newer gear was taxing the efficiency of many control systems. In today's environment, control consoles not only are expected to control an increasing number of DMX devices but also are often linked to other controllers (rigging, special effects, midi devices, etc.). They may also tie a console to its backup and can synchronize other control systems that are operated in conjunction with the lighting system. Due to this, several new standards have been introduced to equip DMX512 for the future.

The first advancement makes use of common computer networking conventions to convert DMX signals to standard ethernet cables and routers. This allows for especially rapid transmission of data throughout a networked system. The speed of an ethernet system is not only much faster than traditional DMX control, it more importantly can carry a much larger volume of data and universes than traditional DMX systems. There is also no need to use a control cable for each universe. Most of the network hardware required for these systems is also readily available from computer or electronics stores. Primary components of these systems still communicate through DMX instructions, but the parts of the system that would be dedicated to long cable runs are replaced with ethernet cables. The location of a connection/conversion between a network connection and a standard DMX interface is called a **node.** The resulting network allows for rapid bi-directional communication between the console, dimmer racks, and any other equipment that is contained in the system. Several manufacturers have created their own versions of networking through systems like ETC's ETCLink and Strand Lighting's ShowNet systems. At present, most DMX-controlled equipment uses standard 5-pin XLR cable, and a node converts the networked cable back to the standard XLR fittings. However, some equipment has started to appear with ethernet ports that allow these units to be plugged directly into the ethernet.

Another technique for addressing the increased data demands was to build more in-depth protocols around the existing DMX512 standard. The first revision occurred around 1990, while the current version, known as DMX512-A, was officially accepted in November of 2004. Two new variations in control protocol have more recently been introduced to the lighting community. Both are generating a lot of discussion, as they will become the primary protocols of the future. The first, **ACN (Architecture for Control Networks),** was adopted as a standard in late 2006 and consists of approximately three to five different control protocols that are specific to various types of equipment in a lighting network. These individual protocols are packaged and function together as a whole unit—what some are calling a **suite.** More importantly, ACN addresses the networking problems of interchangeability, as manufacturers have once again developed their own protocols while shifting to the ethernet systems. It is thought that in the future ACN will not only become the primary control network for lighting but also for nearly any other type of entertainment control system as well. This might include hydraulics, lifts, rigging, and special-effects equipment. In fact, all of these systems could run under the umbrella of a single ACN control system. The system also looks to alternative techniques of transmitting control data by providing standards not only for wired networks but also for wireless control and future carriers like fiber optics.

The second aspect of the new protocol, **Remote Device Management (RDM)** functions as a link between DMX512-A and a fully implemented ACN network. In reality, it is a specific protocol that builds on the standard 5-pin DMX networking. First it addresses some of the shortcomings of DMX512-A and then builds on it to provide a number of improvements in the way that data is used throughout a lighting system. Several of the immediate benefits of RDM include a designation of how bi-directional data is exchanged between a console and a device that is plugged into the control system. This communication takes place along the two wires that have not traditionally been used for data transmission and provides bi-directional capabilities for future equipment as well as backward compatibility for older equipment that can be supported by the new protocol. More importantly, RDM has been developed so that it can provide a "plug-and-play" feature that works like our personal computers. Electricians simply plug a luminaire into a network cable, where the console, upon powering up, identifies the equipment and then goes on to determine the number and type of attributes that should be associated with the unit. It also automatically assigns control channels to each of the unit's attributes. This can virtually eliminate many of the burdens associated with soft-patching, addressing and setting up a console. Most importantly, it ensures that the console and lighting equipment are communicating properly. While this sounds wonderful, skeptics point to the early days of Microsoft Windows plug-and-play technology, when computers more times than not failed to correctly identify and install new pieces of peripheral equipment like printers. In reality, like with Windows, the worst that can happen is that we would have to continue to upload support files or use **firmware** for installing fixtures on our consoles. In time, the practice will more than likely shift to a relatively seamless process. Also, through the bi-directional communication, more features will be incorporated into many control systems. Information like lamp hours, housing temperatures, and homing positions might all be monitored by using this control system. While ACN deals primarily with those aspects of control associated with the ethernet, RDM addresses issues related more to the traditional (DMX-based) elements of the control network. Both are much more sophisticated than DMX512-A and will lead us into the next generation of communication between consoles and the equipment that they control.

ACCESSORIES FOR CONVENTIONAL LUMINAIRES

The largest drawback of traditional luminaires lies in the fact that a fixture can only be dedicated to one function at a time. This cannot be altered without climbing a ladder and changing something at the lighting instrument. As the control problems associated with using more luminaires were overcome, light plots grew exponentially with more and more units being used in productions. Eventually, a point was reached where it was physically impossible to squeeze all the lights into a given location, and innovators looked to modifying a luminaire's functions remotely throughout a performance, on demand.

Scrollers

The first devices that provided changes to conventional lighting instruments usually allowed a designer to change the color of a light. The earliest devices were effects related and included **color wheels** that placed a revolving disk of several colors in front of a light. Fire effects were often created through these mechanisms. Later devices, because of their manner of operation, are known as **color scrollers** and have a series of gels (a **gelstring**) taped together into a scroll that is loaded onto two rollers. A color is selected by moving the gelstring to different positions along the scroll. A designer simply specifies the gels and order in which they should be placed when ordering a gelstring. Most scrollers require a power supply that provides both the power and control data for the devices. Each scroller can be assigned to its own DMX address or may be operated together with other scrollers by having a shared DMX address. Each color or position is associated with a specific intensity level for the assigned channel. Even the simplest scrollers provide

12 to 16 colors while more sophisticated models can mix color by combining two overlapping gelstrings that are independently controlled. The dual gelstring units can typically mix over 400 different colors.

For many years, more expensive automated lights have mixed a seemingly infinite number of colors through a color mixing technology called **CYM mixing** (also known as **CMY mixing**). CYM mixing allows a designer to manipulate three dichroic disks or leaves (cyan, yellow, and magenta) through individual channels that can mix the light to virtually any desired color. In reality, each of the filters produces a new color through being inserted to varying degrees into the optical path of the light. Some designers take issue with this method of producing color because it can be difficult to project the same color uniformly throughout the entire light beam. Also, because the resultant color is a product of mixing, the colors aren't usually as intense or saturated as those produced with filters. On the other hand, in addition to providing so many colors, you can also cross-fade directly between colors, which can't be done with scrollers. Another innovation in color accessories involves placing a CYM mixing module in the body of an ETC Source Four fixture. This accessory, called the SeaChanger Color Engine is produced by Ocean Optics and brings full CYM mixing to any Source Four. The basic operation is much like any other CYM mixing technology with the exception that a fourth disk (a green one) is added to the cyan, yellow, and magenta plates. This provides more variety and stronger saturation in some of the colors that it produces. Both methods of modifying color are illustrated in Figure 9.1.

Moving Yokes

Probably the most desired variable that lighting designers want in their luminaires is the ability to redirect a light's focus. In the past, this required designers to commit to automated lights that were often too expensive for many theatrical productions. The units were also quite large and could generate an incredible amount of fan noise, making them less than desirable for theatrical applications. This led to manufacturers experimenting

a.   b.

FIGURE 9.1 Color Changing Accessories a. Wybron CXI IT: A scroller with two gel strings that are used in combination to mix up to 432 different colors. b. Ocean Optic's Seachanger Color Engine: An accessory that is placed in the optic path of a Source Four roughly at the position of the gate. The accessory allows a full range of color mixing through inserting various combinations of four different color leafs into the path of the light. *Photo credit:* a. Wybron, Inc.; b. PIXELTEQ Inc.

with the idea of creating an accessory that allowed traditional fixtures to be mounted in a specialized yoke that could be repositioned by remote control. The result was the creation of a relatively inexpensive **moving yoke** accessory that allows a luminaire's focus to be adjusted on command. The movements are completed through DMX instructions and a series of servo motors that adjust the tilt and pan settings for the fixture. Moving yokes have become a popular accessory and have seen widespread use in Broadway and regional theatres as well as in spectacle productions like Las Vegas revues and nightclubs. City Theatrical's AutoYoke® is one of the more popular moving yoke accessories that are available to a designer.

Moving Mirror Accessories

Moving an entire luminaire through a device like an AutoYoke® can create torque, resulting in a lot of stress on the moving parts of a unit as well as movement in hanging positions like battens that are not mounted rigidly. The forces have also caused problems in returning to a specific focus point on a repeated basis. An alternative to moving the entire fixture is found in placing a movable mirror at the front of a luminaire. By moving the mirror, focus can be re-directed in much the same way as moving the entire fixture while avoiding the problems of actually moving the lights. These devices are placed in a unit's gel frame holder and are called **moving mirror accessories.** While moving mirrors provide less torque and stress to a lighting system, the fixture and accessory must be mounted in a position that results in the range of movement being more limited than with moving yoke accessories. The Rosco I-Cue Intelligent Mirror™ is an example of this type of accessory.

Gobo Rotators

Gobo rotators (or just **rotators**) provide an effect where shadow projections are animated to produce moving effects. Fire and water effects are commonly produced with gobo rotators. In the simplest rotators, a single motor with an independent speed control is plugged into a non-dim circuit, while more complex units have additional controls that are powered by a special power supply. Each type of motion is usually controlled by a separate channel. Gobo rotators are inserted into the gate of a fixture and some (**double rotators**) may create composite effects by overlaying two different gobos on top of one another. Motion can then be initiated to either or both gobos. Not only the speed, but also the direction, of each pattern can be varied by making adjustments in the channel levels. Through **indexing rotators,** a gobo can even be instructed to stop at a specific point in its rotation, allowing gobos to be stopped in an upright orientation.

AUTOMATED LIGHTING

One of the most important advances in the lighting industry has been the appearance of automated lighting. Developed primarily by the concert industry, the ability to move beams of light freely throughout a venue while also providing numerous effects that couldn't be created with traditional equipment is what drove the development of these luminaires. Rental costs for additional equipment, transportation costs, and setup time are additional factors that played a role in driving concert promoters towards automated lighting. In the early days, many crews referred to these units as **moving lights** or **wiggle lights,** while we now prefer to call them either **automated** or **intelligent lighting.** One of the first attractions to automated lighting came with its ability to replace a number of individual specials. A fixture could focus on one person and later be redirected to another position and focus. The effect of moving the light around a venue while producing color changes, beam zooming, and gobo-related effects soon led to automated lighting becoming an expected element of the spectacle of concert lighting. On the other hand, one of the dangers of automated lighting is in not letting it become a distraction and not to use

Common Automated Lighting Effect Cues

Strobe Sequences	Luminaires programmed to flash in rapid succession—flashing may be within a single fixture or could flash between multiple fixtures.
Color Rolls	Luminaires moving through a series of color changes.
Chasing	A series of luminaires turned on and off in a sequence that forms a pattern.
Sweeps	Moving the light from one location to another while the lamp is lit.
Fans	A group of luminaires moving together either toward or away from a reference point—an example being lights pointed straight downward and then moving upward and outward away from the stage.
Kicks	A single unit sweeps from a downward position to an upward position where it is extinguished as another fixture repeats the motion, moving much like a dance kick line.

the units solely for effect. Every automated luminaire comes with a predetermined number of attributes or features. The actual number and type will vary from model to model and manufacturer to manufacturer, but several of the most common attributes associated with automated fixtures include shutter, color (1 channel for dichroic filters, 3 for CYM color mixing), gobos (spot units only), intensity, pan, tilt, and speed. Additional attributes might include a second color or gobo wheel (with or without rotation), zoom, and focus. Some will have both fine and coarse pan and tilt controls. Other units can have 20 to 30 attributes or more. Sidebar 9.4 lists several choreographed moves that are popular in automated lighting.

Due to the spectacle associated with automated lighting, much of the initial development of these luminaires was directed towards producing effects. Features like number of gobos, whether they rotated, number and range of colors, and strobing capacities as well as movement became important options for making comparisons between different luminaires. The fixtures also usually use short arc sources that cut through the light of traditional luminaires, which along with their higher color temperature allows them to easily establish focus when used with traditional fixtures. For all of the above reasons, plus expense, automated lighting wasn't practical for theatrical venues in their early years. They also tended to be noisy (both servo motors and fans). By their very nature, these units are expensive (many are $3,500 or more) and the more attributes that they provide, the pricier they become. Even if used in a more subtle manner, the fixtures are heavy (typically weighing in at 25–50 lbs., with some weighing in at over 100 lbs.), which can create a fair amount of swing in the electrics.

While expensive when compared to conventional fixtures, the costs of automated units have dropped significantly over the years, making them affordable for organizations and applications where they wouldn't have appeared ten years ago. Sophisticated features like programmable shutters, composite gobos, and a number of effects have also been introduced to the fixtures. More importantly, their once questionable reliability has stabilized, and consistent performances can now be expected of them from show to show. Due to influences like these, variations of automated luminaires have become popular in virtually all areas of lighting design. Most concert plots now contain a substantial number of automated luminaires, and in some cases, shows are lit entirely by automated rigs. Industrial shows, awards shows, television programs, and even churches have come to rely on these fixtures. *The Tonight Show* uses them, large spectacle events like the opening and closing ceremonies of the Olympic Games use them, and sporting events like the half-time extravaganzas of bowl games rely heavily on automated lighting. In fact, I can't think of a recent television awards program that hasn't made extensive use of automated lighting. In architectural applications, automated fixtures and scrollers have even been placed in protective housings so that they can be used to light building facades and other outdoor features and events. Use of these luminaires is growing and we can assume that we will see continued growth in their applications.

Moving Heads (Moving Yokes)

Moving heads form a specific group of automated lighting in which the actual luminaire or head moves. The earliest automated luminaires were primarily of the moving head variety. The units were large and heavy due to the number of mechanical devices and motors that were used to control the attributes of the fixtures. The company that led the early innovations of automated lighting was Vari*Lite, Inc. They introduced the first moving head fixtures with the 1981 "Abacab" tour of *Genesis*. The fixtures were so revolutionary that Vari*Lite went to unusual lengths to guard the trade secrets of their technology. For the first 10 or so years, the units could not be purchased and had to be rented directly from the company. In fact, only Vari*Lite employees were permitted to work on the luminaires, and they even provided the technicians who ran and maintained the equipment as part of the rental agreement. It took several years before the competition introduced automated fixtures that didn't infringe on the patent rights of Vari*Lite. However, a key philosophical difference was introduced when other manufacturers allowed their fixtures to be purchased. Since then, companies like Clay Paky, Coemar, High End, Martin, and Robe along with Vari*Lite have developed numerous automated luminaires. During the early years, control of the automated lights was done through a special console while all of the conventional fixtures were run through a traditional console. More recent models are operated using a standard console along with the conventional fixtures.

We also break the moving head luminaires into two additional groups (Figure 9.2). The first, **spot luminaires,** are used as spotlights and have beams that can be focused to a sharp edge. Many of these units contain effect devices and one or two gobo wheels that can hold up to five or more gobos each. This allows the gobos to be composited on top of one another or spun in the same way as a gobo rotator might be used. Many spot luminaires also have an attribute that allows the focus to be softened or sharpened on demand. In most cases, color is produced through CYM mixing although a color wheel with dichroic filters may also be used. Some of the more advanced luminaires even have shutters that can be positioned through DMX control. The second type of luminaires are **wash luminaires.** Unlike spot luminaires, these have a soft edge so that a series of them can be blended together to produce washes. Another difference between these and the spot luminaires is the lack of features like gobo wheels and shutters.

Some of the accessories that are available for these fixtures incorporate features like laser pointers that allow easy focus spotting during programming and infrared systems that can track a performer's movements. Over time, manufacturers have worked to modify the fixtures for theatrical venues and there are now units that work reasonably

a.   b.

FIGURE 9.2 Automated Luminaires (Moving Head) a. VL3000 by Vari*lite (a spot luminaire) b. Studio Color 575 by High End Systems (a wash luminaire) *Photo credit:* a. Vari*Lite; b. High End Systems—a member of the Barco Group

FIGURE 9.3 ETC's Source Four Revolution *Photo credit: Electonic Theatre Controls, Inc.* •

FIGURE 9.4 Martin MH-10 Scanner *Photo credit: Martin Professional, Inc.*

well for these more subtle applications. Improvements have included: substitution of the arc sources with incandescent lamps, the units have become smaller and weigh less, fan noise has been reduced, and the costs have dropped to within reach of more theatrical organizations. The Vari*Lite VL1000 is specifically designed to blend in with conventional fixtures while bringing the benefits of automated lighting to theatrical applications. Another example of an automated luminaire that has been designed around the needs of theatrical designs is the ETC Source Four Revolution (Figure 9.3). This luminaire is based on a modular design that allows several components or modules to be added or taken away from the unit as needed. The heart of this luminaire is based on the needs of silent operation and an incandescent light source that blends well with conventional fixtures. The basic unit also has a 24-color scroller assembly, a zooming feature, and an internal dimmer. Other accessories that are available for the Source Four Revolution include a remote controlled iris and shutter accessories.

Scanners (Moving Mirrors)

Scanners or **moving mirrors** (Figure 9.4) are another form of automated luminaires. Rather than moving an entire head, only a mirror is moved to adjust the pan and tilt of a moving mirror luminaire. The mirrors are relatively small and light-weight, resulting in a much more economical means of redirecting the light beam. The luminaires are also hung in a stationary position that results in much less stress and movement being introduced to the trusses or battens from which they are hung. Scanners typically work better as a spot luminaire because the focus is usually set only at the fixture itself. Scanners come in a variety of sizes and have many of the same attributes that are found in moving head luminaires. Pan and tilt, color, dimming, and gobo patterns are frequently provided in these fixtures. The units also cost less than moving head fixtures, with the tradeoff being that the range of tilt and pan control is more limited. Despite this drawback, these luminaires are quite popular, and most designers have learned to work within their limitations. If more extreme angles are desired, the unit can be hung in a modified position that allows the light to hit those areas of a stage where required. Scanners have become very popular in bar and dance club venues due to their size and ease of maintenance. They're so popular in nightclubs that many are equipped with audio sensors that change the attributes to the beat of the music.

NON-TRADITIONAL SOURCES

While the incandescent lamp has been the most popular light source for most theatrical luminaires, there has been increasing interest in using alternative light sources in theatrical productions over recent years. Energy efficiency has driven the architectural markets towards fluorescent sources, while the need for higher intensities and specific light qualities have led to the acceptance of many short-arc sources for several special duty applications like retail lighting or exterior applications such as street and roadway lighting. Even theatrical applications are making use of HID and other non-traditional light sources.

Ballasted Fixtures

In theatrical applications, non-traditional sources are usually used to introduce a different quality of light to a stage. Qualities like color temperature and color rendering can vary considerably from one light source to another, and one of the most significant differences of non-traditional fixtures is that most of these units make use of arc sources—with the added requirement that a ballast is required for each unit. This also means that electrical dimming of these sources isn't possible. If dimming is required, the units must be equipped with an accessory that functions as a mechanical dimmer. Lighting instruments that may have ballasts include HMI sources in fresnels, ERSs, and follow spots, and they may use sources like xenon or other short-arcs for specialized effects. Most moving lights also make use of HMI sources. High pressure sodium and mercury sources have also been used in productions of major operas as well as other theatrical events. In architectural and film productions ballasted fixtures are often preferred because of the **red shift** and changes in color temperature that dimming can cause. In these cases, intensity is controlled by varying the wattage of the source or placing filters or **scrims** over the front of the fixture.

Strobes

Other advanced sources include **strobe lights,** which are specialty lamps that can be set to a rapid on-off sequence that produces a stop-motion effect. Most strobes are equipped with a high-intensity xenon lamp that creates a bright high color-temperature flash. Older models had an independent control unit that allowed an operator to manipulate both the speed and intensity of the flashes. Contemporary strobes are controlled through DMX signals that allow a designer to pre-program the intensity, rate, and duration of the flashes. More importantly, while these fixtures can still be used to produce standard strobe effects, they can also be programmed to produce more random effects like lightning flashes or explosions.

Fiber Optics

Fiber optics have not made a strong appearance in theatre applications due to the relatively low intensity of the light that they produce. However, beautiful stardrops and other effects are made possible through this innovation. Fiber optics have even been worked into scenic, prop, and costume designs. There are two variations of fiber-optic cable that are popular in entertainment applications. The first, **end-emitting fiber,** conducts light throughout its length until it emerges at the end of the fiber with relatively no light being emitted from its sides. The second, **side-emitting fiber,** conducts light along its length but also radiates it outward along its sides and glows like a neon tube. In fact, side-emitting fiber is used quite effectively to simulate neon signs. In either case, the fibers are joined together at one end, where a manifold connects the bundle of fibers to a light source. The source is called an **illuminator.** In addition to the source, many illuminators also house devices like color wheels and patterned disks that produce color variations and shimmering effects in the light. The majority of the heat produced in these systems is confined to the illuminator.

Architectural and display applications have made use of this technology for many years. Stars have been created in plaster ceilings and poster board displays, and even model theatres may use fiber optics for creating illumination. Side-emitting fibers have been especially effective as a decorative element for lining objects like steps, buildings, and pool perimeters, while museums use end-emitting systems and specialized heads to direct light to heat-sensitive areas of a display. Particularly interesting uses of fiber optics are as a design tool while making presentations and as an aid to educational lighting. Here, model theatres are outfitted with miniature fiber-optic heads and a control system that allows a set designer's model to be lit on a miniature scale. LightBox (Figure 9.5) is a particularly successful product that uses this technology.

LEDs

A more recent innovation that is creating a lot of interest in the industry is the development of **LEDs.** In the past, these did not produce enough light to warrant their use in any applications other than as an indicator type of device (e.g., the power or signal strength indicators of electronic devices) where we observe the LEDs directly. Later developments led to increased intensities that allowed LEDs to be put to more common uses like in traffic lights, signage, and large video screens like the ones found in Times Square. The intensities of LEDs have continued to grow brighter and now produce enough light to be used as an actual source of illumination. More importantly, by creating clusters of differently

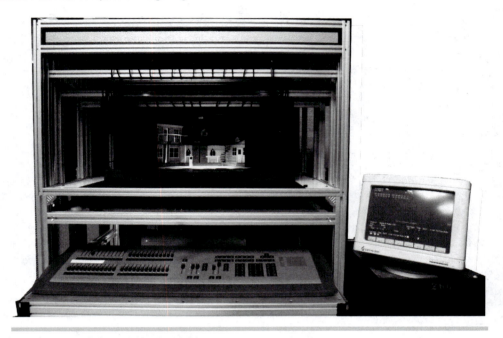

FIGURE 9.5 LightBox by Thematics A miniature fiber-optic model theatre using LIGHTBOX Model Lighting System for Syracuse University. Scenic models are placed within the structure and are lit by miniature fiber-optic heads that are scaled optically to actual stage luminaires. The system can be colored and is controlled by a standard console that allows the actual cues to be pre-programmed and simulated. *Photo credit:* LightBox Method for Model Lighting System for Syracuse University

colored LEDs, additive color mixing is used to produce a variety of colors in the light that emits from these units. Each color is controlled by a separate DMX channel. Typical colors for LEDs in these clusters include red, green, and blue (the primaries) but may contain up to seven channels of color (adding colors like amber, cyan, and possibly white). ETC's Selador units use the primaries plus amber, red-orange, cyan, and indigo in its X7 LED Striplights. The individual LEDs are mounted in clusters that are spaced regularly along the luminaire. These clusters in themselves do not produce much light, but through creating an array of clusters, the light becomes strong enough to warrant packaging the arrays into lighting fixtures. Some of these fixtures produce a compact source similar to a floodlight or soft-edged spotlight like PAR luminaires (Figure 9.6), while others function as linear luminaires that are designed like traditional striplights. A typical control arrangement for these units uses a separate channel for each of the LED colors plus an additional channel for overall intensity and strobing functions. Striplight versions of LED units often have separate channel controls for each segmented array that is formed along a unit's length. This allows the units to be used in complex chase effects. Two issues that are often associated with the fewer channeled fixtures are the inferior color rendering and especially high color temperature of these units' white light.

Companies that specialize in LED technology, such as Philip's Solid-State Lighting Solutions, Inc. (Color Kinetics), have become instrumental in developing luminaires that provide color mixing as part of a designer's toolkit. The color rendering is improving and the intensities of these units are now getting strong enough to be effective on stage, although they are still priced beyond the financial limitations of many would-be users. On the other hand, the units keep getting more powerful and the costs keep dropping, so it is only a matter of time before we see them making regular appearances on theatrical stages. In applications where intensities don't have to be as high, and throw distances not so great (e.g., museum, architectural, and display niches), these fixtures are already appearing in numerous applications. The LEDs have incredibly long life cycles, produce little heat, and

FIGURE 9.6   An LED Wash Luminaire: Philips Solid-State Solutions' (Color Kinetics) ColorBlast® 12 Powercore   *Photo credit:* Philips Solid-State Lighting Solutions, Inc.

can provide full color mixing, while they are also rugged and can withstand many of the environments where traditional light sources don't fare so well (extreme cold, for example). They can also significantly cut the costs associated with the energy for and maintenance of a lighting system. We are rapidly approaching a point where luminaires using LED technologies warrant serious consideration as legitimate light sources. It is also hoped that in the not-too-distant future a compact white LED will replace the incandescent lamp as a primary source of lighting throughout much of the lighting industry.

A special variation in white LED technology has been created by Rosco in the form of its LitePad products. These illuminating panels come in a variety of sizes (3" × 3" to 12" × 12") and are lit from one side by a row of white LEDs. Like in side-emitting fiber optics, these panels transmit light along the flat surface of the panel, which makes them an extremely compact light source for situations where there is no room for conventional fixtures. These units also operate on a 12-volt system that can be powered by transformers or batteries and may even be plugged into a car's cigarette lighter.

Lasers

Lasers have typically been used only as an effect for entertainment purposes. The beams are too well defined, directional, and concentrated for them to be considered as a practical source of general illumination at this time. While some may be operated through the lighting console, most laser effects are both designed by and placed under the control of a laser specialist. In nearly all cases, this operator must have a license as well as a specific permit for operating a laser during a given performance. These stringent rules are due to the hazards that are associated with a laser's operation.

THE PERSONAL COMPUTER

Lighting designers quickly discovered the advantages of using personal computers and became the first design discipline to use them as a regular part of the design process. Lighting, more so than any other area of design, deals with a huge amount of information or data that must be organized into a variety of repetitive yet different formats—a task particularly well-suited to computers. Computers are now making a huge impact on all areas of design, and designers are using them for more complex applications all the time. The only innovation that may arguably be more significant to the lighting industry than the personal computer is the laptop computer. Laptops have made computers easily accessible to designers, who can now take their work directly to the theatres and hotels for completing much of the design process. I personally carry a laptop almost everywhere that I travel. Laptops have had such a profound impact on our profession that it isn't a bit unusual to see several of them on the design tables that are scattered throughout a theatre.

Computers and the lighting software that we use are evolving faster than anyone can imagine. In many cases, there are exponential gains every year or two in the complexity and speed with which tasks can be accomplished by a computer. Computers that we couldn't live without several years ago quickly become obsolete, and programs that were helpful 5 years ago may not even exist in the current market. Because of this, I have chosen to address just a few of the more popular applications that are important to lighting designers. These are organized primarily by type of application, with the major classifications being design analysis, computer-aided drafting(CAD), design paperwork, control and off-line editing, communication, and visualization. In some cases, several applications work together as part of a suite which performs tasks in several categories.

Finally, there is the never-ending debate of **Mac** versus **Windows** and the PC (Personal Computer). Both platforms are used extensively throughout the industry, but much of the determination as to which platform a designer uses is personal. One major consideration that every designer must examine when determining which platform to purchase lies in choosing the software they will be using. Some applications will run seamlessly between both platforms, some will require some form of file translation with varied degrees of success, and others may not be at all compatible between the different platforms. Some designers own and use both platforms. DOS PCs of the past tended to be complicated to operate and more difficult to setup or install applications on, while Macs had a much friendlier user interface. Much of this has changed with the Windows operating system. Windows PCs, on the other hand, tend to be more affordable, and you often get more bang for your buck. However, because of their popularity and the number of different applications that they must address, they also have a reputation for crashing and becoming infected with computer viruses. Many of these issues have been addressed, and the machines have improved significantly over the years. Today, the platforms appear to be merging closer together in regard to their overall operation and features. There are even Mac computers with Intel® processors, dual processors, or simulation software that can be operated using either the Mac or Windows operating systems. Other than specific software choices, most of the other considerations tend to be personal. As a rule, the computers that work best for any lighting applications should be equipped with the fastest processor, most amount of memory, and largest hard drive that you can afford. Other features that you will most likely want to invest in are a speedy DVD/CD drive with recording features, a fax modem, ethernet port, and wireless network options. While we previously used floppy drives for recording our data (3½" or 5¼" in the really old days), we are now storing and moving data between our personal computers and lighting consoles with USB flash drives, CD-ROMs/DVDs, and server options. A good optical mouse is also helpful for data input (especially for working in CAD).

CAD and Drafting Applications

Next to using the computer for design paperwork, **CAD** or **CADD** (computer-aided design and drafting) applications form one of the earliest uses of computers in the lighting industry. CAD is especially useful to a lighting designer because of the number of repetitive activities associated with creating a light plot. Light plots also tend to be very mechanical and precise, making use of a number of straight lines, lots of lettering, and precise spacings. All of these are managed quite easily in CAD. Mistakes are completely erased and a final output will always appear clean and unmarred as a perfect print of the final plot despite the complexity of a design or drafting. More importantly, CAD packages have tools like copy/paste and **block** commands that allow the repetitive tasks of drafting a light plot to be shortened extensively. There are also more sophisticated versions of CAD programs that work in three dimensions which are known as **modeling programs.** Full three-dimensional models with realistic materials lit by real-world photometrics are now possible in CAD design. It is even possible to create images with a photographic quality where the CAD image itself becomes the final design—a **virtual design**. Film sequences may also make use of mattes or models that have been created through computer modeling or animation. Films like the *Harry Potter* series have made regular practices of combining animated elements with the actual props, scenery, and actors. There are even feature-length films created entirely by computers (*Toy Story, Ice Age, Shrek,* and *Up*). The two most popular CAD programs currently being used in the lighting business are *AutoCAD* and *Vectorworks Spotlight*.

One of the best features of CAD comes with the ability to copy elements of a drafting. This could mean copying an element as small as a single line but more often means that complex objects like lighting fixtures, scenic floor plans, master theatre plans, or even entire drawings can be used as a reference and copied. More importantly, objects can be copied between different drawings. Once an object is drawn, it never has to be redrawn again . . . it is simply copied and modified as needed. In a real time-saving method, entire draftings called **prototypes** or **templates** can be used as base drawings for other draftings. The tasks of redrawing the theatre, title block, key, and notation can be forgotten as a prototype for the entire drafting is copied and used to add specific details and luminaires to a project as needed.

One issue that must be dealt with when using CAD is how to create a physical copy or **plot** of the light plot. To plot a large-scale image of a light plot in the traditional ½"=1'−0" or other acceptable scale requires a large format printer or **plotter** (often as wide as 36"–42"). Most designers do not own a plotter and must use a service to produce finished copies of the light plot. The costs and availability of these services must be considered, and even though times are changing, these services are rarely available 24 hours a day or on weekends—in smaller communities they may not be available at all. In a pinch, plots can be printed on a personal printer as a PDF file or as an assembly of tiled images that are printed on standard paper and then taped together. On the other hand, an advantage to digital or electronic design lies in the fact that the draftings can be transmitted to other members of the design team through simply attaching the drawing files to an e-mail.

Design Paperwork

Design paperwork forms the area where lighting designers first discovered the power of the personal computer. Before then, all of our schedules had to be completed by hand. In the 1970s and early '80s the total number of units in a lighting design wasn't that significant, but as the size of the rigs grew, the task of assembling all of the associated paperwork became more difficult. As the shows got bigger, the potential for mistakes grew, while the penmanship of the designer or assistant usually got worse. Since most paperwork follows the format of a table, it didn't take long to discover that computers could generate the majority of the schedules and paperwork quite easily. Since many lighting schedules follow the format of a spreadsheet, a number of designers simply used their favorite spreadsheet software to develop the schedules. The real advantage to these applications comes in that all of the data is entered into the computer only one time. Once entered, the software can manipulate the data to generate the instrument schedules, hookups, and inventory lists that a designer needs for displaying the lighting data. Also, if the paperwork needs to be changed, the data is easily edited and a new set of accurate forms can be generated by simply reprinting the forms.

There are a number of lighting designers who use applications like Microsoft's *Excel* or *Works* for producing their paperwork. There are also applications that have been specifically written to meet the needs of lighting professionals. Unique tools found in these programs include menus and questioning formats or input dialogue boxes that relate specifically to entering lighting data, ways of duplicating the input of repeating data, and lighting speciality tools like determining the total sheets of color or making power/load calculations. The standard for this software has been set by John McKernon's *Lightwright* software, which works on both Mac and Windows computers. In addition to creating standardized forms for paperwork like hookups and instrument schedules, the program has additional features such as lists for work notes, inventories, and comprehensive focus charts that can be stored in the computer. Other companies like Rosco and Stage Research, Inc. (formerly Cresit) also offer paperwork software.

A type of lighting software that has been introduced fairly recently comes in the form of a virtual magic sheet. This software, called *Virtual Magic Sheet*™ by Goddard Design (Figure 9.7), contains a series of tools like ovals, squares, and circles that can be laid out, colored, scaled, and arranged in much the same way as a traditional **magic sheet.** Along with the basic shapes, the designer also assigns a label or function (downlight, area light, John special, scroller, etc.) and associated channel to each shape. The magic of the software comes when the personal computer containing the virtual magic sheet is interfaced with a lighting console using a DMX input. This produces an interactive display in which the magic sheet and its associated intensity levels for each channel are shown within the shapes and functions that have been previously defined by the designer. This gives the designer access to the control channels by function while also providing immediate feedback regarding the levels of the functions that are displayed by the magic sheet. This software is also designed for both Mac and Windows platforms. Another software package uses a specialized spreadsheet to track the focus points used with automated lights. This software, *Focus Track,* allows every attribute of automated fixtures and their focus points to be documented throughout a design. It, too, has an interface that allows the spreadsheet to both trigger and respond to changes between the software and the console.

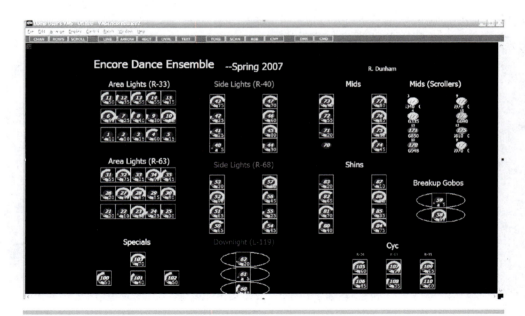

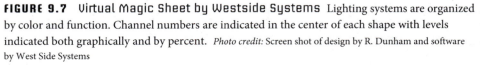

FIGURE 9.7 Virtual Magic Sheet by Westside Systems Lighting systems are organized by color and function. Channel numbers are indicated in the center of each shape with levels indicated both graphically and by percent. *Photo credit:* Screen shot of design by R. Dunham and software by West Side Systems

Control and Off-line Editing

Over the years, there have been several attempts to use personal computers and specialty software to convert computers into a basic lighting console. In each case, specialty software was loaded onto the computer and an interface or black box was connected between the computer and the dimmers. On occasion, an accessory containing a limited number of manual faders (a **wing panel**) could be added to bring some form of manual control to the console. Both Rosco's Horizon and Sunlite's lighting control system combine many of the features of more expensive consoles into a user-friendly interface that operates under the Windows environment. While there are a number of Horizon installations, Rosco no longer distributes these products. More importantly, Rosco distributed the software for free through a CD-ROM or download that was readily available from the company's Web site. This availability permitted designers to run the software on their personal computers for pre-cueing or blind editing without the actual lighting console. Once programmed, the show file could be transferred to a computer at the theatre that was equipped with the DMX interface and the design would be ready to go.

Off-line editing has become a very important tool that allows designers to download software that simulates a lighting console. In off-line editing, show files are created and edited without having to complete the work in the theatre with the actual lights and console. This software is useful in cases like touring, when a production has already been designed and a designer needs to modify a design for each venue. Off-line editing is particularly helpful when the designer is prevented from programming a show live in the actual performance space. Entire shows can be pre-written or roughed-in outside of the performance space using this technology (writing a show **blind**). The pre-written cues are loaded into the console once you get to the theatre and are then **tweaked** or edited once they are seen in rehearsals. Manufacturers of all the major lighting consoles provide off-line editors that are free through downloading the software from their Web site. There are even utilities that can translate data from one manufacturer's console to another. Manufacturers of more complex consoles that are heavily oriented towards the moving light industry supply off-line editors that provide excellent simulations of their consoles.

Communication and Training

One of the primary means of transferring information from one person to another is now through the personal computer. Messages between members of the design team are often done by **e-mail,** and draftings and other visual images are frequently sent back and forth by attaching files **(attachments)** to e-mail messages. Master plans of a stage or performance facility can also often be downloaded from the Web sites of many venues. In some cases, master drawings, research images and photographs, and sketches can be posted to dedicated **Web sites** (Google Groups, Facebook, and Picasa). At the University of Georgia, we use Facebook and Google Groups to link members of a production team to the research that our designers are producing for our productions.

Another area where the industry has changed significantly relates to the manner in which manufacturers and distributors make product literature available to lighting professionals. Several shelves of my office bookcase are lined with product binders containing cut sheets for virtually any theatrical lighting product available. At my home office I actually have a whole bookcase devoted to product binders for just a few of the many architectural luminaire manufacturers—small in comparison to most architectural lighting firms that have a whole room dedicated to shelving product binders. This method of distributing literature is rapidly going the way of the dinosaur as companies shift to distributing their catalogues on **CD-ROMs/DVDs** or through Web-based **online catalogues.** In addition to cut sheets, these Web sites also provide aids to using the products, designer testimonials, price lists, and other resources related to a company's products. In the case of architectural luminaires, many companies even include application tools that help a designer determine which products are best suited for a given situation and create the actual specifications for a project. More importantly, these sites can be updated at any time and are available whenever needed. In addition to catalogues, many companies also provide technical support, product manuals, and learning tools for their equipment. I have found these sites to be particularly valuable for getting operating information for shows that I have done in theatres that use automated lights—often with any literature for these units long being lost. By going to the Web sites, you can quickly find critical information like a listing and order of the unit's attributes, setup requirements, and the striking (startup) and shutdown sequences needed for getting the fixtures up and running.

Design Analysis

Software that is created predominantly for design analysis helps a designer to see and understand light in a given application. While this software may be used as part of the design analysis for a specific situation, these products also form excellent learning tools for designers who are just beginning to work with photometrics and color theory. Although some of these packages, especially in the case of architectural applications, are designed around a particular company's product line, there are others that are representative of the entire industry. Even equipment that is still around despite a company not being in business any longer is included in most of these packages. The first area in which designers used design analysis software concentrated on the effects of distribution, throw distance, and the photometrics of a design. A luminaire is selected and placed at a given trim and distance from a target, while a cone of light resembling the beam is drawn in a particular view (usually sectional). The program plots the beam pattern and uses photometric data to calculate the intensity (footcandles) that would be present at the target. By examining the distribution patterns and intensity levels, a designer can make an appropriate selection of both luminaire and hanging position for a given situation. Finally, additional details like lamp combinations, hanging weight, and accessories are also provided, along with the photometric data. McKernon's *Beamwright* and Crecit's *Light Shop* are examples of this type of software.

One of the most difficult tasks for beginning designers is making appropriate color choices for a production. Not only are the individual selections important, but more importantly, we are interested in how the light from different gels and angles will react and mix with one another and the other colors that will be found on a stage. Two popular programs that simulate the effects of color mixing and angle distribution are *Virtual Light Lab* and *Light Grid*. Both allow a designer to place lights on a grid that is designed to simulate a number of the fundamental lighting angles. Each light is then assigned a gel from any of the major filter suppliers. Not only can the designer study the effects of the gels mixing from the different angles but the intensity of each light can also be varied as an element of the simulation. In some cases, gobo breakups and scenic backgrounds can also be entered into the program and evaluated. Virtual Light Lab even allows a designer to paste bitmap images like a scanned paint elevation into the background of a simulation. By experimenting with different filters, hanging positions, and intensities a designer should be able to get an indication of how a particular combination of these variables will affect the appearance of the subject.

The final area of design analysis comes in the form of creating simulations or **renderings** that provide an image of how an object or environment might look when placed under a given set of lighting conditions. Originally, these were not linked to photometric data and were nothing more than an elaborate storyboard based on what the designer hoped the final design might look like. Paint and illustrating programs like Adobe's *PhotoShop* were among the first programs that were used to suggest what a designer hoped to achieve in their lighting. These images aren't linked to photometric data and we continue to use these products for storyboarding even today. On the other hand, CAD programs have grown into three-dimensional modeling packages that can create virtual images with quite accurate renderings of both the materials and the lighting of a subject. Both AutoCAD and Vectorworks have lighting and materials modules in their basic programs, while products like *3D Studio (Max or Viz)* and *Lightwave* are more complex programs for modeling and rendering light, but once again, the image isn't necessarily linked to photometric data. These images are called **computer renderings** (Figure 9.8). The advantage to programs like 3D Studio is not only in their modeling, but also in their ability to create animation. This includes their ability to create a

FIGURE 9.8   Scenic design and VectorWorks rendering by Michael Helmstion

walkthrough or **flyby** where an observer either is directed through a view down a previously determined path or may navigate through the virtual world themselves.

Visualization

Visualization is a more sophisticated form of computer rendering. In some cases, an image might be so accurately calculated that it depicts a photometrically correct image. This might be just what is needed in the case of making a presentational rendering for a major architectural project, but such images take an immense amount of time and expense to create. In entertainment situations, this is rarely possible—plus, unlike architectural projects, stage images are dynamic and constantly changing. Even if there is time to do such visualizations they are often limited to either a single image per scene or a couple of important moments of a production. On the other hand, there is another variation of visualizations that generates images without using photorealism. More importantly, they work within the framework of real time. With these, accuracy and detail are sacrificed so that a complete animation can be made for a project. The entertainment industry has arrived at a point where these visualizations can account for most design decisions that a designer would use in an actual theatre—even illustrating the transitions between the cues. Entire virtual theatres can be created where model sets are lit with virtual luminaires hung in lighting positions that completely mimic the real plot that will someday be hung in the theatre. The luminaires replicate the photometrics of the actual fixtures and are virtually focused and gelled as they would be in the theatre. Hookups and channel assignments are created automatically and will match the actual plugging of the show in the theatre. Finally, cues are written using the virtual image just as if the production were being lit in the actual space. When the virtual programming is complete, the cues have been roughed-in and the show is ready to be loaded into the console after the rig has been assembled in the theatre. This process saves immense amounts of time in the venue and has become so beneficial that virtual studios have started to pop up across the world where lighting designers rent the computer and software on an hourly or daily basis. The first popular theatrical visualizer was Cast Software's *WYSIWYG (What You See Is What Your Get)*. WYSIWYG is a stand-alone program that even contains its own CAD program. This software not only creates design visualizations, but also aids designers in drafting the plot and section, keeps track of inventories, and generates all of the design's schedules and paperwork.

An even more powerful application of computer visualization connects the personal computer to the lighting console through some form of DMX/USB interface. This allows the virtual program to drive the console in the actual venue. When a change is made in the virtual world, the change is immediately reflected in the real rig. As a further form of sophistication, the communication between these systems is bi-directional, and changes made

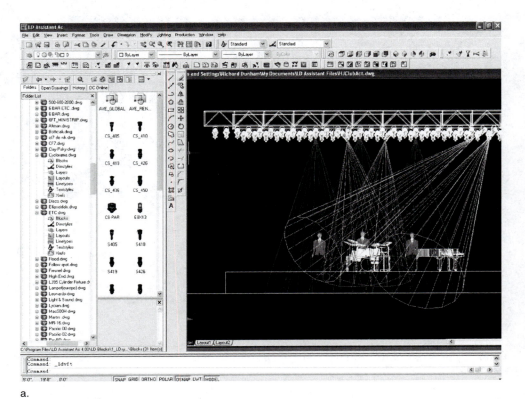

a.

b.

FIGURE 9.9 LD Assistant by Design and Drafting a. Software interface illustrated along with block navigator and wire-frame model of a nightclub design. b. A rendering of the nightclub design. *Photo credits:* Screenshots of design by R. Dunham and software by Design and Drafting

through the lighting console will also create changes in the virtual lighting. Over the years WYSIWYG has evolved into this type of visualization tool and has been bundled into many of ETC's consoles as part of the *Emphasis*® product line. This type of visualization has opened up to other manufacturers and an increasing number of consoles are now being shipped with some form of visualization software. Another visualization package that is comparable to WYSIWYG is *LD Assistant* by Design and Drafting (Figure 9.9). This software comes with a large symbol library (not only lighting instruments but also props and other stage equipment) and also produces all of the draftings, inventories, and other paperwork required for completing a lighting design. It, too, can be equipped with a DMX module that allows the personal computer to interface with a console. The primary difference between this product and WYSIWYG is that LD Assistant is designed around AutoCAD and therefore has all the tools and sophistication of AutoCAD while WYSIWYG uses its own CAD program.

Entertainment designers tend to reserve the term "visualization" for systems that display rendering results in a real or live timeframe/mode, while in reality, visualization can just as easily pertain to static images as well. Visualization techniques tend to be used most often in situations like concert lighting or big spectacle events where complex demands are placed on automated luminaires and where there is a limited amount of time to work in the actual venue. A real advantage to using visualization software comes in its ability to deal with the movements of automated lights. In addition to creating the different cues, a bigger attraction comes in how easily this software can be used to redirect moving lights to new focus points or to work out the choreography of the moving light beams. Timing of these moves can be checked against a piece of music while the accuracy of the moves can be plotted from one stage to another without stepping foot in a venue. Software that is used to create architectural visualizations tends to be more sophisticated than in entertainment applications, but these images also tend to be extremely detailed (photorealism is the most popular style) and are based on true photometric calculations. Three of the most popular architectural visualization and design analysis packages include Lighting Technologies' *Lumen Designer* and *Lumen Micro* as well as Lighting Analysis' *AGi32*.

FOR FURTHER READING

Cadena, Richard, *Automated Lighting: The Art and Science of Moving Light in Theatre, Live Performance, Broadcast, and Entertainment* (Burlington, MA: Focal Press, 2006).

Essig, Linda, *The Speed of Light* (Portsmouth, NH: Heinemann, 2002).

Huntington, John, *Control Systems for Live Entertainment*, 3rd ed. (Burlington, MA: Focal Press/ Elsevier, 2007).

Mobsby, Nick, *Practical Dimming* (Cambridge, UK: Entertainment Technology Press, 2006).

Mobsby, Nick, *Practical DMX* (Cambridge, UK: Entertainment Technology Press, 2006).

Mumm, Robert C., *Photometrics Handbook*, 2nd ed. (Lousiville, KY: Broadway Press, 1997).

Sandström, Ulf, *Stage Lighting Controls* (Oxford: Focal Press, 1997).

Schiller, Brad, *The Automated Lighting Programmer's Handbook* (Burlington, MA: Elsevier, Inc./Focal Press, 2004).

Simpson, Robert S., *Lighting Control: Technology and Applications* (Burlington, MA: Focal Press, 2003).

Essentials of Lighting Design

10

Good lighting design doesn't simply happen. It is the result of many hours of planning that leaves little room for chance or random occurrences. Every luminaire, its placement and focus, its color (by color temperature or filter selection), and its intensity are decisions that should be considered prior to moving into a venue. Lighting design involves a process that entails a number of specific steps—many that are shaped specifically by the working methods of an individual designer. While we all go through roughly the same process, we each have our individual ways of approaching a design. Part One of this book examined the nature of light, and Part Two focused on the technology and tools of lighting. Part Three examines the process of lighting design. While this part of the book provides essential information relating to the design process, it also goes on to present a number of specific techniques that you might consider working into your own personal methods of designing. Some come from practices that have worked for me personally, while others come from my observations of other designers. Feel free to use, adapt, or disregard any of these suggestions in your own personal practices. Even though all lighting designers go through similar stages in the evolution of a design, it should be noted that there is no single formula that will work for everyone. The process is personal and one that you will need to experiment with . . . adapting, revising, and refining it throughout your career. In fact, you will often modify your process based on the specific needs of a given project.

This chapter begins with the process of lighting design and focuses on the task of establishing a vision or **lighting scheme** or **lighting concept** for a project. Although entertainment designers and illuminating engineers may have different approaches to designing, both ask questions that will guide their decisions as they design a project. The task of establishing a vision or image of a project forms an essential first step in the design process, and all of the design decisions will ultimately refer back to this part of the process. These stages in the early development of a design are commonly called **analysis** and **conceptualization.** Several popular names that may be given to the vision itself include **lighting scheme, lighting concept, image of light,** or a **point of view.** In each case, these are nothing more than an image of the lighting that is envisioned for a given project.

SPECIAL CONSIDERATIONS IN LIGHTING DESIGN

One of the most difficult elements of lighting design lies in the fact that we don't get a chance to actually work with our medium (light) until very late in the design process. Everything that a lighting designer produces up to moving into a facility can only indirectly represent a design. A **light plot** or **lighting plan** is just a tool for hanging the lights, while **storyboards** and photographs represent our intentions through another artistic media—but not light. **Mock-ups** and **light labs** form a limited representation of a design, and computer **visualizations** only represent the design in yet another indirect way of presentation. Despite all the technical knowledge that a lighting designer must master, most of it only allows a designer to indirectly control or experience the medium of light. It isn't until we work in the venue with the actual luminaires that we begin to truly design with the real medium of light.

Time and budget form another set of conditions within which a lighting designer must work. In the best situations, a lighting designer will be brought onto a project at an early stage and will have lots of time to be part of the team and to plan the project. However, lighting often isn't given serious consideration until much later than the other production elements. Areas of a production can also fall behind schedule or could become more costly than initially planned and the lighting department will often be asked to help make up for the shortages which these other areas have produced. I can't remember the number of times that my focus or cue writing sessions have been cut short or even been eliminated due to problems that occurred from the load-in of the scenic elements of a production. Despite these compromises, the lighting must still be created in a manner that brings justice to the production and it does no good to whine about the problems. The first performance or opening must go on as scheduled, and the lighting designer needs to remain cool and collected during these stressful rehearsal times. Most importantly, they must remain flexible so that they can adjust to the bumps in the road that frequently occur in the production process.

The best remedy for coping with these unexpected occurrences lies in being completely familiar with your design and to be comfortable in your decisions throughout the design process. It is imperative that a lighting designer have a well-developed plan so that they can react to changes as they develop. Much of this planning must happen well before moving into a facility. Time in the venue is at a premium and every decision that can be made outside of the theatre allows a designer to concentrate more fully on the actual lights and levels that they are setting during the limited time that is assigned to lighting rehearsals. During these times, only decisions that require actual observation of the lighting should be dealt with and anything that could have been set earlier, outside of the venue, should have already been worked out—maximizing the time that a designer can spend working in the actual medium of light. I've frequently observed lighting designers at the design table suffering from the consequences of not making decisions like determining cue placements prior to their cue-writing sessions. Another consequence of this lack of preparation can occur when a designer creates cues alongside a director during a cue writing session. In these cases, I've witnessed the director actually creating the cues while the designer became nothing more than a translator for converting the luminaires into control channels. So, in all fairness to yourself, you have to come to the design table as well-prepared as you possibly can be.

DIRECTORS AND COLLABORATION

Unlike fine artists, lighting designers do not operate in a vacuum. We are part of a team and don't shut ourselves away in a studio as a fine artist would when creating a sculpture or painting. Our art is only one aspect of a much larger art form in which other individuals are also charged with particular aspects of a project. More importantly, as part of a design team, we must work together to create cohesive projects under the guidance of a leader who has a master vision for the final product. In entertainment projects, the director or producer fills this role. As lighting designers, we only control one aspect of a project and must work to help unify our work with all the other designers. In the entertainment world, this team most often involves a director and designers in the specialty areas of scenery and costumes as well as lighting. Other specialists who are also usually considered to be part of the team include, sound designers, media and projection designers, property designers, and choreographers.

While each individual is charged with a given specialty, everyone works together to complete a design project. This type of teamwork is called **collaboration** and forms a very different process than that followed by traditional artists. Each member of the team responds to the ideas of the other team members, and everyone works together to produce a superior product in which all of the individual elements are tied together. Through collaboration and the guidance of a director, the designers work through an approach to a project and make decisions that reinforce one another. Topics such as style, color palettes, themes, and historical detailing form just a few of the considerations that a design team will discuss in regard to a project. Practical concerns like budgeting, scheduling, and sharing resources such as rigging and cabling locations are also dealt with by the team members. In theatre, we often make reference to **unified productions,** in which all of the individual elements come together as a single cohesive project.

A director is charged with the most important responsibility as the team leader in these collaborative projects. While every member of the team is expected to make contributions and bring their personal ideas to a production, the director is ultimately responsible for accepting or rejecting anything that each designer brings to a project. The director must also be capable of motivating and inspiring their team in a way that produces the best solution for a project. While directors want to encourage the full participation of their team, ultimately, if the director cannot be convinced to support an idea, the designer must defer to the director's judgment and should accept the director's decision to reject that idea. While directors often receive the most credit for successful productions, when a production fails, it is also the director who bears the largest amount of responsibility and bad press.

THE INFLUENCES OF LIGHT

Light influences all things. You might recall that at the beginning of the book I made a statement to the effect of, "nothing would be visible without light." In a designed environment everything that we see is due to the manner in which light is used to reveal that environment to us. The specific manner in which a subject or environment is lit can make a significant contribution to the way in which an observer responds to the environment and anything that is contained within it. In the performing arts, light is used to reveal and modify performers, their costumes, the scenery, and anything else that is associated with a production. Light might even become a design element in itself through instances such as when fog or haze are used in concerts or aerial productions. In fact, we rarely see the true physical qualities of many objects . . . only those qualities as influenced by a given set of lighting conditions. If the lighting changes, so will the appearance of these qualities and the associated objects. At this point, it is wise to review several of the basic influences of light.

Controllable Qualities of Light

From earlier discussions I noted that all light can be described through four specific qualities. The specific combination of these qualities makes any light unique. If any one of these are modified, the lighting itself will be changed and the response that it creates in an observer will also be modified. Some of these variations can produce dramatic changes, while others may be quite subtle. These controllable qualities include **intensity** (brightness), **distribution** (angle and overall quality such as harshness or texture), **color,** and **movement** (changes). In reality, the first three are used to describe the actual lighting of a given moment while movement addresses changes or transitions of the lighting from one moment to another. These qualities are used consistently as a means of describing the unique characteristics of any light throughout all areas of lighting design.

Each quality has an influence on how we perceive an object. Intensity can be used to make a subject more or less visible, direction can be used to create a more dramatic impact or to reveal textures in an object's surface, and color can be used to modify the perceived colors that are observed in an object. All the controllable qualities can be manipulated by a lighting designer to create a desired response to a subject. A designer must fully understand how to manipulate these qualities since they ultimately become the lighting designer's equivalent to a fine artist's palette of paint and brushes.

Functions of Lighting

Whether designing the lighting for a play, client's garden, house of worship, or the Radio City Music Hall's *Christmas Spectacular*, lighting is counted on to create numerous functions within the scheme of a typical design project. Through manipulation of the controllable qualities and attaining various lighting functions, a designer can provide a positive experience for anyone who witnesses a production. Unfortunately, just as there are good examples of lighting, there are also many examples of bad lighting where for one reason or another a designer missed the primary intent of a project and the controllable qualities were not utilized in a way that was particularly beneficial to the design. Again, as a form of review, I want to briefly mention several significant functions of theatrical lighting. **Visibility** (or selective visibility), **establishing a scene** (setting a location or appropriate environment), **modeling** (sculpting/revealing form), **mood** (producing an emotion response), **focus** (bringing emphasis), **composition** (an arrangement of elements that may or may not unify an image), **style** (conforming to a specific visual representation), **staging the story** (facilitating the progression of events), and **rhythm** (patterns of design elements or transitions) all form specific functions that lighting can produce for a given project. A lighting designer uses the qualities of light in order to fulfill these functions. A lighting designer should always keep these functions and the controllable qualities of light in mind as they work through any design project. How can an image envisioned for a particular project be established through each of these functions and qualities? What type of mood must we create? What is the central focus of the image? How realistic does the image have to be? Is there a time frame to consider? All of these and many more questions should be considered as a designer works through the specifics of any design project.

ANALYSIS FOR LIGHTING

When I discuss analysis I am referring to defining the specific needs of a lighting project. In the entertainment area this most commonly is associated with some form of **script analysis.** Some areas of entertainment such as opera or musical theatre may require a designer to read a score, libretto, or lyrics rather than a script (although all perform the same function). In entertainment areas that do not make use of a script, like in dance, a design is developed through observations of rehearsals and conversations with the rest of the team of associated artists. Even without a full script, some form of synopsis, project scheme, or storyboard will usually be available to aid a designer throughout the design process. While a script may play a significant role in the analysis of a dramatic production, additional elements of observation and discussion are also important to the development of a production, even more so if a script does not exist. A designer needs to become familiar with all of these techniques of analysis to ensure that the most effective design is developed for a project. Even architectural projects that at first glance appear to require little analysis benefit from a more careful examination of the design problem and a detailed analysis of the needs of a specific project. Analysis forms the first step in the development of a lighting scheme or concept for any project or production.

Script Analysis and Entertainment Designs

Lighting analysis for most entertainment events comes about through a combination of several different processes. The script, if one exists, forms the first place where a designer should begin their work toward developing a lighting scheme. Other elements such as attending rehearsals and production or design meetings will also help a designer grasp the approach that a director is taking for a specific production. Rehearsals allow a designer to personally observe blocking relationships, character associations, and specific interpretations that the director has brought to a production. This additional work is intermixed with further script analysis to determine the details that will emerge and

Brian MacDevitt

Brian MacDevitt is an award-winning lighting designer who works primarily in Broadway and other commercial venues such as touring and regional theatres. He spent nearly 10 years designing in downtown Off- and Off-Off-Broadway theatres where he honed his skills before landing his first shows on Broadway. While he lights predominantly dramas, he also lights musicals, dance, and other projects. He even worked on the film *The Cradle Will Rock* as Director of Photography. Several of his more significant Broadway and other New York credits include *The Color Purple, The Pillowman, Into the Woods* (2002 Revival), and *Urinetown: The Musical.* New York theatre companies that he has designed for include Shakespeare in the Park, The Round-about, Circle Repertory, Public Theatres, Playwrights Horizons, and the Manhattan Theatre Club. Several regional credits include the Mark Taper Forum, Kennedy Center for the Performing Arts, and the Yale Repertory Theatre. His lighting designs have won a number of awards, including multiple Drama Desk nominations, a Drama Desk award, an Obie, a Bessie Award, over half a dozen Tony nominations, and three different Tony Awards for Best Lighting (*The Pillowman, Into the Woods,* and a shared award for *The Coast of Utopia*). MacDevitt also served on the faculty of SUNY Purchase and the Tisch School of Drama at New York University and is a frequent speaker at seminars like the Broadway Masters Classes.

MacDevitt's formal training came through pursuing a BFA in Lighting at Purchase College under the training of Bill Mintzer. Mintzer strove to prepare his students to enter the field after completing their BFA degree and felt that the MFA was unnecessary. Most of his training came informally through on-the-job training by assisting Mintzer and other designers like Francis Aronson. On the other hand, he didn't want to get pigeonholed as an assistant and soon broke out to design lighting on his own. He started doing projects downtown (in lower Manhattan and in the village) and used Off and Off-Off Broadway as his training ground. "A major part of my training was the downtown theatre . . . watching dance . . . understanding how to explore dream states . . . figuring out how the subconscious and unmotivated lighting could be explored through dance and other areas of lighting design." It was over this time that MacDevitt began to work with Tere O'Connor who has been one of his closest collaborative partners over the last 25 years. When he finally got his opportunity to work on Broadway he was ready for it. "It's the same thing I had been doing for 10 years . . . just a bigger audience and more production money at stake. On the other hand, Broadway gets all the resources . . . I feel spoiled now." To remain fresh he goes back to his roots and continues to light projects in small venues when he has an opportunity and where resources can be stretched, and he may even have to carry ladders around with the assistants.

Brian believes that it is important to get a good liberal arts background. "Art, music, and architecture are all important to lighting. Theatre makes use of my background in music and art history . . . they apply to every play that I do and I am thankful for my study in these other arts. However, there still has to be that association in how it fits with the theatre. While working on *American Buffalo* . . . I wanted to know about what was happening in Chicago at that time . . . the historical facts of that era . . . . I needed to understand what was meant by the term 'American Buffalo.'" MacDevitt also believes that much of a designer's work comes through the circle of associates that you keep company with. "My work comes mostly through being recommended by producers or other people that I have worked with. I want people to feel that I can light anything . . . to be comfortable in how I interpret the work and communicate it to the audience through light." He adds, "It doesn't matter what you light . . . lighting a Bar Mitzvah should have challenges to it . . . find something out about the kid and the family . . . then channel that into the room or gallery." Location also has something to do with the type of work that a designer gets. "There's even something to your address. Many theatres want to see a New York address on a designer's resume—even those outside of New York. In fact, some may even want to see a Manhattan address. I actually weighed the issue when I was trying to decide between living in Manhattan or Brooklyn."

MacDevitt considers light to be an amazing medium. "We bring and reflect energy across a stage . . . we are painters who illuminate and compose with light and bring shape and form to what already exists on a stage." He also likes the sense of control and adrenaline rush that accompanies his sitting at the design desk. "I love being in the hotseat and riding the edge . . . the burst of energy and ability to think clearly throughout a very stressful tech process. In many ways it's about being in the moment and trusting yourself. Light is an emotional medium and our profession is in many ways about instant gratification . . . something that is very different from most jobs in the real world." Something that he worries about is that he feels that at times Broadway is becoming too homogenized. "Sometimes we try too hard to second guess the audiences . . . becoming too commercial . . . catering to the ticket-paying crowd. These days, it's easy to get locked into the commercial part of the business . . . especially anything based on music. The juke box musical now seems to be the most popular formula for gaining an audience."

One of Brian's cardinal rules involves the issue of carefully paying attention to the play. "You've got to read the play . . . it's all about the play or all about the score. There's a lot of work out there that has a different agenda than serving the piece." Another pet peeve relates to his observation that its not about the gear. He believes that moving lights are starting to dictate what is happening in color palettes on Broadway and other stages . . . he wants designers to be able tell manufacturers what gear we need for the theatre rather than having to use fixtures that have been developed for other markets like rock and roll. "The equipment is dictating our choices rather than the artist making a decision based on the required qualities of light. Time is also at a premium in commercial theatre . . . you don't get invited back if you can't work within the constraints that are assigned to a show regarding crew calls and rehearsal schedules. There simply isn't time to experiment in these situations." He recommends that if you are just getting started that you err on the efficient side. "Simplify and be prepared . . . get everything that you can in place before showing up at the theatre. Good paperwork is essential and needs to be complete . . . the electricians will see right through shoddy paperwork and plots." When building cues he suggests approaching the design in the same way that a painter would work. "Start with the sky and then work forward to the performers and settings that lie in the mid-ground and then the foreground. Finally, add specials to pop out whatever has to be highlighted." Brian usually likes to light the scenery first . . . then adds in the actors and their lighting. He also takes pride in not stopping rehearsals very often to deal with lighting issues, fixing problems while the actors are working in the actual scene, especially when changing marks for moving light cues. All in all, he likes the speed and works best on the fly. In reality, many of the problems get ironed out during the previews. With the newer generation moving lights MacDevitt finds that he frequently places a half-dozen of the incandescent movers on many of his shows. These are then used in a very subtle manner to move light to where it is needed on stage—in effect using them as refocusable or momentary specials. "In many situations the moving lights need to be used in a more subtle treatment . . . using them only to pop someone out as needed."

In closing, Brian shares his attitude toward work and the associates that he has come to work with over the years. "I have reaped the rewards of being surrounded by a number of good colleagues. When there is a problem in the lighting area, I'll take the blame, if it is warranted, because I lead the area." He also believes that you can still be a "good guy" in this business—to be trusted and honest is what's important. "Don't undermine other people. I probably could have been more demanding at times, but I'd rather be known as a good guy who can pull off a successful design while still making the experience worthwhile as opposed to being someone who uses confrontation to make their points and pull off their art. I think that you get better results and cooperation when you treat people decently. The work must be fun and people need to come into it with a positive attitude . . . it's infectious, and when someone comes in with a good positive attitude, the production itself will also often do better as a result of this positive interaction."

shape the unique qualities of the show. If a script is not part of the design process a designer must concentrate even more diligently on the information that they receive through observing rehearsals, listening to soundtracks, and having conversations with the rest of the design team. Even if a performance event does not make use of an actual scripted text, you should still be able to analyze the piece since nearly all performance events follow some form of storyline or plot that can be analyzed in regard to themes, moods, characters, etc. Even modern dance pieces, which have a reputation for being abstract, have a conceptual framework and some sense of storyline that the choreographer is usually more than happy to share with their lighting designer. Since most productions begin with a script, the next several pages examine ways in which you can create a successful process for analyzing scripts.

A script analysis is nothing more then a careful study of the script. A designer must evaluate many issues relating to how the script has been crafted, and while a director interprets the script, it is the playwright who actually created the event. It should be obvious that the designer must find an understanding of the plot or storyline of the script, but in reality, the script analysis must go considerably beyond this initial treatment. A designer must also understand the characters, their associations and motivations, the themes and stylistic intentions of the playwright, and many other qualities that may not necessarily be apparent to an audience member who will most likely only view the production once. In short, this detailed understanding of the script forms the parameters that will ultimately shape the decisions that drive the designing of the production.

Most script analysis begins with an initial reading of the script. It is important to approach this first reading from the perspective of an audience member. It is the only time when you can approximate the reactions of an audience. Once you have read the script more than once, you begin to gain a familiarity with the script that the majority of your audience members cannot have. You must try to create an experience during the first reading that bests creates the same type of conditions that an audience member might experience for the play. Therefore, during the initial reading you should focus on reading the script for enjoyment. Do not be concerned with a formal script analysis or writing down any specific references to light. Try to imagine the action in a way that allows you to experience the play in a way that would be similar to how an audience might experience it. Most importantly, try to complete this initial reading in a single sitting and remove any distractions that could interrupt your reading of the play. The script isn't something to be read on a bus or subway during a daily commute or in half-hour intervals when you have a moment of spare time between other activities. Interruptions should also be minimized because they prevent you from experiencing the pace and tensions that build in the script and its associated actions.

After the initial reading, designers will read and analyze a script for more specific details during each subsequent reading. With each reading, more specific details are discovered that will be used to refine the designer's response to the text. More significant elements affecting the lighting design will be discovered in earlier readings, while it may take three, four, or even more readings to establish some of the less apparent details of a script. A fairly typical process for many lighting designers calls for reading a script three or four times. However, the actual number of times that a designer reads a script can vary considerably from one project to another and can also change based on the type of project that one is designing. Regardless of how many readings that a designer performs, each additional reading exposes more details that will lead to more effective decisions for creating a production's lighting. Several tasks often associated with a second reading involve responding to specific images that you might imagine while reading the script and creating a **scenic breakdown** that lists the locations and time frames for each scene. Sidebar 10.2 provides an example of a scenic breakdown for Arthur Miller's *The Crucible*.

Further readings require the lighting designer to look at specific references to light. The designer should identify specific staging requirements such as motivational lighting needs, lighting effects, and character associations for more specific lighting demands. Places in a script that provide such information include scene synopses, stage directions or business, and any additional notes found throughout the script that document the original production. Line references, where characters make direct mention of lighting conditions, form one of the most important clues to the specific lighting needs of a production. Some of these references may be direct, such as when a character states, "Look at that burning building over there," or when they describe a specific quality of light, "Look at the golden glow of that sunset." Other references may be inferred, such as when a character speaks of a specific lighting condition ("It's now 7 pm and I don't know where John has gone.") or when a synopsis lists a scene taking place in a particular location or geographical region, a specific type of room, or if a particular weather condition is indicated by the script. The designer should also be sensitive to the mood or emotional elements that are present throughout a script. All of these examples create conditions that provide clues to successfully light a play. The following paragraphs address several specific areas of script analysis that a lighting designer can use to get a better understanding of the lighting requirements of a given play.

GENRE   Genre is perhaps the first place to get clues to the lighting style that might be appropriate for a given script. Genre can best be understood as a broad classification of dramatic style. The genres that most people are familiar with include comedy and tragedy. Several other genres that are less familiar to a typical audience member include melodrama, farce, and musicals. Each genre reflects general stylistic elements or conventions that can be considered to be characteristic of that particular form of theatre. Through simple association with a given genre a specific production style may become an expectation of the final lighting design. A familiar association between lighting and genre that was

---

SIDEBAR 10.2 Scenic Breakdown of Arthur Miller's *The Crucible*

Scene #	Location/Time Reference	Light Reference
Act I, Scene 1	Bedroom in Parris's House Salem, Mass. Spring 1692	Dawn
Act I, Scene 2	Common Room of Proctor's House Eight Days Later	Dusk
Act II, Scene 1	The Wood Five Weeks Later	Night
Act II, Scene 2	Vestry of a Salem Meeting House Two Weeks Later	Middle of day
Act II, Scene 3	A Cell in a Salem Jail Three Months Later	Pre-Dawn

followed for many years involved using brightly illuminated scenes and pink or other warmly colored gels for lighting comedies. More serious plays such as tragedies were typically associated with dark shadowy lighting and were characteristically lit with cool colors like blues, greens, and lavenders. Genres are very broad classifications of drama, and lighting decisions should not be based solely on the specific genre of a production. To put things simply, be familiar with what these associations may mean for a lighting design and then go on to a more detailed analysis to further refine your design decisions.

THEMES   One of the most important areas of script analysis lies in an examination of the themes that a playwright chooses to address. Most importantly, what is the author's meaning of the play? The playwright was most likely trying to convey a message to an audience. What are the major themes or message of the play? Which themes are emphasized? Should one theme be played against another? Does a theme keep recurring throughout a script? These theme-related questions can have a significant impact on the lighting of a production. A director may choose to ignore an obvious theme of a script while choosing to focus on some of the more obscure themes that might also be present in a given piece. Symbolism may be used as a means of drawing attention to themes when elements of the play represent other larger concerns or problems. A designer should also look to see if any of the themes play to universal concerns. Plays often address issues such as aging, sacrifices of war, selfishness or greed, broken relationships, power and corruption, love interests, and abusive behaviors—all forming examples of universal themes. Are the themes of a play written or set in the 16th century pertinent to today's audiences? Themes form a manner in which a playwright presents a message to an audience and communicates to society. The entire design team should explore the themes as a means of aiding the playwright in delivering a message to an audience.

DRAMATIC FORM (STRUCTURE)   Plays are generally crafted in a manner that provides an organizational structure for the script. This structure creates a mechanism by which information is presented to the audience while also allowing for a logical progression of events that move the play toward its conclusion. One manner of examining a script's structure is through observing various informational events that typically occur at various points throughout the play. Most plays begin with an *exposition* in which the playwright introduces the audience to the themes, characters, and other essential information that they will need for viewing the play. The exposition often presents background information by having characters recall or talk about events that have occurred prior to the start of the play. The exposition forms a frame of reference for the play's action. Once the playwright has provided the necessary background information, they usually shift to providing the remaining information through using actual onstage action to present the event to an audience (what is frequently called the *point of attack*). We also examine a play based on its actions—both physical and emotional. The play must create some form of *conflict* in which a desire of a character may or may not be realized. We call these *objectives,* with the major dramatic conflict being the *super-objective.* What drives the action is the conflict that exists between achieving or not achieving this goal or task. Will Oedipus discover who is responsible for the plague in his kingdom? Does Godot in *Waiting for Godot* ever show up? Will a given social injustice be righted? Will the guy get the pretty girl? All of these situations form questions that can represent conflicts within a play. We may refer to these issues and actions as events that form the *dramatic spine* or *major dramatic question* of the play. Each conflict is used to draw upon an audience's inquisitiveness and to lure them into forming an interest in the play. A good play and production strives to have an audience interact with the play and have empathy for at least some of its characters. That point in the play where an audience is exposed to the major dramatic question or primary conflict is commonly called the *inciting incident.* It is at this point where the audience discovers what the play is truly about and what the major conflict of the play will become. Throughout the play, forces will work toward either achieving the primary objective or major dramatic question or preventing it from happening. The playwright then goes on to create a series of events or *actions* through which the emotional responses and tensions of an audience will vary based on how closely we come to achieving the major dramatic question. As the characters face a given conflict, the tension rises until the conflict is temporarily resolved. Then a new action and tension is introduced that will once again move toward creating further conflict within the play. We often refer to these variations in tension or emotional responses as *rising and falling action*. As a play progresses, the conflicts generally become more intense, while the overall level of tension also steadily increases. At some point, the primary conflict of the play must be resolved and the characters either achieve or do not achieve their primary objective and the dramatic question is answered. This point in the action is called the *climax* of the play. Once the play has reached its climax the tension will be lowered and the playwright will bring the play to a conclusion by wrapping up any remaining unfinished details or situations. This final portion of the play is typically known as the *resolution*. Figure 10.1 illustrates an example of the rising and falling action that might exist for a theoretical production of a script.

STYLE   Style relates to the overall manner of presentation for a production. In reality, the style of a production comes about through the combination of a number of individual elements. The acting, directing, and visual styles are several of the primary elements that contribute to the overall sense of style for a production. It is also important for each of the individual styles to reinforce all the other elements of a production. One common method of examining style is based on the concept of realism, and we often use the degree of realism as a means of comparing one production to another. An extreme form of realism, **naturalism,** attempts to present an event in as realistic a manner as possible—down to the last detail in materials, speech patterns, acting styles, etc. On the other hand, as you move in the opposite direction from naturalism, style becomes more simplified and symbolic, becoming more **stylized** or abstract. In this manner, elements of a production are modified in ways that move away from a realistic mode of representation. In

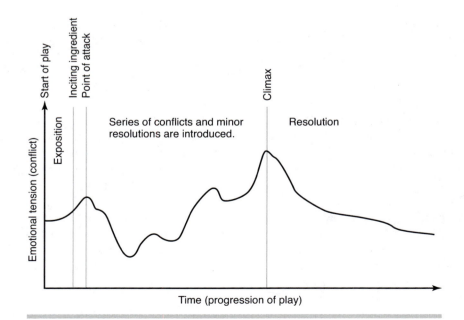

FIGURE 10.1 Rising and Falling Action This graph plots the emotional tension (conflict) through a series of dramatic events. The actual conflicts are theoretical and only illustrate the overall relationship between conflict and a play's structure.

some cases, the images and overall style can become quite distorted. The artistic movements that were represented by schools such as impressionism, expressionism, and surrealism along with many others were nothing more than a group of artists who agreed to work within a given set of parameters of style. Because of this, their work shares a set of similarities or conventions. We may also look at **period style** as a manner of establishing or placing a production within a specific time frame. For instance, if we were to suggest that a production be set in the Renaissance, the director would look at Renaissance acting styles, while the designers would look at the clothing and architecture of that period for inspiration and historical research. A lighting designer would examine light sources of that time and how productions would have been lit in that era. One of the primary tasks of a director is making sure that there is a consistent style being presented between each of the different elements of a production.

There are many places where a lighting designer can use the script as a resource for determining the overall style for a specific production. Scripts written in verse or rhyme suggest a different approach to presentation than those written in prose. Using a narrator requires a different approach than a script where all the information is presented through the characters. What is the progression from scene to scene? Do scenes progress in chronological order or are there flashback conventions used throughout the script? Are there ritualistic or symbolic elements within the text? How are these to be presented? All of these issues have an impact on the overall style that would be used to illustrate a script. While several broad elements of style may be determined through the general type or genre of script, most scripts can be produced through a variety of different styles, and the director has the responsibility for determining the overall style for a given production. Shakespeare's plays form great examples of where many different stylistic approaches have been used successfully for the production of a given script. A designer should also look beyond the script to other productions of the play, as well as to other scripts that have been produced or written by the same playwright, since these plays often make use of similar styles. Style relates very closely to convention, the next form of analysis, because conventions form the rules by which a team agrees to present a production—with many of these rules ultimately determining the overall style of a production.

CONVENTIONS   Every play creates a series of experiences that expose an audience to an event created by a playwright. An audience views these experiences and becomes accepting of various techniques or conventions used by the playwright and production team in order to make the presentation of the event possible. In short, **conventions** are methods that allow the team to present the story to an audience. Using a narrator to describe events that are not re-enacted for the audience, using simultaneous scenes on stage at the same time, or using blue lights for scene changes or to simulate night all form examples of common conventions that audiences are willing to accept as a normal part of a theatrical event. How might time progression be illustrated within the production? How does a team solve the logistical problem of creating all the scenes required for a production when time, space, and money are in short supply? Different styles of production can often be associated with the use of specific conventions. For instance, most Shakespearean productions make use of *aside* techniques (where an actor comes to the edge of the stage and directly addresses the audience). A lighting designer will often place a special light on the actor during the time that an aside is delivered. Both conventions are widely accepted techniques for the production of these plays. Another popular lighting convention is to create a blackout between adjoining scenes. While there are a number of conventions that can be associated with the specific work of various playwrights or groups of productions, what is more important is that a production remain consistent in those conventions that are adopted throughout its presentation. The conventions form a set of ground rules or parameters within which both the creative team and audience agree to work. Making exceptions or not sticking to the conventions can often create confusion on the part of the audience.

CHARACTERS   Other than the major dramatic question, the characters are probably the next most important element of a play or performance event. Designers need to have a thorough understanding of each character, their motivations, and their relationships between other characters in a play. It's their struggles, conflicts, and relationships that the audience follows and it is the characters with whom the audience will develop a relationship of either empathy or hate. Is this character controlling another? What is the personal relationship between the two characters? Does this character belong to a larger group of characters? Which character is most important at any given moment? Why does this character appear in a play? What is their dramatic function? What's this character's motivation? A designer should also develop an understanding of the personality traits of each character. Are they a slob? Are they a flirt? Are they the favorite or least favorite child of the parents? Are they soft spoken? Should the audience like or dislike this character? Should we feel empathy for this character? If not, who should we feel empathy toward? Much of this information can be gathered through what is said in the dialogue of the play and the specific situations that the characters face. Even if unique character traits are not specifically expressed in the script, it is often helpful to create your own background information for the characters, as long as the information is consistent with the material already presented in the script. By creating a full history for the characters, designers can go on to use this information on *character development* as a means of approaching specific design decisions. One character may become associated with a softer or more romantic quality of lighting while another may be tied to a particular tint of color. Characters that bring conflict to a scene might be connected to a harsher, more intense form of lighting, while some roles might be identified with a particular group of characters and a specific color or mood that is shaped by the lighting. The character analysis provides a context for the design and decision-making process.

MOOD   Plays often create a specific emotional response in an audience. While there may be an overall general mood or response to the play as a whole, it is also true that the mood of an audience will change throughout a play. The mood may even change several times in a single scene. You can often find an association between the individual conflicts of a play and the moods that are created throughout the play. If a play is based in comedy, the mood will generally be light and airy. The lighting and other design areas will respond to this by creating designs that produce appropriate moods for specific times throughout the production. The dark, foreboding shadows that a lighting designer might produce for the final crypt scene of *Dracula* produces an appropriate atmosphere or mood for this particular scene. On the other hand, these qualities would most likely be inappropriate for the comedy scene mentioned earlier. A lighting designer must be able to identify the situations in the script that are associated with these emotional changes and needs to manipulate the lighting in a manner that reinforces these qualities. While some mood changes may be abrupt, many are subtle, and the lighting designer must learn to modify the lighting in a manner that gently enhances these changes without necessarily calling attention to the fact that a change has been made in the lighting.

SPECIFIC REQUIREMENTS   While I have chosen to leave specific requirements for last, they probably form the easiest area of analysis for a lighting designer and are often the first area of script analysis that a lighting designer might complete. Specific requirements are nothing more than the lighting requirements that are actually specified by the script. This may be done through either a direct or inferred reference to the lighting. Much of this area of analysis is presented later in this chapter through the discussion of **motivated** and **non-motivated lighting.** The most obvious examples are specific lighting needs that are named directly by the script. A synopsis or stage direction that describes the lighting or a specific reference to lighting in a line stated by a character form the most common examples of these demands. When a character refers to the "golden color of the sun," or the "broken patterns of light cast by an overhead tree," the lighting must reflect these qualities. Action may also dictate specific lighting changes. When a character turns on a lamp or opens a window shade, the lighting needs to respond to these changes. Not quite as easy to spot, but just as important, are those lighting qualities that are inferred by a script. The lighting of a scene that takes place in mid-July is quite different from the same scene taking place in November. Time of day and season play an enormous role in the lighting of a scene. Weather conditions form an example of inferred lighting and geographical location indicates yet another area of inferred references that play a significant role in lighting a scene. Is the scene set in London or Los Angeles? What happens if we set the location in Panama? How might we differentiate between interior and exterior scenes? What are the light sources in the scene? Is there a characteristic image of light associated with the environment in which a scene takes place? How does the lighting for a hospital room, Gothic church, or manufacturing facility differ from one another? All of these form specific demands that a lighting designer must consider as they design a given project.

In summary, the script forms the basic blueprint of the dramatic event and is the first place a lighting designer should explore the lighting requirements of a production. While there may be direct references to lighting within a script, much of what a designer needs to know is not immediately recognized and must be gleaned through multiple readings and a more detailed analysis of the script. Many times these less obvious details don't come into focus until after further discussions with the director or direct observations of the actors in rehearsals. The principles of analysis discussed over the last several pages hold true not only for plays that make use of scripts, but for any event that uses some form of written text—the scores and librettos of musical theatre and operas are texts that can be analyzed like a script. Even if no text or script exists, most performance events tell some form of story and can be analyzed in a manner that is similar to what has been outlined over the last several pages. Ballet and even short modern dance pieces are good examples of this visual form of storytelling, in which a designer's analysis will not be based on a written text. With experience, one can become familiar with how each of these events is analyzed, ultimately leading a designer to more effective designs.

STYLE IN LIGHTING

Even though style forms a specific function of lighting it is especially important to understand style as a guiding principle in determining the overall image for a project. Style on the whole relates to combining visual elements that produce a characteristic quality for the production or project. Style is something that is determined through discussions with the entire production team and not something that a lighting designer should develop on their own. We may also use style as a means of comparing and contrasting one project with another. The previous section spoke to a number of variants that are used to define the style of a production: degree of realism, themes, genre, structure of a play, etc. All of these have an impact on the overall style of both the lighting and any other components of a performance event. Are we simplifying our image so that it only contains those elements that are absolutely essential to the action? Is historical accuracy important to the piece? Should there be a limited color palette? How are the traditional elements of design (line, form, texture, etc.) characterized? All of these questions form examples of issues that will help the lighting designer and other members of the design team define the style for a given project. Each of the designers and the director need to share a common definition of a show's production style in order to create the **unified production** that produces a successful project—each element reinforcing all the other elements of a production.

In addition to the overall visual style, lighting design can also be broadly characterized by two specific types of lighting style. These can work within any other style that might be used for a particular project. The first, **motivational lighting,** seeks to anchor the lighting in a realistic element. As a rule, it has a naturalistic quality and attempts to approach the lighting from a perspective that represents how the light would appear if coming from a natural light source. Luminaires are linked to actual objects such as sunlight, an overhead chandelier, or a fire effect, and the resulting lighting is suggestive of how these sources are observed naturally. Colors, highlights, shadows, and any movement would be based on the natural occurrences of these light sources, and the lighting should appear to be created or driven by these sources. A special form of this lighting is represented by those occasions when the light sources can actually be observed on stage. These are known as **motivating sources** or **motivating light,** and several common examples include placing candles or lanterns on stage, having actors use flashlights, locating a fire somewhere within a setting, and placing lighting fixtures such as wall sconces, table lamps, or chandeliers directly on a set. While these sources are in plain view, motivational lighting does not necessarily require an observer to actually see the light source. In these cases, the lighting may simply give the appearance of coming from a particular source without actually revealing the source itself on stage. This is called **motivated lighting** and is represented by examples like sunlight streaming through a doorway or window, a room being lit from above despite the lack of an overhead fixture like a chandelier, or a field being lit by the sun that has been located somewhere behind the audience from the rear of the auditorium.

Motivated lighting may also be used to reinforce any motivating light sources that are present in a given setting. This is common since many motivating light sources either are too weak to produce a level of illumination required to light a theatrical scene on their own or produce too much glare as a concentrated light source when lit as part of a stage composition. I always take several precautions when I use **practicals** (working light sources) on stage. First, I assign the practical fixtures to a dimmer so that I can control the brightness and glare of the source. I also often replace the fixture's lamp(s) with one(s) of relatively small wattages as a further means of not only avoiding glare but also of providing a larger range of control through the dimmer (higher wattage lamps at very low intensity settings have a tendency to flicker at levels below 10–15%). The independent dimmer assignment also allows me to control the light through the console, making it less difficult to coordinate actions with any performers who are required to turn the associated lights on or off. If at all possible, it is always better to create a system where the performers only mimic any changes to the practicals or light switches on a stage. This setup also prevents the problems associated with tracking whether a switch's position is on or off at any specific point in a performance and should eliminate the need for resetting switches between scenes or act breaks. Most importantly, I add stage luminaires as a form of **accent lighting** that supplement the practicals that are seen on the stage. These luminaires provide the light that is actually required for producing the effect of the practicals and are hung in a way that suggests that the light is actually coming from the practical light sources. Through these techniques, light can be made to appear as if it is coming from the practicals while at the same time avoiding the drawbacks of using the actual sources alone to create this illusion.

Finally, there may also be **non-motivated lighting** where the lighting is not tied to an apparent light source at all. In this case, the lighting is based on an emotional response, mood, or symbolic element of the play and the designer isn't overly concerned with producing a realistic response in the design. Instead, the lighting is approached more from a thematic or symbolic basis. The lighting observed during most pop concerts or frequently associated with events like Cirque du Soleil productions, in which the production is clearly presentational or contains a high degree of spectacle, form good examples of this non-motivated lighting style. In reality, just as there are degrees of realism, there are also extremes at which lighting may exist between motivated and non-motivated lighting styles. A designer may even begin a lighting scheme based on a motivated design approach that eventually becomes exaggerated and shifts to a more abstract non-motivated variation of the initial style.

CONCEPTUALIZATION

Conceptualization relates to an approach to a design problem. Issues such as style, themes, and overall framework of a production are determined through conceptualization. In the entertainment world, the person in overall charge of the project is typically a director who is responsible for guiding the team through the conceptualization process. Initially, the director presents a series of guidelines or personal interpretations of the script or event, which are then used to shape each of the other team members' contributions to the production. Often this is presented through a statement known as a **director's concept** where issues such as themes and meaning, character analysis and associations, placement of the time and locale of the production, and a specific interpretation of the script are presented. The degree of realism or amount of stylization or abstraction and any symbolism within a production will also be considered in most directors' concepts. Production teams may also make use of **metaphors** as a manner of representing specific meanings within a script—a metaphor being a figure of speech in which an object or series of words are used figuratively to represent or make comparisons or create meanings between various objects.

The **concept** forms a series of parameters or conditions through which the team explores and answers specific production demands for a project. Simply put, the concept gives the context for which all other elements of the production are shaped and becomes an approach to a production. As an example of working with a concept, consider a director who might wish to equate the character of Juliet in a production of *Romeo and Juliet* with an association of light. Light could be thought of as a metaphor for truth or knowledge or as a symbol of innocence and first love. Regardless of personal interpretation, each of the members of the design team would search for manners to associate Juliet with the element of light. A scenic designer might provide scenes in which she is featured with structures that reinforce natural lighting conditions, even to the point of working practical light sources such as torches, firelight, or lanterns into Juliet's scenes. The scenic designer might also introduce warm color tones into those scenes in which Juliet plays a significant role. A costume designer could clothe her in colors that are suggestive of flame or fire, while the lighting designer could tint all of her scenes with warm light. The lighting designer might go even further and could place her in specials that are gelled in pink, orange, or yellow colored light. If the design team remains true to the director's approach or concept, each member forms an individual design concept that reinforces the director's concept, which in turn should produce a unified project. All individual design decisions should then be examined and based upon information that supports the design concept.

ADDITIONAL PREPARATION

While it is important to understand the script, score, or written text and underlying needs and principles of a particular design, there are a number of additional areas that a designer should also explore as they create the lighting scheme or concept for a given project. Even though the script forms the basis of the design, it by no means should be the only source of input for a design. Discussions with other members of the design team, rehearsals, and design research are additional areas where further analysis is required for completing a successful design.

Design Research

Research is an important element of the design process and is most commonly displayed through developing some form of visual research for a project. Verbal descriptions or examples of lighting can be used but may cause confusion and can often be misunderstood. This can lead to unwanted surprises as it becomes apparent that the director and designer have had a different understanding of the lighting. The best way to get an accurate response and understanding between a designer and the rest of the production team is to expose them to a number of examples of visual research. By doing this, the designer will not only be able to identify their personal preferences for a design, but will also be able to narrow down specific choices with a director as comparisons are made between different images. Photographs or illustrations of similar productions, examples of art for visual inspiration, or even technical data all form different areas of research that should be explored each time a designer approaches a new assignment. Visual research is especially important for providing examples of an intended lighting effect. Important information can also be learned through carefully listening to the responses that a director makes to a particular visual reference. The old familiar saying, "A picture is worth a thousand words," is especially appropriate for lighting design since conversations often leave plenty of room for misinterpretation and we rarely have the means to illustrate or experiment with our choices in actual light. These visual illustrations form one concrete manner of communicating our intentions to a director while also providing a sampling of our design analysis for a production.

VISUAL REFERENCES   Visual references form the most important area of research that a lighting designer can provide to a director or client. In an area where verbal communication can lead to bad communication, a photograph can provide a clear picture of an intended lighting condition. While it is rare that a single visual source will reflect the exact qualities that a designer may want to bring to a specific project, the reference still provides an opportunity that allows the director and designer to talk about the lighting in a more tangible manner than through only describing a mental image of light. More importantly, through comparing images, a director and designer can come to a common understanding of the specific look that the designer envisions for a particular scene or moment. Paintings, photographs, sketches, films, and videos all form examples of sources that a designer may explore for specific images of light. It is common for me to present numerous images to a director, which we then use as a means of sorting out what qualities of light they think would be most appropriate for a given moment, scene, or overall image for a play. Directors can also contribute to the process by providing their own examples of visual research for a lighting designer. When I lit a recent Off-Broadway production of *The Maids*, the director asked me to become familiar with images of the film noir style. These were black and white films produced in the 1940s and '50s whose lighting made use of a rather harsh quality, strong contrasts, well-defined shadows, and up-light as common lighting qualities. Films such as *The Third Man, Double Indemnity,* and *The Big Sleep* were films that the director asked me to look at prior to our first meeting. Visual references are not only good for communicating ideas to the rest of the design team but also for exposing a designer to a variety of images that can serve as inspirational images for a design. These images can then be used to help discover appropriate choices that might influence or be incorporated into a final design.

PERIOD RESEARCH   Period research simply relates to examining a project within the context of the time period in which the event is to be set. If a play is to be set at night in a Depression-era farm house, the interior lighting would most likely reflect the qualities of kerosene lanterns. If the setting is changed to nighttime in ancient Greece; the lighting designer will need to become familiar with the torchlight that these plays would have been presented under. I once designed a production that was based on a historical presentation of the ancient Kuttiyattum rituals that are traditionally performed as the temple dramas of India. These productions are typically performed only in temples under a single light source in the form of an oil lamp that is placed on the floor at the extreme down center location of the stage. The lamp is also lit and extinguished as part of the ritual of the performance. Therefore, the lighting for the production had to appear as if it was tied to this motivational light source. While the most common form of historical research relates to identifying how the light may have appeared or been created for a given time period, there are other elements of period research that a lighting designer should also consider when lighting a project. What were the performance conventions for a given time period? Were chandeliers hoisted into place at the beginning of a performance? What were the conventions for illustrating nighttime? Does the play fit within a period that dictates a given style of presentation (e.g., the demands of an expressionistic play versus a realistic play)? How does this play relate to other plays that have been written by the playwright or others of a given era? All of these form examples of when period research should play a significant role in the design process.

TECHNICAL RESEARCH   Most designers conduct technical research as a way of facilitating the practical decisions of translating a lighting concept into an actual design. The most common form of technical research is going to the product literature while making selections of the actual luminaires that will be used throughout a design. **Cut sheets** are used to identify specific lighting instruments with optical qualities that will match the requirements of a particular concept. Issues such as quality of light, beam distribution, luminaire output, and throw distances are easily compared from one unit to another by using these materials. If a designer does not have a particular binder containing the specific cut sheets for the fixtures that are under consideration for an application, the information can still be obtained in a variety of other ways. Single cut sheets can be obtained through a request to a lighting distributor or manufacturer but more often are now readily available directly from a manufacturer's Web site. There are also specialized references such as Robert Mumm's *Photometrics Handbook* or John McKernon's *Beamwright* software that provide comparative data for luminaires from different manufacturers. In both cases, the data is presented in a common format that allows easy comparisons to be made between different luminaires. Reference literature and materials are also not limited to the luminaires themselves—information is also available for dimmer specifications, lighting consoles and control equipment, gel, and even wire and other electrical hardware. There is also not only specification literature but application guidelines, testimonials, safety information, data studies, and a host of other reference materials available to help a designer throughout the design process.

In addition to researching specific lighting equipment a designer must also conduct research in regard to the physical characteristics of a venue that they will be mounting a design within. Most facilities that are a home to a production organization or function as a road or touring house have a standard informational packet that provides floorplans, sections, and other critical information that a designer will need to know in regard to designing in that venue. Today, many organizations have this information posted on their facility's Web site. In addition to the master plans, hanging positions, number and location of in-house circuits, lineset schedules, and the dimming and control equipment available form several of the more obvious areas in which a lighting designer needs to gain important information about a particular performance facility. Just a few of the additional technical areas that should be examined include the power and company switches available, any in-house lighting inventory, arbor capacities, crewing requirements, budget, and loading access to the venue.

Design and Production Meetings

Design meetings and **production meetings** form some of the most important opportunities for a lighting designer to gather information that will shape the design of a project. These meetings are attended by all of the principle individuals who are involved in a project. Design meetings occur fairly early in the process and form an opportunity for the entire design team to share and discuss a project. While a director is generally responsible for facilitating the meeting, each individual designer is expected to bring something to the table. Other designers will present renderings, sketches, plans, or even models to communicate their design intentions to the rest of the production team. A lighting designer is often more reactive during these presentations since other parts of a project must generally be agreed on prior to determining how to light the project. However, the lighting designer should still respond to these designs and must feel free to become an active participant in the discussions. They should add to the collaborative effort by expressing their ideas and concerns while providing insight into how the lighting might impact the other designs. Once farther along, these meetings form a place where a lighting designer can share their ideas for lighting a project through making presentations that illustrate their personal research and design intentions. These meetings are critical for developing an understanding of the visual representation of a project. The overall concept, along with the individual design concepts for each area, form a primary area of discussion during these meetings. More importantly, issues related to unity and how the individual production components fit together as a whole become major objectives of these meetings. Although design and production meetings bring all of the individual collaborators together, these meetings cannot replace additional one-on-one discussions between the director and other designers.

Production meetings follow design meetings and are generally more concerned with the practical elements of mounting a production. While topics related to artistic concerns may come into these discussions, the majority of these meetings are concerned with the logistics of getting a project up and running. Scheduling, practical issues related to working out details between production areas, and progress reports form typical concerns that are addressed during these meetings. Production meetings occur much closer to the completion of a project and are frequently scheduled on a weekly basis. Design meetings are scheduled on a more irregular basis much earlier in the production process. Often, several weeks are allowed between design meetings to give designers time to work on designing their specific elements of the project. In most cases, design meetings are completed and the designs are finalized before a project moves into actual production. After that, the team shifts to conducting regular production meetings.

Rehearsals

Rehearsals are another important opportunity for a lighting designer to gain a more in-depth understanding of a play. It is through rehearsals that a designer can directly observe actor movements and blocking, methods of line delivery, and specific staging that a director has chosen for a play. Rehearsals also allow a designer to gain an understanding of the moods, focus, pace, and transitions that a director is developing for a piece. On the whole, the more rehearsals that a lighting designer can observe, the more prepared that they will be for lighting a production. However, to be truly efficient some rehearsals are much more productive for a lighting designer to observe than others. As a rule, *working rehearsals* are not productive for a designer and should generally be avoided. It does a designer no good to spend an entire rehearsal watching a director work and rework the same three pages of a script over and over. It's not only a waste of a designer's time, but can also lead to confusion in how the final version of the staging was set or locked-in. Instead, a lighting designer is much better served by attending **run-through** rehearsals in which a segment of the play is run from beginning to end without interruption. A run-through doesn't necessarily require that the entire play be run but might involve the rehearsal of an entire act, several adjoining scenes, or even a single scene. Designers should understand that it is a luxury to observe actors working on the actual set or within the theatre where a production will be mounted. While many universities can provide this experience, most professional situations operate using the more economical practice of minimizing the time in which the actual theatre is made available to a new production. This is due to the simple fact that every day of renting a theatre without a paying audience means lost income to a production organization. In most cases, rehearsals are conducted in rehearsal halls and studios where rental fees are substantially lower than those of a theatre. The traditional practice is not to move into the theatre until just before the first technical rehearsal.

While university theatres typically have an open rehearsal policy where a designer may come and go as often as desired, this frequently isn't the case in commercial theatre operations. Even though directors are happy to have a designer at as many rehearsals as possible, economics generally prevents this from happening. This is especially true when a designer is being brought in from out of town. There just isn't money to pay for the transportation and other related costs of putting up a designer for many days outside of the time that they are actually required to be in residence for the technical and dress rehearsals as well as the preview performances. Due to this, a lighting designer must develop a method of recording the rehearsal information that they will later need to create the light plot and other materials related to a lighting design. This must also be done in as fast and efficient of a manner as possible. Directors will not stop a rehearsal to repeat a segment of action or to respond to a question posed by a designer. Personally, I am often brought in to observe only one or two, if that many, run-throughs prior to moving the lights into a theatre. Often, I have had to develop the light plot without seeing a run-through at all. In this case, I have to rely very heavily on my personal script analysis, research, and the conversations that I have had with the director and other members of the production team.

I have used a number of different manners of documenting rehearsals over the years but have found that the two most effective techniques are relatively simple. Both provide me with the information that I will later need to reconstruct the events or actions of the production as I work through the design somewhere away from the rehearsal hall or theatre. Video often provides one of the easiest means of recording the movements of the performers and documenting these rehearsals. When I have designed for dance while being located away from rehearsals I have often been mailed a video copy of the ballet or other pieces to be performed for a given production. This allows me to get the information that I require even though I could not be brought in to observe the actual rehearsals. This also provides a complete record of the event and can be very useful not only for keeping track of the movement patterns but also the transitions and mood changes that exist throughout a piece. The biggest disadvantage with using recording techniques is that it may be difficult to locate specific moments in a piece, which means that the information isn't immediately accessible. You must also have the video gear around to gain access to this information (e.g, How many video recorders have you seen at a design table?).

A second technique that I use for documenting rehearsals is based on a variation of dance or blocking **notation** that produces floorplan sketches of a scene while forming a record of the movement patterns of the performers. This manner isn't much different from the method in which the blocking might be recorded in a prompt script by a stage manager. A method that works particularly well for me involves dividing a page in half vertically while going on to create six to eight floorplan sketches of a scene on each side of the page. Room is left between each sketch for written notations that will also be made in regard to the blocking. As I observe a rehearsal, all major actor movements are sketched on the floorplans through lines and arrows that document the blocking while also giving me an understanding of the physical location of each of the principle characters for every moment of the play. Principle characters are generally indicated in their location by a letter within a circle that indicates the initial of the characters name. Secondary characters or extras are simply marked with an "x" as a means of documenting the stage picture. If a sequence of movement patterns occur within a single image, numbers will be added to indicate the progression of events. The page number(s) of the script that correspond to each major composition are recorded to the left of each image and additional details may be noted just below each diagram. Figure 10.2 illustrates this notation. While you don't have the complete record of a rehearsal that a video can produce, this method forms

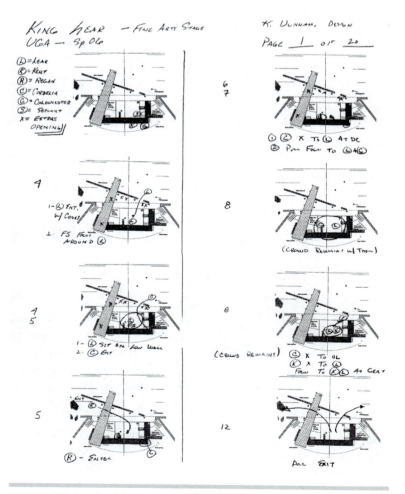

FIGURE 10.2 Blocking Notation for Lighting Design A page of notation from a production of *King Lear*.

an excellent method of documenting the primary compositional moments of the play. When working through the notation later to write a cue synopsis or when actually working on the cues in the theatre, this method allows specific moments of the play to be quickly identified. It also provides a direct reference to the corresponding script. The system is especially useful for productions such as musicals where the stage composition undergoes frequent changes. It is a technique that will take practice, but with time, most designers perfect the technique and become ever more proficient at recording the movements of the performers. In most cases, I can get a solid record of most, if not all, of the performer movements during a single run-through—even complex dance or musical pieces.

DEVELOPING LIGHTING SCHEMES AND CONCEPTS

A **lighting scheme** or **lighting concept** is nothing more than a specific approach to a lighting project or problem. Lighting schemes tend to be associated with architectural projects, while lighting concepts tend to be connected to performance or entertainment-related events. Once an overall concept has been developed for a project, the lighting designer will go on to develop the specific lighting concept for their design. This is discovered through a more detailed analysis of the play, observing rehearsals, and having in-depth discussions with the director and other team members. The lighting concept should be based on the overall production concept while going on to outline the particular manner in which the transitions and individual scenes will be lit by the designer. A general discussion of the qualities of light for the major moments or scenes should form the most significant portion of a lighting concept. What is the overall lighting style? What's the mood? Is it realistic? Where are we geographically? What time of day is it? What season is it? What's the weather like? If the lighting is motivational, what are the light sources? If not, what is driving the lighting? Are there symbolic connections to be expressed through the lighting? How are transitions managed? What lighting conventions will be established for this production? These all form specific considerations that a lighting concept should address. At this point in the process, individual lighting qualities should be described visually rather than becoming overly technical. This is not the place to discuss whether a luminaire is gelled with an R-83 or L-120. Instead, reference should be made to a deep blue color for the light. The lighting concept represents an approach for lighting a project and once completed will be used as a point of reference for the designer to work from while actually designing the lighting and making specific selections of fixtures, colors, and hanging positions. Every lighting project, whether for an entertainment event or permanent installation, should make use of a lighting concept for providing guiding principles for the realization of the design. Projects that have weak concepts are frequently not as successful as those projects in which a carefully considered scheme or concept has been utilized.

LIGHTING KEYS

One of the first concrete decisions that a lighting designer often makes in regard to a lighting design can usually be traced to creating some form of **lighting key.** A lighting key is a visual representation of the primary lighting angles and colors that would be used as an overall scheme for lighting a scene or project. A typical lighting key presents a plan view from directly above a central point that represents a performer or subject. This reference point is generally indicated with a hatch mark. Directional arrows are then drawn around this point to indicate the directions from which light will be focused onto the subject. A designer will also make an indication of the colors of the lights that will be coming from each of these angles. This color may be expressed in terms of a general hue or color description but is more commonly indicated by a specific color of gel (by gel number). In some cases, designers may go further and might also indicate an approximate intensity level (by percent) for the light coming from each direction. Figure 10.3. illustrates two different lighting keys. These keys are representative of the basic **washes** that strike a subject

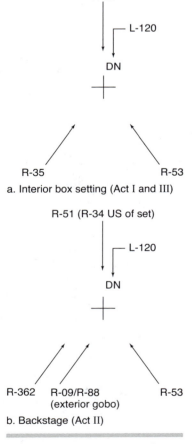

FIGURE 10.3 Color Keys for a Production of *Noises Off*

and should not be thought of as an indication of individual luminaires. The actual choices of angle and color that are used in a lighting key should be directly related to the lighting concept that was developed earlier. While the most common view associated with lighting keys is from above, I have found that the technique may be expanded to include two sectional views that provide additional views of the subject from the front and side. In a situation where there is a single overall lighting scheme, such as what might occur in a single setting where there are no significant lighting changes, the lighting key is illustrated through a single diagram. On the other hand, in a production with multiple scenes, where there are several lighting schemes, a different lighting key may be developed for each scene or significant **moment** of the show. A moment represents a single point in time where all of the elements of a stage image are frozen or recorded—much like taking a snapshot of the stage composition. Another common technique involves providing a general or overall composite lighting key for an entire production rather than creating lighting keys for each scene or crucial moment. It is not necessary to create a lighting key for every moment; the gaps and transitions between these moments are dealt with at a much later time.

The lighting keys become important elements for guiding the designer through the process of creating the light plot—the next step in the design process. Everything related to the lighting and its design ultimately should begin with this vision of light. Even if a lighting key is not formally represented on a piece of paper the lighting designer should have completed the process of creating the lighting key in their mind. This approach to lighting design is significantly different from earlier approaches in which basic illumination was developed through a couple of set formulas or techniques and then modified for the needs of an individual production. What is important at this stage is that the designer has a strong image for guiding the rest of the design process.

COMMUNICATING DESIGN IDEAS

The majority of this chapter has focused on a number of ways in which a lighting designer analyzes a design problem and works through the process of determining a specific image of light for a project. This design may remain static but more often is dynamic and can change many times over a given period of time. Regardless of whether a project remains dynamic or static, each image relates to a specific combination of lighting qualities that the designer believes best represents or enhances the needs of a production at any given time. Even with the best analysis and concept, a design may still fail due to a designer either not being able to realize or produce the intended image(s) or through not successfully communicating the proposed lighting to the other collaborators. Although the following methods are best known for communicating a lighting designer's intentions to the rest of the design team, they can also be used by the lighting designer themselves as a tool for discovering and specifically defining the qualities of light associated with particular moments of a play. Again, it must be emphasized that communicating lighting intentions through any other means than actual light increases the chance for miscommunication of the design idea.

Storyboards

Storyboards are pictorial representations of all the stage components, including the lighting, for a specific moment of a production. These images are based on a perspective sketch of the stage and often take on qualities that are similar to a miniature rendering. A typical format for a storyboard is between a 4" × 6" to 8½" × 11" in size. The images may be produced in full color but can also be represented by simple black and white value studies. In the latter case, white represents light while black and the grays represent shadow areas and surfaces and textures as illuminated by the light. Common media for creating storyboards include pastels and colored pencils with which light can be quickly rendered without much need for elaborate proficiency with the media. Markers may also be used for producing storyboards. While some designers may use white paper as a base for their storyboards many lighting designers tend to prefer to use black paper or illustration board because of the increased theatricality represented by the negative space. In this case, each line or shaded area can be equated to an illustration of actual light as it strikes and reveals an object. The lighting key is used as a resource for determining the specific lighting qualities that are reflected in a storyboard. It is common for lighting designers to produce a collection of storyboards for several of the most significant moments of a production. Figure 10.4 illustrates two storyboards that were done for two different scenes for a

a. Cliff's apartment

b. Finale

FIGURE 10.4 Lighting Storyboards for Music Theatre North's Production of *Cabaret*

production of *Cabaret*. Variations of this technique make use of computer software like PhotoShop to create storyboards. In this case, digital photographs are taken of the scenic model (or the renderings are scanned), which are then manipulated to produce electronic storyboards that can be printed or e-mailed to members of the production team.

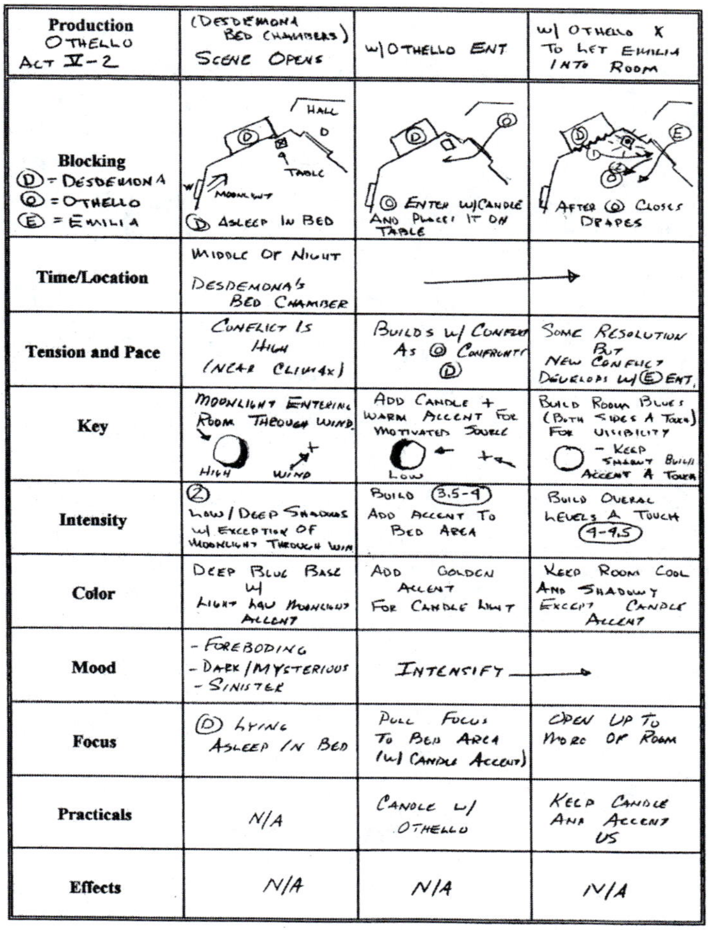

Production OTHELLO ACT V-2	(DESDEMONA BED CHAMBERS) SCENE OPENS	W/ OTHELLO ENT	W/ OTHELLO X TO LET EMILIA INTO ROOM
Blocking Ⓓ = DESDEMONA Ⓞ = OTHELLO Ⓔ = EMILIA	HALL, D, TABLE, W/, MOONLIGHT; Ⓓ ASLEEP IN BED	Ⓞ ENTER W/ CANDLE AND PLACES IT ON TABLE	AFTER Ⓞ CLOSES DRAPES
Time/Location	MIDDLE OF NIGHT DESDEMONA'S BED CHAMBER	→	
Tension and Pace	CONFLICT IS HIGH (NEAR CLIMAX)	BUILDS W/ CONFLICT AS Ⓞ CONFRONTS Ⓓ	SOME RESOLUTION BUT NEW CONFLICT DEVELOPS W/ Ⓔ ENT.
Key	MOONLIGHT ENTERING ROOM THROUGH WIND. HIGH WIND	ADD CANDLE + WARM ACCENT FOR MOTIVATED SOURCE LOW	BUILD ROOM BLUES (BOTH SIDES A TOUCH) FOR VISIBILITY - KEEP SHADOWY BUILD ACCENT A TOUCH
Intensity	② LOW / DEEP SHADOWS W/ EXCEPTION OF MOONLIGHT THROUGH WIN	BUILD (3.5-4) ADD ACCENT TO BED AREA	BUILD OVERAL LEVELS A TOUCH (4-4.5)
Color	DEEP BLUE BASE W/ LIGHT LAV MOONLIGHT ACCENT	ADD GOLDEN ACCENT FOR CANDLE LIGHT	KEEP ROOM COOL AND SHADOWY EXCEPT CANDLE ACCENT
Mood	- FOREBODING - DARK / MYSTERIOUS - SINISTER	INTENSIFY →	
Focus	Ⓓ LYING ASLEEP IN BED	PULL FOCUS TO BED AREA (W/ CANDLE ACCENT)	OPEN UP TO MORE OF ROOM
Practicals	N/A	CANDLE W/ OTHELLO	KEEP CANDLE AND ACCENT US
Effects	N/A	N/A	N/A

FIGURE 10.5 A Lighting Score This score plots the first few moments of Act V, Scene 2 of *Othello,* in which Othello murders Desdemona. Each column represents a new moment, while the rows provide specific information regarding each moment and their associated qualities of light.

Lighting Scores

While storyboards require a lighting designer to be more proficient at drawing and rendering, there are alternate ways of communicating your design intentions for those who consider themselves challenged in traditional artistic skills. For these designers, one method of working around this is to spend time developing a single good line drawing of the image, which is then photocopied onto a number of individual pages (including black construction paper). These are then used as a base drawing upon which the lighting is added. By using this technique, much of the time (and angst) involved in drawing and redrawing the scene are eliminated, and the lighting designer can both experiment and churn out a number of storyboards, discarding those that they feel aren't successful. As an alternative, **lighting scores** may provide an avenue where a lighting designer can communicate the specific lighting qualities found on stage at any moment while avoiding the need to become proficient in the use of art media. A lighting score (Figure 10.5) is best represented in a table format and lists specific moments or scenes along one axis while associated lighting functions and properties are identified and characterized along the opposing axis. Several functions that are commonly found in a lighting score include time of day, physical setting, sources, intensity, focus, primary light source or key, and mood. Many of these qualities, such as intensity or key, may be represented with a simple visual representation or diagram.

Light Labs

Light labs can be created in either a full or miniature representation of the lighting for a stage. Most university theatres have some form of light lab where luminaires can be hung and gelled with the actual colors that would be used for a design project. These labs also usually provide a manner for dimming the luminaires so that a designer can play with color mixing and the contrast ratios between different light sources and the red-shift effect of using lamps at lower intensities. Since the lab actually works with light, it forms a much more accurate means of displaying the intent of a lighting designer. More importantly, light labs allow a designer to experiment and to make comparisons between different design solutions while also studying the effect of the lights on other design elements like costumes and scenic materials. Size of the lab is irrelevant, and while many light labs make use of regular theatrical luminaires, the actual space can vary considerably. What's important is having the option to work with light, regardless of size. In addition to the luminaires, a lab usually provides a control system of six to twelve theatrical dimmers set within a space that has an easily accessible grid (approximately 8'-0" in height). In more limited situations, I have created labs using birdies or inkies in a space as small as a stairwell with dimmers that were bought off the shelf from a hardware store. In these cases, materials are simply placed on a table top while the dimmers are powered from a common wall outlet. A relatively new light lab technique makes use of specialized heads that are outfitted with fiber-optic cables (see LightBox—Figure 9.5). These labs work on a miniature scale and are often used in conjunction with the scenic models that the scenic designers have built. Architectural practices also use light labs and **mockups** for experimenting with fixture designs, wattage, and color temperature specifications, along with mounting positions that are being considered for a given design application.

Computer Visualization

A final manner of both communicating and experimenting with lighting design involves the use of computer rendering and **visualization** software. While much of this form of illustration is relatively new, each year brings amazing advances that produce ever more accurate renditions of computer-simulated lighting for specific applications. Computer visualization works from the principle of creating a three-dimensional model of an environment within a virtual or simulated space. This may take the form of a single room, exterior facade of a building, or fully developed scenic design for a production. After the model is completed, along with assigning its textures and materials, the lighting designer goes on to add lighting fixtures and accessories to the design. The luminaires in a computer model can be modified or manipulated in much the same way as the luminaires would be used in the real world. Images can then be created which give an indication of what the final design might look like based on the calculation power of the computer. While initial versions of visualization software were relatively crude, newer editions have become so accurate that the final image can approach the quality of a photograph. Some of the software packages are even capable of creating cueing sequences that can produce a sequence of virtual events which can be preprogrammed and imported directly into a lighting console. Electronic Theatre Control's (ETC) *Emphasis* system and Design and Drafting's *LD Assistant* are two examples of visualization software that are in popular use due to their abilities to interface with lighting consoles (see also Chapter 9).

With the rising costs of rehearsal time and ever growing number of parameters that must be programmed into a typical production there is an increased desire to use pre-visualization software throughout many areas of the lighting industry. In fact, pre-visualization studios are popping up in major cities all over the world. These studios allow programmers to develop virtual creations for upcoming tours and productions in a studio where there aren't the immediate pressures of designing in a theatre where a production is set to open within hours. With the increased use of intelligent lighting and their ever-increasing number of attributes pre-visualization has become not only an option but in some cases a necessary part of the design process. The finished program is simply loaded into the console and the designer performs a series of final tweaks to fine tune the settings for the venue and actual lights.

FOR FURTHER READING

Ball, David, *Backwards and Forwards: A Technical Manual for Reading Plays* (Carbondale and Edwardsville, IL: Southern Illinois Press, 1983).

Essig, Linda, *Lighting and the Design Idea* (Fort Worth, TX: Harcourt Brace College Publishers, 1997).

Ingham, Rosemary, *From Page to Stage* (Portsmouth, NH: Heinemann, 1998).

McCandless, Stanley, *A Method for Lighting the Stage*, 4th ed. (New York: Theatre Arts Books, 1958).

Mumm, Robert C., *Photometrics Handbook*, 2nd ed. (Louisville, KY: Broadway Press, 1997).

Palmer, Richard H., *The Lighting Art: The Aesthetics of Stage Lighting Design* 2nd ed. (Englewood Cliffs, NJ: Prentice-Hall, Inc., 1994).

Rosenthal, Jean and Lael Wertenbaker, *The Magic of Light* (New York: Theatre Arts Books/Little, Brown and Company, 1974).

Tharp, Twyla, *The Creative Habit: Learn It and Use It for Life* (New York: Simon & Schuster, 2003).

Thomas, James, *Script Analysis for Actors, Directors, and Designers*, 4th ed. (Boston: Focal Press, 2009).

11 Basics of General Illumination

One of the most important functions of lighting is to provide illumination or visibility to a subject or space. Not very long ago, most lighting designers were concerned solely with this function and strove to bring ever-increasing intensities to a stage or environment. As lighting design has evolved, designers have gone on to consider many more criteria than just brightness for creating quality lighting. In fact, it is often desirable to illuminate only what has to be seen—and only to the degree that a viewer gains an understanding of a subject or environment (**selective visibility**). A scene where Frankenstein is pursuing several teenagers wouldn't be as successful if lit with day-like lighting as when lit with the low intensities and shadows of a night scene. However, even though we now consider a number of additional factors for creating quality lighting, visibility still forms one of the most important functions that a designer must fulfill. This basic provision of visibility is frequently created by **general lighting,** and the principle holds true for both entertainment and architectural applications.

This chapter provides some general guidelines for developing lighting systems that create the basic illumination or visibility for an environment. One of the most important aspects of these systems is that rarely will a single light source be sufficient for lighting an entire environment. In practice, the light from most luminaires is directional enough that they can only light a limited amount of space. As one moves throughout the space, the angle of the light appears to change because not enough distance exists between the source and the subject to create parallel light throughout the space. We therefore use additional luminaires as a way of duplicating the light of a selected source, creating the appearance that the environment is lit by a single source. Even though much of this chapter is devoted to theatrical practices, the principles can be adapted and modified for many other areas of lighting design as well. In this chapter I present several methods for developing general illumination and discuss working with resources like sections and floorplans.

LIGHTING THE SUBJECT

The **subject** represents the object that must be lit. In theatrical applications this is usually the performer, while actors in the video and film business are called the **talent**. In architectural applications we make reference to the type of work or **task** that must be accomplished in an environment. On stage, a certain level of visibility must be achieved so that the audience can gain an understanding of the play. Older people require higher levels of illumination for visibility than younger people. It has been a long understood principle that people who can't see a stage's action also have difficulty hearing the performers. When we provide general illumination, we provide a base level of light so that visibility is accomplished. Sometimes we make a distinction between **general lighting**, which typically washes the entire stage, and **area lighting,** which is broken down into more specific areas that combine together to produce general illumination.

When we examine illumination, what we actually see is affected by a number of factors that relate to the light that is used to illuminate an environment. One of the most important elements relates to the sheer intensity, or brightness, of the light. In reality, the range of intensities that we observe on stage is immense compared with what can be conveniently recorded by film or video. More importantly, since what we see is based on perception, stage designers light for what they see, not necessarily a recommended level of footcandles. The problem with this is that people have varying degrees of light sensitivity—while a 20 year old may be quite comfortable with a dimly lit scene, a 50 or 70 year old may struggle to see the same scene. While there are no hard and set rules for illuminating a stage, cameras usually require that a given intensity level be maintained. Cameras also have a much narrower range of **contrast ratios** that they can process. Fortunately, both restrictions have improved with each generation of film and video cameras. Even though illumination levels may vary significantly in live entertainment, the *IESNA Lighting Handbook* still offers several guidelines related to footcandle levels that are considered characteristic of stage applications. On stage, a basic level of 50–100 footcandles is considered adequate for many performances, while 185–200 footcandles or higher is often required to bring significant focus to a subject or performer. In reality, these levels can vary considerably based on the size of a venue and the physical proximity of an audience to a stage—not counting design issues like trying to establish specific moods or settings.

The **inverse square law** plays a significant role in the illumination of an environment, and the farther away a light source is placed from a subject, the weaker it becomes. In fact, the rate of intensity drop is exponentially related to the distance between the source and the subject. In most performance facilities, the locations used for hanging luminaires are set at specific distances from the stage and a mismatched lighting unit can result not only in a luminaire's light being spilled uncontrollably over a larger area, but also in a loss of base level illumination (footcandles) since the same amount of light is spread over a larger area. If using a luminaire equipped with shutters, we could shutter the light to the desired size, but this does not change the reduced intensity of the beam nor the fact that a greater portion of the light now becomes trapped in the luminaire and is converted into heat.

A designer may light a subject from almost any direction, with each angle creating a characteristic effect on the subject (**distribution**). Backlight produces a different image than sidelight, while an up light creates a different mood than light coming from a steep angle. A designer learns how to associate these angles with viewer perception and creates different moods and effects through using various combinations of angle and other lighting properties in a design. Distribution not only plays a role in the shadow and highlight patterns that are found on a subject, but also in revealing which surfaces are illuminated and the amount of color mixing and revelation of texture that occurs on a particular surface. Distribution plays a significant role in how a subject is perceived by an audience.

Once a designer develops an understanding of what they wish the lighting to accomplish, they go on to analyze the specific combination of angles, colors, and intensities that will produce the desired effect. In reality, this happens by working with the **lighting concept** and developing a **lighting scheme** or **lighting key** for a production. In a very real sense, this is how the subject will actually be lit. Using this information, a designer goes on to develop the general lighting for a project.

TYPICAL THEATRICAL LIGHTING POSITIONS

Luminaires need to be mounted from solid structures so that they will remain in their focused positions. In a theatrical facility, these structures or **hanging positions** are found as a series of horizontal and vertical pipes that are mounted throughout a theatre. Some are welded in permanent locations, such as in the ceiling above the audience, while others are characterized by moveable positions like **battens** (pipes located above the stage). Some theatres even have hanging positions mounted to winched catwalks (**light bridges**) that hang directly over a stage. Some battens have permanently wired circuits attached to them, but most do not—although many theatres have provisions for adding circuits to these positions. It is also possible to have battens that are not moveable and are simply hung at a given height above the stage (**dead hung**). In arenas, convention centers, and gymnasiums temporary frames constructed of tubular metal called **trusses** are often hauled into place above a temporary stage and used to create hanging positions for a show's lighting equipment. Trade shows and the concert industry make extensive use of trusses.

Proscenium Theatre

For many years the proscenium theatre has been considered the most popular form of performance facility. We divide the hanging positions of a proscenium theatre into two broad categories: the **front of house** or **FOH,** which is located in the audience or auditorium areas, and the **onstage** positions, which are located upstage of the proscenium wall. The onstage positions may be further broken down into **overheads**, **booms** or **torms, set mounts** and **floor mounts.** The overheads are located on battens above the stage while the booms or torms are typically located to the sides of the stage in the wings. Set mounts are physically mounted to a set, while floor mounts are placed on the floor or deck. The names of the hanging positions (see Figure 11.1) may also change in different regions of the world.

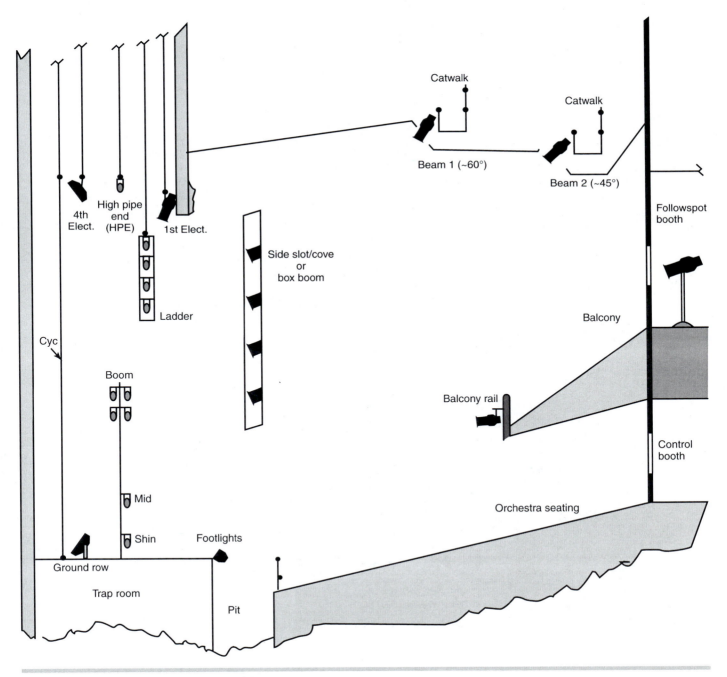

FIGURE 11.1 Proscenium Lighting Positions

SIDEBAR 11.1 Hanging Positions and Lighting Distribution

Projection Booth (Spotlight Booth)
These positions are typically located at the back of the house at the uppermost level of a theatre. They may also be found on the orchestra level at the rear of the house. They are often used for follow spots (offering relatively flat angles) and also frequently house sound gear and the lighting console.

Balcony Rail
This position is common in many older theatres and is nothing more than a pipe that extends along the front of a balcony. Additional balcony rails may be present in theatres with several balconies. The traditional balcony rail provides a very flat lighting angle. While the angle can produce extreme shadows behind a subject, it is good for creating relatively distortion-free projections and for washing the entire stage with just a few fixtures.

Beam or Port
Beam positions are horizontally mounted pipes that run across the width of an auditorium in the ceiling above an audience. Catwalks are often located behind the beams to help facilitate the hanging and focusing of the instruments. Sometimes, rather than a full beam, ports housing four to six instruments each are found in these positions. Beams are among the most important positions for creating general illumination for a stage. The most common beam positions create roughly a 45° vertical angle with the front of the stage. A second popular angle creates a steeper 60° angle and is found closer to the stage. Beam positions are assigned numbers that get progressively larger farther away from the stage.

Footlights
A footlight is a lighting position across the very front edge of the stage at stage level. The position is historical and is associated with the way in which stages were lit in the days of candles and oil lamps. Footlights create an unnatural uplight that can be good for washing the stage, filling in shadows from the overhead lighting, or bringing a unique effect to the stage. Musicals often use this angle by placing striplights along this position.

Box Boom, Slot, or Cove
These are vertical lighting positions consisting of a boom that is traditionally mounted in the box seats of an auditorium. **Box booms** create front diagonal lighting for a stage. In some theatres, there may be two or three box boom positions on each side of the auditorium. In older theatres that do not have beam positions, the box booms and balcony rail form the only source of front light for a stage. In this case, these positions can become quite complex and may contain pipe arrangements that allow 20 or more luminaires to be hung in a single position. Many theatres built after 1960 do not have box seats at all and front diagonal lighting is provided through vertical coves or slots that are cut into the walls of the auditorium. Like beam positions, we assign box booms numbers that get larger as we get father away from the stage while also noting the side of the stage that they are located on (e.g., SL Box Boom#1 or SR Box Boom#2).

Electric
An electric is a hanging position directly above the stage that consists of a pipe or batten running horizontally across the stage. Most stages have several electrics flown from different line sets at various depths throughout a stage. Their **trims** are usually adjusted from the fly rail. The battens are lowered to three or four feet above the deck for hanging, gelling, and circuiting and are then flown to their normal or **working trims** once everything is working properly. Permanent raceways contain pre-wired circuits every foot or so along the length of a batten, while temporary electrics have their circuiting supplied by **drop boxes** or circuits that have been cabled between electrics **(married).** In some cases, circuits may run directly from the unit all the way back to the dimmers **(home run).** Downstage electrics generally provide frontal lighting for the mid- and up-stage portions of the stage while, upstage electrics are usually used for backlight. Mid-stage electrics can be used for either backlight or frontlight depending on what portion of the stage they are focused to, while virtually any electric can be used for downlight. The extreme ends of electrics may be used for high sidelight—what we call **high-pipe-ends (HPE).** Electrics are numbered progressively upward from the electric closest to the plaster line toward the upstage wall.

Booms or Ladders
These hanging positions allow luminaires to be hung in vertical positions that are usually located to the sides of the stage, in the wings. The positions provide a variety of sidelight angles. A **boom** usually consists of a single pipe mounted in a vertical position from the stage floor, while a **ladder** (similar to an extension ladder) performs the same function but is hung from the end of a batten or the grid, allowing sidelight to be created without getting in the way of deck traffic patterns like a boom might create. Another variation, the **dance tower,** uses a truss-like structure to support the sidelights. Booms and ladders are identified by their side of the stage and relative positions from the plaster line, once again numbering progressively higher as you count toward the upstage wall. In many theatres a special boom is found just upstage of the proscenium opening. These are commonly called **torms** (SL Torm and SR Torm), short for tormentor. We characterize sidelight by height, with the highest angles coming from the high-pipe-ends and tops of the booms (12 to 16 feet or higher off the deck), standard sidelight is roughly in the 8- to 12-foot range, head height (about 6 feet), often called **mids,** and low sidelight from below 2 feet (**shins,** short for **shin busters** or **shin kickers**).

Ground Row
A series of luminaires that are mounted on the floor and which run parallel to a cyc or backdrop. Striplights and cyc lights are frequently used in ground rows to wash scenic backgrounds from below.

Black Box Theatre

Black box theatres allow the performance and audience spaces to be modified from one production to another. This flexibility requires that the lighting also be set up in a flexible manner. Most luminaires in black box theatres are hung from a network of intersecting pipes called a **grid** that is usually permanent and extends over the entire theatre. The pipes are generally spaced about 4 to 6 feet apart. In especially friendly theatres, a **suspension** or **tension grid** consisting of a mesh of woven aircraft cable is provided that allows electricians to walk almost anywhere above the theatre, giving them easy access to the luminaires.

Variations

In some cases, performance facilities may make use of a combination of flexible positions and a permanent grid. The most obvious example is in thrust theatres where a grid is provided over the thrust portion of the stage, while a fly loft with battens and moveable electrics are provided in the upstage areas. Catwalks with more traditional hanging positions are often placed over the audience and are oriented so that they are parallel to the edges of the stage.

FLOORPLANS AND SECTIONS

As we create a lighting design we need to be able to make calculations in regard to throw distances, beam spreads, and distribution angles (e.g., determining hanging positions) associated with the luminaires that will light a space. **Beam spread** relates to the angle at which light spreads away from a lighting instrument. Through using floorplans and sections along with information regarding the physical properties of a luminaire, the light that it produces can be translated into graphical data that illustrates the light's behavior in a specific situation. The **floorplan (groundplan)** provides a scaled top view of an environment that can be compared to a map of a room or theatre with its roof removed. The **section** provides a drafting of a space from a side view that is typically drawn along the centerline of a stage. Floorplans aid lighting designers in determining beam spreads and throw distances throughout the width and depth of a stage, while sections are used to determine the vertical angles, heights, and beam spreads based on the trim positions of the luminaires. Sections are also used to determine the **masking** positions for a production. The **light plot** or **lighting layout** will be based on a detailed study of the floorplan and section—especially in the planning of the general lighting systems. This chapter only focuses on how they are used in developing the general stage illumination.

BASICS OF GENERAL ILLUMINATION OR AREA LIGHTING

The majority of lighting designers would agree that the most essential task of any lighting design is to provide general visibility for an environment. **General illumination** was developed to bring this visibility about. In most cases, this means providing a system of luminaires that creates a consistent even coverage of light across the entire stage. While we tend to refer to **general lighting** as being characteristic of washes that light an entire stage, **area lighting** tends to be more specific in that in addition to providing basic illumination, it also provides an opportunity to control specific areas of the stage separately. For a proscenium stage, area lighting generally relates to a series of instruments that light the stage from above the audience in a frontal direction. In other facilities, the issue of area lighting becomes more complex. If we consider a distant light source like the sun, the distance that the light travels is so great that the light appears as parallel rays when viewing objects that are in close proximity to one another. Any objects viewed under such a source share similar qualities in terms of highlights and shadows, shading, and the shadows that they cast. If the objects are separated over great distances, changes may be noted in their appearances, but for most circumstances, the differences are insignificant when they are a great distance from the source. We try to re-create this condition in most general or area lighting systems and simply use multiple lights to create the illusion that the area is being lit by a single distant source.

In one form of general illumination, often called the **single source system,** a single light source is used to illuminate an entire scene. This can be highly dramatic, but is often not the best solution for creating general visibility on a stage. It can cause shadows and other lighting characteristics to change as a performer moves through a space and is usually considered undesirable because it can cause distractions. The effect is even more critical and unwanted in architectural lighting. For this reason, lighting designers usually work to provide a lighting system that creates the illusion of light coming from a single distant source rather than actually using a single source lighting system. In order to accomplish this, we divide the stage into a series of smaller spaces **(lighting areas)** that are all illuminated with as much duplication as possible. In doing so, each area is lit by the same type of luminaire, shares a common light source, and will be colored by the same color media. Just as importantly, each luminaire is placed so that its distribution patterns (beam spreads) and lighting angle are consistent with all the other luminaires that are lighting similar areas of the stage. The net effect produces a well-lit stage that gives the illusion of being lit by a single distant light source. This combination of luminaires that produce similar qualities and functions of light in adjoining areas form what is called a **wash,** while the overall combination of luminaires that are used to create the unified appearance throughout the environment (i.e., the whole stage) is a **lighting system.** Most general illumination is based on a variation of these approaches.

In order to develop an area lighting system a designer needs to examine several issues related to a space and how they will light it. Factors like type and number of luminaires in the inventory, hanging positions, required illumination levels, and desired amount of control form several of the more important considerations for determining how a stage is divided up into smaller areas. When we talk about **area control** we are making a determination of how many areas a designer divides a stage into. After observing a production's blocking, a designer will decide whether they will need to pull into very specific areas of the stage (requiring more acting areas) or if they can make do with fewer, but larger, acting areas. While a luminaire or two may, in theory, cover an entire stage, the resulting intensity may not be high enough to provide a sufficient level of illumination. An example of this is seen in playing a flashlight on a wall and observing how the light spreads over a greater area while also becoming dimmer as the light is moved farther away from the wall. In a similar way, if a designer chooses luminaires that have beam spreads that are too large, the units will spread their light over a much greater area with a resultant loss in intensity.

An acceptable acting area size is based on a diameter of 6 to 10 feet. The center of these circles becomes the focus point, while adjoining circles should just touch edges with one another. The diameter of an acting area is not set in stone, and it should be emphasized that their size can vary considerably from one design or even lighting system to another. It is also common for the diameters of these pools to vary even within a given lighting system. A large stage requires more acting areas, while a small stage may require as few as six or nine areas. Designers usually attempt to establish acting areas in some version of a grid system that produces planes set at even spacings throughout a stage's depth. In an open stage, such as for dance production, area lighting is often indicated by a rectangular array of lighting areas while a production containing scenery requires that the layout be modified so that it is consistent with the scenic elements of a production. Two methods of naming these areas include assigning a letter or number to each area or identifying the areas based on stage positions (Figure 11.2).

The general lighting comes together by combining the lighting key with the area lighting breakdown for a stage. Each area is lit with a combination of units that are based on the directional and other visual requirements of the lighting key. Once the focus point of

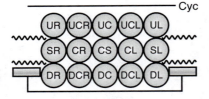

Open stage with
stage designations

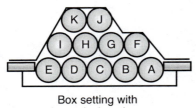

Box setting with
letter designations

FIGURE 11.2 Typical Area
Lighting Layouts

a lighting area has been identified, the designer only needs to use the master floorplan to plot a line from the focus point to a lighting position along an angle that is consistent with the angle found in the lighting key. At this point, a luminaire with an appropriate beam spread is matched to the diameter of the acting area and **throw distance** associated with the given lighting position. By using an acetate or vellum template (Figure 11.3) a designer can make a determination of which beam angle (and associated luminaire) best matches the diameter of an acting pool from a given position. This technique is easily adapted to computer-aided drafting where the angle templates can be inserted temporarily into a drawing to make decisions regarding hanging positions and instrument choices. Lighting designers consider beam angles rather than field angles in these determinations so that the most intense light is concentrated on the acting areas. As a result, the added coverage provided by the larger field angle allows the dead zones between the acting areas to be lit adequately. The combination of these effects should produce an even coverage of

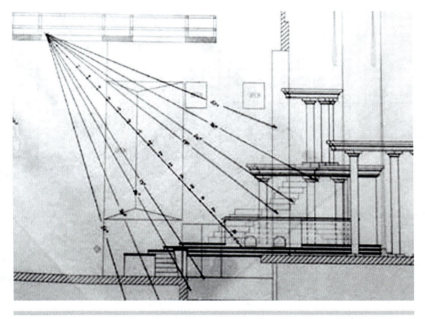

FIGURE 11.3 Determining Relationship Between Throw Distance and Acting Area Size Area coverage based on beamspread angles using a homemade acetate template. The template is also used to determine coverage in plan view.

light across an entire stage. The diameter of a light pool can also be determined by looking at a fixture's **multiplying factor** (found in product literature and references like Mumm's *Photometrics Handbook*) and multiplying this by the throw distance. However, the most accurate determination can be calculated by using the following formula:

$$\text{Beam Diameter} = \text{tangent (Field Angle/2)} \times \text{Throw Distance}$$

Once a luminaire and hanging position have been identified, they are plotted and the process is repeated for the other acting areas. A variation of this approach is used by some designers when using **flat field luminaires** like the Source Four®. The layouts are determined as above but diffusion or frost is added to the units once they have been focused. This fills in the shadows between the adjoining areas. A third method of creating area coverage is based on overlapping only the areas of an instrument's beam associated with the field angles of adjoining instruments. This, too, provides overlapping coverage between neighboring fixtures. Figure 11.4 illustrates each of these area lighting options. It is important to note that the plane in which the lighting is planned is usually 5 to 6 feet above the deck (at the actors' faces), not on the stage floor.

When developing a lighting system where both the acting areas and hanging positions share similar locations, the choice of luminaire is usually the same for all the areas. The designer, therefore, places identical units at locations along the hanging position that are consistent with the angle indicated by the lighting key—the lines representing the throw distances should be parallel with one another. While a protractor or adjustable triangle might be used to plot the intersection of these angles with the hanging positions, another technique allows the designer to locate the fixtures through simply placing them at the same spacing interval as the distance between the areas. If the distance between the centers of each acting area is 10 feet, the placement of the luminaires along the hanging position should also be 10 feet. The result is a combination of luminaires that cover the stage in light beams that are essentially parallel with one another—the illusion of a single distant light source. While luminaires used for general illumination are typically identical across a given hanging position, angles and distribution patterns often change as different planes and hanging positions are used throughout a design. Angles must also often be cheated when approaching the

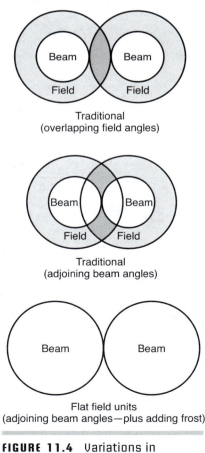

Traditional
(overlapping field angles)

Traditional
(adjoining beam angles)

Flat field units
(adjoining beam angles—plus adding frost)

FIGURE 11.4 Variations in Creating Area Coverage

extreme sides of a hanging position. To ensure proper vertical coverage, the same principles are applied to the sectional drawing to check the vertical angles and beam coverage of the luminaires. This process is then repeated for each lighting angle of the lighting key.

PRIMARY FORMULA APPROACHES FOR AREA LIGHTING

Using the basics of general illumination, several methods have been developed to aid lighting designers in achieving good area coverage for a stage. While most lighting designers now relate many of their choices of area coverage back to a lighting key that is created for a specific scene or production, these formula approaches can be used to help beginning designers as they create general illumination for a production. A lighting designer may also develop modified versions of these systems to suit their needs.

Single Source System

Single source lighting gives the appearance of light emitting from a single light source. It is one of the most desirable illusions that we create as lighting designers—an example being the light that comes from the sun. However, the problem that occurs in most cases of single source illumination is that the source cannot be placed far enough away for the light to take on the parallel qualities that allow the objects to share common features like shadow and highlight definitions. Instead, the highlights and shadows change as you move the subject around the stage. At times, this type of illumination may be desired, and a single source is used to provide a very directional distribution for the stage. This form of illumination is useful for establishing a specific light source for a scene and is often associated with lighting styles that are anchored in **motivational lighting.**

A designer generally arrives at a design solution through one of two approaches when attempting to create lighting that is suggestive of a single source. In the first situation, a designer simply uses an actual single light source that is positioned on or off stage in a location that creates the desired shadows and coverage. A particularly successful use of this technique can be observed when designers place an actual light source like a fireplace, table lamp, or chandelier on stage (Figure 11.5). These units may become the only source of illumination for a scene, and the light spreads out away from them in a naturalistic manner. More distant single sources are less common but may include the suggestion of a street light or some other light source somewhere out of view from an audience. Despite the fact that the actual source is not seen, the light still goes on to illuminate the stage as if it were visible to an audience.

FIGURE 11.5 Effect of a Single Light Source Across a Stage Note how both direction and length of shadows change with stage position.

The second approach is accomplished through hanging a cluster of lighting fixtures around the apparent center of a desired light source. The multiple instruments allow the designer to accomplish the additional lighting angles that would be suggestive of the single light source. An example where multiple instruments can be used effectively involves the depiction of light coming from a chandelier mounted at center stage. Here, multiple luminaires are hung around the intended chandelier (imaginary or actual) to suggest that light is radiating away from the chandelier in all directions (Figure 11.6). A second example includes hanging a cluster of instruments with a coverage that fans outward and away from a light source. This might be used to create the effect of a street lamp.

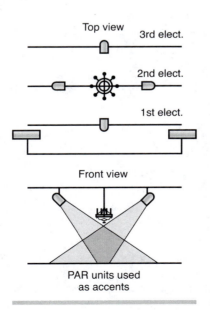

Top view
3rd elect.

2nd elect.

1st elect.

Front view

PAR units used
as accents

FIGURE 11.6 Luminaires Around a Chandelier (Single Source)

Wash System

The **wash system** (Figure 11.7) is actually the system that I have already described as the basis for creating much of the general illumination for a stage. The stage is divided into areas that are then each lit in a duplicate manner. Each group of luminaires that share common qualities is known as a **wash.** Washes typically share basic beam distribution patterns, lighting angles, and colors. In many earlier approaches to lighting design, washes were developed to provide full coverage of the stage from essentially four primary angles (straight front, back, and each side). Multiple colored washes were often provided from each of the angles. Early concert lighting made heavy use of color wash systems, and dance lighting to this day is solidly based on providing warm and cool colored washes from many of these directions. These washes may or may not be oriented in the principle 90° orientations of traditional theatrical wash lighting. In fact, a wash can be provided from almost any angle that a designer desires.

The McCandless System

One of the earliest problems that theatrical lighting designers struggled with related to creating lighting that provided a naturalistic appearance for the performers. Prior to the advent of electricity, stage personnel were more concerned with achieving visibility than the aesthetics of a lighting design. With electricity becoming the basic means of control, it didn't take long for pioneers to develop several formula design approaches for creating basic visibility for a stage. One such pioneer; Professor Stanley McCandless (Yale School of Drama), developed a system for producing area lighting that would have a profound impact on the lighting industry. His formula was introduced as "A Method for Lighting the Stage" in his publication of *A Syllabus for Lighting the Stage*, and became so influential that people have referred to it as "**The Method.**" Simply put, the **McCandless System** relates to a method for creating a realistic image in the general illumination of a stage. The historical significance of this approach is that it came at a time when spotlights were first capable of achieving the longer throws associated with placing luminaires in an auditorium and as hanging positions above the audience first started to be incorporated into theatre designs. McCandless's system became so successful that entire auditoriums and circuiting systems were built on his concept.

One of the compositional problems of theatrical lighting is that it is often difficult to distinguish the mass or depth of objects and performers while they are on stage. As lighting positions began to shift to the Front of House (FOH), McCandless noted that light coming from straight front washed out the dimensional features of a performer and determined that to create a more naturalistic quality a subject needed to be lit by two separate sources from opposing directions. He stressed that the opposing sources should reveal more of the sides and dimensional qualities of a subject as well as that color could also be used to emphasize dimensionality in the lighting. As you may recall, most lighting environments include a combination of the actual source or **key light** and varying degrees of ambient or **fill light.** In a theatre, where most surfaces are painted black and purposefully kept so that they absorb light, there is often little, if any, ambient light on a stage, and a designer must often use artificial sources to create this ambient lighting. By providing light from both directions, a designer has a much better ability to reveal form while also providing clues to the directionality of the implied light source.

McCandless also recognized that most naturalistic lighting involves light sources that are located above as well as to either side of a subject. He went on to incorporate this into his two-instrument method of lighting as well—one instrument would be representative of the key (source) light while the other would be associated with the fill. In his method, McCandless broadly characterized these light sources as coming from a location at about 45° from above and 45° to each side of a subject. Additionally, he realized that he could enhance this effect by creating some color contrast through gelling each light differently. By using complementary tints, he could produce a naturalistic quality in which each side of a subject was influenced more directly by one of the two sources while the subject's front was lit through additive mixing of both sources, which essentially produced some variation of white light. This basic system of two light sources with complementary tints located at 45° from above and to each side of an acting area has become the general formula for the McCandless Method (Figure 11.8). This basic distribution is then repeated throughout as many lighting areas as required by a design. The system had many ramifications throughout the lighting industry and formed a standardized approach to lighting

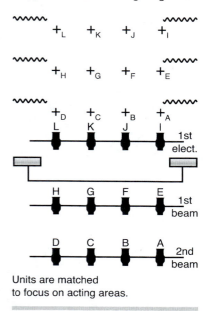

Units are matched to focus on acting areas.

FIGURE 11.7 A Typical Wash System

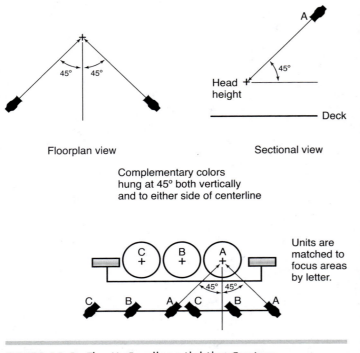

Complementary colors
hung at 45° both vertically
and to either side of centerline

Floorplan view   Sectional view

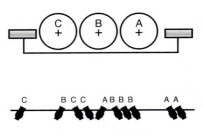

Units are
matched to
focus areas
by letter.

FIGURE 11.8 The McCandless Lighting System

Units are matched to
focus areas by letter.

FIGURE 11.9 Double and Triple
Hanging Areas A, B, and C
essentially follow a McCandless hang
with one unit each coming from SR
and areas A and C being double-hung
from SL while area B is triple-hung
from SL. Each additional unit could
provide an additional color, angle, or
focus to an area.

for much of the 1900s. Even today, it is still used or slightly modified as a basis for general illumination in many lighting designs.

Double or Triple Hanging

While double or triple hanging do not truly relate to formula lighting systems, they do reflect an approach to lighting design. Due to the limitations in numbers of dimmers and lighting instruments, it was common for lighting designers to only create a minimal lighting scheme for a production. This often provided only a single wash or basic McCandless hang for each area of the stage and placed large restrictions on the number of choices that a designer might have for lighting a production. As a way of providing more variety, a lighting system or collection of instruments representing a given wash might be duplicated (**double-hung**) while modifying one or more of the specific qualities of the wash. The most common example of this comes through providing a second system of luminaires that duplicate every element of a lighting system except color (See Figure 11.9). Matching instruments would be hung next to one another and would be colored and controlled as two separate systems. Each light of the second system is focused to the same spots as the original units. Double-hanging is most commonly used to provide a warm and cool color option from the same angle. If used in a McCandless hang, where a neutral color is hung from the opposite direction, this provides not only an opportunity for alternating the warm/cool relationships between either side of a subject but also a full range of color mixing and gains higher intensities through the combined output of lamps coming from the same direction. For example, if one wash is colored in pink while the other is in blue, not only can a designer provide pink and blue colors from an angle, but also a diverse range of lavenders through mixing various proportions of the two colors. It's a fairly common practice to specify double-hanging throughout a number of lighting systems in a lighting design. While most double hanging is associated with providing additional colors, other possibilities include changing the angle of the light (e.g., steeper angles or wider-set angles) and creating more tightly or narrowly defined focus areas. A **triple-hang** provides a third alternative for a wash. **Color scrollers** have become an especially helpful accessory for eliminating double or triple-hanging.

Area versus Color Control

In an ideal world a designer would have enough circuits and dimmers to provide independent control for every luminaire and area contained in a lighting design. This is rarely possible, and fixtures with common functions are often assigned to the same circuits and dimmers so that fewer dimmers are required for a design. The designer must evaluate whether it is preferable to have independent control of a smaller area of the stage or to have more control of the individual colors of a design (**area versus color control**). There was a time when both cross-lights (with different colors) in a McCandless hang were ganged together to a single dimmer because designers wanted control of each area. A shortcoming of this is that the intensity proportions of the paired lights can not be varied and that the color mixing will always have the same proportional values, often muddying the colors at medium to low dimmer levels. Today it is more popular to gang a single color from several adjoining areas as a means of lowering the number of required dimmers because designers tend to prefer color over area control in many of their lighting systems. In reality, the decision greatly depends on the given situation. I frequently design shows where I have created some systems with more stringent controls based on color, while other systems were designed with a stronger concern toward area control. Personally, I usually prefer to keep color and distribution angles together and will almost always choose to combine adjoining areas into larger portions of the stage as opposed to combining lights of different colors or angles.

ALTERNATIVE SYSTEMS FOR AREA LIGHTING

Over the years, a number of formulas for creating general illumination for theatrical productions have been put forward. Most have been developed for the proscenium stage. While many of today's lighting designers follow a general approach to developing area lighting systems, most don't adhere to a strict formula approach to their lighting anymore. Instead, design decisions are based primarily on the specific image that a designer envisions for a scene or production. Through referring back to the lighting concept and lighting key, many designers will develop very specific distribution patterns and general lighting for a production. Despite the current trend to avoid design formulas, a student should still be familiar with the more popular approaches because they do form techniques for lighting a stage that have proven themselves over time.

Key and Fill

Key and fill lighting had its beginnings in the film and television industries but is now often used as a design formula and general reference throughout the entire lighting industry. In its inception **key light** was associated with the primary or most intense light source and was often equated with the motivating light source for a scene. In the early days of video and film lighting the cameras and film had very low light sensitivities, and if intensities fell too low, areas of the image would appear dark and unlit. The lights had to be capable of creating a high enough threshold of illumination simply to allow the subject to be seen by the cameras. Just as on a stage, where there is little or no ambient light, these cameras also had a problem of not being able to see into the shadow areas. As a way of compensating for the relatively low or non-existent light in the shadow areas, additional luminaires, **fill lights,** were added for filling in the shadows and providing a base level of illumination so that these areas wouldn't go completely dark. Once a relationship is established between the distribution angles of the key and fill light, the system is repeated through a series of adjoining areas just as is done in area lighting. Today, most general lighting makes some use of the key/fill principle with light coming from at least two different directions. Each pair of luminaires work together to create a key/fill relationship that provides an indication of the light source in one direction and enough shadow illumination to sustain visibility in the other. In reality, the McCandless Method is a variation of a key/fill application.

The Washed Stage

The **Washed Stage** formula dates back to before the days of electricity and to lighting fixtures that were primarily of a wash/flood variety. Spotlights did not exist yet, and the sources were typically candle or lantern flames. The method was based on horizontal strips of luminaires that were hung above and across the stage or along the front edge of the *apron* in the form of footlights. Additional luminaires were mounted on stands in the wings and provided sidelight across the stage. The washed stage was often lit primarily for the benefit of revealing the scenery even though the illumination levels were often so low that much of the lighting was actually painted into the scenery. In later years, performers might have been highlighted by a spotlight like a limelight but for the most part the stage was illuminated in a soft low-intensity manner. Because much of the lighting came from above, it was common to have unnatural shadows on the performers' faces. This was compensated for by placing a strong emphasis on light from the footlights, which filled out and softened the harsh shadows of the overhead lighting. The lighting style had the tendency to make the actors appear flat and two-dimensional while also

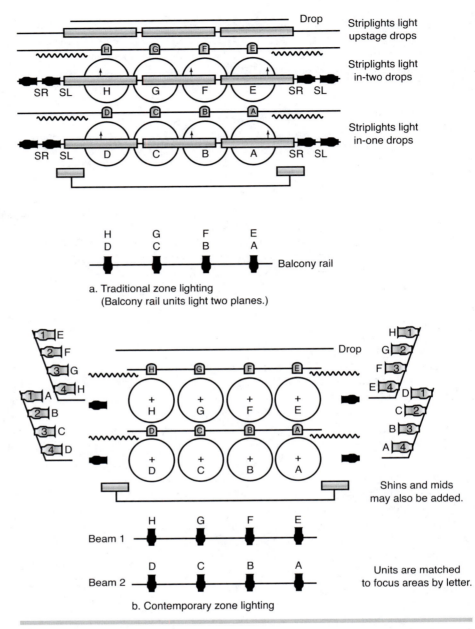

FIGURE 11.10 Zone Lighting

making it difficult to separate the performers from the scenery. The balance of intensity between the overhead washes and footlights was critical because exaggerated shadows could be cast onto the scenery if the intensity of the footlights got too high.

Zone Lighting

Zone lighting forms a special variation of the washed stage and is used in designs where a layered effect is created in the scenery. Productions making use of drops and wing/border settings such as those found in musical theatre or ballet are often associated with this type of lighting. Zone lighting makes use of wash luminaires used to light the scenery from above which are then supplemented by other sources of light. To emphasize the sculptural quality of the performers, high-angled sidelight (usually high-pipe-ends) is used to light across the stage. The sidelight is usually the dominant source in a zonal system and is often hung in a minimum of two colors (warm and cool), which adds variety to the colors from a particular angle. Backlights are often added to push the performers forward and to help separate them from the background. In a zonal system, most units are focused into the planes that are created by the drops/legs or depth of the stage. The final element of zone lighting includes a wash of light (typically from straight front) that is used to soften the shadows created by the sidelight while adding some front fill to provide visibility for the performers' faces. Dance companies make common use of zone lighting because so many choreographic patterns fall within the planes that are created between the leg sets that are placed throughout a stage. Recent variations of zone lighting, particularly those found in modern dance and musical theatre, have shifted much of the sidelight from the high angles associated with the high-pipe-ends to lower angles that are created through using booms that are set within the wings of the stage. These booms are usually placed just upstage of each set of legs. Figure 11.10 provides an illustration of a basic zone lighting system layout.

Jewel Lighting

Jewel lighting is a more recent version of zone lighting where the emphasis is placed on the higher intensity levels of more recently developed lighting equipment. The most important revision from traditional zone lighting is that the primary source of the lighting shifts to relatively low-angled sidelight that is hung mostly from booms positioned along the sides of the stage. In addition to the basic washes, jewel lighting adds accents and specials to bring more interest to a design. It gets its name primarily from the fact that a variety of angles and colors are used to light a subject—the effect being compared to light being reflected and re-fracted by the many facets of a jewel. Tom Skelton was one of the earliest advocates for this type of lighting. A significant change from other approaches lies in a dominant use of front diagonal lighting as more units started to be placed in the front of house positions. In addi-tion to traditional booms, the front-diagonal angle is achieved through placing booms in the box seats of many theatres. This allowed additional instruments to be brought to the front of the house (now capable of side lighting the apron) to support the strong sidelight systems of the onstage booms (Figure 11.11). In many theatres dating before the 1950s, box booms form the only frontal lighting positions outside of the balcony rail. Contemporary theatres generally provide vertical slots in the auditorium walls for the front diagonal angle while overhead catwalks or beams are used for the more frontal lighting positions. Broad-way theatres must often create these frontal positions through rigging a temporary **truss** that is hung for a specific production. Jewel lighting has become a characteristic quality of Broadway musicals.

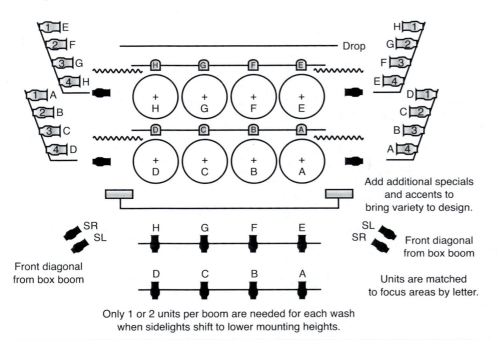

FIGURE 11.11 Jewel Lighting

BUILDING ON GENERAL LIGHTING

Even though area lighting provides the basic source of illumination through most of a stage, there are also specialized needs that must go beyond the provisions of general lighting. Some form additional washes while others have very specific functions in a lighting design. The following categories represent special areas of lighting that are used to supplement the general lighting systems. The majority of these are created through washes that come from different locations throughout a theatre. The most significant washes are associated with the primary directions of a stage and include straight front, front-diagonal, a variety of sidelight angles, downlight, and backlight. The number of luminaires required to complete a wash is a function of the size of the stage, the angle that the wash strikes the stage, and the beam spreads and throw distances of the associated units. In most cases, the stage is divided into zones such as planes where a single wash will require anywhere from one to five or more units per plane. As few as one or two lights are all that most sidelight systems require. The near throw units usually have the widest beamspreads, while the units that are focused to the center or far side of the stage will have more narrow beamspreads. The diagrams illustrated in Sidebar 11.2 are for a relatively small stage where only two lamps are required to cover many of these washes. For larger venues, a third lamp with an intermediate beam spread is inserted midway between the existing lamps while the focuses are spread out evenly across the stage.

Special Areas

While the majority of a stage is lit through area lighting, there are often locations where it is impossible to achieve basic visibility using the area systems alone. One of the biggest distractions that can occur in stage lighting comes as a result of having a performer's appearance (in terms of lighting composition) change as they move throughout a space. As an actor moves up a stairway, the lighting should appear consistent even if the area lighting at this point is no longer based on the main level of the stage. Nooks, balconies, hallways, and locations where walls come together in a way that the area lighting becomes obstructed form examples of these problems. Even though these situations do not permit the general systems to light them, they must still appear to be lit by the same sources as the rest of the room. We accomplish this by making minor modifications in hanging positions and instrument choices to produce a best attempt at continuing the general lighting systems as **special areas.** The overall goal is to produce the appearance that the special areas are part of the same lighting environment as the rest of the surroundings.

Sculpting and Modeling Accents

With general lighting systems lighting the stage from mostly frontal angles, there is significant potential for creating a flat, two-dimensional quality to anything that is lit in this fashion. The effect becomes even more critical as the area lighting becomes flatter. To enhance depth perception, we add side and back lighting not only to supplement the area lighting but to also emphasize the sides and backs of the subjects. These systems are commonly called **modeling/sculpting systems** and are characterized by washes that come from the back and sides of the stage. Sidelight may come from a variety of angles while back light tends to be relatively steep angled due to having to be set at trims high enough to prevent the lights from either blinding or being seen by an audience. Many designers refer to the light that etches or rings a subject from these angles, particularly the backlight, as **rim lighting** because of the rimming effect that they can give to a subject. These washes bring a three-dimensional quality to a subject and help push them forward while separating them from the background.

Blending and Toning Accents

At times it may be desirable to provide a wash over the entire stage to complete a specific design function. Several examples of this might include **toning** or coloring a stage in a full color wash or using an overhead wash to fill in or soften (**blending**) any shadows in

SIDEBAR 11.2 Focus Patterns for Common Wash Systems

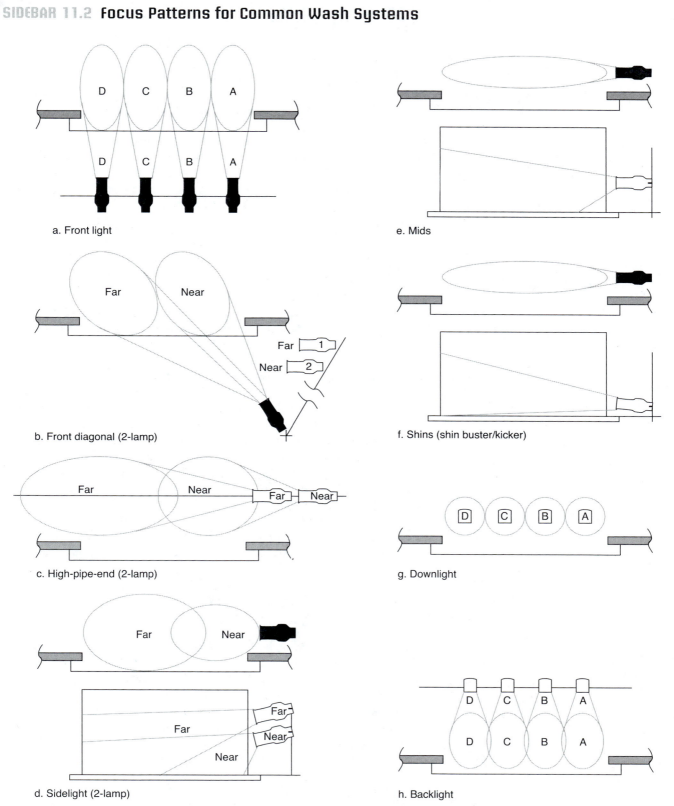

a. Front light

b. Front diagonal (2-lamp)

c. High-pipe-end (2-lamp)

d. Sidelight (2-lamp)

e. Mids

f. Shins (shin buster/kicker)

g. Downlight

h. Backlight

the general lighting system. Blending and toning accents can be particularly effective when there are limited resources or where the area lighting isn't as well-developed as one might desire. Blending and toning accents typically use wash luminaires like striplights or scoops that cover a wide area. Two scoops might be all that's required to effectively cover a moderately sized stage. A common application of toning can be found in many high school auditoriums where a series of striplights are hung directly above the stage, with the primary purpose of coloring the stage in a variety of colors. While the colors may be quite extreme, such as in the case of using just the blue circuits for a night scene, it is more common to use a combination of colors to supplement the area lighting while creating subtle variations in the overall color of a scene. These accents may come from any direction but are most commonly located directly above the stage or from the front of house. Even though wash luminaires have been described primarily for this function, it doesn't prevent a designer from creating a blending or toning system using spotlights whose sole purpose is to create a wash. Many of the washes from the balcony rail form examples where spotlights are used to fill in the performers' faces or to tone a stage.

Motivational Accents

There are times when a lighting designer may wish to provide a clear indication of a specific light source on a stage—what we call **motivational lighting.** One of the problems associated with area lighting is that it commonly becomes a generic design solution that although accomplishing the task of visibility, doesn't necessarily make a significant statement or contribution to the specific needs of a production. By using only area or visibility lighting, a designer will struggle to achieve a unique image for a given situation, and one design might not change that much from any other design. Therefore, a designer needs to carefully examine how a general lighting system might be modified so that it can make a unique contribution to a moment on the stage. While an indication of a specific light source might be accounted for within the general lighting systems, this in itself might not be enough to make a representation of the desired effect. In order to support the motivational light source, a designer should attempt to add additional luminaires and washes that enhance or provide a clear indication of the given source. These accents are known as **motivational accents** and may be as simple as a single instrument, such as light coming from an imaginary street lamp or a full-stage wash representing light coming from a distant setting sun. Many of the special lighting requirements discussed earlier relating to motivated lighting (e.g., the chandelier) can be created through motivational accents. Motivational accents are a key element to adding variety to the lighting and should be used fairly liberally throughout a lighting design.

ADDITIONAL LIGHTING DEMANDS

All of the lighting solutions discussed to this point share a common quality in that they provide a form of illumination that covers a significant portion, if not entire stage. This last group of tasks relates to a number of specialized needs that a designer may have to address while lighting a production. Although many of these solutions can be quite specific, making them a unique element of a design, many can appear in virtually any show that a designer works on. These demands are usually solved through a more limited application than creating wide-spread systems like full-stage washes, and often just one or two luminaires can fulfill the needs of a particular design problem. We refer to a lighting instrument that is used for a specific need or design function as a **special.**

Special Visibility

Special visibility relates to providing luminaires for a specific function of illumination. This may happen when the area lighting does not provide adequate coverage of a given feature, or there is a special quality of illumination that can not be provided by the general or accent lighting systems.

Performer/Actor specials are luminaires that are dedicated to revealing performers in a special manner. The obvious use of this technique is when a lighting designer provides a single light for a performer to use during a specific moment of a performance. General lights may fade away, leaving a performer in a single spotlight, a performer may be revealed from the blackness through bringing up a single light, or a performer may walk into an isolated area of light at a particular moment of a play. These techniques are often used when a performer addresses an audience directly (an aside or narrative moment) or when a designer is creating a more dramatic image for the stage. Specials do not have to bring full visibility to a performer and might even be more effective if they only provide partial visibility to a subject (e.g., an actor in a backlight for a final tableau). Actor specials can also be used in a subtle manner to punch up or add focus to an area of the stage where special visibility is required. Two examples of this include placing specials on doors to draw focus to entrances and adding instruments to cover seating clusters where actors may gather for an extended time.

Scenic specials come in a variety of shapes and sizes. In some cases, a single fixture fulfills a lighting need, while in others, an entire wash or accent system might illuminate a particular scenic element. The most common examples place specials on statuary or paintings to bring a highlight or focus to special features of a set. Others will be used to make symbolic statements. Scenic needs may also include adding sidelight to emphasize the three-dimensional elements of a set or grazing lights to enhance the texture of a surface. Another use of scenic specials is on signage.

Lighting for Costumes

The decisions of a lighting designer can have an immense impact on how costumes are revealed to an audience. While we may worry about skin complexions of the performers and how they might be modified by the lighting and makeup, much of how a performer is revealed relates specifically to how the costumes are illuminated by the general lighting systems. For this reason, it is rare that a lighting designer has to create any specialty lighting based solely on the costumes of a production. Instead, we address the majority of the costume needs as we set up the general lighting and accent systems for a lighting design. The most essential rule relates to the fact that a lighting designer should be making choices that have a complementary effect on the costumes. Colors should in general appear rich, not dull or grayed, and there shouldn't be significant distortion in the perceived color of any costumes unless there is a logical reason for allowing the shift to occur on stage. If a costume designer uses a wide color palette, the lighting designer will on the whole have to use more tints to avoid graying down some of the colors. On the other hand, an intense color choice on the part of the lighting designer may cause some costume colors to "scream" and become almost neon-like, while others might actually appear to be black. Finally, a designer may want to tone down the color of given fabrics or paints and could purposely choose colors that would prevent particular colors from appearing too vibrant. Lighting can also be used to reveal textures both within the fabrics themselves as well as through the manner in which they are draped or swagged. If a heavily swagged costume is lit with a deep blue downlight from above and also accented with a more natural pink light from the side, from front, the deeper portion of the folds will most likely be lit by the downlight, while the raised surfaces will be highlighted by the pink sidelight.

It is imperative that a lighting designer become familiar with the fabrics that the costume designer has chosen for a production. At the very least, the costume samples or swatches should be examined under gel-swatches of the colors that a lighting designer anticipates using on a project. If possible, they should be viewed under lights containing the actual gels that are being considered for a production. One of the benefits of viewing costume swatches under gel and actual light is discovered when hidden dyes cause a fabric to behave differently from what is anticipated. This often occurs when dark brown or black fabrics are viewed under saturated blue light—the blue filters often allow a high transmission of not only blue- but red-colored light as well. The dyes used to create these dark fabric colors often contain a high concentration of red pigment and while the fabric may appear black under normal lighting, under the blue light the red dye is enhanced, causing the "black" fabric to appear reddish-brown or even maroon. These principles hold true for scenic design as well. Similar effects can be observed in patterned or plaid fabrics where the patterns will actually appear to change or even disappear as a result of being exposed to different colors of light. Regardless of design area, the effects of various color combinations can be significant, and it is important that the lighting designer and other designers be in agreement as to how much distortion is acceptable for a given design.

Lighting for Scenery

In many cases, the general lighting systems are often sufficient for lighting a production's scenery, and there are frequently few, if any, additional demands for lighting the scenic elements of a show. In other cases, entire systems must be devised for lighting the scenery.

ARCHITECTURAL FEATURES Often, the ambient light created by the area lighting is sufficient for lighting many architectural features and no further instrumentation is required. However, elements of the set may need to be emphasized, colors might have to be modified, and specific textures/patterns may need to be highlighted or toned down. One example of this is disguising wallpaper patterns in the painting of a set. Here, one wallpaper pattern is revealed under one set of lighting conditions while a second is revealed under another lighting condition. As a rule, the primary focus of a setting should be kept in the lower 8 to 10 feet of a set (where the performers are) and there is seldom a reason for lighting the walls completely evenly. If the walls are lit too evenly, it can diminish the perception of the corners and jogs that are contained in the set. It is also preferable to let the light progressively fade into shadow toward the top of a set. A cornice being lit as well as a door entrance can steal focus, while features like a picture rail can be used as a place to cleverly shutter light that falls onto a wall.

Special types of architectural features are found where entrances lead from the main setting to other areas of a stage **(maskings)**. Here, the scenic designer is often trying to create the illusion of an adjoining room, and a lighting designer must reinforce the illusion by lighting these areas so that performers don't appear to be coming or going into a dark void. This is called **lighting the maskings,** and we hang luminaires to specifically light these walls and the performers that use these areas. The instruments may be hung from overhead electrics but are frequently mounted to the offstage faces of the walls of the principle setting. While maskings may be lit using any type of lighting instrument, many designers prefer the soft, even distribution of flood luminaires like scoops for completing this task.

CYCLORAMAS (CYCS) AND DROPS Cycloramas form a special type of lighting concern. Most cover a significant area of the stage opening and form a neutral backdrop that is found in an upstage position. Cycs are used in combination with lighting to create an illusion of a panoramic background for a stage. A true cyclorama, rarely found today, is a plastered wall that curves around the upstage corners of the stage and is painted white. Cycs are now more commonly formed of fabric that is stretched across the width of a stage and may, or may not, curve or wrap around the upstage corners. Due to their neutral color (an off-white), lights can be played upon them to create scenic backgrounds that are easily modified through lighting changes. Dance productions make significant use of cycs to produce a variety of backgrounds for their dancers. These drops may also be used to reflect or bounce light downstage to light other drops from behind. In this case, you may hear stagehands referring to a **bounce drop** rather than a cyc. A special variety of cyc is the **sky drop,** which for all practical purposes functions the same way as a cyc, with the exception that it is colored light blue.

The most common application of cyc lighting involves placing a series of wash luminaires (striplights or cyc lights) across the length of a cyc so that the units hang parallel to the fabric with their beams overlapping and mixing evenly between adjoining units. In most cases, three or four different circuits/colors are provided across the width of the cyc, each being colored in one of the primary lighting colors (red, blue, and green). A designer

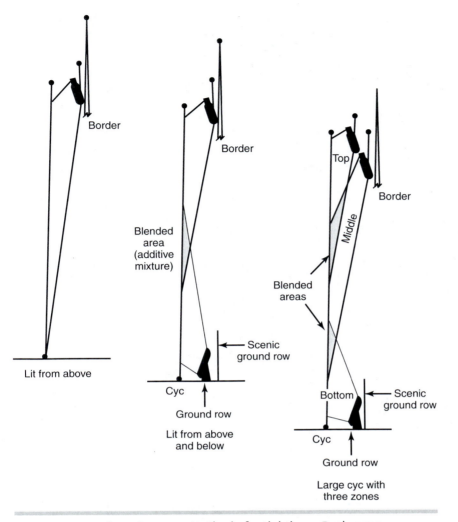

FIGURE 11.12 Three Common Methods for Lighting a Cyclorama
Cyc lights or striplights are hung along an electric that runs parallel to the cyc/drop.
Distance from the drop will vary with specific units but is typically between 1 and 3
or 4 feet.

may also choose to use any colors they wish based on the specific needs of a production.
Cyc lighting is usually done from an overhead batten that is just downstage of the cyc,
focusing the units so that the light washes down the cyc toward the floor. Sometimes a
designer may want additional flexibility or the cyc is large enough that the light does not
carry all the way to the deck. In these cases, the cyc is divided into zones. A top zone and
bottom zone are the most common arrangements, with the top zone being lit from the
traditional top angle while the bottom is lit by a second set of fixtures that are set on the
floor (**ground row**). Sunset images are produced in this manner. If it is impossible to
place a ground row in front of a cyc, the additional instruments lighting the lower portion
are hung above the stage and are focused to the lower portions of the cyc (Figure 11.12).
In extremely large cycs a third (middle) zone may be required.

Although most cyc lighting is done through creating washes over most, if not all, of
a cyc, not all cyc lighting needs to be of a wash nature. The cyc can also become an effective area for projecting simple scenic images such as gobo clouds or sophisticated projections containing slide or video images. I've also played beams of light across different
parts of cycs to create geometric patterns, pulled lenses from Fresnels and focused the
light to create setting suns, produced luminescent moons by back-lighting cycs with spotlights or **moonboxes** and **shadowboxes,** and have even used the cyc in combination with
projectors and gobos to create star-fields of distant stars and galaxies. One of the issues of
lighting these scenic elements is in preventing performers from casting shadows on a

drop or cyc. Techniques that help to avoid this include creating a neutral lighting zone several feet in front of a cyc/drop, taking care to avoid angles that are so flat that the light spills directly onto these scenic elements, and being mindful of any light that could reflect off of a floor back onto a drop or cyc. These side effects might be softened or eliminated through placing a scrim downstage of a cyc or drop.

Scenic drops are often lit in the same way as a cyc but typically have a couple of additional restrictions that must be addressed. First, since a drop contains some form of scenic art, the lighting designer must pay attention to the colors that are found in a drop and should strive to enhance, not distort, the drop through its lighting. Second, while a drop may be hung at the rear of a stage like a cyc, many drops are placed in clusters throughout the depth of a stage. Because of this, lighting designers typically opt to light drops from above and place striplights just downstage of the first drop in a given cluster. There are times when this too, cannot be accomplished and a designer will have to use alternate methods of washing a drop(s) by focusing a series of wash luminaires like scoops or even spotlights with soft focuses to different parts of a drop. Finally, specific parts or features of a drop may also be accented with scenic specials.

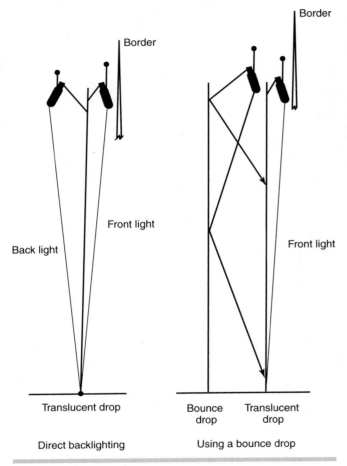

FIGURE 11.13 Lighting a Translucent Drop

TRANSLUCENT DROPS Translucent drops form a special classification of scenic materials. These allow light to pass through them while not allowing you to see through the scenic material itself. A number of translucent materials may be used on a stage—frosted plexi-glass, treated plastics, RP screens, and even muslin can be used to create translucent drops. Through using a bounce drop or by placing lighting fixtures upstage of these drops and shining them directly onto a drop's back surface the translucent material will glow and project light (Figure 11.13). Although a translucent drop may cover an entire stage, it is more common to cut portions of a traditional drop out and replace the missing areas with a translucent material. An alternate technique back paints or masks out those areas of a drop that must have an opaque appearance. The artwork of the translucent areas is then painted with either scenic dyes or light washes (glazes) of paint that allow the light to be projected through them. Stained-glass windows, moonlit rivers, and nighttime city skylines form just a few examples of where this technique can be particularly effective.

SCRIMS Scrims have an open mesh-like fabric that allows them to take on either an opaque or transparent quality. Because of this, we use them to "magically" reveal objects. They are frequently hung across the entire width of the stage and are often colored white or black. As a general principle, scrims appear opaque if lit from the front and there is no light present behind them. As light is added behind the scrim, we see through the mesh holes and anything behind the scrim is revealed. Figure 11.14 illustrates the relative placement of the luminaires in regard to lighting a scrim. Scrims work best if the light in front of them is relatively steep so that the light striking the individual thread elements is reflected upward rather than passing through the material and lighting the objects that the scrim is hiding. In most practices, lighting designers attempt to create a neutral lighting zone directly in front of a scrim while trying to avoid hitting the scrim with any light at all. We frequently shutter lights off of scrims and try to avoid using any lights that strike a scrim while it is in use. However, there are times when scrims are treated with scenery and must be lit. In these circumstances a lighting designer must take care to ensure that any front light for the scrim comes from a fairly steep angle. If the angle is too flat, light passes through the mesh and continues upstage to strike whatever you are trying to hide. Even when precautions have been taken, spill can still occur upstage of a scrim, and it might become necessary to create a neutral zone behind the scrim where performers and scenic elements shouldn't be placed. In extreme cases, a **blackout drape** or **curtain** may even have to be placed upstage of a scrim until just before the effect is initiated. Finally, anything viewed through a scrim tends to have a soft, hazy quality that makes them particularly effective for fantasy sequences like the dream ballets in musicals like *Oklahoma*.

A white scrim may actually be painted with dyes so that the pores of the fabric are not filled despite creating extensive scenic images on a scrim's surface. When lit from the front, the scene on the scrim appears opaque, while on cue it will dissolve as light comes up behind the scrim and reveals the upstage setting. This technique is called a **scrim-through.** You may also reverse the process with a **scrim-back** where the upstage areas fade as we restore to the scene that is painted on the scrim's surface. This effect is used quite effectively for musicals where a show-drop is painted onto a scrim and a scrim-through is used to transition into the opening scene during the overture. Although it is common for scrims to cover the entire stage, they may also be used in smaller applications like in a flat or photograph. I once did a production of *Dracula* where a piece of scrim was placed in a wall section that was painted to look the same as the rest of the walls. The wall appeared solid under normal lighting but revealed Dracula once light was added behind the scrim section of the wall.

In order to stop bounce light from the front light spilling up onto a cyc or to create a completely black surround for a stage, a black scrim is often hung several feet in front of a cyc. This is especially common for dance productions. By using this technique, a cyc can have the appearance of going black while still being able to be lit with a variety of colors. When a scrim is used in connection with a cyc (or drop), the luminaires used to light the cyc must be located between the cyc and scrim.

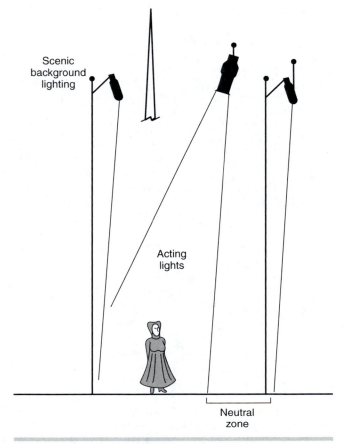

FIGURE 11.14   Lighting a Scrim High-angled cyc lights or striplights wash the scrim from the front, while lights upstage of the scrim are used to produce the reveal effect.

IMPLIED SCENERY   There are times when lighting may be used to suggest scenery if for one reason or another it becomes impossible or undesirable to use a physical structure. More importantly, there are times when the style of a production might be better served through providing suggestive rather than realistic scenic elements. In these more stylized modes, it is quite possible for lighting to be primarily responsible for establishing a scene. Some of the simplest examples of using luminaires as implied scenery include shuttering a spotlight's beam into a rectangle that suggests that light is coming through a doorway or window. Some of the most popular sources of implied scenery come through using **gobos.**

Effects Lighting

Effects lighting can take on a host of different needs for a lighting designer. A special concern regarding this type of lighting is that while effects can add to the theatricality of a production, they can also become a distraction and should be considered very carefully in a lighting design. If an effect must remain visible throughout a scene, the designer has the added problem of determining how prominent it must be. Often an effect will be quite strong when it is first introduced and then fade into a less prominent focus once it has been established. This usually helps to prevent it from becoming a distraction to a scene. Many effects, like fire, can be made through using several low wattage lamps and simply programming a random chase effect into a lighting console.

Jeff Davis

Jeff Davis has worked very successfully in several disciplines of lighting design over the years. His career has gone through phases where he has been associated primarily with a given area of lighting even though he has actually designed for a variety of lighting disciplines throughout most of his career. His early career is characterized by theatrical productions through designing a number of Broadway shows (*Play On!*, *Born Yesterday*, *The Man Who Came to Dinner*, *The Musical Comedy Murders of 1940*, and others), Off-Broadway designs, national tours and pre-Broadway trials, and a number of regional credits. The second phase of his career shifted to a strong association with television lighting where his credits are found on many of the major networks (ABC, CBS, NBC, FOX, and PBS, as well as many specialty networks like TBS, ESPN, and CNN). Many of these credits were for special events like the *Gore/Bradley Debate*, *Nancy Kerrigan's Christmas on Ice*, or *Skates of Gold*, while others were for network daytime productions like *One Life to Live*, *All My Children*, *As the World Turns*, or the syndicated *The Maury Povich Show* and the *Sally Jesse Raphael Show*. Several of these designs earned him Emmy nominations. His television experience opened the door for his third career phase, which is predominantly in opera design and began with his becoming Resident Lighting Designer for the New York City Opera—the television experience paying off with the company's need to adapt its productions' lighting for the popular *Live at the Lincoln Center* series. Davis relit a number of operas for television as well as designed 25 new productions for the company and soon gained a reputation that led to designing for opera companies throughout the country (Washington National Opera, Pittsburgh Opera, Opera Company of Philadelphia, Indianapolis Opera, and more) and internationally. He continues to design in these areas while also lighting a number of industrial or corporate productions with clients like Coke, Honda, Minolta, Johnson and Johnson, and Wendy's. He has also lit unique projects like the productions on the cruise ship *Disney Magic* (Disney Cruise Lines).

Davis lights within a variety of disciplines but currently lights primarily plays and operas with an occasional return to television. He graduated from Northwestern University with a degree in Speech (the theatre department was within the School of Speech). His informal training came from working as an assistant to Tharon Musser and later as an associate designer to Jo Mielziner. "Tharon gave me my start and introduced me to the particular workings of Broadway production. More importantly, she taught me how to be a proficient and effective collaborator." He goes on to offer several tips for preparing for a career in lighting design. "The study of painting and art history has truly helped me to understand foreground, middle ground, and background as well as composition. Learning photography was also helpful in developing a sense of visual composition . . . and

I learned how to read music, which is essential to designing opera. I cannot play music, but I can read it." When asked how he came to work primarily in opera he shares that he more or less fell into it. "I have enjoyed opera since I was introduced to it as a teenager by my grandmother, attending performances at the Santa Fe Opera. I mostly designed plays and occasional musicals for Broadway and regional theatre until I was hired as the Resident Lighting Designer at New York City Opera in 1991. I feel that there were other designers who applied for the position who had more opera experience than I, but believe that I was selected because of my television experience." At the time, New York City Opera productions were being televised for *Live From Lincoln Center* and *Great Performances*, programs on PBS. Jeff shares an interesting story about being "typed" as a designer. "After NY City Opera, it took 7 years before someone hired me to design a production where people only spoke. Producers did not realize or remember that until 1991, I had almost exclusively designed plays." Currently, his work is three-quarters in opera design, but this depends on the year and how the individual projects line up.

Jeff sees one of the fundamental differences between working in opera and other entertainment genres being related to the scale of productions. "Opera, by its nature, is larger than life, even though the human emotions are the same as in a play. They are simply expressed in a larger emotional way . . . singing and orchestration makes it larger . . . the scenery also follows the bigger than life emotion. Thus, the lighting follows. Opera is driven totally by music and the way that light moves is totally aligned with the music." Despite the issues of scale, time is also a unique consideration in opera design. "Opera is large in every way, and time in the theatre is very expensive." Most opera companies operate in unionized houses—add stagehands, musicians, and singers and an average opera can employ 70 to 80 people who will be directly involved with the production in the theatre. "Time is the enemy (financially)." The companies are very tightly budgeted and have a finite amount of time (and money) for rehearsals in the theatre. "The production must be completed in the allotted amount of time." A typical schedule in regional opera has the production loading-in on a Sunday or Monday and opening the next Friday. "As a lighting designer, I must know how much equipment I can hang and focus in the amount of time that is scheduled. More importantly, I must have a very clear idea of the lighting and visual look of the production because my time for lighting is very limited. More often than not, I am lighting over staging rehearsals and have no other time than these rehearsals to create light cues." A typical situation involves cueing a production over two 3-hour staging rehearsals and a 4-hour session without the cast. "You do not have the time to discover the concept and look of the production with the director in the theatre. This speed of production is not for everyone." While time constraints are a challenge, what he likes about working in opera is that, "Producers pay me to listen to pretty music. I also feel that there is more respect in the opera community for the contribution of the lighting designer than in other disciplines." When pressed to comment on what he considers an essential rule for working in opera he states, "For me, it is the same as in any theatrical venture . . . we must tell the story and support the emotion of the piece at every moment. Lighting tells the audience how to see and where to look. Lighting is cinematography for the theatre."

To remain current, Jeff continues to work in both opera and theatre so that he knows the trends, current tastes, and artistic vision of the various companies that he designs for. He also tries to keep up with the equipment by reading trade magazines, visiting manufacturers and the lighting shops, and finally trying to see as much theatre as he possibly can. He offers the following as a final bit of advice, "Go to the theatre. Go to museums. Light anything, within reason!"

Photo credit: Jeff Davis

Other lighting effects include visual chase sequences or other patterns of illumination that aren't necessarily created by a specific set of specials but by cueing luminaires that are already a part of a lighting design. A cyc sequencing through various color combinations in a dance recital forms an example of this type of effect. Lighting effects also do not necessarily have to involve motion; a scene may shift into green light for a specific reason (a symbolic connection to greed), a designer may want to create a visual connection or reaction to a character (the symbolic lights used when Salieri talks to God in *Amadeus*), or a series of specials may be used to create specific points of focus (specials for asides). Finally, projections also form a special area of lighting effects. The projected images may be either realistic or stylized.

FOR FURTHER READING

McCandless, Stanley, *A Syllabus of Stage Lighting*, 5th ed. (New Haven, CT: Yale University, 1941).

McCandless, Stanley, *A Method for Lighting the Stage*, 4th ed. (New York: Theatre Arts Books, 1958).

Mumm, Robert C., *Photometrics Handbook*, 2nd ed. (Lousiville, KY: Broadway Press, 1997).

Palmer, Richard H., *The Lighting Art: The Aesthetics of Stage Lighting Design* 2nd ed. (Englewood Cliffs, NJ: Prentice-Hall, Inc., 1994).

Pilbrow, Richard, *Stage Lighting Design: The Art, The Craft, The Life* (New York: Design Press/Quite Specific Media Group, Ldt., 1997).

Shelley, Steven Louis, *A Practical Guide to Stage Lighting* (Boston, MA: Focal Press, 1999).

Warfel, William B., *The New Handbook of Stage Lighting Graphics* (New York: Drama Book Publishers, 1990).

Plotting the Design   12

The **light plot** or **lighting layout** is a scaled drafting of an environment (top view) that illustrates critical information related to a lighting design. Light plots are used in entertainment lighting, while lighting layouts are used in permanent installations like themed and exhibit designs as well as architectural projects. The light plot and lighting layout can be compared to a road map where every luminaire is placed in a location directly related to where it will be hung in the installation. In addition to identifying the type and location of each instrument, the light plot also provides essential information relating to the wiring and accessories that are associated with each fixture. Some of the more essential information contained in most light plots includes gel colors, instrument numbers, and control channels. Additional information might include dimmer numbers, focus notations, lamp size and type, and circuit numbers.

Everything discussed to this point in the design process has been purely theoretical. When we arrive at this stage; a designer should have completed the majority of their research, developed their lighting concept, drawn lighting keys, and explored a number of potential options regarding a design. It is when the designer gets to this point, when they begin to create the actual light plot, that they start to commit to specific choices that will ultimately dictate the outcome of the final design. Light plots and layouts fulfill two very important functions. First, in rough form, they are used as a worksheet for lighting designers to develop their ideas and translate their images into specific design decisions. They explore which hanging positions are best for a given angle of light, examine how much coverage a luminaire and throw distance might produce, and explore issues related to the relationship between the luminaires and the settings or performers. Second, and more importantly, the light plot is the principle form of communication between the designer and electricians who will hang and wire the lights for a production.

Every plot should be drawn from the perspective that it could be hung without the designer being present for the actual **load-in**. In fact, it is quite common to send a plot ahead of a designer with the intention that the hang will be completed and ready for focusing once the designer comes to town. Neat drafting skills are essential to completing this aspect of a lighting design. On the other hand, the plot is a tool for producing the design and should not be thought of as the final product in itself. While good drafting practices are important, they alone will not produce a successful light plot or final design. I have seen many well-drafted plots with critical problems relating to issues like luminaire selection and placement, angle distributions, and color selection despite having an attractive drafting style. This can be especially misleading in CAD (Computer-Aided Design and Drafting) plots. The light plot forms an extremely important step in the overall process of a lighting design. If a designer makes a major mistake when they create the plot, there may not be much that can be done to fix the problem once the load-in at the theatre has been accomplished. If all the angles of a wash system are too severe, the only practical way of solving the problem will most likely require moving the units to new hanging positions, which may or may not be possible once a show is hung in the theatre.

It's an even bigger issue in architectural applications where openings, mounting hardware and conduits are involved. One final area of concern lies in that the plot is still only one aspect of designing a show. Even with the best plot, lighting designs have failed miserably due to the failure of the designer to produce appropriate cues and transitions for a show.

This chapter and the light plot form an essential step in the design because it starts the process of converting the vision of the designer into physical decisions that ultimately determine the outcomes of a lighting design. The process of creating a light plot is a very personal one that many designers tailor to their individual ways of working. Factors such as time allotment, type and scale of project, collaborators, facility, and the number of tech and dress rehearsals all play a role in the way in which I approach a design. Throughout this chapter I discuss a general process and several specific techniques that I use to translate the mental images of a concept into the physical demands of a light plot. This information should provide beginning designers with a starting point and overall methodology for approaching a light plot. While the techniques presented here will work for many individuals, you should feel free to adopt and revise them so that they work with the specific manners in which you work as a designer.

TRANSLATING CONCEPTS AND LIGHTING KEYS INTO PRACTICAL DESIGN CHOICES

One of the most important functions of a light plot is in aiding a designer in turning their images into actual choices that control the properties of light. We have spent the last several chapters developing an image for a production. What should the lighting look like? Are there motivational lighting elements? Are there practical sources on the stage? Where is the light coming from? What is the quality, color, texture, and intensity of the light? Lighting functions should also be considered as part of this process. Is a particular environment or atmosphere called for? How much visibility is required? What direction is a motivational light coming from? How strong must a focus be and where should it be established? What is the mood? These and questions like them should be addressed in the **lighting concept.** When we get to the light plot, the job of the lighting designer is to convert these conceptual images into practical design choices like luminaire selection, hanging positions, focus points, and color choices. No matter how a designer solves these issues, the answers to all of the questions should be determined in a manner that supports or is founded in the concept—it forms the basis for all your decisions.

Many designers create visual methods for representing specific moments or images of a production. In Chapter 10, I introduced **story boards** and **lighting scores** as two methods of communicating this information to other members of the production team. We might even create computer renderings of these moments. In addition to supporting the concept through story boards or lighting scores, many designers choose to illustrate the lighting compositions through **lighting keys.** A lighting key may be developed for any moment of a production but is used most often to illustrate the full wash systems that cover the majority of a stage. More importantly, they provide a tool for matching the specific intentions of a concept to practical choices of luminaire, hanging positions, and color associations for a plot. It is common to have separate lighting keys for different scenes or acts of a production. Often, the lighting keys become the foundation for the layout of the general illumination or area lighting systems for a show.

WORKING WITH FLOORPLANS AND SECTIONS

As we move toward creating a lighting design we need to make calculations in regard to throw distances, beam spreads, and distribution angles that are associated with the luminaires that will light a scene. By using scaled plans, the unique physical properties of light emitting from a particular luminaire can be translated into graphical data that represents how that light should perform in a given situation. Lighting designers have come to rely on two key draftings for working through this part of a design project. The first, a **floorplan** or **groundplan,** provides a scaled top view of an environment, while the second, the **section** or **sectional view,** provides a variation of side view for a facility.

Floorplans or Groundplans

Floorplans (also called groundplans) are usually considered the most important drafting for many design applications. In lighting design, the floorplan is frequently used as a template for the **light plot,** which forms the single most important design document that a lighting designer produces. With these plots, we do not typically illustrate the entire auditorium, only the stage and adjoining spaces. Many floorplans also indicate a portion of the house or audience areas and FOH lighting positions as well. Several features found on virtually all master floorplans include: the proscenium or stage opening; the edge of the stage; all architectural walls, columns, and doorways; an indication of any permanent lighting positions like torms, box boom positions, beams, and the pre-wired electrics; and a schedule that provides the location and identification of all the flown equipment (scenic, lighting, and maskings) and their associated **linesets.** Common reference lines like the **centerline** and **plasterline** are also indicated. Other information that is often found on a floorplan includes references to a facility's sightlines, inclusion of scaled rules that allow for the measurements from either side of a centerline or plasterline, and labels or notes that clarify information relating to any unique features of a space. When a designer is first contracted to design in a facility they should obtain a packet of information that includes a set of master drawings containing the floorplan and section of the performance space as well as any special information regarding a facility (e.g., circuit layout, number and capacity of dimmers, lighting inventory, etc.). A special variation of master plan that is especially helpful is the **circuit layout.** This drafting includes all the information found in a floorplan plus an indication of all the circuit locations throughout a facility. Most theatres have this information readily available and often post it on their websites.

For a floorplan to be truly beneficial to a lighting designer it should make a clear indication of every permanent hanging position throughout a theatre. In a theatre equipped with a fly house, all of the linesets should be indicated and labeled with whatever is to be hung on them (electric, scenery, maskings, and even empty). This is a **hanging section,** and each of these linesets should be placed in their actual positions throughout the depth of the stage. In those theatres that have a substantially large auditorium, it is common to compress or shorten the distance between the FOH positions and the stage to produce more economically sized draftings. Floorplans may be created using conventional pencil and paper drafting techniques or computer drafting and CAD (Computer-Aided Design or Drafting). Lighting designers, in particular, have embraced CAD due to the repetitive nature of many of the tasks associated with drafting a light plot.

The scale of these drawings may vary due to a variety of issues like the amount of detail required, facility size, and complexity of a design. The issue of scale usually balances between being large and detailed enough so that the electricians can easily read all the specification information while at the same time being small enough that the plot doesn't become awkward to carry around and use throughout the design process. Popular scales in hand-drafting include ¼-inch and ½-inch to the foot scales. The ½-inch scale provides good clear information but can produce a plate or drawing that is too large to handle easily. On the other hand, a ¼-inch scaled drawing reduces the details to such a small size that vital information might be missed. A common compromise is to break the space down into smaller areas using separate plates with larger scales like ½" = 1'–0" for areas like the **overheads** (area directly over the stage) and the **FOH** hanging positions. With CAD drafting, scale has become less of an issue since it is so easy to change the scale of the finished print of a drawing.

Floorplans are an essential tool for helping lighting designers determine the **throw distances** and **beam spreads** of luminaires. The throw distance represents the line of sight distance between the luminaire and its target. Beam spreads are an important element in a lighting design because they effectively determine how much coverage is created by a luminaire. If a lighting instrument is chosen with a particular beam spread, a variety of different sized light pools are produced as the instrument is moved between different hanging positions. As the unit is moved farther away from the stage, its throw distance is increased and the resultant beam gets larger. However, even though the light covers a larger portion of the stage, it is also weakened by being spread out over a greater area. Through using a manufacturer's **cut sheet** and other photometric data regarding a specific luminaire, a lighting designer can determine both the pool size and resultant intensity of a lighting instrument at different distances between the stage and various hanging positions. A designer can make an approximate determination of throw distance simply by drawing a line between the location of where the lighting instrument will be mounted to the location that corresponds to the point where the light will be focused. The resultant line represents an approximate throw distance (in scale) between the two points. The throw distance can then be referenced to a manufacturer's cut sheet to determine the photometric output (in footcandles) and size of its associated pool at that distance. If a designer wants to increase or decrease the brightness of the light, they must either move the luminaire to a different mounting position (closer or farther away) or should select a luminaire with a different output (more or less footcandles for a given distance). For more accurate determinations, a geometric construction can be made that illustrates the throw distance as the hypotenuse of a right triangle. The height of the luminaire **(trim)** is plotted along the vertical axis of the triangle, while the floor distance between the luminaire and target is plotted as the horizontal axis. This allows the true throw distance to be determined using the Pythagorean Theorem ($A^2 + B^2 = C^2$). As a rule, the base of the triangle should be placed at about 5 to 6 feet above the stage floor so that the focus point is at the approximate head height of the performers.

As discussed in Chapter 11, an important first step in many lighting designs after completing the conceptual framework of a production is breaking the stage into specific areas that will each be lit by individual luminaires. A practical size for these lighting areas ranges from 8 to 12 feet in diameter, with many designers using 10 feet as an average-sized area. By creating a simple template, lines can be constructed that represent the beam spread(s) of a given luminaire(s). These angles are split symmetrically across a central line representing the axis of the luminaire and shortest path or throw distance between the luminaire and target. The template is laid over the floorplan with the originating point being placed over the location of the luminaire and the line representing the throw distance oriented so that it passes directly over the target or focus point of an acting area. A second line is then drawn perpendicular to the line representing the throw distance so that it intersects both the focus point and lines that define the beam spread of a given instrument. The length (in scale) of this resultant line represents the diameter of the light pool at that distance from the light source. Pool size is a function of the throw distance, mounting position, and the beam spreads of the luminaires. On the other hand, if a circle representing the diameter of a lighting area is drawn around the focus point, the template can also be used to determine which beamspread and associated luminaire will best match the size of a lighting area from a given hanging position (i.e, which beam spreads on the template come closest to intersecting the full diameter of the area circles). If the luminaire is moved to a closer position, the resultant beam diameter will be smaller, while it will increase if the luminaire is moved farther away from the target. By working with various combinations of hanging positions and beam spreads a designer can determine the most effective luminaires and hanging positions for producing light pools of a given size. While a template can be made as simply as through placing lines representing the throw distance and beam angles on vellum or acetate, commercial templates are also available. Particularly helpful software packages like John McKernon's *Beamwright®* allow a lighting designer to examine pool diameters, lengths of shadows, beam spreads, intensity measurements, and other photometric data. The information is modified based on the data of a specific luminaire and various mounting parameters (trim and floor distances) that are associated with its location. *Beamwright®* contains data for most luminaires associated with the entertainment industry and allows a variety of instruments reflecting different model types and manufacturers to be compared with one another.

Regardless of the way in which a designer prefers to work with a floorplan, what is most important is that the designer uses this material to identify the most effective positions and luminaire choices for a given application. These distances, even as approximations, are usually accurate enough for making comparisons between most luminaires and mounting positions. However, two important exceptions exist where the scale of the drafting can be compromised through issues like using conventions such as compressing the FOH hanging positions. In the first case, one must remember to adjust the location of the luminaire origination points in a FOH position to reflect the true distance of the hanging positions from the stage. The second case comes when a unit is used in a relatively steep angle like downlight, when the floorplan distance is much shorter than the actual throw distance.

Sections

There are two especially important reasons why a section is vital to a lighting designer. First, sections provide the same information in a vertical orientation that a floorplan displays in the horizontal or plan view. Beam spreads, vertical angles, and length of shadows can all be determined from this drafting. Second, the section provides a means by which a lighting designer can determine the **trims** or heights of the electrics while also studying the **maskings** that will be hung from above a stage. A properly masked show will usually block an audience's view of the electrics while still allowing clear shots from the luminaires to their targets. Some lighting designers skip this step in the process—and get burned. I have witnessed issues like electrics being placed at trims that, once masked, caused backlight to point directly into the back of borders as well as upstage platforms that could not be hit due to the trim of a border falling lower than anticipated by a designer. A lighting designer should always take time to complete a section for a lighting design. The more levels that appear on stage, the more important the section becomes.

Sections are typically drawn with the centerline being the cutting-plane through which the view of the theatre is taken. In most cases, it extends from the back wall of the stage to a location somewhere in the house. All vertical elements of a stage are indicated in this drawing. While a master section only illustrates the physical theatre, scenic designers should provide a lighting designer with a section of the scene design for a production. If the scenery warrants, the cutting-plane and associated view may be taken from almost anywhere across the width of the stage. Study of lighting angles, beam spreads, and photometric data are done in the same manner as for floorplans with the exception that the analysis is now done in a different plane—where height becomes a critical determinant in the analysis of the luminaires and hanging positions. Again, most target points are placed at a height 5 to 6 feet above the floor, which aligns the hot spots with the performers' faces rather than their feet. More importantly, by using the same template of beam/field angles, a designer can get a clear indication of the coverage of a lighting instrument in sectional view. This time, the origin of the template is located at a position corresponding with the hanging position, while the line representing the throw distance is oriented directly over the corresponding focus point (at head-height). Figure 12.1 illustrates the use of a section for determining lighting angles and beam spreads for the principle hanging positions used in a production of *Measure for Measure*.

Just as important as determining mounting positions and beam patterns are decisions related to masking a show. This ensures that the trims of the electrics and borders are set so that audience views of the electrics are blocked ,while also ensuring that the luminaires can hit their targets. To establish the proper maskings, an extreme sightline is indicated on the section that is based on the head height of an audience member seated in the first row of the audience. This point is used as an origin point for sightlines that extend from it to the bottom edge of any maskings that are hung from above the stage (e.g., borders). These sightlines are extended beyond the borders so that the electrics can be placed above the sightlines and out of view while also being low enough that the units

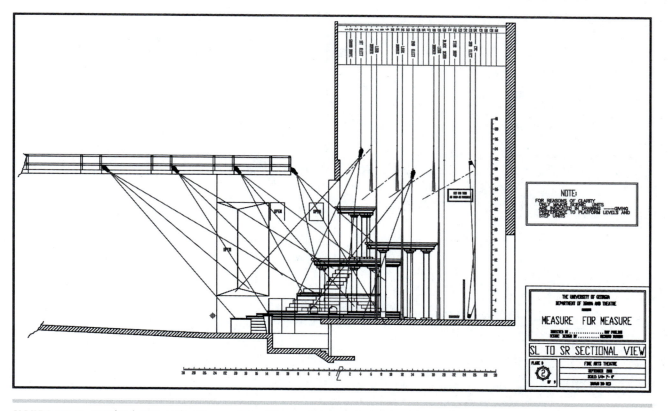

FIGURE 12.1 Vertical Determinations of Position and Beam Spread with a Section

can hit the parts of the stage where they will be focused. Figure 12.2 illustrates the use of the same section to set the border and electric trims for *Measure for Measure*.

Just as a scenic designer provides the lighting designer with a scenic floorplan, a section should also be included in the scenic design packet. This section should include the placement of each border and any other maskings that are hung from above the stage. Other scenic elements like platforms, wall and scenic unit heights, and flown elements with both high and low trim markings should be indicated in these plans. Specific hanging positions and trim heights are often discussed between scenic and lighting designers, and there have actually been a number of times where I, as the lighting designer, was allowed to mask and set the trims for a show. If a scenic designer does relinquish control of the trims and maskings to a lighting designer, it is important for everyone to understand that it may not be possible to go back and change the masking and trim placements once a show has begun its load-in and focus. There are also times when it may be desirable to place electrics in full view of an audience. On these occasions, the section helps a designer to once again determine the best positions for these trims. I designed a production of *Noises Off* in which the electrics were fully masked in Acts I and III, where the setting took place from a traditional audience perspective, while for Act II several of the electrics and borders changed trim to bring the electrics into view to suggest that the audience's perspective had been switched to backstage. I used a similar technique in *Tommy* to expose many of the electrics for creating a concert-like experience. Even though experienced designers may have lit many productions in a given facility and have a good understanding of which luminaires work best from different house positions, it is still important to study the floorplan and section due to the unique requirements of a particular scenic design. The section becomes especially important the first time that a designer works in a space. It also helps, if possible, to arrange a site survey where personal observations and measurements can be made of a stage prior to developing a light plot.

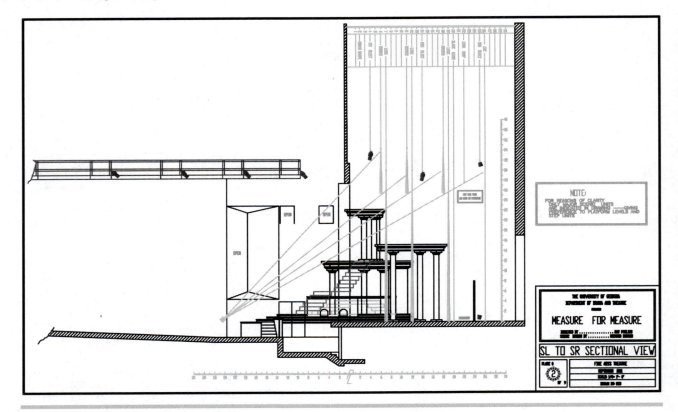

FIGURE 12.2 Setting Borders and Trim Heights with a Section

AN APPROACH TO PLOTTING A DESIGN

Throughout this discussion I use a production of Moliere's *The Miser* as an example of how to apply a design process to creating a light plot. This production was designed as part of the 2005 Jean Cocteau Repertory Theatre season at the Bouwerie Lane Theatre in New York City. This production was of a limited scale, which should make it easier to analyze throughout the process. While I may modify this process based on individual projects, there are several essential steps that are taken for nearly every design that I complete—whether in some formal methodology as presented here or only intuitively as part of the design process. For designers with relatively little or no experience, these steps should provide a more practical way of approaching a design, while those who are more experienced may use these suggestions to review their personal design process. I will continue to use this production as an example in Chapter 13 as we move the production into the theatre.

Preliminary Tasks/Preparation

When I discuss preliminary tasks, I am referring to the acquisition of background materials that will be needed to execute the planning stages of a lighting design. This information should be gathered and fully understood prior to making any specific decisions regarding the light plot. In reality, some of this information will be available, while some will remain unknown due to tight rehearsal schedules and the fact that it is common for a light plot to be completed before a company moves into a venue. The designs that I have completed for the Atlanta Lyric Theatre have always required that the plot be mailed ahead of my seeing a single run-through of a production. In cases like this, a lighting designer must rely heavily on the conversations that they have with the director and other members of the artistic team.

A key step at this point in the process is determining the lighting scheme and concept and creating the storyboards and lighting key(s) for a project. These were discussed extensively in previous chapters and form the basis for most of the decisions that a designer will make in regard to a light plot. Other essential information that the designer should assemble before attempting to work on the light plot include copies of the master floorplan and section of the facility, a copy of the scenic floorplan(s) and section for the production, color indications (swatches, paint elevations, and renderings) from the costume and scenic designers, and a lighting specifications package for the facility. Lighting equipment inventories are an important part of this list. Although most productions must work within set inventory limitations, there are occasions when an inventory might be supplemented or even fully supplied by gear that is provided by a rental house or through combining equipment from other resources. Frequently, equipment provided by a facility is fairly limited, and it is the production's responsibility to provide most of the lighting equipment. Even the dimmers and console are part of many of these rental packages. Most Broadway and touring houses operate in this fashion.

Rehearsals

Rehearsals give a lighting designer the opportunity to view an event prior to moving into the performance venue. While it is common in educational theatres for rehearsals to take place in the actual space where the performances will take place, this is more often the exception when you work on productions outside of an academic setting. Most rehearsals are conducted in rehearsal halls or studios so that the time used in mounting a production in the actual theatre is kept to a minimum. Even if an organization owns its own facility, it is common to rehearse outside of the theatre so that other shows can complete longer runs. Additional issues, like how long a producer can afford to have a lighting designer in residence, also determine how many rehearsals a lighting designer gets to see. Usually, a lighting designer is only brought in for the last week or so of the production process. This eliminates per-diem checks, hotel or room costs, and additional transportation for when the designer is in residence. In many cases, light plots have to be completed even before the designer sees their first rehearsal. This type of scheduling requires a heavy reliance on developing good communication skills with the director.

The significance of observing rehearsals is in becoming familiar with a production. A designer makes important discoveries regarding the performers and director's interpretation of a script when attending rehearsals. However, what is most important is understanding the movement patterns of the performers. In addition to understanding the physical relationships between the actors, the designer should also evaluate the scenes for focus as well as for pace, mood, and transitions. **Run-throughs** are much more beneficial to see than working rehearsals for making these observations. Even if a lighting designer can only see several scenes, they will still gain an understanding of the actions, the way in which the director uses a space, and a feeling for the moods and transitions of the associated scenes. At these rehearsals I take care to make accurate records of the **blocking notation** (Chapter 10).

For *The Miser,* my preliminary design discussions were conducted with the director through e-mail and telephone conversations before I left town for New York. The lighting inventory, plans, and technical specifications for the theatre were also sent to me earlier. In reality, I already had many of the materials since I had lit a production of *The Maids* in the same theatre a year earlier. Even though I had this information, it was important to verify what had changed from the last time that I had worked in the space. In this case, the Cocteau had upgraded to a new lighting system of 60 high-density dimmers. The inventory was also revised to include a number of new luminaires that were purchased as part of the same grant that the organization had received to upgrade its lighting equipment.

The Wish List

Once I have completed my analysis and research for a design, developed the lighting concept, had discussions with the director and other artistic staff, and hopefully been able to attend a run-through or two, I am at a point where I can begin to develop the actual plot.

While there are many different ways of working, I have found that developing a **wish list** for a production forms an excellent manner for allowing me to identify those elements of a design that I believe are most essential. It also allows me both to prioritize and translate all of the lighting needs into specific choices that will ultimately be drafted into the final plot. By the time that I finish working with the wish list a number of the major decisions regarding the design will have been committed to and the design will be ready to enter into a preliminary or rough light plot. Later, this will be converted into the final drafting. Throughout the entire process, the lighting concept and visual references like the story boards or lighting scores and lighting keys are used as a basis for evaluating each task within the wish list.

In creating a wish list, a designer simply makes determinations of those lighting features that they would like to provide for a production. Issues like number of color washes from various locations, amount of coverage or area breakdown required, director-requested specials and images, lighting of scenic elements, effects considerations, accents, and other personal design choices all form part of these considerations. The lighting key plays a significant role in identifying the components of the general or area lighting that will appear in the wish list. The actual list is simply jotted down on a notepad and listed in such a way that the item or "wish" can ultimately be translated into a specific choice of luminaire, color, and control (channel and dimmer). Area lighting and other wash systems are further broken down into the number of area components or zones that the designer will ultimately hope to use for each lighting system. If a designer wishes to use a system with a breakdown of five areas across and three deep, this is indicated in the wish list. If there is even a hint of a desire for a particular special or specific lighting feature I list it somewhere on this list. As I create the list, I try to group each demand into areas of the list that match related lighting needs (i.e., groupings like area lighting, accent washes, specials, cyc lighting, etc.). Those elements of the design that I consider most important are placed further up the list. In many cases, my wish list may contain five or six pages (often more) of specific demands that I hope to incorporate into the lighting design. Basic components of the design in terms of color and angle distributions, area/zone breakdowns, and specific needs like accents and specials form important elements of the wish list. Figure 12.3 provides a partial listing of the wish list for the Cocteau's production of *The Miser*.

A designer must be realistic about the demands that they place in a wish list. Availability can be restricted due to an actual inventory, amount of rental budget, or the amount of time and number of electricians available to hang and focus a show. Most design decisions come about through restrictions in the number of dimmers or luminaires that are available for a design. One question that a lighting designer needs to address early in this process is in the determination of which of these two limitations is ultimately going to be the primary restriction on a design. In a theatre where there are many instruments and relatively few dimmers, the number of dimmers will ultimately shape a design. This was the manner in which most of us had to design prior to dimmer-per-circuit systems. Today, since we commonly have theatres with hundreds of circuits and dimmers, it is more common to have design restrictions based on not having enough inventory to fulfill all the wishes of a lighting design. Even with dimmer-per-circuit dimming, it is still possible to run out of dimmers in a complex design.

Making a Design Practical

Once all of the demands of a design have been placed on the wish list, the next step in the process is assessing the practical limitations of the inventory. I already made reference to the fact that most of today's designs are limited more by luminaire rather than dimmer limitations. Therefore, the inventory is used in combination with the wish list to establish practical solutions for each demand of the list. By working thorough this process most, if not all, of the demands will be addressed and hopefully worked into the final design.

The first step is establishing a complete inventory of each lighting instrument that is available for a production. To work through this, I have developed a table with a format that indicates several key sources of information relating to the luminaire inventory. The

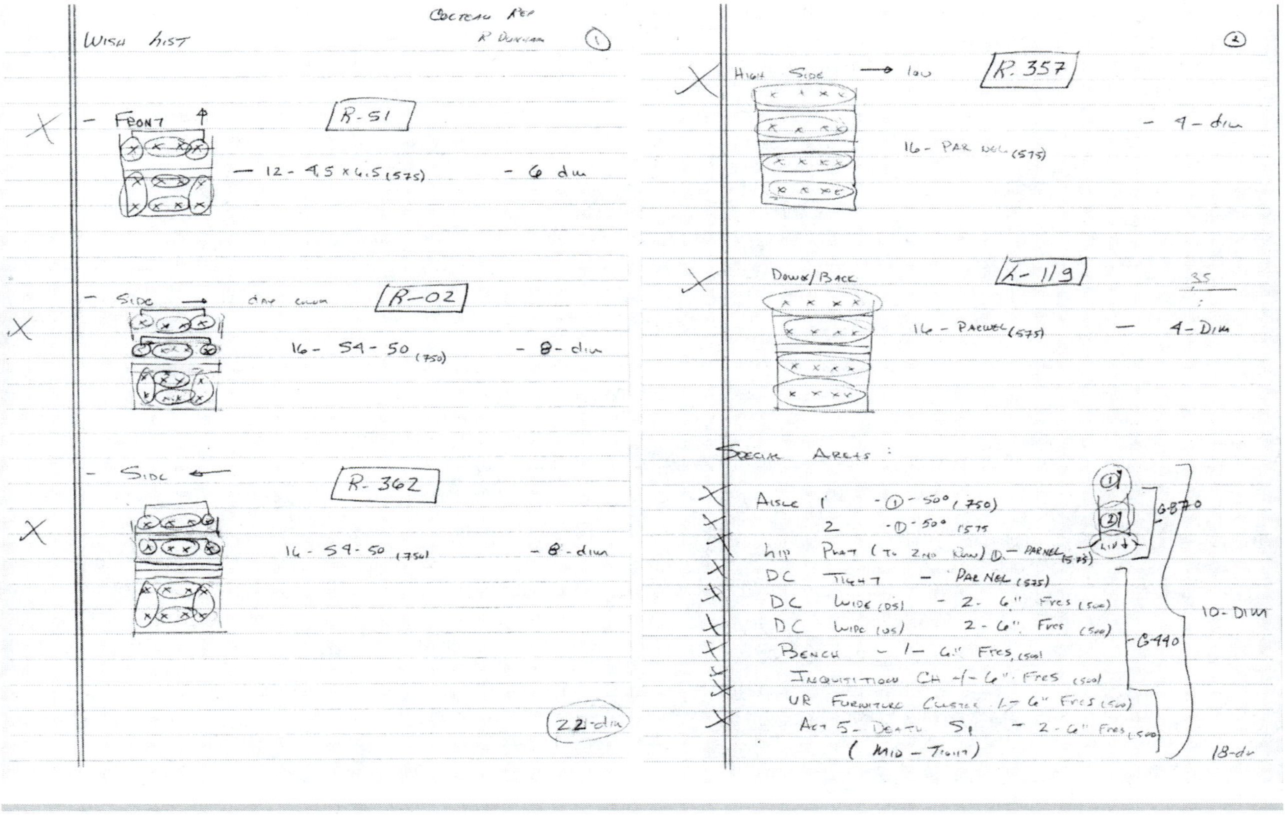

FIGURE 12.3 *The Miser* Wish List (Partial)

first column lists the type of luminaire while the second lists the wattage of the units. The next column provides the total number of units of a particular instrument type that are available for a production. The form also makes a distinction between luminaires of the same type but of varying wattages or from different manufacturers. The next area of the worksheet lists the specific uses of each light that is used from the inventory. Finally, the last two columns indicate the number of each luminaire type actually used and the remaining units still available.

The next step in the process is crucial and involves matching the lighting needs of the production outlined in the wish list with the luminaires that are available through the inventory list. Washes are established with common luminaires, throw distances and beam spreads are matched to hanging positions, and specific specials are matched to instruments that best emulate the characteristics desired in that special. The designer should begin with assigning luminaires to the most important tasks first and then move through the wish list matching luminaires to specific purposes on a priority basis. A general listing of priorities that extend from most to least important would normally include area or general lighting systems, accents and other wash systems, critical specials, motivational units, scenic specials, and finally additional accents and subtle specials. When making luminaire assignments, a floorplan containing the lighting positions and set design is used along with a section to help match the specific needs of beam spread and throw distances to particular lighting fixtures. As a lighting instrument is assigned to a specific function, a tick mark is placed in the "Used" column, while the actual function and number of units assigned to that function are listed in the "Specific Use" column of the inventory worksheet. Additionally, the type and number of luminaires is also listed next to the need/function in the wish list to cross-reference the information between the two forms. Once a function has been assigned to specific luminaires, a check mark is placed on the wish list to indicate that the particular need has been addressed. More complex systems may use graphical illustrations to indicate the specific instrument layouts.

As a designer works through the lists, the decisions become more difficult—as instruments of a specific type become depleted, the designer has to make sacrifices in order to achieve as many of the needs as they can for the design. Instruments may be substituted with luminaires that aren't as good a match with the initial intentions of the designer, two or more specials might be combined by dedicating both functions to a single instrument, an insufficient number of dimmers might require that specials be **re-patched** through common dimmers, individual area control may be sacrificed by ganging several luminaires from different areas to a single dimmer, or in the worst case scenario, specific wishes are simply cut. The process is easy at first but becomes more grueling as fewer instruments remain and more compromises must be made to complete a design. The advantage to this process is that it provides a means for accomplishing many of the wish list demands that could have been too easily dismissed. When the wish list and inventory have been matched as closely as possible, the design has been brought within the practical limitations of a production.

If the number of dimmers is of concern, these too, can be matched to the specific needs of the wish list. By doing this, it is possible to identify those functions where higher capacity dimmers must be specified. Together, both of the above processes allow the needs of the wish list to be translated into specific choices of luminaire and dimmer control while at the same time bringing the design into the practical limitations of a given situation. Last, if not already established through the lighting key or other color assignments, each lighting function is assigned a specific gel color based on the research and lighting keys. These, too, are indicated somewhere on the wish list. By following these procedures most of the decisions affecting the design will be addressed and many of the wishes of a designer will be fulfilled as originally intended. Later, this information is used to create a tentative or rough light plot for the design.

The Tentative Hookup

The next step in the process comes in developing a **tentative hookup** for the production. The **hookup** is nothing more than a listing of all the luminaire and control information of a design placed in a table format. This information is always organized by control data, which more specifically is identified by either the channel, control number, or dimmer assigned to a particular function or purpose of light. The hookup begins with channel or dimmer one and then moves sequentially through each of the channels or dimmers that will be used throughout a show. If a hookup is organized by channel number it is called a **channel schedule** and if done by dimmer, a **dimmer schedule.** It is the designer's preference as to which format is actually used, although the dimmer schedule tends to be preferred in cases where dimmers become the limiting factor in a design. Today, with many theatres using dimmer-per-circuit lighting systems, the channel schedule has become the most popular format and designers often don't have to worry about individual dimmer or circuit assignments, preferring to let the electricians make the assignments as they hang a show. The exception comes when a lighting system contains dimmers with multiple capacities and where the designer has to keep track of how many dimmers are used in each of the different capacities.

Now, through **soft-patching,** most designers organize their console and hookups based on the function of the lights, and channels can be assigned with no regard to dimmer loads. This allows luminaires with similar functions and their channels to be organized into patterns that make sense to the designer. For example, all of the pink area lights associated with a 12-lamp system can be assigned to channels 1–12. The designer can also leave channels unassigned to provide more logic to their assignments. Continuing with the *Miser* example, the lavender area lights associated with the same focus points are assigned to channels 21–32. The singles digit essentially corresponds to a location of the stage for both lighting systems, while the tens digit designates different color systems. Downleft would be lit by channel 1 in pink and 21 in lavender, while down right might be lit with channel 4 for pink and 24 for lavender. One of the benefits of carefully assigning the channels is that it makes the operation of the lighting console easier and more efficient, eliminating keystrokes when inputting console data. In the above example, rather than having to call out and input each of the individual channels, a board operator could simply make use of the "thru" command (Channels 1 thru 12 would be entered to bring up the entire pink system).

A tentative hookup is nothing more than a series of worksheets that list the control channel in the first column and then all the other pertinent data regarding the luminaires and their assigned functions in subsequent columns. Other data typically displayed in a tentative hookup includes instrument types and wattage (to determine dimmer loads), purpose or function of the light(s), and color. If dimmer or circuit information is critical to the assignments this information may also be added to the tentative hookup. Actual placement and unit numbers are not entered at this point in the process even though the wish list should have already established which luminaires and hanging position will be assigned to a particular function. In working through the tentative hookup, the designer simply assigns each of the functions and associated luminaires to a particular control channel. The most important needs are usually assigned to the lowest channel numbers, while luminaires with more limited functions are given higher channel assignments. Most designers tend to assign their area systems to the lowest numbers. If any special area lighting is called for it too is often assigned along with the generals. After all the area systems have been accounted for, designers usually go on to make control assignments for the other washes and accent systems (sidelight, front-diagonal, back, etc.), often working progressively from the front toward the back and downlight angles. Multiple colors or washes of similar lighting systems are traditionally grouped together like the pink and lavender area lighting examples that were presented earlier. Once the washes have been allocated, assignments of specific specials and finally any large scenic washes such as cyc lighting are worked into the hookup. As a function is assigned to the hookup it is once again checked off the wish list. Once completing the tentative hookup, the only step that remains is determining the locations of where the luminaires will actually be mounted in the theatre.

The Rough Light Plot

Although I know lighting designers who don't create rough light plots, I have found that it is usually more beneficial to do a rough plot where you can work out a design and don't have to worry about creating a beautifully drafted plot. You should feel free to make changes, correct mistakes, and try various options while you plot a design. There was even a product at one time (Marcplot, distributed by GAM) that allowed colored magnetic symbols of lighting instruments to be placed on a board on which the lighting designer would have previously drawn a floorplan and hanging positions with erasable markers. This permitted lighting designers to easily shift luminaires around as a plot evolved in much the same way that a child's magnetic board is used as a spelling primer. Once all the decisions have been worked out on the rough plot, the designer moves on to drafting a final plot with virtually no need for making corrections or changes. This philosophy has changed somewhat as designers have shifted to using computer-aided drafting (CAD) and the relative ease with which many of the luminaire changes can be made in these programs. More importantly, the units can be moved easily and edited as the design evolves. Even then, issues like juggling instrument locations around due to space limitations and having to renumber them frequently occur. In fact, many CAD programs can renumber the units of a lighting position through a simple command. In conventional drafting, it is best not to number the units until all of them have been placed.

While napkin sketches can play a role in some of your design development, the rough light plot should be an actual drafting. It must be to scale and should show all the critical elements of the theatre in the same fashion that you would illustrate them in the final plot. Once a batten has been identified as an electric it should be drawn as a single line on the plot just as any other permanent lighting position. Many designers will also add small hatch marks along the battens at 18" intervals from either side of the centerline for marking positions where the luminaires might be located. The 18" spacing allows most neighboring instruments to have full pan control without bumping lens barrels. While the scale does not have to be the same as the final plot, scale is an important element of the rough plot, and luminaires are drawn to scale so that the designer can determine whether there is enough space to hang all of the units that they want in a given location. I often find that a 1/4" scale works fine for the rough plot and will then shift to a 3/8" or 1/2" scale for the final plot. Many designers also like to add an indication of the major scenic elements on a rough plot as well. This is done by lightly tracing the outline of the scenic components onto the plot or transferring the scenic design to the plot with colored pencils. Designers may also choose to place a copy of the scenic design under the plot or use clear acetate to lay over the rough plot. The final step in preparing the rough plot before the addition of the actual instruments is in identifying those primary focus points associated with the area lighting systems. Most designers indicate the focus points with a simple hatch mark. These are further identified by placing a letter or stage designation next to them (e.g., A, B, C, or DC, CL, etc.).

The process of creating the rough plot is actually quite simple. The designer simply goes through the tentative hookup one channel at a time and places the associated fixtures on the rough plot. Those channels associated with luminaires that have more critical placements are transferred to the plot first, while those with less particular placements are added later. In order to ensure that the luminaires are created at the right size, a designer will use a specialized stencil called a **lighting template** (Figure 12.4) to draw scaled representations of the instruments on the plot. A lighting template contains a basic silhouette of the sizes and shapes of the primary lighting units. The drafting/symbol standards in the entertainment industry were established through a special review process by USITT (The United States Institute for Theatre Technology). In addition to the symbols, USITT has also indicated a manner (notation) in which information like unit number, channel identification, color, and focus are to be noted on a light plot. Figure 12.5 illustrates several common representations of the USITT standard (Recommended Practice), while Appendix C provides the full USITT RP-2 Lighting Graphics document.

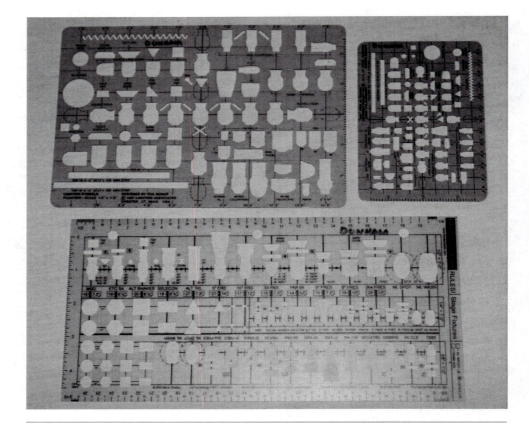

FIGURE 12.4 Lighting Templates

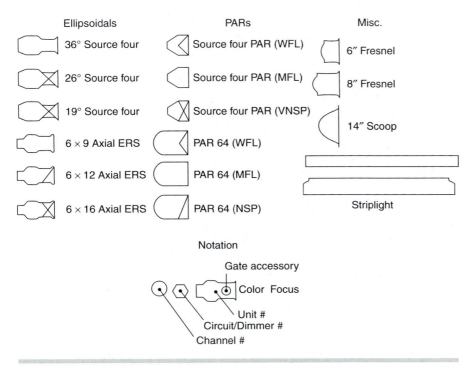

FIGURE 12.5 Common USITT Luminaire Symbols and Notation

As a lighting designer examines the tentative hookup they should be able to identify and prioritize those luminaires that require a more critical placement. Lighting design is not an exact science, and specific hanging positions may have to be altered slightly from the lighting key due to issues like the hanging positions being too close to or far from a subject, obstructions or sightline issues created by scenery or theatre architecture, and even other luminaires that may already occupy a space. The designer should approximate these positions and should not be overly concerned if a luminaire has to shift even as much as several feet either side of its intended position. In fact, there are circumstances in which the luminaire, if it remains on its central axis, can actually shift forward or backward 6 to 10 feet to completely different hanging positions with little noticeable effect on the stage. On the other hand, there are occasions when only a few inches might determine whether an instrument can hit its target. Once a unit's position has been identified, its associated symbol is drawn on the plot, and other data such as its channel, color, and focus or purpose are also noted by the luminaire. The one set of notations that are purposely avoided are the unit numbers. After all the channels and associated luminaires are entered on the rough plot, the unit numbers are finally added as the last element of the plot. This ensures that the units are listed in an accurate order without having to renumber them several times throughout the design process. This also encourages a designer to approach the drafting based on the needs of the hookup, since any changes that may be needed are easily made through shifting luminaires around as problems like space limitations become an issue. Once the rough plot is completed, virtually all of the design decisions have been made, and the information is simply transferred to the final plot, resulting in the final plot being drafted in a way that is both neat and accurate.

DRAFTING AND THE LIGHTING DESIGN

The drafting of the light plot and section serve an important role in communicating the intentions of a lighting designer to the electricians. In many cases the light plot, section, and associated paperwork will be sent ahead of the designer and needs to be detailed enough that the hang can progress without their presence. This scenario should provide a guiding principle in that a designer should indicate as much information on a plot as the electricians will need to complete the hang in their absence. At the same time, it also

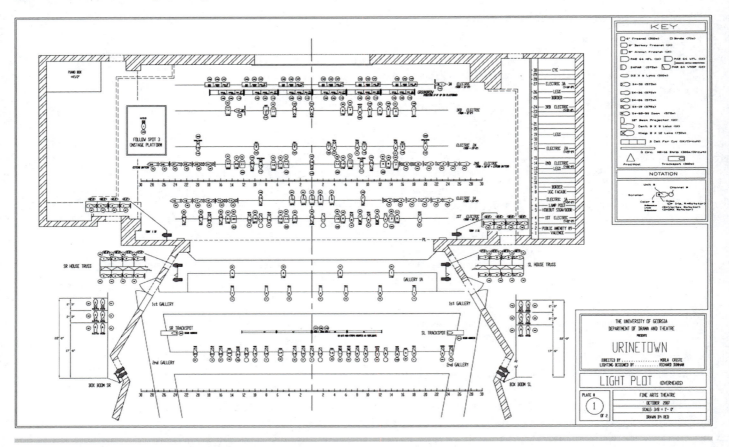

FIGURE 12.6 Overhead Plot from University of Georgia Production of *Urinetown—The Musical*

needs to be clear and concise. In addition to the plot and paperwork for *The Miser,* I have also included a more extensive plot for a production of *Urinetown—The Musical* as an example of a plot that can be referenced throughout the following sections (Figure 12.6).

Drafting Light Plots

If the rough plot has been done properly, all that needs to happen to create the final plot is to simply transfer the information to the new drafting while using the industry's symbols and conventions. Care must be taken to display the information so that the lighting data is easily accessible and important details don't get lost in the sheer volume of information that is represented in a final plot. While USITT makes provisions for indicating virtually any property that you may want to provide for a luminaire, most designers only provide several of the most important elements of information on a light plot. The principle guiding these decisions usually relates to how much information that the designer feels that the electricians need to accurately hang their production. Regardless of what may be indicated on the plot, all essential information for each unit will be found and cross-listed in the design paperwork. The three current schools of thought on what information for each luminaire should be indicated on a plot include: 1. nothing more than unit number, instrument type, and associated accessories; 2. the items listed in 1 plus anything that the electricians need to know to hang/circuit the plot (unit type, number, color, and channel indication); and 3. an academic approach where all of the above along with dimmer, circuit, and focus notations are also indicated for each luminaire. Additional information like manufacturer designations, lamp types, and wattage can be indicated on the plot as well. Designers have their personal reasons for using any of these or other variations of these standards. I personally prefer the second method since it provides the electricians with all the information they need to hang my show without getting too detailed.

Everything on the light plot should be in scale. This gives an accurate depiction of how all of the elements, including the luminaires, fit into a facility and their associated hanging positions. Without using scale, a designer might find that they have squeezed too many luminaires into a given position, making it impossible for the electricians to hang that aspect of the show. The next several segments of this chapter will take you through a typical process of developing the final light plot. The order of these steps is not critical and designers should work in any way that they think works best for them. What's important is that the information presented in the next several pages makes its way into the final light plot. The methods do not change significantly from hand to CAD drafting, although there are many shortcuts that make the drafting of a CAD light plot much less time consuming and tedious. Regardless of how a plot is created, the designer should never give away the original drafting and should only send copies (bluelines, large format photocopies, or prints of a CAD drafting) to a venue.

THE BASICS   The first step in creating the final light plot relates to picking a scale that will present the information in a clear way without becoming so large that it is unmanageable. The more information that you choose to indicate about each unit, the larger the associated scale that you should draft in. On the other hand, if you are designing for a large facility, a large scale could make the plot awkward to both draft and carry around during a light hang. As an alternative, designers may still choose to use a large scale but may opt to create several smaller plots for a design—each illustrating a different part of the theatre. I often create two plots (an **overhead** and **front-of-house**) for several of the larger facilities that I design in. On occasions such as when I designed *Tommy*, I have even created a third plot that was used solely for the ladders and booms or sidelight. The most common scales that most designers draft in are 1/4" (to the foot) for small and 1/2" or 3/8" for large scales. In some limited setups, especially in location shooting for film or video designs, 1/8" scale may also be utilized. Once the scale of the plot has been determined, the designer chooses a sheet of velum or drafting paper that is of an appropriate size to not only illustrate the architectural features of the stage or facility but also leaves ample room for additional features like the **title block, key,** and other information.

PRIMARY INFORMATION   This gives the electricians the essential information they will need for interpreting the material that is presented in the light plot. It also gives them a frame of reference through identifying specific information relating to the facility. Some of the initial information that is first included in a light plot is of the same nature as in any other drafting. A borderline is drawn around the perimeter of the page and a title block is created that clearly indicates key information about the production. The title block is typically located in the lower right-hand corner and includes information like the title of the production, producing organization, name of the theatre where the production is being mounted, title of the drawing (e.g., Light Plot), month and year, your name as designer, and most importantly the scale of the drawing. Additional material that could also be included in the title block might include the name of the director, name of the master electrician or assistant designer, the initials of the draftsperson, and contact information such as cell phone number or e-mail address for the designer. If a designer is union, they will also place their union stamp somewhere around or within the title block.

One of the most important elements to include is the floorplan of the theatre. This is marked in relatively heavy lines and includes the walls of the theatre, the edge of the stage, the pit (if one exists), smoke pockets, and any other physical obstructions within the stage areas. Added to this is the hanging or lineset schedule, which is drawn to coincide with any battens that are hung in the facility. Most designers both identify the line number and list what is actually hung on a particular lineset in the hanging section. Both loaded and empty linesets are included since batten assignments might have to be changed at some point in a load-in. If possible, this schedule should be located in the wings, preferably in the same location as the flyrail, but might even be placed outside of the theatre if the wings are filled with other equipment like booms or ladders. Regardless of the placement of the hanging section, the placement of each lineset should be accurately depicted throughout the depth of the stage. Other general information that is drawn into the plot at this time are reference lines like the centerline and plasterline and scaled reference lines (scales or rules) that extend across both the width and depth of the stage. The horizontal rule crosses the centerline and is marked with hatch marks or ticks on 12- or 18-inch spacings (moving outward in each direction from the centerline) and allows electricians a quick way to identify the placement of luminaires along the electrics without having to use a scaled rule. A similar scale is also constructed through the depth of the stage with the plasterline forming the beginning point. A lighting designer may also include light-weight reference lines that trace the outlines of the primary scenic elements of the production. These lines are often added once the plot is nearly finished because they are frequently broken as they cross any information related to the electrics.

KEY AND NOTATION   The **key** can be compared to one used on a road map and simply matches the drafted symbols with the actual lighting equipment. It is an area of the plot that lists all of the symbols that the designer has used throughout the drafting. The USITT *RP-2 Recommended Practice for Lighting Graphics* forms the standard symbol guidelines within the entertainment industry, while IESNA has established a common set of symbols for the architectural community. Regardless of how a designer illustrates their symbols, they should be clearly labeled as to the type of luminaire that they represent in the key. Wattage is commonly indicated through variations in the basic symbols. Additional items that may appear in the key include lighting hardware and accessories like barndoors, scrollers, and templates. While the key provides identification of the various luminaires, the **notation** provides an explanation of the information that is related to a lighting instrument. The notation may be labeled as "typical" by some designers. Information that is usually indicated in the notation includes unit number, channel and dimmer number, and color. Some designers show more information (e.g., dimmer or focus/purpose) but regardless of what is shown, the notation explains each piece of information associated with a luminaire's symbol.

LUMINAIRES   Each instrument from the rough plot is neatly transferred to the final plot using a template and the scaled symbols previously identified by the key. Additional information regarding color, hookup information, and accessories are also indicated throughout the plot. Each hanging position is marked where it is actually located in the theatre with the exception of FOH positions like beam positions, which typically have the distance between them compressed as a way of saving space. If this is done, a note calling attention to the compression is placed somewhere near the FOH positions. Each lighting position is laid out lightly with a barely perceivable guideline that is then used to help place the luminaires. There are two schools of thought in regard to orienting the luminaires on the plot. The first orients the units in the actual lines of focus, while the second places the units only in the four primary directions (straight front or back and to either side). Advantages of the first system are that it is easier to spot where a unit is focused as well as whether the barrels of neighboring units will interfere with one another. The major shortcoming of this system is in the more chaotic arrangement of the notations associated with each unit. Two ways of reducing this confusion lie in using a standard spacing interval such as placing the instruments on 18-inch centers and using the 90° orientations. The lighting symbols are drawn in medium- to dark-weight lines since they form the most important element of the light plot. Additional data such as channel and color information can be added at this time and are typically drawn using light-weight lines. Gel numbers are placed at the front of the symbol, while control channels are typically placed in a circle located at the back of the symbol. Once all of the units have been placed along the hanging position the lines between the units that represent the batten can be darkened to the same line-weight as the luminaires. Each lighting position is then labeled and is also noted with its trim height (if applicable). Often, a listing of all the luminaires used in a position is added near this label. This aids the electricians in pulling the inventory for a hanging position. On occasion, designers may also list the minimum number of circuits that will be required for the given hanging position. The luminaires are then numbered so that every instrument has a unique number that makes it clearly identifiable from any other unit on the plot. Most instruments are assigned a number

SIDEBAR 12.1 Common Numbering Practices

LIGHTING POSITIONS

Beams/FOH Horizontal Positions	Begins with 1 closest to the plasterline and number away from stage with the highest toward the rear of the house.
FOH Booms/Slots	Identified as SL or SR and begins with 1 closest to the plasterline and highest toward the rear of the house.
Electrics	Begins with 1 closest to the plasterline and number toward the upstage.
Onstage Booms/Torms	Identified as SL or SR and begins with 1 closest to plasterline and highest toward upstage.

UNIT NUMBERING

Horizontal Positions	Begins with 1 SL and ends with highest SR.
Onstage Booms	Facing Boom from onstage with 1 at top closest to plasterline and assigning higher numbers for each unit moving upstage through all units at the same height and then jumping down to the next tier while again numbering from plasterline towards upstage, progressing through the lower tiers.
FOH Booms /Slots	Facing Boom from stage with 1 at top closest to centerline and then assigning higher numbers for each unit moving offstage through all units at the same height, then jumping down to the next level, progressing downward through the lower tiers.
Floor or Set Mounts	Designer's preference, but typically done with some form of order such as numbering progressively from SL to SR.
Multi-Circuited Units	Each circuit is given a number, while the entire unit is given a letter designation (e.g., a three circuit striplight with circuits A1, A2, and A3 while successive striplights in a row like a ground row would be assigned letters B, C, D, etc.)

based on their hanging position. Sidebar 12.1 provides information relating to the most common numbering practices for both the hanging positions and the individual luminaires. If a luminaire is added at some point after the plot has been numbered (such as at tech/dress rehearsals or later stops in a tour) the unit is simply drawn in the location where it is to be hung and assigned the same number as the lowest unit number next to it plus an added letter component. If more than one instrument is added between existing units additional letters will be assigned to the instruments (Unit 23, 23A, 23B, etc.). Booms and other vertical hanging positions are plotted in two orientations—the first gives a bird's-eye view and is used for placing the boom (often illustrating only the top row of luminaires) and is hatched or shaded, while the second is an elevation view and provides information regarding the mounting heights of the units (a dimension or elevation marker that is taken from the deck to either the center of the luminaire or to its associated sidearm). Additional features such as floor mounts, set mounts, and practicals will finally be added to the plot as it nears completion. These may be indicated through placing a symbol at the actual location of a unit or could be listed in a table that is located somewhere else on the plot. At the discretion of the designer additional elements like scenic components, focus areas, maskings, and other information are also added to the plot. Figure 12.7 illustrates a detailed area of a light plot that depicts conventions that are typical for drafting the electrics, while Figure 12.8 illustrates conventions that are typical for displaying booms and ladders (*Tommy* plot details). Figure 12.9 provides the final light plot for the production of *The Miser* that has been used as an example throughout this chapter. It also provides an example of a plot that follows a slightly different format than

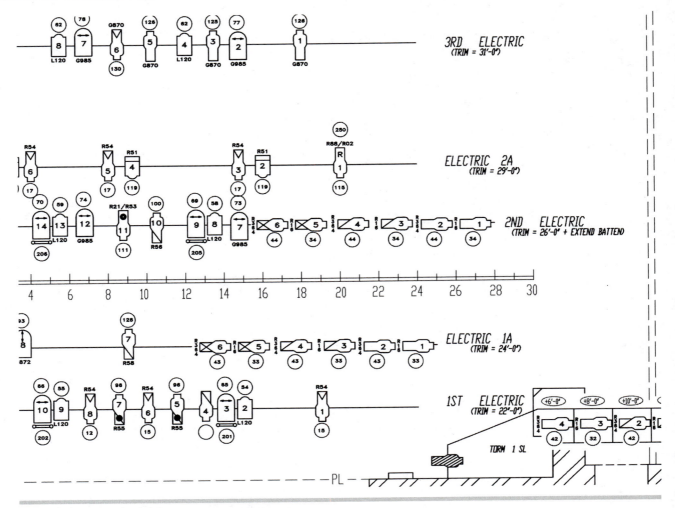

FIGURE 12.7 Sample Electric Layout and Notation

the more traditional plots that have been illustrated through the *Urinetown* and *Tommy* light plots.

Drafting the Section

Drafting the section isn't that much different from drafting the light plot. The exception being that the section is more concerned with positioning the trims of the hanging positions and maskings as opposed to providing specific information about each of the luminaires. While designers can pull off a decent design without doing one, the results of not drafting a section can be disastrous. It could lead to problems like creating hanging positions and trims that can't possibly hit their targets, luminaires that are impossible to mask, and lighting angles that become deceptively steep or shallow from what may be expected. For all of these reasons the section forms an important document that shouldn't be skipped.

While the section doesn't necessarily have to be drawn to the same scale as the light plot, references and comparisons are more easily made if a common scale is shared between them. Once again, 1/4", 3/8", or 1/2" scales are the most popular scales for drafting sections and the drafting of a section follows many of the same practices followed while drafting a light plot. Borderlines and title blocks are indicated but there is no key or notation for a lighting section. The section typically follows a cutting plane along the centerline of the theatre and illustrates information that would be needed regarding the vertical elements of the design. Scales are provided along the depth of the stage (both forward and backstage of the

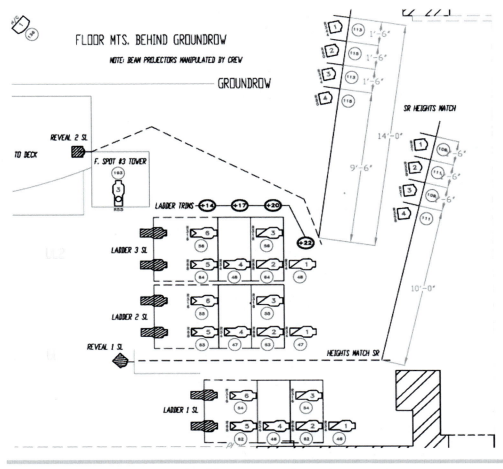

FIGURE 12.8 Sample Boom and Ladder Layout and Notation

plasterline and along the height of the stage). Heights of any scenic elements and the trim positions of the electrics and borders are also drawn in a section. Vertical maskings are checked through drawing partial sightlines from the critical seat (critical sightline) across the bottom edges of the borders to illustrate what may or may not be seen by an audience member from that location. Lighting angles and distributions are checked and illustrated by placing focus points at head height within each plane of the acting areas and drawing a line representing the throw distance between this point and the hanging positions from which that area will be lit. Lines representing the beam spread of the fixtures are then drawn along the line representing the throw distance to indicate how much coverage a given luminaire will provide for the associated focus points. Some designers will choose to show the throw distance in their final sectional drafting while others only show the beam patterns of the luminaires. This process is repeated for each plane of focus as well as for each angle (e.g., front and backlight), and unique areas of a design (e.g., elevated areas like balconies or towers). Figures 12.1 and 12.2 illustrate these principles.

LIGHTING SCHEDULES AND DESIGN PAPERWORK

Light plots tend to be large and bulky, making them hard to carry around and work with. While it is important to use them throughout the initial hang, most designers and electricians find it more helpful to have the information repeated in various table formats that are smaller and more easily carried around. These tables (**schedules** or **paperwork**) list all the same information as the light plot but organize the data on standard-sized pages that can fit on a clipboard. Each type of schedule organizes the

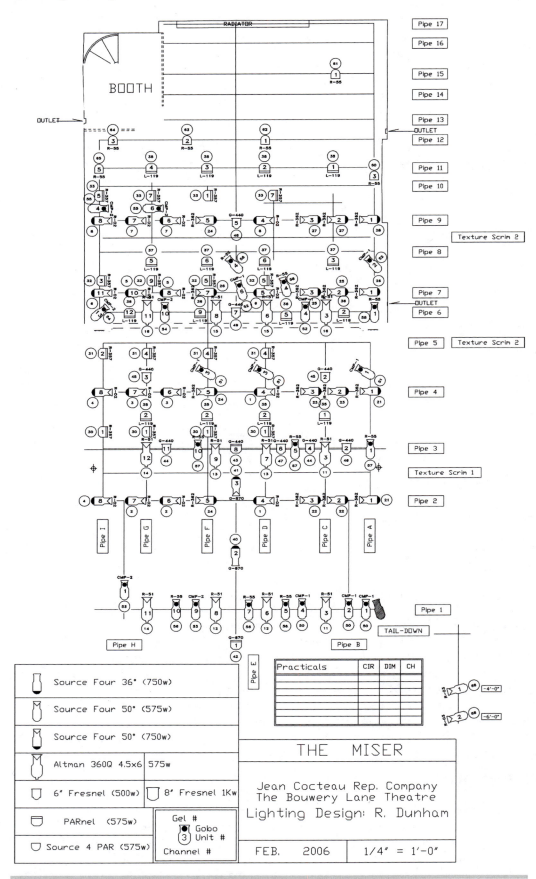

FIGURE 12.9 CAD Drafting of the Final Light Plot for *The Miser*

data in a different manner and is beneficial to the designer or electricians at different stages of the design. About the only information that a plot can provide that the schedules won't is the actual physical location of the luminaires. Often, the paperwork becomes the only complete record of much of a design since many designers prefer to place only a limited amount of information on the actual plot while the schedules go on to list all of the data that a designer specifies for the luminaires. Typical data provided throughout the paperwork includes instrument number and location, luminaire type and wattage, wiring data (circuit, dimmer, and channel), focus/purpose information, color, and accessories (barn doors, templates, etc.). Lighting schedules often grow to many pages for each of the different schedules.

With lighting designs growing from fifty to hundreds of luminaires, the creation of the paperwork for a production became a monumental task that often required an assistant who was charged with monitoring and revising the paperwork throughout the production process. With the advent of affordable personal computers, it didn't take lighting designers long to figure out that all of the repetitive data in these schedules could be entered into spreadsheet programs like Microsoft's *Works* or *Excel.* Today, many lighting designers use programs like these to organize a production's lighting data. In fact, many lighting designers use a specialized spreadsheet application created by John McKernon called *Lightwright,* which has been designed around the special needs of lighting designers. Over the years this program has evolved and not only creates paperwork but can also track problems such as overloaded dimmers or circuits, make determinations of phase loads, keep records of focus/shutter patterns, check for errors like using bad dimmers or assigning circuits/dimmers to two channels at a time, track inventory lists, and even determine cut lists (with or without an existing inventory of gel). Other software packages also exist—some even produce the paperwork as modular elements of computer-aided design (CAD) packages. *Vectorworks Spotlight®, LD Assistant,* and *MacLux* all have the capability of producing not only a light plot but also its associated paperwork in a seamless manner that directly inserts the data into the appropriate schedules.

Hookup

The **hookup** is probably the second most important document that a designer produces after the light plot. The hookup takes all the information related to the luminaires and presents it in a table format using control information as the primary form of organization. The first column relates to the control element used to operate the associated instrument(s). The two most common forms of hookup organize the data by either channel (**channel schedule**) or dimmer number (**dimmer schedule**). While the channel or dimmer number must be placed in the first column, the rest of the data can be organized in any fashion that the designer thinks is most appropriate. This additional information usually includes hanging position, unit number, unit type, wattage, color, accessories, and its focus or purpose. Designers may wish to include more classifications or could drop some based on the particular needs of a production. Hookups are helpful for troubleshooting wiring problems, dealing with lamps that don't come up, and for completing **dimmer checks** prior to a rehearsal or performance. Figure 12.10 shows the first page of the hookup (channel schedule) for the Cocteau production of *The Miser.*

Instrument Schedule

Instrument schedules (see Figure 12.11) follow the same format as the hookup but are organized according to hanging positions and unit numbers. This piece of paperwork becomes especially helpful when an electrician is working on a particular hanging position. They can walk along a position like an electric to check circuit assignments or can pre-stack the gel for easy insertion along an entire batten. In addition to the information presented in the hookup, many designers also like to list a gang column in instrument schedules. This allows electricians to quickly identify those instruments

The Miser

CHANNEL HOOKUP

The Jean Cocteau Repertory Theatre
The Bouwerie Lane Theatre
R. Dunham, Designer

Channel	Dim	Position	Unit#	Type	Wattage	Color & Template	Purpose
(1)	4	PIPE 2	4	S4 -50	750w	R-02	SIDE -DL
	"	PIPE 4	"	"	"	"	"
(2)	11	PIPE 2	6	S4 -50	750w	R-02	SIDE -DC1
	"	"	7	"	"	"	"
(3)	13	PIPE 4	6	S4 -50	750w	R-02	SIDE -DC2
	"	"	7	"	"	"	"
(4)	12	PIPE 2	8	S4 -50	750w	R-02	SIDE -DR
	"	PIPE 4	"	"	"	"	"
(5)	57	PIPE 7	8	S4 -50	750w	R-02	SIDE -CS
	"	"	10	"	"	"	"
(6)	38	PIPE 7	5	S4 -50	750w	R-02	SIDE -SL AND SR
	"	"	11	"	"	"	"
(7)	49	PIPE 9	6	S4 -50	750w	R-02	SIDE -UC
	"	"	7	"	"	"	"
(8)	43	PIPE 9	4	S4 -50	750w	R-02	SIDE -UL AND UR
	"	"	8	"	"	"	"
(11)	5	PIPE 1	3	4.5x6	575w	R-51	F. WASH -DL
	"	PIPE 3	"	"	"	"	"
(12)	21	PIPE 1	6	4.5x6	575w	R-51	F. WASH -DC1
	"	"	8	"	"	"	"
(13)	17	PIPE 3	7	4.5x6	575w	R-51	F. WASH -DC2
	"	"	9	"	"	"	"
(14)	24	PIPE 1	11	4.5x6	575w	R-51	F. WASH -DR
	18	PIPE 3	12	"	"	"	"
(15)	37	PIPE 6	6	4.5x6	575w	R-51	F. WASH -UC
	"	"	8	"	"	"	"
(16)	53	PIPE 6	3	4.5x6	575w	R-51	F. WASH -UL AND UR
	"	"	11	"	"	"	"
(21)	1	PIPE 2	1	S4 -50	750w	R-362	SIDE -DL
	"	PIPE 4	"	"	"	"	"
(22)	2	PIPE 2	2	S4 -50	750w	R-362	SIDE -DC1
	"	"	3	"	"	"	"
(23)	34	PIPE 4	2	S4 -50	750w	R-362	SIDE -DC2
	"	"	3	"	"	"	"

Richard Dunham/Lightwright 4   (1) thru (23)

FIGURE 12.10   A Partial Channel Hookup for *The Miser*

that are two-fered together and helps them to use fewer circuits. For a designer, the instrument schedule is extremely beneficial during a show's focus. The designer can move quickly down a pipe, focusing each unit in order through having easy access to the channel and focus needs of each instrument while avoiding the time losses associated with shifting a lift or ladder more often than absolutely necessary. Instrument schedules are often organized with each hanging position being kept to its own page(s). This allows several people (e.g., a designer and his assistant) to focus different areas of the plot at the same time.

The Miser   INSTRUMENT SCHEDULE   Page 2
25 Feb 2010

PIPE F

U	Purpose	Type/Acc	W	Color	Template	Di	Ch
1	HIGH SIDE -DS1	PARNEL	575w	R-357		14	(30)
2	DOWNLIGHT	PARNEL	575w	L-119		36	(35)
3	GOBO LEAVES -SCRIM 2	S4 -50	575w	R-13, R-88, R-356	G-294	35	(51)
4	HIGH SIDE -DS2	PARNEL	575w	R-357		20	(31)
5	HIGH SIDE -MIDSTAGE	PARNEL	575w	R-357		39	(32)
6	DOWNLIGHT	PARNEL	575w	L-119		44	(37)

PIPE 6

U	Purpose	Type/Acc	W	Color	Template	Di	Ch
1	GOBO LINES -SCRIM 3	S4 -50	575w	R-55	G-673	56	(58)
2	DOWNLIGHT	PARNEL	575w	L-119		48	(36)
3	F. WASH -UL AND UR	4.5x6	575w	R-51		53	(16)
4	GOBO LEAVES -SCRIM 3	S4 -50	575w	R-13, R-88, R-356	G-294	54	(52)
5	DOWNLIGHT	PARNEL	575w	L-119		48	(36)
6	GOBO LEAVES -SCRIM 3	S4 -50	575w	R-13, R-88, R-356	G-294	54	(52)
6	F. WASH -UC	4.5x6	575w	R-51		37	(15)
7	CS SP	6" FRES	500w	G-440		52	(49)
8	F. WASH -UC	4.5x6	575w	R-51		37	(15)
9	DOWNLIGHT	PARNEL	575w	L-119		48	(36)
10	GOBO LEAVES -PERFORMERS	S4 -50	575w	R-54, R-87	G-218	59	(54)
11	F. WASH -UL AND UR	4.5x6	575w	R-51		53	(16)
12	DOWNLIGHT	PARNEL	575w	L-119		48	(36)
13	GOBO LEAVES -PERFORMERS	S4 -50	575w	R-54, R-87	G-218	59	(54)

PIPE I

U	Purpose	Type/Acc	W	Color	Template	Di	Ch
1	HIGH SIDE -DS1	PARNEL	575w	R-357		14	(30)
2	HIGH SIDE -DS2	PARNEL	575w	R-357		20	(31)
3	HIGH SIDE -MIDSTAGE	PARNEL	575w	R-357		39	(32)
4	GOBO LEAVES -PERFORMERS	S4 -50	575w	R-54, R-87	G-218	50	(55)
5	HIGH SIDE -UPSTAGE	PARNEL	575w	R-357		46	(33)

PIPE G

U	Purpose	Type/Acc	W	Color	Template	Di	Ch
1	HIGH SIDE -DS1	PARNEL	575w	R-357		14	(30)
2	DOWNLIGHT	PARNEL	575w	L-119		36	(35)
3	DC WIDE-2 SP	6" FRES	500w	G-440		31	(45)
4	HIGH SIDE -DS2	PARNEL	575w	R-357		20	(31)
5	DOWNLIGHT	PARNEL	575w	L-119		44	(37)
6	GOBO LEAVES -PERFORMERS	S4 -50	575w	R-54, R-87	G-218	50	(55)
7	HIGH SIDE -UPSTAGE	PARNEL	575w	R-357		46	(33)

Richard Dunham/Lightwright 4   PIPE D thru PIPE 6

FIGURE 12.11   A Partial Instrument Schedule for *The Miser*

Magic Sheets

Magic sheets are a special form of paperwork that designers use when they set levels or program a show. There are a number of formats for creating magic sheets, and each designer has a preference in what format they adopt for their personal use. Magic sheets do not contain all of the information that the other schedules provide—they are abbreviated and only contain the information that a designer will need to set levels or cues. The only material presented in many magic sheets is just the control channel, color, and purpose/focus of the luminaires. At this point, the designer doesn't need to worry about the actual instruments creating an effect or the manner in which they have been wired, only the effect and its control channel. The magic sheet reduces volumes of paperwork down to as little as a single page of key data that the designer will need for setting cues. While some designers prefer a table-like format (Figure 12.12a), many of us feel that this too closely approximates a hookup and that if a number of channels are involved in a design, the format becomes inefficient. Instead, a graphical format (Figure 12.12.b) is frequently used that traces the directional or focus patterns of the lights onto a schematic representation of the set or stage. The control channels are then illustrated in a manner that links them to a functional pattern or description of the light. Magic sheets are also used for dimmer checks, with the understanding that if a problem is found, the electricians can go back to the instrument schedule or hookup to look up the additional information they need to troubleshoot a problem. Yet another version of providing control information is through a cheat sheet. A **cheat sheet** (Figure 12.13) also follows a table format and lists all of the control channels in sequential order along with additional information relating to the purpose and color associated with a cue and each channel.

Magic Sheet   R. Dunham, Design

The Miser—The Cocteau Rep.   Page: __1__ of __2__

		DL	DC1	DC2	DR	MID-ON	MID-OFF	US-ON	US-OFF
Area	R-02	1	2	3	4	5	6	7	8
	R-51	11	12	13	14	15	16		
	R-362	21	22	23	24	25	24	27	28
HPE-SR	R-357		30	31		32		33	
DOWN	L-119		35	36		37		38	
GOBOS -SR	Mixed		50			51		52	
GOBOS -SL	Mixed		56			57		58	
Specials	DC tight	45							
	Bench	46							
	Inquisit.	47							

a. Magic Sheet in Table Format

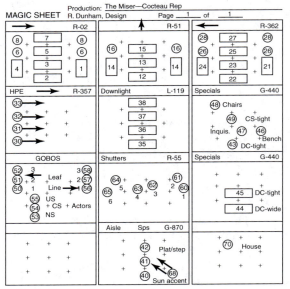

b. Magic Sheet in Visual Format

FIGURE 12.12   Magic Sheets for *The Miser*

Production: THE MISER   Company: COCTEAU REP

Cue #: 6   Count: 4 / 8   Preset: B

R. Dunham, Design

Chan	1	2	3	4	5	6	7	8	9	10	11	12
Purpose	AREA R02	AREA R02	AREA R02	AREA 02	AREA R02	AREA R02	AREA R02	AREA R02	✕	✕	AREA 9 R51	AREA 4 R51
Level	7	8	8	7	7	6	6	6	✕	✕	5	6

Chan	13	14	15	16	17	18	19	20	21	22	23	24
Purpose	AREA 1 R-51	AREA 1 R-51	AREA 1 R-51	AREA 1 R-51	✕	✕	✕	✕	AREA R.362	AREA R.362	AREA R.362	AREA R.362
Level	6	5	6	5					4	5	5	4

Chan	25	26	27	28	29	30	31	32	33	34	35	36
Purpose	AREA R.362	AREA R.362	AREA R.362	AREA R.362	✕	HPE ① R-357	HPE ② R-357	HPE ③ R-357	HPE ④ R-357	✕	DOWN L-119 ⑤	DOWN L-119 ⑥
Level	3.5	3.5	3.5	3.5	✕					✕	4	4

Chan	37	38	39	40	41	42	43	44	45	46	47	48
Purpose	DOWN L-119 ③	DOWN L-119 ④	✕	AISLE SP ①	AISLE SP ②	AISLE SP ③	DC (TEXT) SP	DC (W) SP	QS (W) SP	BENCH	INQUIS.	UR CHAIRS
Level	4	4								6	5.5

FIGURE 12.13 A Designer's Cheat Sheet Note the similarities between this form of paperwork and the tracking sheet discussed in Chapter 13.

Shop Orders

Shop orders are an inventory of all the materials and equipment that will be required to complete a lighting design. Often a designer will not have to complete a shop order because they are working in a facility where the console, dimmers, circuits, and even luminaires are permanent elements of a space. Here, the designer only needs to make sure that the design falls within the listed inventories and that they have ordered the **perishables** (expendables) for a production. Perishables include items like gel, templates, tie-line, and gaffers tape, which are either disposable or unable to be returned once they have been used.

When designing for a touring production or rental facility that is completely stripped, the lighting designer is responsible for specifying each element of the lighting rig. This includes the dimmers and console, luminaires, cabling (circuits are not typically installed in these facilities), and hardware/accessories, along with the perishables. It is important to be completely accurate in this document because failing to include a single piece of key equipment could result in the entire rig not working. The shop order also forms the primary document that is sent to rental houses when a show is put out for bids.

The first page of a shop order usually lists specific information relating to the production. Items like the show title and name and address of the theatre or where the equipment will be delivered are important elements of the first page. Key individuals for the production and their contact information are also provided on the title page. The producer or production organization, lighting designer, and master electrician are individuals who are often identified here. One last bit of information usually included here is the rental period for which the equipment is required. This is specified with a load-in date on which the equipment will be picked up or delivered to the theatre and a second date for the strike and return of the equipment. Most rental houses bill their rentals on a weekly basis using a Monday-to-Monday schedule. The highest fees are charged during the first week, but are then reduced over additional weeks depending on how long the equipment is rented. If doing a single weekend gig, you can usually expect to pay the full weekly fee if you tie up a company's inventory for more than 3 or 4 days. On the other hand, if you are a regular client, many rental houses will cut you a break where they can. Also, the representatives for most rental companies are extremely knowledgeable in how their equipment functions and are glad to help you with technical support both as you place your order as well as throughout the rental period.

The shop order is traditionally broken down into several key areas that list specific components of the lighting package. The first area, the **instruments** section, contains a complete listing of all the luminaires that will be required for the production. Instrument types, lamp wattage, and general luminaire specifications will be included here. The overall specifications are often given as a general note that includes a statement identifying how each of the fixtures should be equipped (e.g., each unit must be equipped with a color frame, safety cable, and C-clamp). An especially important specification is the connector type that the units will have. Once all the luminaires have been specified, a second area (**control**), is completed. This part of the order simply lists the console and associated hardware and cables (e.g., number of monitors, etc.), the number of dimmers and their capacities, and the number of feet of control and feeder cable that a rig requires. The third area, the **irons** section, lists all the pipe, hardware, and accessories that will be required for the production. Sidearms, boom bases, top hats, and hanging irons form some of the gear that is ordered in this portion of the shop order. Pipe lengths for each individual boom or other hanging positions are also specified in the irons section. A fourth area of the shop order lists all of the **cables and two-fers** required for the production. There are numerous manners by which an electrician may determine the lengths of these cables, but two important points to keep in mind while specifying these cable runs include remembering to include the trim heights in your cable runs and that most rental houses only provide cables in increments of 5 or 10 feet. It is also good to add a 10% safety factor to ensure that your estimates do not fall short. The shop order then lists the number of pieces of each length of cable and number of two-fers, three-fers, and other specialized cables that are required for the hang. The final part of the order relates to ordering the **expendables** or **perishables.** These materials must be purchased. Gel will be broken down into a **cut list,** which specifies the number of cuts and frame sizes that are required in each color as well as the number of sheets of each color that will have to be ordered. Other items that are often included in the perishables include items that help facilitate a hang. Extra connectors for practicals, tie-line for securing and dressing cables, and gaffers and spike tape are just a sampling of these materials. One last item that should not be overlooked is to specify spare lamps for the production. Most designers will request that a spare lamp inventory of between 10–20% be made available for a production. When lamps burn out in rental fixtures, especially in the case of a long running show, it is the responsibility of the renter, not the rental house, to replace the lamps. Each lamp type that appears in the design (even if there is only one unit making use of a particular lamp) should be covered by a minimum of at least one or two spare lamps. Often, different luminaires are lamped with the same model lamp.

CAD DRAFTING AND LIGHTING DESIGN

CAD (Computer-Aided Design and Drafting) was discussed fairly extensively in Chapter 9 and a few highlights are mentioned here to emphasize several of the more important elements that this tool brings to a lighting designer's drafting. In all fairness, one can say that the computer has revolutionized the drafting of light plots. Due to the repetitive nature of much of this drafting, lighting designers were among the first in the entertainment industry to embrace CAD drafting. Lighting symbols are easily copied and pasted into locations throughout a plot, while primary features of a facility can be made into a master drawing known as a **prototype.** Prototypes permit drawing features like the borderlines, title block, auditorium or stage outlines, hanging schedules, and reference lines to be stored in a common file that is simply opened each time that a designer wants to draft in a particular venue. Probably the most important single attraction of CAD drafting lies in the ability of this software to store a host of pre-designed symbols. These symbols contain an outline drawing of a luminaire as well as a host of other information regarding that particular lighting instrument. We call these symbols **blocks.** What makes them so attractive for lighting designers is the ability to insert a symbol for a given instrument (**attributed block**) into a drawing and to then add specific data (**attributes** such as color, channel, focus, etc.) that is unique to the particular unit and posted automatically with the associated symbol. Despite all of its advantages, a CAD plot is in an electronic format that can be completely lost if backup precautions are not taken. Also, there's the issue of converting the digital data into a hard copy of the plot. In this case, a large format printer (plotter) is required to print the drawings to a scaled format. Most of the plots that have been illustrated throughout this chapter have been created through CAD.

FOR FURTHER READING

Mumm, Robert C, *Photometrics Handbook,* 2nd ed. (Louisville, KY: Broadway Press, 1997).

Shelley, Steven Louis, *A Practical Guide to Stage Lighting* (Boston: Focal Press, 1999).

Warfel, William B., *The New Handbook of Stage Lighting Graphics* (New York: Drama Book Publishers, 1990).

moving into the venue

13

All of my discussions regarding lighting design to this point have been primarily about preparation. In fact, it is quite possible to get this far into the design process without having touched a single lighting instrument. Much of this chapter, like the two previous chapters, is also concerned with preparation. However, you should feel some sense of accomplishment because we are now finally ready to move into the facility and will soon be working with the actual medium of light. Having said that, there are still several critical steps in the design process that must diligently be completed before moving on to actually designing with the lights in the theatre. At this time, luminaires are hung and circuited, colored, focused, and assigned or patched to controllers associated with the lighting console(s). While this is happening, scenery, maskings, props, and costumes are also being assembled in the theatre as the final steps of preparing a production come together. It is at this point, as we move into a theatre, that we are finally free to begin the most important step in lighting a project. It is here that light and its controllable qualities are used to produce a variety of functions and effects and the true artistry of a lighting designer comes into play as you make design choices that are appropriate for every single moment of an event. The lighting designer is not only responsible for providing an appropriate combination of design choices for a given moment or **cue,** but also for the transitions that are made between each cue. All the work to this point has been related to preparation and creating the palette that the lighting designer will ultimately use to design from. Some lighting designers have even come to refer to this part of the process as **painting with light.**

This chapter provides information related to the tasks of a lighting designer and lighting crews as they move a production into the facility in which a show will be mounted. While the entire process plays a role in the final outcome of a design, the majority of the tasks associated with moving into a facility are once again technical and in themselves not the final design. It is only once all of these tasks have been completed and the designer is sitting at the design desk ready to **set levels** that the real process of lighting a show actually begins. Now, as light is created for each cue, the designer manipulates the intensities, colors, and instrument selections in order to produce the effects required by the concept. As lighting is added to the other production elements the lighting designer helps create the appropriate atmosphere, mood, and focus suggested by the performers, script, and other design areas. If done correctly, the preliminary work should pay off and the designer will find themselves with the proper tools to create what is required for the project. A designer can only do so much with a plot, meaning that if the tools aren't in the plot an effect may not be able to be realized. On the other hand, even a perfect plot (if there is such a thing) doesn't guarantee a successful design and might very well be used ineffectively when setting the levels for a production. This aspect of relativeness is especially important in lighting design where what works well in one design or even moment may be completely inappropriate for another moment or design.

This chapter will take you through the process of getting the lights into the air, focused, and finally cued in combinations that are appropriate for any given moment of a production. Since lighting does not exist alone, at this point in the process, we combine it with the other elements of a production to complete a full composition as we create the world of the performance event. This is done through a series of specialty rehearsals that are discussed toward the end of this chapter. By the conclusion of this chapter we will have designed the lighting and linked it in an appropriate manner to the concept, the performers, and the other design elements that are associated with a project. Due to space limitations, this book cannot begin to address all of the details associated with moving into a venue and will instead provide an overview of the process. For a more thorough explanation of the load-in process you should refer to Stephen Shelley's book, *A Practical Guide to Stage Lighting*, a wonderful source of tips, procedures, paperwork, and common practices that can be used in bringing a lighting design to the stage.

FINAL PREPARATIONS FOR THE LOAD-IN

Many of the final steps in preparing for a **load-in** are completed as the lighting designer produces their **design packet** for a project. This packet includes all the information that the designer needs to communicate to the electricians who will actually hang the show. The design packet most importantly contains the light plot, other draftings related to the electric's department (e.g., the lighting section and plates containing signage or other scenic pieces containing practicals), the lighting schedules, and inventory lists and shop orders. This informational packet is often created as close to the load-in as possible so that the plot can address the latest needs of a production. If a show is to be sent out for bids, this material may have to be produced well ahead of the actual load-in date, but regardless of the individual conditions that a designer is working under, it is important that the material be assembled in a timely manner so that the load-in can proceed on schedule. When designing locally it is common for the packet to be hand-delivered to the master electrician or shop so that it can be reviewed and prepped prior to the day of the actual load-in. It is also common, especially in the case of touring productions, for the design packet to be mailed to the performance venue using carriers like FedEx. Today, it is even becoming fairly common to send these materials by electronic methods like e-mail attachments. Regardless of how the materials are delivered, most electrical departments and master electricians need to have the design packet at least several days before the actual load-in.

Although much of the final preparations of a lighting designer are related to creating the lighting packet and getting the technical information together for the electrical crews, another area that should not be neglected is observing any rehearsals that are conducted in the final days before a load-in. This allows a designer to become more familiar with the blocking, moods, and transitions. These rehearsals are great sources for noting the specific placement of actor specials, getting a sense of pacing, and noting various transitional timings. More importantly, these rehearsals will help the designer document much of the information that they will later need for creating appropriate cues for the production. The more familiar that a designer becomes with the production, the easier and more successful the later cue-writing sessions will become. Visits to the scenic and costume studios at this time will allow the lighting designer to check the final color and texture treatments of these elements. These visits will also provide an opportunity to observe any unique conditions that may not be readily apparent from the plans and renderings that the other designers may have provided to the lighting designer.

Time is a luxury in the entertainment industry and producers cannot afford to spend any more time than absolutely necessary on the load-in process. One of the most important elements regarding final preparations for a load-in is in making as many decisions outside of the theatre as you possibly can. This is particularly true in lighting, where we can't tell exactly what our final design is going to be until all the other elements of a production have come into place. Opening night is rarely delayed and all too often time is lost during a load-in due to a scenic or other production element taking more time to install or work into a performance than originally anticipated. Unfortunately, problems like these generally result in the lighting department having to pay the price in terms of lost time. A lighting designer should always strive toward having the most amount of time possible for sitting at the design desk actually creating the cues. They should come into the cue-writing session with as many decisions already committed to as possible— prior to the load-in if they can, so that when they begin writing cues they will have the maximum opportunity to actually work and design with the medium of light. Decisions such as cue placement should be committed to well before the cue writing session so that the designer can concentrate not on where the cues go, but on the actual look of the cues. Transitions and cue counts should also be completed prior to the cue writing session as yet another way of making the cue writing process more productive. By using these guidelines the lighting designer will maximize the amount of time and opportunities that they have for working with the actual lights in the venue.

THE CUE SYNOPSIS

The **cue synopsis** (Figure 13.1) is another piece of paperwork that is created by a lighting designer but unlike other schedules and paperwork, the cue synopsis functions as a guideline for the actual creation of a production's cues. It does not contain the technical information that other forms of paperwork provide, but instead assigns a cue number to every cue or look in the production, and then provides specific information related to each cue. A typical cue synopsis contains a cue number that allows easy identification of each cue (progressively numbering the cues in order), **counts** (transition times between cues), the execution point (specific action or line at which the cue is taken), and a visual description of each cue.

A cue synopsis forces a lighting designer to consider each of the images or looks of a production from curtain up to curtain down. As a means of supporting the lighting concept, many designers think about specific moments of the play and then go on to answer questions that relate to the controllable qualities of light at those points in the action. Lighting functions are also considered as part of this process. What color should the light be? Is the entire stage washed in this color? Is there a specific direction or source suggested by the lighting at this moment in the script? What is the overall quality or mood? How much visibility does the scene require? Where should the focus be established? How strong must the focus be? In many cases, lighting designers produce visual references such as color keys, storyboards, lighting scores, and even virtual images to assist in their creation of the cue synopsis. The blocking notation is another important aid to the designer at this time. The designer must consider the lighting image for each moment of the production. Cue placements can be tried and retried, transition times can be imagined and revised, but most importantly, a visual description is created for each cue of the production. As a rule, cues should be described using visual language and the controllable qualities of light, with the discussion of the individual channels kept to a minimum. This is done for two reasons. First, it eliminates the need of translating specific light sources into channel numbers (saving time), and second, designers often discover that the image that they are ultimately happy with may or may not be created with the same channels that they initially thought would produce the required look. If the cues are always written through a descriptive manner these revisions will not cause the cue synopsis to become irrelevant since revisions are made in the construction of the cues. Therefore, the cue synopsis can continue to be used successfully throughout the design process despite any changes that may develop in actually producing the desired effects.

The key advantage to completing a thorough cue synopsis is that it requires the lighting designer to make design decisions regarding the specific treatments of the lighting outside of the theatre. Cue sequences can be imagined and rehearsed in one's mind where they

Cue Synopsis				Urinetown -The Musical	
R. Dunham, Designer				University of Georgia -Fine Arts Theatre	
					10/15/2007
CUE #	Count	Page #	Execution Point	Description	Notes
0.5	5		Prior to house opening	Preset --Glow of scaffolds w/sidelight. Dark blue skyline. Blue Downs. Low overall levels....more sculptural in overall quality.	
HS	5		When Set	House to Half	
1	5		With appearance of musical director	Build musical director special and pit band.	
			Overture begin		
2	10		About 30 seconds into overture	X-fade to deep blue shadowy quality over entire stage. Add some cool accents here and there. Slight build of area around Amenity 9 -- especially gobos. X-light cool scaffolds. Scrollers in lavender.	
HS	5		w/ LQ-2		
3	10	1	With music change to lead-in to Urinetown	Pull to deeper cool blue plus boost lavender backlight. Pre-dawn	I-1 Amenity #9
	4		Following LQ-3 Just before Narrative		
		1		Lockstock (L) --body	Frame 5
		1	...hear people referring to a lot ↓ through the show.	Slight build light around Amenity and where Penny (P) is setting up shop. Chorus is on all levels --even the top.	
				Spots should include Little Sally (LS) with L when needed	
		2	What's that Little Sally. ↓ w/people coming to life.	Suble build of Amenity areas as sunrise approaches	
		2	...central conceit of the showw!	Build all more for vocal w/ L. Warm it some...shift more lavender..	
		3	...never bother with ↓ jail.	All build, keep cool...add front diags. And cool footlights	
		3	You won't need bail.	Restore LQ-6 but not quite a full pull-down to LQ-6 levels.	
			w/ LQ-9		
10	4	3	Visual w/ Hope enters (Aren't we all)		
FS1↑		3		Add FS1 to Hope	Frame 4
11	2	4	The gleaming tower↓ on the hill?	Add UGC tower special.	
12	4	4	...directions and such. Bye	Tower drop to medium glow.	
FS1↓			w/ LQ-12		
13	6	4	...to Urinetown (the musical)!	Restore LQ-8 Plus slight build.	
14	4	5	Often is a line.	Build backs and cools.	

FIGURE 13.1 A Cue Synopsis Page 1 from *Urinetown—The Musical.*

can be worked out successfully without the pressure of keeping up with a rehearsal. By having a good cue synopsis many decisions involving the design become nothing more than punching instructional sequences into the console at the actual cue-writing session—avoiding the need to make decisions regarding much of the more mundane information required throughout the cue-writing process. A cue synopsis is particularly helpful for entering repeating cues (**restore cues**) and counts into a lighting console. Productions with complicated cue sequences, such as musicals or dance performances, benefit greatly from a well thought out cue synopsis. In the case of musicals, a copy of the sound track can prove especially beneficial, as sequences can be played as many times as needed to time cues to the music and to work cue transitions out well ahead of time. More importantly, once in the theatre, the designer can focus on those aspects of the cue-writing session that deal with the actual use of lights and their associated intensity levels. The more time that the designer can actually work and observe the lights, the better chance that they have of creating a successful lighting design. Probably the most common cardinal sin of beginning lighting designers is in coming to a cue-writing session without a solid cue synopsis. Time is wasted making decisions that could have easily been made outside of the theatre when the designer wasn't under the pressures of the time constraints and fatigue that are associated with the cue-writing process. There is nothing more unproductive than watching a lighting designer and director sitting in a dark theatre struggling to decide on the placement of a given cue. More importantly, without this preparation the designer may find that they have designed themselves into a dead-end alley, which could result in having to go back to previous cues to make corrections or even having to discard cues and entire sequences that were created while going down the wrong path (and losing the time invested—even if it's hours). A complete cue synopsis also allows the lighting designer to maintain control of the lighting session by providing a detailed plan for lighting the production. The director will be able to understand if the designer is on the right path and discuss any issues ahead of the actual cue-writing process. The cue synopsis also provides a manner for the designer to pace themselves during the cue-writing session. If you're 4 hours into a 6 hour cue writing session and you're on cue 90 of a 200-cue show it becomes quite apparent that you'll have to pick-up your pace or find some manner of simplifying your show. It is easy to spot designs where the team ran out of time as evidenced by the contrast between the number of cues that exist between the beginning and end of a piece. Finally, the cue synopsis can also be given to the stage manager so that the cues can be entered into the prompt script prior to the cue-writing session. By doing this, valuable time in the cue-writing session is not lost transferring cue placements to the prompt script. Simply put, the cue-writing session should be a time where the lighting designer can focus on looking at the cues and transitions, not on making decisions about the general description or placement of the cues.

The cue synopsis can be created at any point in the process but is best done at a point where the designer believes that the blocking of the play is set and when there probably won't be any significant changes in the overall actions of the play. You don't want to do this too early because significant changes in the blocking could trigger changes in how you might light a given scene. However, you can also use any later rehearsals to check the cue synopsis along with the placement and counts of the cues that you are creating for a production. Cue descriptions can also be checked at this time. Through checking and rechecking the cue synopsis the cues can be refined even before the show moves into the venue. In some cases, due to limited rehearsal time, the cue synopsis may not be able to be completed until after the show has been loaded into the venue. When this happens, the designer will benefit from seeing the blocking as actually spaced in the theatre, but will also find themselves in a more extreme time crunch. As an alternative, there are some lighting designers who complete the cue synopsis even before they create the plot and paperwork for the production that they are lighting. Regardless of when the synopsis is created, it is important that it be checked, if at all possible, against at least one run-through prior to writing the actual cues.

THE LOAD-IN

When we discuss a **load-in** we refer to the time period in which all the scenery, costumes, and lighting equipment arrive and are installed or set up at the venue. The time that a load-in may require can vary considerably. In summer stock, where a new production must be performed for an audience in a day or two after closing the previous production, the load-in will typically be completed in less than 48 hours. In touring productions the load-in is often shaved down to 6–10 hours. On the other hand, in situations where elaborate production needs may be required, the load-in can extend to a week or two, if not more. No matter how long a load-in is scheduled, it is important for the lighting designer and their team to be productive and well-organized throughout the entire process. The lighting team must remain on schedule and cannot delay other aspects of the load-in. They must also remain flexible due to unforseen issues that may develop as the show comes together. For the lighting team, the process of loading in a show involves moving the lighting gear into the theatre, setting up and completing the power distribution and tie-ins to the dimmers and control systems, hanging and circuiting all of the luminaires, loading the color, and focusing the production. Many refer to the whole process of arriving at the venue and preparing the production as the load-in. Others think of the load-in as being only the physical setup of the equipment and will recognize additional calls like hang and circuiting calls, focus calls, and cue-in or cue-writing calls or sessions.

Proper scheduling during the load-in is extremely important to the overall success of this part of the process, and even more time must be allowed for the load-ins of productions that are being mounted for the very first time. The additional time is used for working out any kinks that may be discovered as the production is assembled for the first time. In touring productions, the load-in time will be trimmed down significantly due to everyone both being familiar with the exact tasks that have to be performed as well as the creation of a number of specialized tools that will be used to streamline the load-in process. A production such as a touring dance company that has been on the road for a while can accomplish a fairly sophisticated lighting setup within the space of 4 hours or less. Some of the techniques for trimming down the repetitive tasks of loading-in productions such as these are discussed in more detail later in Chapter 14. The pool of labor must also be examined as part of this process. Are there enough electricians to get the production hung and focused in the time allotted by the producer? How many electricians does the house require for a focus call? Are the electricians union? A common guideline that many designers use for estimating crew calls and numbers involves using an estimated time of 3 minutes for the hang and focus of each luminaire in the plot. Some units will take longer, some shorter, but this estimate accounts for all the tasks related to loading-in lights for a given production. Are there student or union electricians involved in the load-in? If using students, the time estimate should be extended. Finally, other departments must also be considered in terms of load-in estimates. Where is the electrical gear in the trucks? What part of the stage will the carpenters use at any given time during a work call? Are there any in-house luminaires that can be set up prior to the load-in? Whose job is it to load-in and set the trims of the borders and other maskings? All of these questions are related to issues that will have an impact on the load-in process.

It is rare for electrics, or any other department, to have the entire stage to themselves for any extended amount of time. For the most part, all departments need to share the stage, and efforts must be made to coordinate the needs of each of the departments throughout the load-in process. The production manager and technical director (in consultation with the master carpenter, rigger, and master electrician) are most commonly placed in charge of this process and related scheduling. The number of crew assigned to any department will also vary throughout a typical load-in. The largest number of stagehands and electricians will be employed for the initial load-in and setup, while the crews are made smaller for completing later portions of a load-in. I design regularly for the Atlanta Lyric Theatre and my call for electricians during the initial load-in typically consists of a minimum of 8–12 electricians. The initial lighting call must also include a flyman or two so that the battens can be operated and weighted throughout the load-in process. For the Lyric's focus calls the number of electricians will be reduced to 4–6, and by the time I start my cue-writing sessions the crews will be reduced again only to those electricians who will be running the production (the console and followspot operators). If the production doesn't use followspots, even those electricians are pulled. The role of a lighting designer can vary significantly during a load-in. In some cases, the designer may have to function as their own master electrician or may be expected to coordinate the electric's crews during the load-in, possibly even taking on large elements of the physical hang and focus personally. In other situations (most significantly facilities under union control) the designer may not be involved with the physical load-in at all. Even if the designer is not permitted to participate physically in the load-in, they or an assistant should still be in attendance and readily accessible for answering questions and resolving unforseen issues that come up during the load-in.

The first items of business for the lighting designer to complete at a load-in should be a quick survey of the theatre and a discussion with the house representatives, master electrician, master carpenter and technical director for the production. Any surprises resulting from undocumented plans (more common than you might expect), issues related to the plot, production changes, and other items affecting the load-in are discussed at this time. Everyone should also review the hanging schedule or lineset assignments to make sure that the lines are positioned as everyone had thought and that any changes in assignments can be made prior to beginning the actual load-in. The 15 minutes spent here are time well spent. There is nothing more frustrating than having to move equipment from one batten to another because something had to change in the hanging assignments. Many times the crew can simply enjoy their morning coffee and donuts while this discussion is taking place. As a rule, electrics tend to take the stage first. This is done so that the overhead electrics can be brought down to 3–4 feet above the deck where they can be easily loaded, colored, and circuited from the ground. The electricians should also test and troubleshoot the electrics at this time since any problems will be much easier to trace and fix while the batten is near the ground. By beginning with the overhead electrics on the deck, valuable time can be saved by not having to use a lift or ladder—any work done from a ladder multiplies the time for completing a task by several factors. While I know designers who prefer to load the color during the show's focus, I think that it is far more beneficial to have the color placed in the fixtures during the initial hang. Problems such as sorting through a stack of color frames and looking for a particular gel in the dark, juggling color frames or running them up a ladder to the electrician, media falling out of its frames, and bumping units out of focus while dropping color are all eliminated. Most pastel–medium saturated colors can be easily focused with the gel in place, while any deeply saturated colors that make it difficult to see a unit's beam or fixtures that demand an especially critical focus can have the gel pulled and then dropped back in after the unit has been focused. Those designers who think that it is easier to focus lights without the gel can still pull the color on an individual basis or have the gel organized into stacks that are given to the focusing electrician who will place them in the units once a particular light has been focused.

Once the electrics have been loaded and flown out of the way the carpenters start the assembly of the scenic elements. The first scenic elements to be put in should always be the maskings and any soft-goods like drops and scrims. This is often done during the same time that the electricians are working on the overheads because the stage is as open and as clear as possible. As the carpenters take over the stage, the electrics crew will shift to hanging and circuiting the front of house (FOH) and any positions such as booms or ladders that would be located in the wings. Much of the load-in must be carefully coordinated between both departments so that maximum efficiency is accomplished for the entire load-in. Another common arrangement involves having the carpenters work upstage while the electricians work downstage or vise-versa. Through a coordinated effort both departments will share the stage and complete the load-in process faster. Any permanent scenic elements are assembled last, after the overhead electrics have been completed and flown out of the way. In looking at a typical schedule for the Atlanta Lyric Theatre; the first call begins at 8:00 a.m. on Sunday mornings and consists of just electricians. The electricians are called from 8:00 a.m.–noon and use that time to hang and circuit the overhead electrics. They break for lunch at noon, which is also when the carpenters are first called and the trucks with the scenery are scheduled to arrive at the theatre. The carpenters will have the stage for the rest of the day. The electricians come back from lunch at 1:00 p.m. and work until 5:00 p.m. completing the front of house, pit areas, sidelight, and any practicals associated with the production. By the end of the day the electrics will be completely functional and ready for focusing on the next day.

The schedule presented in Sidebar 13.1 is quite typical, yet in reality, schedules can vary considerably from one situation to another. While this is a common schedule for the Atlanta Lyric Theatre, other organizations have the luxury of additional technical rehearsals such as a **dry tech rehearsal** and a **tech with actors** and as many as three or four dress rehearsals. In other cases, technical rehearsals may be nonexistent and there may only be a single dress rehearsal for a lighting designer to light a show. When I designed for the Brunswick Music Theatre (Maine State Music Theatre now) we would strike one production following a Sunday matinee, do a complete **changeover** throughout the next 24 hours, and would have a single run-through of Act I from 7:00–11:00 p.m. on Monday night and Act II on Tuesday afternoon from 12:00–4:00 p.m. An audience would show up for the first performance later on Tuesday evening. I would cue the productions in the middle of the night with full work lights and house lights at about 50% as the carpenters worked on the settings, which were typically from completely different scenes than the ones that I was trying to light. More importantly, these two limited rehearsals afforded the closest thing that we could ever get to a dress rehearsal for observing what I had created with the performers. This represents the most compact of load-in schedules.

Even though schedules will vary, a lighting designer must learn how to be extremely efficient through this stage of the production process. Organization and preparedness are essential to running a successful load-in. Decisions should be made before entering the venue if at all possible, and the designer must remain flexible while maintaining the ability to make snap decisions based on any issues that may come up during the load-in process. Those who can remain calm and make quick rational decisions, despite all the other tensions that typically arise at this point in the process, will do well in the business. A critical skill for a lighting designer to learn is in determining where compromises must be made and when it is appropriate to move on. On the other hand, they must also be able to identify those times when it is necessary to take additional time to work out a problem and to hold on to a specific element of a design. In some ways, inaction can actually be worse than making a wrong decision. Making decisions is an important part of the process, and you learn from your mistakes.

THE FOCUS CALL

Once all of the lighting equipment has been installed and tested the lighting team moves on to focusing the luminaires. When we discuss **focusing** we are referring to pointing the luminaires to the exact locations that the designer has planned. Electricians also adjust any other optical controls that may be provided by a lighting unit at this time. Pan and tilt, soft or hard edges, focus of any gobos, spot/flood settings, and shutter cuts form typical adjustments that can be performed on luminaires. It's also a time in which a lighting designer checks for consistency between units that form washes and works with the electricians to even out any shadows that fall between individual lighting areas. Frost or diffusion media may also be added to help even out washes and to soften any units that have hot spots or hard edges. The time scheduled for focusing is commonly named a **focus call.** In most cases, the gear is installed on one day with focus calls being scheduled for the following day. However, in the case of one-day events or touring productions the focus will often be done immediately after the units are hung and circuited, since a performance will be scheduled for later that evening. If the hang and circuiting of a production takes longer than anticipated it is quite common for a portion of the crew to go ahead and start focusing while the remaining electricians concentrate on finishing up the circuiting and troubleshooting of the equipment.

SIDEBAR 13.1 A Typical Load-in Schedule

DAY 1

8:00 a.m.	Electrics Load-in Overheads
	Carpenters Hang Masking/Flying Scenery
12:00 p.m.	Lunch
1:00 p.m.	Electrics Hang Front of House and Booms/Wing Units
	Carpenters Assemble Platforming and Main Stage Scenic Units
5:00 p.m.	Crews Released for Day 1

DAY 2

9:00 a.m.	Electrics Focus Call, Wire Additional Practicals, and Troubleshooting
	Carpenters As Needed
12:00 p.m.	Lunch
1:00 p.m.	Continue Focus
5:00 p.m.	Crews Released for Day 2

DAY 3

9:00 a.m.	Electrics Cue-Writing Session
	Carpenters as Needed
12:00 p.m.	Lunch
1:00 p.m.	Cue Writing Continued
6:00 p.m.	Dinner
7:00 p.m.	Tech/Run with Performers and Lights
11:00 p.m.	All Released for Day 3

DAY 4

6:00 p.m.	Touchup Call and Notes
7:00 p.m.	Dress Rehearsal

DAY 5

6:00 p.m.	Touchup Call and Notes
8:00 p.m.	Performance

*Schedule Continues Through Performance Run

The lighting designer plays a vital role in the focus of a production. Only the lighting designer can truly evaluate if a luminaire has been adjusted to a point where it is achieving exactly what had been envisioned. Often, compromises will have to be made, and only the designer is in position to decide whether a given adjustment will be acceptable or not. There are times when parts of the plot or even the whole focus may be entrusted to an assistant or associate lighting designer. This is more the exception in original productions but is quite common once a show has already been produced and is being remounted. This is especially true for touring and repertory productions. The assistant or associate designer will coordinate the day-to-day operation of the production and will make any decisions regarding compromises that must be made in regard to the different venues that the production will be staged in. A good assistant or associate will do this in way that appears to be consistent with the original production.

The number of individuals involved with a focus call may vary considerably from one production to another. A fairly typical arrangement involves the lighting designer, a board operator, the electrician who will actually focus the luminaires, and two additional electricians assigned to moving the ladder or lift that supports the focusing electrician. In fact, there are times when several teams of electricians may be organized for a single focus call. This will allow the designer to work several areas of the theatre at a time. I commonly use two focus teams and will alternate between them so that one team is focusing while the other is moving their ladder or lift to another position. I can also move on to focusing with the second team when the first team encounters a problem with a fixture. The Metropolitan Opera in New York City's Lincoln Center completely mounts and focuses a minimum of two different operas nearly every day (one in rehearsal or matinee and another for the evening performance). The overheads are frequently focused while the audience is gathering in the house and a number of the operas even require some focusing during intermissions. What is important during a focus call is that a logical order be established so that efficiency is stressed throughout the call. Designers have to learn to make judgment calls in regard to what portions of the stage need to be focused first, how to move through the order of the focus, what elements of a luminaire's beam quality are critical and worth spending time on, and when to move on when an electrician struggles with an uncooperative unit.

There are several items from a designer's perspective that can be done to help move through a focus in an efficient or productive manner. Probably the most important time-management rule for coordinating a successful focus involves focusing in such a way that creates minimal moves of any ladders or lifts. You don't want to be constantly moving the ladder from one side of the stage to another—in doing so, you spend your valuable time shifting the ladder around instead of focusing the lights. Most designers try to focus all the lights from a single hanging position at a time as a manner of building efficiency into their ladder moves. Quite often the first light to be focused from an electric will be at its extreme end. The position will then be focused progressively from one end to another. The Instrument Schedule becomes a critical source of information for the lighting designer during a focus call because it arranges the luminaire's technical information by hanging order (unit number) and position. While I usually begin the focus at one end of an electric there are times, such as when focusing critical washes, that I may begin to focus a position from the center (such as a FOH catwalk). This helps ensure that I can create good coverage through the central part of the stage. If the coverage is spread a little thin it allows the light to be tapered off at the edges as opposed to causing dips or shadows in the central portions of the wash or coming up short on the far side of the stage. Booms, likewise, can be focused more efficiently if focused from the top downward.

The most common practice of focusing is having the designer stand at the exact focus point to where a luminaire will be focused. Experienced electricians will have already prepped the unit to make sure that all the shutters have been pulled and that the pan and focus bolts aren't excessively loose. Once the designer is in position the electrician should point the center of the pool of light or **hot spot** onto the designer's face or head. The designer then provides fine-tuning instructions to the electrician to ensure that the hot spot falls in the exact location desired. How designers observe the hotspot varies from designer to designer. Many of us vary our technique depending on how bright the light source is, how many hours we've been focusing, or how fatigued we are. One common practice is to stare into the lens of the fixture and to look for the dot of the lamp's filament. If the dot is centered in the lens, it can be assumed that the hot spot of the luminaire is focused on your face. Variations of this technique involve wearing sunglasses or facing away from the unit and observing your shadow within the beam of light. Facing away from the lamp and observing one's shadow is the safest manner of focusing a unit. Staring directly into a lamp can create temporary blindness that can cause accidents like tripping or falling into the pit and may also have long-term effects like producing cataracts. There are even some designers who stand or sit in the audience while observing the effect of the light on an assistant or electrician who has been placed at the focus point. For those of us who are of average height there is no need to compensate for height differences, but if you are taller or shorter than most performers you will need to adjust your focus position by moving several steps closer to the fixture (taller) or away from the unit (shorter) as a means of compensating for your height difference.

Hand signals are often used for communication between the designer and focusing electricians because of all the noise that is associated with a load-in. I personally use thumb signals for fine-tuning the focus—a thumb-up means to bump the focus up slightly while a thumb-down or to one side means to drop the unit or to inch it over to one side or another. It is important to understand that movements of the unit of only fractions of an inch can translate into movements measured in feet on the actual stage. Once happy with the focus, the electrician is instructed to **lock the unit down.** On this instruction the pan and tilt adjustments are tightened up by the electrician while taking care that the focus doesn't drift or drop. These units don't have to be tightened down so securely that they'll remain in place for the next 50 years, but they do have to be snug enough that gravity or vibrations from air-conditioning or heating systems won't cause them to drop focus. There is no excuse for having to go back to fixtures to focus them a second time because an electrician didn't lock them down properly at the original call. After the luminaire is locked down and the designer is happy with the position of the hot spot the designer will have the electrician set the actual focus of the unit. We often set ellipsoidal reflector spotlights with their barrels all the way out or forward (**running the barrel**), which usually produces the softest edge and focus to the pool of light. This is done to blend the edges of the beams from different luminaires together. On occasions, such as with gobo patterns, a designer will want a sharper edge or focus for a unit. In these cases, the point at which the edge or pattern is sharpest will usually be found somewhere between the extreme points of the unit's focus adjustment. It is also at this time that many designers adjust any zoom or spot/flood controls that a luminaire may be equipped with. After the unit has been focused, the final adjustment is in making shutter cuts (if the unit has shutters) and shaping the beam as well as shuttering the light off of any unwanted objects. It is important to remember that shutter cuts are made through manipulating the opposite shutter from what is observed on the stage. I use open hand and arm motions for communicating shutter cuts and their orientation to the electricians. The arms are used to create the angle that the desired shutter should be adjusted to (think kids and imaginary planes) while the hands are used to coach the in and out placement of the shutter. In lieu of hand signals many facilities now give the designer and electricians wireless intercoms to use throughout a focus call. This is particularly helpful for focusing FOH positions that are far away from the designer and where heat or air-conditioning equipment can cause communication problems.

While the designer is observing the actual focus and overall shutter cuts of the luminaire the electrician should watch for any unwanted spill onto objects like borders or the edge of the proscenium. These problems are often hard to see from the designer's perspective. Once a unit is focused the designer will refer back to the instrument schedule to mark it off and to bring up the channel of the next luminaire that is hung in the position. At the same time that the designer asks for the next luminaire, the unit that was just completed will be shut down or **saved.** With luck, the ladder will not have to be moved, but even if so, the move is usually only several feet along the path of the electric to the next cluster of luminaires. Occasionally the board operator or an assistant may monitor the focus with the plot or paperwork and will call out the channel for the next unit to be focused. We often call this **riding the plot.** After a unit or two sharing a common purpose have been focused, electricians will often add additional steps to their prep by roughing in settings such as the spot/flood position or running the barrel prior to focusing the actual instrument. Even though these simple operations only take a few seconds the cumulative effect can shave a significant amount of time off the focus call. In a successful focus session a rhythm will develop between the electricians and the designer as the team steadily moves through the theatre until every instrument has been focused. The last items that are generally dealt with in a focus session are any set mounts and practicals that need to be made operational prior to the cue-writing session. When the focus session is complete, the designer should have a good idea of exactly what each luminaire is accomplishing within the design. It is at this point, after we have moved beyond the theoretical qualities of the plot and paperwork, that the first significant step is completed in the physical realization of the design.

THE LEVEL-SETTING OR CUE-WRITING SESSION

Everything that a lighting designer has done up to now has been in preparation for arriving at this point in the design process. The **level-setting** or **cue-writing session** forms a time in which the lighting designer actually creates the images or cues for the production. In addition to creating the cues the designer also determines the transitional times and related effects that are used to go from one cue to another. We may also refer to this process as **setting levels** or the **cue-in.** The cue-writing session is the phase of the design process where the lighting designer truly becomes a full-blown member of the creative team. It is here, in the dark theatre, where the lighting designer uses all the tools that they have assembled through the plot and focus to actually light the production or to "paint with light," as many of us would say. The design may be created with just a few lamps or hundreds of luminaires but in the end the lighting designer is revealing, modifying, modeling, directing focus, and creating the composition and mood of the stage for every moment of the event. How bright a stage must be is actually dependent on a number of factors. A level of between 100 and 150 footcandles is often considered enough to provide adequate illumination for many stage situations. However, depending on mood, size of facility, and other factors like material reflectance, it is quite permissible to have illumination levels that fall both well above and below this range. Film and architectural lighting will have an entirely different range of illumination levels that will be associated with particular applications. In reality, theatrical designers design for perception and by what they see.

Preparation is key to a designer's success at this stage of the process. As stated earlier, a complete and thorough cue synopsis will make this part of the design much easier for a designer. If this has been done properly, the designer will have no need to consider many of the more mundane tasks of the cue-writing session. This is also a time when many designers start to grow fatigued from having endured several hours or days of long hours from the load-in and focus sessions. The two most important documents that are required for the level-setting sessions are the cue synopsis and magic sheets. In reality, once I get to the cue-writing session, I can often light an entire show using just these two documents. This doesn't mean that I don't keep a copy of the plot, paperwork, and script near me as I work through the cue-in process—they are still kept as reference materials in case they are needed.

Several additional forms of paperwork may also be introduced at the level setting session. If not introduced here, they will become part of the production process at some point in the rehearsals that follow the cue-writing session. In many cases, these too, are completed by the designer prior to the cue-writing session, often as the cue synopsis is completed. The first are cue sheets for any followspots that are associated with a production. These provide essential cueing information such as who to pick up, the color frame assignment, size of the spot, and any other information that the operator might need to know. We often tie the spot cues to the lighting cue numbers so that the information is more easily communicated to the spot and board operators by the stage manager. An example of a followspot cue sheet is presented in Figure 13.2. In another example, a facility may not have a sufficient number of dimmers for a production, which results in the need for reassigning dimmers throughout a performance. Here, a dimmer will be assigned to an initial circuit but will at some point have another circuit patched and reassigned to it (often following the completion of a certain cue). This is called **repatching** and these reassignments may be done several times throughout a performance. We often assign specials to repatching as long as they aren't used at the same time as any other luminaires

	Follow Spot Cues				Urinetown -The Musical		
	R. Dunham, Designer				University of Georgia -Fine Arts Theatre		
		Followspot #	1				
							10/15/2007
CUE #	In/Out	Count	Frame #	Pickup	Notes:		
4	In	4	5	Lockstock (L) --Body	Just before narrative.		
					Spots should include Little Sally (LS) with L when needed		
9	Out	4					
10	In	4	4	Hope (H) --Body	w/her entrance		
12	Out	4					
20.5	In	6	6	Penny (P) --Body			
25	Out	4					
33	In	5	1	Cladwell (C) --Body			
47	Out	4					
51	In	2	4	Lockstock (L) --Body			
60	Out	6					
65	In	4	1	Hope (H) --Body			
73	Out	10					
80	In	8	4	Penny (P) --Body			
87	Out	0					
91	In	7	4	Cladwell (C) --Body			
100	Out	4					
106	In	4	3	Bobby (B) --Body			
127		5			Random searching sequence		
128		1	3	Lockstock (L) --Body	Lands on Lockstock at end of search		
129	Out	0					
				INTERMISSION			
137	In	2 + 4	2	Hot Blades (HB) --Body			
138	Out	2 +3					
140	In	2 + 6	4	Lockstock (L) --Body			
142	Out	2					
146	In	4	2	Josephine (J) --Body			
150	Out	3 + 6					
152	In	3	4	Lockstock (L) --Body			
155	Out	3 + 6					
157	In	2	4	Hot Blades (HB) --Body			
160	Out	2					
170	In	6	5	Bobby (B) --Body			
180	Out	3 + 6					
189	In	1	3	Cladwell (C) --Headshot			
190	Out	1					
194	In	2 + 4	4	Fipp (F)			
195	Out	4					
209	In	4 + 10	5	Little Sally (LS) --Waist	She's sitting on deck.		
211	Out	4					

FIGURE 13.2 Followspot Cue Sheet A partial cue sheet for Followspot #1 for a production of *Urinetown—The Musical.*

that may be assigned to a given dimmer. There must also be sufficient time to make the actual wiring change before the new special is illuminated. Obviously, the designer must track each of the specials that are assigned to a repatching dimmer in order to ensure that the repatching occurs while the dimmer is off. Repatching may occur at the patch bay, the actual circuit outlet, or at the end of a given cable run. While the electricians must ultimately keep track of the actual circuit numbers many times we simply assign letters or colors to the circuits to make the repatching easier for the running crews. An example would be in labeling a circuit and its repatches as Red 1, 2, and 3 or A 1, 2, and 3. The practice of repatching can go a long way toward helping a designer bring additional elements to a production, provided that there is time for the electricians to swap the circuits around.

One of the more important goals of the level-writing session involves creating the cue sheets for the light board and its operators. This has actually been pretty well eliminated in many theatres since most cue information is now stored electronically in the memory of computer consoles. While there was a time when none of us trusted the computer and we were paranoid about losing a show, technology has advanced to the point that we now have confidence in these consoles and any backups that we make as we go through the cue writing process. However, the only certain manner of safeguarding your cues and the time that it took to program a show is through creating a printed copy of the cues. Most of today's consoles provide a function that will print a copy of the cues onto paper using a conventional computer printer. The essential information that is provided through these printouts includes the timing of each cue along with the intensity levels for every channel/dimmer for each cue of the show. This is what we call **tracking** a show. At one time, an assistant was assigned to write down the levels and other settings for each cue. Figure 13.3 illustrates a typical track sheet. In situations where a designer is using a manual board, which is still fairly common for specific types of productions, the level-writing session also becomes the time in which the cue sheets are written for the operators. Sometimes the designer or their assistant will create the cue sheets, while at other times the operators are expected to write their own cue sheets. In

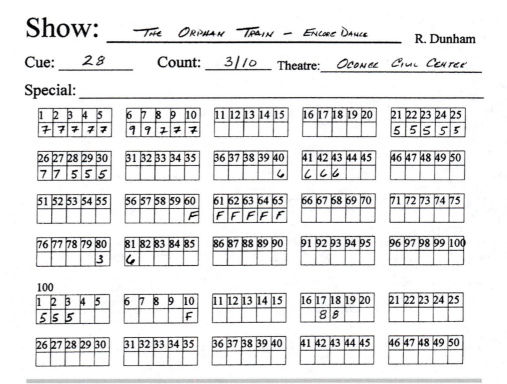

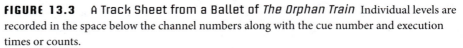

FIGURE 13.3   A Track Sheet from a Ballet of *The Orphan Train*   Individual levels are recorded in the space below the channel numbers along with the cue number and execution times or counts.

the case of manual boards, like the older piano boards, it was common for the operators to simply write down the actual action and levels that took place during a cue. In preset systems, master cue sheets (Figure 13.4) are frequently created that display rows of the dimmers in a series of presets that allow the levels to be written in a box just below each dimmer number. The levels portion of the each cue listing is then supplemented with another section that documents the action to be taken during a particular cue. Such actions would include the cue number and count, which preset was becoming active, the cross-fade assignment required to complete the cue, and any special instructions such as manual or independent assignments.

The amount of time allowed for a designer to write or program the light board can vary considerably from one situation to another. Sometimes the designer has the freedom to create the lighting with the help of only the board operator, while at other times the director may sit by the designer throughout the entire process. Sometimes cues are set with the proper scenery on stage and at other times this is not possible. In the most extreme cases the cue-in will take place with the actors in attendance and posing in their blocked positions. Obviously, the more elements that a lighting designer has in place the more accurate the initial cueing will be. However, due to costs, this is seldom done outside of those situations where money is not a factor or where the producer is willing to pay for making sure that things are done properly the first time (some academic programs and Broadway). Unfortunately, lighting designers must often come up with the best lighting that they can under significant time limitations and less-than-ideal working conditions. Sometimes cue-writing sessions are set outside of the traditional rehearsal schedule, while other times they are worked into the schedule through a series of special rehearsals called technical rehearsals. A **technical rehearsal** is a rehearsal in the performance venue with its focus on the technical elements of a production and issues like scene changes, light cues, sound cues, and their transitions. Performers are often not called to all the technical rehearsals. Time to cue in the actual theatre is scarce and a designer must find ways to be both quick and efficient. In some cases, the designer may choose to write the cues **blind,** or program the console prior to entering the theatre. This saves time because the cues will be roughed in prior to seeing them on the stage and you won't be starting your cue-in from scratch. This means that they only have to be tweaked or edited in the theatre—but you can also find yourself out in left field when writing a show blind. In reality, the more experience that you have, the more confidence you will gain and the better that you will become at using pre-cueing for a show. Today's visualizers can make the process even easier.

Show: ___Encore Dance—Spring 2006___   Theatre: ___Morton Theatre___   Page: _3_ of _12_

Cue #: _5_   Count: _3_   Preset: _A_   Special Instuctions: _____

1	2	3	4	5	6	7	8	9	10	11	12	13	14	15	16	17	18	19	20	21	22	23	24
F					F					6	6			4	4	4					8		

Cue #: _6_   Count: _2/5_   Preset: _B_   Special Instuctions: _Split-Fade_

1	2	3	4	5	6	7	8	9	10	11	12	13	14	15	16	17	18	19	20	21	22	23	24
3	3	3	0	0	0							4	4				9				5	3	

FIGURE 13.4   A Preset Cue Sheet

By the time that a lighting designer completes the level-setting process they have cleared a second hurdle of realizing their design. Even though this is perhaps the most stressful part of the design process it is also the most fun and rewarding aspect of the experience for most designers. It is at this point that the designer turns all the tools (plot, focus, etc.) into an actual design in light. The objective of a cue-writing session should be to get something programmed into the console for every major moment of the production. If there isn't sufficient time to program all the cues, only the major images should be programmed so that you can get a sense of how successful the base cues will be when the lights are first viewed with the performers. The skipped cues can be programmed into the board at a later time. By following these guidelines the cues can be evaluated during a rehearsal within the context of the moment—with the performers in their proper positions, compositional elements in place, and moods easily identified. Transitions should also be evaluated through this process. More importantly, if a designer has followed this technique they will not only be able to evaluate the success or failure of a cue based on the context of the moment, they will also be able to tweak or refine it based on observations that they can make in rehearsal. Issues like whether focus is properly established, if the color is too saturated, if there is enough visibility, or whether the proper mood is created are easily evaluated and fixed if there is something in the board to evaluate. Another mistake commonly made by beginning designers occurs when they run out of time when setting levels. In this case, the designer will not have anything to evaluate or react to beyond a given point in the rehearsal. When plotting ahead, even if the recorded levels are completely wrong, you at least have something to evaluate and will be able to make some concrete decisions in regard to how to fix the remaining cues. What's important is getting something to look at—the absence of information will always be wrong, but any information, even if bad, gives you an opportunity to make corrections. In some cases, true inspiration actually comes out of cues that were simply plugged into the console for the sake of just getting something to look at for that first rehearsal with the performers. With the advent of automated lighting, the number of additional variables that a lighting designer must consider when cueing a show has grown astronomically. Because of this, it is common for shows making use of automated lighting to require more tech time for setting up a console and programming a show. In fact, a specialized technician (**programmer**) has appeared whose primary function is setting up and programming all of the intelligent lighting.

CUEING AIDS FOR MEMORY CONSOLES

Despite the variations between specific boards and manufacturers there are still a number of techniques that many designers and operators use to help make cueing more efficient. Even though the specific manners of achieving these concepts may vary from board to board, a designer should be aware of how they can streamline the cueing process and should trust the local board operator for the specific techniques in which a particular board may operate. These local programmers use the boards day in and day out and are the people who will be most familiar with their console. They have most likely already been asked to create some unique effect or use some buried board feature from another designer who has passed through at an earlier time. Use your console operators and trust them; they're a terrific resource for getting through the cueing process. The following pages will not give you the specific keystrokes for a timesaving measure but will discuss several essential cueing practices that will help minimize the number of keystrokes that it will take to achieve a cueing sequence.

Many consoles are equipped with features that enable the operator to be more productive in their cueing. Many of these were discussed previously in Chapter 8. **Tracking** or **cue only** modes, the **wheel, blind mode, submasters, groups, independent masters,** and **blackout buttons** are just a few console features that are used to help reduce keystrokes during the cueing process. Also, as discussed in Chapter 12, the designer can play a role in eliminating keystrokes through paying careful attention to the manner in which he or she lays out the hookup of the production. Even beyond this organization and the specific console features, there are additional techniques that will lead to further efficiency in writing cues. Sidebar 13.2 provides a listing and explanation of just a few of these aids to cueing.

REHEARSALS IN THE VENUE

Once a production has been focused, a series of special rehearsals are scheduled in the theatre or venue in which a show will be performed. This usually entails a series of **technical rehearsals** where the technical elements of a production are developed (including the lights) that may or may not include the performers and a series of **dress rehearsals** that emphasize getting the show into its final form and ready for an audience. The amount of time allotted for these rehearsals can vary significantly from one organization to another (e.g., touring productions have no need or time for any of these rehearsals) while additional specialty rehearsals may also be added (e.g., preview performances) for other productions. The following pages address rehearsals that would be typical for most productions. The specific number and lengths of each type of rehearsal may also vary considerably between different organizations.

Technical Rehearsals

Technical rehearsals are dedicated to working out the technical elements of a production. Scenic changes, flying sequences, special effects, and the cueing of the lights and sound are all dealt with in these rehearsals. Different organizations have different manners of coordinating technical rehearsals. In most situations productions receive a minimum of two technical rehearsals. The first, typically called **first tech** or **dry tech,** may actually be the cue-writing session for some organizations. However, it is more common for the cues to be written ahead of time and to have the lighting designer simply present the cues (without performers) to the director and other members of the production team. It's a time where reactions to the cues are discussed and revisions will be made based on comments from the director and other team members. Questions regarding the placement of the cues can also be addressed, and more elaborate sequences might be practiced and revised. Board operators will also experiment with the manner in which they must operate a console to properly execute a cue sequence. In especially sophisticated productions the team may schedule an additional meeting called a **paper tech** where cue placement and sequences are simply discussed sometime prior to going into a full-blown technical rehearsal.

In many organizations a second technical rehearsal is scheduled in which the performers are added into the mix and the cues are refined based on how the lighting interacts with them. This is called a **tech with actors** or in some cases a **wet tech.** The emphasis of this rehearsal should not be on performance issues but rather on how well the cues work with the actors. This rehearsal is typically long and tedious and is often scheduled as a ten out of twelve (working 10 hours over a 12-hour period) day. If time is spent properly at these rehearsals to iron out any technical issues; the focus of the director can shift back to the acting and overall appearance of the production at the later dress rehearsals. These rehearsals should not be rushed, or pushed through simply for the sake of getting through them, because valuable time will be taken away from later rehearsals as the same mistakes continue to reappear from one rehearsal to another. Issues such as determining whether there is enough base level illumination, an appropriate mood is achieved, a particular actor has a strong enough focus, or if a crowd is lit consistently enough are just a few of the issues that are examined during technical rehearsals. Once again, lighting levels are refined to accommodate the needs of the production, and transitions from one cue to another are examined and modified so that the cues flow with the action and pace of the performance.

In the best of all possible worlds a lighting designer would be provided with an opportunity for at least a tech with the actors. However, in many situations this is not possible and the first time that the lighting designer sees their lights with the performers will be at a first dress rehearsal. With the ease with which computer consoles record cue

SIDEBAR 13.2 Cueing Aids

Block Cues	These are sometimes also called **hard blackouts.** These are cues placed throughout a program that have every channel recorded at a level of zero. A logical place for the location of a block cue is at the end of a scene where an actual blackout is required. Block cues are created as a means of preventing tracking channels from continuing to make changes past a given point or scene.
Check Cues	A check cue is created to check or verify that particular actions have taken place prior to the beginning of a show or act. They are commonly created before the preset cue for the beginning of an act or during an intermission sequence. An example would be a cue that would bring up all the repatch channels to a glow to verify that the circuits have actually been replugged at intermission. A **blackout check** that plunges the theatre into complete darkness to check that all grid, fly, and worklights are out for the top of a show forms another type of check cue.
Cue Blocks	Cue blocks establish and number sequences of cues together as a group. The most common forms include creating blocks where each act of a production begins a new numbering sequence (i.e., Act 1 begins with Cue 101 while Act 2 begins with Cue 201). I often use cue blocks for dance concerts where each dance will be assigned a block of 10–20 cues. Dance 1 will begin with Cue 11, while Dance 2 will begin with Cue 21, andDance 6 will begin with Cue 61, etc. The base cues (in this case 10, 20, or 60) form preset cues for each dance. By using this technique dances can be cued in any order (which often happens—be sure you stay in cue-only mode or set block cues) or for when dances are shifted around into any performance order in a repertory situation.
Fixture Keys	Fixture keys are specialty keys on consoles that are user-friendly for automated lighting and provide an operator easy access to an automated luminaire's multiple attributes through previously addressed assignments to the console's encoders and submaster pages.
Focus Points	Focus points are a variation of a palette assignment (see palettes below) that provides pre-assigned channel settings for pan and tilt attributes of automated fixtures that correspond to specific locations or points on a stage. Individual cues and pan/tilt assignments are referenced to these points so that if a point is relocated all the cues can be instantly updated through a simple redefinition of the focus points.
Library Cues	On many occasions a designer may find that they may want to go in a different direction for a cue or cue sequence but may feel unsure that the new cues they are creating will be any better than the first version. Rather than simply recording the new cues over the old cues, the old cues are moved to an unused area of the console and are reassigned new cue numbers. For instance old Cue 135 could be stored as Cue 535 (well after the last planned cue number) and then a new Cue 135 can be created. If the replacement cue isn't effective, the old cue can be used to simply overwrite Cue 135.
Move Cues	Move cues are created immediately before or after a cue utilizing a unit with moving attributes such as scrollers or automated lights. These specialized cues preset any attributes that must be assigned before the unit is illuminated. Move cues provide a means of preventing an audience from seeing lights slide into position or color scrolling through a series of colors as the gelstring shifts to a new color. These are also called **mark cues.**
Palettes/Pages	As a means of making all of the attributes and channel functions more easily accessible, common attribute assignments are preprogrammed into a console in predetermined combinations of channel assignments for each of the units. Faders or encoders can often take on multiple assignments or functions that can be changed through a simple page command. Color assignments, gobo combinations, or zoom settings all form fairly common palettes that are often created for a production. This technique has become extremely popular with programmers who work with automated lighting. In fact, many programmers carry their own personal disks with predefined palettes that they tend to use on a regular basis. Quite possibly the most common palette used is the focus palette, which preprograms pan/tilt instructions or combinations to specific points on a stage.

changes most designers prefer to **edit** their cues or make most of their revisions live while a cue is in the context of the moment. During a dress rehearsal actors are in their staged positions, moods can be set appropriately, and focus assessments can be easily compared from one part of the stage to another. It is especially important for a lighting designer to maintain a calm, efficient manner of editing the cues and to make quick changes **on the fly** while the action continues uninterrupted. This is not a job for people who get flustered easily or who do not respond well to being under stress. Any changes that cannot be made while the action is running must be carefully noted and fixed at some time when the performers are not rehearsing—what we call taking a **note.** Most designers will maintain at least two sets of notes. The first list, **worknotes,** relates to technical issues that will require an electrics crew and deals with problems such as refocusing, bad color assignments, or non-functional instruments. The second relates to cue issues and includes notes that require some form of cue editing that could not be completed while the rehearsal was running, notes for the stage manager that relate to cue placement and calling the show, and finally notes that relate to director input or questions. I personally like to keep a tablet for each area of specific notes. I know other designers who like to place their notes on 3×5 cards, which they then sort and distribute to each of the related areas. An honest effort should always be made to address all of your board notes before the next rehearsal. I have found that the best time for doing this is immediately after a rehearsal as the actors are getting out of costume. At that time, not only will the director still be available to answer any questions, but more importantly, any problems that I have experienced during the rehearsal are still fresh in my mind. I can also respond to any of the director's questions at that time. By fixing your cueing problems between rehearsals you can avoid repeating the same mistake at consecutive rehearsals. At the very least, even though the cue may not yet be right, you will have ruled out several potential solutions for a particular problematic cue or sequence. Actually, you will often find that the new cue, even if not perfect, moves you closer to a solution for the given situation. Technical notes will often have to wait until the next time that there is an electrics call. It's a fairly common practice to collect the technical notes over several days without bringing a crew in until later so that a number of notes can be completed at the same time and excessive labor costs in the way of minimum calls can be avoided. In situations that are not bound by minimum calls, the notes should be done at the earliest convenience so that you don't have to continue to see the same old problems.

Dress Rehearsals, Previews, and Openings

DRESS REHEARSALS Dress rehearsals form a time where all the final elements of a production come together to create the performance that the audience will come to experience. As much as possible, the team works together to produce rehearsals that continue to approach performance conditions. Additional elements that have not yet been introduced to a production will be added during the dress rehearsals. Most commonly, costumes are introduced at the first dress rehearsal, while makeup will often be added on the second or third dress. As a team progresses through subsequent dress rehearsals the production is continually refined until it is ready for an audience. **Previews** are a special type of dress rehearsal where an audience will be in attendance.

From a lighting designer's perspective dress rehearsals form an extremely important time for fine-tuning a production. Performers often have weeks to develop and refine their actions and delivery of a given set of lines or scene, while lighting designers are not afforded this luxury. It is important for a lighting designer to achieve a final tweaking of a production's cues during these rehearsals. Just as important is the task of ensuring that the transitions between cues are accomplished in a way that appears to flow with the action of the show. As a rule, most production teams like to concentrate on running the production during dress rehearsals, and stopping a rehearsal is avoided except in those circumstances in which there are severe problems or a condition is created that could be potentially dangerous for the performers or backstage personnel. As with anything else, each dress rehearsal proceeds to get better than the last, and notes become more minimal and more specific as the team goes through the process. Most organizations have two to three dress rehearsals plus an additional **final dress** rehearsal. The final dress rehearsal is conducted so that the production is presented as if it were under performance conditions—with the exception of an audience.

Just as with technical rehearsals, board notes should be completed live within the context of the moment if at all possible during a dress rehearsal. This requires good organization skills and an ability to act quickly since each moment is quickly lost. By focusing on the largest problems first, a steady improvement will be observed from one dress rehearsal to the next. Magic sheets with clearly identified systems or channels and a good cue synopsis become critical to a lighting designer's success during dress rehearsals. The most successful designers use their dress rehearsals to modify and refine the cues to the best point possible. Speed and the ability not to get frazzled are essential skills required at this point in the process. As a designer works to modify cues during dress rehearsals they should not cause any major distractions for the director and performers and must take care not to create any unsafe conditions like an unexpected blackout while the performers are working on the stage. If a cue cannot be fixed before another cue is advanced or played back the designer should make a note of the problem so that they can go back and edit the cue(s) at a time that will not interfere with the rehearsal. When making changes it is extremely important that any cue revisions get recorded prior to hitting the "go" button for an upcoming cue. Not observing this practice will result in losing any changes that you may have made, or even worse, having the board record a cue that reflects some sort of transitional state that exists between the two cues that you were working on. To avoid this I always try to record the cue when I hear the stage manager call the standby for an upcoming cue. As a rule, the initial dress rehearsals tend to focus on level-setting problems, while the later ones tend to be more involved with the transition and execution of the cues. In most cases, the assistant lighting designer is responsible for keeping the lists of notes so that the designer is free to watch the stage and make corrections during a rehearsal. These changes should be programmed by the actual console operator (if at all possible) so that the designer is free to concentrate on their paperwork and the stage. The very last dress rehearsal, the **final dress,** tries to replicate an actual performance condition, and in most cases lighting designers are discouraged from making changes while this rehearsal is in progress. In fact, the design table and intercoms that are assigned to the lighting designer and their staff will often be struck for the final dress rehearsal. Notes from this rehearsal will be collected and then fixed sometime following the rehearsal.

PREVIEWS AND OPENINGS   Previews form a special type of dress rehearsal in which a paying audience is in attendance. This allows the performers and production staff to get a sense of how an audience will react to a show while also providing further opportunities for the team to refine the production. Even though the company may reserve the right to change or even stop a performance during previews, most teams tend to treat previews as an actual performance, and the audience usually gets the chance to see the production in much the same form as the audience who will attend the opening performance. The number of previews associated with a production can vary considerably from one organization to another. Some theatres may choose not to offer any previews at all, while others like many Broadway productions offer 2 or more weeks of preview performances. The companies that I have designed for in Atlanta typically offer one or two preview performances, while the Off-Broadway theatres I have worked for often have 1 week of previews. In some situations, the entire production is treated as a preview where the production is tried out in a smaller, lower-cost market such as Off-Broadway houses or out-of-town theatres. These early productions are called **out-of town tryouts** or **pre-Broadway runs,** and cities like Baltimore, Boston, Philadelphia, Chicago, Cleveland, and Washington have often served as a testing ground for new productions. Regional theatres also produce many new works that will eventually be transferred to Broadway. The recent Broadway production of *The Color Purple* was first produced at The Alliance Theatre in Atlanta. Other regional theatres like The Longwarf Theatre (San Diego), The Guthrie (Minneapolis) and The Arena Theatre (Washington, DC) have become regular contributors to the Broadway stage.

Opening nights are a magical moment in a production's history. With the coming of opening night comes the celebration of all the work and preparation of the performers and production team. It's often the first time that the show is presented to a live audience and marks a pivotal point in determining whether the team has a hit or flop on its hands. It is also the first time the production will be reviewed by critics, and with that, both the artistic and financial success or failure of a project will soon be established. For the lighting designer, it should be a time to observe and enjoy the production along with the rest of the team. A few notes might be completed following this performance but as a rule the night is reserved for supporting the show and celebrating its opening. A cardinal sin that a designer should not commit is missing the opening of a show that you have designed. Yes, you might be exhausted, but you insult your fellow team members by choosing not to support your own production. While your teammates will understand if you have another out-of-town commitment, simply not attending your opening is one of the surest ways to get yourself removed from the network of artists that you have just collaborated with. Once the production has officially opened and gone into its performance **run** the lighting designer's role in the production is over. The master electrician will work to maintain the show, keeping track of lamp and gel burnouts, touch-up focuses, and any other problems that may develop, while the stage manager will maintain the execution of the show. When you arrive at opening night your contract ends and you are free to move on to the next project. In the case of a long-running production, the designer may be brought back occasionally to ensure that the production has remained consistent with how it was left on opening night. If it runs beyond a predetermined number of weeks, the designer may even be entitled to further compensation through **residuals.** These are nothing more than a weekly fee based on a percentage of the box office receipts that was agreed upon as a part of the initial contract.

RUNNING AND MAINTAINING THE PRODUCTION

When we discuss the run of the production we are simply referring to the production entering a period of regular performances. There are many different formats that a run may follow and each will have an impact on the type of crew and the role that a lighting designer may play in the performance run. In most cases, the crews take on all the responsibilities of the lighting once a production has opened. The most popular performance runs involve a straight run, in which the production is contracted for a predetermined number of weeks and performances. Typical runs extend from 6 to 8 weeks with regular performances (five to eight) throughout each week. When the run ends, the production will be **struck** and a new production will open in its place. This format is used at most regional, academic, and summer stock production companies. Runs are often shortened to as little as a week or two in the case of academic or summer stock theatres. The run of a production may also be extended by adding performances or weeks of performances if the production has met with success. Any run lasting longer than 6 to 8 weeks is often called an **extended run.** There are several exceptions to the lighting designer being finished once a production enters its run. The most notable is in the areas of touring, when a production must maintain a consistent look from one venue to another even though the performance facilities might vary significantly from one another. In these situations the lighting designer may be retained to ensure that the plot, focus, and levels are modified so that the lighting will be consistent from one venue to another. When a lighting designer is not available or unwilling to travel, an **assistant** or **associate lighting designer** or a **lighting director** is often hired to take the designer's place. This individual has the responsibility of not only making the design functional in a variety of performance spaces but must also faithfully reproduce the design as closely as they can to the original designer's intent.

Regardless of the type of situation that may exist when a production enters into a run, there are several issues that must be addressed in order to keep the show maintained and consistent from one performance to another. Those audiences who see the show in week 4 are entitled to the same experience as those who were lucky enough to attend the performance on opening night. This principle should hold true even when a show goes into an extended run of months or years. While the designer is seldom involved in the actual run of the show, other members of the electrics team take on a variety of responsibilities to ensure that every audience receives a similar experience. The most important person in maintaining the electrics in most organizations is the

Beverly Emmons

Beverly Emmons is a renowned lighting designer who fits into the third generation of lighting designers, having assisted both Tom Skelton and Jules Fisher. She has a solid reputation in dance, drama, and opera lighting design. She has also lit a number of *avant garde* productions and projects. Her credits include a varied collection of collaborations with many of the most influential companies and performing artists of the last 30 years. She has lit for Broadway and prominent regional theatres, a number of the most significant dance companies in the world, and both national and international opera companies. A brief sampling of directors and choreographers that she has collaborated with include: Robert Wilson, Merce Cunningham, Martha Graham, Bill T. Jones, Trisha Brown and Joseph Chaikin. Her opera lighting has been seen at La Scala and the Welsh National Opera and she is the recipient of numerous lighting awards that include seven Tony nominations (*Jekyll and Hyde, Passion, Les Liaisons Dangereuses, A Day in Hollywood/A Night in the Ukraine*, and *The Elephant Man* among others). She has also been honored as a USITT Distinguished Lighting Designer, won an Obie, a Lumen Award (*Einstein on the Beach*), and two Bessies for her dance lighting. She has served on the graduate faculty of Columbia and Yale, is a regular panelist of the Broadway Lighting Master Classes, and frequently speaks and designs as a guest artist throughout the country. Even with such an active professional life she has had a successful family life while also shepherding a series of important projects by serving as the artistic director for Lincoln Center Institute and creating the Lighting Archive Project, which is developing the Theatrical Lighting Database for the New York Public Library for the Performing Arts.

Emmons received a combination of both formal and informal education. Her formal training came through studying dance composition with Bessie Schonberg at Sarah Lawrence College. She also studied lighting at the Lester Polakov Studio. Informally, she assisted Tom Skelton and Jules Fisher in the early part of her career. She has not been pigeonholed as a lighting designer associated with a particular area of lighting, preferring instead to light a variety of projects, which allows the types of lighting designs that she creates to vary significantly in any given year. Emmons shares that, "An important interest of mine is not to be typed into any particular area of the profession. To be moving from one area to another keeps life lively." Originally, Beverly was a dancer who got involved in the backstage through her associations with Tom Watson and Tom Skelton. "I was interested in the process of how dances were created in the quiet concentration of a studio . . . and then how to make the transition to performance on a stage. I was interested in minimizing the chaos of that process by having the stage preparation properly planned so that the lights were hung and focused and the floor washed in the scheduled time so the dancers could begin in a calm concentrated way." While working at the summer dance festivals she had the opportunity to observe some of the best dancers and choreographers in the world and eventually became more interested in the technical areas and stage management than in performing. So, like many other lighting designers, she began her shift to lighting through becoming a stage manager. Dealing with the technical elements of the lighting, as well as calling other people's cues, were part of the job. Her early design experience came from recreating her own lighting on the road, where she had to problem solve and think on her feet to re-create the lighting for a variety of spaces that were often quite different from the original facilities and equipment. Her first lighting design position came when she was hired by Merce Cunningham. "My work with Merce Cunningham 'vetted' me for a wide range of '*avant garde*' artists like Robert Wilson, Meridith Monk, and Joseph Chaiken. Many of these artists were moving off in a different direction from the more saturated lighting and color treatments that were fairly common at that time . . . rebelling from the style of the day and shifting to a cleaner, less intense association with color—insisting upon a white-light, no-color treatment of their work."

Beverly speaks fairly specifically about some of the differences between designing in different areas of the profession. "It is part of a designer's job to understand the aesthetic needs of each art form. The economic and structural differences between the genres are also very important. . . . Dance has to be quick . . . opera also has little time but adds advantages as well as additional restrictions. Dance usually has to work with a rep plot and you can't change much, while opera has rolling rep which can be confining with only hours to refocus and recolor the plot day after day. You have to understand the realities of each situation . . . especially the economic implications of time with crews and money. Commercial theatre is more flexible in that you can put equipment any place it needs to be . . . rent and use any lights available in the shops, and once the show opens the lights are maintained exactly as you left them. In terms of the design, you do the plot before the rehearsals start and you have to be flexible because at that point you don't know what you're lighting and you need to have many options. Most importantly you learn to trust and listen to other people." Emmons adds that each genre has different cueing needs. "Opera cueing relates to the music . . . dance is all about movement. A Broadway musical has so many cues: sound and scenic moves as well as lights, requiring that some of the standbys and cues are called with light switches."

Emmons, like others, sees both good and bad in working on a variety of different projects. While working in different areas of lighting keeps things fresh and exciting, it also means that there is much more material in which she must stay up to date. She believes that one of the best ways to remain current is by "seeing productions and observing what other designers are doing." She advises students to "look at light . . . look at how it behaves . . . look at it striking objects . . . observe the sky." She also advises that, "You have to decide what you want. There's good lucrative work for both designers and electricians, but you have to decide what you want to be. If you are a technician, learn how to program and fix moving lights. There is well-paid work in these areas . . . but you have to be good at it. If you want to be a designer . . . be an assistant. Assisting is a wonderful way to learn. You have to figure out where you want to get your experience . . . and then when you're designing be brilliant . . . be organized . . . do more than required. Get the other artists and the organization to think they could never do another show without you. Being present in the moment is what we do. Every project is important and one must always do one's best. Pay attention to beauty . . . pay attention to the art part of what you do . . . the problems will always be there and the way that you become successful is by recognizing the problems in advance and defusing or dealing with them . . . know that they never go away."

Photo credit: Blanche MacKey

master electrician. This person also often operates the lighting console during the run and along with the stage manager is responsible for ensuring that the cues are executed properly from one performance to another.

The most important task for maintaining a design is in completing a **dimmer** or **channel check** immediately before every performance. To complete a dimmer check the board operator simply steps through each dimmer or channel, one at a time, bringing each channel up to a level of full. While the channel is up, the electricians check to make sure that all of the instruments assigned to that channel are operational, that each unit has maintained its proper focus, and that the gel has not burned out. If any problems are discovered, they are noted before moving on to the next channel. After going through the entire hookup the notes are addressed and fixed—all to ensure that the plot is restored to its original condition. Dimmer checks should be completed when the crew is first called so that there is time to troubleshoot and fix any problems prior to opening the house to an audience. The channel check also allows the crew to check items like repatches to ensure that all of the patches have been restored for the top of the show. Many beginning electricians get sloppy during dimmer checks and tend to only check that a light is coming up. In reality a dropped focus or burnout of a deep blue gel can cause even bigger disruptions to a performance than a lamp that doesn't come up. I've even witnessed performances where FOH luminaires that had dropped focus continued to come up in scenes only to light audience members who were seated directly below them.

Another important task that should be completed prior to opening the house for any performance involves creating a blackout cue so that the theatre can be checked for complete darkness (**blackout check**). This ensures that light sources like worklights, gridlights, and lights from other adjoining spaces like catwalks are not accidently left on. Additional preset cues can also be programmed that will allow the crew to check items like the **focus points** of automated lighting gear. If a problem should occur during a performance, it is the master electrician, along with the stage manger, who will have to determine how to make the correction and continue with the show. Some burnouts that occur during a performance will not cause significant problems and can be replaced at the next dimmer check, while the loss of a critical special might require the board operator to find a way of sneaking an alternate light into a scene that would have been lit by the failed lamp. All problems that develop during a performance require a solution that comes from sound judgment and quick actions on the part of the team. Occasionally, larger problems such as a console losing its memory or **dumping a show** can happen, but these are infrequent occurrences and the data can usually be restored both simply and quickly through reloading the show from a backup disk. A full backup system will exist in those situations where a failure cannot be tolerated.

FOR FURTHER READING

Bellman, Willard F., *Lighting the Stage: Art and Practice,* 3rd ed. (Louisville, KY: Broadway Press, 2001).

Pilbrow, Richard, *Stage Lighting Design; The Art, The Craft, The Life* (New York: Design Press/Quite Specific Media Group, Ldt., 1997).

Shelley, Steven Louis, *A Practical Guide to Stage Lighting* (Boston: Focal Press, 1999).

Watson, Lee, *Lighting Design Handbook* (New York: McGraw-Hill, Inc., 1990).

Variations on Essential Theatrical Design

14

This chapter builds on the general principles of entertainment lighting that were presented throughout the last several chapters. While the earlier chapters addressed primarily design process and the proscenium stage, this chapter expands to include considerations for other performance spaces, the nature of an event, and the role of genre and presentation style on a lighting design. The focus of these discussions is centered on performance events like drama, although the concepts can be expanded to include opera, dance, and musical theatre.

All of the processes discussed previously can be applied to lighting designs across a variety of specialties. The techniques are simply adjusted so that they apply to the needs of a particular project. We generally categorize these adaptations as belonging to one or more of essentially three groups. The first relates to the type of space that an event is being produced in. The role of space relates primarily to the relationship that is created between the performers and the audience. While the scale of a venue has an impact on the design, the real consideration lies in the orientation that an audience has with the stage or performers. The most obvious examples come with moving an event to a venue that has a different physical form than a proscenium theatre. Rather than having an audience facing a single direction, the stage may be surrounded by an audience on three (**thrust theatre**) or four sides (**arena theatre**). Arena theatre may also be called **theatre-in-the-round,** while thrust theatre may be called **3/4-staging.** In the most extreme cases, the audience and performers may even be intermixed (**environmental theatre**). Each of these theatre arrangements requires a different approach to successfully light an event. There are also **black box theatres,** which are nothing more than a large black room with an overhead lighting grid. Sometimes we call these **flexible spaces** since they can be reconfigured in any manner that's appropriate for a production. Another consideration for designing in black box theatres is that a designer must frequently specify the house lights (often theatrical luminaires like fresnels) due to the flexibility of the spaces.

Due to the variety of audience perspectives, sightlines become important issues for a scenic designer and director as they work in these other performance spaces. The more that a stage is surrounded by an audience, the more critical the effect becomes. Additionally, thrust and arena theatres aren't usually equipped with mechanisms for shifting scenery. These two effects tend to force scenic elements to become more minimal as productions move progressively towards arena orientations. Lighting is often used to compensate for these scenic compromises and will play a larger role in establishing the setting of a scene, while the role of the scenery shifts to becoming more of a neutral background. The lighting designer must also consider the specific nature of the event. Is the production to be mounted only once? Is the production touring? Will it be one of several productions in repertory? Finally, the role of genre and the specific nature of the performance event will also shape the way in which a production is lit. Each art form has an associated design aesthetic—dramas are lit in a way that is different from the way that operas or dances are lit. Some of these qualities relate to style, while others are associated with the conventions that are characteristic of a particular type of event. Design choices that might be considered typical for a dance production will often be out of character for an event like a play. Regardless of the nature of a performance event, each can be designed through modifications in the techniques that have been discussed up to this point.

THRUST AND ARENA PRODUCTIONS

Most plays can be performed in a variety of audience relationships. Some are very formal and distant (proscenium productions), while others explore a more intimate relationship between the performers and audience (arena and environmental). There are essentially two effects that must be considered when lighting productions in which the performers are surrounded on more than one side by an audience. The first relates to the varying perspectives of the seating areas, while the second relates to the proximity of the audience to the performer(s). Both reinforce the role of the performer as the major element of the stage composition and de-emphasize production elements like the scenery.

Audience perspective should play a critical role in how a lighting designer lights a production. The lighting is relative and must be considered differently for each of the audience perspectives. In a thrust stage, a single front special that creates a wonderful face light for a monologue will be seen as a sidelight by audience members seated on either side of the stage. In an arena production, the audience on the opposite side of the stage will actually see the performer in silhouette. In some situations this may be acceptable, while in others it would become a distraction that could take away from an audience's experience. A lighting designer must consider the relative views of each seating location while also ensuring that each area is well-lit throughout the entire production. A designer should understand that each perspective will be unique and should not attempt to duplicate the lighting from one perspective to another. It's amazing how different a design can appear through the different perspectives. Accept the fact that each will be different and simply work on achieving an acceptable solution to lighting each of the audience areas. On the other hand, it is imperative that a design be fully examined from each audience perspective for the entire show. I achieve this through moving the design table to different seating areas for different rehearsals. More importantly, the practice allows me to check each cue within the context of the play while also providing me with an opportunity to fix any problems that might not have been apparent when I lit the piece from the initial perspective. My assistants also often view a show from different perspectives for me. Because these productions are viewed from multiple directions, the number of luminaires and dimmers required to provide the general lighting is also normally quite a bit higher than those required for proscenium productions. Other issues that relate to audience perspective include the fact that luminaires are typically hung in full view of an audience with little attempt to mask them. We can also look beyond the stage to see other audience members who are directly within our view. Therefore, the audience becomes a part of the visual composition of the stage. These effects require a lighting designer to pay particular attention to issues like **glare** and **spill,** which normally have a much smaller impact on proscenium productions.

Proximity of an audience also plays an important role in how a lighting design is conceived for a thrust or arena production. With audience members on three sides, these theatres typically have steeply raked seating areas that allow the patrons in the nearest rows to be as close as close as 3 to 4 feet from the stage. Even the most distant viewers are often only as far as 50 to 60 feet away from the stage. In arena productions, the theatre seats patrons on four sides and may be as small as having seating areas of only three or four rows—some are even smaller. Theatres like this form an intimate event where the audience and performers can clearly see and react to one another. This intimacy requires a lighting designer to be sensitive to issues that could distort the performers, and several different trends can be observed between the way in which a designer must light thrust or arena productions from proscenium productions. Strong color saturations and extreme angles (both steep and flat) have to be used with care in arena and thrust spaces so that any distortion of the performers is based solely on the needs of the script and not by the general lighting. On the whole, subtle choices are better for thrust and arena designs, and strong choices such as steep angled specials, dominant downlighting, or deep color saturations are better left for those occasions when a specific effect is called for. The more intimate environment also usually requires smaller area lighting pools than those associated with proscenium stages. This allows the general lighting to be more controllable. Shorter throw distances are common in thrust and arena theatres, which results in the use of luminaires that tend to have wider beamspreads than those used in proscenium productions. Because of the need for more area control and a desire for avoiding audience spill, steeper angles also tend to be more common to thrust and arena productions. Other tendencies relate to spill forming a significant issue in thrust and arena designs when light continues past its target and spills into audience areas or is reflected off the stage floor. Glare from luminaires that light the stage from the opposite direction also becomes a consideration, and a designer should avoid situations that force audiences to look directly into lighting instruments that are focused towards them from across the stage. All of these effects are even more critical in environmental designs where performers are intermixed with an audience. Here, a certain amount of spill is usually unavoidable and a designer must simply work to make it acceptable. Each of these conditions result in more top hats and barndoors being used in thrust and arena lighting.

When designing the area coverage in thrust or arena productions, a designer should work to establish a minimum of two face lights coming from two different directions for each of the audience perspectives. By using two or more luminaires from different angles, both color and intensity can be better used to manipulate the sculptural qualities of the performers. Since color is seen as a relative lighting quality, coloring each unit differently creates a warm/cool relationship that will enhance the modeling effect of the two lights. While I know designers who focus a single light from each audience area to each acting area from straight-on, the approach tends to produce less shadow definition and can create a flat, uninspired form of illumination for a production. Instead, by following the practice of establishing a good key/fill relationship between the two face lights, a solid sculptural effect is created on the performers. Color choices for the area lighting are generally less saturated than those associated with proscenium productions and it is common for **pastel tints** to be used in many area lighting systems that are created for thrust and arena designs.

Once the general illumination has been planned, there are also additional demands that the lighting designer must meet that are layered on top of the general illumination scheme for thrust and arena productions. Unlike proscenium facilities, thrust and arena stages have aisles called **vomitories** or **voms** between audience areas that allow performers to pass through the audience as they enter and exit the stage. These aisles have to be dealt with specially so that the entrances and exits are lit and spill does not strike the neighboring seats. Instruments that are used to light these entrances are often hung along the axis of the aisle so that their light can be directed along the path both toward and away from the stage. Also, low lighting angles such as sidelight are hard to create in a thrust or arena environment, and it is within the voms that this low-angled lighting is typically arranged. This also helps to prevent audience members from having to look into the fixtures that are used to create these low lighting angles. If a designer wishes to use booms and low-mounted positions like shin-kickers they are almost always located within the voms or across the upstage area (thrust theatres). An important issue to keep in mind when comparing specials used in proscenium theatres with those used for thrust or arena designs relates to the fact that while a single luminaire can be used as an effective special in a proscenium design, this may not be the case in a thrust or arena designs. In thrust and arena design such an effect commonly requires two or three specials to achieve the same result due to the varied audience perspectives.

The following sections provide several specific techniques for creating workable lighting designs for thrust or arena productions. These techniques represent several formula approaches that have been proven over time. On the other hand, while these will satisfy the needs of producing a general illumination scheme for a production, designers should not think of these approaches as the only means for lighting thrust or arena events. Environmental productions generally follow design principles based on those used for arena productions with additional concern placed on the issue of audience spill. As a designer gains confidence, they will learn to modify these methods in ways that will create unique responses for a given production. There are few set rules to lighting any production—only that the design be appropriate for the given moment and event.

Thrust Productions

Thrust productions are unique in that the audience is situated around the staging area on three distinct sides. The fourth side, often complete with a proscenium, generally becomes a scenic background for the performers. In many cases this upstage area will have a small staging area, wings, and possibly a full flyhouse and rigging system. In addition to the three different audience perspectives these venues tend to have steeply raked seating areas that allow the audience to look down on the stage while having a more intimate or closer proximity to the stage and performers. The floor often becomes a major scenic component in thrust theatres. Thrust theatres may also have balconies that are oriented along the three different perspectives of the stage. Aisles or voms are located between each of the seating areas, and performers often enter and exit the stage from these positions. More importantly, these locations often become transition areas as different scenes unfold for an audience. In some cases the voms are built under the second tier of seating so that audience members may actually sit directly over the voms.

HANGING POSITIONS Thrust theatres (Figure 14.1) may be constructed as permanent facilities or as temporary structures in a flexible space like a blackbox theatre. In the most simple arrangements, pipes are simply hung over the stage and used to hang both the

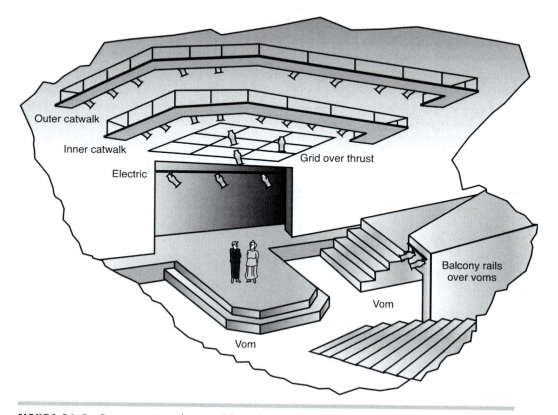

FIGURE 14.1 Common Hanging Positions in a Thrust Theatre Catwalks may be masked by clouds or valences that are hung on the offstage side of the catwalks. Stagehouse hanging positions can include: electrics, torms, booms, and ground rows.

luminaires and any scenic elements that need to be supported from above. In most cases, the scenery does not raise or lower and is **dead-hung.** In more elaborate systems, a grid is hung from above the theatre. A grid consists of two perpendicular sets of pipes that are mounted on even spacings that typically range from 3 to 5 feet. In a permanent thrust theatre a grid is often located directly above the stage, while traditional battens are located in the upstage area of the flyhouse. Additionally, thrust theatres frequently have a series of catwalks that contain mounting pipes and circuiting that run parallel to the edges of the stage and seating areas. These catwalks are the primary hanging positions for much of the area lighting for a thrust theatre and often contain some form of cloud or baffle mechanisms that help mask or conceal the instruments from the audience. If a thrust theatre has a balcony there are often additional mounting positions across the front of the balconies in the form of **balcony rails.**

Low angles can be a challenge in thrust or arena stages. One obvious limitation relates to the fixed trim height of a grid. In cases where luminaires must be hung from a lower height, designers will mount additional pipes that hang below the grid—a practice that is called **tailing down.** As stated earlier, voms are usually lit through positions that are mounted along their axis from above or from booms placed just offstage of their entrance area, allowing light to be shot along the path of the entrance. Other hanging positions that may exist in a thrust theatre include torm positions that are mounted just upstage of the proscenium and additional wall mounted vertical pipes or booms that might be located around the perimeter of the theatre.

GENERAL LIGHTING TECHNIQUES FOR THRUST DESIGN   I've already discussed the importance of providing two face lights for each of the audience perspectives. This becomes critical in thrust design because it helps model the performers as highlight and shadow are used to create depth and visual interest throughout a design. In addition to the benefits of increased modeling, hanging positions based on variations of a 45° orientation with the seating and oriented more or less with the voms help to reduce glare and bounce of unwanted light into the audience and upstage areas. With spill being a major consideration of thrust design, the designer should choose mounting positions that are steep enough to avoid light spilling into adjoining audience locations. A common solution to this problem is to slowly increase the steepness of the mounting angles as one moves across the stage toward a given audience area (Figure 14.2). Audience members in the first rows should also be protected from looking directly into lights from across the stage. The steeper angles (especially if supplemented with barndoors or top hats) will help avoid this source of glare.

Audience members seated within the first several rows of most thrust or arena theatres will often be lit to some degree simply due to ambient light. When an audience area

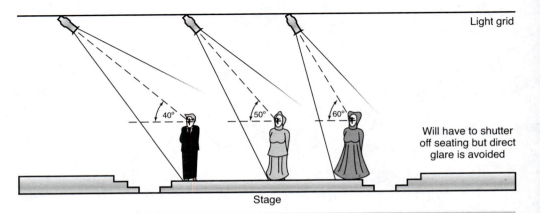

FIGURE 14.2 Using Progressively Elevated Angles to Avoid Spill and Glare While elevating angles helps to avoid spill and glare, it also creates a side effect of highlighting the forehead and browline and can cause eye sockets to go into shadow. The secret is in finding an appropriate balance between these two extremes.

is particularly close to the stage care must be taken to shutter the top of the light so that the performers' heads will remain fully lit when standing at the edge of the stage while at the same time avoiding spill on the adjoining audience areas. I often try to shutter the light so that it is cut off the seats from about waist level for anyone seated in the first row—lower if possible. Barndoors and top hats are also frequently used to control spill and glare in audience areas. While all of the above provide some general principles for developing the lighting for a thrust production, the following paragraphs provide several formula approaches that can be used or modified to fit the needs of a specific project.

One of the most popular techniques for lighting thrust productions makes use of three area lights for each acting area. The lights can be mounted at almost any vertical angle although 45° to 60° forms the most common range of angles. The three luminaires are then arranged around the area or focus point at approximately 120° from one another. The most common orientation places one of the luminaires as a direct backlight for the center or primary seating area. In this way, the flatness associated with hitting a subject from straight on will be avoided since no audience is located in this position. This approach is often called the **three-point system** or **three-point lighting.** In more complex variations, the orientation of the three luminaires might be rotated in relationship to the audience or the angles between the luminaires could vary to include both more acute and obtuse angle variations. The vertical angles may also be varied from one unit to another. Another variation is the more complex **four-point lighting** system, which requires an additional instrument for each lighting area. This system is discussed in arena lighting since it forms the most common system for lighting arena productions. The orientation of the four-point system for thrust stages is generally in such a manner that the lights are oriented with the voms of the theatre with each of the units being placed 90° from one another.

There is a common practice for assigning color in the three-point lighting system based on the principle of color perception (Figure 14.3). This technique establishes some form of warm/cool or key/fill relationship between the three luminaires that light each acting area and makes use of different colors for each of the lighting instruments. Two units will be assigned colors that provide a distinct warm/cool relationship with one another, while the third color is a neutral color that appears cool when compared with the warm colored lamp and warm when compared with the cool colored lamp. By using this principle, the relative sense of color can be used to create a sense of highlight and shadow from every audience perspective. The warm color is commonly associated with the key light for a scene and its color is often chosen to reinforce the primary light source for a scene. In many cases, the neutral color is placed in the luminaire associated with light coming from the upstage direction. A common example of this color scheme might involve using a pastel pink for the warm color, a pale blue for the cool, and some variation of lavender tint for the neutral colored gel.

Ideally each area and luminaire of a wash or area system would be controlled separately from one another. In reality, this is usually not practical, and a lighting designer must consider the most effective way of ganging instruments together in order to consolidate circuits and dimmers. Just as in working with proscenium systems, we refer to **area control versus color control,** and how a designer chooses to combine luminaires is very much dependent upon the specific needs of a production. In some washes, luminaires from adjoining areas will be able to be two-fered together, while in others independent control will have to be maintained. The one condition that a designer should try to avoid if at all possible is ganging luminaires of different colors. Even though this may appear to be an attractive means of providing area control, the loss of the ability to control the key/fill ratio and color proportions isn't usually worth the sacrifice.

Arena Productions

Arena productions become even tricker for the design team because the designers and director have to consider audience perspectives that completely encircle the stage and performers. The issues and considerations are quite similar to those of designing for

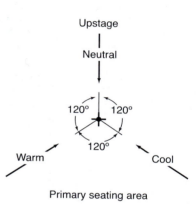

FIGURE 14.3 Three-Point Lighting with Color Associations
Placing the neutral color in the upstage position is fairly common, but color may be assigned to any of the 120° angle orientations.

thrust productions but become more delicate since arena theatres offer an even more intimate environment between the performers and an audience. In addition to the fourth audience perspective, the closeness of seating areas becomes an even more critical issue in regard to spill and glare. Arena staging is often done in a black box theatre consisting of a central performance area with seating in the four surrounding areas and voms at each of the four corners.

HANGING POSITIONS   As in thrust theatres, the grid forms the most common method for mounting luminaires in an arena format. Many arena stages are located in black box theatres with a full grid that covers the entire theatre. While the simplest grids are nothing more than a network of perpendicular pipes that may or may not have an associated catwalk system (to facilitate the hanging and circuiting of the luminaires), there are two additional grid systems that a designer may encounter when lighting in a black box theatre. The first is a **tension** or **suspension grid** and consists of a series of tensioned aircraft cables stretched across the entire theatre in two perpendicular directions on roughly 2-inch intervals. This allows electricians to walk directly on the grid and greatly facilitates the hanging and focusing of the luminaires. The instruments are either mounted to the grid with special hardware or more commonly are hung from horizontal pipes that are temporarily mounted above the grid across vertical uprights. The instruments hang just above the mesh grid and are easily focused and maintained by the crew. Due to the closeness of the lens barrel to the grid, light from these luminaires passes directly through the grid and the mesh pattern is not seen by an audience. However, if a lamp is mounted too far above the grid, the shadows of the individual cables can become visible and will produce a gobo-like effect across the stage. Also, when looking up, not only will an audience see the circle of light associated with the lens of a lighting instrument but also a secondary ring of light that is cast onto the surface of the grid, which is shaped according to the angle at which the light strikes the grid. The electricians must also take special care not to bump previously focused units and shutters when climbing around the grid while working, which can become a challenge when crawling under or trying to step over pipes that contain a number of luminaires and their associated wiring.

The second form of grid is an **egg-crate grid,** which consists of a series of portholes that are created on a regular grid pattern directly above a stage. These grids look like an egg crate and generally cover the entire ceiling of a theatre. The portholes, which are actually fashioned into the ceiling design of the theatre, are typically 2 to 3 feet square and contain a pipe or other hardware that allow several luminaires to be mounted in each opening. A particular issue associated with many of these grids is in the depth of the ceiling and size of the ports, which can result in luminaires not having as much clearance with the sides of an opening as a designer may wish. This can limit the angles in which the luminaires can be mounted.

GENERAL LIGHTING TECHNIQUES FOR ARENA DESIGN   Once again a designer should strive to provide two face lights for each audience area. Proximity and spill become an even more important element to consider throughout these designs, while distortion of any type must almost always be kept to a minimum. While the three-point lighting system can be used when there is a limited inventory of luminaires or control, most designers prefer to use some variation of **four-point lighting** for lighting arena stages. In a textbook example, four luminaires are arranged at 90° intervals from one another with their principle orientation being 45° from the central axis of any seating area (Figure 14.4). In this way, the luminaires are essentially oriented with the voms of the performance venue. The essential angles and overall orientation may once again be modified according to the needs of the project.

Just as with the three-point system, color is designed based on its association with perception and the relative sense of color. There are essentially two models that can serve as guides for color selection in a four-point lighting system. The first places a set of the same colored warm and cool gels across from one another on opposing diagonals that together create a warm/cool contrast and key/fill relationship for each of the audience

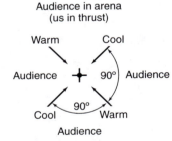

a. Units are ganged (two-fered) with warms together and cools together

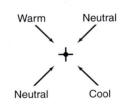

b. Units are typically under individual control. If the neutrals are the same color they are often ganged together.

FIGURE 14.4 Four-Point Lighting with Color and Control Options

perspectives (although warm and cool relationships will be inverted from one side to another). This system works particularly well if there are a limited number of dimmers or circuits because matching colors can be ganged together for each area, providing a constant mechanism for controlling the key/fill ratio. A second method that is generally more effective but requires a larger number of dimmers places a warm color directly across from a cool colored luminaire while the two remaining lights on the opposing diagonal are gelled with a common neutral colored gel. This provides a true warm/cool relationship throughout the entire design and best replicates a situation where a directional or strongly motivated light source might be desired. The color of the key light is based on the primary light source that the designer wants to create for the scene. In terms of control, it would be best if each light as well as each area were placed under individual control, but this is rarely possible. A common compromise involves ganging the neutral colored lights together while providing separate control for the warm and cool luminaires. This again provides good control of the key/fill relationships. A possible color layout that follows this approach might include using a gold for the warm color (linked to a motivation source like the sun), a light blue for the cool or shadow color, and two light lavenders for the neutral tints that are used to tone the performers from the other directions. Like the other approaches that I have outlined, it is generally preferable to gang similar colors from adjoining areas rather than to gang different colors from the same area together. The four-point lighting system is also commonly practiced in thrust lighting designs where there are ample luminaires and control possibilities.

A final variation of general lighting used in many thrust and arena situations involves the addition of a downlight for each of the lighting areas. This may be referred to as a **five-point system.** The downlights can provide a strong sense of isolation for each area but can also cause severe shadowing. They are more commonly used to add strong color toning to the stage. The deep blue downlight washes that are often used to create night scenes are frequently produced in this manner. Gobo breakup washes can also be effective from this angle. Finally, several different downlight colors may be included in the basic illumination of an acting area to create additional flexibility through additive color mixing. Any one or all of these systems can be modified by angle, orientation, color, and control to make an appropriate statement for a design. A designer should not feel that they have to adhere rigidly to any of these approaches, and with experience, most designers go on to create their own variations based on the specific needs of a production.

OUTDOOR DRAMAS AND FESTIVAL PRODUCTIONS

Outdoor festivals have several unique qualities and conditions. First, in most cases there is no cover over the stage. While this is great in terms of providing a natural background or landscape for the productions, it also eliminates any overhead lighting that a designer would have through traditional hanging positions. Backlight and downlight are virtually impossible to create in many outdoor venues. The emphasis then shifts to front lighting, which may be done in one of several different ways. In the most desirable situations, lighting towers or some other form of front hanging positions will be located somewhere behind the audience. At one outdoor theatre where I have designed, the FOH facilities were located in a barn behind the audience and the FOH units were hung on pipes that were set into the windows of the barn that faced the stage. Whether using a structure or towers, these luminaires must usually be equipped with narrow beam angles and high-powered lamps because of the long throws that they have to the stage. Unfortunately, these angles often tend to be a bit flat—an effect that can become even more of an issue since backlighting is often not possible. Sidelight is located where it can be positioned on booms or towers to the sides of the stage but it too is difficult to provide in many outdoor venues. When possible, sidelight should be used to help sculpt or model the performers. In many outdoor theatres towers are erected to either side of the stage near the front of the audience area. These are comparable to the box boom positions found in traditional proscenium theatres. In some outdoor theatres, these two side towers are the only FOH hanging positions. If this is the case, the general lighting is approached in the same manner as a proscenium theatre whose only front lighting positions are the box booms. If you are fortunate enough to have front lighting positions in addition to these towers you can go on to treat these positions more as sidelight positions through using more saturated colors in these towers/booms. The front towers would then be gelled in less saturated tints for the general lighting. The basic technique approaches that of the jewel formula that was discussed in Chapter 11.

In addition to the hanging positions, a designer should also be aware of still other concerns regarding the lighting of an outdoor venue. The most obvious ones relating to weather and waterproofing. Outdoor festivals can age your equipment especially fast if you take no precautions to protect it from the elements. C-clamps and shutter plates rust, connectors become stressed, and corrosion can develop in much of your gear. As many of the electrical components as possible should be placed indoors or in some sort of sheltered location. Control consoles and dimmers form the most obvious example of equipment that should be located indoors. In festivals where there is no permanent shelter, measures should be made to create a temporary shelter for as much of this equipment as possible. A tent cover, tarp, or even the portable stage will help protect the equipment in times of inclement weather. If you don't have cover, be able to seek temporary cover easily—storms can blow up in almost no time. Understand that producers must often take a chance regarding the weather and will often only decide not to let an event go on or continue if the situation actually becomes dangerous. Outdoor events have a tendency to continue when under threat of a storm with the hope of getting the show in before the sky opens up. I can't count the number of shows I've had to continue with in a drizzle or even steady rain during the performance. In the case of an actual storm, you must be prepared to shut down and get any vital gear out of the elements as soon as possible. Lightning should be one of your biggest fears and any close hits should be an immediate signal to start the shutdown process. It is also quite common to pick up a performance from where the show was stopped or to have a rain delay that could push back the performance by an hour or so. Special precautions regarding weather include proper insulation and weatherproofing of all your electrical connections, building shelters to protect the luminaires on the towers or other mounting positions, and adding brads to all the gel frames to prevent the wind from blowing the gel out of the lights. If your luminaires do get wet, proper care must be taken to ensure that lenses and lamps do not shatter as a result of the cold rainwater hitting the hot glass. Once wet, precautions should be taken to ensure that the instruments are dried properly before continuing with the show. Make sure any standing water trapped in the luminaires is removed and slowly burn off the remaining moisture by heating the lamps by powering them up in increments of approximately 10–15% over a half hour—a procedure that many of us call **burning-off** the moisture. This allows the moisture to evaporate with little chance of cracking a lens or shattering a lamp.

Other unique elements of outdoor festivals involve the mist that is often found in the air that accompanies summer evenings. This can produce the same effect as a hazer and is a result of small particles of water vapor reflecting the beams of light that come from the luminaires. The effect is quite dramatic and can add an element of spectacle to a performance. If a designer is aware that such a condition is likely to exist, they can make use of the natural haze to produce lighting effects that add to the production. Another unique quality of outdoor lighting relates to the fact that warm colors appear to be richer and more vibrant in an outdoor venue than they would in an interior setting. Finally, consideration must be made regarding the location of the sun and the time of day at which the performance is presented. Most outdoor programs begin around dusk, and the overall intensities of the lights have to be pumped up to be seen against the effects of the dwindling daylight. As evening progresses, more of the lighting becomes dominated by the theatrical luminaires and the intensities of these lights will not have to be as high to give a sense of a particular intensity level. Also, the length of daylight progressively changes from day to day and must be a consideration for outdoor productions that run for an extended period of time. If designing for one of the history dramas that run for the entire summer, the designer must consider how much daylight is present at a given time in June versus July or August. A lighting effect that was successful at an early point in the summer might become completely washed out by natural daylight 2 weeks later.

TRANSFER PRODUCTIONS

When we discuss transferring a production we are referring to moving it from one theatre to another. Most productions are mounted once and enjoy a **limited run** of performances that continue for a set period of time. A common run in many regional theatres extends somewhere between 6 and 8 weeks, while the runs of other venues such as summer stock productions last on the order of only 7 to 15 days. If the theatre is free, a successful production may be **extended** beyond its initial run. These extensions may range from adding a single performance to months or even years as in the case of a successful Broadway show. Many productions are first mounted in one theatre where costs are minimal and then upon becoming successful transfer to a larger, more prestigious theatre. Years ago, many of the productions that ultimately landed on Broadway were first produced in cities such as Boston, Philadelphia, or Baltimore, where the costs of producing the shows weren't as high as in New York. Today, untried productions are often mounted by Off-Broadway, Off-Off-Broadway, or regional theatres which upon becoming successful will transfer to more prestigious venues like Broadway. The recent Broadway hit (8 Tony Awards) of *Spring Awakening* was first produced at the Off-Broadway Atlantic Theatre Company. Other companies such as The Alliance Theatre in Atlanta, The Goodman Theatre in Chicago, Arena Stage in Washington D.C., Mark Taper Forum in Los Angeles, and Actors Theatre of Louisville have become regular proving grounds for new Broadway successes. Other organizations make a regular practice of transferring productions between several theatres. When I designed for the Broadhollow Theatres on Long Island (New York), nearly every mainstage production was transferred between two of the company's three or four theatres as a means of allowing the company to reach different audiences throughout Long Island. Other companies may pool their resources and mount the same production on each company's stage—using the same scenery, costumes, and even actors for their productions—although the lighting has to be modified for the different theatres and lighting inventories. The Gateway Playhouse on Long Island commonly shared productions with the Candlewood Playhouse in Danbury, Connecticut. Touring productions represent an extreme form of remounting where shows can be re-produced within as little as 6 to 8 hours and productions typically play different theatres every night. On the other hand, a major repertory company such as the Metropolitan Opera might retire an opera for 10 or 15 years before bringing it back for a public performance. In this case, the records from 10 years ago become an essential element in re-creating the lighting for the production. Whether transferring a show or prepping it for a tour, the record keeping is essentially the same. The more that a team can document of a design, the better the second and subsequent load-ins will be.

When a producer makes the decision to transfer a production the design team may or may not have much advance warning. In the best situations, the team will be aware of the transfer well before the first production has been mounted. Whether the lighting designer is aware of an upcoming transfer or not shouldn't have an overwhelming impact on the manner in which a production is designed. However, if they even have a hint of a transfer, the designer should take extra care to maintain good paperwork and to fully document their design. In order to make a transfer as easy as possible every element of the lighting must be documented as thoroughly as possible. This includes a fully revised plot with all the changes noted from the original production, updated paperwork, track sheets and other cue-related documentation, and a set of **focus charts** that provides a record of the focus and shutter cuts for every single luminaire in the design. By making sure that the plot and paperwork are kept up to date a detailed set of plans be created that will form a sound basis for the remount and any subsequent designs that will be based on the original production. On the other hand, sloppy paperwork and undocumented changes will make a production more difficult to remount and some of the mistakes that were corrected in the first production might even be repeated. Something that further complicates the process of transferring a production comes as a result of producers not wanting to take the same amount of time to load-in and tech/dress the remount as they did in the original venue. In reality, the tech/dress time can be shortened significantly for a remounted production, but it's also not realistic to expect a designer to load-in and relight a show in too short a period of time either.

There are several practices that a lighting designer can use to help a transfer occur more smoothly. First, and most important, the designer must document as much of the original design as possible. This means making sure that the plot reflects all of the revisions, the paperwork is clean and up to date, and the cues and cue synopsis are tracked and completely accurate. If the designer is not aware that a transfer is going to take place until sometime during the run of the original production they should revisit the production and complete any documentation and record keeping that isn't up to snuff as well as add any additional information that will be needed for remounting the production. While there is often no time to completely document all shows in every manner possible, if you know that the show will be transferring, additional time should be taken to complete focus charts and track sheets as part of the original design process. These tasks are frequently skipped when a production is not being considered for a transfer because they usually require that an additional assistant be hired. If the designer is aware of the possibility of a transfer, most will go ahead and complete the additional documentation as part to the original design process. Focus charts are completed during the focus sessions and track sheets are produced once the show has finished its dress rehearsals and been completely cued. With today's consoles, track sheets can easily be sent directly to a printer to create a hard copy of the cues. In addition to the track sheets the designer should also retain at least one or two copies of the show files and disks. If you are lucky enough to be using the same type of console for the second production, you can cue the show through simply loading the show disk and associated file into the console and then fine-tune the cues as needed.

In the best situations the designer will be moving the production to a facility that shares a nearly identical footprint as the original theatre, the hanging positions will be similar, and the console and luminaires will be the same. In some cases, the lighting package will be rented and used as an exact copy between the different theatres. While having theatres that are essentially the same is ideal, this is generally not the case, and facilities and hanging positions like the front of house often differ from one venue to another, power supplies may vary, equipment may not be the same, and there might be conditions in the new space that will require significant modifications to the original design.

When revising a plot for new venues the designer doesn't worry so much about creating an exact duplication of the original plot as trying to recreate the same lighting systems and specials that are required by the original design. Therefore, function or purpose becomes a driving force in making these design decisions. It doesn't matter so much that Source Four 19° units are used over Source Four 26° units for front light as it does that you have the same number of acting areas, basic angles, and colors as those in the original design. It also doesn't matter so much that any front washes shift from one beam position to another or even to the box booms if there are no beam positions in a given facility. It is more important to provide the systems and as much of the function of the original design than to slavishly try to produce an exact copy of the original plot. Channel assignments are the one element of the design that the designer should make all efforts not to readdress if at all possible. This is because all of the channel assignments are linked to the cues, and if these remain the same, the designer will be able to get the base cues loaded into the lighting console through simply loading the original show file into the new console. By using the soft-patch feature the new circuits and luminaires are easily assigned to their original channels and the cue list that was loaded with the show file is finished, complete with cue numbers and counts or transition times. The production is now ready for fine-tuning with much of the preliminary effort of cueing already completed. Even if you are using a console that isn't compatible with the first production, it is easier to transfer the cueing information from the track sheets to the new console than to completely relight the show. By using techniques like the ones outlined above, a designer should find that productions can be transferred from one venue to another with relatively few hassles.

In order to document the focus of a production lighting designers produce a set of forms called **focus charts** (Figure 14.5). These forms are often completed by an assistant lighting designer as the focus is being conducted for the original production. Information that is typically recorded in these documents includes each luminaire's focus position (hotspot placement based on distances from centerline and plasterline), beam characteristics (spot/flood settings, harshness/softness of edge/focus, etc.), and the lighting instrument's shutter positions. The form is usually based on a graphical record and includes several different diagrams for recording a fixture's data. As a reference, the stage is broken down into even measurements (often 2-foot increments) that extend from the

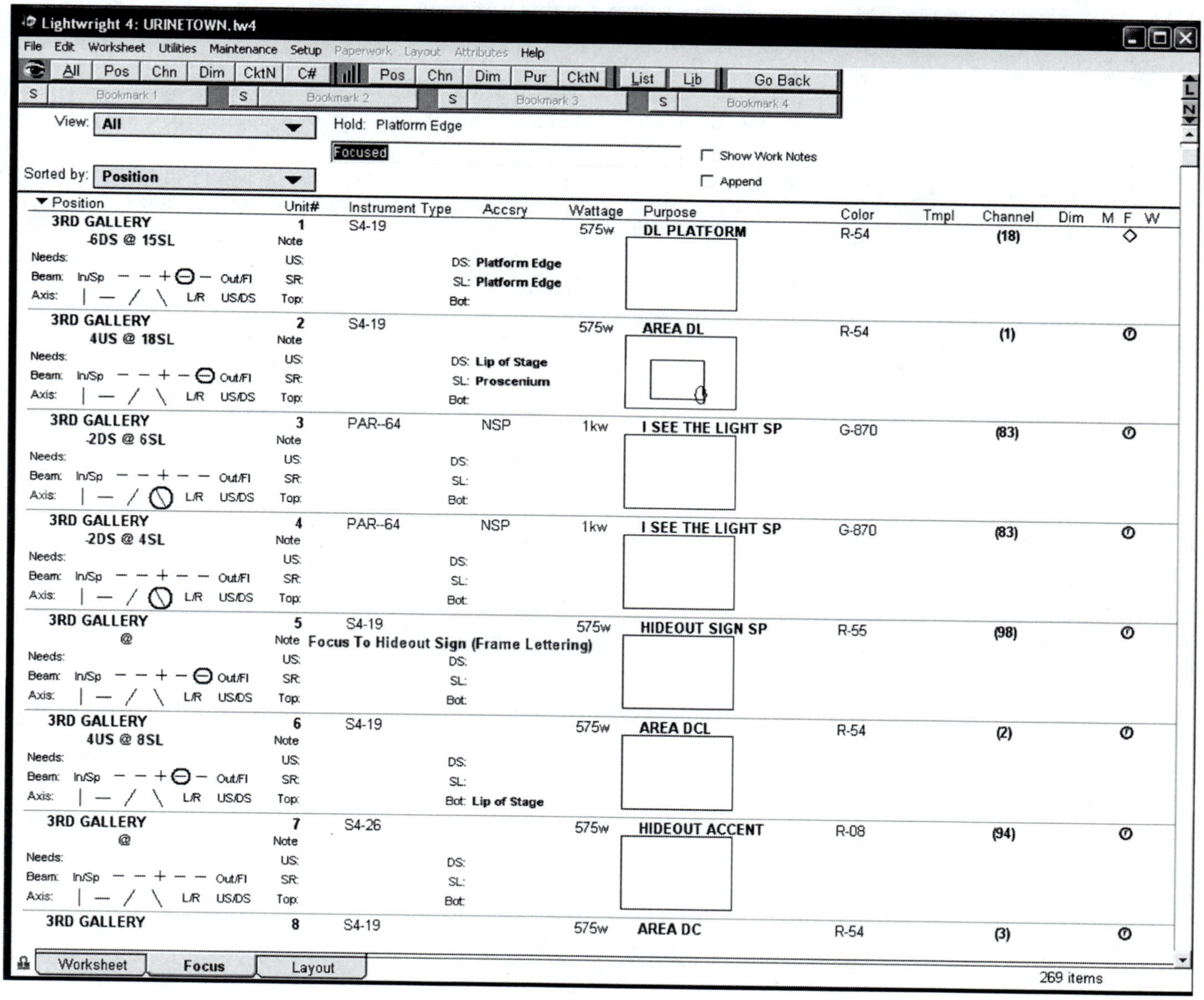

Lightwright 4: URINETOWN.lw4

File   Edit   Worksheet   Utilities   Maintenance   Setup   Paperwork   Layout   Attributes   Help

All | Pos | Chn | Dim | CktN | C# | Pos | Chn | Dim | Pur | CktN | List | Lib | Go Back

Bookmark 1 | Bookmark 2 | Bookmark 3 | Bookmark 4

View: All   Hold: Platform Edge   Focused   ☐ Show Work Notes
Sorted by: Position   ☐ Append

Position	Unit#	Instrument Type	Accsry	Wattage	Purpose	Color	Tmpl	Channel	Dim	M	F	W
3RD GALLERY 6DS @ 15SL	1 Note	S4-19		575w	DL PLATFORM	R-54		(18)				◇
Needs: Beam: In/Sp − − + ⊖ − Out/Fl Axis: │ − / \ L/R US/DS	US: SR: Top:		DS: Platform Edge SL: Platform Edge Bot:									
3RD GALLERY 4US @ 18SL	2 Note	S4-19		575w	AREA DL	R-54		(1)				⊘
Needs: Beam: In/Sp − − + − ⊖ Out/Fl Axis: │ − / \ L/R US/DS	US: SR: Top:		DS: Lip of Stage SL: Proscenium Bot:									
3RD GALLERY 2DS @ 6SL	3 Note	PAR-64	NSP	1kw	I SEE THE LIGHT SP	G-870		(83)				⊘
Needs: Beam: In/Sp − − + − − Out/Fl Axis: │ − / ◯ L/R US/DS	US: SR: Top:		DS: SL: Bot:									
3RD GALLERY 2DS @ 4SL	4 Note	PAR-64	NSP	1kw	I SEE THE LIGHT SP	G-870		(83)				⊘
Needs: Beam: In/Sp − − + − − Out/Fl Axis: │ − / ◯ L/R US/DS	US: SR: Top:		DS: SL: Bot:									
3RD GALLERY @	5 Note	S4-19 Focus To Hideout Sign (Frame Lettering)		575w	HIDEOUT SIGN SP	R-55		(98)				⊘
Needs: Beam: In/Sp − − + − ⊖ Out/Fl Axis: │ − / \ L/R US/DS	US: SR: Top:		DS: SL: Bot:									
3RD GALLERY 4US @ 8SL	6 Note	S4-19		575w	AREA DCL	R-54		(2)				⊘
Needs: Beam: In/Sp − − + ⊖ − Out/Fl Axis: │ − / \ L/R US/DS	US: SR: Top:		DS: SL: Bot: Lip of Stage									
3RD GALLERY @	7 Note	S4-26		575w	HIDEOUT ACCENT	R-08		(94)				⊘
Needs: Beam: In/Sp − − + − − Out/Fl Axis: │ − / \ L/R US/DS	US: SR: Top:		DS: SL: Bot:									
3RD GALLERY	8	S4-19		575w	AREA DC	R-54		(3)				⊘

Worksheet | Focus | Layout   269 items

FIGURE 14.5   Focus Charts and Documentation of Lighting Instruments' Beam Qualities This is a page from a focus chart that has been generated by *Lightwright*.

plasterline upstage and outward from the centerline in each direction. When the designer moves to the location of the stage where they wish the light to be focused, the assistant records the position on the form (e.g., 8' SL, 4' US). Once the position has been documented the assistant goes on to complete the remaining areas of the form as the focus is completed. Degree of focus, spot/flood settings, and even a diagram of the individual shutter cuts are provided for each luminaire. *Lightwright*^{TM} provides very workable focus forms that have the added benefit of being able to complete them within a computer (including shutter cuts). In fact, the latest versions of *Lightwright*^{TM} even allow a designer to import digital photographs as part of the focus chart options that are then used as further references for documenting the design. In today's production environments, much of this record keeping is done on a personal laptop by one of the lighting assistants.

While show data files can often be transferred between different console models made by the same manufacturer, they rarely transfer between consoles of different manufacturers. Unfortunately, the only manner of making this happen usually involves typing the data for each cue into the new console by hand. Although it's unfortunate that the data will have to be re-entered, a hard copy of the original cues or **track sheets** will become quite beneficial for turning this data transfer into an exercise of simply re-entering the data from the previous design. In addition to the channel levels, each cue's personal execution information is also fully documented by the track sheets and includes up and down fade times, delays or waits, auto-follow or cue-linking information, and any effects that are related to the show. Not long ago, when we were under the constant threat of dumping shows, we used to track all of this information by hand. In fact, it was generally one of the lighting designer's assistants who tracked or wrote down every setting for each cue of the production. Today most consoles can be connected to a printer to generate a full set of tracking documents. In recent years, our consoles have become quite stable, and many designers now forgo hard copies of the track sheets, opting instead to keep digital files of the show that are stored on disks in a safe place or on their personal computers. These files can actually be edited through console simulation software that replicates the console on a designer's personal computer. This type of software is an **off-line editor.** While digital files should be kept, nothing is as safe of a backup as having an actual printout of a show's data. Floppy disks are known to go bad over time, and many designers are discovering that shows for which they had even multiple backup copies are lost because they didn't get an actual printout of the track sheets or the disk format is no longer compatible with the newer consoles.

TOURING PRODUCTIONS

Touring productions do not vary that much in their approach and execution from transferring a production between theatres. Touring deals with transferring productions on a regular basis—sometimes weekly, sometimes nightly and the time between stops can vary significantly. What remains constant is the need for moving in and out of the theatres in a timely manner. As when transferring a production, organization and detailed record keeping are key elements for becoming a successful tour designer. In the best touring situations, the production will carry a lighting package that is easily adapted to each theatre but which remains in nearly the exact configuration for every single show.

When a lighting designer sets up a design for a touring production they should attempt to create a lighting package that for the most part remains the same for every stop along the tour. As a rule, the designer designs for the smallest theatre on the tour, while larger stages on the itinerary will **tab-in,** or move the torms toward the centerline and lower the grande teaser to create the same sized proscenium opening. This results in the tour always playing within a standard-sized opening, a practice commonly known as **closing-in** a stage. This opening will also dictate the locations of the legs and borders along with the trims of both the borders and electrics. The plot and production are then designed around this opening. In most tours, the lighting designer sends a copy of the touring plot to the local electricians several weeks before the tour is scheduled to perform in a facility. The local electricians review the plot and work with the designer to satisfy as many conditions of the plot as possible. This may result in the substitution of luminaires based on the local venue's inventory, revised FOH decisions based on the hanging positions that are present in a facility, and modifications based on the power and circuiting options that are available in a particular theatre. In most touring arrangements the tour will provide the lighting equipment used on and above the stage, while the local theatre provides the FOH equipment. Occasionally local crews will completely hang and circuit a show using a facility's inventory and the designer will be able to walk into the venue and go right into the focus. In those cases where the local facility cannot provide the equipment required for a design, the local producer is usually expected to rent the additional gear from a rental shop.

Finally, there are measures that have been developed by electricians that provide a significant time savings for remounting touring productions. Dance and concert tours form the most common examples of productions that follow this format. In each case, steps are taken to package the lighting so that much of the work becomes a matter of assembling modular units rather than individual components of luminaires and cables. In this way, the redundancy of many of the load-in activities along with the time consumed in dealing with all the smaller elements is eliminated. Concert lighting has set the standard in regard to creating structures like **trusses** that eliminate the need for hanging individual luminaires each time that a rig is assembled. These and other elements of concert design are discussed in detail in chapters 16 and 19. More traditional touring productions, like dance companies, that use standard batten layouts can also make use of several time-saving measures to help the crews become more efficient as they move between facilities.

Several of the most common techniques that touring electricians use to shorten load-ins include packaging their luminaires in road boxes that are organized by hanging position so that they can be rolled off the truck to their assigned positions and packaging the dimmers in rolling racks that are simply tied into a theatre's company switch. One significant time-saving measure involves the creation of **batten tapes** for a production. These are nothing more than a piece of scenic webbing that is secured to a batten and marked with a centerline and an additional mark and label for every luminaire that is to be hung on the associated pipe. Some electricians prefer to use different colored spike tape to signify different fixture types, while others prefer to write the unit type directly onto the webbing with a black marker. The batten tape is the first element to be secured to a batten and is referenced so that its centerline corresponds to the centerline of the batten and theatre. By using batten tapes the time-consuming task of measuring each luminaire's distance from centerline is eliminated. In addition to the fixture type, some electricians also provide information such as circuit numbers (for a bundle), unit number, and gel labels on the batten tape as well. As a further means of speeding up a touring load-in, gel is secured to its color frames with brass fasteners and each frame is then marked with not only the color (R-57, G-870, L-120, etc.) but also the electric and unit number that the frame should be inserted into. This allows the color to be easily sorted and stored in stacks organized by hanging position that are transferred to the instruments by electricians who simply walk down a pipe dropping the color. In some cases, like in rock and roll touring, the luminaires are shipped fully mounted, gelled, and already wired in manufactured truss structures.

One of the problems of many light hangs arises when eight electricians gather around a single plot waiting to get some information relating to the individual position that they have been assigned to work on. One way that much of this waste can be eliminated involves the creation of **hanging cards** that break each of the plot's hanging positions out into individual cards. Each card is a partial copy of the plot and contains all the information that an electrician will need to hang that position. In this way, an electrician working on the third electric would be given the hanging card for that position while those working on the first electric or a stage left boom would be given those respective cards. Some electricians may even laminate the cards or place them on cardboard backings so that they can stand up to the abuses of touring.

One last area where electricians have greatly improved the efficiency of a load-in involves creating pre-assembled **bundles** for cabling each of the primary hanging positions. These bundles begin at the dimmer racks where the individual cables or circuits are plugged directly into the dimmers and terminate along a hanging position that the dimmers are powering. The entire bundle is tied directly to the electric after the luminaires have been hung and individual circuits drop out of the bundle at a place directly above the unit that they are powering. This allows the luminaires to be plugged to their associated circuit with no further cabling. Both ends of each circuit are clearly labeled so that it is easy to identify all of the individual circuits. All of the two-fers and individual cables are tied together into the bundle in such a way that the bundle becomes a single entity that greatly reduces the time that would be required for running individual cables to each unit.

Up to this point I have only discussed manners in which prep work can eliminate some of the hassles of touring a design. There are also a number of practices that can help the design to be mounted more efficiently even after the trucks arrive at the loading dock of a new venue. Speed is of the essence in the world of touring—not haphazardly fast, but simply being efficient and methodical. Excess speed can be especially bad in touring situations when crew members get overly zealous running road boxes that weigh several hundred pounds each in and out of your trucks. Speed in touring relates to how quickly and efficiently you can conduct a load-in as well as in the sense of being able to quickly size up a situation and make decisions regarding the lighting and local facility. Can the first electric be hung on line six or eight? Should I leave the fourth electric out in the truck because there isn't enough power? Do I use the house dimmers or the touring dimmers for the FOH? Is this shutter cut close enough or do I have to keep fussing with it? You have to learn to be flexible when you're on the road. Understand what elements of the design are absolutely essential and where compromises can be made that will not have a huge impact on the design. Know where you have to be insistent with a local crew and when you can back off and go with the flow. Pick your battles and know how to both motivate and work with strangers. Finally, you have to be able to remain calm and cool under stress. The show still needs to go up at 8:00 P.M. even though the trucks got lost and you're running 2 hours behind in your load-in. The locals want your production to be just as successful as you do . . . understand that you and they are on the same team and that they are there to help you. Locals are extremely good resources to a touring designer because they know the town and their facility. Local crew members can recommend everything from a local gel distributor to the best burger and bar within walking distance of the theatre—even a local dentist (I've received tips on all of these from local crews). Use them, respect them, and have fun with them!

REPERTORY PRODUCTIONS

Repertory productions form a unique area of lighting where a single plot must satisfy the needs of several different productions. There are a variety of formats in which repertory theatres may operate but most follow some variation of scheduling with overlapping performances of two to five productions. A common approach to many repertory operations is to introduce new productions to the performance schedule on a regular basis (every week or so as an example). At some point the organization will have a set number of productions performing in repertory and shows will eventually start to be rotated out of the schedule as new productions are added. While most repertory organizations confine their productions to a single season, others like the Metropolitan Opera in New York will store productions as part of their repertory for many years. In the case of the Met, a production may be brought back 20 years after the original production was mounted.

In approaching a repertory design a lighting designer will face some added quirks in the design process. First, you have to understand that your design is only one of several designs that must be supported by the rep plot. The more productions contained in the repertory, the less individual flexibility you will have for the design of a given production. This can be further complicated by the fact that different designers will frequently be lighting the productions that are contained in a repertory. On the other hand, there are a number of techniques used in repertory designing that add flexibility to a plot so that a unique quality can still be created for each production. As a rule, repertory plots tend to grow in sophistication and number of luminaires and dimmers because of the additional lighting systems that are added to these plots for providing more options for the individual designs. The repertory plot for the Metropolitan Opera (Figure 14.6) is extremely complex and contains several hundred luminaires and projectors. A designer is free to select, refocus, and repatch virtually any unit in the plot. The Met also provides a stock inventory of hundreds of additional units for supplementing the rep plot with more electrics, booms/ladders, and specials that can also be added to a specific design. While the Met supports so many designs primarily through the sheer size of its rep plot, most repertory situations do not have this option available to them. The following paragraphs provide several techniques that can be used to add more flexibility to designs that must be lit in a repertory situation.

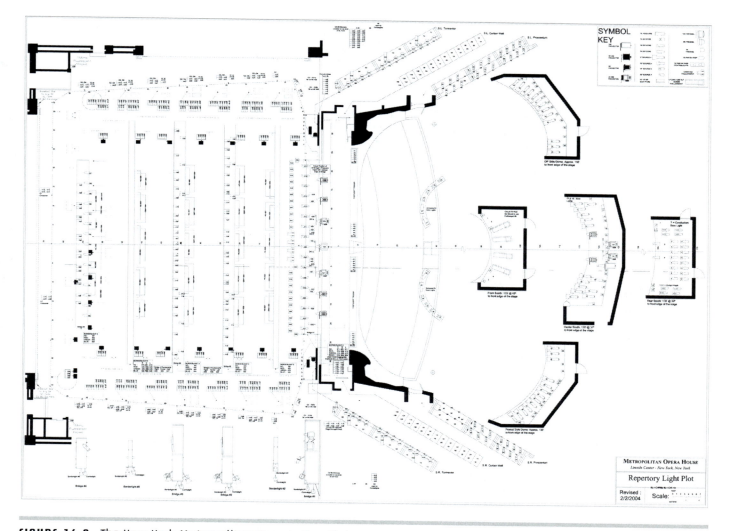

FIGURE 14.6   The New York Metropolitan Opera's Rep Plot   *Credit:* Courtesy of Wayne Chouinard, Resident Lighting Designer

Maintaining flexibility is the key to repertory design. While adding more luminaires and lighting systems may work in some cases, it is more common for designers to create flexibility in rep plots through using other techniques. This is due to expenses, changeover schedules, personnel, or any number of other factors that may make the addition of more luminaires an unfavorable option. If you cannot hang a plot that incorporates all the needs of each of the individual shows, you will have to find a means of combining the requirements of each production into some common denominators. As a first step, lighting systems that can be used for several if not all of the productions should be developed. In many cases, general washes such as those used in downlights and area lighting can be used by all of the productions. These washes may also be double-hung or regelled as a means of adding flexibility to the designs. Multiple lighting systems provide increased variety for the individual designs and the more of these that a designer can include in a rep plot; the more potential that the plot has for creating unique images for each of the productions. Dance lighting is often built on many basic lighting systems and a variation of repertory design. Many designers also use relatively new technologies like color scrollers, moving mirror accessories, and even automated luminaires to bring further flexibility to their rep plots. Once the area lighting and general washes have been developed, any accents and specials required for the individual designs are added and layered on top of the general layouts. Most rep plots are also designed with a given number of specials that are dedicated to each of the individual productions.

Assuming that there are a limited number of luminaires available for a rep plot, additional flexibility can be built into a plot through having a lighting crew make limited modifications in the plot for each of the productions. This is a **changeover** and can result in crews refocusing, regelling, or repatching portions of the plot between performances of each production. The amount of changeover that can occur between two productions is dependent on both the number of crew members and amount of time that is allocated to a changeover. The Met has enough crew members that the plot can be completely changed from one production to another twice a day (two shifts of twenty or more electricians each). On the other hand, many repertory theatres need to be able to complete a changeover in less than an hour or two with only one to three crew members. This then dictates what is reasonable for a crew to accomplish during a changeover. The easiest changes to complete during a changeover involve repatching the luminaires, which is particularly effective for specials where lamps that are unique to each show can be assigned to common dimmers or channels for the different productions. This may be done through swapping the circuiting at the patchbay or switching some of the cabling at some other location within the theatre. If possible, the designer should try to avoid any re-circuiting that would require an electrician to use a ladder. If the specials are fortunate enough to be circuited to their own dimmer, the repatching can be as simple as changing the softpatch when the new show is loaded into the console. If the changeover time is not as big a consideration, the designer may consider additional options like regelling several of the common systems or refocusing different luminaires within the plot. Often a series of specials are designated within a rep plot with the intention that each can be regelled and refocused for each production. If possible, it is best to keep any re-coloring and focusing to easily accessible areas like catwalks or electrics that can be flown in to the deck.

DESIGNING FOR SPECIFIC GENRE

The final area of consideration for an overall design scheme by a lighting designer relates to approaching a project based on the **genre** of the performance event. Genre relates to the specific type of event. The most obvious form of genre is drama and consists of traditional plays. We may be even more specific through referring to several types of drama such as comedy, tragedy, melodrama, etc. What is important to each genre is that specific performance conventions, including expectations of the lighting, are associated with the particular type of event. Farce would never be played or designed in the same manner as a Shakespearean tragedy. Melodrama is significantly different from docu-dramas. Manners of characterization, visual style, degree of realism, and acting style are all shaped with a common range of qualities that can be characterized as belonging to a given genre. Genre is perhaps the most important overall design consideration to examine because it sets some general parameters for a production. Audiences and other artistic team members will have certain expectations about the overall approach and conventions that the

DESIGNER PROFILE

F. Mitchell Dana

F. Mitchell "Mitch" Dana has an extensive background in repertory lighting and has lit almost 600 professional productions in addition to working as a technical director, head prop man on Broadway and on tour, stage manager on Broadway and Off-Broadway, and production manager. He is head of lighting design at Mason Gross School of the Arts at Rutgers University. Dana received his M.F.A. from the Yale School of Drama, and his many Broadway credits include: *The Suicide, Freedom of the City, Mass Appeal, Monday After the Miracle, Once in a Lifetime, Man and Superman, The Inspector General,* and *Oh Coward.* His opera credits include *La Rondine* for the New York City Opera, *Turandot* for the Royal Opera at Covent Garden, *The Magic Flute* and *The Merry Widow* for the Cleveland Symphony, *Carmen* to open Expo'92, seven operas for The Los Angeles Opera Company, and ten seasons with the Opera Festival of New Jersey. He is vice president of United Scenic Artists, USA 829.

Mitch lit his first production, *Riders to the Sea,* for the Catholic Youth Organization in the gymnasium of a Catholic Church with RBG strips, six fresnels hung from a basketball hoop support, six dimmers, and three on/off switches. He went on to light everything that came his way until he was about 22. His formal training began at Utah State University, where he initially was a Forestry major. Grades in organic chemistry and spending too much time doing shows for the theatre department convinced him to change majors. His mentor, Ferd Manning, advised him to stay at USU to study theatre since it was a small department with good people and he would be the only one doing lighting. In hindsight, he sees this as excellent advice. For 3 years he acted, built, stage managed, performed, and lit an average of three shows a week, ranging from Peter, Paul, and Mary with two followspots to piano thesis performances, and even the Mormon Tabernacle Choir. Then it was on to the Yale Drama School to study with Harvey K. Smith, Eddie Kook, Donald Oenslager, Ed Cole, and Charles Elson.

When asked about how he broke into repertory design Mitch relates the following story. The American Conservatory Theatre (ACT) in San Francisco had their set and lighting designer hired on a Broadway show who left ACT precipitously. ACT called several lighting designers to fill the job and all were unavailable, which led to one of Dana's former students (who had become a producer) suggesting him for the job. At the time, he was on tour filling a number of roles (including lighting designer) for a production of *A Doll's House.* The tour was in Philadelphia when he got the call, on a Friday, with ACT going into tech rehearsals for *Anthony and Cleopatra* and *Caesar and Cleopatra* on Monday. He was already scheduled to load the tour into the Kennedy Center on Sunday with an opening at the Eisenhower Theatre with President Nixon in attendance on Tuesday. After checking with his producer he told ACT that he could be there by Wednesday. ACT had no other choice, and he was brought in and lit both shows in 10 days. He established a good relationship with ACT and the result was 54 productions with ACT in San Francisco, Hawaii, and the Soviet Union—and a reputation for rep which led to lighting seven seasons at the Pittsburgh Civic Light Opera, thirty-six productions in rep for the Opera Festival of New Jersey, two rep seasons for the Los Angeles Opera, seven seasons at the Muny in St. Louis, and six shows at the Mark Taper Forum.

Dana relates that lighting design for repertory theatre differs from other forms of lighting, in that the design becomes part of a larger system of crew, maintenance, finances, scheduling, and a multi-year plan. It is not all about the lighting design for one show. A single show can focus on the design alone; it has no larger systemic concerns. In repertory light planning, one considers several shows over a longer period of time, potentially over several years. "At ACT, the one area that I had to consider more than others was the life of my crew—it meant time for their family and a better chance that a wife would put up with the crazy hours that repertory required." With an hour and a half changeover for all design elements, they could not do frilly things, so he learned how to pare down to the essentials of a production. Complicated things that might be less reliably recreated each time that a show was mounted were also dropped—if they failed, the audience might be cheated. "We learned to throw out good ideas that were only 90% reliable because only the artistic team missed them and the audience never knew what they were missing . . . we focused on 'less is more.'" He also relates to the KISS acronym ("keep it simple stupid") for repertory design as well as the 7P rule ("Proper Prior Planning Prevents Piss Poor Performance"). But the fundamental principle is KISS. Another consideration of repertory design relates to the issue of the equipment being in the air most of the time—how can it be maintained? Producers do not allow time to do maintenance so

(Continued)

the owned equipment deteriorates, and the tax laws do not allow a not-for-profit to rent the entire rig each year. So roughly every 10 years the lights are replaced by a grant from some contributor, with the resulting problem that for at least 5 of those years most of the equipment is not efficient, or even desirable.

Mitch likes the brain exercise required in thinking about the many scenarios that he may run into when designing a series of repertory shows and how to accommodate them all. "It is a great four-dimensional chess game: all physical dimensions and time. How can I make more possible? Is it the equipment, location, or control? How do I accommodate the more modern musical styles of shows like *Aida* and *Miss Saigon* as well as the older styles that are required for shows like *My Fair Lady* and *South Pacific?*" He likes the speed required for lighting a production. "Let's get on with it and not spend forever discussing things. I am action oriented and this career appeals to me. My wife says I'm an adrenaline junkie and she's not entirely wrong." Ironically, what he likes least is the lack of time. There is little time to explore a production. "You have to hone in on the core issue, and go directly at it, which is both good and bad." He also feels that sometimes designing has become more of a job and less fun. "There's no time for taking the

loving care that we would like to have at the MUNY and I dislike the fact that it is so fast that it dilutes my contact with other theatre professionals, such as actors. I like and respect many actors and miss the sense of community that I had while in residence at ACT. That is why I will work for directors and producers that I like, even for less money than I am worth. It is less of a job and more fun. Most of us theatre folks are 'people folks' at heart, and communication is our meat and drink."

"The goals of good theatre have not, and probably will not change—only the techniques. Without clear goals there can be no well-directed, efficient, and effective result. Today's technology puts a premium on training, and an intelligent crew is necessary for the execution and reliable recreation of a design. In reality, the technology allows a lot of things to happen that often should not. Choice is still the major tool of the designer. We research, select elements, and then arrange those elements to tell a story that shines a light on a specific human condition so that an audience might be able to understand it. Even with all the technology available, the artist is still the one who must make the choices that clearly communicate an essential truth."

Photo credit: Tanya Dana

lighting, or any other design area, should follow when an event is associated with a given genre. Opera is performed in a very different manner from dance, and the lighting designer will usually light each event quite differently. Once a designer understands the genre that a project belongs to they can work within the conventions of that genre to produce a unique design for a given project.

Since genre and the type of performance event plays such an important role in the overall approach to lighting a project, the entire fourth and fifth parts of this book have been written to address lighting design in a number of specialty areas. This last section of the book is devoted solely to lighting applications. The first several chapters (15–17) provide a general introduction to these lighting specialties (as well as a chapter on projection—Chapter 18), while additional online chapters (19–27) provide a detailed examination of a variety of specific lighting applications. Many of these remaining chapters address specialty areas of lighting that have only recently come into widespread acceptance as lighting specialties. These represent fertile new ground and markets for lighting designers who can apply their design skills to these emerging disciplines. At the same time, they can also provide financial rewards and a relatively secure profession for those lighting professionals who venture into these other markets.

FOR FURTHER READING

Bellman, Willard F., *Lighting the Stage: Art and Practice*, 3rd ed. (Louisville, KY: Broadway Press, 2001).
McCandless, Stanley, *A Method for Lighting the Stage*, 4th ed. (New York: Theatre Arts Books, 1958).
Palmer, Richard H., *The Lighting Art: The Aesthetics of Stage Lighting Design*, 2nd ed. (Englewood Cliffs, NJ: Prentice-Hall, Inc., 1994).
Shelley, Steven Louis, *A Practical Guide to Stage Lighting* (Boston: Focal Press, 1999).
Watson, Lee, *Lighting Design Handbook* (New York: McGraw-Hill, Inc., 1990).

15 Traditional Areas of Theatrical Design (Drama, Dance, Opera, and Musical Theatre)

Lighting design, like any other design discipline, needs to be appropriate for a given situation. In theatre, we often make reference to **conventions** or a set of rules or practices by which we create theatrical presentations. One of the most popular examples of a theatrical lighting convention that most people are familiar with is the use of blue light to indicate night or darkness. This effect is rarely seen in real situations outside of the theatre but forms a method in which an audience can see in the dark. Audiences are usually very accepting of most conventions that a production team might establish—they only need us to remain consistent with them once we establish a particular set of ground rules for a production. While there are occasions when a convention might be changed for dramatic effect, it is usually better to establish the conventions early in a performance and to remain consistent with them so that the audience can buy into them and become engaged in the show. The longer that we take to establish these rules, the longer an audience will be left to try to figure them out. In the meantime, they might miss other information that is essential to their understanding of the play. Likewise, if we choose not to follow our conventions, audiences may struggle with how to process the information and can become confused. Once confused, they may get frustrated or lost and break their engagement with the production. Often, good productions can be separated from mediocre or poor ones simply based on whether or not the conventions have been adhered to.

One of the most important issues that any designer needs to consider relates to the fact that every type of performance event has a given set of qualities and conventions that are characteristic of that mode of performance. Some of the more common qualities that can be associated with a particular event relate to the type of action, visibility of the performer, presentation style, subtlety of cueing, transitional mechanisms, and overall performance mode that an audience expects from a given form of entertainment. These qualities are often related to the conventions that are expected or associated with a particular type of event. This chapter presents information related to lighting more traditional forms of entertainment. These have been around pretty much since the inception of theatrical lighting and include drama, dance, opera, and musical theatre. Each of these specialty areas is discussed in the following pages with regard to conventions that make each area unique, special issues or considerations related to lighting each type of event, and several techniques for lighting these events. While each of the upcoming segments presents a number of guidelines for lighting a given discipline, there is no such thing as a universal approach that will work 100% of the time. There will always be exceptions to any common practice, and what worked in one situation may not be at all appropriate for the next one. Lighting is relative, as is the overall style of a production, and every event needs to be lit based on the specific needs of a given script and concept. On the other hand, the overall approach to lighting any of these events will not vary that much from one specialty to another, and the general design approach that was presented in Part Three can be used and modified for each of the disciplines that are featured in the remaining parts of this book. While I know many lighting designers who work predominantly in a single discipline, most designers work within several, if not all, of the areas on a fairly regular basis. Each year I typically light several dramas, one or two dance productions, and a few more musicals or occasional operas/light operas. It is rare for a lighting designer to work exclusively in a single discipline unless they are on the permanent staff of a company and unable to complete projects outside of that organization. However, most of us do have one area that we tend to acquire a reputation in—for myself, this is in musical theatre, where I do the majority of my freelance designs.

LIGHTING FOR DRAMA

Drama accounts for the majority of traditional entertainment and is most commonly associated with plays. Even within drama there are a variety of genres of playwriting and dramatic production. Each can be associated with specific production styles and conventions that are considered acceptable for that genre. The most common genres that most people are familiar with are **comedy** and **tragedy. Docu-drama, farce,** and **melodrama** form several other popular genres of plays, each with defining characteristics that are considered unique to each type of drama. It needs to be emphasized that there is no single approach to lighting that will always be correct for every script or genre of production. In reality, there will be a variety of design solutions that will be completely acceptable for a production—some will be better than others, some may even be great—while others may be unacceptable and can actually fail. Most of the design approach presented in Part Three of this book was written from the perspective of designing for dramatic productions, and that information is not duplicated here. However, there are a number of manners in which this process can be refined so that it is more applicable to the production of plays, which focus on the performance of a script. The following sections address some of the more unique considerations related to the production of plays and introduce several design solutions that are considered to be relatively good guidelines for lighting plays and other dramas.

Performance Considerations

There are several performance qualities that are unique to the drama experience. Most noteworthy is the fact that the predominant mode of presentation is through dialogue. The performers themselves are a major element of the presentation, and what they say is critical to an audience's understanding of a play. The audience must be able to hear the actors to follow the storyline, make observations about character relationships, and understand the themes, meanings, and motivations of a play. An audience tends to have a more difficult time hearing if they can't see a performer's face. This condition goes back to a basic psychological phenomena where involving a second sense (e.g., sight and sound) results in more information being observed and understood by an individual. When this principle is applied to theatre, sight and sound are found to be directly connected to the understanding of an audience. A major requirement for lighting most plays therefore relates to establishing enough visibility that performers' faces can be easily observed by the audience. In addition to providing a reinforcing environment for the verbal elements of the play, increased visibility also allows nonverbal communication like facial gesturing to become a more significant element of the communication between a performer and an audience. The less physical action demanded by a play and the more that it is based in dialogue, the greater the need for good visibility. On the other hand, just maintaining visibility can lead to a design that doesn't add anything to the theatrical experience. A design that only provides general visibility is often perceived as boring or uninspired and will often fail to make any real contribution to the overall production. On the other hand, lighting shouldn't bring unnecessary attention to itself either. Lighting cannot upstage the action of a play—if elements of the design take an audience out of the world of the play, that, too, is a disservice to the production. One school of designers even claims that the best lighting should go unnoticed by an audience. My personal feeling is that such lighting often fails to add anything to a production and that a designer should strive to use their lighting to enhance a production rather than to simply illuminate it. The secret to good lighting is in creating an appropriate environment for the production, which can at times become as important, if not more important, than simple visibility. The argument of **selective visibility** should be a major consideration of any lighting design because it relates to the specific needs of a production.

Production style forms a major consideration in determining the overall success of a lighting design for a production. The most significant element of style relates to the degree of realism in which a play is being presented in. Chapter 10 presented a fair amount of material regarding production style, and you should recall that an overall principle guiding the definition of style relates to placing levels of realism along a scale. While **naturalism** is an extreme form of realism, the most extensive forms of **abstraction** or **stylization** are found at the opposite end of the scale. In drama, the range of production styles can be extreme, and while some plays are better performed in a very realistic fashion, others are meant to be dramatic and heavily stylized. Much of the determination of an appropriate performance style for a given script is based on the specific genre that the play is associated with. Comedy is produced differently than tragedy, and issues such as when a play was first written, the writing style of the playwright, and traditional approaches of producing a play automatically start to define the degree of realism with which a production will most likely be produced. The production team's definition of realism also goes on to define many of the conventions and expectations that an audience will need to accept for a given production. These expectations, and whether a design team chooses to accept, ignore, or experiment with them, often determine the success or failure of a production right from the start of the design process. While taking chances on ideas that lie outside the normal conventions can lead to innovative productions, this more commonly results in audiences having problems understanding the reasoning behind the choices and intentions of a production team. As a result of that misunderstanding, the audience fails to connect with the play. Trying to present a naturalistic production of a Shakespearean play is probably not a good choice simply because of the unnatural speech patterns and stylization demanded by the Shakespearean dialogue. In addition to writing style, there are a number of other elements that help define a production—acting style, directing style, visual style, and period style all bring specific qualities and conventions to the overall style of a production. While general qualities and conventions can be associated with the major genres of theatrical production like comedy or tragedy, even further expectations and conventions are typically associated with more specific artistic movements like farce, melodrama, expressionism, etc. In all cases, the lighting needs to take on specific qualities and conventions that reinforce the other production elements of a production.

Design Techniques

Visibility is a major consideration in lighting a typical play. Therefore, through selective visibility, a lighting designer plays an essential role in allowing an audience to see what is needed for their understanding of a play. If a lighting designer fails to do this properly, issues such as fatigue, eye-strain, restlessness, and a lack of communication can become factors in whether an audience becomes engaged in a play. The best chance for providing a successful lighting design for plays relates to developing good overall area lighting systems that can deliver an acceptable amount of visibility to each member of an audience no matter where they are located in the theatre. Such systems must work for audience members located in the last balcony as well as for those located in the center section of the orchestra seating area. Likewise, in facilities like arena or thrust theatres, visibility must be accomplished for each of the different audience perspectives. Chapters 10 and 11 presented a number of techniques for producing lighting systems that could provide general illumination for a proscenium stage, and Chapter 14 expanded on this to include solutions for thrust and arena stages. While some of these techniques, like the **McCandless System,** were quite specific in approach; others are more flexible solutions for lighting an entire stage. These techniques for accomplishing general visibility are often modified by designers based on their creativity and specific needs of a production.

It is critical for a lighting designer to learn what lighting conventions are associated with a given performance style and genre of drama. The presentational style required for an expressionistic play with saturated colors, shadows, and harsh angles will be completely out of place for a more naturalistic play such as *The Miracle Worker,* which chronicles the life of Helen Keller. It can become challenging when a precise production style isn't defined by a director or production team and the lighting designer must venture into creating their own conventions based only on the needs of a particular script. However, in many ways, this is what good lighting design is all about . . . creating an appropriate response to a given script and concept. Once, the general visibility systems have been laid in place, the designer can go on to refine a design based on the specific needs of a production. A relatively safe approach to lighting plays is in developing the area systems first, lighting specialty areas and scenery second, then layering on top of these the accents and specials that are based on motivational elements like practical light sources or light entering from windows or doorways. Finally add accents based on mood, specific actor specials, and any other needs of a play.

When comparing the lighting of plays or dramas to other forms of entertainment lighting the design choices are on the whole more subtle. The good visibility required by the majority of these productions generally calls for moderate to bright intensity levels, less saturated colors, and an overall use of more conservative lighting angles. If you must talk absolutes, lighting levels for a well-illuminated scene are frequently somewhere in the 100–150 footcandle range. In reality, we often use levels much lower than this where visibility is relative and more of a function of contrast between intensity levels for different areas of a stage. For the majority of the performing arts, perception of intensity is much more important than absolute intensity levels. Cueing for plays also tends to be less dramatic and often involves transitions that may be barely perceptible to an audience. Subtle shifts of focus and mood are popular in lighting this type of entertainment. These productions also tend to be lit from a more naturalistic perspective than other forms of entertainment lighting and are often grounded in the use of **motivational lighting** and **motivated** light sources. As a play becomes more stylized, the lighting elements become more stylized and will take on qualities that are less subtle, more dramatic, and have fewer connections to motivational elements. In the end, it is the appropriateness of the design decisions and how they mesh with the other elements of a production and concept that will in many ways determine the overall success of a lighting design.

DANCE LIGHTING

Dance is unique in that the entire body of the performer is used to communicate a message to an audience. The story is moved along by movement and music. Some dances are short and can be performed in a space of 3 to 10 minutes, while others may contain a number of movements and can take several hours to perform. In ballet, the dances are used to tell a complete story. Famous ballets like *Peter and the Wolf* and *The Nutcracker* are popular throughout much of the world, and most people over the age of 10 can probably recall the basic plot and outcome of the stories that these dances tell. Almost all dances and their related **choreography** tell some sort of story while creating a performance event for an audience. In dance forms like modern dance, the story may not be as well-defined as in ballet and may become more representational of a particular feeling or expression, but these, too, are often constructed in some storyline fashion.

Performance Considerations

Because the emphasis of dance is placed on the body and not on the voice as in drama, communication of themes, character relationships, and plot are of a very different nature than in performing a play. The choreography becomes the manner by which the story is presented to the audience through gestures, positioning of a body, body movements, and even the relationships that are created between different performers. This broader, more dramatic quality of performance requires that the lighting be modified to allow for good revelation of a body's form and that a more modeled/sculptural quality ultimately be present in dance lighting. Side and backlight are important to performing this function. This also leads to a less subtle performance event that by its very nature becomes a more stylized form of entertainment. A lighting designer is often free to use a variety of angles and colors as a way of creating flexibility in a dance design. Also, mood, emotional responses, and dramatic images are often major elements of dance lighting, while at the same time, lighting is often the only visual element other than the performers and their costumes for many dance events. Lights are usually cued to change both frequently and more dramatically as a means of enhancing a performance, and a variety of spectacle elements are often associated with this type of lighting. Use of lighting to change mood, create isolation, provide texture, and direct focus are just a few of the more important functions that lighting typically performs in dance designs.

Dance, like drama, also contains different forms or genres. Each can often be associated with a particular style of performance. The work of Mikhail Baryshnikov's classical ballet is very different from the work of Jerome Robbins (ballet and musical theatre) or Michael Bennett and Bob Fossie's styles of musical theatre. This holds true of not only the performers and choreography itself but also of the visual style in which a dance is presented. Lighting, as well as the other design areas, will be shaped by the demands of a dance genre. Conventions that may be appropriate in one form of dance may be inappropriate for another type of dance. Several unique genres of dance include: ballet, modern dance, ballroom dance, spectacle/entertainment dance (tap or jazz), and ethnic dance (based on customs or regional qualities). The flashy lighting of a Vegas revue or *Follies* production will be quite different than that of a ballet. Ethnic-based dances and companies like the *Ballet Folklorico* companies will be different from ethnic-based dances of other nationalities or cultures. Even within a given ethnic grouping, style can vary considerably—an example being the simplistic overall presentation of clogging versus the highly spectacle presentation of clogging that has become famous through the work of Michael Flatley and his *Lord of the Dance* and *Riverdance* programs.

Another unique consideration of dance performance relates to the manner in which a group of individual dance pieces are presented to the public. While there are productions such as ballets in which the entire event is based on a single story, the majority of dances are presented as a collection of different pieces that are performed together in a single program. A typical dance concert or recital often contains a half-dozen or more individual dance pieces in both halves of a 2-hour program. There have been occasions where I have personally lit up to 30 different pieces for a single concert. A variety of dance styles are usually represented by these dances because it is typical for the majority of the pieces to be choreographed by different choreographers. Due to this, the lighting must have a large degree of flexibility so that a designer can develop a unique creation for each dance. The best manner of achieving this flexibility while keeping the changes between the dances manageable is through the use of **repertory light plots.** The key to successful dance designing is in finding ways to use the same tools of the plot over and over again while adding some flexibility for initiating changes that will create unique images for each dance. This is particularly true in rep plots that are used in festivals that will present the work of numerous companies and performers over an extended period. Recoloring and refocusing form the two most common methods of adding flexibility to these plots. A more extensive discussion of repertory lighting was presented in Chapter 14.

One final consideration of dance lighting lies in the extensive touring that dance productions are associated with. While some dance companies may have their own resident theatre, most rent theatres for a limited time based on a week or two of performances several times a year. Even if a company is associated with a home theatre, most dance companies tour on a regular basis. This means that a lighting designer must design a plot that not only addresses the many needs of the dances contained in a company's repertory, but that it must also be capable of touring and being set up and struck in a very limited amount of time. Dance companies are notorious for conducting tours that operate primarily on a one-night-stand basis, and a lighting designer associated with such a company must be especially adept at making changes and going with the flow. Working fast, making quick evaluations of a space, being flexible, and committing to decisions that will allow a performance to go up in a safe, efficient manner, on time, are important traits of a lighting designer working in dance. They must also be able to do this without compromising the artistic quality of the event in any significant manner. A common schedule for many dance tours involves loading a show into a theatre between 8 and 9 in the morning (hang and focus), writing and tweaking the cues so that the stage is ready for a spacing rehearsal in the late afternoon, presenting a performance at around 8 P.M., and then striking the show and being on the road again by midnight. This is repeated several days a week and often contains back-to-back performances in different cities with several hundred miles between each venue. It is also very common for a lighting designer to function as the stage manager or even technical director for these companies, most often **calling** their own cues or shows.

Design Techniques

Probably the most important element of dance lighting lies in revealing the form of the dancers. This leads to a strong emphasis on side and back lighting in light plots that have been developed primarily for dance production. Front light should still be worked into the plot because facial expression can remain an important element of some dances. However, in most cases, front washes tend to be used predominantly for softening some of the severe shadows created by the side lighting elements of the plot. Due to the emphasis on side and back lighting, many designers attempt to provide as much variety in these angles as possible. This happens by providing a number of both angle and color choices from these basic directions. In a typical dance plot, two, if not more, full-stage color washes (preferably a warm and cool) are provided from each of the primary lighting angles. This typically includes: straight front, both front diagonals, both sides, downlight, and backlight. Since revelation of form is so critical, designers then go on to develop a variety of side lighting angles for the stage. These typically include washes from a high angle from the offstage ends of the electrics **(high-pipe-ends),** medium **sidelight** (from **booms** or **ladders** 8 to 16 feet off the deck), **mids** (about head height), and **shins** (within a foot or two of the deck). In touring situations the booms may be replaced by **dance towers** (a variation of vertical trussing), which provide a relative permanent manner of mounting the sidelight that is easily transported from one venue to another. Figure 15.1 illustrates a simple repertory dance light plot. If possible, two color systems are used in each of the higher mounting positions while flexibility is created in the mids and shins through regelling them between each piece in the program. A short break of several minutes is often given between each dance so that the dancers can change into new costumes as the electricians regel the shins and mids for the next piece. To make the process even simpler, lighting designers are now placing **scrollers** in the shin and mid positions. Regardless of how or where the sidelights are mounted, it is important that the light spreads evenly across the stage and that there are no holes or shadow zones between each of the leg sets. It is just as important that no hot spots are cast on the performers as they enter the stage. These conditions can usually be avoided by making sure that the booms are positioned far enough offstage that the light can open up and fully illuminate the dances as they enter the stage. Making sure that the beamspreads of the luminaires are large enough to spread out and cover the area between the legs is a second consideration which will help a designer avoid holes and hot spots in the sidelight. A final issue relates to the need to consider a higher overall focus for lighting dance. This is due to the *lifts* that will take place throughout a performance. Sometimes lifts will be confined to specific locations and can be covered with specials, but if done throughout the whole space, it is better to cheat the focus of most of your instruments a bit higher than normal so that the dancers aren't lifted out of their light.

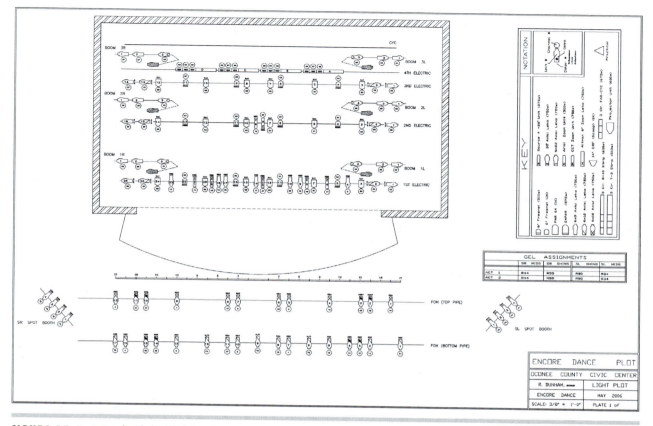

FIGURE 15.1 A Basic Light Plot for Dance

Lighting designers and technicians should also be aware of several unique precautions that are often taken to help guide and protect the safety of the performers in dance and musical theatre. The first is in taking care to mark and glow-tape each of the booms to protect dancers from running into these units as they exit the stage. Generally, a couple pieces of glow-tape placed on each edge of the gel frame clips/holder in the mids and shins will prevent performers and crew members from striking these instruments. If using boom bases rather than flanges, it is also wise to tape out or mark these as well. Second, in ballet and several other areas of dance it is important for a dancer to be able to *spot* or determine very quickly which direction they are facing. This can be especially hard when performing the fast pivoting movements associated with many dance forms and being surrounded by a number of sidelights. In order to help guide and orient the dancers, a small low-wattage lamp (usually red) is placed at the rear of the auditorium on the centerline of the theatre. This lamp, called a **spotting light,** is left on throughout the entire performance and is used to help the dancers spot front and center.

Since dance is based on movement, cueing is also based on movement, and it is up to a lighting designer to completely understand the choreography of any dance that they are lighting. Since there is no script, a designer must find a manner of becoming familiar with and tracking the movements and stage positions of the dancers. Most of us have developed variations of dance notation that allow us to draw schematic diagrams of the actual movements of the performers. While some designers use classical dance notation and symbols that are fairly universal to choreographers, many of us with limited dance training have devised our own methods of documenting these movements. Several examples of notation were introduced in previous chapters. In the end, all that is really required is that you understand the system for yourself so that you can have a meaningful discussion with the choreographer and can place the cues properly. When the lighting designer must later perform the role of stage manager, this notation becomes an especially important tool for calling a show. In calling a dance, a designer must be extremely sensitive to the timing so that the transitions are perfectly synchronized with the performers.

Just as important as revealing form and providing a variety of color and angle choices is the issue of being able to isolate portions of a stage and to draw focus to different dancers at various points throughout a performance. To accomplish this, many of the wash systems discussed earlier are broken down into channel assignments that will allow a designer to isolate different areas of the stage. While in an ideal situation every luminaire in a system would be controlled by a separate dimmer, this is rarely possible due to the massive number of dimmers that would be required to light even a moderately sized stage. Instead, designers usually combine several luminaires of a wash system to economize on the number of dimmers that are required for a production. More importantly, these groupings allow a designer to isolate the stage into regions or areas that are based on the movements of the dancers. While some systems such as a front wash system may often retain individual control of each luminaire (in effect creating a special for every stage area), most lighting units are combined in a variety of ways that follow the movements of the dancers.

Several of the more important grouping patterns that are worked into virtually all dance plots include **planes, corridors,** and **diagonals.** Planes form pathways across the width of the stage and are located between each set of legs throughout the depth of the stage. This allows a designer to limit the lighting to a single row of dancers at a given stage depth or to light dancers differently when they are placed in different planes. Many designers also refer to planes as **zones** and reference each zone by its relative location in stage depth (**in-one** being the plane closest to the audience and farthest downstage, **in-two** being the next one upstage, then progressively . . . **in-three, in-four,** etc.). Corridors follow movement patterns that form a narrow pathway that extends from an extreme upstage position to an extreme downstage position. These allow a designer to isolate movement patterns across the width of the stage (i.e., dancers can be treated differently in stage left, center, and stage right positions). The last of the major groupings, the diagonals, form diagonal pathways that extend from the extreme downstage corners to the opposite upstage corners of the stage. These groupings, along with a series of generic specials, often form the heart of a good light plot for dance. Figure 15.2 provides illustrations of these movement patterns. Several common generic specials that are often included in a dance plot include both a wide and narrow downlight at centerstage, downlight specials at the quarter or third lines and centerline along the downstage portion of the stage, and tight front specials in these same positions. Not all designs make use of all these specials or groupings and in many cases additional systems can also be introduced to the plot based on the needs of the designer. For instance, I often like to include several full-stage gobo breakup washes within my dance plots. These, too, add variety to a designer's toolbox for lighting dance pieces from a repertory plot.

Because dance usually requires that the stage be kept as open as possible, scenery is often not incorporated into many of these productions. One common exception to this is ballet, where the scenery is usually quite limited. Even in these instances much of the scenery is two dimensional and comes as painted elements that are hung in the form of drops and wing and border sets. Any three-dimensional scenic elements required for these performances are almost solely confined to small units and props such as furniture pieces that are placed around the perimeter of a dance area. The majority of dance productions actually make use of no scenery at all and are designed against a neutral background. This background is typically either a set of black maskings and **traveler** drape or a **cyclorama/skydrop.** The cyc provides a canvas for creating a variety of lighting effects through projections and color washes which function as key ingredients for creating unique images throughout a dance program. As a means of creating even more variety, many designers like to place a black **scrim** directly downstage of a cyc and any lighting ground row so that the stage can be easily changed from a colorfully lit cyc into a formal space with a black background. The scrim also helps prevent unwanted reflections from bouncing off the floor onto the cyc. Even recent Broadway hits like the revival of *Chicago* (Figure 15.3) are making use of these more simplistic staging conventions and use of a cyc.

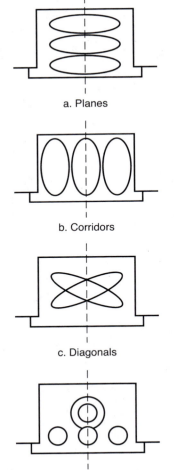

a. Planes

b. Corridors

c. Diagonals

d. Centerstage (tight and wide down specials) and other generic specials (down and front)

FIGURE 15.2 Dance Control and Grouping Patterns

FIGURE 15.3 Drawing Focus in Dance Lighting *Chicago:* Lighting by Ken Billington (Broadway Revival) *Photo credit:* Ken Billington

Since dance lighting doesn't necessarily require strong visibility, a designer can often be more expressive and dramatic in the way in which they light a piece of choreography. Mood often plays a strong role in the design, and many times the music (if any) can be used as a clue for developing an overall emotional response to the dance. Be forewarned that the music may also be chosen to work in direct opposition to the movements of the dancers. Regardless of the role of the music, conversations with the choreographer and observation of rehearsals will provide a means for correctly interpreting the meaning of a dance and what the lighting should contribute to it. I am often provided a video of a dance in rehearsal when I am not in residence with a company. This, along with my conversations with the choreographer, helps me to develop an effective plot before I am brought in to complete the final elements of a design in the theatre (focusing and cueing).

The illumination of a performer's face often isn't as important in dance as it is in drama, and this can lead to additional freedom on the part of a lighting designer. More contrast can be introduced into these designs and gobo washes may be added to bring additional interest and texture to a lighting design. On many occasions the patterns are focused directly on the performers and include full-stage washes. In those cases where facial expression is important, additional light can be added to bring further illumination and focus to the featured dancers and their faces. Additional light can come from either picking up the levels of the general lighting systems or preferably through placing additional light onto just the featured performers by using specials or other techniques. In ballet this is often done through assigning followspots to the featured performers so that they are slightly highlighted while the modeling created by the sidelight isn't washed out by bringing up the front lighting systems. These followspots are often used in such a subtle manner that the audience may not even be aware that they are being used at all— what we call running **ballet dim.** While it is possible to create a design that is overly dramatic and intrusive to a dance performance, most lighting designers welcome an opportunity to work in dance because of the additional freedom and creativity that they can bring to a performance.

Jennifer Tipton

Jennifer Tipton is an internationally renowned lighting designer who designs primarily within the areas of drama, opera, and dance. She is probably best known for her lighting of dance and has lit many of the premier dance companies of North America. Just a few of her dance credits include: The New York City Ballet, the American Ballet Theatre, Twyla Tharp Dance, The Paul Taylor Dance Company, and choreographers Mikhail Baryshnikov and Jerome Robbins. Her dance lighting has been further recognized by being awarded two Bessies and a Laurence Olivier Award. Her opera designs have also taken her throughout the world and include national credits with The New York Metropolitan Opera, Houston Grand Opera, and the Chicago Lyric Opera. She has lit numerous stage productions over the years and holds two Tony Awards for Best Lighting (*The Cherry Orchard* and *Jerome Robbins' Broadway*). She also is a recipient of the USITT Distinguished Lighting Designer Award. In addition to her busy freelance career, she is an adjunct professor of lighting at the Yale University School of Drama where several of her former students include lighting designers Don Holder, Christopher Akerlind and M.L. Geiger among many others. In 2008 she was further honored by being named one of the prestigious MacArthur Foundation Fellows as well as a US Artist Gracie Fellow.

Tipton received a B.A. in English from Cornell University but had always been involved in dance. Upon graduation, she began her professional career as a dancer but ultimately transferred her knowledge of dance to lighting when she became a lighting designer. She shares that she actually had no formal training in lighting. "I learned my craft on tour with the Paul Taylor Dance Company from 1963–1970 and the craft of lighting ballet with the Joffrey Company as Production Supervisor from 1970–1972." Her most significant mentor in her early career was Tom Skelton. "He was terrific. He always pushed me but never farther than I could go without losing confidence." She lit *Celebration: The Art of the Pas de Deux* at the Spoleto Festival in Italy for Jerome Robbins in 1972. This resulted in numerous offers for lighting theatrical productions, some of which led to both Broadway and Off-Broadway. Once again, she learned through "simply doing it." After lighting the Broadway production of *Le Bete* in 1990–'91 she was asked to light opera and began working in that area of the profession as well.

Jennifer feels that, "Lighting in any discipline asks the same questions and poses the same problems. The challenge is to answer in a way that is appropriate to the production at hand. I try to find a new vocabulary (light landscape) for each thing that I do." She also feels very strongly that, "Lighting onstage is the music of the eye and must follow the same rules of form and structure that music follows. If you establish a theme then it should be developed throughout a piece." What she likes most about lighting for dance is, "Grappling with the questions that arise about the form and structure of each piece that I do . . . it has kept me young of mind and very much in love with the art of light. What I like least is the focus . . . probably because it is so critical. It's the one chance you have to do it correctly; if you do it incorrectly there is often not enough time to go back to do it over again." She considers the most important rule of lighting to be in providing "visibility to tell the story."

When asked to comment on how she remains current she provided the following insightful response. "I have never worried about staying "current." I use the equipment that I have available to light the production that I am doing in that space. If rental is possible, it may give me more freedom in my choices, but so often the sky is not the limit." On the other hand, "Of course I do what I can to stay knowledgeable about new equipment, and since I am a teacher, I also learn along with my students."

Finally, Jennifer speaks very candidly about how her attitude and passion have helped in providing such longevity in her career. "When I first began as a designer I was always worried that my interest and passion would not last for my lifetime. I have discovered that by making each thing I do a new experience that I have no need to fear. I have had a long, productive, and rewarding life working with this mysterious stuff that is the measure of our universe. I feel very lucky."

Photo credit: Lois Greenfield

OPERA AND OPERETTA LIGHTING

Opera is a variation of entertainment where the majority of the communication with an audience is through music and singing. With the exception of an occasional phrase or word, virtually all of an opera's dialogue is presented through song. Opera is almost always associated with a large scale of production. Tragic plots are also frequently, though not necessarily, found in this form of entertainment. The works of Richard Wagner are especially associated with this grand scheme of production, but other composers like Mozart, Puccini, and Verdi are also noted for creating operas that are known for their epic qualities. In fact, many refer to this type of opera as **grand opera** simply based on the extreme scale that they represent. Much of the scale relates to the fact that these productions make use of a full orchestra (which can be over 100 pieces) and the large number of chorus members (30 to 50 or more). Because of the sheer number of performers (chorus and orchestra) it takes a large venue to accommodate the needs of simply getting all the people on stage. Also, the nature of much of the material written by opera composers tends to call for a sense of epic scale and proportion. The sense of greatness, universal qualities, and conflicts of epic proportion are reflected in all areas of opera design. The costumes are massive, heavily adorned, and textured, and the scenery can be monumental, overpowering, and stylized. It is all "bigger than life," and the essence of opera usually equates it with a form of entertainment that is created through spectacle. Just as with the other production areas, lighting, too, takes on these spectacle qualities and can become a major element of these productions. **Operettas** are a smaller version of opera that are often written from a more comic perspective. They tend to have a shorter length, smaller orchestras and casts, and are generally of a much smaller scale than grand opera. Therefore, they also have fewer production requirements. Many of the works of Gilbert and Sullivan are examples of operettas that are produced on a regular basis.

Most opera production is extremely costly due not only to the massive demands of the visual elements of these productions but also the special needs of the performers. In addition to the large commitment of paying salaries for the large casts and orchestras, most star performers must also give their voices a day's rest between performances. Unless there is double casting (rare since most audiences come to see a particular performer in a given role) an opera quite often must go **dark** or be without a performance every other night. Most companies avoid going dark by producing several operas at a time and having the performances scheduled through some form of alternating or repertory performance schedule. Companies like the Metropolitan Opera in New York have operas that have been part of their repertory for 30 or more years. Opera stars will usually be jobbed in by a company for performing a given role, the company chorus will perform the chorus and minor roles of each opera, and the scenery and costumes will be brought out of storage and once again assembled on the stage. The Met can actually rehearse or perform two or three different operas in any given day during their repertory season. This is an extremely large company and there are even several different shifts of electricians to complete the usual twice-daily changeovers.

Performance Considerations

Like dance, repertory design is often a large part of working for large opera companies. On the other hand, many smaller cities have companies that cannot afford to operate on a repertory basis. These companies typically engage in limited runs of an opera that often last only a week or two. The heart of the company is the chorus, which is typically made up of any number of local company members, while the principle or star roles are usually jobbed in and performed by singers who only make an appearance during the last week of rehearsals. In fact, there are many opera singers who perform a limited number of roles and make a career of flying all over the country performing these same roles over and over again. This can, and has, led to problems between local directors and those performing these star roles in regard to the interpretation and staging of these local productions. The orchestra is also typically formed from local musicians.

While the majority of the performers may come from a local talent pool, the scenery and costumes used by many opera companies are often rented from other companies. This is predominantly due to the massive demands and scale of these designs, which ultimately equates to the exorbitant costs of producing these sets. Most opera companies only own a few set or costume collections that they produce and use for their own productions. More importantly, they use these to generate additional income through renting the set and costume pieces to other opera companies. While some companies may rent and store a number of their past productions, storage fees are costly, and many companies find that it is more economical to keep and rent only a few of their best or most frequently used designs from past productions. When a company arranges to rent these settings they usually pay a weekly rental fee plus the trucking costs associated with transporting the scenery and

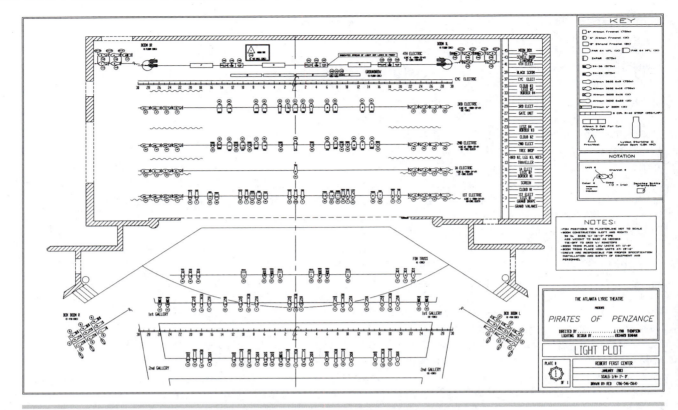

FIGURE 15.4   An Opera Light Plot   *The Pirates of Penzance* (Atlanta Lyric Theatre)

costumes to and from the original company. When lighting a production that makes use of rented scenery, a lighting designer should pay particular attention to the floorplans and other documentation that is provided for these designs. Figure 15.4 provides a light plot from a production of *Pirates of Penzance*. A couple of words of caution should be noted here in that these designs often aren't documented properly and there can be serious discrepancies between the plans and the actual finished setting. Unfortunately, you often don't find out about these problems until the scenery is loading into the theatre and your electrics have already been loaded and run to trim. In yet another worst case scenario, artistic directors have been known to make decisions about renting a set based solely on production photographs that they have seen of the set as it stood in the original theatre, without any sense of true scale. One opera company I know was involved in a production of *The Barber of Seville* in which the company rented a beautiful setting from the Houston Grand Opera. The major scenic element was a full-stage turntable that contained several stories that ended up having to be located in such a way that platforms were added to the pit so that the last several feet of turntable could fit the stage and roll out over the musicians.

The essence of the opera experience is both in the visual and more importantly the musical elements of the performance. The most important element is the character(s) singing at any given time. This could be a solo as in the case of an *aria,* a *duet* between two lovers who are embraced together, a duet or *trio* between different characters in two or more different worlds or time realms, or an entire chorus of over 100 voices. In each case, the lighting designer has the important task of drawing an audience's focus to that one important voice that must be isolated from the masses. Creating layers of focus becomes an extremely important consideration of opera lighting design. As a general rule, the principles with the aria or duet will always require the primary focus, while the chorus takes on a secondary role and is often lit in a more sculptural subtle manner, except when the chorus shifts roles and becomes the major vocal and visual element of the staging. On the whole, especially in the epic tragedies, the audience usually only needs to be aware of the presence of the chorus as opposed to being able to see each face clearly.

FIGURE 15.5 Scale in Opera Design   *Don Giovanni*: Lighting design by Jeff Davis.
Photo credit: Jeff Davis

Scenery, although often monumental in scale, needs to be treated as a background, and while it should be lit in an interesting fashion, it cannot be lit in a way that upstages the rest of the image—sometimes a difficult task, since these massive elements are often treated in decorative manners that often demand attention. The sense of scale that is found in opera is demonstrated in Figure 15.5.

Opera has traditionally not provided much physical action on the part of the performers. In fact, many traditional opera singers performed their roles by taking an extreme downstage position to sing the role, while the chorus and remaining characters simply became part of the background. This practice has changed over the last 20 years and many opera singers now receive actor training and incorporate much more physical action into their performances. This trend will continue to produce a more natural performance style as singers who have received this training mature and become more popular in the larger roles.

Two other considerations that are often dealt with when producing opera relate to the use of projections and slides in opera performances. Many scenic designs in opera use large areas of the cyclorama as a means of creating huge expanses of background for the opera settings. In many cases, these expanses are created through projections. These projections form an important element of these operas, and the lighting designer needs to understand how to vary the stage composition so that the projections are presented in the most successful manner possible. Chapter 18 deals extensively with projections, and specific information relating to them can be found there. A special type of projection that is often used in operatic design are **titles.** Most operas are performed in German, French, or Italian, and the majority of an English-speaking audience are not able to translate the words of the opera's native language. Titles are nothing more than a line-by-line translation of the text projected onto a screen that is located either directly above or below the proscenium opening of the stage. Several newer solutions involve placing miniature LCD or LED screens in the backs of auditorium seats, much like the screens that are popular on planes that are used for cross-country flights. This permits operas to be performed in their native language while also providing a way for an audience to understand the musical phrases. A lighting designer needs to know if a production will be using titles as well as the location of any screens that will be used for displaying them so that they can take steps to ensure that spill can be kept off of the screen's surface.

Design Techniques

Composers have traditionally not worried about the scenic shifting needs of a production and have consistently asked for large epic settings that may change several times within a single opera's performance (usually at intermissions). With the need for additional sets comes the need to store them when they aren't on stage. While some stages have wonderful fly, trap, and wing systems; most theatres have much too little space to accommodate all of the storage required by these productions. I know of theatres that even hoist scenery up into the wings to gain extra floorspace for storing additional scenery that is no longer required on the stage. Regardless of the size of a stage's wings, they are usually the most common location for storing scenery on stage, which makes the placement of booms and other mechanisms for creating sidelight a problem. In order to avoid the complication of hitting and moving scenery around booms, many designers simply move the sidelight to higher elevations, making high-pipe-ends and ladders popular mounting positions in opera designs. While many designers like to **deadhang** the ladders from the grid to save linesets, further flexibility can be created by hanging the ladders off battens so that the ladders can be flown out of the way while a set is changed and then lowered back in to their working trims once the scenery has passed beneath them. When a company cannot use ladders, the lighting designer's primary source of sidelight may have to shift to creating several systems of high-pipe-ends. If a lower angle of sidelight is required, we can often place one or two luminaires on a small boom that is equipped with dollies so that it can be rolled into place as needed **(a rover).**

I already spoke to some degree about creating levels of focus on an opera stage. This is accomplished primarily by setting appropriate lighting intensities to establish different levels of focus within the stage composition. What's brightest will usually receive the primary focus. Other levels of focus can be created by placing progressively lower intensities on less important subjects throughout the stage. Other techniques, such as using the relative sense of color or a variation in lighting angle can also be used for focus control. The huge scale of opera makes this especially important since an audience will often have problems trying to distinguish who on a 50-foot-wide stage and cast of sixty is actually singing at any given moment. Followspots are used quite often to establish the primary focus in an opera. How hard an edge that these are used with depends on how stylized the production may be. Most followspots used in opera design are of a more subtle nature, often just adding a bit of an extra glow to the principle singers. The chorus often takes on a secondary focus while the scenery is lit in a fashion that makes it unobtrusive. Use of textures and lighting of a sculptural nature, as in dance lighting, form a visual element that is often desirable for a number of opera designs. The rule, once again, lies in a determination of whether any specific design choice is consistent with the styles and conventions required by the given opera.

In situations where followspots are not used, a lighting designer has to take precautions to make sure that he or she knows the precise location of every aria and major piece of dialogue delivery. With this knowledge, cues are built where lights are brought up around the area where the performer will be located when delivering the given aria, duet, etc. Many times the general lighting systems are broken down into specific areas that are consistent with the manner in which much of opera has traditionally been staged. One consistent pattern involves placing solos directly at the downcenter position of the stage and placing duets in which performers do not share a common space or time in positions that would be equivalent to the down center-right and down center-left positions. This translates to an area breakdown that provides isolation at centerstage and each of the quarter or third lines and generally means creating an area layout that consists of an odd number of acting areas spread across the width of the stage. With large stages this would mean developing area systems of five or seven areas across the width of the stage. While this can often be less intrusive than using followspots, it takes care in cueing and also leaves the lighting designer at the mercy of the performer, who may or may not choose to remain in their light. At one time opera performers were notorious for changing their blocking and going to areas of the stage that were outside of any light that had been added for a specific moment. As a means of covering ourselves, many lighting designers choose to use followspots in a subtle manner so that the performers are covered whether they follow their blocking or not. For an even more subtle use of followspots, designers may place them upstage of the proscenium on a light bridge or other elevated position behind the performers. These positions create a nice rimming effect on the performers and can help separate them from the scenery and chorus. A fairly extensive use of specific specials is also often associated with opera designs. These, too, can be used to provide the proper degree of focus and illumination for a given area of the stage at a particular moment.

One final issue that a lighting designer must consider if they are going to light operas relates to the fact that the lighting cues are always set to the music and are therefore placed in and called from the *score*. The score differs from a *libretto* in that the score contains the actual music and orchestration while the libretto only contains the words to the songs or music. While I know designers who have designed in this area without being able to read music, it puts a designer at a real disadvantage if they cannot do so. The cues are set to the music (e.g., two beats after measure 46), the counts are tied to the music's tempo, and even the stops and starts during a rehearsal are communicated through the music (e.g., the second repeat after 97). This understanding of music will not only help a designer during rehearsals but will also become extremely beneficial when following a recording of an opera when completing tasks like pre-cueing a show on paper. At the very least, a designer should be able to follow the melody of the music. If you can't follow music, the libretto often gives you enough information to light the majority of the piece, although you might still have some confusion in places of long orchestrations or transitions such as in overtures and large movement sections like **dance breaks** where there is no singing. It will also be more difficult to identify the exact point of musical entrances and cutoffs.

LIGHTING MUSICAL THEATRE

Musical theatre is the single largest contribution that the United States has made to the world theatre scene and is the form of entertainment that has become most often associated with the Broadway theatre of New York. Musicals are a mixture of narrative scenes like plays **(book scenes)** that are alternated with segments of song and dance. These musical elements can be small and intimate, such as in the case of a **ballad** or reflective song performed primarily as a solo or duet, or a large **production number** that brings the entire company together in a flashy, high-energy song and dance. The traditional form of musicals began in the first quarter of the 1900s but was really perfected in the 1940s through 1960s. Individual composers and teams like Cole Porter, Richard Rogers, Lerner and Loewe, Rogers and Heart, and Rogers and Hammerstein are credited with writing an incredible number of musicals that can all be associated with the American theatre scene. Hits like *My Fair Lady, Hello Dolly, Anything Goes, The Sound of Music, Camelot, Carousel,* and *Oklahoma* are just a few of the many musicals from this era that are still produced on a regular basis even today. In the 1970s, a newer variety of musicals appeared that were characterized by a strong blending of all three elements (dance, song, and scenes) into a powerful production that was tied together through a strong plot or storyline. These musicals had a very strong visual aesthetic associated with them and have become known as **concept musicals.** Musicals like *Cabaret, Jesus Christ Superstar, Evita, Gypsy,* and *Sweeney Todd* are some examples of these musicals. Later musicals of the 1980s and '90s continued to grow in scale, becoming known for their lavish production elements, and are typically associated with an immense amount of spectacle. Musicals such as *Tommy, Cats, Les Miserables, Phantom of the Opera, Miss Saigon,* and *The Lion King* are examples of these spectacle musicals. Multi-million dollar set and costume budgets, flashy dance and song numbers, and expressive lighting make up the important elements of these productions. Currently, most new musicals appearing on Broadway are getting away from the strong reliance on concept and spectacle and are often remounts of older musicals or based on the songs of pop artists. In the latter case, songs that were written for the music industry are simply worked into a theatrical presentation that showcases a given composer's work. These songs are then linked together in some form of plot or storyline. Recent hits like *Mamma Mia!*, *Movin' Out*, and *Jersey Boys* chronicle the songs of ABBA, Billy Joel, and the Four Seasons, respectively. Other musicals based on the songs of popular song writers include the work of Johnny Cash, The Beach Boys, and Billy Elliot.

Performance Considerations

Musical theatre combines qualities from all three forms of entertainment that have already been discussed throughout this chapter. At times, during the book scenes, a production will take on a quality more in line with a play, while at other times the production will shift to a form of presentation that is more commonly associated with dance or opera productions. The lighting should also take on these qualities at various points throughout a performance. The key to successful design in this mode of entertainment is in developing a plot that will allow the lighting to easily shift between these different presentational styles. Musical theatre tends to reflect an overall stylized approach because of its spectacle quality and more theatrical methods of presentation—we don't normally break into song upon losing or gaining a lover. Scenery and costumes are often stylized, even to the point of sometimes having cartoon-like appearances, and the overall manner of presentation is seldom subtle. Lavish settings, bold use of color, flashy lighting sequences, presentational acting, and exaggerated costumes all make up production qualities that are typically associated with musical theatre. Performers can also step out of the reality of the production and interact with an audience directly. This form of entertainment is seldom created for generating any serious thought and is instead usually presented primarily for the pure entertainment of an audience. Other elements of this presentational style include a strong association with moving lights and followspots, which may be used in a subtle manner, but more commonly are used boldly with no attempt to hide the hard-edged beams that are formed around the featured performers or on the set.

Stage arrangement is a major element in the determination of how a given musical will be lit. Musicals are notorious for the number of different settings that might be required for a production. *Gypsy* requires somewhere around a dozen settings for each of the two acts. There is actually one sequence where Gypsy Rose Lee enters a time progression in which the setting changes to three or four different stages in the space of a single production number while she's onstage performing a striptease throughout the whole sequence! In many musicals, especially the traditional ones, the scenery is designed to work in a series of planes or zones just as in dance. Those scenes requiring the most scenery are designed as fullstage settings and use the depth of the stage, while those that can be designed in a more minimal fashion are staged against drops or backgrounds that correspond with various leg openings or depths of the stage. A setting like Henry Higgins' study in *My Fair Lady* will be created as a fullstage setting, while scenes like the streets of London or the Ascot scene have virtually no scenic requirements and can be set against a simple painted drop that is located near the front of the stage (traditionally in-one). These small scenes are often created to shorten the time required for scene shifts of more elaborate scenes that are set up behind the drop while these other scenes are being performed downstage. In the extreme form, **cross-over scenes,** the performers literally walk from one side of the stage to another, delivering a minimal number of lines or a single song while the scenery is changed upstage of the drop or curtain that is flown in behind the performers. If all goes well, the setting is changed by the time that the song has ended, and as the performers exit the drop flies out to reveal a completely new scene. Because of these shifting demands, the lighting often plays a significant role in aiding these transitions from one scene to another.

Due to the sense of spectacle associated with musicals, cueing becomes a major element of a musical's lighting design. Cues are almost always timed to the music and can become as complex as following the actual beats of an orchestration. Cues in musical theatre are rarely subtle and are often anchored in expressing moods and focus for a given stage moment. Rhythm and counts are extremely important to the cue structure of a musical, and while a drama may require 80 to 100 cues, a musical will often have 100 to

200 cues at a minimum. I typically design musicals with well over 100 cues in the first act alone. A production of *Hair* that I designed in the early 1990s had over 600 cues—without even counting any of the chases or effects! In designing dramas, there is often plenty of time to tweak a cue between the time that it and the next cue have been executed, while this is seldom the case in musical theatre. In correcting a single cue you may find that several additional cues may have passed you by. Because of issues like this, precueing and making efficient use of your tech time are especially important elements of lighting musicals. In many ways it can make the difference in getting through the cueing process successfully and with a minimal level of stress.

Design Techniques

Many of the principles for lighting a musical are based on the techniques used to light dance productions. This is predominantly due to two issues. First, the dance elements of a musical are best lit from the same perspective as a dance, and second, musical theatre staging is traditionally organized into a zone structure that is used to support the shifting scenic elements of a production. The multiple settings and relatively flat approach to scenic design through using drops and cutout pieces allows booms to be placed fairly easily between each of the leg sets while isolation is created between the zones by the layered scenery that defines each plane. While some designers may add a layer or two of general lighting systems based on a variation of the **McCandless Method** to create a more naturalistic lighting for the book scenes, many designers prefer to place their emphasis on the development of a good **zone** or **jewel** approach for lighting musicals. These systems place an emphasis on sidelighting and on the modeling qualities that are required by the dances. Good backlighting is also essential for separating the performers from their backgrounds. In addition to modeling, these methods also allow for better control of spill and focus while also permitting an overall use of more saturated colors throughout the plot. Extra visibility is achieved where needed with followspots. This is particularly true for the musical numbers, especially in the case of picking out the solos or featured performers. In all, this emphasis on sidelight aids in making the overall style of musicals more theatrical and interesting to an audience. The basics of all of these lighting systems were discussed previously both in Chapter 11 and in the dance lighting segment of this chapter. Figure 15.6 illustrates two of the three light plots (the majority of the FOH units are on a third plot) for the University of Georgia production of *Tommy*.

While dance is an important element of a musical, a designer cannot ignore the book scenes and songs that form the solos, duets, and ballads that are also a characteristic part of musical theatre performances. As a matter of overall approach, the sidelighting discussed in the last paragraph does not work particularly well for these circumstances and some form of front lighting must be used to bring a more natural quality to the book scenes. As already suggested, front lighting systems are frequently worked into a musical's plot for supporting the book scenes. Followspots are also often used to add visibility and focus to characters who are of significant importance at particular times throughout a production. Because of their frequent use, followspots are an accepted convention of musical theatre and often play an important role in most of these productions. They are not only used to create the primary source of visibility on the principle performers, but also allow the other theatrical elements of the lighting to be carried out more successfully in the background. Regardless of whether the followspots are used with a hard or soft edge or whether they are added to a scene in a subtle manner, they form a significant part of the musical theatre experience. In a fullstage production number where an entire company is singing and dancing, the lights are typically fairly bright over the entire stage, and a followspot may be the only thing bright enough to draw focus to the star at that given moment. In fact, I have witnessed shows where the followspots weren't powerful enough to cut through the rest of the lighting, causing the principles to be lost in the rest of the crowd that had been assembled on the stage. If obtaining more powerful followspots isn't an option, the solution is in getting the intensities of the rest of the stage low enough that a proper balance can be maintained between the followspots and the rest of the lighting (something that may not be possible because the difference is too

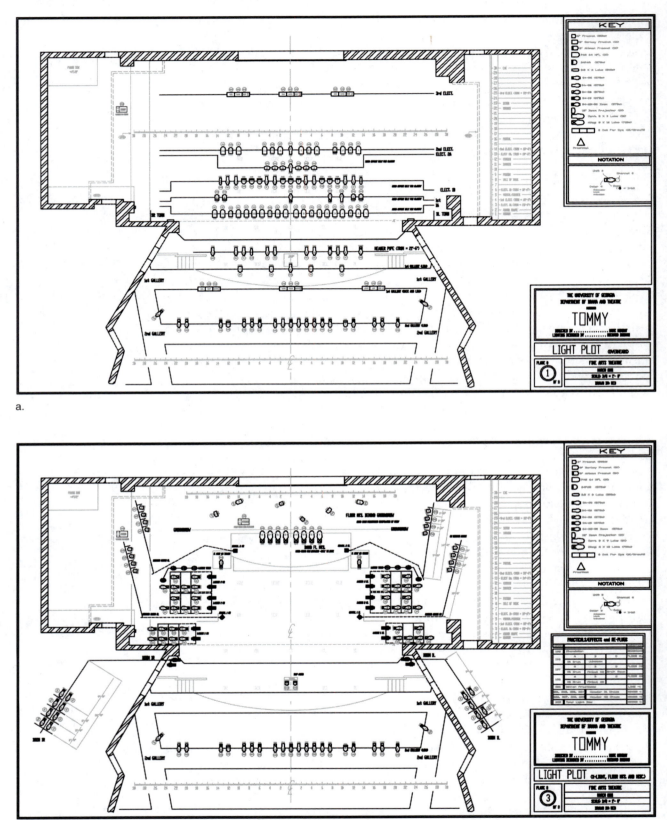

a.

b.

FIGURE 15.6 Light Plots for the University of Georgia Production of *Tommy* a. Overhead plot b. Sidelight and set mounts

great). The most common practice for using followspots in musical theatre involves using them in solos and ballads for bringing a sharp focus to the principle(s) while the rest of the lights are dimmed. This dimming is often to a full or partial **blackout.** I personally prefer to dim the stage to a variation of the existing lighting or some version of a **blueout** rather than a full blackout at these times. Followspots are frequently used in pairs, and if located to either side of the house, the **pickups** should be assigned so that the spots cross over one another at the center of the stage as much as possible, meaning that a followspot mounted in the stageleft house should pick up performers entering from stageright. This provides an angle that places more light on a performer's face for a larger portion of an audience. If at all possible, a pickup by followspots from both sides works best because not only does each light cover the front of the performers face but also each side of the face will be lit. While designers will vary the size of spot for a variety of reasons, a typical body shot usually tries to light the performer to about knee level. If there is a natural line, like the bottom edge of a skirt, this will often be taken as the place to draw the iris to. In the case of a duet, where the performers are relatively close together, it is usually better to open the iris a bit more to cover both performers with each of the spotlights. If the pair starts to pull so far apart that the size of the pools get so large that they become a distraction, one spot should be assigned to each performer using the traditional cross-over conventions. Most musicals are designed using two to four front followspots, while others, as in opera, may add additional followspots from a relatively steep location somewhere directly to the side and upstage of the proscenium from light bridges or towers erected elsewhere backstage. Regardless of how many, or where the spots are located, followspots are a classical element of musical theatre.

Musical theatre tends to be associated with one of the most presentational forms of entertainment lighting, not only because of the manner in which the plot is created or its heavy reliance on followspots, but primarily due to the way in which it is usually cued. Cueing in musical theatre is typically complex and follows the rhythms, emotional qualities, and momentum of the music. Mood and focus are critical elements of cueing for musical theatre. Not only is the look important, but also the manner of transitioning or getting between the different images. More than a few good lighting designs for musicals have been wrecked because the designer was not sensitive to the musical transitions. A stage manager who can't **call a show** can also destroy an otherwise great design. In these cases, either the person calling the cues will need to be replaced or the cueing will have to be simplified. Once again, it is best if a lighting designer can follow the score of a production, but since most musicals are published with a libretto it is still fairly easy for a designer who doesn't read music to cue a musical. If a designer is cueing only from a libretto, it is important to find an alternate manner of documenting and cueing any portions of the musical that aren't based on the text (e.g., overtures, entr'actes, dance sequences, and dance breaks). Precueing and the development of a solid **cue synopsis** makes up an extremely important step in the design process for designing musicals. I personally use a CD or cassette recording of a musical's soundtrack for assisting me in precueing every musical that I design. Other methods include downloading soundtracks to an iPod or MP3 player. The best part of this process is that it allows me to work on sections of the lighting over and over again, outside of the theatre, until I am finally satisfied with the sequences. There are a variety of special cueing techniques that have come to be associated with musical theatre productions. While these aren't limited to musical theatre, they have become characteristic of this type of designing. Sidebar 15.2 provides a description of several of these cueing techniques.

Musical theatre can represent a significant challenge for a lighting designer because of the complexity that these shows bring to the theatre. Speed, preplanning, and efficiency are three important principles for succeeding in this design environment. Organization needs to be done thoroughly and pre-planning is central to working in this area of performance. Anything that can be decided or committed to prior to loading into the theatre should be done ahead of time while the designer is fresh. In this way, valuable time isn't wasted making decisions that could have been made earlier in the design process and without the effects of being tired from spending numerous hours in a dark theatre. It is especially hard for an inexperienced designer to make the transition into this field because of the constant threat of

---

SIDEBAR 15.2 **Common Musical Theatre Cueing Terminology**

Ballyhoo	A theatrical use of a followspot(s) to create sweeping movements in a figure-eight pattern that pans across an audience or stage.
Blackout	A cue where all lighting intensities are changed to zero in a zero count.
Build	To add intensity to a scene. Often used in association with the building music as a song moves towards its climax and finale.
Bump	A cue done on a zero count.
Button	A dramatic cue (usually with a zero count) that is executed on a specific beat of music. This is usually done to add visual emphasis to the music. Popular examples include shifting the color of the cyc or shifting the lighting's focus with the final cutoff of a song.
Button-in	A variation of button cue that pulls the lights into a tighter focus (e.g., using the button to pull the lights and focus to the principle character(s).
Button-out	A variation of button that opens the focus of the lighting back out to a larger portion of the stage (if not the entire stage).
Chase Effect	A variation of cueing often done as an effect that automatically sequences a series of individual light changes. The simplest chase is a progression of two or three individual looks and would include something like the chasing lamps in a marquee effect. This technique can be expanded to include any progression of cues such as alternating the colors of a cyc.
Fade to Black/All Fade	A cue where all intensities are faded to zero. The count can be anything.
Pile-on	To add additional lights, an effect, or a second cue on top of a cue that already exists on the stage.
Restore	Returning to a previous cue. Many times variations of a look will be created on stage with a common look separating them. The best example would be in creating a common look for each chorus of a song with different variations or looks for each of the verses.
Rolling Cues	A variation of chase-like effect that creates a repeating sequence such as a series of repeating color changes in a cyc or other wash system. The sequence is typically programmed to roll by itself with predetermined timings for both the duration of the entire sequence and the time between each step in the sequence. Each step is typically timed to change to the beat of the music.

---

becoming overwhelmed. The best method to begin working into this particular area of design is to observe and work with designers who have mastered this design format. Watch how they create a plot, look at how they structure cues, observe their preparation, watch how they build cues, and most importantly watch how they handle stress and work through the tech/dress process of building and tweaking their designs. This can be done from performing any role where you can observe a master designer in action—being an assistant, board operator, master electrician, or even running a followspot. Regardless of the challenges and stress, lighting musicals can be extremely fun and an immensely rewarding design avenue to pursue. It is also important to note that even though the lighting can form a significant element of the overall spectacle and style of these productions, you still have to take care that you don't upstage the entire performance—to do so is still a disservice to a production. My personal reputation is predominantly connected to musical theatre, and I can honestly say that I find it to be one of the most personally rewarding areas of design that I work in.

FOR FURTHER READING

Palmer, Richard H., *The Lighting Art: The Aesthetics of Stage Lighting Design* 2nd ed. (Englewood Cliffs: Prentice-Hall, Inc., 1994).

Pilbrow, Richard, *Stage Lighting Design; The Art, The Craft, The Life* (New York: Design Press/Quite Specific Media Group, Ldt., 1997).

Rosenthal, Jean and Lael Wertenbaker, *The Magic of Light* (New York: Theatre Arts Books/Little, Brown and Company, 1974).

Watson, Lee, *Lighting Design Handbook* (New York: McGraw-Hill, Inc., 1990).

16 Non-Traditional Entertainment Design

This chapter introduces a number of entertainment lighting specialties that employ lighting professionals and designers outside of the more traditional areas of theatrical lighting. Many of these specialties are closely related to theatrical design, with the most significant difference being simply one of scale. Others, like concert lighting and especially film and video lighting, have a number of unique features as well as specialized equipment that are associated with them. This chapter will introduce some of the essential elements of each of these design areas.

During the last 50 years, lighting professionals have come to work between these disciplines on a fairly regular basis. In reality, the broadening of their horizons helps them to land more design projects. Some dabble within several different areas of lighting design while others establish themselves as specialists in a given niche such as lighting televised programs or special events. I have thought for some time that it has become necessary to provide more of an introduction to these disciplines than to simply mention that they are areas of lighting that are alternatives to working in the theatre. This chapter provides an introduction to some of these lighting areas as well as a series of interviews with designers who have established a reputation in particular specialties of the lighting industry. On the other hand, these lighting areas are specialties in themselves and entire books have been written in regard to the specific needs, equipment, and design practices that are characteristic of any given lighting application. The depth of information required to provide a full reference to someone who has taken on a project in these areas is well beyond an introductory book like this and can't be dealt with here. However, a series of followup chapters have been created as a part of the online resources for this book that present a full chapter (per topic) of additional material for the speciality areas that are introduced in this and Chapter 17. While these chapters can't present all that one needs to know in regard to a lighting specialty, the more detailed information should provide a solid bridge between a designer's theatrical experience and the more specialized materials of a particular lighting discipline. The specific contents of these online chapters are listed in the table of contents, while the introductions are characterized by the headings that are found in this and the next chapter (e.g., The Music Scene—Chapter 19; The Spectacle Performance—Chapter 20; Trade Shows, Industrials, and Corporate Events—Chapter 21; and Film and Video Basics—Chapter 22). In addition to more detailed information, the online chapters also provide a listing of more topic-specific references that can be used as a starting point for assisting anyone needing further information on a given lighting specialty.

THE MUSIC SCENE (REVUES, CLUBS, AND CONCERT LIGHTING)

The musical areas of entertainment are some of the most cutting edge and challenging yet rewarding disciplines in which a lighting designer may find employment. Production styles associated with these forms of entertainment are commonly stylized and frequently contain many theatrical and presentational elements. Like opera, the scale of these events is often quite large, providing a larger-than-life experience for both the performers and audience. Spectacle plays a significant role in these productions, and a designer often has a fair amount of latitude in responding to the performers and their music. The bottom line lies in finding a balance between heightening the experience so that it enhances the performer(s) and their music while at the same time creating a stimulating visual environment that brings interest to a show, especially for patrons who are in the most distant seats from a stage. Lighting is a primary component of most concerts and forms a major element of a typical concert experience. In fact, most people would say that lighting should become a significant part of a concert performance. Mood and focus play especially important roles in this type of lighting, and in most cases the lighting is dominated by relatively bold design choices. Saturated colors, extreme contrasts, distortion, and visual effects are not only common but frequently dominate these performances. Cueing plays an extremely important role in these designs and it is quite rare for cues to remain on stage for more than a minute or even seconds at a time. Subtlety is relatively rare, and the transitions between cues are usually very apparent to an audience. Even though a designer is given an immense amount of freedom, choices must still be motivated by the music and the performing artists. It can be easy for a lighting designer to get swept up in the emotion of a performance and care must be taken to not misdirect an audience's focus by either upstaging the artists or losing track of the rhythmic elements of the production. The top designers who work in these areas usually have some form of music background and a keen sense of rhythm and timing. Bad cueing in these events is much more noticeable than in more traditional areas of lighting and can therefore have a greater impact on the overall success of a performance.

Musical Revues

A **musical revue** is a production based on a collection of songs and dances (usually from a variety of shows) that are performed in much the same manner as in a traditional musical—with the exception that the **book scenes** are removed or replaced with brief elements of narration. Many revues showcase the work of a particular time period or artist, such as a choreographer, director, or songwriter. *Jerome Robbins On Broadway* presents the choreography of Jerome Robbins, while *Side by Side by Sondheim* showcases the musicals of Stephen Sondheim. A revue may also showcase a particular theme or talent. The Follies programs that are associated with the show girl productions in Las Vegas or the performances by the Rockettes at Radio City Music Hall form examples of these revues. *Tintypes* is an example of a musical revue based on the music and events of a particular time period—that of Charlie Chaplin and Theodore Roosevelt and the late 1800s to early 1900s—while *Sugar Babies* is a tribute to vaudeville and burlesque performances.

Most revues are presented by an ensemble of performers who take on the many roles represented by the musicals or other source materials that are used throughout the revue. Revues are created as a means of presenting the most memorable song and dance numbers of a particular interest. The storyline, if there is one, is often weak because the primary reason for the show's existence is simply the performance of a variety of song and dance routines, not necessarily connecting them together. This produces a wide range of performances that alternate between ballads and small intimate numbers, medleys that link a half-dozen or so songs together, and large production numbers that involve the entire company (traditionally the opening and closing numbers for each act). The lighting of musical revues doesn't change that much from lighting traditional musicals since nearly all of the performance elements come from musicals. However, there are several unique issues that a lighting designer must consider in order to create effective lighting for this type of entertainment. First, unit set designs are quite popular for these productions because of the amount of variety that must be included in these settings. It is also quite common to place the musicians on stage as part of the show. Due to issues like these, the lighting takes on a more central role in creating the variety that is required for each of the many routines. Lighting is also used as the primary vehicle for creating an appropriate atmosphere or mood and unique image for any song or dance that is performed as part of these programs. Additionally, lighting plays a critical role in moving an audience through the transitions that occur between the musical numbers, and cueing becomes a major component of these productions. The **cyc** is also frequently used as a major element of these designs. Finally, visual effects like **strobe lights, blacklight, fog** or **haze,** and **chase lights** also find their way into the lighting of many musical revues.

Nightclubs and Dance Club Lighting

These areas of lighting are unique in that the major focus isn't always on the performer or band but can shift to the audience, which is also usually lit. Contact with the audience, and even full audience participation may be encouraged. The primary difference between a **nightclub** and **dance club** lies in whether a dance floor is present and whether or not dancing is encouraged while a band is performing. Nightclubs tend to provide a lounging area with tables for drinks and snacks and conversation along with a stage for the performers. Audience members are usually not encouraged to participate too fully in the event other than through applause and clapping along to the music at various points in a performance. On the other hand, a dance club may still use table and seating areas but the club's activities are centered around a dance floor(s). Dance clubs are meant to achieve the full participation of the patrons, encouraging them to become immersed in the music and dancing. A significant amount of the lighting equipment is typically focused onto the dance floor so that its effects can be played over the dancing patrons. Many clubs have live entertainment performing on a stage that faces a dance floor, which allows patrons to alternate between dancing to the band's live music and recorded music that a DJ plays while the band is on break, maintaining the best of both worlds.

In most clubs, a stage is part of the permanent facility and is equipped with a basic selection of lighting and sound equipment. The artists traditionally provide their own instruments and personal amps, while the venue uses a repertory plot and house sound system to provide the primary lighting and sound needs of each act. Typical club lighting rigs provide a series of washes from several different directions like front and back lighting along with some specials and a short-throw followspot. In the smallest clubs or lounges, this may be as limited as having several different colored PAR-38s focused to each member of the band. As clubs grow, so do their lighting rigs—many to the point of providing a reasonably well-equipped rig featuring PAR-64s for several different color washes of front and back light, automated fixtures, and even LED instrumentation. In the smaller venues a house employee typically designs and runs the lighting **on the fly** while more established bands may have their own lighting designer. While the stages of many bars and nightclubs are lit primarily with theatrical equipment, dance floors are typically equipped with a wealth of specialized gear. Virtually all of it related to effects lighting that is designed to energize and stimulate the patrons. While some of the lighting illuminates architectural elements of the club, the majority is based on throwing moving patterns of light and color not only throughout the venue but most importantly on the guests who are dancing on the dance floor. Much of this specialized equipment and its layout are discussed in Chapter 19 online.

Concert Lighting

Concert lighting is one of the most expressive areas in which a lighting designer can work. On the other hand, it also comes with a number of demands that make it a particularly stressful area to work within. Because of the immense role that a lighting designer plays in the overall success of a concert, most designers are expected to tour with the performers and personally run the console during each performance. Also, the followspots for these performances are typically run by local operators who are not familiar with the show, and the lighting director typically **calls** or gives instructions to these operators throughout a performance. Even though there are a number of individuals who get beyond their thirties or forties and can still handle the rigors of touring, once reaching this age, many designers move on to other areas of lighting so that they can settle into a more traditional lifestyle and spend more time with their families. In those cases where a designer has been lighting a performer for many years it is common for the designer to light the show and go out on tour for only a brief period (the **shakedown**) and then turn the tour over to someone else who supervises and runs the lighting from one performance to another. With the lucrative financial rewards of the music industry and strong touring emphasis came the fact that these shows were rarely produced in properly equipped theatres. This was due to the increased costs of producing shows in larger venues with more seats in order to help keep the costs of the individual tickets more reasonable. In the early days, the artists typically toured with only their instruments and amps, much as they had when performing the club circuit, and the burden of transforming a gymnasium or venue into a performance space was left to the promoter. This frequently resulted in a range of successes (and failures) in terms of providing what was considered acceptable by the artists. As a result, the whole touring movement became a leader in the development of portable staging equipment. Lighting and sound companies rose to the occasion in fulfilling the specialized needs of the concert business and placed a strong emphasis on developing equipment that was not only portable but also reliable and could hold up to the pace and rigors of touring. **Trusses, chain motors, automated lighting, rolling dimmer racks** and **power distributions, PAR units,** and **portable generators** are only a few of the more important innovations that developed out of these needs. In fact, many of the most significant innovations of the entire lighting industry can be attributed to solving problems that were faced by the concert industry.

Once bands began touring with their own or rented equipment they did not compromise their tour itineraries, often maintaining a schedule that required back-to-back performances on a daily basis. Likewise, the shows also grew in sophistication. Many bands averaged five or six shows at as many venues each week. Even despite the larger technical demands, the **one night stand** still forms the most popular form of touring. This puts increasing demands on the crews in regard to the speed and ease in which the gear can be transported and assembled on a new site for each performance. Speed is everything to the touring electrician, and the concert industry developed a number of innovative manners of modifying stage equipment so that it could be set up, struck, and transported as efficiently as possible. Much of the speed of loading-in and loading-out this gear relates to prepackaging the lighting and sound equipment—making much of the equipment modular so that many of the steps to the equipment's assembly are done prior to moving into a venue. The bottom line in most concert applications relates to speed and flexibility. Conditions are constantly changing from venue to venue, and a touring designer must be capable of quickly sizing up a situation and making decisions that keep the momentum of a show moving forward. Learning the difference between when a compromise is necessary and when to push for a specific production requirement form critical assessments that a touring lighting director must be capable of achieving.

PAR-64s form the workhorse for much of the concert industry in conventional touring rigs. They are generally laid out in circuits of different colors that simply wash the entire stage. Most of these are hung from trusses that are placed directly downstage and upstage of the band. Backlight forms an especially important element of concert productions. Specials are also commonly added as back diagonals for the drum kit and lead vocalists or instrumentalists. These provide additional accents and focus for these musicians. Washes may come from the front, back, side, down, or front diagonal. In most cases, the washes are nothing more than a repeatable color sequence of PAR-64s that are arranged along the length of a truss. One unique quality of concert lighting is its heavy reliance on followspots. These allow the principle artists to be given focus at any given time while the rest of the stage is bathed in washes of color or effects. In many traditional setups, the followspots formed the only lighting that came from directly in front of the

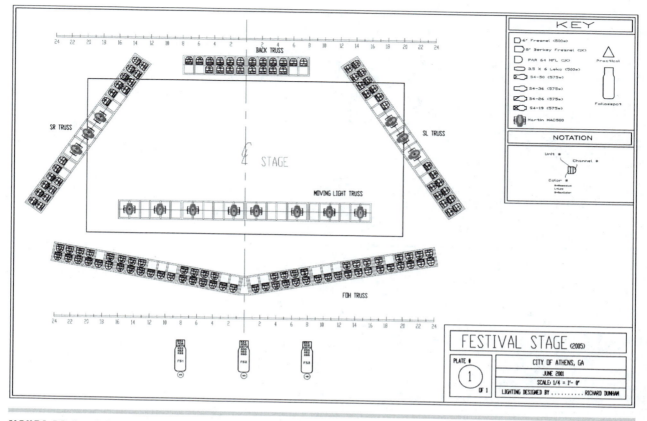

FIGURE 16.1   A Contemporary Concert Plot

band. Designers may also choose to place followspots in the upstage trusses to produce steep angled backlight from behind the performers. Figure 16.1 illustrates a more contemporary concert plot where the trusses aren't simply arranged across the width of the stage and contain automated lights in addition to the PAR-64 washes.

Cueing is the most challenging yet rewarding aspect of lighting musical events. You have to get your head into the music and know the artists, their music, and their routines as well as you possibly can. The majority of a concert design is based on intuition, and improvised lighting is popular even if you have already established a general series of cues for a song or entire event. The element of improvisation comes not only from a lighting designer's perspective but also from the band and the nature of the concert experience itself. I've often experienced times when musicians go off on tangents with solos and jams that occurred simply because the crowd provided some good feedback and everyone got a bit more into the show. This is some of the fun of working the concert scene. I've also had experiences where I've had no warning, other than the lead-in, of a band launching into a song that wasn't even on the **set list** but was pulled from the band's repertory and may not have been played in days or even weeks. A concert lighting director must be able to go with the flow when things like this happen and should try to enjoy the spontaneity of a performance. If you panic when an extra chorus gets played or a set list gets switched around, this is probably not the business for you. There are also a fair number of occasions where I have been the house man or have run lights for festivals where I had never worked with or, for that matter, even heard, any of the music from the bands that I was lighting. In these cases, you learn to use a number of standard looks and effects and to improvise along with the band. By not doing anything too drastic you can usually run an effective show by simply improvising along with the music. When working in situations where you are not familiar with the artists or their work it is good to hesitate a few seconds when a group breaks into another number to evaluate where the song is heading before doing anything too drastic with the lights.

Lighting plays a major role in any concert event, and while there may be a significant amount of stress associated with mounting and running these productions, this career can also form very valuable and fulfilling experiences for anyone who chooses to work in this area of lighting. The pace is fast and the challenges can be stimulating, but no other form of lighting allows the work of a lighting designer to have such a significant role and impact on a performance. For a much more detailed treatment of concert lighting, I urge you to examine Chapter 19 online and then go on to explore Jim Moody's book, *Concert Lighting: Techniques, Art, and Business.* Mr. Moody is one of the pioneers of the concert lighting industry and provides thorough discussions and examples relating to his work and experiences throughout this book.

SIDEBAR 16.1 DESIGNER PROFILE

James L. Moody

James L. "Jim" Moody is currently Head of Technical Theatre and Design at The Theatre Academy at Los Angeles City College. He is a truly diversified lighting designer with credits in concert, television, theatre, Vegas shows and reviews, corporate productions, and film. He has designed over 200 productions at Regional Equity theatres as well as for a number of college and universities as a guest artist. Jim is considered one of the founders of concert lighting and received the very first Concert Lighting Designer of the Year Award. Several of the concert acts and tours that he has designed include: America, David Bowie, John Denver, The Eagles, The Fifth Dimension, Dolly Parton, Kenny Rogers, Linda Ronstadt, Rod Stewart, The Supremes, and Stevie Wonder. Also active in television lighting, he has earned two Emmy nominations and one team win for his lighting for video. He served for ten years as Director of Photography on *Entertainment Tonight* and then switched to *Jeopardy!* and *Wheel of Fortune* for 12 years. He has also lit a number of corporate productions with a client list that includes Apple Computers, Sony, Wendy's Restaurants, The Sunkist Growers Association, Epson, Goodyear, Disney, Mercedes-Benz, Coca-Cola, Federal Express, and Bank of America. In addition to the Emmys, his designs have earned him numerous other awards, including: The USITT Distinguished Achievement in Lighting Award, Drama Logue Awards, and IESNA Achievement Awards. He has written many articles for a variety of lighting publications and two books, *The Business of Theatrical Design* and *Concert Lighting: Techniques, Art, and Business* (now in its 3rd edition).

Jim holds a B.S. degree from Southern Illinois University and an M.F.A. in Theatre Lighting Design from UCLA, and has completed his doctorate in Educational Management. After college, he needed work, and began his lighting career in manufacturing as the assistant to the president of a rather small lighting manufacturing company while designing theatre at night. His venture into concert lighting is best told in his own words. "After 10 years, I left a good paying job to try full-time professional theatre, but it just didn't pay much. Concerts were new back then and I had a music

background, so when I was offered a chance to do one I tried it and liked it. I made a lot of contacts very quickly and started going on the road with bands within the year. My first tour was with Rod Stewart and Small Faces, which had Ronny Lane as the guitarist before he joined the Rolling Stones. My second tour was for David Bowie and the Spiders from Mars on his first American tour." When asked about how he prepared for working in the concert industry Moody relates that he had no advanced preparation for concerts because nothing existed at the time—it was a brand new media. "That is why Bob See, Tom Fields, Bill McManus, and I are considered by many as the founders of the concert lighting style. We all helped 'teach' each other. The Las Vegas shows came with my concert artists being signed to do shows in the casinos and I went with them." His crossing into film and television came later. "I worked in L.A. on non-union shows between tours and built up my knowledge of working in these mediums on the job and eventually got my International Alliance for Theatrical Stage Employees (IATSE) local #600 Director of Photography card. Corporate and Las Vegas shows are so much like theatre musicals that the transition to designing for them was pretty easy." Now that he is a full-time professor, his responsibilities to his department take the majority of his time, but he continues to design professionally, with the work being about 70% theatre, 10% architectural, 10% television, and 10% concerts.

Moody credits two individuals with helping him break into the business. First, Joe Tawil (President of GAMProducts), the man he went to work for when he finished college, would become a real mentor and friend to him. Second, Joe would introduce him to famed Broadway lighting designer Julies Fisher whom he later assisted for two shows. "That was my second big break. Julies is a great teacher as well as designer and really 'trained' his assistants—not just demanded that they go for coffee and pick up the laundry." Several unique considerations of designing for concerts, as well as for Vegas revues and corporate shows, is that a sense of timing (musicality) is more critical than that needed in theatre. Jim also claims that working in this area is great training for theatre because of the time pressure that is imposed on these designs. "Theatre now seems to me like we are walking at half-speed because I got used to the much tighter scheduling of concerts." In designing for film and television, he says that, "You have to give up the notion that you, as the LD, control what the audience will see and accept that the director determines which shots will be used. In multi-camera setups, the DP must allow each of the angles to be lit properly, not just one angle. Film and television lighting also require a heightened awareness of the needs of a director and an ability to be two steps ahead of them. Finally, knowledge of the technical requirements of the media, such as light levels and contrast are a must." Unique considerations of working in the concert industry relate primarily to time. "Scheduling, load-in, focus, calling the show, and strike all have to happen in 12–14 hours. Staying on top of everything and total advance planning are some of the keys to a designer's success. Not being afraid to make a decision when things are moving very quickly is another must-have skill." What he likes most about concert lighting is the immediate gratification. "Decisions must happen on the spot and the ability to think on your feet is essential. You must never be wed to a single idea. Be flexible and keep a clear vision of what your end design wants to be and then focus on getting as much as you can under the time, space, and financial constraints."

What he dislikes about the business is hardly anything. Sometimes the inability of a booking agency to lay out the tour far enough in advance or incomplete advance work can cause headaches. Worse, dates and venue styles can change at the last minute, such as from an arena to a few mixed dates in theatres. That can cause a situation where your rig won't work as you planned and you have to make quick decisions on what to drop or modify in a design. He believes that remaining totally *flexible* is the most important rule to consider when working in these areas. "You must have a plan and that plan must be open enough to have options that have already been considered so that when a change is necessary you are ready." He also suggests being bold. "There is no right or wrong way to light concerts—those who are successful are the ones that take chances."

In closing, Jim shares that "I am a great believer in learning about *all* areas of lighting because cross-pollinated ideas from other media help make the most creative decisions possible. The added exposure will give you access to more creative tools. Even if you have no desire to work in these alternate media, the broader aspect of knowledge will always serve you well."
Photo credit: Beatrice Huguet

THE SPECTACLE PERFORMANCE

Spectacle performances usually relate more to scale and number and types of effects used during a performance than to anything else. The size of a facility that an event is produced within, the lavishness of the design elements, the size of the budgets, the number of cast members, and technological sophistication of a show also play into the degree of spectacle achieved by an event or production. While scale is one of the most common means of attaining spectacle, it is not the sole measure of spectacle. There are many technologically advanced spectacle performances that take place in relatively small venues. The numerous Blue Man Group productions that are appearing in many cities form examples of these spectacle productions that are presented in more intimate environments. At the other extreme are huge extravaganzas like the halftime shows for the Super and Orange Bowl celebrations or the opening and closing ceremonies of the Olympics. Spectacle raises the expectations and experience of an audience. There should be elements of surprise and some element of "wow" factor connected with these performances. Selective use of spectacle becomes an ever important element of designing these events. Yet a designer should not go overboard and simply produce one effect after another. Too much **flash and trash** can become nothing more than flashing lights and can fail to make any positive contributions to a performance. In fact, such techniques might have a detrimental effect by creating issues like a misdirection of focus or not providing enough variety in a performance.

Headline Acts

Headline acts are shows built around a given artist—one who is typically associated with having risen to a superstar status. The act may be an individual or a group of performers such as a rock band and can be mounted in a more traditional theatrical or concert-like format. In many ways they are a good transition between the events covered by musical revues or concerts and some of the mega-productions that are examined in the following paragraphs. In many cases, these acts are presented in theatres that have been especially equipped to handle the given show. Some people in the business refer to these theatres as **showrooms.** The casino shows that feature Vegas acts like Bette Midler, Barry Manilow, or Cher (for your parents), and Elton John or Celine Dion (for the younger crowd) form popular examples of these productions. The majority of these events are music acts, although magic and other popular forms of entertainment may also be represented in this format. Siegfried and Roy (remember the tiger attack?) along with Penn and Teller are two popular

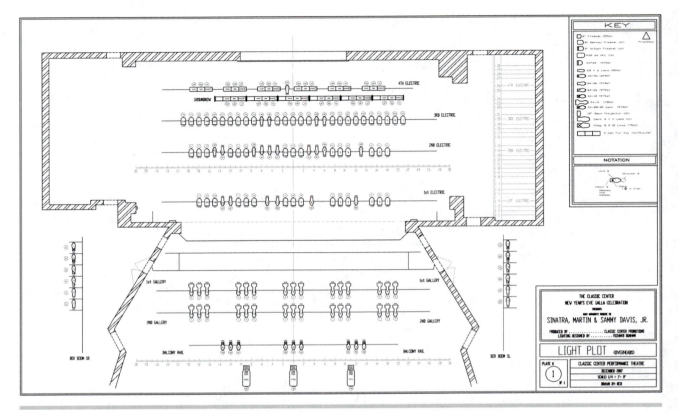

FIGURE 16.2   A Light Plot for a Headliner Revue

magic acts that perform regularly in casino hotels in Las Vegas. Other popular casino cities that produce headline acts include Atlantic City, Reno, Lake Tahoe, and Branson, Missouri. These productions are frequently treated as permanent installations, and shows are presented on a regular basis, often daily, with two shows in a single evening.

In regard to lighting design, every choice should showcase the headliner even though effects and spectacle are often major components of these shows. The spectacle elements should also not distort or make the artist look unattractive in any way. Although many acts are billed around a single artist—most have accompanying vocalists, dancers or chorus members, and an orchestra that must also look attractive to an audience. At the same time, focus needs to be clearly maintained on the star performer. Followspots and color washes play an essential role in this form of entertainment. Figure 16.2 represents a plot designed for a touring revue of Rat Pack impersonators. Outside of the larger scale and the need for establishing a strong primary focus, most of the remaining elements of lighting these events follow the same principles that concerts and musical revues might use.

Arena Productions and Stadium Productions

Arena and stadium productions relate more to a physical space for mounting a production than to an actual entertainment event. Once an event grows to a size at which it is no longer profitable to produce it in even the largest theatres, other venues need to be secured that allow for a greater number of audience members. This ultimately keeps the ticket prices more affordable. Rather than spreading the costs over a 3,000-seat auditorium, the audience for a single event can be increased to 5,000, 10,000, 50,000, or even more seats. Much of Chapter 19 deals with concert tours where shows are produced in arena environments. Once concert promoters had the proper equipment and knew how to produce their shows in arena formats, other large-scale productions like circuses also began to move into these venues, using the same techniques that had been perfected by the concert industry. The most popular method of producing these events is by trucking your own or rented equipment to a facility and setting the show up in the arena for a limited period of time. This may be for a single performance or could stretch to 2 or 3 weeks. In most cases, the performance period is restricted to only a couple of days—spending about a week in a given city and venue. Once again trusses, chain motors, rolling dimmer racks, PARs, and automated luminaires are common elements of these productions. The equipment is usually rigged from the steelwork or superstructure of the building and can be assembled and struck in a matter of hours. A concert in a sports arena on one evening can be followed by a basketball game the next day. In addition to concerts, many ice shows, children's programs, and even televised awards programs are conducted in these arena formats. In general, arena programs are lit with much fewer luminaires than a concert, and more care is taken to provide a series of washes that cover the performance space in a variety of tinted colors. Throw distances are typically fairly long, which results in the beam angles of many of the luminaires being relatively small. Followspots are frequently used to draw focus and once again form a significant element of these productions.

Stadium productions raise the level of expectation and spectacle still further by providing an even larger venue and audience—audiences of 60,000 to 100,000 people or more are quite common to stadium events. Events that characterize this type of spectacle include the very largest concert events like The Rolling Stones or Garth Brooks concerts and other special events like the half-time celebrations associated with the Orange or Super Bowl and the opening and closing ceremonies of the Olympic Games. The cover of this book displays an image from the Opening Ceremonies of the 2010 Winter Olympic Games in Vancouver. Scale once again becomes a major factor that drives these productions. Choices must be bold and a significant amount of the lighting is used to emphasize the bodies of the performers. Washes are a common approach to providing general area coverage for the event, while focus and the lighting of the stars is best done through followspots, often with the aid of large format projection screens and live camera feeds using **I-Mag** technologies. These events often contain not only spectacle lighting and performance qualities but may also include audience participation, pyro and fireworks displays, and even laser shows. In the largest of these events; celebrity performers, hundreds of dancers, and thousands of audience members might participate in the event. These events are nearly always televised and therefore have yet another layer of complexity placed on them.

There are also additional issues (not only scale) that relate to lighting a production in the exterior environment of a stadium. While inclement weather may become an obvious concern, there are other factors that can actually have a more profound effect on a performance than the weather. First, it is usually more difficult to light events at dusk through twilight than after the sun has dropped below the horizon due to the relative high level of ambient light that exists in these facilities. Deep shadows will also form in these venues due to the specific location of the sun, which can cause contrast problems in different areas throughout the stadium. There are also no rigging points in a stadium and all overhead gear must be rigged with either ground supported systems or by some sort of crane device. Mounting luminaires along the front tiers of the seating areas may also form alternative hanging positions. Moving lights have become an especially attractive element for these events because of their ability to both move and change physical parameters through use of a lighting console. This is especially helpful with the shortage of mounting positions that are typically associated with these venues. These events tend to represent some of the most costly events that we ever produce.

Dedicated Venues

Dedicated Venues are facilities for which an entire performance space has been created around the needs and artistic demands of a particular show or performance group. The best examples of this include the many Cirque du Soleil productions that have been mounted in cities like Las Vegas. These productions cost millions of dollars and months if not years to produce. Scale is huge, and monumental production elements like fantasy costumes and elaborate set pieces and gymnastic apparatuses are characteristic of these productions. An immense amount of time is spent on creating a fully spectacle world around the performers. One of Cirque du Soleil's productions, O, is conceived around a playing space that is formed predominantly by a huge pool. Lighting is unique for each

Jeff Ravitz

Jeff Ravitz has been involved in lighting for over 30 years and entered the profession through designing concerts. He was introduced to video lighting through both adapting his live shows for a television audience and following his concert clients to light their music videos. His reputation is now found primarily in lighting television studio and live events for broadcast and music-based entertainment. Several notable clients that he has lit for broadcast specials and concert tours include Bruce Springsteen, Cher, Usher, Shania Twain, Rush, and the Superbowl XXIX Halftime Show. His lighting has won awards, including both an Emmy Award and second Emmy nomination. His program credits include *Larry the Cable Guy*, *Caesars Challenge*, *Personals*, *Wheel of Fortune* and *Jeopardy!*, ice shows, a feature film (*The Manchurian Candidate*), and a number of infomercials and other special events.

Jeff holds a theatre degree from Northwestern University but points to 30 years of experience as an important element of his training. "Trial and error, taking risks, learning from mistakes, observing the masters, and endless conversations and debates with friends, colleagues, and teachers are all important to my learning and staying current in the business." After college, he embarked on a theatre career but found that he missed his days as a musician. When an ad appeared in a local paper seeking a lighting designer for a local recording artist he applied and landed the job. He states that, "I had the time of my life combining my theatre, lighting, and music skills and found myself at the ground floor of an exploding new area in entertainment production." After several years, Ravitz was exposed to the emerging field of music videos as well as lighting live concerts for broadcasts. "I watched the crews and production teams that were brought in to create the videos and TV specials for my concert clients and learned much of the process. When it became common to have I-Mag projection of our shows onto large screens for the benefit of the audience seated farthest from the stage I had the opportunity to see the effects of lighting for the camera while I watched the results of the live action compared with the images that appeared on the screens. I got a sense of what worked, or didn't, and developed my own style and standards. With a few lucky breaks and the confidence of my clients, I was eventually given the opportunity to be the television LD on a few shows and my resume and reel began to take form." Jeff's next break came when he partnered with renowned designer James Moody to form a design firm. Moody had already made the transition from theatre to concerts and then into television lighting. "Jim often had multiple opportunities (that is to say, he was frequently double and triple booked!), and I had the chance to sub for him on shows like *Wheel Of Fortune* and *Jeopardy!* as well as for sitcoms and newsmagazine shows. Jim is a most generous teacher and shares his experience and knowledge liberally. This partnership brought me to a new level of skill and confidence, and with the purchase of some really good meters I had the impetus to seek work as a lighting designer specializing in televised entertainment."

An event that really shaped Ravitz's career was his televised lighting of the Bruce Springsteen E-Street Band reunion at Madison Square Garden. The show was shot in high-definition video, which was new at the time, and they spent a lot of time adjusting the show's lighting so that it was balanced for the camera while retaining the excitement of the original touring design. "The resulting show was broadcast on HBO and I was honored with the Primetime Emmy for Outstanding Lighting Design along with my tour lighting director, Gregg Maltby. This gave me credibility as a TV lighting designer and I soon began to get more chances to design shows for live broadcasts and to adapt other designers' shows for the camera."

Ravitz suggests becoming an active member of professional organizations that service special areas of the lighting industry when crossing into other disciplines of lighting. "I have been an avid member of the International Cinematographers Guild, the American Society of Lighting Designers, the Designer's Lighting Forum, and the Illuminating Engineering Society of North America (IESNA). These organizations hold seminars and workshops that allow for person-to-person exchanges of ideas and experiences. I have also taken courses in architectural lighting and read everything that I have time for: trade publications, books, and articles." Jeff also believes that maintaining a dialogue with your peers is important, from crew members to directors, producers, and senior members of the design community. "Talking to these people and sharing experiences continues an oral tradition of passing information along." Finally, he notes that just *doing* it is the most important way to improve and develop. "Trying out the newest equipment or techniques and doing your best to squeeze the most out of them is the best way to learn and grow."

Jeff shares that the main thing that separates television lighting from theatrical lighting is the wide gap between the sensitivities of the human eye and the camera. "The ability of the eye to simultaneously see many things of vastly different intensities and to assimilate them comfortably into a whole picture is far superior to that of a camera." Another major difference is in the camera's tendency to put the viewer in the front row or even nose-to-nose with the subject. "The live audience sees a full frame from one end of the stage to the other and a lighting designer draws attention to the most important elements in a way that is similar to how a cinematographer goes from a wide shot to a close-up. However, the closest that a live audience member ever gets to a subject is still a minimum of 20 feet away. Things simply look different and the detail is not the same as when you view someone's face from 1 foot away in an extreme close-up. More importantly, the techniques that a lighting designer uses to make things look good, dimensional, and simply visible in a large house for a live show often exaggerate shadows and other features that would appear somewhat grotesque if you were to suddenly change camera angles and shift from a wide-angled shot to a close-up. In lighting for the camera, there is much more emphasis on using angles that are flattering to the face." He also shares that it is not unusual to allow areas of the stage to fall off into darkness in live performances, which can be a problem in camera work. Multi-camera productions must be especially careful in paying attention to the different angles that can be simultaneously captured. "From a tight close-up to a wide shot, from a view of what is behind the talent to a view of what is off to their side in the far distance—it all has to be considered. That is why we spend a lot of time analyzing the wings in TV production and how they will look in the background of certain side- or cross-shots. We also tell our clients that it is our mission to make the show on the screen appear as close to the live show as possible. But, in order to accomplish this, we also tell them that we will have to make some changes to the live show that will alter the experience for the in-house audience." Though he dislikes the technical limitations of the camera, he enjoys the new challenges that the medium poses and claims that they have kept his approach fresh while allowing him to cross-pollinate between different parts of the lighting industry. "There is no doubt that my TV lighting style is greatly affected by my years as a live show designer. I can draw from things that work, or don't, from each area and can then use them to extend my palette and broaden my tool chest."

Photo credit: Jeff Ravitz intensityadvisors.com

of these productions, and care is taken to produce a design that not only speaks to the individual performers but also connects to the show as a whole. Stunning visual images have often been associated with these productions. The lighting is very specific, even to the point of adding hanging positions as specifically required by the designer.

Additional Areas of Spectacle

Two final areas of spectacle include events like the fountains used in **dancing water displays** and **aerial shows** where light is projected into the air and sky. The fountain shows are frequently found in the gardens or atriums of upscale hotels while the aerial shows are often associated with community festivals or celebrations. In both cases, specialized luminaires are used to project light onto the surfaces of either water or clouds (smoke in the case of fireworks) and other large scale structures. Most dancing water displays contain water fountains that use a variety of water jets, sprays, and fountain heads to create artistic displays of pulsating water that are timed and choreographed to a soundtrack of music. In order to add more theatricality to the event, the fountains will be lit and programmed to change color in response to the music and fountain choreography. In the aerial shows, light is played off of clouds and smoke that is produced through fog and haze machines or even fireworks. More sophisticated techniques might include the aerial displays like those associated with a bowl event like the Super Bowl or an outdoor celebration like the re-dedication of the Statue of Liberty. Just outside of Atlanta, there is a park called Stone Mountain that produces an event that combines choreographed lights, fireworks, and lasers into nightly shows throughout much of the summer. It has the reputation for being the largest aerial laser show in the world. On a more somber note, the memorial that was created for the Twin Towers attacks in New York City, which produced two shafts of light upwards from Ground Zero, forms yet another element of aerial spectacle. In this example, two grids of narrow-beamed luminaires were directed skyward in two columns that were symbolic of the former towers.

TRADE SHOWS, INDUSTRIALS, AND CORPORATE EVENTS

Many professionals refer to these productions or events as **corporate theatre**. The lighting of these events follows design practices that are similar to those used in other lighting applications. In some cases, such as in trade shows, the designs are more in line with what you might expect for a display or exhibit in a retail environment, while other corporate events are so driven by theatricality and spectacle that they can be compared to theatrical events that rival Broadway shows. Examples include product showcases associated with trade shows and other special events like press conferences, new product introductions, and business meetings. Political conventions (see Figure 16.3) are another example of these types of events. Because many of these events are conducted in hotel ballrooms and

FIGURE 16.3 The 2004 Republican National Convention with Lighting by Bill Klages *Photo credit:* Bill Klages

convention centers or arenas, much of the equipment and production practices come directly from the concert industry. Most companies that produce corporate events produce only one, or at most just a few, of these events each year. Due to this, virtually all of the equipment for these productions is rented from local theatrical rental houses. The annual car and boat shows that introduce the latest model cars and boats or the seasonal fashion shows produced by premier clothing designers are examples of these events. Although trade shows and corporate events may be open to the public, many are created and reserved for a select audience—employees who are members of a company's regional or national distribution system, sales representatives, or members of a specific profession.

Corporate Mentality

Whether lighting trade shows, industrials, or any other type of corporate event, the most important element to working successfully in this programming is making the product and its corporate sponsors look as good as possible. Because these events are produced predominantly by sales and commercial representatives there are several important differences in how a designer is expected to work in this area of production. Probably the most significant difference lies in the fact that your producer is the company and that the people who are responsible for working with the design team often have limited backgrounds in theatrical production. This can lead to a number of situations where decisions are made by individuals who do not understand the ramifications of their choices. The best corporate producers have some background in the theatrical business and know how to be involved in the process while trusting their designers to create the most effective presentation possible. Finding an effective way of communicating with those who aren't versed in theatrical terminology or practices becomes an important task for any designer working in corporate theatre. Visual illustrations and photographs are important and can go a long way toward creating an understanding of what you intend to produce for an event. Another issue comes in the question of who is really in charge of a corporate production. While the production team may have worked extensively with an individual or team that represented the company throughout the planning stages of a project, someone further up the executive chain like a vice president or board chairman who has not been a part of the process may come in at the last minute and make demands of the event and its designers. Such situations can be frustrating and can add an incredible amount of stress and expense to an event as designers scramble to accommodate the changes being demanded by these people. I know of corporate shows where designers had to re-color and re-cue significant parts of a production due to revisions in a script or move entire stages and their related lighting rigs to different locations in a venue. I have even heard of an occasion where all of the lighting fixtures and trusses were repainted a different color just hours before the beginning of an event—all on the insistence of a corporate player further up the company ladder.

On the whole, most corporate events are produced very quickly with time being an important limitation of these productions. A fashion show may load into a ballroom or mall location on a given morning and can be presenting shows as early as 10:00 or 11:00 A.M. On the other hand, organizational, design, and production meetings for many corporate events can occur months ahead of the actual production. Some companies begin to work on their next annual productions only shortly after completing their current show. Regardless of amount of planning, the physical load-in of an industrial typically follows an abbreviated work schedule. While the number of days in a venue are kept to a minimum, the time is well-organized, and a flurry of activity can occur at virtually any time of the day or night when actually producing these events. Ballrooms are expensive, and companies frequently don't want to pay the additional rent and labor costs associated with providing time for an extended load-in and rehearsal process. Often, these are one-time events, and it is hard to justify the costs associated with several days of load-in and rehearsals for a single 1- or 2-hour show. In many smaller productions, the load-in occurs in the morning and the event takes place later that day or evening. Often events are presented and quickly followed by a few hours of setting up and rehearsing for the next event, which is then presented and followed by yet another period of preparation before moving on to the next event in the production schedule. A designer is paid to be quick and efficient throughout the load-in and design process. You are also not done with a corporate production until the final performance is over. Perhaps more importantly, one must create a certain amount of flexibility in these lighting rigs so that when changes are demanded, you can quickly adapt to the new needs of your client. As a rule, you should always make sure that you cover yourself with a couple of backups or options so that you can react to the new demands that are bound to develop with corporate productions. Again, visual images that are presented to a client before you get into the venue can help ensure that you are on the same page as the client. Pre-show visualization tools like *WYSIWYG, Martin Show Designer*, and *LD Assistant* are extremely beneficial for this type of work because you can pre-cue and run animated sequences to illustrate your lighting to the client.

Another important issue relates to money. Most corporate producers do not understand the shoestring budgets associated with many theatrical productions and as a result spare little expense in producing as effective a show as possible. The amount of money that marketing teams are used to spending on ad campaigns and the promotion of their products far exceeds what most of us would associate with theatrical budgets and by comparison can be considered very generous. This is especially true when comparing the number of performances that each type of production is associated with. Many corporate events are conducted for a single performance, and even if connected to a series of events, it is rare for these productions to last more than a week at a given location. Even if a show is moved between different regions of the country, like those associated with regional sales meetings, most corporate events are produced in fewer than half a dozen locations. Design fees and production budgets can also be very attractive in comparison to those found in theatrical circles.

Corporate image is a final distinction between these areas and designing for more traditional theatrical venues. Where jeans and t-shirts are an unquestioned wardrobe for concert designers, a designer working in a corporate setting must fit in with the clients that they are serving. While you may dress more conservatively than the typical suit and tie associated with most corporate dress codes, you do need to dress appropriately for the occasion and corporation for which you are working. This often requires a dress shirt and slacks or skirt, dress, or pant suit that gives a professional image to a designer. With some clients, this dress code could still include a coat and tie. Being well-groomed without displaying distracting body piercings or tattoos is also part of this professional

SIDEBAR 16.3 DESIGNER PROFILE

Betsy Adams

Betsy Adams began her lighting career in theatrical design. She is a graduate of Smith College and assisted Tharon Musser for several years in the mid-1980s. She went on to design lighting for a number of regional and NYC productions before moving into corporate lighting where she is a founding partner of the corporate design/production firm of Blue Hill Design. She continues to be active in both areas. She has notable theatrical credits with The Guthrie, Denver Center, Mark Taper Forum, Arena Stage, and Paper Mill and La Jolla Playhouses in addition to many others. Opera companies that she has designed for include the Seattle and San Diego Opera Companies, among others. A few of her more prominent clients in the corporate world include Saturn, Pfizer, IBM, Gillette, Ford, Kodak, Canon, and Pepsi-Cola.

Ms. Adams had gained a number of professional design credits at reputable theatre companies across the United States and was well on her way to a very successful theatrical career when an incident occurred that would change her professional life. A company which had contracted her to light four productions folded on the night before she was to begin techs for the first production. This left her with a large hole in her immediate design schedule and employment. She contacted everyone she knew who might be able to send some design work her way. One friend introduced her to the head of the staging department at a company that produced corporate events, and that led immediately to work drafting for several technical directors in the company. After a short period of time she was given the opportunity to light her first corporate production, which ultimately led her to a whole new area of lighting design. While the percentage of corporate versus theatrical projects varies from month to month, she consistently finds that corporate events typically forms about half of her design work in any given year. She notes that the state of the economy has a bigger impact on corporate projects: when the economy slows down, there are fewer corporate events, and those that exist tend to have smaller budgets.

When asked to discuss several of the significant differences between designing for corporate and more traditional forms of theatre, Ms. Adams singled out venue and schedule. "Most corporate events are produced in hotel ballrooms or convention centers. There is a lot more rigging involved, and lighting positions are dictated by rigging points. There is also a lot of creative truss design that goes hand-in-hand with the lighting design of corporate events. Once you get past the mechanical aspects, the design process is very similar in both worlds. Adjusting to the corporate world has more to do with getting used to the speed at which these events happen and expanding my vocabulary." She also emphasizes preparation and being able to deal with stress effectively. "The time pressure in corporate events is severe; one of the significant differences is that a corporate event has no previews and often only one rehearsal. The pressure of putting together a successful show is magnified many times."

Adams goes on to add several additional tips that are fairly unique to working in corporate theatre. The design needs to work with the theme graphic of an event, which calls for close attention to both color and template choices. "You must know each company's corporate colors. Ford blue, Gillette blue, and IBM blue are all different. If you don't have the ability to change color with color-mixing equipment you must choose your colors with extreme care. It is also useful to know the color of the competition; this way you will not end up using Fuji green in a Canon show unless it is to support a moment where it is used to make a point or to get a laugh." Video is often a part of corporate presentations through I-Mag (Image Magnification). If I-Mag is being used, the lighting must work for the camera as well as for the audience. A single person at a lectern is often projected onto a screen that is 7′ × 15′ or larger. Backlight is important, while downlight is rarely used because the shadows are much more apparent to the camera than to the naked eye. The background also needs to be visible. While a black velour drape behind a speaker may be perfectly acceptable to an audience, on screen, the speaker will appear as a floating head if no light is placed on the dark background.

On the positive side, budgets and fees are larger than they are in the theatre and often give a designer an opportunity to try new equipment long before it becomes affordable in the theatre. It is also important to remain abreast of changes in the profession. "Keep in touch with colleagues, read the trades, go to rental houses or manufacturers' open houses to see demos of new equipment. It is a very small world, and we have all survived in it because we are good at what we do. There is a confidence and camaraderie that grows out of this type of work that I really enjoy." On the downside, schedules are extremely tight, and there is rarely enough time to really polish your work. When asked what she believes to be the most important principle for lighting with the corporate environment Adams states, "Rule #1—Make the client happy. The lighting must support the structure of the event, whether that means a smooth opening sequence, an exciting awards segment, or a flawless speech by the CEO. The design process is all about being well-prepared when you walk into the venue and being able to do your job well and fast under high pressure on site. You have to think on your feet, adapt to changes, stay calm, and keep your sense of humor."

Photo credit: Robert Murphy

image. This image should be presented at every occasion in which you are dealing with the client, which includes not only design meetings but also at all times when you are in the venue dealing with the company and general public. A designer's communication skills should reflect those used in the business world and are yet another important element of working successfully in this niche of lighting design.

E-mails create an important paper trail regarding the progression of corporate events, and messages must be returned promptly. This also holds true for phone messages. A designer should have a cell phone and must subscribe to a good voice messaging system. All messages that you place on your answering service for incoming calls should have a professional quality, and you must get into the habit of checking your services at least once or twice daily—even when on the road or in rehearsals or performances. Messages should be checked even more often if you are expecting or are expected to provide important information to a client. Any e-mails that you create should also reflect a professional image, and the slang and abbreviated language that one might use while e-mailing or text-messaging friends should be avoided.

FILM AND VIDEO BASICS

Film and video lighting can vary significantly from that of live theatrical production. These distinctions may be large or small and since there is an indirect manner in which they produce their images, many professionals like to refer to both film and video as **media.** One of the most significant differences between lighting for film or video and other forms of entertainment lighting is that you are lighting for a camera and not the human eye. This holds true not only in the manner in which a designer must approach a project, but also in the type of equipment that is used in a design. On the other hand, many of the concepts of good lighting that one learns through theatrical applications are also applicable to these areas of lighting design. One of the more significant differences between designing for media and live theatrical events lies in the philosophical difference between the aesthetic and artistic forces that drive traditional forms of entertainment and the often more commercially driven requirements of film and video production. This is not to say that creating good art is not important in these media, but that much of these industries is centered around a more commercial attitude due to the increased costs of these productions, especially television work. A design team needs not only to produce satisfactory results from an artistic perspective but must do so efficiently under time and cost restraints. On the other hand, video and film productions aren't typically produced as frugally as most theatrical productions. However, considerations must still be given to the scheduling and rental rates of a studio or sound stage, the size and **calls** of crews, and any number of special issues like transportation of the crews and equipment for when a project is shot **on location.**

Even though **Directors of Photography (DP)** through **gaffers** or **head lighting technicians** and **Lighting Directors (LD)** through **electricians** design and control light, they deal with it in a rather indirect fashion, having to rely not on what they see on set but how the image finally appears on the screen (film) or master monitor (video). Even though the name of gaffer is still used, these professionals are usually now called head lighting technicians. Both are affiliated with the film industry. While the DP generally has the overall vision for a film's lighting, the head lighting technician is actually responsible for the majority of the lighting decisions and deals with the selection and placement of the equipment along with maintaining the desired intensity levels. Another group of professionals, the **grips,** are in a way comparable to theatrical stagehands and are responsible for setting up and assembling most of the equipment that will be used on a shoot, including scenery and camera equipment (e.g., dollies, cranes, and booms) along with rigging and setting up many of the stands, reflectors and other accessories that are associated with the lighting. The DP is also concerned with camera positions and angles, lens choice, exposure settings, and the overall look of a scene. In reality, they provide the broad vision for the lighting and describe it (direction, intensity, character, mood, ambiance, etc.) to the gaffer, who then translates this information into an image by selecting and placing the equipment properly. This forms a sense of collaboration between these professionals, with one of the most important jobs of a gaffer being simply anticipating the needs of the DP.

Lighting Directors (LD) are traditionally associated with video work and have responsibilities and a role in productions that are quite similar to that of the lighting designer in theatre. They work with the **Video Engineer** or **Video Controller (VC)** to produce good quality images for a program. Together they work to ensure that no under- or over-exposure situations occur and that issues like color balance, exposure requirements, contrast ratios, and image matching are accounted for when shifting between different shots and cameras. One of the most important considerations of their jobs is in being accountable for image resolution and the contrast ranges of the images. The VC's main monitor displays what the final image will look like when broadcast or captured to tape or DVD. It is because of this need to work so closely together that the LD and VC generally sit next to one another in the control room for many studio productions like game shows and sitcoms, music videos, or live events. This is especially true when multiple cameras are used. The LD is quite involved with the technical elements of lighting a video project—choosing luminaires, coloring, making determinations of intensity levels, contrast ratios and ranges, etc.

Light and the Camera

Film and video cameras are pretty similar in regard to the principles in which they function. Both make use of lenses and apertures to focus and control the light and images that they produce. Film cameras focus an image onto a photosensitive substance **(film)** made up of chemical emulsions, or layers, that are applied to the surface of a plastic material (celluloid in the past). The emulsions respond to different wavelengths (red, blue, and green) as the film is exposed to light. Once developed or processed, the film forms a record of the associated images. A video camera works in much the same way with the exception that the film is replaced by photoelectric sensors that convert the light into a series of corresponding electrical signals. While films use emulsions for recording the various wavelengths, a video camera captures three separate video signals—once again, each associated with a different primary color of light. The overall exposure recorded by a camera is a result of three different factors: the sensitivity of the film or video sensors, length of time that an image is exposed, and the amount of light allowed to enter the camera at any given time.

Film and video lighting come under a number of unique influences as a result of using cameras. Cameras see light in a different way than the human eye, and a lighting designer must be aware of several properties that may change between the lighting that is observed in a studio or location setup and how it actually appears in the final image. To make matters more difficult, many of these changes can only be detected through an experienced eye or through the aid of special equipment like light meters. Chapter 22 provides a detailed discussion of several factors that can have this kind of an impact on a film or video image. Several of these include color temperature, color rendering, speed of exposure, and aperture or f-stop considerations. All of these provide specific controls in how light is captured by a camera. Two of the most important considerations relate to producing lighting levels that fall within the sensitivity ranges of a film or camera. The intensities must be strong enough to actually record the event (the **threshold exposure**) while not being so strong as to overexpose the image. The second quality relates to producing appropriate **contrast ratios** in an image. Contrast ratios simply relate to the ratio between the brightest and darkest parts of the image. Cameras and films are not as sensitive as the human eye and cannot respond to contrast ranges or ratios that are too wide. On the other hand, a camera may also pick up variations in intensity that we cannot perceive with our human eyes. Trying to expose a camera or film to too great a contrast ratio results in parts of the image either going into extreme darkness or becoming so bright that they are overexposed and appear burned out.

Contrast ratios can also be described in terms of the relationship between the intensity of the **key light** and that of the base or **fill light** for a given scene. This tie to key and fill is quite popular in video production, and a lighting director often refers to **lighting ratios** when making comparisons between the intensities of the key and fill light. If the key light for a scene is measured to be 100 footcandles and the fill is metered at 50 footcandles the contrast ratio will be 100:50 and therefore 2:1, or a one-stop difference between the light levels. This represents a fairly flat or even lighting ratio. A more dramatic contrast ratio would include a two-stop or 4:1 ratio. Sometimes professionals working in video will speak of high key and low key lighting. **High key** relates to images in which there is little difference between the intensity levels of the key and fill light—those with a small lighting ratio (1:1, 2:1, or 3:1). **Low key** is more dramatic and reflects higher contrast ratios and a greater difference between the two lighting levels (5:1, 8:1, 10:1, etc.). Lighting ratios approaching 9:1 or greater tend to make the difference so drastic that the fill lit areas may appear to be in complete darkness. A bright sunlit day can often have contrast ratios along this order. The famous film noir movies of the 1940s and 50s are great examples of low key lighting. At the other extreme are the 2:1 lighting ratios that are fairly common for many television talk and news programs. Contrast ratios may be great or small, but the larger the degree of contrast, the more dramatic the image and the greater the potential for encountering problems in your overall exposure settings.

Key and Fill Light

The actual system of key/fill lighting had its beginnings in the film and television industries but is now often utilized as a design formula throughout the entire lighting industry. This approach has already been introduced through the discussion of theatrical lighting formulas in Chapter 11. In its initial inception, **key light** was associated with the primary or most intense light for a scene and was usually equated with the scene's motivating light source. In the early days of video and film lighting, cameras and film had very low light sensitivities and if the intensity levels fell too low, areas of the image would appear dark and unlit. Luminaires had to be capable of creating a high enough threshold of illumination simply for objects to be seen by the camera or film. Just like on a stage where there is little or no ambient light, cameras also have a problem seeing into shadow areas that are not lit by the key light. More importantly, since cameras have a more limited range in contrast ratios, they frequently have an even larger problem in recording scenes where there is a significant difference between the darkness of the shadow areas and the areas that are illuminated by the key light. As a means of compensating for this, additional luminaires (**fill lights**) are added to fill in or soften the effect of these shadows. This additional lighting provides a base level of illumination that prevents portions of the subject from going completely dark when seen through a camera. In the early days of video lighting some referred to fill light as **base level lighting** or **base light.** If not careful though, this can also produce low contrast lighting that will ultimately create a flat uninspired image.

Once a relationship has been established between the distribution angles of the key and fill light, the pattern is re-created through a series of adjoining lighting areas just as is typically done in area lighting for the stage. However, this repetition, unlike theatrical area lighting, is often limited to a much smaller portion of a studio (e.g., the anchor desk for a news program) and it is rare that an entire studio will be lit in this fashion. These systems are also based on the camera placement and angles that will be used during a filming or taping sequence. Film and video designers also need to be more conscious of the contrast ratios that exist between the key and fill light of a scene. Today, most film and video lighting makes some use of key/fill principles and light the subject from at least two different directions. Each pair of luminaires creates a key/fill relationship that provides an indication of light coming from a given direction with enough shadow illumination to sustain visibility throughout a scene. Even the McCandless Method becomes a specific variation of a key/fill application.

Control Elements

Historically, dimmers have not been used that heavily in film or video lighting due to the combined effects of **amber shift** on a lamp's color temperature and the fact that these media are especially sensitive to color temperature changes. Also, due to the lack of exposure sensitivity in older cameras, much of the lighting for film and video of the past was concerned with simply providing a base level of illumination that could be recorded by the cameras. Rather than using dimmers, many luminaires used in film and video lighting make use of "**hot**" or **continuous light sources** that are simply plugged into a power source. These luminaires may also be equipped with multiple lamps or lamps with several filaments that can be turned on or off in different combinations to control how much light that a luminaire produces. The number of luminaires that use ballasts and arc sources in film and video lighting have also contributed to the lack of dimmers being used in these industries. A head lighting technician may also use one of several alternate methods to modify the intensity of a luminaire. **Scrims, silks** and **diffusers,** and **mechanical dimmers** make up several of these solutions. Film is especially sensitive to color temperature variations as a result of dimming and it is often desirable to simply not use dimmers at all in these applications. Video setups, on the other hand (especially in studio production), often use dimmers. Initially they were used primarily for controlling ganged light sources rather than for dimming, but they are now often used to adjust contrast ratios and to balance or boost/drop intensity levels and draw focus to particular subjects that are found throughout a scene. **Scrims** are made of a screen mesh (usually metal) of different densities and are slipped into the front of a luminaire in a frame where the gel would be located. The resultant light that passes through the scrim will have its intensity dropped by a given proportion without having an effect on the lamp's color temperature. The higher the density of the scrim, the more light it will absorb and the greater reduction it will have in a unit's light output. These scrims are quite similar to the dimming screens that are discussed in museum and exhibit lighting. Scrims are not specified so much by their density as by the number of f-stops in which they reduce the light. A single scrim reduces the light by about half an f-stop while a double reduces the light by a full stop. A color system has been created that allows scrims to be quickly identified by the color of their associated frame (green for a single and red for a double). Scrims are often grouped into a kit or pouch containing a basic selection of different density scrims that fit a given luminaire and are stored through hanging the entire kit on or near the unit. **Neutral Density Filters (ND** or **NDF)** are used in the same way that scrims are used. These are special filter media that are similar to gel in that the light's transmission is dropped without affecting the color temperature or overall spectral composition of the light. Each of the gel manufacturers makes a range of neutral density filters. Indirect light may also be introduced to a scene by reflecting light off panels or fabrics like silks and into a scene (Figure 16.4).

Filters aren't used to the same degree in television or film lighting as they are in theatrical lighting. In fact, a significant amount of shooting is done with little or no color except for the use of color correction filters. While there are occasions when the use of more saturated colored filters are appropriate (linking the light to a specific motivational light source or for theatrical effects), they are usually the exception rather than the norm. Perhaps the most important aspect of working with filters in lighting for film and video relates to a series of specialty filters known as **color correction** or **conversion filters.** The most common use for these filters is in correcting the color temperature of a luminaire or light source so that it matches all the other light sources in a setup or matching the source's light with the

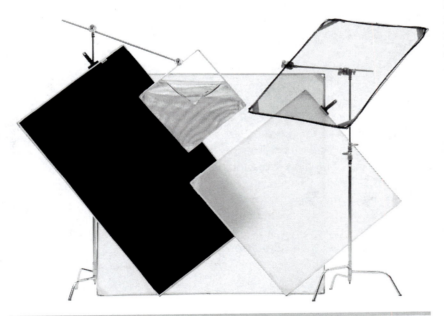

FIGURE 16.4 **Diffusion and Reflector Equipment** Chimera panel kit (a selection of frames and C-stands as well as diffusion and reflective cloths and a carrying case). *Photo credit:* Chimera Lighting

particular needs of a camera or film stock that is being used. Unmatched color temperatures result in the color balance of a film or video being distorted and shifts in color within the final images. A gaffer or LD will typically match the color temperatures of the different luminaires throughout a setup by making a selection in correction filters that match or color-correct all the sources to the same color temperature. A common example of this might include shooting an interior daytime scene where the exterior light coming through a window is quite different from that of the room's interior. In this case, the interior lights and most likely all the production luminaires will be lit to an interior color temperature based on tungsten-halogen sources (approximately 3,200° K), while the daylight would have a color temperature more on the order of 5,600° K or higher. This will cause exposure problems between the differences in color temperature of these two sources. The typical solution for this is to simply place a specialty filter over the window surfaces to correct the daylight color temperature to that of the interior lighting. Specifically, this would call for a **CTO (color temperature orange) filter.** Likewise, when interior sources or luminaires having low color temperatures need to be raised to match a high color temperature source a **CTB (color temperature blue) filter** can be used to correct the color temperature of the light. You will also hear these called correct-to-orange and correct-to-blue. In addition to the standard sheets, color correction filters also come in sizes as large as 4 by 8 feet and in rolls. This allows the filters to be fit to large surfaces like windows and glass doors. A number of different CTO and CTB filters are available that allow sources of different color temperatures to be corrected to a standard color temperature like tungsten or daylight. These additional filters are indicated by values such as 1/4 CTO, 1/8 CTB, or 1/2 CTB, etc.

Key Elements in Film/Video Illumination

As discussed earlier, video and film cameras have a different way of "seeing" and the resultant image produced by a camera can be significantly different from what is seen by the native eye on a set or in the studio. Another set of differences relates to the proximity of the lighting and camera equipment for shooting film or video setups. Unlike theatrical situations where audiences have full view of the entire stage, a video or film shoot is staged only to the scale that encompasses the viewpoint of the camera angles that will be used for a scene. If a setup only consists of close-ups, then the lighting will be placed close to the talent and just out of view of the cameras. Due to this, the manner of providing general illumination can vary significantly in film or video shoots, being dependent on the type of action, distance to talent, and camera angles that a scene will require. Also, if camera angles change, then the lighting needs to appear as though it is consistent from angle to angle. Sources that once appeared to be in front of the talent must appear as if they have remained in the original location and that only the camera has changed position.

In addition to key and fill light we also speak of hard and soft light in film or video lighting. This is sometimes called **coherence. Hard light** is often associated with the key light for a scene and is quite directional. It is usually responsible for producing the strong highlights and sharp, well-defined shadows in a scene. **Soft light** is associated with diffuse illumination and can be characterized by not having any prominent shadows. It is often used as a fill light to soften shadows that may have been created by the key light and frequently provides a base level of illumination for the shadow areas of a subject. Hard light is frequently created by compact light sources that produce a very concentrated directional beam while soft light is produced by luminaires that create a soft, widely-distributed pattern of light. Soft light, because of its relatively large source, also tends to wrap around a subject and fill in shadows that would be associated with the surface texture of the subject—something that is a real benefit when a performer's skin might have wrinkles or other imperfections. Many video and film lighting professionals prefer to shoot with soft light unless there is a specific need for the more dramatic shadows of a hard lit scene. Soft light also allows a camera to be opened up a bit more, which gives more control over the **depth-of-field** of an image. Whether a light source is perceived as a hard

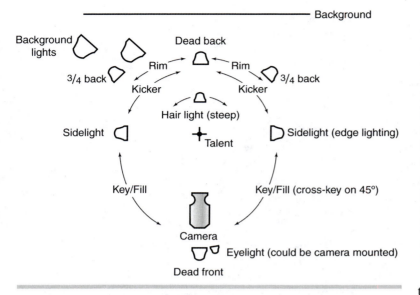

FIGURE 16.5   Directional Distribution for a Camera

or soft source generally comes down to a combination of two variables. Most important is the relative size of the light source in comparison to the size of the subject (soft sources are large). Also significant is the distance between the source and the subject. In reality, even though we may refer to hard or soft light luminaires, a luminaire could actually become either one depending on the specific combination of how large the light source is and how far away from the subject that it is placed. The key to producing soft light is to create diffuse light from a relatively large light source, which creates parallel rays that wrap around the surfaces of a subject. In fact, a soft light could in effect become a hard light if the source is placed far enough away from the subject where the rays would no longer appear parallel.

Distribution in video and film lighting follows the same principles as found in other areas of the lighting industry with two minor adjustments. First, the camera is not always as sensitive to the directionality of the light as our eyes may be, and second, lighting professionals have given unique names to a number of specific lighting angles that are used in film and video lighting (see Figure 16.5). These angles are based on the camera's location and are referenced from the camera being placed directly in front of the subject or **talent**. Lighting with a single directional source is also quite rare in video or film setups because cameras have traditionally struggled with the extreme contrast created between those areas of the subject that are lit brightly and those that fall into shadow. As additional luminaires are introduced to a scene, the lighting director must become concerned with the contrast or lighting ratios that exist on each of the illuminated surfaces that are revealed by the lighting instruments. Typical distribution angles for video and film production include **dead front** and **dead back, sidelight, cross key** positions on the front diagonals, **3/4 back** on the back diagonals, and **offset angles** that fall just off the dead front/back positions. A sidelight may also be aimed so that it grazes the surface of a subject and produces extended shadows that emphasize the texture of a subject's surface **(edge lighting)**. **Backlight** forms an important element of camera lighting because of the need to separate subjects from the background and usually comes from directly behind the subject. Other important angles that produce specific effects include **face** or **eyelight** that is relatively flat light coming from about the same angle as the camera (often camera mounted), which enhances the performer's face and brings life or sparkle to their eyes. **Hair light** is used to add highlights to the talent's hair (it is a variation of steep backlight). The **kicker** and **rim light** are more confusing because they can mean different things depending on who you talk to. Most professionals agree that they are both variations of backlight that are shifted to the side to provide more modeling than a straight backlight. The **kicker** is a backlight that is offset to one side but can come from any direction above or below the subject (it is often used to simulate motivated sources and to produce dramatic effects). Kickers are often called 3/4 backlights because their positions are shifted slightly to the side and around more of the subject. They also tend to wrap around the face of a subject, while **rim lights** have a higher elevation that edges (rims) the subject rather than wraps around it. Rim lights are often used to help separate a subject from the background. **Background lights** don't light the subject at all but instead wash the background behind it and are used for maintaining a proper balance and establishing contrast between the subject and the background. An additional form of lighting that may or may not focus on a subject is **effect lighting,** which is used to produce effects such as the projections of patterns like windows or doors, accents for fire light or moonlight, or any other lighting effect.

SIDEBAR 16.4   D E S I G N E R   P R O F I L E

William L. Klages

William "Bill" Klages is one of television lighting's pioneers. Primarily associated with lighting special events that are televised to millions of live viewers, he has lit a variety of stars (Frank Sinatra, Barbara Streisand, Dorothy Hamill, John Denver, Bette Midler, Patti LaBelle, Mikhail Baryshnikov, and Barry Manilow to only mention a few) as well as numerous televised programs throughout the more than 50 years of experience that he brings to his design projects. His designs have won him seven Emmy Awards and approximately 30 other awards and nominations over the years, including the USITT Distinguished Lighting Designer Award. Several significant television programs that he has lighted include *The Kraft Music Hall, The Perry Como Show, Entertainment Tonight* and *Fairie Tale Theater*. Just a few of the special events that he has designed over the years include: The Closing Ceremonies of the L.A. Olympic Games; The Atlanta Olympic Games; The Kennedy Center Honors broadcasts; Emmy, Grammy, Tony, and Country Music Awards; The Statue of Liberty Celebration; and several national political conventions like the 1992, 2000, 2004, and 2008 Republican Conventions. In recent years he has created a television lighting consultancy through forming the New Klages, Inc. where just a few of his impressive projects include the Mormon Church's Assembly Hall in Salt Lake City (a 21,000 seat worship center with television production services), Joel Osteen's 16,000 non-denominational Lakewood mega-church in Houston (where both broadcast and in-house video form important elements of the services), and a number of broadcast studios in the top-40 market.

In part, Klages's entry into television lighting can be attributed to simply being at the right place at a time when the industry was in its beginnings. He never had any formal training in lighting because people coming to work in the broadcast industry at that time came from electrical engineering backgrounds. "Lighting Director" was the term that was first used for the individual that is now better described today as a "Lighting Designer." It took many years to erase this incorrect designation. Bill recounts his entrance into television through a series of opportunities that emerged early in his career. "My career in television started very early (1948 to be specific). I was hired by NBC in New York as a result of having an Electrical Engineering degree, a requisite at the time. I was heavily involved in the technical aspects of television broadcast, which was then in its infancy." After a year or so, he moved to the operating group as a Video Control Engineer, where he developed an interest in lighting and the manner in which visual quality was obtained in this (then) mysterious new medium. "As a result of this interest, and a set of unusual circumstances that could have only transpired at the time, I became a Lighting Director." His first show was the largest-budget live drama series that NBC had presented to date and was called *Playwrights 56*. The year was 1955. "My only training for the job was from observing and analyzing from the video control

position how the Lighting Directors practiced their craft at that time and how they obtained images that I either liked or didn't like. It was with the confidence of youth and my inexperience that I believed that I knew how it should be done and could prove it. Thankfully, there were disappointments and reverses along the way that humbled and matured this view."

Klages believes that the abilities that define a person as a lighting designer are not confined to one lighting discipline. For example, "I have been able to work in many areas: feature films, facility design, traditional theatre, architectural lighting as well as my primary field, television production. All that the designer must do is discover what unique technical requirements or techniques make the unknown discipline different from his own familiar and more comfortable discipline. This is illustrated when a theatrical lighting designer is asked to adapt and translate his efforts to a video production. If the designer exercises his imagination and observations, he will immediately be aware that the two audiences require rather different lighting methods and that his "bag of tricks" may fail in a very disappointing way when used for the television medium. He will also have to make the difficult decision about which discipline will take precedence." On the other hand, "The great joy is seeing an end result that is even better than what you had in your mind. The worst is when the end result does not meet your expectations." We are bombarded with trade publications and press releases that help us remain abreast of industry developments in all the lighting disciplines. However, he also suggests "swallowing your pride and watching other talented designers' efforts as well."

"Lighting for a camera is much more complicated as a result of all the numerous changes of state that might be present (optical, electrical, and chemical, as well as heavy manipulation of the electrical signals before the final display of a visual image). Characteristic elements of the lighting system will demand techniques that cannot be as simplified as say, using a warm/cool approach (although it has been tried). Predicting the end result may be difficult and must be learned, but is not impossible if this skill is approached open-mindedly." If Bill had to offer a cardinal rule, it would relate to creating proper exposure and the balance of values ("brightnesses") that are found between all of the elements in each camera view. When Klages got his break, there were no established methods. "Everyone was learning, known rules were few, and those that we assumed to be true were not necessarily true. Every day could bring not only a new revelation but also a different job experience. The personal associations made at this time would continue and expand like an enormous family tree throughout my entire career." He recalls that even in the early days he was obsessed with the idea of how to obtain images on video that duplicated what he saw in feature films. "It has taken more than 50 years for the video system to finally get to a point where this is actually possible. The end result of having video acquisition replace film is a very practical reality of today."
Photo credit: Bill Klages

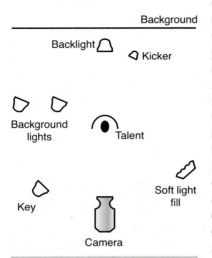

FIGURE 16.6 Three-Point Lighting (Video Variation) This formula lighting approach is actually a misnomer because the three basic angles (key, fill, and backlight) are frequently supplemented with additional units like background lights and kickers.

THREE-POINT LIGHTING

One common method of creating general illumination for a video or film shoot involves **three-point lighting.** Though the basic system may be modified, the essence of the three-point system lies in providing several luminaires that are placed around the subject. This is a simple formula approach that is treated in much the same manner as the McCandless Method in theatrical productions. In fact, critics of the system believe that it has produced many of the same negative influences in the film and video industry as the McCandless system brought to the theatrical community—namely, that it has led to uninspired lighting when such an approach hasn't been necessary, especially with the sensitivity of today's cameras and films. Figure 16.6 illustrates a typical three-point lighting setup. The basis of the system lies in providing a key light that is from the front and offset to one side of the subject and camera, with a second light (the fill light) placed on the opposite front side of the subject and a third unit used as a backlight placed directly behind the subject (often in line with the camera). The backlight is used to separate the subject from the background while a fourth light is often added to light the background. The method is quite adequate for producing basic illumination but at the same time can come off as uninspired and mechanical. With today's cameras and films a LD or head lighting technician can create their own variations of a three-point system that provides a unique solution to a particular setup. In fact, there are other popular lighting formulas based on variations of this system that use four or more lamps per area. In one system the units are oriented approximately 45° from one another and provide a variation of key/fill light for virtually any angle in which a camera might be placed. Some variation of three-point lighting is often used to light the talent or performers that are found on a set. More importantly, decisions regarding the key light placement should be based more on the motivational lighting elements of a scene than on a formula approach that is now somewhat dated. This newer technique of linking the lighting to motivational sources and a more dramatic quality of lighting is called **following source** and is a direct result of the improved contrast ratios that have come to camera designs since the 1980s. Since then, the industry has steadily been shifting towards low key lighting as this ability to sense larger ranges of intensity and contrast ratios have improved. It has also brought more effective use of shadowing and stronger dramatic qualities to the lighting of today's film and video productions. However, regardless of how inexperienced one is, the three-point-system still forms a place to start from and will produce satisfactory results in most situations.

FOR FURTHER READING

Illuminating Engineering Society of North America, *An Introduction to Light and Lighting (ED 50)* (New York: Illuminating Engineering Society of North America, 1991).

Illuminating Engineering Society of North America, *IESNA Lighting Education 100 (Fundamental Level)* (New York: Illuminating Engineering Society of North America, 1993).

Illuminating Engineering Society of North America, *IESNA Lighting Education 150 (Intermediate Level)* (New York: Illuminating Engineering Society of North America, 1993).

Illuminating Engineering Society of North America. *IESNA Lighting Handbook,* ed. Mark Rae, 9th ed. (New York, NY: Illuminating Engineering Society of North America, 2000).

Illuminating Engineering Society of North America. *IESNA Lighting Ready Reference,* 4th ed. (New York: Illuminating Engineering Society of North America, 2003).

More detailed references relating to each of the specific lighting applications are found at the conclusion of each of the online chapters (Chapters 19–27) that have been written on the specialty areas.

17 Additional Lighting Applications

This chapter introduces specialties that employ lighting professionals outside of the entertainment lighting industry, although elements of entertainment design may still be present in some of these applications (e.g., themed design). Many of the specialties have been around for less than 50 years and have typically been designed by individuals whose backgrounds are quite different from that of entertainment lighting designers. This is due to these designs often being based on more of an engineering perspective than theatrical design. This also requires that the equipment in these areas and the training of those working in them be more specialized than what most theatrical designers are familiar with. In fact, many of the lighting professionals who work in these areas are trained as **illuminating engineers** who approach lighting designs from a more quantitative perspective than theatrical lighting designers would use. Despite this, these specialties use the same controllable qualities and functions of light as theatrical lighting—it's just that they are used in somewhat different ways from how we might use them in entertainment applications. The design practices of these specialties and theatrical lighting have also moved much closer together during recent times, and as a result, more theatrically trained lighting designers are moving into these other disciplines. Topics like retail and museum lighting, architectural and landscape lighting, themed design, and even virtual lighting form several of the specialties that are examined in this chapter.

Like Chapter 16, this chapter provides an introduction to some of the more unique elements of working in these lighting applications. Once again, I also present interviews of lighting designers with established reputations in these specialties as well as a series of online chapters with more detailed information on each of the specialty areas. For more specific information on a given discipline, the best place to begin, beyond the online chapters, is with an examination of the *IESNA Lighting Handbook* and the particular IESNA (Illuminating Engineering Society of North America) guidebooks or recommended practices for a particular type of project. The specific contents of the online chapters are listed in the table of contents while their introductions are represented by the headings of this chapter (Display/Retail and Exhibit/Museum Lighting—Chapter 23, Architectural Lighting—Chapter 24, Landscape Lighting—Chapter 25, Themed Design—Chapter 26, and Virtual Lighting—Chapter 27). The online chapters also provide more specific references for each of the lighting specialties.

RETAIL AND MUSEUM LIGHTING

Retail and museum lighting are unique because they contain elements based on both entertainment and architectural lighting, yet the subject (a product, artwork, or artifact) cannot be displayed in a way that is too theatrical or distorts its appearance. There are a number of architectural lighting principles found in display (or retail) and exhibit (or museum) lighting. Despite this, display and exhibit lighting can still form very creative areas in which a lighting designer might find work. Traditionally, the lighting in these disciplines fell to illuminating or electrical engineers. However, in recent years these industries have moved toward more creative lighting treatments that emphasize the thematic and aesthetic aspects of displaying an object rather than simply illuminating it. Some notable comparisons between retail or museum lighting and entertainment lighting come from the fact that the approach to lighting these areas is usually more subtle than that of entertainment lighting. Colors must be chosen more carefully, movement cannot distract or distort a subject, and intensities and other lighting elements must be manipulated to reveal the subject in the best way possible. Throw distances are also small compared to those found in entertainment and architectural applications. The smaller distances, sometimes smaller than 1 foot, result in these luminaires typically having lower wattages and larger beamspreads than those used in other applications. Care must also be taken not to harm the subject through exposure to excessive heat or other forms of electromagnetic radiation that can come from the light sources.

Lighting Layers

Both retail and museum lighting are based on the principles of **layering.** This relates to creating several different lighting systems that provide a variety of functions within a given space. In many ways, these systems aren't that much different from those developed in entertainment lighting—in fact, many of the same principles apply here too. The heart of the lighting for most stores and museums lies in the development of two different lighting systems. These include the **primary** or **general circulation** and **secondary** or **accent lighting systems.** The primary system may also be called the **ambient lighting system.** The primary lighting aids customers in moving around in a store or museum and creates basic visibility throughout a space while the secondary systems are used to accent or draw focus to displays or exhibits. In nearly all situations, several different lighting layers must be created due to the various visual tasks that are performed in these environments. For example, even though a jewelry store best displays its merchandise with cool-colored light (light that enhances gems and silver), this particular light is unflattering to skin tones, and a designer should also provide some form of incandescent lighting where potential customers can evaluate the jewelry as they wear it. While the secondary systems are primarily associated with accent lighting, other types of lighting can be broken down into more specific functions. When evaluating the lighting for architectural and display or exhibit applications we worry not only about providing a given quantity of light on flat surfaces like table tops **(lighting the horizontal plane),** we are also concerned about the quantity of light hitting vertical surfaces like walls and shelving or display units **(lighting the vertical plane).** Both are measured by the amount of light that strikes a surface (footcandles). In many stores, lighting the vertical plane may be more important than lighting the horizontal plane because most products are arranged along vertical shelves and displays. Also, many luminaires used in retail and museum lighting are of a decorative nature, which includes thousands of designs for bringing a unique character to an environment.

While dimmers are used in accent lighting, it is usually preferable to adjust lighting intensities through selecting lamps of different wattages rather than through using dimmers. The main reason for this lies in avoiding **red** or **amber shift** as lamps are dimmed. On the other hand, when a store or museum uses dimming, it is common for those dimmers operating at the highest levels to seldom run over 90%, resulting in a color shift that creates an appropriate ambiance for an environment. This also saves energy and increases lamp life. Wire mesh screens **(dimming screens** or **reducing screens)** of various densities may also be placed over the front of a fixture to reduce the light output of a given lamp. This has the benefit of lowering the intensity while having no effect on the color temperature of the light. These work in essentially the same way that **scrims** are used in the film and video industry. Figure 17.1 provides several examples of dimming screens. Accent lighting, through intensity control, is a primary element of display and exhibit lighting because these systems direct customers and visitors to merchandise and exhibits where subjects can be examined more closely.

Essentials of Retail and Museum/Gallery Lighting

Since both retail and museum and gallery lighting are variations of architectural lighting at least some of, if not all, the elements that make up a design are subject to various code guidelines and enforcement. Areas that need to be specified by a lighting designer or electrical engineer with training in these specialties include elements like **general circulation systems** (area or ambient lighting), **specialty areas** and **accent systems** for proper illuminance levels, **electrical distribution,** and **power densities.** You will find further details regarding these and other architectural lighting practices in Chapter 24 online. Museums tend to have fairly permanent displays and are more often designed by lighting specialists, while retail installations typically have the overall lighting systems designed by specialists, with the individual displays lit by the sales staff. In many cases, the professionals who do the general display or merchandising work for a store are trained in basic retail lighting and often light their own displays. Occasionally a store will have lighting specialists who light the majority of their displays and who may even travel regionally to light displays in similar stores as part of a retail chain. However, the day-to-day modification of a design that accommodates the routine changes of exhibits and displays often falls to members of a retail or museum staff who produce mixed results because they have not received sufficient training in lighting. Galleries also tend to use their own staff to work with the curators and artists for lighting specific shows, while permanent exhibits or collections are often designed by lighting specialists. A cardinal rule in retail lighting is in illuminating a product or display in a way that best enhances its features. This practice should relate to an object's color rendition, texture, and detailing. The two most important issues relating to lighting a retail environment are drawing attention to the products and revealing them in the best way possible.

Museum and gallery environments are lit in much the same way as retail establishments. On the other hand, several principles of lighting these areas are quite different from those of retail lighting. Perhaps the most important difference relates to protecting the artifacts and artwork from being lit with too much exposure to radiant energy (visible light, ultraviolet radiation, and heat). This is considered critical when lighting one-of-a-kind artwork, artifacts, and other rare or historic objects. Another significant difference is in the attention that is placed on determining the circulation patterns or visitor flow in museums and gallery settings. Rather than crowded sales floors, a series of individual galleries, halls, or exhibit chambers are set up throughout a museum or gallery that are each lit appropriately. In fact, the illumination of the general lighting layers are kept much lower in museum and gallery designs—some designers even argue that an ambient layer isn't even necessary in some museum applications. Also, unlike retail environments that use more horizontal displays, the majority of museum and gallery exhibits consist of vertical displays that are hung along walls or in cabinets. Finally, mood and ambience play a large role in museum layouts, which also tend to be lighted in more dramatic styles than galleries or retail establishments (see Figure 17.2). Galleries tend to approach lighting from a neutral perspective, creating an environment that reveals the artwork in a natural manner that lets the work speak for itself. Museums tend to have different

FIGURE 17.1   Dimming Screens *Photo credit:* Philips/Lightolier Lighting

FIGURE 17.2   Dinosaur Museum Exhibit (Carnegie Museum of Natural History) *Photo credit:* Christopher Popwich/C&C Lighting, LLC

Cindy Limauro

Cindy Limauro designs lighting for theatre, opera, dance, and architecture. In addition to designing professionally, she leads the lighting program at Carnegie Mellon University and holds a visiting professorship with the Higher Institute of Architectural Sciences, Henry van de Velde, in Antwerp (Belgium). She is a member of United Scenic Artists (USA) and the International Association of Lighting Designers (IALD), and was named a Fellow of the Institute by USITT. Several notable companies that she has designed for include The Pittsburgh Opera, Opera Columbus, Burt Reynolds Theatre, The Pittsburgh Public Theatre, the Cincinnati and Pittsburgh Ballets, and the Barter Theatre in Virginia. Her international credits include work with Teatro Vascello in Rome and a series of architectural installations throughout Prague coordinated with a group of international lighting design students. Her movement into architectural lighting has produced a business partnership with her husband, Christopher Popowich (also a lighting designer), that has produced such creations as the lighting of the *Hall of Dinosaurs* exhibit at the Carnegie Museum of Natural History.

Cindy's formal training includes a BA in theatre from the University of Michigan and an MFA in lighting design from Florida State University. She became interested in theatrical lighting when Arthur Miller visited her undergraduate playwriting class (she originally majored in creative writing). "I also found an emotional connection to storytelling in the lighting course that I took and became a double major in English and Theatre. I was so mesmerized by the power of lighting and how it impacted an audience's experience that I chose to become a lighting designer after graduation." Following graduation, she worked a couple of years and then went to graduate school, where she was introduced to the worlds of dance and opera. "I developed a love for all three areas and vowed that my career would follow this passion." After graduate school she primarily lit theatre and dance. Her first opportunity in lighting opera came from an artistic director who saw her dance work. Years later, her introduction to architectural lighting came from architects who saw her theatre work and wanted a more dramatic approach to lighting one of their projects. She estimates her current design work to be about 60% theatre, opera, and dance and 40% architectural lighting.

While Limauro continues to both work and teach in a number of areas of lighting, she has found that her skills were readily transferred from one discipline to another. Even with the larger shift into architectural lighting she relates that, "It was a natural transition going from theatre to architecture. The design process is very similar. I did take an IES workshop on architectural lighting but it mostly dealt with technical issues like lighting calculations and daylighting. My theatrical training has served me well in crossing over." In discussing the similarities and differences between lighting for theatre and architectural projects she feels that the processes aren't that different from one another. "As a designer I ask the same questions. What kind of mood am I trying to create? Where is the focus? How do I create contrast and visual interest? In the theatre, I'm trying to reinforce the director's vision . . . in architecture, it's the architect's vision. Space is about people whether it is characters in a play or people in the real world. How is the space being used? Both disciplines also require collaboration and everyone working towards a common goal. The only real difference is that theatre lighting is temporary, while architectural lighting is permanent, and you have to be aware of additional issues like codes. While the lighting principles are the same, there are different fixtures and lamps in architectural lighting, but this, again, is something that a lighting designer can easily adapt to." Several other unique considerations of architectural and display lighting relate to the specific conditions that you must work within. "Every city is different in regard to code issues. Also, if you are lighting a historic landmark there will usually be very strict rules about what you can and cannot do. Architectural lighting designers must also strive for energy efficient designs and need to think about issues like sustainability."

What Cindy likes most about working in the theatre is that it is a live event with an audience. "You never know how they are going to respond or if a show will run flawlessly." What she likes most about working in architecture is the permanence of the work. In all areas, she loves the collaboration with different people. What she dislikes most are the time and budget constraints facing today's arts. "While lighting technology is getting more and more sophisticated, the amount of time necessary to create a polished design is becoming less and less in the theatre. As a designer, you often have to work with speed and efficiency rather than enjoying a process of experimentation." What she likes least about working in architecture is how slow the process can be. "Projects require a much longer design period, and budgets can be cut at any time in the process."

Limauro remains current by attending both LDI (Lighting Design International) and Lightfair (the architectural and display lighting professionals' equivalent to USITT) trade shows or conferences and reading many of the lighting industry trade journals. In offering a bit of advice she suggests, "Whether working in theatre or architecture, always start from a black void. Add the first light and ask is this enough? If not . . . what do I need to add next? Too often people overlight." She also has a strong interest in bringing students from different cultures together and wants them to be involved in the communities where they live. These ambitions have been realized through projects like the Antwerp experience where students researched and created a design presentation for a museum and neighborhood for an architectural lighting installation. They did full-scale mock-ups and made a presentation to the city and museum staff who were impressed enough that the design was actually installed that summer. She is currently working with students to create a Master Plan of Light for the Carnegie Mellon campus and collaborating with the Pittsburgh Cultural Trust on branding the downtown area with light.

Photo credit: Christopher Popowich

lighting levels from one exhibit space to another, and a lighting designer must work to ensure that proper **transition zones** are created between spaces with large variations in their lighting levels.

Two specialty areas of retail lighting are unique because they combine elements of theatrical production and retail design. These are *retail shows* and *themed stores*. In retail shows, actual performances or some variation of a production are created around a product, product line, or corporate/sales event. *Fashion shows, trade shows,* **product unveilings,** and **corporate sales meetings** are examples of these events. These projects usually take place outside of the retail environment and are frequently presented in ballrooms and conference or convention centers. They are known for their spectacle and sizable budgets and form another area of design known as corporate theatre/productions or industrials, which were introduced previously in Chapter 16. Themed stores are another specialty area of retail design where customers are immersed in a designed environment. Building decor, layout, displays, music and sounds, and even costumed sales clerks can contribute to this immersive experience. Several retailers that make use of heavily themed stores include the Disney Store, Build-a-Bear Workshop, and LEGO stores. Restaurants often make use of themed environments as well. Themed design is a specialty area that will be discussed in more detail later in this chapter.

ARCHITECTURAL LIGHTING

Architectural lighting relates to lighting buildings and structures. We often break this into several different, more specialized, areas of lighting design. The two most common specialties are **interior** and **exterior lighting.** Although these make up the most obvious specializations, other specialties like **landscape lighting** and **street** or **roadway lighting** have also emerged as specialties in this part of the lighting industry. Many architectural lighting designers work in several of these or even narrower specialties like **residential, hospitality** (hotel and restaurant), **health care, office,** and **house of worship** (church) design. **Themed lighting** goes further and brings a unique blend of architectural and entertainment design into a specialty that some call **architainment.** We also look at architectural lighting as a fairly permanent solution to an illumination problem that can be expanded to include the lighting of public monuments and statuaries, roadways and parking lots, and bridges as well as buildings.

Most lighting designers approach the lighting of buildings from one of two perspectives. The first approaches a design from a quantitative perspective in which minimal visual standards are determined based on the visual **task** (type of activity or work being done) and the specific needs of an environment. From this information, a design is developed through creating a lighting system that delivers the required level of illumination to the environment in which the task is to be completed. The second method is based more on aesthetics and is less concerned with specific illumination levels. In reality, every project draws on a combination of both approaches. The first can be quite complex and is often planned by individuals with mostly electrical-engineering backgrounds (illuminating engineers), while the second brings people into the design process from a variety of backgrounds like interior design and theatrical professions. Even though there are illuminating engineers, most individuals coming from an engineering background only design lighting as one element of all of a building's electrical systems.

Unique Qualities and Demands of Architectural Lighting

Unlike entertainment lighting, most architectural lighting is designed on a permanent basis. In fact, a significant problem lies in that many installations are not properly maintained and once-beautiful designs are destroyed through issues like burnouts and dirty luminaires. Other common problems include burnouts being replaced with lamps that don't follow the original specifications or **fixtures** not being refocused once a subject has been moved. It is also important to note that design decisions related to architectural lighting are in a sense etched in stone. Fixture placements require that conduit runs and electrical boxes be placed within ceilings or walls where construction materials like drywall or plaster are built around a unit's housing. A mistake in calculating a mounting position or beam specification can result in lighting that is either too dim, misplaced, or mismatched to a given application. This can further lead to safety issues, a costly fix, or a mistake of a permanently mismatched luminaire to design application. Another important difference lies in the timeline of architectural projects. While entertainment projects are designed over a period of weeks and months, an architectural project typically takes months, if not years, to complete. While there is collaboration in architectural lighting, the collaborators also come from a variety of professions. The lighting designer is usually employed by a client who is either the architectural firm designing the project or the *end user* or owner of a building. Other collaborators can include interior designers, planning and space consultants, electrical engineers, and engineers of specialty building systems like plumbing or heating and air-conditioning (HVAC) systems. Once a project has been put out to bid, the lighting designer will also work with the general and electrical contractors that are hired to install a project.

Another difference lies in the immense variety of fixture designs that are available in architectural lighting. The next section identifies several ways of classifying these luminaires. Also, because of their extended operation, reliability, maintenance, and efficiency become major factors in architectural applications. The fixtures must also be aesthetically pleasing because they are frequently in full view and may even bring decorative elements to a project. Finally, since most fixtures are mounted with a single purpose that will rarely change, the units are specified and manufactured to tolerances based specifically on what each fixture must accomplish for a particular task. This has led to manufacturers creating thousands of very tightly specified luminaires for architectural lighting, which is very different from the few general-purpose luminaire designs that are associated with entertainment lighting.

Architectural Luminaire Classifications

One way architectural luminaires are classified is by application. Applications might include **wall-washers, task lights, downlights,** etc. Wall washers create a wash of light over the surface of a wall, while task lights place light in a localized area where a specific task is completed (e.g., a desk, table, or reading lamp). You might also distinguish luminaires by their light source (**incandescent, arc or HID, fluorescent,** etc.). Two other methods of classifying architectural luminaires are based on their mounting arrangements and beam distributions. The five categories of fixtures named by the **Illuminating Engineering Society of North America (IESNA)** based on mounting arrangements (see Figure 17.3) include **surface-mounted** (mounted directly to walls and ceilings), **suspended** (luminaires hung below a ceiling from a **pendant,** wire or other device), **recessed** (mounted within a wall or ceiling with the face of the fixture being flush with the surface), **semi-recessed** (mounted partially within a wall or ceiling), and **track** luminaires (mounted to an electric path/rail or raceway) that are suspended below an architectural surface. Fixture classifications that are based on the distribution pattern of a light source have also been defined by the IESNA (see Figure 17.4). These classifications assume that a fixture is mounted directly downward and include the following: **direct luminaires,** where 90–100% of the light is directed downward, **indirect luminaires,** where 90–100% of the light is directed upward and reflected off the ceiling, **direct-indirect,** where light is directed upward and downward roughly equally, **semi-direct,** where a significant amount of light is directed upward (10–40%) but the majority of the light is directed downward (60–90%), **semi-indirect,** where 10–40 percent of the light is directed downwards while 60–90 percent is directed upwards, and **general diffuse** where light is directed outward in virtually all directions.

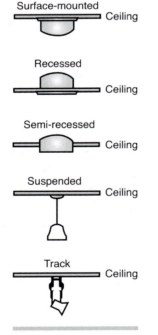

FIGURE 17.3 IESNA Mounting Classifications of Architectural Lighting Fixtures

Key Elements in Architectural General Illumination

The process of lighting architectural spaces is largely based on perception and how **occupants** are affected by the way in which an environment is revealed to them. All architectural lighting is designed through providing several different functions within a lighted environment. This is essentially the same layered approach to lighting that was discussed for retail and musum design—one in which each layer provides a different function. Variations of this approach have been discussed in many other areas of lighting already presented throughout this book. The concept of providing a base level of illumination over an entire area and adding simple **accents** or additional work lights to specific areas creates a popular example of this layered approach—with the assumption that each of these functions will most likely be satisfied by a different group of luminaires. While a project may have several different layers of lighting, the most important aspect of any architectural project is the **task lighting.** This is the lighting that provides the critical level of illumination for a specific job or task. In areas where more critical activities take place, a higher level of illumination is called for and specified. Illumination levels may also vary throughout a facility. Hallways and stairwells are not lit to the same levels as locations where more critical activities take place. One significant difference between architectural applications and other areas of lighting is that the illumination levels for most architectural applications are dictated by specific building codes and recommendations. A second type of architectural lighting is the **ambient lighting** or **general illumination** that is provided throughout a space. Some designers call this **fill light,** while others may refer to it as **general lighting** or **base level lighting.** It is typically diffuse and provides a basic level of illumination for a space. It is also common for the task and ambient lighting to be created by the same luminaires in many environments.

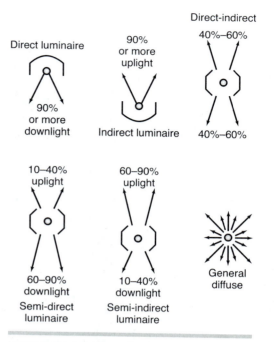

FIGURE 17.4 IESNA Distribution Patterns of Luminaires

The challenges of designing general lighting systems for architectural projects can become quite complex even though the basic manner of laying out an architectural design is quite similar to creating the area lighting for a stage. The major difference is primarily that luminosity levels must actually be calculated for the task(s) that will take place in an architectural space. Considerations are also made for the visual acuity, reflectance levels of the surface materials, and the fact that luminosity levels are measured precisely rather than taken only from general observations. Once the illumination levels are calculated, the lighting designer goes on to match luminaires and their beam patterns to the layout of a room in much the same way that stage lights are assigned to a stage. Through this, fixture layouts (**lighting plans** or **lighting layouts**) are generated in much the same way as theatrical light plots are created. A lighting layout for a condominium lighting project is illustrated in Figure 17.5. The general lighting for an architectural application is more complex not only in that the luminaires must deliver a prescribed quality and quantity of light, but also because the luminaires need to be considered from an aesthetic point of view. They must also be arranged neatly and should reduce effects like spill and glare.

Even though it is common for architectural spaces to be lit almost exclusively by task lighting systems, other lighting elements are often added on top of a basic lighting design. Lighting may be used to direct attention and draw focus to a building's architectural features, lure occupants throughout a space, and to establish a particular mood for an environment. Other lighting elements may be used solely in decorative ways like modifying the appearance of a building's architectural features (e.g., grazing a wall to add texture) or being a design element in themselves (a chandelier or wall sconce). There are a variety of lighting techniques that are used to light architectural environments. Several of these include task and ambient lighting (discussed previously), as well as **accent lighting, cove lighting, decorative lighting, grazing, space manipulation,** and **wash lighting.** Chapter 24 provides a significant discussion regarding each of these lighting classifications. Luminaires can also bring visual interest, like sparkle, to an environment.

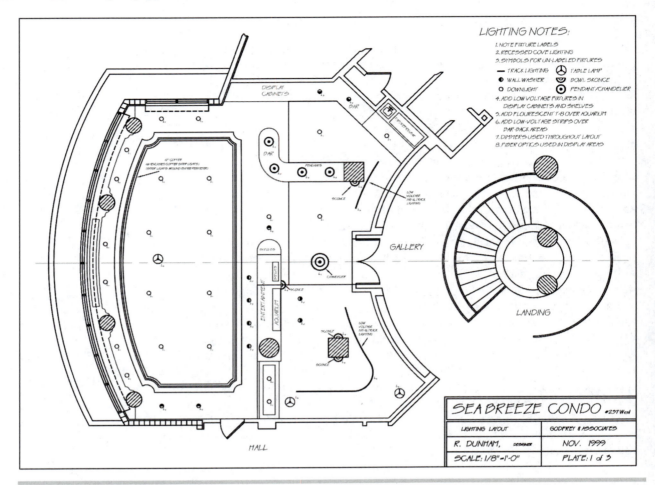

FIGURE 17.5 A Lighting Layout

SIDEBAR 17.2 Lighting Design Questions

How does the lighting relate to the architecture and interior design?

Does the design satisfy the aesthetics and primary needs of the client?

Does the lighting contribute to the ambience or mood of the room or project?

Are appropriate illumination levels created by the lighting?

Does the design satisfy the needs of the primary visual task? Secondary? . . . etc.

Is there an appropriate level of control for the lighted environment?

Does the lighting enhance the architecture and other elements of a space?

Do the luminaires and other fittings blend in with the rest of the design elements?

Are different levels of focus or accents established appropriately?

Does the design comply with all applicable codes?

How does the design satisfy lighting economics and energy use?

Does the design satisfy the budgetary needs of the client?

The Architectural Lighting Design Process

In the last 60 to 70 years we have become much more energy conscious, resulting in some of the first elements of true architectural lighting being instituted to maximize efficiency and to conserve power. The popularity of fluorescent lighting in commercial buildings is a direct result of this. This economical influence continues to play an ever-increasing role in architectural lighting. However, a second significant influence is in the philosophical shift of lighting spaces in a more aesthetic rather than quantitative manner. The movement began roughly in the 1970s and the argument of **quantity versus quality** has since led to a rethinking in how the lighting of most buildings is conceived and designed. This new approach has expanded to include nearly every area of architectural lighting and is now considered not only as a functional building system but also as an integral part of a building's total design. This has led to the introduction of numerous carefully designed yet highly visible lighting fixtures, especially for public spaces like municipal buildings, stores, hospitality properties, corporate headquarters, and churches.

Even though there's much more consideration of aesthetics in a lighting design and the design solutions are more strongly based on the unique needs of an individual project, maintaining minimal illumination standards and following a set of general guidelines are still very much a part of the process of architectural lighting design. The newer approach has, however, resulted in a modified use of design guidelines for the architectural lighting community since 2000. The 9th edition of the *IESNA Lighting Handbook* addresses these changes and incorporates them into the design process while still providing the required recommendations on illumination levels for any visual task. The IESNA also publishes design-specific guidelines that address unique areas of the lighting industry through a series of booklets called **recommended practices.** These provide guidance to the special needs and concerns of particular types of lighting installations. Recommended practices have been written and published by the IESNA for topics like hospitality design, health-care facilities, museums, and schools and other educational buildings, as well as for offices and many other areas of lighting design.

Regardless of application, many of the general principles of architectural lighting can be used for virtually all of the specialized applications that are presented in Chapter 24. Specific lighting areas that are addressed there include residential lighting, hospitality lighting, public buildings, houses of worship, commercial and industrial lighting, lighting for educational and healthcare facilities, and exterior structures. Identification of the principle tasks, layering, and a solid use of basic lighting practices can result in the creation of energy-efficient lighting that satisfies the needs of any application while bringing visual interest to a project (see Figure 17.6). In many instances, several lighting tasks may be addressed through a single lighting system—many lighting environments contain as few as one or two layers. This also helps avoid issues like **ceiling clutter.** Sidebar 17.2 lists several lines of questioning that can be asked of almost any architectural project. Public and commercial buildings will also have additional lighting systems like **worklights** (for after-hours cleaning) and **emergency lighting** systems that become active when the principle lighting systems fail.

The actual method of designing the lighting for an architectural project can vary considerably from one designer to another, and while designers may refer to these steps differently (or recognize additional steps), there are essentially four steps that a lighting designer completes for most architectural projects. These are: 1. Determine the design needs, 2. Determine the luminaires (light source, photometrics, and actual luminaire selection), 3. Create the layout, and 4. Provide the control system(s) for the design. It should be noted that these steps relate only to the design of the lighting, which is different from working through the construction phases of a project. Just like a lighting design for a theatrical production requires a concept, an architectural project also requires a lighting concept. Many in architectural circles prefer to call this a **lighting scheme,** which is nothing more than the architectural equivalent of a lighting concept. Finally, as an architectural lighting designer makes choices in specific luminaires and where to place them, they develop a scaled plan (lighting layout) that functions in much the same way as a theatrical light plot. A variation of the lighting layout may also specify control data like switch locations and circuiting information that identifies which luminaires share a common circuit. Once the lighting layout has been completed, additional forms and tables are developed that provide essentially the same type of schedules and control/fixture information that a theatrical designer's hook-up and instrument schedule would provide.

a. An interior project

b. An exterior project with several layers of lighting

FIGURE 17.6 Architectural Lighting a. Accenting the reception area with multiple layers of luminaires b. Note revelation of both exterior and interior as part of the "total" design.

SIDEBAR 17.3 DESIGNER PROFILE

Robert Shook

Robert Shook began his career in theatrical lighting but was introduced to lighting architecture when he was asked to consult on a couple of architectural projects by Chicago architects who had seen his theatrical designs. He now works almost exclusively in architectural lighting and partnered with fellow lighting designer Duane Schuler in 1986 to form the architectural lighting firm of Schuler Shook. Bob holds both the IALD (International Association of Lighting Designers) and LC (Lighting Certified –National Council on Qualifications for the Lighting Professions) designations and has consulted on numerous architectural lighting projects throughout the world. Several high-profile projects he has designed include O'Hare International Airport, the Chicago Master Lighting Plan, Wrigley Field, The Historic Water Tower (Chicago), John G. Shedd Aquarium (Chicago), Cathedral of the Immaculate Conception (Ft. Wayne), Second Street Bridge (Columbus, Indiana), and numerous university projects (Rice University, Northwestern University, Valparaiso University, and DePaul University). His lighting has won him many awards (IESNA Int'l Illumination Design Awards, IESNA Illumination Design Awards, an IESNA Int'l Illumination Design Award of Distinction, IALD International Illumination Design Awards, and a GE Edison Award of Excellence).

Shook was trained in theatrical lighting design and received a BFA from the Goodman School of Drama and an MFA from Ohio University. He was working in the Chicago theatre scene following his graduate work when he was first approached to offer advice on how to light architectural projects. "My reputation as a theatrical lighting designer in Chicago led some clients to call me to help them with architectural lighting challenges. As a theatrical lighting designer, I welcomed the opportunity to design lighting that would be more permanent." His initial break came when Chicago architect John Vinci hired him for several small lighting projects—this being before he had established a reputation in architectural lighting. This introduction to the field of architectural lighting was extremely helpful in gaining entry to other projects with additional architects throughout Chicago.

In 1980, he met his future business partner Duane Schuler while working for the Chicago Civic Theatre and Duane was resident lighting designer for the Lyric Opera of Chicago. They worked together consulting on a number of architectural projects and eventually formed their own lighting firm.

Bob's preparation for architectural lighting came primarily through his participation in the many educational seminars that are conducted through IALD and IESNA. Even with many years of designing architectural lighting, he tries to attend as many educational opportunities as possible. "The IALD and IES offer excellent seminars that are sources of information to help you remain up to date in the discipline." In describing several unique differences between lighting for theatre and lighting for architecture he points out that, "Architectural lighting design differs from theatrical lighting primarily by its permanence. In most cases, once luminaires are installed in an architectural environment, there's no moving them around or adding or subtracting to make corrections or refinements in a design. There's also no rehearsal process and little opportunity to test ideas. A lot more up-front research and calculation must be done to assure that the design will meet the client's requirements and expectations." He also shares that, "Architectural lighting must conform to local and national energy codes, so designs must utilize energy-efficient sources like metal halide, fluorescent, and LED. Designs must be tested for energy usage in addition to illumination levels, architectural integration, and artistic concept."

What Shook likes best about designing in architectural lighting is that every project is completely different in regard to the artistic requirements that it will have. He also likes the collaboration that takes place over the lifetime of a project and believes that, "Lighting designers must discover how best to relate lighting to each architect's personal artistic process." This attitude also ties into what he considers to be one of the most essential principles of working in this area of lighting—that, "The lighting must be completely integrated into the architecture and that the lighting and architecture must be seen as one complete design."

Photo credit: Dan Rest

Daylighting

The light sources discussed to this point in the chapter have been artificial or man-made, and light has been manufactured through converting one form of energy into another. Daylight, on the other hand, is natural, and while we can't create it, it can be manipulated to enhance or supplement the lighting of an environment. It can also have detrimental effects on an environment as well. **Daylighting** uses natural sunlight to illuminate a space. Although sunlight isn't a typical consideration of entertainment lighting, it's becoming an ever more important element of architectural lighting. While there are aesthetic considerations for using daylighting as a supplemental light source for a project, energy conservation forms a major factor in the increased role that daylighting is playing in many architectural designs.

There are two daylight components. The first relates to **direct sunlight,** while the second relates to the effect of light scattering in the atmosphere and sky. This scattering creates a diffuse source of illumination called **skylight.** Direct sunlight is usually more of a problem than a benefit to architectural projects due to issues like the extreme contrasts and glare that it can produce. It also produces a greenhouse heating effect once trapped in an interior. Sunlight is also fairly unreliable due to the extreme variation that it displays and is therefore usually only considered as a supplemental light source for a building. Skylight is more consistent and has an overall predictability that direct sunlight does not. Just a few of the many daylight factors that have an impact on a building's daylight exposure include: time of day, geographical location and orientation of a building, seasons, weather, and even cloud cover.

Lighting Green and Lighting Economics

From the energy crisis of the 1970s on, lighting professionals have searched for ways to reduce our need for power, examined alternative energy sources, and looked to a variety of technologies for conserving and protecting our resources and environment. One of the programs in the construction industry that emphasizes environmentally friendly building practices is the **LEED (Leadership in Energy and Environmental Design)** certification program. This program provides certification of a building through earning qualifying points by practicing environmentally sound building practices. Lighting is only one area that affects the certification process but can earn over a dozen points toward the certification score of a particular project. While other parts of our society focus on conserving gas, commuting, recycling, and eliminating waste, the lighting industry has focused on issues like energy conservation, luminaire and power efficiency, and elimination of hazardous materials in its daily practices. While much of the interest in conservation is tied to making the earth a better place to live, an even larger part of the effort is economically based and relates to finding methods to lower a client's power and lighting-maintenance bills as electricity and other sources of energy become more expensive.

Unlike entertainment lighting systems, architectural lighting systems are in operation for many hours a day. When considering a commercial building this may mean that a considerable amount of power is consumed as the lights perform their daily tasks. This becomes even more significant as buildings get bigger and expand into large square-footage or multi-level structures like warehouses, industrial complexes, and high-rise apartments or office towers. Most economical concerns that relate to lighting are aimed at either reducing the power demands of an installation or making determinations of how long it takes for an investment in new lighting equipment to pay for itself. These economic issues are addressed through a series of practices that are collectively called **energy management** and **lighting economics.** Energy management relates to finding ways of reducing a building's power demands while at the same time causing a minimal loss in quality to the lighting and other building systems. In large commercial buildings, lighting is often one of the most energy-demanding systems to operate. It can also have serious impacts on other building systems—for instance, using more light sources can raise the temperature of a room which forces the air-conditioning units to work harder. Power conservation has become so important that there are now energy codes that dictate how much power a lighting design may use over a given time period. This is expressed in **power densities** that relate to the watts/square foot that a building system consumes. The most widespread energy code that specifies power densities is the **ASHRAE/IESNA 90.1** code, which dictates the maximum number of watts/square foot that a lighting design may use for a given application. This and other energy codes will increase or decrease the allowed power density specifications based on the activities that take place in a given environment. The maximum power density for a hospital is higher than one allowed for a hotel, while the power density allowed for a school or office building is higher than those of an adjoining parking garage. Nearly every building or renovation project must now be designed to be in compliance with these power density requirements—and several states, like California and New York, have even more stringent power codes. In lighting economics, we are concerned with an issue called **payback,** where the costs of installing and operating lighting systems are compared to one another. The basic principle involves adding up all of the costs of installing (costs of the equipment and labor) and maintaining a lighting system and making a determination of how long it will take for a system to pay for itself through the energy savings that are created by operating the system on a daily basis.

In addition to power consumption, lighting green also relates to recycling resources: raw materials are returned to a resourceful use instead of taking up space in a landfill, and hazardous materials are disposed of in a safe, environmentally friendly manner. Several specific ways in which the lighting industry recycles include the conversion of old luminaire housings to scrap metal or retrieving copper wiring and cables from old installations. Many older luminaires and wiring have hazardous materials like asbestos that must be removed and disposed of in specific manners. An even larger problem lies in the disposal of traditional fluorescent lamps that contain mercury, which is defined as a hazardous material. While lamp manufacturers now make mercury-free versions of these lamps, the earlier lamps are one of the most popular lamps used in commercial applications and should be disposed of in a prescribed manner.

LANDSCAPE LIGHTING

Landscape lighting is a special discipline of architectural lighting in which the lighting of a building's exterior and surrounding grounds combine to enhance a property's appearance. Items that are typically lighted as part of a landscape design include the vegetation (trees and plants), pathways, sculptures, water (pools and fountains), exterior building surfaces, and other architectural features of a property. Landscape lighting has been around for a number of years but has often been limited to commercial or high-end residential applications. Now, with advances in low-voltage equipment, landscape lighting is flourishing. Corporations draw the public to their buildings through creating an inviting image that begins with viewing their property and its buildings from the street. Home owners use landscape lighting to create curb appeal that increases the value of their homes while also making their yards usable for more activities over a greater portion of the year.

Lighting Landscapes

Landscape lighting provides a number of functions that are important to a building owner—many go well beyond creating an aesthetic response or providing greater use of a property's outdoor spaces. A unique element of landscape lighting relates to the fact that the primary subjects of these designs are usually a property's plants and trees. This is very different from lighting for a building's occupants and creates several special considerations that must be examined while completing these projects. Despite this, lighting for particular types of visibility still forms an important element of these designs. Many refer to this as lighting for **safety.** Another important function of landscape lighting falls to providing **security** for a property. While some security lighting is provided through simply flooding a property with floodlights, a more desirable approach can often be found that provides a more creative solution to security lighting than simply flooding an area full of light. In the end, prowlers are usually more concerned with the absence of light than the way in which a property is actually lit.

There are two additional issues that a landscape lighting designer must contend with that are unique to this area of lighting. Both are related to the special needs of the luminaires that are used in this area of lighting. First, the fixtures are exposed to the natural elements. Extreme shifts in the weather, prolonged exposure to ultraviolet radiation, exposure to moisture from rain and irrigation systems, and even harm from careless landscapers all have detrimental effects on these luminaires. Second, the means of powering these systems can be either **line-voltage** (120 volt) or **low-voltage** (most commonly 12 volt). Line-voltage systems deliver plenty of power but are more dangerous and require special safety practices in their installations. On the downside, low-voltage systems have issues related to **voltage drop** where the wires to the fixtures farthest from the power undergo additional resistance that causes their lamps to glow more dimly than those located closer to the power source.

Essential Approaches to Lighting Landscapes

Unlike many other forms of lighting design, appropriate landscape lighting intensities become more of a relative than absolute determination from one installation to another. First, as a rule, the intensity levels of garden or landscape lighting are relatively low when compared to most other lighting applications. Overall intensity levels of a project are also partially determined by the relative amounts of light associated with the neighboring properties and environment. Excessive **glare** should also be avoided since people circulating throughout a property might be blinded by poorly aimed luminaires. For the most part, landscape lighting is best utilized through creating **accents** that focus on specific elements of a landscape, not on creating uniform lighting throughout an entire space. This selective use of darkness brings contrast and visual interest to a design. Landscape lighting is also not limited to lighting trees and plants. In fact, many of the more effective elements of these designs involve lighting objects other than foliage. The plants or growing elements are called **softscape,** while architectural features like footbridges, pathways, and sculptures are called **hardscape.**

Landscape lighting is usually designed from several different perspectives. While there's often a prominent view, there will be features that are also highlighted for those who see a project from other directions. One must also consider the lighting from within a property. Many restaurants offer choice seating where windows provide views of the landscaping and surrounding areas. Finally, landscape lighting designers must design with the idea of planning for the future. The vegetation is constantly growing and the lighting must evolve as the landscape matures and changes. Lighting saplings from below with in-ground fixtures will work nicely for a couple years but only until the branches of the trees extend beyond the beams of the fixtures. To correct this, the fixtures have to be refocused or moved to extend their coverage of the maturing branches.

a.

There are a number of distribution patterns or functions that landscape lighting can provide for a property. Just a few of these include **area** and **pathway lighting, accent lighting, security lighting, spotlighting,** and even **contour** and **background lighting.** Some landscape lighting is based on familiar techniques like **cross lighting, grazing, uplighting,** and **downlighting,** while others like **shadowing, mirroring, perspective lighting, moonlighting,** and **vista lighting** are unique to this specialty. Several of these techniques are demonstrated in Figure 17.7.

Principles of Landscape Lighting

There are many ways that a lighting designer can use light to create a unique exterior environment that is suited to the specific needs and tastes of a client. Many of these variables are based on factors like the personal preferences of a property owner, the types of plants being lit, and the intended use of the exterior spaces. Contrast plays an important role in landscape lighting designs. This is most apparent through making a comparison between **soft light,** which is generally more diffuse and less defined, and **hard light,** which has a hard, clean edge that produces relatively sharp shadows. Hard light is typically created

b.

FIGURE 17.7 Landscape Lighting Projects
a. Uplighting of trees with path lighting along sidewalk. Both lead to the building's entrance lobby. b. Moonlighting with area lighting of flower beds.

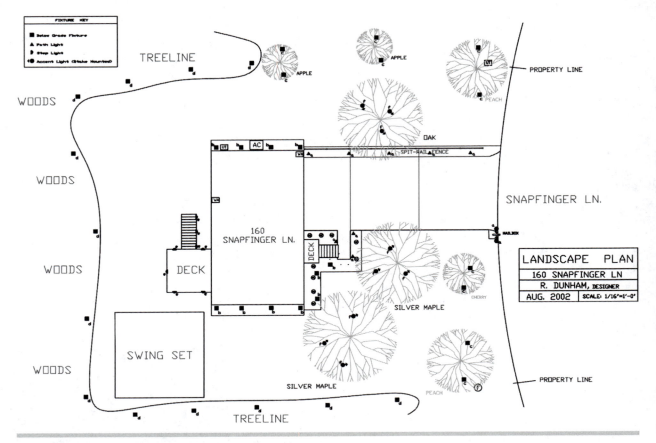

FIGURE 17.8 A Site Plan with Lighting Indicated

from point light sources and is often used to direct focus and add sparkle to a scene. In pathway lighting (especially in public areas), issues like the base or minimum intensity level of a project may be dependent on local governance. A designer should also consider the effect of how much **light trespass** or spill is coming from other properties and the immediate neighborhood. On the flip side, a designer must also be considerate of light trespass onto neighboring properties. While an uplight may be perfect for lighting a tree near a property line, you could create a problem if the spill or glare from that light enters a neighbor's bedroom.

Perhaps the most important element of the design process, as with architectural lighting, is getting to know the client and understanding their likes and dislikes, how they intend to use the exterior environment, and the items that they want to feature. After gaining an understanding of the client's expectations, the designer moves on to looking at the property and landscaping features or **site plans** to develop a concept and eventual **lighting plan** or **layout** for the project (Figure 17.8). Control and fixture schedules are also completed as part of the design package. The lighting layout becomes the equivalent of a light plot and not only provides the luminaire specifications and locations but also the location of the circuiting, power sources (like transformers), and control devices (like timers).

THEMED DESIGN AND SPECIALTY LIGHTING

Themed design relates to creating some form of entertainment experience for patrons who share in an event. While theme parks are the most obvious example of themed designing, it should be noted that theming techniques have moved into many areas of our lives. Several of the more popular applications include the design of hotel and resort attractions, many upscale restaurants, and a host of retail establishments. In the purest sense, themed design seeks to create a story-like experience for anyone who is exposed to the themed event or environment. A truly themed attraction is organized and designed around a more significant experience and attempts to involve the guests in a story, even to the point of being participants in the action. There are many elements of our lives that are influenced by some form of theming, even though they may not be truly themed experiences in themselves. One only has to go to the nearest mall to find restaurants like Outback, Cracker Barrel, and Red Lobster or stores like The Disney Store, Build-a-Bear Workshop, LEGO Imagination Center, and Bass Pro Shops to see the effects of themed design. There's even a grocery chain in Connecticut (Stew Leonard's) that places *animatronic* animals and games throughout its stores. Many restaurants, especially in tourist areas, make use of themed design. Popular examples include Planet Hollywood, Rainforest Café, and Chuck E. Cheese restaurants. On a smaller scale, themed design can appear in retail displays like the room settings of furniture stores like Rooms to Go or the clothing displays of Ralph Lauren or Christie Brinkley that are found in department stores. While this area of lighting has traditionally been called **themed lighting,** professionals are now referring to this type of lighting as **specialty lighting.**

The Story

One of the most critical considerations that must be examined when completing a themed design is the story that is developed for a project. Not only is the story important in its own sense, it becomes the mechanism for connecting guests to the attraction on an emotional level. The story is used to define the event, and every design decision should be evaluated on how well it supports or ties into the story that is being told. Without it, a project simply becomes a ride or attraction with no greater experience for the participant.

Designers of themed events (especially themed attractions) try to create an all-encompassing experience that immerses the guests in an event. Universal Studio's *E.T. Adventure* doesn't simply take guests on an aerial bicycle ride, it places them in the same chase sequence as the boys who help E.T. escape from the authorities in the film. The ride tells a story while introducing the guests to additional adventurers with E.T. A truly themed attraction attempts to bring as many of a participant's senses into the experience as possible. While sight and sound are the primary senses that are stimulated in these attractions, touch and motion are also addressed through creating vibrations and blasts of heat or air, using motion simulators, and using water and spray technologies to create mists or to otherwise get the guests wet. Disney and other park operators have even gone to the extent of introducing smells to some attractions. The initial interaction with an attraction begins as guests first approach the structure or building that houses the attraction and as they stand in the **queue** waiting for the actual ride. One technique for disguising excessive lines involves designing queues that lead from one chamber to another while revealing parts of the story (*exposition*) leading up to the point where a ride actually begins. Some popular attractions with elaborate queues like *The Amazing Adventures of Spiderman* or *Men in Black Alien Attack* (Islands of Adventure/Universal Studios) and *The Pirates of the Carribean* (Disney) have mazes of tunnels and a half dozen or more chambers that entertain guests while they wait. The queue for *Men in Black* includes being led past a creature break room, a central control/processing area, and a weapons room before entering the staging area where guests are loaded into the vehicles for the actual ride. All of these areas are designed and lit appropriately. Figure 17.9 features a chamber from a themed attraction based on the *Terminator*.

There are a number of examples beyond theme parks where strong storylines are worked into themed environments. Historical sites like Williamsburg and Mystic Seaport re-create entire villages based on themed environments where casts take on the roles of craftspeople who perform re-enactments of life in an earlier time. Museums and

FIGURE 17.9 *Terminator*-Themed Attraction *Photo credit:* Entertainment Design Group, Inc.—Atlanta. Photo by Rick Clark

special exhibits are also gravitating toward more theming in their designs. The *Titanic* touring exhibit goes to the extent of issuing boarding passes to guests containing one of the names of the original passengers that are compared to a survivor list at the end of the exhibit. Some refer to this type of designing as **edu-tainment.** Regardless of the nature of the event, the story becomes the most important theme in driving the rest of the design decisions. Ultimately, it becomes the primary element that determines the success of a project.

Development of a Themed Project

One of the most challenging aspects of themed projects is found in the schedule that they follow. Even a fast-developing project can take 6 months to several years to complete because most of an attraction's development is based on original concepts and equipment that have never been created before. Attractions are also construction projects rather than theatrical ventures and are subject to the more stringent demands of building codes and other time-consuming construction practices. Another significant difference comes in that the equipment that makes a show possible often must be engineered as part of the design process. In fact, the show or ride, with all of its equipment, is usually designed before the building that houses the attraction.

Most themed projects begin with brainstorming—what is called **blue sky development.** After this, a concept is developed and the team works out the details of a project. In addition to entertainment value, there are also concerns regarding economics (budgets, schedules, etc.), volume of visitors per hour or day, duration of an event, crowd control, and engineering requirements that are unique to a project. For the lighting designer, this is the point where a formal **light plot** or **lighting layout, control schedule,** and other aspects of the lighting are finalized. The luminaires are also often mounted on scenic structures and may have to be placed by the designer personally. Finally, much of these installations are permanent, and the layouts must be accurate so circuit boxes and conduit runs can be placed properly by the electrical contractor. At some point, after the majority of the equipment is installed, the lighting team **aims** or

focuses the luminaires and cues the attraction. The lighting, as well as all other elements of the attraction, is then tested and refined over an extended period of time (**shakedown**).

Considerations of Themed (Specialty) Lighting Design

Lighting in most theme parks or any other themed environment must ultimately operate on several levels. The solution to a design is also a factor of the nature of a project. An attraction in a theme park will have more flexibility in the way that it is lit than what can be expected in a themed restaurant, which in turn will have fewer limitations than lighting a collection of products in a retail environment. One thing that is almost certain is that the specific lighting for any attraction will almost always be unique since most themed projects are one-of-a-kind creations.

Much of the lighting in themed attractions goes back to the concept of creating layers of light, each with a particular purpose. The first layer is probably the most important and usually relates to lighting the story elements of an attraction. It should be lit first. What does a guest have to see? How should the focus be directed? What is the dominant mood of each setting? Questions like these relate to how the lighting designer contributes to telling the story of an attraction. Because of the amount of control that many of these tasks require, it's common for theatrical luminaires and control equipment to be used for many aspects of an attraction's lighting design. Some even refer to this as the **theatrical lighting** for an attraction. **Contrast ratios** are especially important in an attraction's lighting because they become the primary means of directing the guests' attention. The lighting equipment associated with much of this illumination is frequently off-the-shelf theatrical equipment that is mounted and wired in a permanent fashion. The most common practice is to run conduit and junction boxes from the dimmer racks to where the units are mounted and wired directly to their associated circuits. While theatrical gels are often used, the extended use requires their replacement on a regular basis—something that often gets ignored until the lighting becomes dismal. Because of this, many designers are specifying dichroic filters as a long-term solution to the gel problem. Maintaining the fixtures (lamp burnouts, cleaning, refocusing, etc.) is another concern for keeping these designs in their best condition.

Once the primary elements of an attraction have been lit there are additional features that will also need lighting. This is done through developing supplemental lighting for elements like the interior and exterior features of the building that houses the attraction. This is commonly called the **architectural lighting** element of an attraction. Even though this lighting is predominantly architectural, it doesn't prohibit these units and equipment from being used for theatrical functions, or vice-versa. This lighting typically provides general illumination for various building components and supports tasks like guest circulation (e.g., lighting building approaches, queues, and waiting areas), illuminating the exterior of the building, and lighting the attraction's landscaping. Often these systems are used in queues to help guests make the transition from the bright exterior sunlight to the much darker interiors of an attraction. Typically, these parts of an attraction's lighting use architectural and landscaping fixtures rather than theatrical luminaires. The architectural systems should also move beyond simple illumination and are frequently used to create moods, set off a building's features, illuminate signs, and make other statements about the attraction.

The final layer of an attraction's lighting design involves **effects lighting** and is used to create special effects throughout an attraction. Gobos can create textured light like that associated with being in the woods, LEDs can be used to create a shimmering water effect, chase and flicker effects are designed for fire effects, and strobe sequences, fiber-optic effects, and black light (with day-glow paints) all form additional lighting effects that are popular in many attractions. While not used as part of the themed lighting, these installations will also have **emergency** and **worklight** lighting systems.

Tom Ruzika

Tom Ruzika has a career that reflects a project list with credits in many areas of lighting design. His designs have been seen on Broadway, in national tours, major regional theatres, and national and international dance and opera companies. He's lighted over 85 productions for the South Coast Repertory Theatre with design credits at other leading companies that include Coconut Grove Playhouse, Hollywood Bowl, Ford's Theatre in Washington D.C., Laguna Playhouse, Los Angeles Civic Light Opera, Opera Santa Barbara, Berkeley Repertory Theatre, and the Mark Taper Forum. More uniquely, he has designed the lighting for numerous attractions associated with theme parks in six different countries and architectural projects that include prestigious hotels, casinos, restaurants, and retail centers covering several continents (North America, Asia, and Europe). His entertainment lighting can be seen at theme parks in six countries and his architectural lighting can be seen across the nation and in multiple Asian and European countries. Just a few of his themed projects include *Backdraft*, *Earthquake*, and *Back To The Future* (Universal Studios, Hollywood); the Main Street Emporium and renovation of the Disneyland Hotel Grand Ballroom (Disneyland); *Batman Forever* and *Maverick* shows at Movie World Australia (Warner Brothers); *Seuss Landing* at Universal's Islands of Adventure in Orlando; as well as five theme parks in Japan and additional attractions at Knott's Berry Farm and other parks. Several of his more visible architectural projects include the Beatles Revolution Lounge at the Mirage Las Vegas, Body English, the Hard Rock Las Vegas Ultra Lounge, two Seminole Hard Rock Hotels and Casinos in Florida, the Hard Rock Hotel San Diego, MGM Mirage City Center Sales Pavilion and Grand Hotel Star Lane in Las Vegas, the South Coast Plaza and Palm Springs Malls, the Los Angeles Music Center, and Universal City Walk's Panasonic Pavilion. He has also consulted on numerous performance facilities (including the new South Coast Repertory Theatre facility) and created an extensive Master Plan for lighting the exterior facades of 104 historic buildings in downtown Los Angeles. His lighting has won many awards across multiple areas of the industry, including numerous Critics Circle Awards, the Lifetime Achievement Award in Lighting from the Los Angeles Drama Critics Circle, Lighting Dimensions Designer of the Year Award, and a number of national and international architectural lighting design awards.

Ruzika's formal training includes a BS in Drama from California State Polytechnic University, Pomona and an MFA from University of California, Irvine. More interestingly, his introduction to theatre came through his playing the organ for choirs in his high school auditorium. "Being backstage, this experience led to my interest in stage lighting. I learned theatrical lighting in high school 'by doing' and continued my training in college." His learning of architectural lighting came about when he was asked to light a shopping mall parking garage to help make women look more attractive. He learned themed entertainment lighting when he was asked to light a portion of a theme park in Japan. There were different people that helped him break into each of the specialty areas of lighting in which he now works: Tharon Musser and Ken Billington (stage lighting), Pat Maloney of Universal Studios Hollywood (themed entertainment lighting), and Henry Segerstrom with the South Coast Plaza Mall project (architectural lighting). Since there are relatively few options for being trained for much of this type of lighting, most of his training came out of "developing knowledge of all styles of lighting via projects that came through my design studio and being in the business for over 25 years." Currently, his design work is comprised of approximately 45% architectural and specialty lighting, 20% themed entertainment, 20% lighting control system design, and about 15% theatrical designs.

Tom states that, "I love everything about working with light. There is great satisfaction in revealing something in an exciting, vibrant way, making it stand out no matter what it is . . . an actor, or a building. This is especially true today with the many new light sources that are available. Our imagination can really soar because we can achieve so many exciting compositions of light." Several unique conditions of working in architectural and themed lighting are the considerations of picking the light sources and luminaires and where you ultimately put the lighting fixtures. "You need to collaborate with the architects in the early phases of the design; there is no lighting plan with specific hanging positions like in a theatre, so you have more freedom, but at the same time you have more constrictions due to building codes, energy restrictions, construction techniques, lamp choices, and the stylistic nature of the architecture that you are illuminating." On the other hand, Ruzika also shares that, "All lighting design is based on the same principles; what makes the difference is in the question of what are you lighting? An actor, a building, piece of art, cartoon characters; the principles are all the same—it's the equipment that's different."

When asked to respond to what he considers to be "Rule #1" for lighting within any of these disciplines Ruzika replies that it has to be about "providing high quality 'selective visibility' to a project or environment—be it an actor, building, or themed scenic element." He also comments on the lack of time that can exist on these projects as well. "You don't always have time for creative or reflective thought on a project. With today's computer aided systems, we get projects on a Friday afternoon and are told that initial design drawings must be finished by Monday. We are given less time to actually design!" Like many other designers he reads the trade magazines, goes to LDI, and observes what other designers around the world are creating as a means of remaining on top of the technology and business. One final thought that he shares speaks to how he has done so well in such a range of disciplines throughout the lighting industry. "Good lighting design practice is based upon knowledge, skill, and collaboration. It is also in accepting challenges, problem solving, talent, and bringing a sense of fun and adventure to a project."

Photo credit: Donna Ruzika

In contemporary society, there is a wide range of design projects that have some form of themed elements contained within them. While theme parks and their associated attractions form obvious examples of these special areas of design, other areas like restaurants, hotels, and retail stores form additional niches where the concepts of themed lighting are put into regular practice. Chapter 26 (online) provides detailed discussions of several different forms of themed projects and how their lighting might be approached by a lighting designer.

VIRTUAL LIGHTING (RENDERINGS, VIRTUAL REALITY, GAMING, ETC.)

Virtual lighting relates to lighting within the simulated or digital worlds of computers and other electronic devices like video games. Since the appearance of the personal computer, many areas of design have seen the potential for using specialized software to present and communicate design information to other professionals and their clients. Entertainment designers, architects, and interior designers all make use of virtual designing in their professions. The best comparison to virtual design is in creating a scenic model that is placed in a model light lab where it can be illuminated. All objects that are contained in a virtual environment are created (**modeled**) as a simulation of three-dimensional elements. While the creation of the initial model is usually quite time consuming, the advantage that computer modeling brings to a project is in the flexibility with which a design may be presented. In traditional rendering, a single viewpoint is taken of a design with a specific perspective view that is then painted or illustrated in a manner that reflects a choice of materials and lighting for a given scene. This rendering is only good for a single combination of features, and if a team wants to make comparisons between different materials, colors, viewing angles, or any other design elements like lighting, additional renderings must be made—each one beginning from scratch. Digital designs allow a single model to be created and saved as a master file, which is then used to generate a number of additional images based on different combinations of materials, views, colors, and lighting conditions. These images are typically called **computer renderings** or **visualizations.** Computer rendering allows many of the repetitive tasks of creating a rendering to be eliminated since only one model is required for exploring the many options. These visualizations have evolved from primitive images to scenes that can illustrate the same amount of detail as a photograph. Design visualizations that depict this amount of detail are often called *photorealistic* or are said to display a high amount of *photorealism.* Due to the speed at which computers can produce new images, animated sequences can create a series of images that follow the changing position of a virtual camera or alter other variables in the models themselves. In some cases, the new images are created **on the fly,** in real-time, allowing an observer to move through a virtual world as environments are rendered around them (e.g., computer action games).

Virtual Design

Virtual design exists through the electronic files of computer programs. In effect, everything created in a virtual design is an assemblage of formulas and mathematical data where the image is a representation of specific values and color associations for a collection of points known as **pixels.** The smaller the pixels, the more **resolution** or detail an image can display. However, the more pixels used to create an image, the more time and calculations a computer must take to generate an image and the more data that is stored in an image file. In the end, a designer must consider the tradeoff between rendering speed and file size versus the amount of detail and resolution to be depicted in a final image. If a single photorealistic image of an architectural rendering is desired, it would make sense to use a very large resolution for its rendering. However, if the same image were part of an animation, it would be better to lower the resolution so that the sequence could be rendered more quickly. The average viewer will not be able to see the difference in quality as the animation is played using the lower resolution images. With computer processors getting faster and the amounts of RAM increasing, we can now use much higher resolutions than even a few years ago. This allows us to create more detailed animations that are rendered more quickly. The final images are bigger and look better, but expectations have also gotten higher. So, what took a long time to render for the look that we produced at one time still takes a long time to render today because of the higher levels of detailing that we expect in today's images.

A variety of special applications in virtual design are presented in the online chapter that has been written in regard to this material (Chapter 27). Several of the more specific topics presented there include using virtual lighting as a tool for visualization, creating virtual elements for film and video production, and virtual game design. A detailed discussion of the different rendering processes is also presented in this discussion.

SIDEBAR 17.5 DESIGNER PROFILE

Chris Wells

Chris Wells is a digital animation and visual effects expert who has been working in digital effects and lighting for over 15 years. He began college in technical theatre in the 1990s and is within a few classes of earning a BA degree from the University of Georgia, where he discovered the world of digital or CG graphics early in his student career. He was one of the first students to forge his own path in the study of digital design but left college in his last quarter and never got around to finishing his degree. His training led to experiences in both filming and digital arts. Chris began his professional career at a small Atlanta based company where he worked for several years developing the skills that allowed him to transition to a more established company based out of New York. During that time, he spent several years working mostly on commercials and television. Later, he moved to Los Angeles to work not only in these forms of digital media but also on motion pictures. Since then, he has helped create or supervise the lighting and effects for numerous projects. Several of his more familiar credits include *The Curious Case of Benjamin Button, The Incredible Hulk, 300, Live Free or Die Hard, The Fantastic Four, X-Men: The Last Stand, Poseidon, Shooter,* and *The Day After Tomorrow*. Currently, he is Visual Effects Supervisor at Hydraulx, which is based in Santa Monica, CA.

Chris's earliest interests in lighting were in theatrical lighting, which is what he began his college studies in. But through taking an introductory animation class as an independent study and the mentoring of one of his professors (Mike Hussey), he was "able to translate my enjoyment of stage lighting into a digital art back in the days when digital classes were almost nonexistent." Wells began his work in the animation industry by working in all areas of computer animation. Even while attending college he "showed a particular knack for replicating photorealistic imagery in his computer animations." While in school, he learned basic skills in both digital imaging and lighting. After graduation he spent several years honing his craft. "From there I started working on projects in the smaller markets but was constantly recruited into the feature film market." Through his work in these markets Chris emerged as a digital artist who specialized in lighting and visual effects. "In my particular profession I get to sit down and light digital scenes for movies, but my main job is to work with other artists to make sure that they are hitting their aesthetic marks, whether that is matching a pre-existing image or creating their own concept for a film." As for training beyond the classroom, Chris states that, "I had to learn about photography. It's good to know how to light a small area or enclosure, but it's better when you know how light in the real world works. Photography allows you study light and to develop an understanding of how it behaves."

When Chris was asked to respond to how this area of lighting is different from other lighting areas he identified several important observations, the most important probably being in his statement of, "it's fake." You can do things in the digital world that are impossible to create in nature, but this can have a cost. "The biggest problem I've noticed with myself and other digital artists is that you have so much creative freedom that it's hard to stay focused on what's important. You don't just 'make light,' you also create the surfaces that are being lit. I constantly remind myself that composition is just as important as the world that I'm lighting or creating." He adds that, "Even though the lighting may be fake, the concepts of how you work with light are the same—instead of wearing gloves and climbing ladders, you sit at a desk and turn on the computer."

What Wells likes most about designing in this area of lighting are the challenges and freedoms that come with most projects. "I really enjoy watching and being part of the evolution of a project." This freedom can also have a downside. "Some projects can be mentally exhausting and I've had to work on some projects for months, looking at the same images over and over again." In order to remain current he suggests observing both nature and other people at work. "Since we work in visual effects, I always encourage people to 'go outside' and see the world. The more you see, the more you'll train your eye for future projects. Things are always changing so it's good to watch what other people are doing to see if their ideas might help you in your future work. There are still many things in the digital world that aren't physically accurate, so we learn tricks to accomplish the same look. Over time, people are figuring out how to make the physics work with newer software that, along with subtle changes, helps make higher-quality images possible." His most important advice is to "know what you want, whether it's a photo-real object or an abstraction—always have a plan for what it is that you want to accomplish."

Virtual Light Sources

Virtual lighting makes use of several groups of virtual light sources with distinct properties that are different from one another. These lights can be altered or manipulated in a number of ways (color, intensity, falloff, etc.) that make each source unique in a given setting—much in the same way that traditional luminaires may be controlled. In addition to normal parameters like being able to adjust intensity or color, some of these sources can go on to produce effects that are impossible to create in the real world. Perhaps the most unique of these is the ability to create a negative lighting effect where a virtual light can be pointed and used to actually remove light from a target area. Also, virtual lights do not necessarily cast shadows, which allows for effects like shining a light directly through one object onto another without producing a shadow (Figure 17.10). More specifics regarding the classifications of virtual lights are presented online in Chapter 27. Some virtual lights have names and properties similar to several traditional luminaires like **ambient lights** and **spotlights,** while others (such as **point** or **omnidirectional lights** and **global illumination**) are unique to virtual environments.

Lighting Techniques for Virtual Lighting

Lighting for virtual scenes is often based on the same principles of illumination as other forms of lighting design. However, there are a couple of interesting twists in virtual lighting that allow a designer some extra freedom to create lighting that is impossible to create under real-world circumstances. Here, a designer uses the software to manipulate the lighting so that the final image displays the effects that they want, whether the result can actually be produced in the real world or not. Several of these techniques of cheating in virtual design have already been discussed. However, one additional quality of virtual lighting that is especially interesting comes in the sense of establishing the **falloff** or **attenuation** of a light source. While the intensity of light in the real world follows the inverse square law and rapidly drops off, the attenuation of a virtual light can be set to the whims of a lighting designer. The intensity can even be set to increase as it moves away from its source or fluctuate if it fits the needs of a project. In most cases, virtual lighting follows one of two models. The first tries to replicate the real world and is used in simulations like architectural renderings where a designer is trying to predict the appearance of a subject and its lighting as accurately as possible (Figure 17.11). The second is commonly associated with animations and is based more on the practices used in film and video lighting. **Three-point lighting** has come to be a staple in many animation sequences, but here, too, the industry is moving away from formula lighting and is shifting towards lighting based on the sources and **motivational** needs of a project. Another unique quality of this form of design is that a scene can often be lit with a single light that is representative of a specific source, and the need to duplicate a series of **lighting areas**

a. Original image and light sources

b. Same lights with key light's shadows turned off

FIGURE 17.10 Faking Shadows in Virtual Reality Note how objects have highlights but may (a) or may not (b) cast shadows.

FIGURE 17.11 Virtual Lighting for an Animation Waterwitch animation project with naturalistic virtual lighting. *Photo credit:* University of Georgia, Dept. of Theatre and Films Studies for Perpetual Motion Films and Port Columbus National Civil War Naval Museum; CG Supervisor, Michael Hussey

as in theatrical lighting isn't usually required in virtual designs. This reinforces the illusion of a single source producing a scene's lighting because it eliminates issues like overlapping light pools and multiple shadows from additional lights.

DESIGNER PROFILE

Christopher Higgins

Chris Higgins is a computer animator who specializes in 3D lighting. He holds a degree in Interdisciplinary Study in 3D Computer Animation from the University of Georgia. He is currently the Director of the CG (Computer Graphics) and VFX Department for the Cartoon Network On-Air Promotions. Two current series that his department produces graphics for are the Cartoon Network's *You Are Here* franchise and *Star Wars: The Clone Wars*. During his career, he's had the privilege to conduct Maya Master Classes for notable conferences such as SIGGRAPH. Prior to joining the Cartoon Network he was a Senior CG Animator for Turner Studios and helped launch programs like *Toonami Reface 2006* and *Miguzi* in 2004. Other clients that he produced animations for include TNT, TBS, Turner South, and Turner Sports. Awards that his animations have won include two BDA Gold Awards (NBA—TNT Signature and *Toonami* "Lockdown"—Cartoon Network), two BDA Silver Awards (*Spy Kids 2*—Cartoon Network and *Power Puff: Be An Artist*—Cartoon Network), a Southeastern Regional Emmy (*Swamp Theater*—Turner South) and a Student Emmy while he was in undergraduate school (*Mamita Rica*).

Chris came to specialize in CG lighting after beginning his animation career as somewhat of a generalist. "For my entire career, I've been a 3D generalist who can cover all areas of animation at any given time. Lighting has become one of my primary specialties, partly due to necessity, as there have been numerous times when it was needed, but mostly, because it's always been one of my favorite areas of 3D." His training combines a mixture of traditional training in animation and design (stage design, lighting classes, and color theory) as well as a lot of personal study of movie and TV production. An even more important part of his training was simply done through a lot of hands-on learning—just seeing what worked and didn't work. In order to stay current, he tries to stay abreast with various 3D trade magazines as well as with the traditional film production journals. He's also always looking for the latest groundbreaking animations to learn from.

His big break came when a former professor introduced his work to a friend who worked for Turner Entertainment and ran the 3D department at Turner Effects.

When asked to respond to how CG lighting is different from more traditional areas of lighting Higgins states that, "The biggest difference is that with 3D, you can do anything with the light that you can imagine, without any restrictions due to the physics of light or the real-world equipment used to create it. You can easily control light as you define your frame and can just as easily animate it and change it over time, by setting a few key frames. It's really up to the lighting artist to define the frame." Chris goes on to also explain that, "Since you aren't limited by the number of lights in a scene, you must always ask yourself the question, 'What does the scene need, and what am I trying to accomplish in making these lighting decisions?' More lights are not always better, and in 3D, every light comes at the expense of slower rendering times, so you must make these decisions carefully." In fact, what he likes least about the profession is that this unlimited nature of lighting can be intimidating. "Since anything is possible, the struggle is often deciding what is really needed and limiting yourself so that you can achieve your result while meeting the deadline." He also loves seeing a scene come to life through focusing the viewer's attention with light and creating an appropriate mood for a scene. "I love the step-by-step process of adding a light, seeing its effect, deciding what's needed next, adding another light . . . rinse and repeat. The process of balancing all of the light within the frame feels subjective and artistic, even if it's a simple logo."

As a final thought, Chris considers contrast to be the most essential element of lighting for animation. "In 3D lighting for Broadcast Television, I think Rule #1 is contrast. While many lighting principles should be considered during the lighting process, the most important for conveying the message to the home viewer is the balance of contrast within the frame. It should be present throughout the animation and should direct attention to whatever is considered most important at that time. If you only do one thing with lights, create contrast."

FOR FURTHER READING

Illuminating Engineering Society of North America, *IESNA Lighting Education 150 (Intermediate Level)* (New York: Illuminating Engineering Society of North America, 1993).

Illuminating Engineering Society of North America, *IESNA Lighting Ready Reference*, 4th ed. (New York: Illuminating Engineering Society of North America, 2003).

Illuminating Engineering Society of North America, *IESNA Lighting Handbook*, 9th ed., ed. Mark Rae (New York: Illuminating Engineering Society of North America, 2000).

More detailed references that speak to each of the specific lighting applications are found at the conclusion of each of the online chapters (Chapters 19–27) that have been written on the specialty areas.

18 Projections and Lighting

Projections cover a wide range of topics. They may be as simple as a shadow projection or as complex as a full-blown video that is delivered in real time. They may cover a limited portion of a stage or may surround the entire stage environment. Sometimes the image is formed from a single projector while at other times a number of projectors are used to form a complex composite image for an event. Projections also don't have to necessarily be a traditional image on a screen—any surface, even performers, can serve as a projection surface. While we may think of many projections as requiring expensive or sophisticated equipment, many can be created very simply. On a grand scale, projection technology seems to be growing in complexity on a daily basis, and a designer who chooses to use this technology has a number of options available to them beyond the traditional slide and shadow projection techniques that have been around for many years. Video walls, digital lights, and laser or holographic images are just a few of the more advanced forms of projection that are now available to a designer.

The question of who is responsible for projections in a production has always formed a gray area in the entertainment industry. At times the scenic designer has been in charge of them, while at other times the lighting designer has been responsible for providing the images. Some even draw a distinction between the projection gear and the **content** being the responsibilities of different personnel. Currently, if projections are a significant element of a production, it is common to bring a projection specialist on board as another designer for a production. As projection has become more complex, these specialists and designs have emerged as a *bona fide* design area. Whether or not a specialist is part of a design team, a lighting designer must be very involved in any discussions regarding projections because of the profound effect that the lighting can have on the final images. Projection design is evolving at an incredibly fast rate. New equipment and technologies appear every year, and the roles of the lighting and projection designers keep overlapping more and more. In many cases, projections become a shared responsibility in which all of the designers need to be sensitive to each other's needs. Collaboration must be especially high when using projections due to the impact that they can have on the other design and performance areas. No matter how insignificant the projections may appear, they can't help but to alter the audience's perception of the scenery, costumes, and other design areas. The more dominant they are in a production, the greater the impact they will have on the other design areas and the more important the discussions with other designers become. Projections can also easily steal the focus of a scene, becoming a distraction rather than a component of a scene or production. Over the last several years the roles of projection and lighting designers have become so nested within one another that many professionals discuss this overlap by means of a special term called **convergence.** This trend will continue as lighting designers work to design the entire lit environment.

This chapter cannot begin to provide a full treatment of projections since this is an area of design that is changing so quickly. The **digital lights** and **media servers** that are revolutionizing the way that we think about projection weren't even around several years ago, and **LEDs** have only begun to have a widespread impact on the industry. While I provide discussion on projection equipment, the majority of this chapter focuses on how to use the technology rather than dwelling on the specific equipment.

A BRIEF HISTORY OF PROJECTION

Some forms of projection have been around since the beginning of time—images of shadows from around a campfire or the Indonesian art of shadow puppetry have existed for hundreds if not thousands of years. However, much about projection remained mostly theory until the 1900s due to a lack of sophistication in optics and light sources. Although designers understood the potential for using light as a major element of a setting, they didn't have the means to produce it in a way that could be considered successful. Scenographers like Adolphe Appia, Edward Gorden Craig, and Robert Edmund Jones saw the potential for using light and projection as significant elements of their designs and rendered them into their sketches and renderings but, had no way of producing the effects that they felt were so central to their designs.

The forerunner of traditional optical projectors was called the **magic lantern,** the development of which is generally credited to Jesuit Father Athanasius Kircher during the late 1600s. This projector is crude and produces a fairly weak image by today's standards but is important in that it provides the principle by which most traditional projectors are designed. In its original form the lanterns were used in pairs of two so that a set of projectors produced overlapping images that could be cross-faded from one lantern to another. Originally the projectors were set in the center of a theatre and were illuminated by oil. Later versions used limelight as their light source and were moved to the back of the stage, where through rear projection much of the "magic" of the scenic effects could remain with the technicians. Variations in the use of magic lanterns became an essential element for many of the epic operas of Richard Wagner as projectors became stronger and motion was added to the projections. Moving clouds formed a principle application of these moving images.

The scenographer often credited with first making use of modern projection technology and developing techniques that could produce the projections envisioned by the earlier scenographers was Josef Svoboda. Svoboda spent much of his life developing projection equipment and techniques that have become the foundation for contemporary projection. Svoboda developed most of his theories during the mid–late 1900s while working on opera productions in Prague. Several areas in which he made significant contributions to the field of projection include his development of light curtains, use of low-voltage lamps, creation of large-scaled projections, and experimentation with techniques for charging an atmosphere with particles that reflect a projected beam of light—the foundation for the **hazers** and fog machines that are in common use today. As time has evolved, projectors have become more powerful and sophisticated even though the basic techniques of projection have not changed and traditional projection still requires the same elements that were used over the last century.

A recent development in projection technology over the last 10 years has been in the use of light and images that are produced through electronic rather than optical methods. In this type of projection the slide is replaced by a digital image and projectors like those that might be used for PowerPoint presentations are used. In the most extreme cases, we may even use automated luminaires (**digital lights**) to project the images. Using this technology, an image can be moved to a new location, focused, sized, and even cropped as needed. Even basic distortion like **keystoning** can be corrected with these projectors. In some versions of digital projection, rather than projecting light onto a surface such as a screen, these new technologies allow audience members to actually view the sources creating the projection. A popular version of this innovation are the **video walls** that are used on many concert tours. A network of video monitors may also be assembled into a configuration where images can be sent to the individual screens or to the entire group as a composite image. Finally, LEDs can be assembled into clusters to form screens of almost any proportion. The LED intensities are controlled by software that allows a large-format image to be produced on the surface of a screen in the same way that a television or computer monitor produces an image. Displays like these are becoming more popular all the time and can be seen in places like Times Square. They can even be large enough to fill an entire side of a building.

PROJECTION CONSIDERATIONS

Whenever a design team considers using projections, every lighting designer should perk up—this is true whether they will ultimately be responsible for the projections or if a projection designer has been added to the design team. While there are many valid reasons for bringing projections to a production, they should not be thought of as a cheap alternative to scenery. In reality, they can be time consuming to create, can require turnaround times that may or may not be under the control of the designer, and often cost more than a typical scenic budget by the time you pay for the specialized equipment and image processing that they require. The projections must be thoroughly planned, though there may be many unknowns that don't appear until the production loads into the theater, resulting in compromises where pre-planning mistakes might have to be lived with. Many novices think that projections form a simple solution to a design problem when, in fact, they have no idea what they are getting themselves into. On the other hand, when the designers are thoroughly prepared and a producer is committed to making the expenditures that will allow the projections to be presented successfully, the images can add immensely to a production. Sidebar 18.1 provides some comparisons related to the good and bad of using projections.

ELEMENTS OF PROJECTION

Most projection is done through projecting an image of an object such as a slide onto a screen or other material. Therefore, traditional projection usually involves three components: the **projector** (with the light source), the **slide** or original material, and the **screen** or projection surface. A projector will contain at a minimum a housing that is outfitted

---

SIDEBAR 18.1 Considerations of Projection Design

ADVANTAGES TO USING PROJECTIONS:

1. Ability to easily facilitate a change to a number of different locations or settings.

2. Transitions between scenes can become quick and fluid using cross and split-fade techniques between scenes and other split-focus effects.

3. Can initiate moving effects and scenic elements.

4. Can add texture and depth to a design.

5. Transporting of equipment and slides for touring is more minimal and easily done than with comparable scenic elements.

6. Can establish focus for an audience.

7. Can create an effective presentation style for a production. They allow abstract style and color to be used as a primary design element while providing an ability to soften or modify the effect as needed.

CAUTIONS FOR USING PROJECTIONS:

1. Maintaining proper contrast and balance between the intensity of projections and the rest of the stage.

2. Cost and time issues related to the projection equipment and preparation of the slide materials.

3. Loss of resolution or clarity when projecting to large full-sized images.

4. Distortion in the form of depth-of-field, focus, and keystoning effects.

5. Determination of the proper density or translucency of the slides for optimal projection of rich colors without having the slides become opaque with an associated loss of transmittance.

6. Can distract or steal focus from the primary action of a scene or production.

7. Loss of stage space due to creating neutral zones where actors will not cast shadows onto the screens or within the optical paths of the projectors.

with a high-powered lamp and some means of attaching or holding a slide. A slide can be created from any translucent or transparent material like glass or plastic that allows light to pass through it with various degrees of **transmission.** An opaque object may be used in place of a slide to cast shadows, as in the famous shadow puppet theatres of southeastern Asia. The slides are typically (although not always) mounted near the front of the projector and parallel to the lamp or back of the housing. Most projectors make use of a set of lenses (**objective lenses**) that are placed in front of the slide to help intensify and sharpen its image. Although most projectors hold a single slide, some models accommodate multiple slides added at various positions to form a composite image. Images produced in this manner create different degrees of focus for each layer, which helps to create the illusion of depth in the final image. It is important to note that images can be projected onto any surface and that screens only form one type of projection surface. Scenery and even actors can become viable projection surfaces if the team feels it is appropriate. The relationships between the light source (projector), slide (size and position), and projection surface (distance and type of material) all play a significant role in the appearance of the final image that an audience will observe. These interdependencies also hold true whether a designer is using front or rear projection. One final concept to consider in projection design relates to the fact that many projections work best in a more abstract format and that these images frequently look better if their focus is softened slightly instead of being in sharp focus. On the other hand, this would be undesirable in a project that provides documentary images or film clips for a production. Here again, success is dependent on the context in which the effects are applied. **Depth of field** (the range of what is kept in focus) can also be used effectively by allowing portions of an image to soften at various locations throughout a stage or screen.

FRONT OR REAR PROJECTION?

One of the most important considerations that must be made at the very inception of a production using projections relates to the consideration of whether the images will be projected from in front of or behind the screen or projection surface. This decision affects not only the projection designer but also the lighting and scenic designers. Too many times projections come off as an added layer of an event rather than as an integral part of the overall production. This is frequently a result of other design areas (most commonly scenic) being designed well ahead of the projections and projection surfaces and without the input of the projection designer. In some cases, the scenic and costume designs may have been completely designed before the projection designer has even been hired. Thankfully, this situation is becoming a lot less common.

The consideration of **front projection** versus **rear projection** is a variable that is dependent on an individual production. At times the manner in which a director envisions the use of a stage will dictate one manner over another, while at other times the nature of the performance facility, the scenic design, or even the available equipment may determine which method is most appropriate for a given situation. As a rule, we try to avoid conditions that cause performers to cast shadows onto a projection surface, thereby often favoring rear projections, but if a director or designer wishes textured projection patterns to fall on the actors or scenery, rear projection is out of the question. In the case of front projection, the projectors may be located either from straight ahead of the screen or from an angle to either side or above the screen. On the other hand, when mounting a projector from any angle other than dead-on, distortion enters the situation through keystoning as well as through issues related to depth of field due to the image being cast to a variety of distances from the projector. On occasion these effects may be desirable, but in most cases some form of correction will have to be made to compensate for the distortion. One manner of reducing effects like these is to mount the screens and projectors in such a way that both remain centered along the same optical axis and that the planes of the slide and image remain parallel to one another. Using front-projector locations has an advantage in that the image will appear approximately the same to all viewers across the entire width of an audience, but this also requires that precautions be taken to prevent performers from casting shadows in the projected images.

Throw distances form a consideration in that the size of any image is directly proportional to the lens combination and the projector's distance from a screen. For a number of reasons rear projection tends to be the favored solution because actors can pass close to the projection surfaces without casting shadows onto the projected images. Since the screens used in rear projections actually glow, rear projection tends to produce more vibrant images than those created through front projection, unless the screen material used in front projection is treated with highly reflective materials like white paint or reflective glass beads. However, it is also rare that a highly reflective screen would blend-in aesthetically with the rest of the elements of a production. Common disadvantages of rear projection might include the presence of a *hot spot* at the center of an image that is related to the lens of the projector and the fact that images tend to drop off in intensity and clarity as a viewer moves toward the sides of an auditorium. Another consideration of rear projection lies in dedicating a sufficient amount of backstage space to a neutral zone to give the projectors sufficient throw distances for creating satisfactorily sized images. If the stage does not have enough depth, throw distances can be increased by using a mirror as indicated in Figure 18.1d. Because rear-screen projectors are out of view of the audience, they can also be mounted in a way that eliminates problems like keystoning. Crews will also have relatively easy access to the projectors and might even be able to troubleshoot them at any time (even during a show).

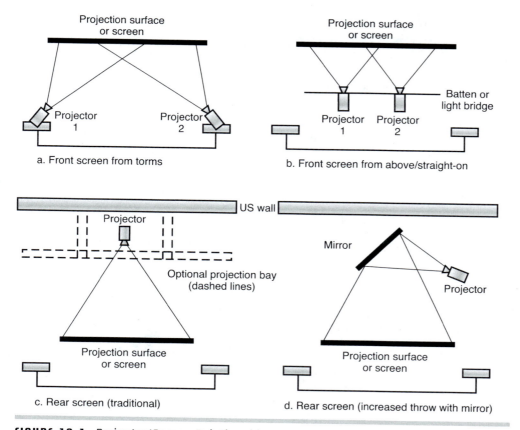

FIGURE 18.1 Projector/Screen Relationships Projectors are typically elevated in each situation to avoid hitting scenery and performers (especially in front projection systems).

TRADITIONAL PROJECTION EQUIPMENT

As stated earlier, the basic elements of projection are the projector, slide/object, and projection surface. All three play a role in the success or failure of a projected image. This portion of the chapter isn't concerned so much with specific equipment as with the general principles, physical properties, and optics that are used within each area of projection design. This segment of the chapter deals with more traditional equipment, while current trends like digital projection are discussed later on in the chapter.

Lensless Projectors

Lensless projectors form the simplest example of projectors and in many cases can be compared to simple shadow projections. The earliest designs were based on variations of the magic lantern. An intense light source is placed at the rear of a housing, which will then have objects or a slide placed in front of it. The smaller the filament and overall light source, the sharper the image that is created by the projector. Some projectors even use the smaller filaments of low-voltage lamps to capitalize on this principle. Slides in these formats may be opaque and used for shadow projections but are more often colored with transparent dyes and high-temperature paints that allow light to pass through them to create a colored image. The less densely that a slide is painted, the brighter the associated image will appear, while the larger the slide, the more detail that can be rendered into both the slide and resulting image. The slides are created from large pieces of glass or plexiglass that are mounted near the front of a projector. The size of the image is directly proportional to not only the distance between the projector and screen, but also the distance between the slide and the light source. The closer that the slide is to the projection surface the sharper it will appear, while the closer that it is to the lamp the larger the image will appear. The best focus occurs when the distance between the screen and slide is kept approximately the same as that from the slide to the lamp. However, if a designer wishes to create an image of any significant size that is in relatively sharp focus, the slide must approach a size that is much larger in order to create the intended image. Limitations such as these result in these projectors being used primarily for more abstract, suggestive projections. A series of composite slides might even be spaced at different depths within a projector to create a layered effect where each slide is progressively more focused than those that are closer to the lamp (Figure 18.2). This can add great depth to an image.

By far the most popular lensless projector is the **Linnebach Projector,** developed in the early 20th century by Adolph Linnebach, a stage engineer from Germany. Linnebach made modifications in the basic design of the lensless projector to create a more effective scenic projector. The results of his efforts produced a more efficient projector that was capable of creating a much larger-scaled image. One of the general

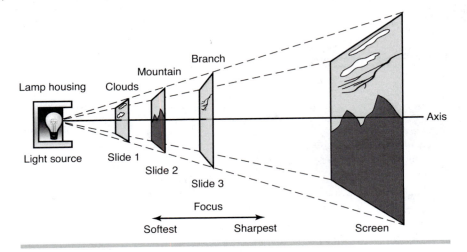

FIGURE 18.2 Lensless Projector with Multiple Slides

design principles of these projectors is that the slide should be placed as far from the light source and as close to the screen as possible. One of the problems with this projector lies in the fact that even with a small lamp, different surfaces of the filament do not perform as a true point light source, which creates a **penumbra effect.** This causes a bit of fuzzing or blurred edges in any image created by this projector. Another issue results from the intensity of the image dropping off at the edges due to the increased distances that the light must travel from the source. Some general rules regarding these projectors relate to using the largest slides you can, using the smallest light source or filament possible, and keeping the distance between the slide and screen to a minimum. On the other hand, the closer that the slide is placed to the light source, the larger the resulting image will be, with the tradeoff being that additional blurring will appear around the edges of the final image. While a Linnebach Projector has a flat front face and makes use of flat slides, a variation with curved sides, the **Cinebach Projector,** is designed to project onto the curved faces of a plaster or wrap-around cyclorama. Slides for these projectors are made of plexiglass, rather than glass, so that they can be bent into the curvature of the projector.

Lens Projectors

Lens projectors have a set of **objective lenses** placed in front of a slide that are used to concentrate and focus the image fairly precisely onto a projection surface. Much of this type of projection produces high quality images that are sharp and well-illuminated. One requirement of most projectors with lenses is a light source capable of producing an intense beam of light. Projectors often have lamps with wattages of several thousand watts, while others can even make use of arc sources. In cases where a projector makes use of an arc, dimming can only be accomplished through some form of dowser or mechanical dimmer. In the majority of projectors, an additional set of lenses (condenser lenses) need to be added between the light source and the slide to both protect the slide from the extreme heat of the light source and provide maximum coverage and illumination of the slide.

The Ellipsoidal Reflector Spotlight (ERS)

Lighting designers are already quite familiar with the simplest form of lensed projector which is the **ellipsoidal reflector spotlight (ERS).** Shadow projections are made through simply inserting a **gobo** into the pattern slot or **gate** of the luminaire. While these are often used to create textured breakups where orientation and distortion are not an issue, there are other occasions, such as when a gobo depicting an architectural detail is projected onto a cyc, where the hanging position and effect of keystoning must be taken into consideration. The majority of the gobos that a designer will use are obtained through purchasing them from theatrical manufacturers who produce a vast collection of different patterns. Custom gobos may be designed through placing a special order with a manufacturer or can be homemade through cutting pie plates or other thin-gauged metal into patterned templates or by etching the design onto print plates using an acid. In the case of enhanced ERSs, they can even be transferred to acetate sheets that are used directly as gobos. All of these methods produce simple projections relatively cheaply. Gobos and their accessories were discussed in detail in earlier chapters.

The 35mm Projector

Another form of lensed projection that is in frequent use is the *35mm Ektagraphic slide projector* by Kodak. The projectors have a variety of lenses that allow them to be modified to a number of different throw distances. More importantly, the projector is fairly easy to acquire and can be used to project full-color photography. There are also accessories that allow a designer to easily complete transitions or **dissolve effects** between two or more projectors. Designers have often modified these projectors through separating the fan and lamp circuits from one another so that the lamp can be assigned to a theatrical dimmer while the fan can run on a non-dim circuit for constant cooling. If this is done, precautions need to be taken to ensure that the lamp is not turned on without having the fan circuit already running. While a designer must take into account the lead time and costs associated with film processing, the slides are for the most part easy to create, and most medium-sized cities have photo labs that can turn your processing around in 24 hours or less—however, do not confuse this type of photo service with the 1-hour processing that is typically found at drug or discount stores. The finished slides are placed in a carousel and are advanced through a simple remote control. When using a number of projections, care should be taken to use the lower capacity (80- versus 140-slide) carousels to help eliminate jamming. For those times when the projections need a bit more intensity, there are power modules available that contain a more powerful lamp and improved optics that slide into the modular design of the projectors and can increase the light output by another 20 to 30%. This format may not be so easy to use in the future because of the trend of shifting away from film toward digital media.

For larger applications the projector can be modified extensively into a more powerful version like the **Buhl Projector.** Buhl Projectors take an Ektagraphic Projector and replace the standard lamp with one of a much higher wattage (from 300 to 1,200 watts) and add a system of heat sinks along with a high-powered fan for extra cooling and a superior set of lenses for producing higher-quality images. These variations of the projector already have the lamp and fan circuits separated and the crews must take extreme care to ensure that the lamp is never turned on without having the fans already running. The heat that can build up in these units is so extensive that permanent damage can be inflicted

---

SIDEBAR 18.2 Calculations Regarding Projectors and Lenses

A. RELATIONSHIP BETWEEN SIZE OF IMAGE AND FOCAL LENGTH OF LENSES

F = Focal Length of Lens   D = Throw Distance

I = Image Size   S = Slide Size

$$F = \frac{D \times S}{I + S}$$

*All units must remain the same (e.g., mm).

*Image and Slide measurements are taken along comparable sides of a slide and image.

To determine the focal length of a lens required to produce a 10-meter-wide image from a 35mm slide for a throw distance of 10 meters:

$$F = \frac{10,000mm \times 35mm}{10,000mm + 35mm} = 34.88 \text{ (or a 35mm lens)}$$

B. RELATIONSHIP BETWEEN THROW DISTANCE AND INTENSITY OF AN IMAGE

I = Illumination Intensity   O = Projector Output

D = Throw Distance

$$I = \frac{O}{D^2}$$

To determine the illumination intensity of an image created by a projector with an output of 2,000 lumens at a distance of 3 meters:

$$I = \frac{2000 \text{ lumens}}{3 \text{ meters}^2} = 222.22 \text{ lumens/meter}^2$$

This same relationship can be used to make determinations of the maximum screen area that can be covered with a specified level of brightness from a projector with a given light output. As an example, if the targeted illumination intensity is 500 lumens/meter^2 and your projector is capable of producing 5,000 lumens:

$$D^2 = \frac{5000 \text{ lumens}}{500 \text{ lumens/meter}^2} = 10 \text{ meters}^2 \text{ or } 10 \text{ square meters}$$

the approximate equivalent of a 3.16 meter $\times$ 3.16 meter screen.

quickly on the projector and slides if a problem develops in the cooling system. Because of the extreme heat of the powerful lamp, any slides placed in a Buhl Projector should be treated by mounting the actual slide between a set of protective glass cover slides and changing the cardboard slide mounts to ones made of either plastic or metal. In reality, switching the mounts to plastic or metal is a good idea for any 35mm slides because they eliminate much of the friction and warping that are associated with cardboard mounts. Buhl Optical has been associated with superior optics for many years and manufactures a variety of lenses for both the Buhl and Ektagraphic Projectors. The designer simply has to match the proper lens to the throw distance and desired image size that they will need for their project. Focal length is inversely proportional to the angle of projection or beam dispersion, and the shorter the focal length, the wider the projected image will be. The overall goal should be to select a lens that will create the intended image size while at the same time placing the projector as close to the screen as possible. This creates projections of maximum intensity.

Scenic Projectors

Scenic projectors are designed for delivering high-quality projections to the stage, and even the least expensive projectors usually represent an investment of several thousand dollars. There are even large-format projectors capable of filling an image over the entire side of a ten story building that can exceed $56,000. Features that set these projectors apart from the smaller projectors include: a more powerful light source (a minimum of 1,500–2,000 watt lamps for incandescent or arc sources), larger slide formats for adding clarity and detail to the images, and superior optics in the objective lens system. Some projectors may also have animation accessories that add moving effects to the projected images. While these projectors may be used to produce less realistic effects, their improved optics and light sources make them ideal candidates for when detail and more photographic-like effects are desired.

Perhaps the most common small-format projector in use is Gam's **Scene Machine.** The basic model provides a modular housing and lamp/reflector assembly equipped with a 1,500 or 2,000 watt lamp. The unit is also equipped with a powerful fan assembly. The Scene Machine is unique in its modular design. Effects like animation disks, slide carousels (actually 4" × 5" format), and film loops form several of the popular accessories that can be snapped into place at the front of this projector. Many of the accessories can be stacked on top of one another to produce composite effects, and the moving effects have speed, directional settings, and remote controls that allow crews to modify an effect as needed. Several of the more popular effects include film loops, fire and rain animation disks, and a large-format slide head. An objective lens selected from a variety of focal lengths is placed beyond the effects **heads** for optimal control of the image. Some of the lenses have extremely wide beamspreads that can be used to cover a large area through a relatively short throw distance, while others are fairly narrow and can be used at considerable distances from the stage. Rosco has also introduced a small format projector, the X-Effects Projector, that makes use of a high-intensity short-arc light source and two wheels that are oriented and rotated in a side-by-side relationship that overlap within the projector's optic path. Traditional, dichroic and textured glass gobos are placed into the wheels to produce a number of animated effects where the speed and direction of the wheels can be controlled independently from one another.

Large-format projectors start to get expensive very quickly and are often not feasible for a number of production companies. Not only are the projectors expensive, but the production of the slides (almost exclusively in large-format glass) can add considerably to the costs of this type of projection. Projection at this scale needs the skills of a specialist who is dedicated to the preparation and execution of the projections and their associated equipment. Projectors of this caliber can deliver a bright image from a significant distance. If a wide-angled lens is used, much of the image can be dispersed over a large area like a cyc. Often, only two of these projectors are needed to cover an entire cyc (one left and one right). The use of large-format projectors is quite popular in opera houses throughout the world. For example, the Metropolitan Opera in New York has no less than 10 or 12 large-format projectors in its repertory plot.

Lamps used in large-format projectors are often rated in the 5,000-watt range with several models even exceeding 10,000 watts. The brightness of even the smallest of these projectors is well over 100,000 lumens, and some can exceed 800,000 lumens. In a number of projectors HMI and arc sources are used, as opposed to incandescent lamps, and a mechanical dimmer is incorporated into the projectors's design. There is an argument for equipping all scenic projectors with mechanical dimmers due to the negative impact that an incandescent lamp can have on an image's color when going through **red-shift** while being dimmed through an electrical dimmer. This change in **color temperature** distorts the natural colors of the slides and images. Pani Projectors, from Austria, provide one of the most popular lines of large-format projectors used in the world today. Along with their superior light sources and optics these projectors can be used in both still and moving effects—even film projections. These projectors are large and bulky, often weighing in at well over 100 pounds and requiring several crew members to maneuver the units into their operating positions. Many of these projectors are large enough that they come equipped with their own mounting frame and caster/dolly system, complete with leveling adjustments. The larger format of the slides (typically 4" × 5" and larger) causes the slides and their preparation to be expensive. One manner of eliminating some of the costs is producing the original slides on acetate or film transparencies and then sandwiching these between two plates of cover glass. Several common slide formats for these projectors include: 3" × 4", 4" × 5", 4" × 6", 6" × 8", and even 8" × 10" and 11" × 14" formats.

SLIDES AND SOURCE MATERIALS

The slide or source material is an extremely important element of any projection and in many cases determines the overall success of a resulting image. The quality of an image can never be greater than that of the original slide—with the notable exception of abstract designs where blurring and less defined resolution can actually work to the advantage of an image. The larger the slide, the more detail and resolution that a designer can build into the image. A variety of methods can be used to produce slides. In the simplest cases, as with gobos, the pattern of the image is simply cut away from an opaque material like a thin sheet of metal. Most slides, however, are designed to produce an image based on the use of some form of translucent or transparent materials. The slide is usually made of glass and is painted with high-temperature paints, markers, or some other etching process. Images may also be painted or drawn on films or acetate and treated as transparencies. Sometimes the images may come from film or other transparencies like photographic slides. Dr. Martin's paints, which have been treated with an additive, or special projection paints from companies like Rosco seem to provide the best results for adding color to these slides. If painting the slides, a designer must pay attention to the density of the materials so that the paint doesn't build any unintentional opaque areas into the slide—these will appear as shadows as opposed to the intended color.

PROJECTION SCREENS

Projection screens are more appropriately called projection surfaces because many projections are not necessarily directed onto a traditional screen. The cyc, scrims, scenery, and even the performers can be viable projection surfaces. In front projection, the surfaces need to exhibit enough reflectivity that the audience can see the images, while in rear projection, the screens have to be translucent enough to allow the image to be seen on the projection surface. Additional conditions that can either aid or obscure projections are in the contrast between the projections and the colors, textures, and overall values of the scenery. Rear projections often appear more vivid because you see the light on the screen's surface as opposed to a reflection of the image. Size and shape of the projection surfaces do not matter as long as they fit within the rest of the scheme and style of a production. Many of the considerations of front versus rear projections were discussed earlier, and only the actual screens are examined here.

Front-Projection Screens

The traditional idea of a projection screen is what comes to mind when we first mention front projection. The basic principle of casting an image on a highly reflective surface that in turn is reflected back to the viewer forms the basis of this screen. The more reflective the surface, the more successful the material will be as a screen. A bigger issue in front projection relates to disguising the screen on a stage. This is an especially important consideration when the screen is being viewed when there are no projections on it. Usual attempts to deal with this issue relate to filling the screen at all times with either projections or washes of colored or textured light. In this way the screen never appears untreated and becomes a part of the overall stage composition. All sorts of materials may be used for front projection systems. Hardcovered wood panels such as masonite that have been painted white, muslin, scrim, and even bed sheets and shower curtains have been used successfully as screens in a pinch. Many screens are made specifically for projection and are crafted from especially reflective materials. Beyond the traditional idea of a projection screen almost anything can become a projection surface. This also holds true of the color of a projection surface where screens can be of any color but with the correlation that some colors are more reflective than others.

One manner of characterizing a screen's ability to reflect or transmit light relates to the **gain** of the screen. The higher the gain, the better the material will perform as a reflector and the better projection surface that it will become. In some cases, such as in movie screens, the gain of a screen has been increased significantly through adhering miniature glass beads to the projection surface. This increases the reflective capabilities of the screen and makes the images appear brighter, but with a negative effect in that the intensity of the image appears to drop off significantly as you move to either side of the screen. These screens work fine when an audience is not spread across any great width, but can present problems in wide auditoriums. This is one of the reasons why movie theatres are often built in a fairly narrow configuration. Matte screen surfaces, on the other hand, are less reflective but tend to have gains that are less affected by viewing angle and are best for working in auditoriums with fairly wide sightlines.

Rear-Projection Screens

There are a number of issues related to front projection that have caused projection designers to consider rear projection as a more successful alternative for creating projections. The most notable issues relate to avoiding the keystone distortion that is common in front projection by providing a straight-on relationship between the screen and projectors. This also helps prevent objects or performers from interfering with and casting shadows in the beams of the projectors. One of the most positive features of using a **rear-projection screen (RP screen)** is that performers can be blocked right up to the projection surface. The biggest negative consideration in rear projection is getting a sufficient backstage throw distance and lens combination for creating the proper sized images. Venues in which there is a known need for using projections are often designed with a cubby-hole known as a **projector bay,** which is an inset that extends several feet into the upstage wall. This allows projectors to be placed directly behind the stage at an additional distance from the cyc and projection surfaces. The Disney Cruise ships use this technique to gain additional throw distances for their scenic projectors.

Almost any material can be used as a projection surface but, in rear projection the designer must pay particular attention to the transmission ability of the material that will be used for the projection surface. A rear-projection screen works on the bases of a certain amount of light being stopped or **diffused** on the projection surface upon which the image is observed. All rear-projection screens must display a certain degree of translucency. If the screen material is too opaque and has too low a **transmission rate** no light will be observed on the front surface of the screen. On the other hand, if the transmission rate is too high, the light will pass completely through the material without having a chance to strike and scatter at the screen to form an image. This is one of the reasons that

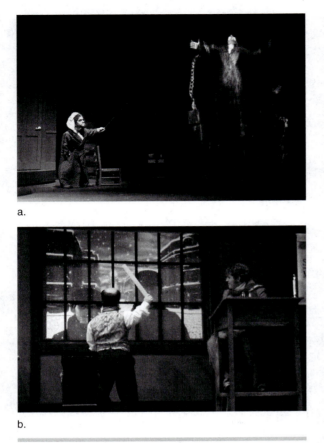

a.

b.

FIGURE 18.3 Projections in the University of Georgia Production of *A Christmas Carol* a. Front Projection of Marley's Ghost onto mesh screen and fog combination. b. Rear-screen projection in shop/office window that combines green screen technology with animation and composite video. *Photo credit:* University of Georgia, Dept. of Theatre and Film Studies

projecting onto fog or haze is not always successful—if the density of the haze drops below a critical level (e.g., the fog dissipates) the light simply passes into space without forming an image. We produced an adaptation of *A Christmas Carol* several years ago where Marley's Ghost was projected onto a combination of fog and crumbled mesh-like material (Figure 18.3a). Initially, the idea was to use just the fog, but when we had problems during techs with keeping the fog from blowing away from the location where the projector was focused, we added the additional material as a means of safe-guarding the projected effect. On the other hand, fog and haze are often used very successfully as a projection surface, from as simple an effect as making the light beams visible at rock concerts, to the rotational effects of spinning gobos in a haze to create textured patterns of revolving light, to full-blown slide projections that appear magically after being cast onto a screen of fog or even water.

Special materials have been created that work especially well for rear-projection screens. These are usually made of relatively thick yet pliable plastic that comes in black, neutral gray, and white colors. The most important aspect of these materials is that they have comparably high gains and can shield an audience from the hotspot of the lens that can be associated with rear projection. The gray and black materials are more popular because they are easier to disguise or blend with a production's scenery. However, as the material gets darker, the images drop off in intensity and are not seen as well by people who are to the sides and outside of a critical viewing angle. This property of lowered appearance is known as **bend.** White screens can provide nearly 180° of visibility for a projected image, while in dark materials this viewing angle can become quite narrow, with people to the extreme sides of an auditorium being unable to see the projected images very well at all. Another consideration of rear projection is whether the lens of the projector becomes visible from behind a screen. This is most commonly seen as a hotspot at the center of the screen's surface. The best way of avoiding this effect is to use a screen or material with a transmission rate high enough that successful projections are created, yet low enough to mask the view of the projector lens, which is most likely located directly behind the screen. Another method involves mounting the projector in a location so that the lens and associated hotspot are out of view of the audience. This may be an easy solution for more abstract projections but will mean that the designer will have to consider distortion corrections in other types of images.

It is best to cover the entire surface of a screen with a single sheet of projection material and to avoid placing any seams across a projection surface if at all possible. A screen exceeding a dimension of more than about 55 inches will have to be assembled from more than one width of material and can be created by joining strips of the material together with clear tape. Precautions must be taken to ensure that a perfect butt joint is created between each strip. If the strips overlap, a shadow will be created, while if the seams don't quite meet, glare and a direct view of the projector's lens will become visible at the gap. Specially sized screens of almost any dimension with no seams can be custom made for a production but are expensive and often out of the question for many shows.

PRACTICAL ISSUES OF PROJECTION

When a design team first considers projections they should be aware that the amount of time and number of issues involved in making successful projections is often misleading. On first impression, they can appear deceptively simple, but in many ways they can add levels of complexity to a show that could have never been imagined on first appearances.

While even professionals can be burned by the process of adding projections into a production, novices should be especially cautious any time that a director casually mentions projections as part of a general production scheme. Issues such as playing space, lines of sight, expensive equipment rentals, projection surfaces, distortion, slide preparation, and turnaround time are all additional elements that must be factored into the production schedules and budget. Projections, on the other hand, can add yet another wonderful layer to a production. The remaining parts of this section relate to several considerations that a lighting designer should examine when designing a production that uses projections.

Two Critical Considerations (Path and Balance)

While there are a host of issues that will contribute to the success or failure of any projection, there are two essential areas of consideration that provide the most insurance for delivering successful projections for a specific project. Both hold true whether a production uses front or rear projection. The first relates to making sure that there is an unobstructed path between the projectors and the projection surface. While a straight-on relationship produces the best results, this isn't always possible, especially in the case of front projection. Therefore, some form of correction must be introduced to deal with the distortion caused by these offset positions. The second primary consideration relates to maintaining a correct intensity or balance between the projected images and the stage illumination. At times, the levels of one or the other may be purposefully increased as a manner of drawing focus to a specific area or feature, but more importantly, both of these must perform together for the entire stage. If the intensities of the projections are too high, they steal focus, and if too low, they cannot be seen appropriately. One of the dangers of using projections relates to having to lower the intensities of the general lighting in order to maintain the proper balance between the overall stage and weak projections. This most commonly occurs when the projectors aren't strong enough for a given situation. The overall effect can cause visibility issues for the entire production while also creating a muddy grayed-out effect in the stage illumination (red shift issues).

Spill and Ambient Light

With one of the primary successes of projections being determined by the balance of intensities between the projections and the rest of the stage, it stands to reason that spill and ambient light need to be major considerations on the part of a lighting designer. Probably more so than anything else, a lighting designer needs to be sure that spill in no way falls onto a screen or projection surface. Several ways of accomplishing this include: tight shuttering and focus control, creating neutral zones that are 4 to 6 feet wide between an acting area and a projection screen, using steeper angles in lighting systems that are focused near the screens, and avoiding low, flat washes from the front-of-house lighting positions. Other techniques that can help include emphasizing sidelighting in areas directly downstage of the screens, placing a scrim several feet in front of a screen (rear projections only), and to avoid blocking the actors to positions directly in front of the screens. A lighting designer has to consider the effect of not only direct spill but also reflected light bouncing off the floor or other surfaces onto a projection surface. One method that can control some of the reflected light coming from the floor is to locate the screens 4 to 5 feet off the floor (even higher if possible) so that the light is reflected into the scenery rather than the screen. Another technique places a scrim between the screen and downstage light sources. Careful consideration of the floor treatment and its finish can also prevent this from happening.

Ambient light is harder to control because it doesn't necessarily strike the screen surfaces directly but instead gives an overall glow to a stage. Most of this is simply due to a general presence of reflected light. The best manner of controlling ambient light is to use only as much light elsewhere across the stage as needed. Don't run excessively high intensity levels on anything and try to avoid full-stage lighting as much as possible. Try to use the lighting to establish tight focuses and keep the light confined to those performers that form the primary elements of a given moment. You might also encourage the scenic designer to use black and matte materials in their masking and other scenic treatments to absorb as much of the stray light as possible. The more that you can control the spill and ambient light, the better chance that you will have of maintaining a proper balance between the projections and the rest of the stage.

Image Size

Another area of concern relates to achieving the proper size for a projection. This is a function of several issues but is most dependent on the lens configuration and the throw distance between the screen and the projector. While it may seem that all you need to do to get a larger image is to increase the throw distance or shift to a wider-angled lens, the increased size comes with sacrifices. The most notable is through the effect of the **inverse square law,** where the same amount of projected light is spread over a greater surface area, resulting in a dimmer image. A way of compensating for this lowered intensity is through dividing the projection into smaller units that are each projected separately. This not only allows more complex images to be created through a composite effect but more importantly allows the projectors to be placed closer to the screen, with each one projecting a smaller portion of the image. This automatically produces an intensity increase in the final image since there are more lumens of light striking the screen through the additional projectors as well as the effect of the shorter throws between the projectors and the screen.

Distortion

The last area of concern relates to **distortion** and other factors that have an influence on how a projection appears to an audience. We tend to refer to distortion as any variation or shift in appearance between the original slide and the projected image. While some distortion may come into the system through any of the three primary components of a projection system, the majority of any image distortion usually comes about through issues related to either the actual slide or the manner in which the slide is projected or strikes a projection surface.

FOCUS Focus relates to the overall sharpness of an image. The original image in the slide should be sharp and in focus. The projector can always be used to soften the slide if necessary. If a slide begins with being out of focus, then its focus cannot be sharpened beyond that point. This principle holds especially true if you are using photographic images. You can never improve the sharpness of a slide through projection—you can only make it worse!

DEPTH OF FIELD Once an image is focused onto a screen, there is an area both in front of and behind the screen where a sharp focus will be maintained (Figure 18.4). **Depth of field** relates to this range in which the image remains in focus. When a screen and projector are kept in a flat-on relationship depth of field isn't a major issue. However, if the screen is placed in a position that is oriented diagonally in relationship to the projector, depth of field can become an issue, as the plane coinciding with a sharp focus only exists at one point throughout the depth of the screen, and some areas of the screen will be closer to the projector while others will be farther away. This results in portions of the image falling in and out of focus depending on what part of the screen the image is actually focused to. The way to correct this situation is selecting a lens that is associated with a large enough depth of field to keep the entire image focused throughout the depth of the screen. The larger the depth of field, the more of the screen that will remain in focus. Lenses with shorter focal lengths (wider angled) will have a larger depth of field. This works well for trying to keep throw distances shorter, but if using narrow lenses to project longer distances, the depth of field will be narrower and more precisely defined. Longer throw lenses also tend to have an overall lower light output than shorter ones. Tilting a

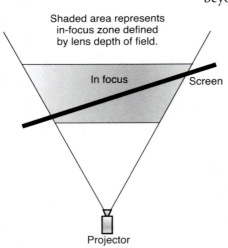

Shaded area represents in-focus zone defined by lens depth of field.

In focus

Screen

Projector

FIGURE 18.4 Depth of Field with Angled Screens Maintain plane of screen within depth of field of lens for good focus control.

screen forward or backward so that more of its surface falls within the depth of field is another way of correcting this problem.

RESOLUTION   Resolution relates to the amount of detail in an image. In most cases, any slide used in a projection application will be magnified considerably. Therefore, any detail (or blemish) will also be magnified significantly in the final image. Because of this, projection designers should provide as much detail as possible in the slides that they create. They should also take special care to avoid careless imperfections as they make any slides that will be used for projections. The amount of required detail in the slide will vary depending on factors like the detail needed in the final image, throw distance, and lens configuration of a projector. In computer-based images special attention should be paid to the resolution of an image so that problems with **pixelation** can be avoided (small rectangular tiles that form the basic component of computer-generated images). In photographic images, this is seen in the graininess of the film: the more grain or the lower the density of the film, the greater a problem this will be for the projection. The more that an image is scaled up, the bigger the issue of resolution becomes. This is why large-scaled projections are created with larger-sized slides.

KEYSTONE EFFECT   When a screen-to-projector relationship is anything but straight-on, a form of distortion takes place called **keystone effect** or **keystoning**. A prime example of this is seen when two sides of an image that would otherwise be parallel appear to tilt in or away from one another. The effect can happen within a single plane or in some cases a double plane resulting in all four sides of an image being distorted. This type of keystoning occurs when a projector is mounted both above and to one side of a screen. The best solution for fixing keystoning is in creating slides that are themselves distorted in such a way that they counter the distortion that would be found in an image. The approach follows the idea of two wrongs making a right. The following methods are typical solutions for correcting keystoning in slides (see Sidebars 18.3 and 18.4):

1. The simplest manner of correcting for keystone effect is as simple as tilting the screen so that it ends up being placed in a flat relationship with the projector lens. If a projector is mounted from an overhead position for a frontal projection, the screen's bottom would be tilted out. This practice of tilting the screen can be done in one or several planes, however, the angle that the screens make with an audience may become an issue. Often, this type of correction for a straight-on or straight-back situation isn't even perceivable to an audience.

2. Photographic film in the form of slides are one of the most popular choices of slide material for many projection designers (withholding digital images). One of the most popular manners of correcting for keystone effect involves shooting a photograph of the original artwork from a perspective (position and angle) that corresponds with where the projector will be located in relationship to the screen. The first step in the process involves plotting the exact horizontal and vertical angles that a projector will make with the screen and then taking a photograph of the original artwork with a camera placement that simulates exactly the opposite of where a projector will be located. While this fixes the angle issues, the designer must also crop the photograph to adjust for the proper distance that the projector will be from the screen. If the projector were located 30° above a horizontal reference line to a screen, then the photograph for the slide should be taken 30° below this reference line. The resultant slide should fully correct for the given projector position. However, this is a one-time solution, and if the projector or screen are relocated in any way a new set of slides will have to be photographed based on the new relative positions.

3. A mathematical construction may be used to plot out and calculate the keystone effect that will occur within any particular screen/projector relationship. Sidebar 18.4 illustrates this technique.

4. In a number of theatres that use projections on a regular basis scenic projectors are often hung as part of a rep plot or from a series of standardized locations. Many large-scale

SIDEBAR 18.3 Keystone Correction

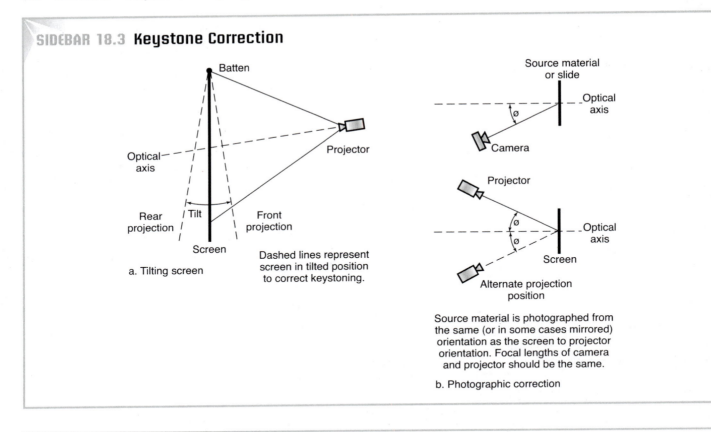

a. Tilting screen

Dashed lines represent screen in tilted position to correct keystoning.

Source material is photographed from the same (or in some cases mirrored) orientation as the screen to projector orientation. Focal lengths of camera and projector should be the same.

b. Photographic correction

SIDEBAR 18.4 Mathematical Grid for Keystone Correction

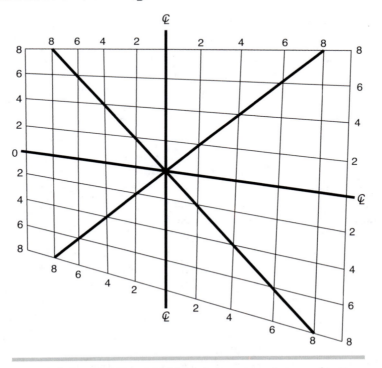

A master distortion grid is prepared for each screen-to-projector combination. The grid is then used as a master template for all slides that will be used for that projector/screen combination. Master grids are frequently made by hanging a gridded drop in the proposed screen location and taking a photograph of the drop and its markings from the proposed projector location.

opera houses throughout the United States and Europe have projectors mounted on a permanent basis throughout their theatres. Companies making use of this system have master slides already configured with keystone guidelines based on the screen positions that a particular projector is typically used for. These master slides contain a skewed grid that is oriented along the axis and planes of a given screen location. The designer then uses the master slides as guides in producing the distorted production slides required for each projector/screen combination. Sidebar 18.4 illustrates a distortion grid that might be used for a master slide.

5. For more abstract projections a designer might paint a portion of a slide and periodically put it into the projector to view it on the actual screen that the image will be projected on. This is a trial-by-error technique that isn't often practical because most of the time the slides have to be completed prior to a show's load-in.

DIGITAL PROJECTORS AND LIGHTS, LCD/LED SCREENS, AND MEDIA SERVERS

Digital projection represents the future for the projection industry. The basis of digital projection is the replacement of the slide that serves as the source of an image with a digital source or computer file and the traditional optical projectors with digital or electronic ones. One of the great attractions of digital projectors is in their ability to display both video and computer images along with the ease with which the images can be modified. This allows immense potential for not only creating but also manipulating source material. Video sequences can be edited and input to a projector, while still images may be created and modified with software packages like Adobe's PhotoShop or Microsoft's PowerPoint that are then sent directly to a digital projector. The sources of these images are readily available through paint programs, image downloads, image scans, and digital cameras (both still and video). No matter how the artwork is created, it is sent by computer to a digital projector that can be set up for either front or rear projection. Duplicate images using multiple projectors can also be created through a process that is as simple as placing a signal splitter and extra set of cables for each of the projectors rather than having to have duplicate sets of slides prepared for each projector.

Another significant advantage to digital projection is in the ease with which the images can be modified, sometimes even on the fly. Today's software allows images to be edited with an everyday computer, even a laptop, while today's projectors can aid us even further with features that can be used to correct issues like a limited amount of keystoning. Most importantly, turnaround times requiring film processing and special labs are eliminated. Sources of media that can be very easily projected through today's projectors include: traditional video tape (VHS cassettes), live video feeds, computer designed graphics and animations, web content, and digital images (still and video) from CD-ROMs and DVDs. All of these sources have led to imaginative new uses of projections in the entertainment business. Several years ago the University of Georgia produced a play (*The Living Newspaper*) that even featured a live chatroom that allowed people online to simultaneously respond to segments of the production that were being presented as a live Web broadcast. To make matters even more interesting, the chatroom conversations (though delayed for 10 seconds and edited if appropriate) were also projected live on a screen that was worked into the scenic design of the production. Through this, the Web audience actually became active participants in the performance event.

Early video and digital projectors were large and bulky while also being marginal in terms of their lumen output. This frequently resulted in placing limitations on the size of a projection screen and a lowering of the overall stage lighting levels so that a proper intensity balance could be maintained between the projections and the rest of the stage. The excitement in digital projection over the last 5 to 10 years relates to a series of innovations in projectors that have made them especially attractive to the entertainment industry.

Among some of the most important changes are reduced physical size and weight, more complexity and ability to deliver higher resolution images, reduced cost, and most importantly a much higher lumen output. While the lumen output of projectors several years ago was relatively low, there are now projectors that are in use in classrooms and business offices that can be purchased through an office supply store that have strong enough lumen outputs to work in many small theatres. These projectors can produce outputs as high as 2,000 lumens. Bigger projectors that are more applicable to the entertainment industry and large-scaled applications have lumen outputs that frequently fall in the range of 5,000–20,000 lumens, while some large-format projectors have outputs that can exceed 50,000 lumens.

The first widely used digital projector was the **CRT (Cathode Ray Tube) projector,** which essentiality projected three overlapping images of red, blue, and green light onto a screen. This technique had a relatively low light output but was all that we had in the late 1970s–80s and was based on the same technology made popular in the first generation of widescreen TVs. Many of these projectors were popular in bars and nightclubs of that time and were used to project news and sports programs to a bar's customers. Newer versions, the **LCD projectors,** combine the output of the three colors into a single high intensity light source that is usually produced through some form of short-arc like a xenon or metal halide lamp. The manner of image creation in a LCD projector is essentially the same as the **LCD screen,** with the exception being that the light source is located behind and projects through the LCD panel or display. Projectors like these have become a popular element of the concert industry, big awards shows, industrial meetings, and trade shows where closeups of the performers or speakers are placed on screens located to either side of, or behind a stage. Many of the mega-churches that are popular today use these displays as a regular part of their worship experience. Two issues that a lighting designer must consider when lighting performers who are being videoed for projections during a live performance include maintaining a proper balance between the illumination of the stage and the screens, and achieving the required illumination levels required for both the stage and cameras throughout the performance.

A final form of projection that is beginning to emerge is in the use of **digital lights.** These are special variations of automated fixtures that not only perform the standard operations of automated lights but also many of the functions of a projector, including projection of both still and video images. When using a digital light, projections can be moved at will to a new screen or surface, then resized and focused as needed, and can even be corrected for the new position's keystoning and individual shuttering needs. These unique projection tools are especially complex and expensive, but with all the features that they bring to a production, more design teams are choosing to use them all the time. One of the most important aspects of these specialized projectors is their ability to be run from a DMX signal that allows them to be operated from a traditional lighting console along with all the other lights. While some digital lights like High End's Digital Light DL.2 or .3 have all the control software actually loaded in the lighting unit (an onboard media server), most digital lights and displays require that their video content be developed and sent to the fixture through a secondary piece of equipment called a **media server.** High End's DL.1 works in this fashion. Media servers are discussed in more detail at the end of this section. The DL.2 and .3 even have a camera that can be used to capture video images or to perform as an infra-red sensor for locating pick-ups and observing an otherwise dark stage. Control can be an issue with these units since all of the many functions and attributes require additional channels—the DL.3 will use up to 170 channels of DMX control. As the projection, video, and lighting fields become more closely married; digital lights will perform more common tasks and will become an even more vital tool in the future.

In the last 10 years the electronics industry has perfected several techniques for generating screened images that are produced through a composite effect. In these technologies a screen is made up of clusters of red, blue, and green light sources that glow at various intensities in order to create a composite image. The final image is a combination of light outputs that work much like a color televison, but on a grand scale. In many ways the process isn't that much different from that used in the pointillism painting technique. While these techniques don't represent a true form of projection since we actually observe the light sources by looking at the screens, they are still becoming a popular means of adding video and other computer material (**content**) to a production. Each cluster of sources becomes like a pixel of the larger image, and the smallness of each, along with how closely they are arranged with the neighboring clusters, determines the overall **resolution** of a screen. The screens may be a single entity or may be formed from a matrix of several smaller screens that produce a tiled effect with each screen carrying a portion of a larger image. **Video walls** are a variation of this tiled treatment. One of the primary screen varieties that make use of this technology is the **LCD (Liquid Crystal Display) screen.** In this case, the output and associated colors of each small element of the screen (**RGB, or Red, Green, and Blue**) are based on the individual reflectance of each of these color elements as varied by a small control voltage. Large-screened versions of this type of media can be seen in advertising screens in major population centers. Times Square is filled with displays based on this technology—even live video is often displayed on the screens. Newer versions of this technology that have been introduced in the last several years use **LEDs (Light-Emitting Diodes)** as a light source that has proven to be yet another major innovation in projection.

One issue that must be considered in working with screens that are based on LCD or LED technology relates to the **pitch** of a screen. Pitch is the size or spacing of the smallest element of a screen (the spacing between the clusters that make up a minimally sized area or pixel of a screen, i.e., each cluster of three-colored LEDs). The pitch is a factor because it determines not only the cost of the screen but more importantly the resolution and optimal viewing distance, or range, of a screen. While a higher resolution or definition screen will be desired for relatively close distances, a lower-definition screen can be used at larger distances. If the lower-definition screen is viewed from too close, the image will be distorted because you will see the individual imaging elements. Another property that affects the appearance of these screens relates to the **color depth** or number of colors that a screen can effectively create. The simplest screens display 8-bit data, which translates to 256 different levels for each of the three primary colors and a total of 16.7 million different colors. A 16-bit screen on the other hand can create 65,000 color levels in each of the primaries for a total of 275 billion colors. LEDs form a special point of interest in screen developments because of their capability to be formed into video walls. One early version of this type of system that was installed in Radio City Music Hall created a complete scenic background for this epic-sized stage. Similar walls have made appearances in several recent Broadway productions as well.

The final element of many digital projection techniques lies in a piece of optional equipment called a **media server.** Media servers are specialized computers (some under Mac, others under Windows) that allow a designer to create and edit media content for any of the digital screens or projectors that have already been discussed. Once the content has been developed in the media server it is transferred to a digital projector or screen. The media content is sometimes run from the server directly and sometimes downloaded to the fixture and run independently of the server. These devices generally come pre-loaded with a diverse collection of video and animation files that can be used either directly or with modifications to produce a number of visual effects. Additional content can also be imported from existing collections found on CDs and DVDs, shared media libraries, Web downloads, or more importantly, digital content that is provided directly to the programmer by the designer or any other member of the production team. Several of the most popular media servers in use today are the Catalyst and Axon Media Servers by High End Systems (the Axon being a second generation media server), the Hippotizer by Green Hippo Ltd, and the Mbox Extreme by Production Resources Group (PRG). These servers are extremely complex and provide an incredible number of variables for creating media content and effects. Media servers can severely tax a lighting control system, but designers continue to use them because of the potential that they bring to a production's media design. As lighting consoles get faster and less expensive and as we become more comfortable with adding additional universes to our control systems we will continue to find media servers becoming a more popular element of entertainment lighting. This area of technology is changing so rapidly that it is nearly impossible to stay on top of the trends and equipment innovations that are related to digital design and projection. To offset this, many manufacturers keep up-to-date Web pages that are dedicated to their equipment as well as online forums where users can exchange information and share ideas.

As production costs continue to escalate, media servers along with LCD projectors, video walls, and digital lights are becoming viable alternatives, or an important supplement, to theatrical scenery. Recent Broadway hits like *Young Frankenstein* and *Ring of Fire: The Music of Johnny Cash* have used media servers to support effects and scenic illusions demanded by these productions. On the down side, a small media server and single associated luminaire may require 70 to 80 channels of independent control simply to achieve the basic motions and projection capabilities that may be required for a projection sequence. More extensive servers can demand over 300 channels of control. This degree of sophistication makes this technology understandably expensive, and more importantly calls for an individual whose sole function is to deal with the projected images. Now that automated fixtures are capable of projecting digital images and video, the lighting industry is once again going through a debate as to what type of relationship should exist between the lighting, scenic, and video designers as these disciplines draw themselves closer to one another—once again, coming back to the issue of **convergence.**

LASERS AND EFFECTS PROJECTION

There are a number of times when projections may be used to create a special effect. The simplest versions of these effects are nothing more than a moving wheel like an **animation disk** that is placed in front of a traditional spotlight. These devices can be used quite successfully for creating effects like rippling water, rain, or fire. I even created a variation of this effect a number of years ago to suggest the moving windmill that Don Quixote/Cervantes attacks in a production of *Man of LaMancha*. Newer versions of animation disks can be found in devices like Rosco's Infinity accessory. The **Scene Machine** and other **effects projectors** mentioned earlier also function in much the same manner to produce a variety of effects. Other projected effects relate to using mirrors with transparent materials like glass or plexiglass and light to reflect images from one place to another. The famous effect known as **Pepper's Ghost** is created in this fashion. If you've ever experienced the *Haunted House* ride at either Disneyland or Disney World you've witnessed a variation of this effect in the last few moments of the ride as several ghosts appear to sit by you in your car.

Several unique forms of projection can be found in the use of **lasers** and **holograms.** Most of these effects are created through an intense directional beam of light that is produced in the form of a laser. Some laser effects are nothing more than projecting and reflecting laser beams off a series of mirrors that have been precisely located and focused or aimed throughout a venue. Many concert tours place mirrors at various points throughout their trusses, and when the air is charged with haze, the laser paths become visible. A special version of laser, called a **scanner,** moves the laser very quickly along a path that traces a shape or outline of a figure or image. This movement is so fast that the eye can not see the tracing action and instead sees the full path or image that the laser has scanned or traced. A hologram is another advanced effect that is produced through a combination of laser and film effects. The unique quality of a hologram is that it can be used to produce an illusion of a three-dimensional image. Many of these effects use lasers that are powerful enough to cause damage to a person's eyes and therefore need to be regulated carefully. As a result, licensed operators and special permits are often required to use lasers in a performance. In order for the majority of these effects to work properly, they, too, need to be projected onto a surface—with haze or fog often becoming this projection surface. However, due to their power and concentrated beam, lasers can also cover large distances. For this reason these effects are quite popular in large arena or stadium productions like rock concerts and outdoor events where they are used to produce a number of aerial effects and projections. In large aerial displays the projection surface may be clouds, or more commonly the smoke associated with fireworks that have also been worked into an event. Near Atlanta, a local event at Stone Mountain Park produces a lavish light and laser show that is accompanied by music and fireworks almost every night throughout the summer. It is thought to be the largest permanent exterior laser installation in the world. The evening fireworks and finale production (*IllumiNations*) at Disney World's *Epcot Center* also forms another example of these laser projections. In this event, a series of lasers are beamed from the world pavilions, from building to building, across the large lagoon that forms the centerpiece of the park. In the grand finale scanning lasers are projected onto the geosphere structure that houses the *Spaceship Earth* ride, which transforms the giant sphere into a large circling image of a rotating earth.

CONVERGENCE

Convergence is a relatively new term to the lighting industry that we are just starting to use to discuss the interrelationships that are emerging between the scenic, lighting, video, and projection disciplines. With the advent of digital projection all sorts of new potential has been introduced to the projection industry. It is also becoming more difficult to separate where any projection issues may fall between each of these varied disciplines. Projection surfaces are often elements of the setting, video is becoming an ever more important element of content, and luminaires are now effectively being used as projectors. While each of these areas will most likely remain as separate disciplines and a "super" designer who designs all of these elements will probably never emerge, convergence does relate to the need for more collaboration and troubleshooting between the different design specialists. Why not a "super" designer? Each design expert came about as a result of increased sophistication and complexity in a given area of design. This trend continues at an ever-increasing pace as a result of an industry that is becoming ever more specialized. All these developments are driving the industry in much the same way that technology in the lighting industry eventually led to the acceptance of the lighting designer as a specialist in the 1950s–60s and the programmer as a specialist around the turn of the new millennium. We have now reached a point where there is a projection design classification within the United Scenic Artists (USA).

For lighting designers, convergence is extremely important for two reasons: first, just as in the past, we are the individuals most responsible for maintaining the balance and overall look of the entire stage composition, and second, our equipment is now being called upon to deliver more and more of the content (especially video) used in contemporary productions. More importantly, the area between lighting and video is becoming more blurred all the time through the continued development of these digital technologies. While many video or projection designers tend to concentrate on content that is more specific for a given situation, there seems to be a tendency for designers coming from a lighting background to use this technology as a texturing tool, much like an advanced form of gobos or animated effect. Lighting designers and programmers are also finding themselves being regarded as the individuals who are responsible for specifying and maintaining this technology, even though the content may have been developed by another member of the production team. Finally, a single designer often sees things differently than if there were two separate designers representing their own areas. In the end, the single designer should be able to maintain balance between the different areas more effectively while creating a more cohesive final image than if the video and lighting designer only worried about designing their own areas. In the 2005–2006 season alone digital technology played a significant role in more than a few new Broadway productions.

A couple of these included: *The Woman in White* (a musical by Andrew Lloyd Webber), *Lestat* (a vampire musical), *Ring of Fire* (the Johnny Cash story), *The Color Purple*, the London revival of *Sinatra*, and a Toronto production of *The Lord of the Rings*. Several additional Broadway productions that have made successful use of digital projection and convergence in the last several years include *Wicked, Jane Eyre,* and the recent revival of *Into the Woods.* Even the new productions by Blue Man Group in Toronto and Las Vegas make widespread use of both digital and conventional projection techniques, not to mention all of the digital imaging associated with the concert industry and spectacle productions like the Beijing Summer and Vancouver Winter Olympic Games. With all these successes, it can easily be concluded that digital projection and screen technologies will continue to play an ever-increasing role in future productions.

FOR FURTHER READING

Bellman, Willard F., *Lighting the Stage: Art and Practice,* 3rd ed. (Louisville, KY: Broadway Press, 2001).

Kook, Edward F., *Images in Light for the Living Theatre* (New York,: Edward F. Kook, 1963).

Kramer, Wayne, *The Mind's Eye: Theatre and Media Design from the Inside Out* (Portsmouth, NH: Heinemann, 2004).

Saxby, Graham, *Manual of Practical Holography* (Oxford, UK: Focal Press, 1991).

Walne, Graham, *Projection for the Performing Arts.* London, UK: Focal Press, 1995.

APPENDIX A
Lighting Periodicals

Entertainment Lighting Design

American Cinematographer (www.theasc.com)

DV—Digital Video (www.dv.com)

Filmmaker Magazine (www.filmmakermagazine.com)

Lighting and Sound America (www.lightingandsoundamerica.com)

Live Design (www.livedesignonline.com)

Projection, Lights and Staging News—PLSN (www.plsn.com)

Theatre Design and Technology—TD & T (www.usitt.org)

Videomaker Magazine (www.videomaker.com)

Archival entertainment publications that are no longer in print:

Lighting Dimensions

Theatre Crafts

Theatre Crafts International

Architectural and Display Lighting Design

AL—Architectural Lighting (www.archlighting.com)

AL LED; a supplement to Architectural Lighting
    (www.archlighting.com)

Architectural SSL (www.architecturalssl.com)

ArchiTech (www.architechmag.com)

Contract Lighting (www.contractlighting.net)

Hospitality Lighting (www.residentiallighting.com/
    %5CHospitality-Lighting-article10705)

Illuminate: Lighting Architectural Spaces; a supplement to
    Architectural Products (www.arch-products.com)

Interiors and Sources (www.interiorsandsources.com)

Lighting Design and Application—LD + A (www.ies.org)

Metropolis Magazine (www.metropolismag.com)

Mondo* Arc (www.mondoarc.com)

Residential Lighting (www.residentiallighting.com)

VMSD (www.vmsd.com)

Online Resources

eLumit (www.elumit.com)

Design Guide (www.designguide.com)

Light Search (www.lightsearch.com)

*Many of these trade publications offer both online and print versions.

APPENDIX B
Lighting Equipment Manufacturers

The companies listed below form a sampling of manufacturers that produce a variety of lighting equipment. Some of these companies specialize in theatrical or entertainment equipment, while others are representative of other specialized areas of lighting, such as architectural or display lighting equipment. The address of each company's Web site is provided so that students may be directed to the most current information regarding a variety of lighting products. There has been no attempt to create a comprehensive list of manufacturers, only enough to aid students in beginning the task of researching the quickly evolving equipment. Many companies also contribute products in more than one of the categories but are listed in only one area as a means of saving space.

Luminaire and Control Equipment

A.C.T. Lighting/M.A. Lighting (www.actlighting.com)

Acclaim Lighting (www.acclaimlighting.com)

A.C. Power Distribution, Inc. (www.acpowerdistribution.com)

Action Lighting (www.actionlighting.com)

Alkalite/Elation Lighting (www.elationlighting.com)

Altman Lighting Company (www.altmanltg.com)

American DJ (www.americandj.com)

Applied Electronics (www.appliednn.com)

Avolites (www.avolites.org.uk)

Barco/High End Systems (www.highend.com)

Chauvet Lighting (www.chauvetlighting.com)

Clay Paky S.p.A. (www.claypaky.it)

Compulite Systems (2000) Ltd. (www.compulite.com)

DmxSoft (www.dmxsoft.com)

Dove Lighting (www.dovesystems.com)

Electronic Theatre Controls (ETC) (www.etcconnect.com)

Electronics Diversified, LLC/Cooper Controls (www.edionline.com)

Galaxia, Electronics Co. Ltd. (www.winvision.co.kr)

ICD -Coemar USA (www.icd-usa.com)

Johnson Systems, Inc. (www.johnsonsystems.com)

KUPO Industrial Corp. (www.moonlightusa.com)

Lehigh Electric Products, Co. (www.lehighdim.com)

Leprecon (www.leprecon.com)

Leviton/NSI/Colortran (www.leviton.com)

Lex Products Corp. (www.lexproducts.com)

Lighting and Electronics, Inc. (www.le-us.com)

Lightronics, Inc. (www.lightronics.com)

Lycian Stage Lighting (www.lycian.com)

Martin Professional (www.martin.com)

Moonlight Illumination Co. (www.moonlightusa.com)

Philips/Color Kinetics (www.colorkinetics.com)

Philips/Strand Lighting (www.strandlighting.com)

Phoebus Lighting and Manufacturing (www.phoebus.com)

PixelRange (www.pixelrange.com)

Robe Lighting (www.robelighting.com)

SGM Technology/Techni-Lux (www.techni-lux.com)

Selecon North America (www.seleconlight.com)

Spotlight S.R.L. (www.spotlight.it)

SSRC (www.ssrconline.com)

Strong Lighting Equipment (www.strong-lighting.com)

Swisson of America Corp. (www.swisson.com)

Techni-Lux, Inc. (www.techni-lux.com)

TMB Production Supplies and Services Worldwide (www.tmb.com)

Vari-Lite (www.vari-lite.com)

Zero 88 (www.zero88controls.com)

Peripheral Equipment and Accessories

Apollo Design and Technology, Inc. (www.internetapollo.com)

Birket Specialty Lighitng (www.birketspecialtylighting.com)

City Theatrical, Inc. (www.citytheatrical.com)

Doug Fleenor Design (www.dfd.com)

Entertainment Technology–a Philips Group (www.etdimming.com)

GAMPRODUCTS, INC. (www.gamonline.com)

GOBOLAND (www.goboland.com)

GoboMan, Inc. (www.goboman.com)

Goddard Design Company (www.goddarddesign.com)

INLIGHT GOBOS (www.inlightgobos.com)

Lee Filters (www.leefiltersusa.com)

RC4 Wireless/Soundsculpture Inc. (www.theatrewireless.com)

Rosco Laboratories, Inc. (www.rosco.com)

SeaChanger by Ocean Optics (www.oceanoptics.com)

SSRC (www.ssrconline.com)

Tempest Lighting (www.tempestlighting.com)

Wybron, Inc. (www.wybron.com)

Lighting Software

AGi32 Software (www.agi32.com)

AutoDesk (www.autodesk.com)

Cast Software (www.cast-soft.com)

FocusTrack (www.focustrack.co.uk)

Future Light, Inc. (www.future-light.com)

LD Assistant (www.ldassistant.com)

LTI Optics (www.ltioptics.com)

John McKernon Software (www.mckernon.com)

Stage Research, Inc. (www.stageresearch.com)

Vectorworks Spotlight by Nemetschek North America (www.vectorworks.net)

Lamps and Light Sources

GE Lighting (www.gelighting.com)

Philips Lighting (www.philips.com)

Osram Sylvania (www.sylvania.com)

USHIO America, Inc. (www.ushio.com)

Architectural Equipment

AC Electronics (www.ace-ballast.com)

Advance (www.advance.philips.com)

Bartco Lighting (www.bartcolighting.com)

Cooper Controls (www.coopercontrol.com)

Cooper Lighting (www.cooperlighting.com)

Dreamscape Lighting, Inc. (www.dreamscapelighting.com)

Edge Lighting (www.edgelighting.com)

Elliptipar Lighting (www.elliptipar.com)

Focal Point (www.focalpointlights.com)

Halco Lighting (www.halcolighting.com)

Hubbell Lighting (www.hubbelllighting.com)

Juno Lighting Group (www.junolightinggroup.com)

LEDtronics, Inc. (www.ledtronics.com)

Leviton Manufacturing Company, Inc. (www.leviton.com)

Lighting Control and Design (www.lightingcontrols.com)

Lightolier/Philips (www.lightolier.com)

Lutron Electronics, Co., Inc. (www.lutron.com)

Neo-Neon (www.neo-neon.com)

Nexxus Lighting (www.nexxuslighting.com)

Prescolite (www.prescolite.com)

Pure Lighting (www.purelighting.com)

SPI Lighting (www.spilighting.com)

Times Square Lighting (www.tslight.com)

Universal Lighting Technologies, Inc. (www.unvlt.com)

Film/Video and Projection Equipment

Airstar America, Inc. (www.airstar-light.com)

American Grip, Inc. (www.americangrip.com)

ARRI, Inc. (www.arri.com)

Christie (www.christiedigital.com)

Dadco (www.dadco-llc.com)

Daktronics/Vortek (www.daktronics.com)

Gerriets International, Inc. (www.gi-info.com)

Green Hippo Ltd. (www.green-hippo.com)

Harkness Screens (USA) Ltd. (www.harkness-screens.com)

Mole Richardson Company (www.mole.com)

Pani Projection and Lighting (www.pani.com)

Photon Beard (www.photonbeard.com)

Robert Juliat America (www.robertjuliatamerica.com)

Sunray Mfg. (www.dadcopowerandlights.com)

The Tiffen Company, LLC (www.lowel.com)

Related Equipment and Manufacturers

Bad Dog Tools (www.baddogtools.com)

Clark Transfer, Inc. (www.clarktransfer.com)

Clear-Com Communication Systems (www.clearcom.com)

Columbus McKinnon Corp. (www.cmworks.com)

Global Truss (www.globaltruss.com)

HME (www.hme.com)

James Thomas Engineering (www.jthomaseng.com)

J.R. Clancy, Inc. (www.jrclancy.com)

Laser Production Network (www.lasernet.com)

Le Maitre Ltd. (www.ultratecfx.com)

Look Solutions USA, Ltd. (www.looksolutions.com)

MDG Fog Generators (www.mdgfog.com)

Prolyte Products Group (www.prolyte.com)

SECOA (www.secoa.com)

Skjonberg Controls, Inc. (www.skjonberg.com)

Telex Intercom Headsets (www.intercomheadsets.com)

TOMCAT USA, Inc. (www.tomcatusa.com)

Total Structures (www.totalstructures.com)

Ultratec Special Effects Inc. (www.ultratecfx.com)

Vortek, a division of Daktronics (www.vortekrigging.com)

Union Connector Co., Inc. (www.unionconnector.com)

Universal Manufacturing Corp. (www.universaltruss.com)

Professional Organizations and Unions

The American Association of Cinematographers—ASC
(www.theasc.com)

Entertainment Technician Certification Program—ETCP
(www.etcp.esta.org)

Illuminating Engineering Society of North America—IESNA
(www.ies.org)

International Organization of Lighting Designers—IALD
(www.iald.org)

International Alliance of Theatrical Stage Employees—IATSE
(www.iatse-intl.org/home.html)

National Council for Qualifications for the Lighting Profession—
NCQLP (www.ncqlp.org)

United Scenic Artists Local 829—USA (www.usa829.org)

United States Institute for Theatre Technology—USITT
(www.usitt.org)

Glossary

Absorption A process by which light (and its associated wavelengths) is absorbed by a material and usually converted into heat.

Abstraction (Stylization) Expressing artistic style in a way that is in opposition to realism. Stylization is more abstract and symbolic, while realistic styles emphasize duplication of the natural environment.

Accent Light A luminaire used to draw focus or attention to a given feature or subject. In entertainment design it is often used to supplement practicals or to suggest other sources that are lighting a scene.

Accent (Secondary) Lighting A form of lighting associated with architectural and museum or retail lighting that provides focus to specific subjects or displays. It's also found in landscape lighting, where it is used to provide sparkle or establish focus. In concert lighting, accent lighting relates to the color accents that come from the backlight and sidelights.

Adaptation A process where the eye narrows its response to a limited brightness range to become more efficient and sensitive within a narrow range of intensities. The eye accepts this as normal and tends to ignore brightnesses outside of this range.

Adapter A short cable with different connector types mounted on each end.

Additive Color Mixing When different wavelengths or colors of light are combined to produce another color. The process can only come about through having different colored light sources illuminating or falling on the same surface.

Add-on A specialty program that is installed on top of a CADD program. The application works within the original program and provides a host of extra tools that are designed for the specific area of design.

Addressing The process by which control/channels are assigned to specific dimmers and the attributes of other lighting/specialty equipment such as automated lights.

Advance To visit a performance venue prior to a scheduled load-in to survey the space.

Aerial Show An exterior spectacle production that typically includes lighting effects, lasers, and fireworks.

After Hours (Cleaning/Maintenance) Lighting See *Worklight*

Afterimages The illusion that appears following the removal of a disproportionally high color saturation or intensity light source or other image/stimulus that remains unchanged for an extended period of time.

Aim To focus landscape and architectural luminaires or fixtures.

Aircraft Landing Lights (ACL) Narrow-beamed lamps adapted from their use in airplanes for theatrical purposes. They are often low-voltage sources that must be used in conjunction with a transformer.

Air Light A reference to lighting in which the actual beams of light become visible due to the effects of haze and smoke (first associated with the concert lighting industry).

Alignment A manner of adjusting the orientation/relationship between a luminaire's reflector and lamp in order to achieve maximum light output.

Alternating Current (AC) A type of electricity developed through electromagnetism that results in the voltage constantly changing both direction and level (voltage) over a period of time.

Amber Drift See *Red Shift*

Ambient (General Circulation or Primary) Lighting 1. General non-directional background light that is a result of scattering and indirect reflections. 2. A retail/museum and architectural lighting system that provides a blanket of general illumination over an environment.

American National Standards Institute (ANSI) A standard's organization that regulates codes and measurement standards.

American Society of Cinematographers (ASC) Professional organization for directors of photography.

American Society of Lighting Designers (ASLD) A society of the film and video industries that represents lighting directors and gaffers.

Americans with Disabilities Act (ADA) A group of construction codes that apply to making a building accessible to people with handicaps.

Amperage (A) The measurement of electrical flow that relates to the rate of electrons flowing through a point at any given time. Its unit of measure is the ampere.

Analog Control A control format where the console creates a constant low-voltage signal that is proportional to the voltage being made available to the circuit.

Angle The direction from which light comes from and strikes an object. Various responses in mood and other overall lighting qualities are associated with the directionality of light.

Angstrom (Å) A unit of measurement for light wavelengths. It is equal to $1/254,000,000$ of an inch.

Animation Disk A moving wheel accessory that is placed in front of a spotlight to create simple motion effects.

Applause Button A console button, similar to a blackout button, that bumps the intensities of all the lights to full rather than out.

Arc A very bright, high color temperature, light source created by an electrical spark that jumps between two electrodes.

Architainment A variation of design that combines elements of architectural design with entertainment. It is another name for themed design.

Architecture for Control Networks (ACN) A lighting control protocol that primarily addresses the formatting of control communications over an ethernet network. It covers several specific protocols that are packaged together as a unit or suite. This protocol supports bi-directional data flow between a console and any networked gear. ACN may also be used as an acronym for Advanced Control Network.

Architectural Lighting Lighting the interiors and exteriors of buildings. It can also refer to the architectural lighting elements of a themed design or other structures.

Architectural Luminaires   A classification of exterior lighting fixtures that are used to bring focus to entryways or other significant features of a building.

Area Control   Creating general or area lighting so that there is an ability to pull into smaller portions of the stage or lit environment. Greater area control allows more specific area selection while less area control is more general and less defined.

Area Lighting (General Illumination)   A means of bringing overall visibility to an environment. This usually means providing a system of luminaires that creates a consistent even coverage across an environment, giving the appearance of being lit by a single distant light source. In landscape lighting this relates to lighting an area with enough illumination that a given task can be performed.

Area versus Color Control   A choice in area or general lighting where specific control of the luminaires is based on whether more specific control is designed into the number of areas that the luminaires light or by the different colors that are lighting an environment.

Aria   A solo that is performed (usually by a principle character) in an opera.

ASA (ISO)   An index of how sensitive or fast a film reacts to light. Values are based on a standard by the American Standards Association (now ANSI) or International Organization of Standardization (ISO). The higher the rating, the faster the film speed and more quickly it can capture an image.

ASHRAE/IESNA 90.1   A document that guides energy codes and the manner in which power densities are determined and specified for architectural lighting.

Aside   A performance technique in which a performer addresses the audience. They are often performed downstage and frequently present a character's inner thoughts.

Assistant House Electrician   The electrician who is second in command of the electrics crews for a performance facility.

Assistant Lighting Designer (ALD)   A personal assistant to the lighting designer whose duties may vary considerably from one situation to another but whose primary task lies in the organization and documentation of a lighting design.

Assistant Master Electrician (AME)   An electrician who is directly under the Master Electrician and is usually charged with specific aspects of coordinating the electrics crews both for a performance as well as the load-in and strike of a production.

Associate Lighting Designer   A personal assistant to the lighting designer who operates at a level of authority just below the lighting designer. The responsibilities of an associate designer can vary considerably but are more along the lines of providing artistic input for the lighting designer.

Astronomical Clock   A control device or computer used in architectural and landscape installations that executes a timing program that instructs lighting equipment to turn on and off at pre-determined times.

Attenuation (Falloff)   The property by which a light's intensity drops off as it moves farther away from its source.

Attribute   A control function of a luminaire or lighting accessory. The most common examples involve automated lights, with attributes like pan, tilt, color, etc. In CADD light plots, attributes relate to notation data like color and channel numbers.

Attributed Block   A library symbol (block) used in CAD drafting that not only contains the basic symbol but also a means of tailoring the data associated with a symbol to the specific block. Lighting often uses attributed blocks to insert luminaires into a drawing while modifying attributes like color, unit number, and channel to the specific unit that is being inserted.

Autofader   A variation of crossfader or splitfader that has a timing device. Times are preset and run at the assigned times once the cue is initiated.

Automated Color Changers   See Scrollers

Automated Lights (Automated Luminaires)   Fixtures that have multiple control features/attributes that allow elements of a luminaire like its pan and tilt to be changed through control commands. Also called intelligent, wiggle, and moving lights.

Autotransformer   A dimmer that harnesses the technology of AC currents and their ability to induce magnetic fields to create a back-EMF that in turn regulates the voltage/intensity of a circuit.

Averaging Meter   A reflective light meter that records the average light level throughout the entire field of a camera. They are good for determining overall exposure.

Awning   An architectural feature that is placed over windows and other glazed surfaces that provides shade and helps block direct sunlight from entering a window.

Axial ERS   A version of the ellipsoidal reflector spotlight (ERS) that places the lamp directly on the back of the housing (on the optical axis) where it is inserted into the center of the reflector. These units were developed in the 1970s and are much more efficient than earlier ERS designs.

Back Diagonal   A direction of lighting distribution that comes from behind an object and gives a rimming type of effect.

Background Lights or Lighting   Luminaires in film and video shoots that light the background behind a subject and are used to maintain a proper balance between the subject and background. Also used as a concept in landscape lighting where more distant or perimeter areas are lit while other subjects are lit in the foreground.

Backing off the Rods   See Ballet Dim

Backlight   An angle that comes from behind a subject and helps to separate and push the subject forward, away from the background. It can produce a rim/halo effect.

Backlot   A collection of many exterior locations that are scenic constructions used for filming movies.

Baffle (Egg Crate)   An optical accessory typically added to architectural luminaires and soft-lights that creates a network of box-like dividers over the face of a fixture. They help block the viewer from direct lamp and reflector glare.

Balance   A consideration of the intensity or illuminance levels between different objects or surfaces. Also a concept in an electrical system where the demands of the entire service are evenly distributed on each of the power legs.

Balcony Rail   A hanging position located across the front face of a theatre's balcony. It provides a relatively flat lighting angle and is often used for washing a stage.

Ballad   A slow, often romantic or sentimental, song that is usually performed as a solo or duet.

Ballast   A transformer-like device that is wired in series with a fluorescent or HID lamp and regulates the current and voltage to the lamp. It also provides the initial voltage needed to start the arc process.

Ballet Dim (Backing off the Rods)   The use of a followspot in such a subtle manner that the audience may not be aware that a followspot is being used. Designers use ballet dim to draw focus without drawing attention to the light itself.

Ballyhoo   A way of sweeping spotlights (followspots or automated luminaires) throughout a venue. A ballyhoo may be done over the stage or audience.

Barndoors   An accessory that provides folding flat panels that can be rotated and tilted inward or outward to block glare and spill or unwanted light.

Base   An element of a lamp that supports the lamp in its proper orientation within a luminaire and provides the electrical contacts that lead to the lamp's filament.

Base Light or Base Level Lighting Another name for fill light used by some lighting directors and directors of photography. Light added to a scene to bring shadow areas to an intensity level that the camera can record. Some refer to the process as base level lighting. Also used to define the ambient light in an architectural application.

Basic Retail Environment A low-end, economical store or retail environment. Lighting is designed predominantly from a visibility or functional point of view.

Batten A pipe that is located and flown from directly above the stage. They are used as temporary mounting positions for lighting instruments, maskings, and scenery.

Batten Tapes A piece of scenic webbing that is secured along a batten and marked with a centerline and additional marks or labels for every luminaire hung on the associated electric. They are frequently used in touring and eliminate the need for measuring the distance from each unit to centerline.

Beacon A specialized fixture that produces a moving effect based on the same effect as the rotating light on emergency vehicles.

Beam A hanging position of horizontal pipe mounted in the ceiling above an audience that runs across the width of an auditorium.

Beam Angle The angle representing the beam distribution of a luminaire where the intensity has fallen off by no more than 50% of the initial intensity.

Beam Projectors A luminaire that uses a parabolic reflector and is the only spotlight that does not contain a lens. Beam projectors produce a very harsh intense beam of nearly parallel rays of light.

Beamspread The amount of coverage that a luminaire creates as a distribution pattern. Beam angle and field angle are two specific ways of expressing beamspread.

Below Grade A manner of mounting architectural or landscape luminaires in a vault or waterproofed box where only the lens (if that) projects above the ground's surface.

Bend A property of rear projection screens where image intensities drop off and are not seen as well by people who are to the sides and outside of a critical viewing angle.

Best Boy The electrician, in video and film production, who is the gaffer's assistant.

Bidding A construction phase where contractors are provided with documents and make offers for providing the lighting equipment and its installation for a set price.

Bi-directional Data Digital control information that is exchanged in both directions between lighting consoles and sophisticated devices like automated luminaires.

Birdies Small PAR luminaires that are designed around MR16 lamps.

Black Box Theatre (Blackbox Theatre) A theatre facility that allows complete flexibility in assigning staging arrangements. Black box theatres are typically painted completely black and have a lighting grid over the entire room.

Blacklight A specialized luminaire or form of light that has the majority of its spectral composition in the ultraviolet range. Special dyes and bleached objects will glow (usually in psychedelic colors) when activated by this light.

Blackout A fade to complete darkness that is done to a zero count (instantly).

Blackout Button A push button switch that allows a control board or console to instantly lower every channel to zero intensity.

Blackout Check A blackout cue that is loaded just prior to opening the house so that a venue can be checked for complete darkness.

Bleed Out Diffused light that smoothly fades out at the edge of a beam.

Blind (Blind Mode or Preview Mode) Programming or writing lighting cues without the benefit of observing the actual lights, environment, or subject(s). A console mode that displays channels and their associated levels for previous or upcoming cues. This allows a designer to work on the cues while another cue is on stage.

Block A pre-designed symbol stored in the invisible background of a CADD drawing that allows simple insertion of the symbol into a drafting. Blocks contain the outline of the luminaire along with a host of other information regarding the unit and how it is to be equipped (color, focus, wattage, control channel, etc.).

Block Cues (Hard Blackouts) Cues that are entered into a console with all channels assigned to a level of zero to create points that stop any tracking instructions.

Blocking Notation A means of drawing graphic diagrams to record or notate the movements and positions of the performers.

Blueout A special type of fadeout in which all of the lights fade to a deep blue as opposed to complete darkness. This assists crews in scene changes and can also make these shifts more interesting from an audience perspective.

Blue Sky Development A form of concept development where a team is given a blank slate and simply brainstorms themes for an attraction.

Board Operator A crew member who helps the designer program the light board and executes the cues as ordered by the stage manager during performances.

Body (Hood or Housing) The actual enclosure of a luminaire. The housing provides for the proper mounting and orientation of all the optical components and accessories of a unit.

Bollard A special form of post light that is frequently used to mark pathways and entrances. They are usually around 3 feet in height and typically have the luminaire and its lenses incorporated into the design of the post.

Book Scenes A type of scene associated with musicals where the mode of delivery shifts to traditional acting without an emphasis on singing or dancing.

Boomerang (Color Boom) A device that allows followspot operators to quickly change a spotlight's color. Most color booms contain six different colors or gels.

Booms (Trees) Pipes extending upward from the stage floor that allow luminaires to be mounted vertically rather than horizontally.

Boom Base A heavy (50 lbs.) metal plate of cast iron that forms the floor base that supports the vertical pipe of a boom.

Borders An overhead masking that stretches across the width of a stage and prevents audience view of the flyspace and any scenery or lighting equipment above the stage.

Borderlights Banks of permanently wired striplights that stretch across the width of a stage. These were popular before the use of spotlights for general illumination and contained three or four circuits of colored roundels (typically red, blue, and white, although circuits of canary or green were often substituted for white).

Bounce Drop A drop that is placed behind another drop (either a translucent drop or one with translucent elements) and to which light is focused and reflected towards the back of the first drop.

Box Boom A hanging position that historically came from a boom mounted in the box seats of a proscenium theatre. The position provides front-diagonal lighting, and we now often refer to any position coming from the side walls of a theatre as box boom positions, box seats or not.

Box-Spot (Plano-Convex Spotlight or P-C Spotlight) Luminaire representing one of the earliest forms of theatrical spotlight and is quite similar to a Fresnel spotlight. It consists of a spherical reflector, light source, and single plano-convex lens. It is still popular throughout Europe and other parts of the world.

Bracketing A photographic technique of taking multiple exposures to increase the chances of obtaining a successful image—one at the exposure suggested by a light meter and then a second and third exposure shot one f-stop on either side of the recommended exposure.

Branch Circuits Individual circuits, with their own circuit protection, that lead from a distribution panel to electrical equipment like lights and outlets.

Break-in An adapter for the male end of a multi-cable that interfaces the cable with other cables or electronic hardware like a dimmer rack. It separates the multi into individual male connectors for each circuit.

Break-out An adapter for the female end of a multi-cable where the cable interfaces with other cabling. The break-out separates the multi into individual female connectors for each circuit.

Brightness Perception A consideration of all the variables that determine the brightness of an object—the amount of light falling on the object, our optical sensitivity, and the degree of reflectivity are all factors in the perceived intensity of an object.

Broad A linear light source used in television and film production that features thin tubular lamps. They are generally considered and used as a soft-light.

Brute A multi-light or cluster light used in film and video that uses an arrangement of nine lamps in a rectangular array.

Buhl Projector An enhanced Ektagraphic Slide Projector where the standard lamp is replaced with a high-wattage one along with a system of heat sinks and high-powered fans for extra cooling. They have superior lenses for better projections.

Build To increase the intensity by either raising the intensity levels of the individual dimmers or by adding additional lighting instruments into a cue.

Bulb The glass envelope of a lamp which creates the appropriate atmosphere for the lamp to operate with.

Bullet Lights A landscape luminaire that is used for both flood and spotlighting. The unit has an inverted-cone shape that has its socket and electrical fittings in the tip of the housing while the lamp's face is exposed through the wider opening.

Bump (Flash) Buttons A momentary switch associated with a controller or submaster that can instantly bump its level to full regardless of the actual controller setting.

Bundle A number of individual cables or circuits that are simply tied together as they run along a single hanging position. They are created for hanging positions like electrics and booms as a way of pre-packing the circuits and facilitating a faster hang while touring. Bundles are often used as an alternative to multi-cables.

Burning-Off Drying out the moisture left in luminaires after a rain by heating the lamps up slowly through powering them up in increments of approximately 10–15% over a period of time.

Burn Out The breakdown of a gel or filter from continued exposure to light and heat. The gel eventually fades in the center and may even melt completely through.

Bus Bars Metal bars that are used in large-capacity applications for moving electricity from one location to another instead of using heavy wires or cables.

Butterflies (Nets or Silks) Large diffusers used in the video and film industry that are made of translucent muslin or silk-like fabric mounted on large folding frames. Smaller versions are mounted on simple frames held in stands that are placed in front of a luminaire. Sizes and materials will vary, which results in a variety of names being associated with these diffusion accessories. Nets are made of a mesh material (bobbinet), while butterflies and silks are made of translucent material.

Cable (Jumper) Technically refers to combining several insulated wires into a single shield or jacket. It is also used synonymously with jumper to describe a two/three conductor cable with a male connector on one end and female on the other.

Cable Lighting A variation of track lighting where the track is replaced by decorative cables that also function as conductors for the low-voltage electricity.

CAD or CADD (Computer-Aided Design and Drafting) Software programs or applications that are designed for drafting. While initially developed for drafting needs, the software has evolved to include full modeling and visualization.

Call A work period for crew members. A call time is when individuals report to work.

Call a Show Providing the cueing commands (i.e., sound or lighting cues) to the crews during a rehearsal or performance. This is usually done by the stage manager.

Camera-Lights (Obie) A variety of portable luminaires used in film and video shoots that are mounted to a camera in order to produce good front fill over a subject.

Camera Rehearsal A rehearsal in film and video setups that would be similar to a dress rehearsal in the theatre. Lighting, costumes, actors, and cameras are all rehearsed and tweaked before the actual shooting takes place.

Camlock (Cam-lock) A heavy duty connector that is used on each individual cable of feeder cables, dimmers, and other power distribution equipment.

Candlepower (Candela) Distribution Curve A representation of photometric data that allows comparisons to be made between luminaires. This data forms a graphical representation of the measured light output (intensity) of the luminaire at various angles to either side of the centerline of a luminaire.

Carbon-Arc Spotlight A spotlight (often a followspot) that has a carbon-arc light source.

C-Clamp A type of mounting hardware that secures a lighting instrument's yoke to a batten or other hanging position or pipe.

Ceiling Cavity (Plenum) The void between the decorative ceiling and the bottom of the overlying floor or ceiling joists. It hides equipment like ducts, conduit, and pipes.

Ceiling Clutter A reference to an unsightly, disorderly arrangement of lighting fixtures on a ceiling of a retail, commercial, or other architectural lighting project.

Cell An individual lamp or reflector along with its associated housing in a cyc light or far cyc. Each cell is gelled and wired independently of the others. Cells are often bolted together and hung from a common yoke. Typical units contain three or four cells that are often colored in the three primary colors.

Centerline An imaginary reference line that passes through the center of a stage, room, or building. Most side-to-side measurements are based on the centerline.

Centerline Section (Section) A sectional drawing that is drawn as if cutting through a facility on a plane along the centerline of a stage. It is a side view of the building along this plane and is used to determine vertical heights and trim settings.

Chain Hoist (Chain Motor) A winch or hoist that is specifically designed for overhead rigging. They are used to support trusses, speaker assemblies, and scenic components, most extensively in the touring industry.

Change Order A contract document used in specifying permanent installations that outlines a revision and amends the original construction documents.

Changeover The time given to making changes from one production to another. While it may relate to the transfer between new productions, it is more commonly associated with the daily changes being made between repertory productions.

Channel A control assignment that provides the actual identity of control that a console recognizes as a base element for assigning control voltages. Channels are typically assigned intensity levels that fall between 0–10 or 0–100%.

Channel Check (Dimmer Check) A check done at various points in the load-in and before each performance where each dimmer or channel is brought up to make sure that every lamp is both operational and hasn't lost its focus.

Channel Schedule A form of designer paperwork that presents all of the luminaire data of a light plot in a table format. It is a form of the hookup that organizes the data by channel number.

Chase (Chase Lights) A programmed effect that produces a rapid sequence of cues/steps that are each associated with a given set of luminaires. Theatre marquees form an example.

Cheat Sheet A table that lists all of the control channels in order and then provides additional information relating to the purpose and color associated with each channel. It performs the same function as a magic sheet.

Check Cues Cues that are placed in a console for checking/verifying that various tasks have been completed. An example would be glowing any circuits that have been repatched at intermission to ensure that they have actually been reassigned.

Chicken Coop/Space Light A film and video soft light that is typically suspended from above and used to create a general level of fill or area lighting over an area. They are built around the concept of a soft reflective canopy using several light sources. The chicken coop is built around a rectangular arrangement of lamps, while the space light is cylindrical and uses multiple lamps in a circular arrangement.

Chief Lighting Technician (Gaffer) A video or film crew member who is the equivalent to a master electrician in theatrical production. They work with the lighting director or director of photography to provide the specified equipment, filters, and power for each shot. They also supervise the lighting staff during production.

Chimera A soft light used in film and video work that is built around the concept of creating a soft reflective canopy containing one or more light sources. They are usually mounted on a stand and used to produce horizontal fill light. They have collapsible hoods of diffuse material that are adjusted to a given situation.

Chinese Lanterns A soft light that is similar to the larger lighting balloons where lamps are placed within a circular lantern-like sphere to create a soft, diffuse light for a film or video setup.

Choke A coil that is wired in an electronic dimmer (usually SCRs) to reduce electronic interference generated by the dimmer.

Choreography The movement patterns and gestures that are established for a dance or other movement-based performance.

Chroma (Saturation) The purity of a color. The more saturated the color, the more specific and limited the range of wavelengths associated with it.

Chroma Key A form of composite or matte photography in which an electronic image of one scene is projected onto a neutral surface in another. The most popular versions are based on the colors of these surfaces and are known as blue-screen or green-screen techniques.

Chromatic Aberration (Color Fringes) An effect of an unwanted prismatic or rainbow effect at the edge of a beam of light. It is usually due to inferior lenses.

C. I. E. Chromaticity Chart A chart that indicates the wavelengths of color radiation given off at various temperatures of a black body radiation. The importance to lighting designers lies in its depiction of the relationships between each of the three primary colors and that fairly accurate color predictions can be made for resultant colors that are formed through mixing different colored light sources.

Cinch-Jones Connector A special multiconductor connector that is used for connecting analog control cables to one another and to control gear like light boards and dimmer packs.

Cinebach Projector A variation of Linnebach Projector where the sides and slides have been curved to accommodate the shape of a curved cyclorama.

Cinematographer (Director of Photography [DP]) Individual who is responsible for creating the entire visual environment for a video or film. Although the director of photography is responsible for the lighting they also have responsibilities in choosing location, determining camera angles and range of an individual shot, and selecting the camera lenses and film speeds.

Circuit A complete cycle of electron flow that follows a pathway from a source, through a device, and back to the source.

Circuit/Control Schedules Paperwork used in landscape lighting that organizes the data by circuit/control assignments (similar to theatrical dimmer schedules).

Circuit Breaker Electrical device that is designed as the weakest link in a circuit and meant to trip or "blow" if the circuit encounters a short or is overloaded. A circuit breaker can be reset once it has blown.

Circuit Layout A floorplan that includes all of the information found in a typical floorplan plus an indication of all the circuits and their locations.

Circulation Lighting A form of architectural or themed lighting that provides enough visibility so that people can move around safely within an environment.

Cleaning/Maintenance (After Hours) Lighting See Worklight

Closed-Backed Window A display window that has a back and is shut off from the store that is behind the window.

Closed Fixture A landscaping luminaire in which a lens and protective gasket are placed over the front of the luminaire to prevent water from entering the unit.

Closing-in A method of making a proscenium opening smaller through lowering the borders and bringing the legs farther onto the stage.

Cluster Mounting A mounting method used in street and roadway lighting where several fixtures are mounted from a single pole.

CMY Mixing See CYM Mixing

Cobra Head A luminaire used with HID lamps in roadway and street lighting that has a distinct shape that resembles the head of a cobra. Most high-pressure sodium, mercury, and metal halide street lamps are of this particular type of luminaire.

Coefficient of Utilization (CU) A factor that relates to the overall efficiency of a luminaire within the Lumen Method calculation. CUs are determined by luminaire manufacturers and are found in tables that make a correlation between the CU, reflectance of a room's surfaces, and the RCR for a given situation.

Coherence A means of describing the overall quality of light in film and video lighting. It is usually associated with the hardness or softness and diffusion of the light.

Cold-Cathode A lamp that produces light as a glow from the discharge of electrons within an enclosed tube. One of the more popular versions gives off a cold cobalt blue light that is often used in cove lighting applications. The tubes can be bent to follow the contour of architectural elements and come in a variety of colors.

Color A controllable quality of light. A perception based on how specific wavelengths of light stimulate the photo sensors in our eyes. Light will have an associated color based on the specific collection of wavelengths being present in its makeup.

Color Adaptation Distortion in color perception when the eyes are overstimulated due to being under the influence of lighting conditions that have remained unchanged for an extended period of time. This results in the perceived color being distorted until the cones become fully functional.

Color Boom See Boomerang

Color-Compensation Scale A specialized scale (actually two scales) used in connection with a Color-Temperature Meter to correct the color temperature of a light. They are used to make a selection of color/gel correction that will make the light appear white on film.

Color Contrast Comparisons in hue and relative warmth/coolness either within or between scenes.

Color Correction (Color Conversion) Filters A special type of color media that filters a light source to change its color temperature. These are extremely important to the film and video industry where it is imperative that light from different sources be modified so that they appear to share common color temperatures.

Color Depth Relates to the number of colors that a video screen or projector can effectively create. The simplest screens display 8-bit data, which translates to 256 different levels for each of the three primary colors or a total of 16.7 million different colors. A 16-bit screen, on the other hand, can create 65,000 color levels in each of the primaries, for a total of 275 billion colors.

Color Extender An accessory that looks like a top hat and has internal slots that allow a luminaire's gel to be placed farther away from a light source.

Color Frame (Gel Frame) A thin square of folded sheet metal with a large hole located in its center used to hold gel at the face of a lighting fixture.

Color Fringes See Chromatic Aberration

Colorist The person that adjusts the color and development of a film to ensure proper contrast exposure and color continuity between different takes and setups.

Color Key A figure that illustrates the approximate angles and color of light that surround a subject. A lighting key may be developed for any moment of a production but is usually used to illustrate the full wash systems of a stage.

Color Media Materials that either filter or modify the light produced by a source or fixture. Gel and color filters are popular names given to color media.

Color Organ A popular entertainment device of the 1970s with audio sensors that could be tuned to specific frequencies which, upon activation, could flash lights to a musical beat.

Color Palette In automated lighting, the color settings used to create a given color are preset so that a previously defined color can be brought back through use of a simple recall or library system.

Color Rendering The ability of a light source to accurately render or light a variety of colors without distorting the natural colors of an object.

Color Rendering Index (CRI) An index number that relates to the color-rendering ability of a source and how accurately it can depict an object's true color. Sources with high CRIs have more individual wavelengths in their composition and enhance a larger range of colors. The maximum CRI possible is 100.

Color Scroller A lighting accessory that places an assembly of color filters (twelve or more) in a scroll-like configuration that is then rolled into various positions to change the color of the light.

Color Temperature A comparison of the sum of all the individual wavelengths of a light source with the color emitted from a black box radiation for a given temperature. Every color of radiant energy can be equated to a referenced temperature on the Kelvin scale, where absolute zero equals 0° Kelvin or -273° Celsius.

Color Temperature Meter Directors of Photography and Lighting Directors use a special light meter to measure the color temperature or overall color output of light. These measure light along two different scales: the first measures red/blue present, while the second measures the magenta/green content of the light.

Color Wheel 1. An accessory that is mounted in the color holder of a luminaire that moves a motorized disk of colored filters through a unit's light. 2. A diagram that illustrates the primary and secondary colors and their relationships to one another.

Combination Circuits Circuits that contain both series and parallel components.

A common combination circuit contains several lights wired together in parallel placed under the control of a single switch that is wired in series.

Commission Starting up the lighting systems in architectural lighting—completing any aiming and programming the levels for an installation as the design team turns the building over to the occupants.

Compact Fluorescent A form of fluorescent lamp that combines the lamp with a ballast in a single unit. They are often being used as a retrofit for traditional incandescent lamps because of their efficiency.

Compact Iodide Daylight (CID) Lamp A special variation of metal halide lamp that makes use of a specific mixture of gases and metal halides to produce a cleaner, brighter light source.

Compact Source Iodide (CSI) Lamp Another variation of metal halide lamp that make use of a specific mixture of gases and metal halides to produce a characteristic quality of light.

Company Switch (Road-tap) A specialized distribution panel or disconnect box that provides the power (typically 200–800 amps of three-phase power) that a touring lighting system or other equipment may be connected to.

Complementary Color A color that lies directly across the color wheel from a color.

Complementary Tint Theory A lighting technique of the stage that is associated with creating a fairly naturalistic style of lighting. The effect is produced if two fixtures containing complementary tints are hung on opposing 45° angles from one another. The lights are to be hung 45° to each front/side of a subject (splitting centerline) with a vertical angle of 45° for each light. The method is credited to Stanley McCandless and is often called a McCandless Hang.

Composite (Matte) Photography An image created through a combination of several individual shots or settings. Blue- or green-screen technology form popular examples of an electronic insertion of one shot into another.

Composition A function of lighting that relates to combining all of the elements of a scene, stage, or environment together into a complete unified visual package.

Compound Reflectors A reflector shaped with more than one principle shape along its surface. This forms a more efficient way of directing light in a primary direction.

Computer Rendering An image of a subject or environment that is created through creating a virtual model, coloring/texturing it, and lighting it through using a computer and specialized software.

Concave Lens   A lens in which one of the surfaces is curved inward towards the center of the lens.

Concept   A manner or method of approach to creating meaning in a production. It relates to an approach to a design problem and addresses the themes, style, and conventions that will be used in a production.

Concept Development   The first design phase of a project, in which a team first lays out the general ideas, concepts, and parameters of a project.

Conductors   Materials that allow electron movement easily and have little resistance to electrical flow. Metals are usually the best conductors.

Conjugate (Secondary) Focal Point   The second focal point of an ellipsoidal reflector to which all light is reflected from a source placed at the primary focal point. Any light or image that passes beyond the conjugate focal point is reversed.

Connectors   Electrical hardware that allows for the easy connection and disconnection of multi-wired cables. Connectors may be male or female.

Conservation   A process of providing limited lighting exposure to materials that are subject to heat and light damage, especially ultraviolet radiation. This is especially important in retail and museum or gallery lighting design.

Construction Documents   A set of documents that contain all the plans (lighting layouts, reflected ceiling plans, details, etc.) and specifications for a design.

Content   The source material for digital images and projections.

Continuity   1. Observing details in video and film shooting to ensure that no discrepancies occur between camera angles and that every take is lit in exactly the same way, providing consistency from one angle to another. 2. In electrical theory, continuity relates to providing a complete wiring path with no breaks in a circuit.

Continuous Fire   A dimming state where an SCR blows in the on position and the dimmer remains at full intensity despite any changes in the control signal.

Continuous Light Sources (Hot Light Sources)   Luminaires used in film and video production that are not dimmed and are designed to simply plug into a power source.

Contour Lighting   Lighting that follows contours or lines. One of the most obvious cases of this is when people line their walkways or pathways with luminaires.

Contract Document Phase   An architectural design phase where the contract documents are created and assembled. The specification of the lighting equipment and installation requirements are done at this point in the design process.

Contract Rider (Rider)   An addendum to the contract for a touring company, band, or artist that lists the production needs that must be provided by the local promoter

Contrast Ratios   A range of intensity variations that compare the brightest to darkest elements within a frame or image. Contrast ratios are especially important to film and video production and relate to these proportional intensities—a camera with a large contrast ratio is capable of capturing a more extreme range of intensities.

Contrast Viewing Glasses   A set of specialty glasses that are used to view a scene through a tinted filter. They allow quick identification of the highest- and lowest-intensity areas and help in setting the lighting/exposure levels of a scene.

Control   Usually used to reference brightness or intensity modifications and control but also relates to determining which luminaires are circuited and wired together. In architectural applications this can also relate to focus and beam control as well.

Control Cable   A low-voltage signal cable in electronic dimming systems that provides communication between a console and the dimmers or other devices.

Control/Circuit Schedules   Schedules in landscape designs that organize the design in manners such as by circuit or control assignments. These are very similar to the dimmer and instrument schedules used in entertainment designs.

Control Schedule   An architectural version of the hook-up or channel/dimmer schedule.

Controller   The actual slide switches or faders found on a lighting console. Controllers may control individual channels or dimmers, submasters, or even the grand master. Controller assignments range from 0–10 or 0–100% in intensity.

Control Specification   A design document that is based on the lighting specification of a project from a control perspective.

Conventionals   A term used to reference traditional luminaires or lighting instruments when they are combined in a rig that has automated luminaires.

Conventions   An approach or use of dramatic techniques that an audience accepts as a means for a playwright and production to present a dramatic event. These are theatrical techniques (e.g., blue light is accepted as darkness) that allow the team to present the story to an audience.

Convergence   An association where the ground between the lighting and video designer is becoming increasingly blurred through digital images, automated luminaires, and projection techniques that are bringing the two disciplines closer together.

Converging Rays   When light rays are redirected in such a manner that they are focused towards one another and a common point.

Convex Lens   A lens in which one of its surfaces curves or flexes outward away from the center.

Cookie (Cucaloris or Gobo)   These were developed in the film and video industry and are custom-made flags or panels (with holes or patterns cut into them) that are placed between a light source and a target. Originally, it was meant as a "go between" and often called a gobo. While this, too, forms a shadow projection it is quite different from placing a template in an ERS as in the case of a theatrical gobo.

Cool Colors   Light that has an abundance of blue, green, and lavender wavelengths and tends to produce psychological responses of calm, contentment, or melancholy.

Corporate Theatre (Corporate Sales Meeting)   A special area of performance events that are produced by corporations to increase sales or to introduce new products.

Corridor   A distribution pattern associated with dance lighting that forms a pathway extending from an extreme upstage position straight downstage.

Count   The timing of a cue, usually based on seconds.

Cove (Slot)   A lighting position that replaces the box boom position. A vertical cut located in the side walls of an auditorium where a boom or ladder-like device is located behind the wall for mounting front-diagonal light sources.

Cove Lighting   A form of architectural lighting where wash luminaires are hidden behind a masking along the edges of a room or perimeter of a tray or other architectural feature. It creates a decorative wash around the perimeter of a room.

Crossfade   To evenly shift from one lighting cue or scene to another.

Crossfader   A specialized fader that allows a board to shift or fade between two or more presets. In one extreme position one preset will be live while in the opposite position a second preset will become live while the first is faded out.

Cross-Key Lighting A variation of film and video lighting in which the camera is located essentially in a frontal position with two luminaires mounted roughly in opposing 45° front-diagonal positions.

Cross Lighting A lighting technique in which two lights are aimed at a subject from opposite directions. This adds dimensionality to an object while also providing a slightly more diffuse lighting treatment.

CRT (Cathode Ray Tube) Projector The first widely used projector, which essentially projected three overlapping images of red, blue, and green light onto a common screen and had a relatively low intensity.

C-Stand A folding stand that is fully adjustable and used for mounting luminaires and grip equipment that is associated with location shooting.

CTB (Color Temperature Blue) Filter A filter used to correct the color temperature of light sources or luminaires with low color temperatures that need to be raised to match the higher color temperature of an exterior light source.

CTO (Color Temperature Orange) Filter A filter typically placed over window surfaces to correct the daylight color temperature to that of interior light sources.

Cucaloris See Cookie and Gobo

Cue (Cueing) A static lighting image or look that creates a given combination of lights and their angles, intensities, and overall mixing. Cueing relates to establishing the looks and recording them so that they can be duplicated from performance to performance.

Cue Blocks A method of numbering cues as a group based on their having similar functions. A common cue blocking technique includes grouping cues from individual dances of a dance repertory into blocks of cues that begin with specific numbers like 10, 20, 30, etc.

Cue-In (Set Levels) The cue-writing session where cues are created through a selection of luminaires, their colors, and intensities. Transitions are also determined during these sessions. Also known as level setting or writing cues.

Cue List (Cue Stack) A series of cues that are stored in a console that can be pulled up and initiated by a programmer at will.

Cue Only Mode A console mode by which any changes made in a cue are performed on that cue only and will not have any impact on any other cues.

Cue Stack See Cue List

Cue Synopsis Design paperwork that functions as a guideline for the creation of a production's cues. It assigns a cue number to each cue and then goes on to describe specific information related to the cues. Cue numbers, counts, execution points, and a visual description of the cues are included in this information.

Cue-Writing Session (Level-Setting Session) See Cue-in

Cut 1. A film and video editing technique in which changes are made in what an audience sees through making switches between camera angles or scenes. 2. To strike or drop something from a production.

Cut-Off A quality of roadway luminaire design that relates to controlling how much light spills above a horizontal plane. Luminaires are characterized in regard to how much glare and spill that they allow above a given reference point.

Cut List A listing of the number of cuts/frames of a particular gel color that will be required in each frame size for a production.

Cut Sheet Reference literature that provides specification data for a piece of lighting equipment. Examples of this data might include photometric data, mounting specifications, voltage/lamp requirements, and control channel capabilities, etc.

Cycle The voltage fluctuation that occurs throughout a single revolution of a generator. Also used to describe frequency comparisons in electromagnetic radiation.

Cyc Lights (Far Cycs) A floodlight that has a significantly large distribution pattern and produces a smooth wash over a large area. Its soft edges allow it to be easily blended with adjoining fixtures. Far cycs are often used as a multi-colored wash luminaire where several cells are gelled differently from one another.

Cyclorama (Cyc) A large, flat, scenic surface used as a neutral background for stages and television studios. The wrapped or curved cyc curves around the upstage corners of a stage or studio and extends back downstage at its sides.

CYM Mixing (CMY Mixing) A technology found in many automated luminaires that allows a designer to manipulate three dichroic filters (cyan, yellow, and magenta) to mix light of virtually any desired color.

Dailies (Rushes) The first prints of film that was shot during a given day. Dailies are often developed during the late afternoon and evaluated after the evening meal or the next day.

Daisy Chain (Straight Run) A popular landscape wiring technique that forms a single chain of luminaires that are wired in parallel along an entire circuit/run. While being simplest to install, it also experiences the greatest effect of voltage drop.

Damper A set of shutters in a followspot that allow an operator to quickly cut the light across the top and bottom beam edges.

Dance Breaks The portion of a song and dance number in musical theatre where the performer(s) stop singing and go into a featured dance routine.

Dance Club A particular type of nightclub in which dance by the patrons forms the primary element of entertainment.

Dance Tower A variation of boom that uses a metal truss-like structure to support the sidelights.

Dancing Water Display A performance event that features fountains with a variety of choreographed jet sprays and colored lighting, which are set to music.

Dark Ride A themed ride in which vehicles move through a darkened environment where only accent lighting is used on given features of the ride. The vehicle passes from one chamber to another through doors that it "bumps" open.

Day-for-Night A filming technique where a filter is placed over a camera's lens that filters the daylight to give the illusion of the scene being shot at night.

Daylighting A consideration of architectural lighting that uses the natural effects of daylight to provide supplemental illumination to an interior space.

Dead Relates to a circuit not having power.

Dead Back A reference to a light that is mounted directly behind a subject.

Dead Front A reference to a light that is mounted directly in front of a subject.

Dead Hang To tie-off or hang something like a batten directly from the grid.

Deck Electrician An electrician who works backstage to connect and disconnect temporary circuits, shift equipment, and make new circuit assignments throughout a show.

Decorative Lighting Luminaires whose primary function is to add to the decor of a space. They often bring glitter and sparkle to an interior design and are illustrated by chandeliers, wall sconces, and floor or table lamps.

Dedicated Controller A lighting console that is designed specifically for operating lighting equipment.

Dedicated Venue A performance facility that is specifically designed around the event that it houses. The Cirque du Soleil programs often make use of dedicated venues.

Depreciation   A reduction in the light output of a lamp or luminaire over time. Factors that cause depreciation might include temperature effects, place in life cycle, dirt and grime, etc.

Depth of Field   A range of focus located on either side of the focal point where objects remain in relatively good focus.

Design Development   A design phase that represents a point at which the team comes to a basic agreement on the design, works out the details, and moves toward finalizing their designs.

Design Meeting   A meeting between the director and all of the designers. Concepts are presented and the team collaborates and refines ideas regarding the designs for a production.

Design on the Fly   A design mode in which a lighting designer runs a console predominately in a manual mode while creating original cues during an actual performance. It is a manner of improvising along with the performers.

Design Packet   An information packet that a lighting designer sends to the venue ahead of their arrival that includes all the information that the crew will need to hang the design. It contains the light plot, other draftings related to the electrics department, the lighting schedules, and inventory or shop orders.

Design Paperwork (Paperwork or Schedules)   A set of standardized lighting forms that organize all the information presented in the light plot in table formats. Each schedule is organized around a given type of lighting data. Instrument and channel schedules or hookups form the most commonly used schedules.

Design Phase   A step in design development that relates to making a determination of the actual image of light. The initial phase relates to developing a concept, while later stages deal with translating this image into practical choices like fixture selection and mounting positions that support this vision.

Desk (Lighting Console)   A computer or automated lighting control device. It is preferred over older terms like light board.

Diagonal   A distribution pattern associated with dance lighting that form diagonal pathways that extend from a downstage corner to the opposite upstage corner of the stage.

Dichroic Filter   A glass color filter that works on the principle of reflecting unwanted wavelengths of light rather than by absorbing them.

Dichroic (Cold Mirror) Reflectors   A recent innovation that permits heat and low-wavelength electromagnetic radiation to pass through the reflector to the back of the instrument while the shorter wavelengths (light) are reflected.

Diffuse   A quality of light that is generally associated with a soft even distribution that does not produce sharply defined shadows.

Diffuser   A piece of glass, plastic, or other material that is placed over the front face of a luminaire to scatter and soften light while also preventing view of the light source.

Diffuse Reflection   A type of reflection where light is scattered in numerous directions.

Diffusion Media (Frost)   Media similar to gel that is used to alter the quality of the light (to soften, as a rule). Film and video designers tend to use more diffusion due to the closer proximity that the luminaires have with the subject.

Digital Control   A control protocol where a burst or packet of information (channel numbers and intensities) is sent to the dimmers and other equipment at a time when a change is required in the channel levels.

Digital Light   A new generation of automated lighting instruments that in addition to having all the functions of any other automated fixture also have the ability of projecting still and video images.

Digital-to-Analog Converter (Multiplexers)   A piece of equipment that acts as an interface for translating the digital signals of a control console to the analog control voltages used by older dimmers.

Dimmer   A control device that adjusts the intensity of the lights. In most cases, a dimmer varies the voltage to control the brightness of the lights.

Dimmer Check   See Channel Check

Dimmer Doubling™ (Multiplexing)   A trademark for ETC technology that allows designers to add additional control to a lighting system through adding specialized hardware to an existing dimmer. These additions effectively convert the single dimmer into two separately controlled dimmers.

Dimmer-per-Circuit (DPC)   A specialized form of dimming in which every lighting circuit is hardwired to its own dimmer.

Dimmer Plate (Plate)   The name given to the physical dimmer assembly in resistance and autotransformer dimming. It contains the coils, mounting plate, electrical contacts, and shoe mechanism.

Dimmer Schedule   A specific form of paperwork or hookup that presents all the luminaire data of a light plot in a table format. It organizes the information by dimmer number.

Dimming   Changes in intensity of a luminaire. Dimming may be both raised (dimming up) and lowered (dimming down).

Dimming Curve   A relationship between how smoothly or proportionally a dimmer controls its load as it progresses from off to full.

Dimming Screen (Reducing Screen)   A lighting accessory with a metal screen that is used in architectural and display lighting to lower the intensity of a luminaire without having an effect on the lamp's color temperature. Different screen densities provide a variety of intensity drops.

Dip   To lower the intensity of a lighting fixture or entire cue.

Direct Component   An element of lighting considered by illuminance at a point calculations for the line-of-sight measure of light coming directly from a luminaire to a particular point on a surface

Direct Current (DC)   Electricity in which the voltage remains steady and relatively constant throughout time. Batteries produce DC current.

Direct-Indirect Luminaires   An IESNA classification of luminaire based on a distribution pattern in which the light is directed equally well in both the upward and downward directions.

Direct Luminaires   An IESNA classification of luminaire based on a distribution pattern where 90–100% of the light is directed downward.

Direct Sunlight   One of the components of daylighting. This relates to the effect of sunlight shining directly into a space or facility.

Director of Photography   See Cinematographer

Director's Concept   A statement presented by a director that addresses issues such as themes, meaning, character analysis and associations, and a specific interpretation of a script. Degree of realism or stylization and any symbolism may also be presented in a concept. The statement provides the context within which the production is to be created and becomes the guideline that shapes all of the interpretations and decisions connected with producing the project.

Disconnect Box   A distribution panel that provides a power source for easy connection to supplemental equipment like a touring dimming rack. A company switch or road-tap are common examples of disconnect boxes.

Display Lighting   An area of lighting that relates to lighting displays associated with retail and museum lighting as well as any other types of displays.

Dissolve Effect An effect that smoothly fades from one photographic image to another.

Distortion A series of properties by which a projection may be deformed. The most common form of distortion relates to keystoning.

Distributed Dimming A form of dimming that uses solid state electronics to shorten individual cable runs through placing the actual dimmers in locations where the circuits would be located.

Distribution A controllable quality of light. Most lighting designers relate distribution to two specific lighting properties: angle or direction and quality.

Distribution Amplifier A device placed on a DMX control line to strengthen the control signal.

Distribution Panels Secondary electrical panels located throughout a building that are fed from the main switchboard and further distribute the power into branch circuits that lead to specific electrical equipment like lights and outlets.

Divergence When light rays are redirected in such a manner that they are focused away from one another and a common point.

DMX 512 The original universal control protocol for digital dimming. It provided a common control signal that allowed control and dimming equipment from a variety of manufactures to work together. A newer variation of the control protocol was updated in the 1990s and is known as DMX512A.

Dots (Flags and Fingers) In film and video lighting these are opaque objects that are placed between the source and the target to block light from an unwanted area. Each variation relates to a different shape and variety of sizes.

Doughnut An accessory placed in the color frame of a luminaire that consists of a metal plate with a hole cut at its center. They are used to sharpen the image of gobos.

Double-hang A manner of providing additional variety by duplicating lighting instruments representing a given wash or function. The most common example is in providing a second color system for a given lighting angle.

Double Rotator A variation of gobo rotator that allows two gobos to be stacked to produce a composite gobo effect. Both gobos may be rotated in either direction at a variety of speeds.

Douser A mechanical dimmer used to dim lighting fixtures that cannot be dimmed electrically. They are found on followspots and other units that use arc sources.

Downlight A distribution angle that comes from directly above a subject and tends to

produce distorted or heightened shadows that can have the effect of shortening or squashing a subject.

Dramatic Form (Structure) The manner in which a play is crafted with specific elements of its structure being presented to an audience at given points in its performance.

Dramatic Spine (Major Dramatic Question) The element or action that will form the major conflict of a play. Examples might include: whether a particular social injustice is righted, if a particular relationship is restored, or if the boy ends up with the pretty girl.

Drop-Boxes A circuit distribution box that is lowered from a stage's grid and provides from three to twelve or more circuits to a new hanging position.

Dry Run (Walkthrough) A film or video first rehearsal in which the actors arrive for a blocking rehearsal and the director establishes their movement patterns.

Dry Tech (First Tech and Technical Rehearsals) A rehearsal that is often associated with the actual cue writing process or first evaluation of the cues by the director. It focuses on the technical elements of a production, not the performers. Lighting, sound, and scenic elements are introduced and integrated into the production at this time. Performers are usually not called unless there are especially complex sequences involving them.

Dumping a Show When a computer lighting console loses it's memory and all of the cues and their related data is lost.

Edit Cues Making revisions or changes in the cues.

Edge Lighting A type of film or video lighting that uses a variation of sidelight to graze a subject's surface to produce extended shadows that emphasize its texture.

Educational Facilities Lighting Lighting that is associated with the illumination of schools and college or university facilities along with other educational buildings.

Edu-tainment A form of themed entertainment that is often used in museums and uses entertainment as a method of teaching.

Effect Lighting 1. Video or film lighting that doesn't directly affect the subject but is used to produce specific effects in a scene (projection patterns, accents, etc.). 2. Lighting in a themed attraction that only exists for effect (strobes, black light, etc.).

Effects 1. Lighting that generates some form of optical effect (fire effects, water reflections, lightning, etc.). 2. A set of menus found on computer lighting consoles that allow a designer to create elaborate cue sequences into pre-programmed effects.

Effects Module A pre-programmed effect like a chase sequence that can be assigned to specific control channels. Operators can usually vary the speed of the effects.

Effects Projector A projector that is equipped with a series of modular motion effects that can be used to create moving effects like rain and fire.

Egg Crates See Baffles

Egg-Crate Grid A lighting grid that consists of a series of portholes that are created in a regular grid pattern directly above a stage. The portholes, or wells, are fashioned into the structure of the ceiling (2 to 3 feet square) and contain a pipe or other hardware for mounting luminaires.

Electric A hanging position for lighting that is found directly above the stage and consists of a pipe or batten that runs across the width of a stage. Many facilities have permanent electrics equipped with raceways and larger counter-weight arbors.

Electrical Contractor The company (or individual), in architectural applications, that is contracted to acquire and install the lighting equipment according to the designer's specifications and building codes.

Electrical Distribution The electrical pathway in which electricity flows from its power source through a series of cables or wires and electrical hardware to its final destination and devices that use it, like luminaires.

Electrical Mastering A form of control in which individual dimmers are assigned or wired together with dimmers of a larger capacity

Electrical Potential A difference in energy levels at two different points. It comes through the addition or gathering of electrons at one of the points and represents a potential for electrical flow.

Electricians Crew members who work around electricity and are primarily associated with the preparation and execution of the lighting for a production. In architectural applications electricians are licensed and install all of the electrical equipment.

Electrics Crew The crew that is responsible for all of the electrical requirements of a production. Their work focuses on lighting and sound but they also provide power to effects, lifts, hydraulic pumps, winches, and other electrical equipment.

Electromagnetic Radiation Energy in the form of electromagnetic waves or radiant energy.

Electromagnetic Spectrum A continuum representing a collection of different levels of radiant energy, like visible light, that are specified by different wavelengths. The longer wavelengths (radio, television, and electricity) relate to lower energy levels, while the shortest (gamma and cosmic rays) relate to higher energy levels.

Electromagnetism A physical phenomenon in which an electrical current can be produced or induced by moving a wire through a magnetic field.

Electronic Control A form of lighting control using semi-conductor electronic hardware in which a low-voltage control signal is used to proportionally regulate the line-voltage that determines the brightness of the lights.

Electronic Dimming A form of dimming in which a low-voltage control signal is created at a light board/console, which in turn regulates a line-voltage power supply that provides proportional power to a circuit and luminaires.

Electronic Mastering A low-voltage form of mastering that became possible through electronic dimming. Electronic mastering provides presetting and a host of other dimming features that aren't possible with manual control systems.

Ellipsoidal Reflector A reflector based on the shape of an ellipse. A unique property of this reflector is that through placing a light source at the primary focal point, the light is focused to and passes through a conjugate or secondary focal point.

Ellipsoidal Reflector Floodlight (ERF or Scoop) The simplest floodlight in use. It creates an extremely wide distribution pattern of soft, diffuse light. The edges are soft and easily blend with adjoining fixtures.

Ellipsoidal Reflector Spotlight (ERS) The most extensively used spotlight, with optics that are superior to other luminaires and produces a crisp, even pool of light. Most have a very sharp, well-defined edge as well as the ability to shape the light through accessories like shutters or gobos.

Emergency Lighting Lighting that comes on and gives a base level of illumination when there is a power outage. It is powered by a battery or generator.

Encapsulated Arc Sources A variation of short arc lamp in which the arc is enclosed in a glass envelope. In film and video setups, these lamps have very high color temperatures (approximately 5,500° K) and are often used to supplement daylight.

Encoder A knob or rotary control found on control consoles that is particularly friendly for programming the attributes of intelligent fixtures

Energy Management Reducing a building's power demands while producing a lighting system that is designed and used in a way that is energy efficient and doesn't have an adverse effect on lighting quality or other building systems.

Enhanced Definition Lens Tube (EDLT) A lens barrel developed by ETC for the Source Four Spotlight that has superior optics.

Enhanced Ellipsoidal Reflector Spotlight (ERS) An improved variation of the ellipsoidal reflector spotlight (ERS) that was developed in the early 1990s. Its improved lamp, shutters, and reflector design produces far superior light than traditional ERSs. It is becoming the luminaire of choice for most designers.

Enhanced PAR A PAR luminaire that is designed around the newer HPL lamp. The light is similar in quality but superior to a traditional PAR, and beam angles are varied through the replacement of lenses rather than by using different lamps.

Entertainment Services and Technology Association (ESTA) An organization of theatrical manufacturers and dealers that provides resources to the commercial areas of the entertainment community as well as a venue for establishing many of the standards of the industry.

Entertainment Technician Certification Program (ETCP) A certification program that helps to insure that individuals have an established level of competency as a professional (rigger or electrician). Certification is granted through passing an exam every three years or going through a series of educational programs.

Establish a Scene A function of lighting in which light is used to communicate specific information about the environment that is being created (time of day, season, geographical location, etc.).

Evaluation Phase A phase of construction that takes place after a client has taken occupancy and where the designer checks client satisfaction, performs fixes or modifications as needed, and helps the client understand how to maintain and operate a design.

Exit Lighting A special lighting system that powers signage that identifies exit routes and doorways in public buildings.

Expendables (Perishables) Lighting materials such as gel, tie-line, and gobos that must be purchased and cannot be returned once used.

Exposure 1. Amount of light used to sensitize or produce an image on film or video. 2. The detrimental effect of heat, visible light, and ultraviolet radiation coming from

light sources (of particular concern in retail and museum or gallery lighting). It can also come from natural sources like daylight.

Exposure Ratios A variation of contrast ratios for video lighting where a comparison is made between the lighting intensities of any two objects or areas in an image.

Extended Service Lamps with longer lamp lives than normal lamps.

Exterior Lighting Lighting of the outside of a building and its entrances. Many make a distinction between exterior lighting and lighting the surrounding grounds (landscape lighting).

Eye-Lash (Half Hat) A variation of a top hat that only masks half the cylinder.

Eye-Light A type of front fill used in film and video work that comes in at a low angle from the front (often mounted on the camera) and provides good facial light while bringing sparkle to a subject's eyes.

Face-Light A frontal source used in film and video that comes in at a low angle and provides good facial lighting. Eye-light is a special type of face-light.

Faders The actual slide switches found on a lighting console.

Falloff Relates to a light's intensity dropping off as you move away from its source. Falloff is directly related to the inverse square law.

Far Cycs See Cyc Lights

Far-Side Key Placement of the key light in film and video so that it is on the side of a performer's face that is away from the camera. Far-side key is usually preferable.

Feeders (Feeder Cables) Large-gauge wires that deliver high capacity power to distribution panels and other dimming/electrical equipment.

Female Connector A connector with one or more receptacles for making quick connections between electrical devices and cables. The female connector provides the source of the power.

Fiber Optics An assemblage of very thin glass or plastic tubes that transport light. There are two popular forms: end-emitting fiber, which conducts light throughout its length where it emerges at the end of the fiber, and side-emitting fiber, which radiates light along its sides that glows like a neon tube.

Field Angle The angle representing the beam distribution of a luminaire where the intensity has fallen off to 10% of the intensity at the center of the beam. Field angles are inclusive of beam angles.

Filament The part of an incandescent lamp that contains the highly resistant material that is heated to produce the actual light source.

Filament Sing (Lamp Sing) A side-effect of early electronic dimmers where the dimmers caused the filaments of the lamps to vibrate and actually produce harmonics that could be heard.

Fill Light Light that is the result of diffusion or scattered reflections—ambient light in many cases. In entertainment and film or video lighting, it is an additional source that adds light to the areas of an object that would be associated with shadows or achieves a base level of illumination that the cameras can record. In architectural and landscape lighting, fill light is a low-level light that provides an overall ambience to an area while tying all the other sources together.

Film A medium in which photosensitive emulsions are exposed to light to record images.

Filtering Placing a material in front of a light source that selectively removes frequencies or wavelengths of light.

Filters A material through which light passes where certain wavelengths are filtered out (absorbed) while others pass directly through. Gel is a generic name for filters.

Fingers See Dots

Fires Relates to the moment of switching on or the sampling point of an SCR dimmer.

Firmware Software that is downloaded to a console, automated light, or other computer peripheral and improves the equipment's performance.

First Team The primary or actual performers in a film or television production.

First Tech See Dry Tech Rehearsal

Five-Point Lighting A system for area lighting design that is based on five luminaires. The most common practice placing four units at roughly 90° from one another and adding a fifth downlight to an area.

Five Times Rule A rule for establishing the validity of using the inverse square law in lighting calculations—the law is less accurate at close distances. It states that the distance between the source and target should be at least five times the largest viewed dimension of the source to provide accurate luminance calculations.

Fixed Capacity An association in which a dimmer (generally resistance) must be fully loaded in order to achieve complete dimming.

Fixture A name given to a luminaire, but more specifically designating a luminaire that is permanently installed or mounted.

Fixture Library A collection of data regarding automated luminaires and their attributes. These can be downloaded and stored in a console to eliminate programming that would be required for setting the units up in a console.

Flags See Dots

Flash Buttons See Bump Buttons

Flash and Trash A reference from the concert industry that alludes to simply flashing lights without any clear thought or consideration towards a lighting design.

Flat Angle A lighting angle that is relatively low and straight-on.

Flat Field A beam distribution pattern in which the intensity of the beam remains fairly consistent and even throughout the entire field or pool of light.

Flat Field Luminaires Newer enhanced spotlights developed since the early 1990s that have relatively flat fields and more efficient light production.

Flatted Reflectors A variation of mirrored reflectors that have a series of prismatic faces over the reflector surface.

Flicker Device An animation device that produces a flicker effect, which is created through placing a motorized disk with open areas in front of a spotlight's beam of light.

Flood Focus A setting for a Fresnel spotlight in which the lamp is moved closer to the lens, which causes divergence and results in the light being spread out.

Floodlight A luminaire that has a soft, diffuse light with undefined edges that washes over a large area evenly. Floodlights do not usually contain a lens.

Floodlighting A type of lighting that creates a soft, evenly distributed light over a large area.

Floor Mount A lighting instrument that sits or is mounted to the deck or floor.

Floorplan (Groundplan) A scaled top view of a performance area or environment that provides an aerial view of a facility as if the roof had been removed.

Floor Pocket A theatrical distribution box located in the stage floor that contains several independent circuits.

Flown Truss (Flying Rig) A truss supported from above by winches or chain hoists.

Fluorescent Bank Luminaires used in the video and film industry that contain a group of fluorescent lamps (often with special properties) that are housed together and used as economical wash luminaires. They can be either a soft or hard light source depending on what other units are used in a setup. Kino Flo units are popular examples of these luminaires and come in a variety of sizes and lamp configurations.

Fluorescent Lamp A lamp that works on the principle of energizing a field of low-pressure gas between two electrodes. Unlike arc sources, whose light comes from the arc, this arc is in the ultraviolet range and energizes another material like phosphorous that glows and actually creates the light.

Flyby A tool used in visualization programs that permits a viewer to experience a virtual world through following a view along a predetermined path.

Flying Rig See Flown Truss

Focal Length A measurement taken from a given point of a lens (its optical center) to its focal point.

Focal Point A point of focus along the optical path of a lens or reflector that coincides with the location from which light rays will be directed to produce parallel light rays. The reverse (where parallel light rays are directed to a focal point) is also true.

Focus 1. A lighting function that relates to drawing attention to various elements of an environment. 2. Aiming and adjusting the beam quality of a luminaire.

Focus Chart A table that documents the focus characteristics of each luminaire in a design. Most importantly, it documents the unit's location of the hotspot and focus as well as the focus settings (hard/soft), spot/flood settings, and shutter positions.

Focusing (Focus Call) A crew call in which the lighting crews aim and adjust each light for optimum performance under the direction of the lighting designer.

Focusing Spots Location luminaires that are relatively small and designed to be mounted on portable stands. They can be open-faced or may contain a lens. In some cases, the reflector may also be changeable.

Focus Palettes (Focus Points) Reference points to which automated lighting fixtures have pre-assigned pan and tilt positions. This allows a programmer to quickly move a light to predetermined positions.

Focus Track A specialized device that is used where a lift or ladder cannot be used due to obstructions to their movement on the deck or over an audience. It essentially places a movable boatswain's chair on a track that is mounted on or near a neighboring electric or truss. An electrician sits in the chair and is moved along the position at trim height to focus lights across the position without having to deal with the obstructions that are below.

Following Source A video or film technique in which the lighting is based predominantly on motivational lighting elements.

Followspot A spotlight that is used to follow performers around a stage or performance area. Most have controls for easy modification of the shape and color of the light.

Followspot Operator An individual who operates a followspot. They typically control pan and tilt, color, and size and sharpness of the beam of light that strikes the performers.

Footcandle A measure of illuminance that is based on the illuminance level found at a one-foot distance from a candle.

Footlights A lighting position at the very front edge of the stage at floor or stage level which provides a wash of uplight onto the performers.

Four-Point Lighting A system for general lighting that is based on four luminaires being placed at roughly 90° orientations with one another. It is a popular formula approach for thrust and arena lighting design.

Four-way Barndoor A control device that is placed in the front of a luminaire and has four individual panels that can be rotated into the beam of light to block or control spill.

Four-wire System (Wye) An electrical service connection where a power utility provides three different hot wires and a common neutral to a given site.

Framing To shape the light around a subject using shutters or other devices. Framing is often associated with architectural, retail, and museum applications.

Framing Projector A smaller variation of ellipsoidal reflector spotlight (ERS) that is often box-shaped and contains superior optics along with shutters and other accessories for manipulating the shape of the light. Framing projectors are used in retail and architectural design, but are more commonly associated with museum, gallery, and landscape lighting.

Fresnel Lens A variation of plano-convex lens that has portions of the convex surface removed. A dimpled texture on the plano surface adds a diffusing effect that masks the concentric rings found on its front surface.

Fresnel Spotlight Named for the inventor of the Fresnel lens, Augustine-Jean Fresnel, the essential elements include a lamp, spherical reflector, and Fresnel lens. Light from Fresnels is moderately harsh, while the edges are soft and not clearly defined.

Frequency A method of measuring waves based on the number of oscillations per unit time.

Front Diagonal A distribution angle which places a light approximately midway between a front light and a sidelight angle. It offers the best of both angles in regard to revelation of a subject.

Front End The portion of a control system that contains the console or light board.

Front of House (FOH) A reference to lighting positions that are downstage of the proscenium or are in the audience area (house).

Front Light A lighting angle that comes from in front of a subject and helps provide visibility and visual clarity. At the same time, it can flatten and reduce the effect or appearance of three-dimensional textures and forms.

Front Projection A form of projection where the projector and source material are placed in front of the screen or projection surface.

Frost See Diffusion Media

Frosted Finish A bulb finish that contains a natural diffuser to help soften the light that a lamp produces.

F-Stop The size of the aperture/opening of a camera lens, which is expressed through a set of numbers that relate to one another logarithmically. Every drop in f-stop equates to allowing twice as much light into a lens.

Funnel A tapered or cone-shaped snoot or top hat.

Fuse An electrical device that is designed as the weakest link in a circuit and meant to trip or "blow" if the circuit should become overloaded. Unlike a circuit breaker, most fuses cannot be reset.

Gaffer See Chief Lighting Technician

Gain A way of characterizing a screen or projection surface's ability to reflect or transmit light. The higher the gain, the better the material performs as a screen.

Gaseous Discharge A form of arc light source where the arc is placed in a specific atmosphere of gases. Fluorescent lamps are an example of this light source.

Gate The area of an ellipsoidal reflector spotlight (ERS) that is located roughly at the unit's secondary (conjugate) focal point. This forms the location where the light is most concentrated and where shutters, gobos, and other accessories are placed.

Gating The process in electronic dimming in which a low-voltage signal is used to control or sample the high-voltage output of a dimmer through triggering an SCR so that it fires or turns on at a given point in a cycle.

Gauge A measurement of the thickness or diameter of a wire. The larger the gauge (number), the smaller the diameter of the wire and the less current or load that it can safely carry.

Gear A term often used by entertainment professionals for lighting equipment.

Gel A color filter originally made from animal gelatin that was tinted to produce different colors. As fixtures improved, gel could no longer stand up to the temperatures of the newer light sources and has been replaced by plastic filters.

Gel Frame See Color Frame

Gelstring A sequence of gels that have been taped together to form a scroll of adjoining colors for a color scroller. Gel strings typically contain twelve or more colors.

General Circulation Lighting See Ambient Lighting

General Diffuse Luminaire An IESNA classification of luminaire based on a distribution pattern in which light is directed equally well in nearly all directions.

General Illumination (Area Lighting) See Area Lighting

General Lighting See Area Lighting

Generator A device that allows mechanical motion to be transferred into electrical potential or power by moving electrical coils through a magnetic field. Portable generators that are used on location shoots for film or video may be as small as lawnmower engine or as large as truck or trailer mounted units. They are often called a "Genny" by people in the business.

Genie-Lift (Genie Tower and Super Lift) Ground supports for trussing that are adaptations of lifts that were designed for the construction industry.

Genny Operator (Generator Operator) The individual who operates and monitors the generator(s) on a location or remote shoot.

Ghosting 1. A dimming condition in which a full out cannot be achieved by a dimmer, despite having a setting that should produce no light. 2. Placing very low levels of intensity on a stage, such as during a near blackout for a scene change or to check if a lamp is working.

Ghost Light (Ghost Load) 1. An additional load of lamps placed on a resistance dimmer to bring it to full capacity while also allowing a full range of dimming for a circuit. 2. A bare bulb lamp placed on a stand and left glowing when a theatre is not in operation. It prevents people from being harmed when entering the space.

Glare The presence of distracting light within a viewer's field of vision. This may come about as the result of an unusually high level of reflectance (snow on a bright afternoon) or when an observer is forced to look directly into a light source.

Glazing   The clear or translucent material used on windows and building facades.

Glitter (Sparkle)   A positive element of glare. We may want to create a limited amount of glare to add visual interest and perhaps some focus to a scene or object.

Global Illumination   A special form of virtual lighting that creates a uniform light throughout an environment.

Goal Post   Grip equipment used in location shooting that connects two vertical stands like C-stands with a horizontal arm or batten to which luminaires and other grip equipment can be mounted.

Gobo (Pattern or Template)   1. A metal or glass pattern that is inserted into the optical path of a luminaire to create a texture or designed image in light. 2. The film and video industries identify gobos as custom-made flags or panels (with holes or patterns cut into them) that are placed between a light source and a target. See Cookie and Cucaloris.

Gobo Rotator   An accessory that generates a rotating motion for gobos.

Grand Master   An intensity fader that provides a mechanism in which the entire system can be controlled by a single fader.

Gray Card   A poster-like reference card that is printed in a middle gray and used for white balancing cameras and color temperature calibrations for shooting film and video under a given set of lighting conditions.

Gray Scale   A reference scale used in film and video lighting that rates light reflectivity and value on a scale of 0 (black or total absorption) to 10 (white or total reflection). It is used for color balancing and exposure settings.

Grazing   Light played across the surface of an object at an extreme angle. This angle is used to enhance the texture of a surface.

Green Bed (Greenie)   A catwalk system of platforms that are hung from the rafters of a sound stage at about 4 feet above a set. They are arranged along the outline of a set and have a series of holes along their edges for mounting luminaires along their perimeters. Power is dropped down to the platforms from above and distributed to the lights as needed.

Green Power   Using conservation methods or "thinking green" as a way of lowering the energy demands of a project and ultimately saving our natural resources.

Grid   A structure at the top of a theatre's flyspace that supports all the blocks and rigging hardware for all the flying equipment (battens, scenery, maskings, and electrics). Also short for lighting grid—a series of pipes

hung over a performance space for hanging luminaires and other objects.

Grips   The crew members for film and video shoots who are responsible for the movement and setup of any equipment required for a production. They are also responsible for the installation and operation of camera gear like dollies and cranes.

Grip Truck   A truck used on location shoots that holds and transports lighting and grip equipment for location production. Studios rent grip trucks that are equipped with a pre-determined inventory of lighting and grip equipment for a standard fee.

Ground   A point that represents the lowest potential for an electrical charge (earth or absolute ground) and toward which all electricity strives to flow. In electrical services, the ground is a safety path or wire that leads from a device to an earth ground and becomes the emergency path for any unwanted electrical flow.

Ground Fault Circuit Interrupter (GFCI)   A device that detects any flow of electricity between the neutral and earth ground. If it detects any, it trips in the same way as a circuit breaker trips. They are typically installed in areas where there is a higher risk of shock and are often found in kitchens, bathrooms, and exterior locations.

Groundplan   See Floorplan

Ground Row   A collection of luminaires (usually striplights) that are floor-mounted across the width of the stage that illuminate a drop or cyclorama from below.

Ground Supported Truss   A truss that is supported from below by towers or lifts.

Groups   A manner of combining channels or dimmers into larger elements with less specific control when using an electronic control system.

Group Relamping   A method of relamping in which lamps are replaced together as a group on a regular schedule. The schedule is based on the number of hours that the system is in operation and the rated lamp life of the lamps. This is especially efficient when luminaires are hard to reach.

Hair Light   A form of film and video lighting (a variation of steep backlight) that is used to add highlights to the talent's hair.

Half Hat   See Eye-Lash

Halogen Metal Iodide (HMI) Lamp   A special variation of HID lamp that makes use of metal halides to produce an arc light source with better color rendering capabilities than other arc sources.

Hanging and Circuiting   Placing or hanging the luminaires and wiring them

according to the specifications of the lighting designer.

Hanging Cards   A partial copy of a light plot that contains the information that an electrician needs to hang a single lighting position. They can be mounted on laminated cards or cardboard so that they can stand up to the abuses of touring.

Hanging Irons   Specialized hardware, with an attached C-clamp, that are used to hang striplights. Two are required for each stripligh—one for each end.

Hanging Position   A permanent mounting position for luminaires located throughout a performance venue. They also usually have permanently wired circuits running to them.

Hanging Section   A portion of a light plot that provides the location and labeling of all the battens/linesets that are hung from above the stage.

Hard Blackouts   See Block Cues

Hard Light   A classification of light in film and video lighting that is often associated with the key source for a setup. It is quite directional and generally the primary source responsible for producing strong highlights and sharp, well-defined shadows in a scene. In landscape lighting, this is the higher contrast light and is marked by clear well-defined shadows.

Hard-Lights   A classification of film and video luminaires that produce a sharp light with shadows. The luminaires are often focusable and have a reasonable degree of control. They form strong shadows and are good directional light sources, making them a logical choice for key lights.

Hardscape   The architectural and sculptural elements of a landscape.

Haze   A low-grade fog or smoke that lightly charges the atmosphere with particles that permit the beams of light to be seen.

Hazers   A piece of equipment that is similar to an atmospheric fog machine that lightly charges the air with a haze rather than filling the air with fog or smoke.

Head   An accessory that is added to a projector to create a specific projection effect.

Head Gaffer   The individual who supervises the entire lighting department for a television or film production.

Health Care Lighting   Lighting associated with the needs of the medical industry. It is one of the more complex areas of architectural lighting and relates to lighting hospitals, long-term care facilities, and medical offices or labs.

Heat Shield   A special form of clear, gel-like material that filters ultraviolet radiation. It is inserted at the front of a unit, between the lamp and gel (leaving a gap for airflow between them) and can help extend a gel's life.

Heat Sink   A metal fin-like assembly for mounting and cooling SCRs and other electronic equipment.

High-Density Dimmers   Small, compact dimmers that can be packaged into a limited amount of space (High-Density Racks). Today's high-density dimmers are small enough that nearly 200 of them can be mounted in a single rack.

High-End Retail Environment   A retail market in which the customer enters an environment where they are made to feel comfortable and catered to as they go through the purchasing process.

High-Intensity Discharge (HID) Lamps. Highly efficient sources that use an enclosed arc to produce light. These lamps require a ballast and have a warm-up period of up to 10 minutes. They are common to architectural applications with mercury, high pressure sodium, and metal halide forming the most common examples.

High Key   A lighting condition in video lighting in which there is little difference between the lighting levels of the key and fill light—those with a small lighting/contrast ratio (1:1, 2:1 or 3:1) and a less dramatic image.

Highlights   Flashes of reflected light that represent areas that are directly illuminated by a light source.

High-Mast Lighting   Mounting street and roadway luminaires on poles over 60 feet tall.

High-Pipe-Ends (HPE)   Luminaires that are hung on the extreme ends of the electrics for high-angled sidelight.

High-Pressure Sodium Lamp   A variation of HID lamp that uses sodium as its primary lamp fill and is often used for street lighting. It is very efficient and can be recognized by its pinkish-orange color.

High-Resolution Mode   A mode associated with the degree of control that an attribute has in an automated luminaire. High-resolution modes are associated with 16-bit/2 channel operation of an attribute. Resolution modes are frequently associated with pan/tilt functions where fine and course adjustments are available for these movements.

Hologram   An advanced projection effect that is produced through a combination of laser and film effects. The unique quality of holograms is that they can produce an illusion of a three-dimension image.

Home (Homing)   A process that automated luminaires go through as part of a startup sequence where the stepper motors are referenced to specific points so that the luminaires share a common reference for their attributes with every performance.

Home Run (Spidering)   A manner of theatrical circuiting where luminaires are wired directly from their hanging position all the way back to the dimmers. This is popular for touring and is often done in road houses and rental facilities.

Hood (Body)   1. The actual enclosure of a luminaire. It provides for the proper mounting and orientation of all the optical components while also providing a way for mounting the luminaire and its accessories. 2. An optical accessory for architectural luminaires that fits over the face of a fixture and helps block viewers from direct glare from a lamp or reflector.

Hookup   Design paperwork that presents all of the information contained in a light plot in a table format. The data is organized by control (channel or dimmer number).

Hospitality Lighting   A variation of architectural lighting that relates to the hotel and restaurant industries.

Hot Light Sources   See Continuous Light Sources

Hot Wire   Wire that leads to the power source for a circuit.

House Electrician   Typically a master electrician assigned to a specific theatre or performance space, which is common in both union and road or touring houses. It is also used to distinguish between a local and touring electrician on work calls.

Houses of Worship (Church) Lighting   A specialized area of architectural lighting that relates to lighting churches, temples, and other religious structures.

Housing   See Body

Hues   The generic name for a color (e.g., red, blue, orange, etc.). Hues become a familiar means of communicating basic color information from one person to another.

I-MAG (I-mag or I-Mag)   A video projection system used in large venues in which live camera feeds are sent to large-format screens that allow the most distant audience members to see the artists more closely.

Illuminance   The density of light that has struck an object's surface and is then reflected. Two measurements of illuminance include the lux (1 lumen per square meter) or the footcandle (1 lumen per square foot).

Illuminance at a Point   A lighting calculation used for determining the illuminance at a specific location rather than the average illuminance over an area. This method of calculation can be used for both horizontal and vertical surfaces and is best utilized for single light sources. It is particularly helpful for determining the illuminance in applications involving wall surfaces like displays and bulletin boards.

Illuminating Engineer   An individual that designs the lighting for architectural projects who comes from an electrical engineering background.

Illumination Engineering   A specialized field of lighting that relates to the design and specification of architectural and other permanent lighting installations.

Illuminating Engineering Society of North America (IESNA or IES)   A professional society that provides services to lighting professionals and the lighting industry. Publications, training, and controlling specification standards and recommended practices for the industry are a few of the responsibilities of this organization.

Illuminator   The equipment that provides the light source for a fiber optics bundle.

Image of Light (Lighting Scheme/Concept or Point of View)   A vision of the lighting for a project. All other tasks related to a lighting design ultimately go back to this initial step in the process.

Incandescence   The most popular method of light production, which is represented by the common light bulb. A metal filament is heated to the point that it gives off electromagnetic radiation and glows.

Incident Light Meter   An exposure type of light meter that is used by standing in the location of the subject and pointing the meter back towards the camera and light source. It measures the level of light striking a subject.

Independent Master   A special form of controller that allows those channels assigned to it to function independently from any other mastering on the board.

Index of Refraction   The relative speed of light moving through translucent materials expressed as a proportional ratio to the speed of light moving through a vacuum.

Indirect Illumination   A form of illumination in which light is reflected off another surface before being used as a source of illumination. Many architectural designs use the ceiling to create indirect illumination. Film shoots use large reflector panels to soften a light source and to provide indirect illumination to a scene.

Indexing Rotator   A gobo rotator that allows gobos to be stopped at precise locations.

Indirect Luminaire   An IESNA classification of luminaire based off of a distribution pattern where 90—100% of the light is directed toward the ceiling, where it is reflected back into the room.

Induced Current   The current that is created in a wire from the pulsations of a magnetic field, as in the case of a transformer.

Industrial Lighting   Lighting facilities that are involved in the manufacturing process.

Industrials   A type of corporate theatre where large spectacle presentations combining performers, theatrical gimmicks like presentational lighting and pyro effects, and large-screen video projections build enthusiasm for a product or company service.

Inky   The smallest version of Fresnel spotlight (a 3-inch variety).

In-one   A plane or zone that forms a pathway across the width of a stage. It is associated with the area between the proscenium opening and the first set of legs. Additional planes include: In-two, In-three, etc.

Instrument   A luminaire. The term "instrument" is more commonly used in the theatrical and entertainment areas of lighting while fixture or luminaire is more popularly used in architectural applications.

Instrument Schedule   Lighting paperwork that organizes the data contained in a light plot by hanging position and instrument number.

Insulated Gate Bipolar Transistor (IGBT) A solid-state component of the newer sine wave dimmers that has the capability of sampling an AC current several hundred times throughout each half-cycle of a dimming cycle—producing a more accurate sampling of the AC voltage than traditional SCRs.

Insulation   Highly electrical resistant material used to cover conductors such as wires.

Insulator   A material with high electrical resistance that forms a barrier to electrical flow.

Intelligent Lights   See Automated Lights or Moving Lights

Intensity   A quality of light associated with the brightness of light.

Interconnection Panel (Interconnection Pachbay)   See Patchbay

Interference Patterns.   A laser image in which the laser is distorted by passing through an irregular piece of material like glass or plastic, which causes its individual waves to become scattered or knocked out of phase with one another. The technique produces colored patterns of light that form simple or more complex organic patterns that are capable of being transported over long distances.

Interior Lighting   An area of lighting that relates to lighting building interiors.

Interlocking Handles   A form of mechanical mastering done through connecting banks of dimmers (resistance or autotransformer) to common shafts and control handles that can be locked together through spring-loaded pin mechanisms.

Intermediate Colors (Tertiary Colors)   An unequal mixture of primary colors.

Intermediate Retail Environment   A retail environment that falls between the high-end and basic retail markets. It contains elements of both markets and would best be characterized by department stores where different departments are lit differently.

International Alliance of Theatrical Stage Employees (IATSE)   The union that represents the lighting and stagehand crews for theatre, video and film, and other production houses and facilities. It is common to hear this union called the IA or local.

International Association of Lighting Designers (IALD)   A professional society that is similar to the IESNA but whose membership is restricted to lighting designers.

International Illumination Design Awards (IIDA)   Design awards that are given annually for exceptional examples of architectural lighting design.

Inverse Square Law   A law that states that the illuminance of a light source is inversely proportional to the square of the distance from the source. $E = I/D2$.

Iris (Iris Kit)   1. A mechanical device or accessory that allows light to be shuttered in a circular pattern that allows an operator to narrow or expand the diameter of the light. 2. The colored part of the eye that adjusts the amount of light entering the eye.

Irons   A category of hanging hardware and accessories. Items like C-clamps, sidearms, and hanging irons form examples of irons.

ISO   See ASA

Island Window   A window display that is surrounded by glass on all sides and allows customers to walk around it to examine merchandise.

Jewel Lighting   A variation of the zone lighting formula in which an emphasis is placed on higher intensity levels and the low-angled sidelight that is hung primarily from booms positioned along the sides of the stage and the front diagonals. In addition to the basic washes, jewel lighting adds accents and specials to bring visual interest to a design, and characteristically lights a subject from many angles.

Jones Box   A lighting accessory that connects all of the individual control cables of analog dimmer packs to an interface of the digital to analog converter.

Jones Connectors (Cinch-Jones Connectors) A special connector associated with analog control cables that provides low-voltage connections between the control cable and the console or dimmers.

Jumper (Cable)   A cable containing two or three insulated conductors that has a single male and female connector on each end. It is often used synonymously with cable.

Junction Method   A landscape wiring technique that attempts to eliminate voltage drop through wiring every lamp back to a single point in the circuit.

Key   1. A portion of the light plot that indicates the specific choice of luminaire with an associated symbol or accessory. 2. The key light or luminaire that provides the key light.

Key and Fill   A system for creating general lighting in which one source (the key) is associated with the primary or apparent source and another (the fill) provides enough illumination to suggest any ambient light required for general visibility. It originated in the film and television industry where cameras required minimum levels of illumination to prevent shadow areas from going completely dark.

Key Light   The light that is the primary source responsible for lighting a scene. It is associated with the source of the lighting and produces the strongest highlights and shadows.

Keystone Effect   A distortion effect that occurs when a projection surface and projector's slide and resulting image are not oriented properly along the same axis. Keystoning causes lines and surfaces to spread outward in a radiating rather than parallel manner.

Kicker   A form of lighting distribution in film and video lighting in which a backlight is offset to one side but can come from any direction above or below a subject.

Knock-Offs   A substitute fixture provided by a contractor for architectural installations that is less expensive than those originally specified and often only meets the specifications minimally. They are used to increase profit margin and are undesirable in most situations.

Ladder   A hanging position that performs the same function as a boom but is hung from above. Ladders often look similar to an extension ladder and allow sidelight to be added while avoiding ground support that gets in the way of traffic on the deck.

Lamp   A device that produces artificial light.

Lamp Alignment   Adjusting the orientation or relationship between the reflector and lamp of a luminaire to achieve maximum light output.

Lamp Flicker When using arc sources (most notably HMI) one must consider that the film or video camera can pick up exposure inconsistencies (flicker) caused by not having the power of the camera and lamp's ballast synchronized properly.

Lampholders A socket and adjustable fitting which is used to mount flood and spot lamps like PAR-38s from the face plate of a junction box.

Lamp Life The average number of hours that a lamp will burn before failing. It is based on trials in which light production drops off by 80% or more.

Lamp Sing See Filament Sing

Landscape Lighting Lighting exterior grounds and its plant and floral life.

Laser A special form of light that contains a limited or even single wavelength of light that is emitted in a concentrated, narrowly defined direction. A laser also emits light in a synchronized or stepping manner that increases its intensity or energy.

Latitude The range of darkness to brightness that a film's emulsion or video camera is capable of capturing. Latitude is often expressed in terms of f-stops.

Law of Reflection The angle of incidence is equal to the angle of reflection. An essential physical property that determines the behavior of light with reflectors.

Law of Refraction (Snell's Law) As light passes into a more dense material, the light is bent toward a normal angle at the surface boundary between the materials, while light passing from a more dense material into one of less density is bent away from the normal angle with the surface.

Layered Design Approach A design approach connected primarily with architectural design (but also used elsewhere) in which different visual tasks are solved through providing several different lighting solutions on top of one another, each one solving the needs of a particular task.

Layering A technique of using contrast to superimpose one or more lighting systems on top of one another (e.g., creating a base level illumination over an area and placing accent specials on various subjects in that space).

LCD (Liquid Crystal Display) Screens and Projectors A projection technique in monitors and screens that are constructed of a matrix of liquid crystals that form an image by having their individual reflectances or light outputs varied through a small control

voltage. These units can be assembled into screens of almost any size. LCD projectors are different from traditional projectors in that an LCD panel is located within the projector, where a high-intensity light source is placed behind the display, which then projects the image onto another surface.

Leap-Frog If a tour is so large that it cannot be set up in the time allotted between stops, a producer may elect to duplicate some of the equipment so that part of the gear only plays at every other stop.

Learning Education Units (LEUs) A unit of course instruction that is given for a specified number of classroom hours of continuing professional education. LEUs are frequently used to maintain certifications like the LC Certification by NCQLP.

LED (Light-Emitting Diode) A solid-state device that produces light through a process in which electricity is applied to a crystal or diode material in a given direction or manner. The result of this creates light in a very limited range of wavelengths.

LEED (Leadership in Energy and Environmental Design) A program in the construction industry that emphasizes environmentally friendly building practices.

Leg (Phase) One of the power sources or hot wires of an electrical power service.

Legs A masking of vertical fabric that is hung to either side of the stage to block audience view of the stage's wings.

Leko See Ellipsoidal Reflector Spotlight (ERS)

Lens An optical device that makes use of refraction to consolidate and redirect light. If a point light source is placed at the focal point of a lens the associated light will be redirected into parallel rays.

Lens Barrel The focusing portion of a spotlight, which consists of a moveable assembly containing the fixture's lenses.

Lens Flare An effect created when backlight accidently hits a camera's lens. It usually causes an undesirable effect through producing internal reflections of the light in the camera but can also be used intentionally for dramatic effect.

Lensless Spotlight A location luminaire that is nothing more than a housing containing a roughly spherical reflector and small tubular tungsten-halogen lamp. It has a wide distribution pattern and provides a good, economical source for the limited power that it consumes.

Level-Setting Session See Cue-Writing Session

Library Cues Cues in a memory board that may not necessarily be part of a cue sequence

but are stored for safekeeping. Storing base cues or an old version of a cue that a designer may wish to go back to form examples of library cues.

Life Cycle Costing A calculation that predicts how much a lighting system will cost to install, operate, and maintain over its projected life span.

Lift 1. A mechanical device (usually with electric or pneumatic power) that is used, like a ladder, for elevating electricians and other crew members to the heights where they can troubleshoot and focus luminaires in their hanging positions. 2. A mechanical device that is used to support lighting gear like trusses from below (the deck).

Light A specific form of electromagnetic radiation that corresponds to the wavelengths of radiant energy that are visible to the human eye. It is commonly known as the visible spectrum.

Light Attic A chamber found in display cases (particularly museum cases) that is added to the top of a cabinet that houses the lamps, diffusers, baffles, or other optical accessories used for illuminating a case. This gives protection through separating the lighting elements from the artifacts or other case contents.

Light Bridge A winched catwalk that contains several lighting pipes (often with pre-wired circuits) that is flown directly over and across the width of the stage.

Light Center Length (LCL) A measurement from the center of a lamp's filament to a specified location on its base. This base location depends on the style of a lamp but remains consistent between all bases of a given style.

Light-Emitting Diodes See LED

Light Grid A network of perpendicular pipes that are hung at regular spacings (3 to 5 feet apart) above a stage or studio. It is used to hang luminaires and scenery from above a performance area.

Lighting Area A smaller portion of an environment or stage created through dividing a larger area into a series of smaller spaces that are each illuminated in a similar manner.

Lighting Balloons An aerial balloon used in exterior location lighting that is flown above a set and contains one or more internal HMI light sources that provide diffuse light to the areas below.

Lighting Calculations A process of using a variety of formulas to determine various lighting properties for an architectural installation. A determination of illumination levels

(Lumen Method and Point at a Source) form the most common calculations, but power efficiencies and economic calculations like payback or maintenance costs are also done for most projects.

Lighting Concept (Lighting Scheme, Image of Light or Point of View)   A mental image or plan that creates a framework that drives the individual decisions for any lighting project. The concept addresses issues such as style, mood, and transitional patterns as well as specific environmental qualities such as location, geographical setting, and time frame. Lighting concepts are more typically associated with theatrical and entertainment lighting projects. Also see Lighting Scheme.

Lighting Certified (LC)   A professional certification for architectural lighting designers by the National Council for Qualifications for the Lighting Profession (NCQLP). To earn the LC certification an individual must pass an exam and/or participate in educational activities on a three-year cycle.

Lighting Console   See Desk

Lighting Designer (LD).   The individual who is charged with the overall design of the lighting of a production, event, or environment. A lighting designer produces an artistic vision for the lighting of a project.

Lighting Director   The individual who has overall charge of the lighting and its design for a film or video.

Lighting Economics   Using calculations to determine the actual costs of installing and maintaining a lighting system. They are also used to determine maintenance and re-lamping schedules.

Lighting Green   To design lighting using environmentally sensitive practices. Lower power densities and consideration toward disposal of hazardous materials (e.g., mercury) form several examples of these considerations.

Lighting Instrument   See Luminaire

Lighting Key   A visual representation of the primary lighting angles and colors that would be used as part of a general or overall lighting scheme for a scene or project.

Lighting Kit   A selection of approximately a half-dozen location luminaires, along with their accessories (scrims, barndoors, flags, etc.), and portable stands and mountings that are packaged as a group in a shipping case.

Lighting Layout (Lighting Scheme or Lighting Plan)   The architectural equivalent of a light plot. It identifies the type and location of the luminaires and also often illustrates the wiring and switch locations that are specified by a lighting designer.

Lighting Plan   See Light Plot

Lighting Pole   A pole used in studio setups that helps a studio electrician pull the luminaires down from the lighting grid to their working heights while also focusing and adjusting them from the studio floor.

Lighting Ratios   In video production, a variation of contrast ratio that is based on the relationship between the reflected intensity of the key light to the base or fill light.

Lighting Scheme (Image of Light or Point of View)   A vision or image of the lighting for a given project. It is the architectural equivalent of a lighting concept.

Lighting Score   A manner of illustrating specific lighting qualities found on stage at any given moment. It is a table that indicates specific moments or scenes along one axis and a variety of lighting functions or properties that are identified and characterized along the opposing axis.

Lighting Specification   An architectural contract document based on a specification of the luminaires that will be used on a project. It is organized from a luminaire perspective.

Lighting Stands   Portable stands used in film and video lighting (particularly location work) to mount luminaires and accessories from the floor.

Lighting System (System)   A group of luminaires that perform similar functions and work together as a group. Washes form popular lighting systems in which a group of lights share qualities like color, hanging angle, and basic instrument type while being focused to different areas of the stage.

Lighting Template   1. A specialized stencil used to draw proportionally scaled lighting instruments on a light plot, section, or lighting layout. 2. See gobo or pattern.

Lighting the Horizontal Plane   Measuring the quantity of light striking flat surfaces (the workplane) that are parallel with the ceiling (e.g., a desk or countertop).

Lighting the Vertical Plane   Measuring the quantity of light striking flat surfaces that are perpendicular to the ceiling (e.g., shelving units and walls).

Lighting Unit   See Luminaire

Light Jockey   The operator who improvises a light show on the dance floor for a club.

Light Lab   A layout of lighting fixtures and a pipe/grid system that allows fixtures to be hung, wired, and experimented upon in a limited small-scale setting, usually with a height of only 6 to 12 feet. The lab is used for experimentation prior to completing a prototype or actually lighting of a project.

Light Loss Factor (LLF)   A factor in lighting calculations that deals with properties that inhibit the delivery of light to an application. This represents factors like the effects of ambient temperature on a luminaire, heat exchange, voltage factors, ballast efficiency, lamp depreciation, burnouts, and the amount of dirt or cleaning that impairs or improves a luminaire's efficiency.

Light Plot (Lighting Plan)   A drafting that communicates all of the information that a crew will need to execute the hanging and circuiting of a design. Typical information contained in a light plot includes choice of type and number of fixtures, hanging locations, gel colors, and control or wiring information.

Light Pollution   A condition in which reflected and misdirected light or glare causes scattering and a general ambience of unwanted light in an area. This can be as limited as spilling light onto a neighbor's property or as large as the loss of a nighttime view of the stars by city glow.

Light Shelf   A passive solar device placed outside window surfaces that is used to reflect sunlight upward through the window and into the room where it is reflected off of the ceiling as an indirect light source.

Light Trespass   A condition in which light spills into an unwanted area or causes unwanted glare. This is a particular issue when light causes problems with neighboring properties.

Limelight   An antiquated luminaire that contained a block of lime that was heated by a gas flame to the point that it created a bright source of light for the stage.

Linear (Wash Light)   Light sources and fixtures that have a long narrow source like a fluorescent tube and are used to create smooth, even washes over an area.

Lineset   A batten and its associated rigging hardware.

Line-Voltage   A reference to electric systems that are operated on normal household currents of 120 volts AC.

Linnebach Projector   A variation of lensless or shadow projector that was developed in the early 20th century by Adolph Linnebach, a stage engineer from Germany. The projector has a single light source placed at the rear of its housing, while large acetate or glass slides are designed to cover the entire front of the fixture.

Live   1. Relates to a circuit having power or current within it. 2. A performance mode where cues are actually on stage and being executed during a performance.

Load   The total capacity requirements of a circuit. It contains the power requirements (amps or watts) of every device contained on a circuit.

Load-In The process by which all of the technical elements and equipment (scenery, lighting, sound, etc.) is transported and set up in a performance venue. In lighting, this usually refers to the hanging, circuiting, and focusing of the luminaires.

Lobster Scope A visual effect that produces a strobe-like property that was developed during the vaudeville era and before strobe lights. It was produced when a followspot operator rapidly passed an opaque panel like a piece of cardboard back and forth in front of the light to produce a flicker effect.

Local See IATSE

Lock the Unit Down A command given by a lighting designer to an electrician during a focus call that indicates that the designer is pleased with the pan and tilt adjustments of a light and that the electrician should tighten down the appropriate set-bolts.

Long-Throw Followspots Followspots used in large venues like auditoriums, arenas, and stadiums.

Look and Light A method of lighting associated with studio lighting in which the designer simply goes into a studio and picks lighting from whatever instrumentation is already hung. Commercials are frequently shot in this manner.

Loop System A low-voltage landscaping lighting technique that reduces voltage drop by having all the luminaires wired in a daisy chain with both ends of the cable or circuit wired to the transformer.

Louvers An optical accessory with baffles or concentric rings that is placed over the face of a fixture to block the viewer from direct glare.

Low-Capacity Dimmer A dimmer with a relatively low-wattage or load rating. Frequently one of 1,200 watts or less.

Low Key A lighting condition in video lighting that is more dramatic than normal and reflects higher contrast ratios (5:1, 8:1, 10:1, etc.) and greater difference between the intensities of the key and fill lights.

Low-Pressure Sodium Lamp A variation of HID lamp which can be identified by its deep yellow color (like bug-lights). It is very efficient but has very poor color rendering.

Low-Resolution Mode A mode associated with the degree of control that an attribute has in an automated luminaire. Low-resolution modes are associated with 8-bit/1 channel operation of an attribute and do not have the same degree of control (fine-control) as high-resolution modes of control.

Low-Voltage Lighting systems that are operated on a voltage of approximately 12 volts

(AC or DC), although other voltages like 24 volts are also used. Display and landscape lighting systems often use low-voltage power.

Lumen A measurement of light that relates to the luminous flux of a light source.

Lumen Maintenance A consideration of how quickly the light output of a lamp drops over the time that it is in operation or ages.

Lumen Method (Zonal Cavity Method) A specific manner of calculating and specifying average illumination levels or lumen density for an architectural lighting application. Properties such as volume of the environment, physical properties of the luminaire, mounting heights, condition of the room's reflective surfaces, and visual tasks all play a role in the illumination levels that are calculated by using this method.

Lumen Output The actual amount of light that is delivered by a lamp or luminaire.

Luminaire The actual lighting fixture. A luminaire contains a light source, reflector, housing, and many times a lens(s). Other names for luminaire include lighting units, fixtures, instruments, and lamps.

Luminance The source's intensity divided by the surface area of the source as observed by the viewer. A directional function that is dependent on the relationship or viewing angle of the viewer.

Luminous Exitance A measurement of intensity that relates to the total amount of light either reflecting off or leaving a surface. It is not direction dependent like luminance. Reflection/transmission factors are introduced to the metric based on the reflective/transmitting qualities of the source or object.

Luminous Flux A measure of the actual flow of energy from a light source. The most common unit of measure is the lumen.

Luminous Intensity A measurement of the ability of a light source to produce intensity in a given direction. It is usually measured in candela.

Magic Lantern The forerunner of traditional projectors whose development is generally credited to Jesuit Father Athanasius Kircher in the late 1600s. Although crude in comparison to today's standards, it provides the principle method by which most traditional projectors are still designed. Light sources could be oil or limelight.

Magic Sheet A type of paperwork that designers use when they set levels or program a show's lighting. It is an abbreviated form that is often created in a visual format and contains only the information that a designer will need to set levels (typically only channel, color, and purpose/focus).

Main Feeders Heavy duty cables that connect a main switchboard to the distribution panels that are located throughout a building.

Main Switchboard The primary distribution center for a building. It is connected directly to the power source that comes from outside the building.

Maintained Illuminance The average amount of light that reflects off of a given surface (usually horizontal).

Male Connector A connector with one or more receptacles for making quick connections between electrical devices and cables. The male connector taps into the source of power.

Manual Control or Dimming A form of dimming in which electricians are responsible for physically moving various components or hardware to regulate the lighting intensities. All cues must be executed in a live state.

Mark Cue (Move Cue) A cue that is created for presetting a moving light attribute or other DMX function so that the move is done without the knowledge of an audience.

Married When circuits and their associated cables are run from one electric or batten to another. This is usually done by running the circuits off the end of one batten onto the same end of a second batten and forming a loop of excess cable between the two pipes. The battens must be flown together when moving either batten.

Maskings Drapes, flats, or other scenic materials that are used to prevent view of the backstage and fly areas by an audience. Legs and borders are common examples of maskings that are found on many stages.

Master Electrician (ME) The technician who plays the most important supervisory role for the lighting installation. They are charged with making sure that the lighting and other electrical equipment is installed and operated in an efficient safe manner.

Mastering A manner of having multiple dimmers or other lighting controls controlled together. There are essentially three types of mastering: mechanical, electrical, and electronic.

Matte Photography See Composite Photography

McCandless System (The Method) A method for providing relatively naturalistic lighting for general stage illumination based on the teachings of Yale professor Stanley McCandless in the 1930s. His technique, often called "The Method" (McCandless did not intend this), is based on dividing a stage into areas that are around 8 feet in diameter, with each area being lit by two luminaires containing complementary tints hung at 45° both above and to each side of an area.

Mechanical Mastering A form of mastering in which some form of physical device is used to mechanically link the control handles of individual dimmers.

Media A reference that is usually made to film or video, where the performance is often recorded in some manner.

Media Server A computer that allows a designer to create and edit digital content for many forms of digital screens and projectors, including digital lights. Material is developed in the media server and transferred to the projectors or screens. These devices come pre-loaded with a diverse collection of video and animation files that can be edited or used directly, but more importantly, content can be imported from collections found on CDs, DVDs, or digital video and animation clips that are provided by the media designer.

Medium Base A specifically sized (1 inch diameter) lamp base.

Memory Control Lighting consoles that actually store cues in some type of memory (long or short term). Computer consoles form the most notable examples.

Mercury Lamp A variation of HID lamp that is cost-effective and used in many security and highway lighting applications. It is recognized by its bluish-green to white light.

Metal Halide Lamp A form of HID lamp that is very efficient and becoming fairly common in retail environments. The lamps contain various combinations of metal halides in addition to the traditional mercury and argon gases. These additional materials produce a better quality of light that is associated with better color rendering and a crisp quality of fairly high color temperature.

Metaphor A means of representing specific meanings where an object or series of words is used figuratively or symbolically to represent or make comparisons or meanings between objects.

Middle Gray A reference on the gray scale that represents the midpoint of the perceived value of white/black as well as an 18% overall reflectance.

MIDI Control A control format (Musical Instrument Digital Interface) that allows one device to trigger actions in another through various digital instructions –such as using a light console to trigger various effects devices or having the lighting controlled by a sound track. Two variations of this include: MIDI Show Control (MSC) where the triggers are controlled by events and MIDI Time Control

(MTC) where the triggers are based on a timing code.

Mids Luminaires mounted on a boom at head height as a special form of sidelight.

Miniature Base A specifically sized (Approximately 3/8" in diameter) lamp base.

Miniature Reflector (MR) Lamp A miniature lamp that is similar to a PAR lamp in that it has a reflector (flatted) built into the actual lamp's construction.

Mini-Striplight A revision in striplight design that is about half the width and height of traditional striplights and based on the MR-16 low-voltage lamp.

Mired (Micro-Reciprocal Degrees) A scale used in film and television production that relates the difference between perceived and actual color temperature by dividing the light's measured degrees in Kelvin by 1,000,000. Mired factors are used to calculate the proper color correction that must be applied to a source.

Mirror Board A special type of reflector or shiny board used in film and video lighting in which the surface of the panel is covered with a mirrored surface.

Mirror Lighting A technique of lighting water features in a landscape project where the water is purposefully kept dark so that the nearby lit structures and related activities can be reflected on the water's surface.

Mockup Mockups create an experimental situation for architectural lighting applications. They use actual design elements like the wall and floor materials or finishes and furniture in a limited fashion so that luminaire choices and design solutions can be examined in a limited but full-scale setting. A mockup may even involve testing luminaires on site.

Modeling A function of lighting that uses light for enhancing the three-dimensional qualities or form of an object. Also known as revelation of form or sculpting.

Modeling Programs A variation of CAD software where three-dimensional virtual models are created in a computer with realistic materials and lighting that produce a reasonably accurate image or rendering of the virtual object(s) or scene.

Modeling/Sculpting Systems A lighting system or collection of luminaires characterized by washes of back and side light that enhance depth perception throughout a stage.

Mogul Base A specifically sized (1½" diameter) lamp base.

Moment A point where all of the elements of a stage picture are frozen and recorded.

It is like taking a snapshot of the stage composition.

Monopole A telescoping pole used to mount luminaires in a studio grid that allows a lighting unit to be quickly brought down to a lower height (from its stored position) for use, or for creating flatter angles.

Mood Mood relates to creating a specific emotional response. Architectural spaces also project moods, much of which can be directly attributed to their lighting.

Moonbox (Shadow Box) A specific type of shadow box that is created to simulate a moon. Shadow boxes are boxes with enclosed light sources that have a translucent front and are used to produce a lighting effect that actually transmits light. Signs are often produced as shadow boxes.

Moonlighting A special form of downlighting that simulates natural moonlight through mounting mercury vapor lamps in the tops of trees or poles so that the shadows and cool color provide a suggestion of moonlight.

Motion Detectors (Occupancy Sensors) An energy-saving switching device that extinguishes lights in areas like stairwells and restrooms that have not been occupied for a set amount of time. They can also be used to restore the lighting when someone enters the space.

Motivated Lighting Often used synonymously with motivational lighting, but relates to light coming from both actual and apparent sources (sources not actually visible to the observer). It is represented by sunlight streaming through a doorway, a room being lit from an imaginary fixture like a chandelier, or a field being lit by the sun from somewhere above and behind the audience.

Motivating Light (Motivating Sources) A special form of motivational lighting in which the actual light source is seen on stage. Examples include placing candles or lanterns on stage, flashlights, a fireplace or fire, or having sconces, table lamps, or chandeliers on a stage.

Motivational Accents Luminaires and washes that are used to provide an indication of a specific or suggested motivational light source.

Motivational Lighting Light that is linked to an apparent source such as sunlight, a given lamp or chandelier, or an effect like a fireplace. It is a realistic style and attempts to approach the lighting from a perspective that represents how light would appear in a natural setting.

Mounting Height The height at which an architectural fixture is mounted. It's used in the same way that throw distances are used in entertainment luminaires.

Move Cue   See Mark Cue

Movement   One of the controllable qualities of light. It suggests changes in the lighting by: seeing the actual light source move on stage (carrying a flashlight), seeing light but not the actual source move (the effect of a followspot), and seeing changes in the lighting over time (running cues).

Moving Head   A variation of automated luminaire in which the body of the luminaire swivels to complete pan and tilt motions.

Moving Lights   See Automated Lights

Moving Light Operator   See Programmer

Moving Mirror (Scanner)   A type of automated luminaire in which a moving mirror is placed at the front of a unit to reflect or direct the light to different locations.

Moving Mirror Accessories   An accessory that provides an alternative to expensive scanners and allows movement to be introduced to conventional luminaires. This accessory and its control components are placed in the gel frame at the front of a luminaire and allows the focus to be redirected by a moving mirror.

Moving Yoke   An accessory that allows a conventional luminaire's focus (pan and tilt) to be repositioned.

M-speed   A control attribute of many automated fixtures that makes use of a speed function for evening out any jerky motions that a fixture might display while moving a light or its attributes during a cue transition.

Multi-cable (Multi)   Cables that are manufactured with a number of independent conductors that terminate in individual male and female connectors corresponding to the number of circuits that are contained in a cable.

Multi-lights   A luminaire used in film and television lighting that consists of an array of lamps mounted in a fixed arrangement on a panel or as groups of lamps mounted in frames that allow several lamps to be focused together. Individual lamps may be turned on or off independently or as a group. One of the most popular multi-lights is the nine-light, which combines nine PAR lamps into a three-by-three grid arrangement. This particular unit may also be called a brute, while other variations are based on the size of the lamps (e.g. a maxi-brute uses PAR 64s).

Multiple-Feed System   A landscape lighting technique where individual cable runs are run from different junction points that in turn have multiple luminaires wired to each junction point (daisy chained or junctioned).

Multiplexers   See Digital to Analog Converter

Multiplexing   See Dimmer Doubling™

Multiplying Factor   A numerical factor multiplied by the throw distance to calculate an approximate pool diameter for light associated with a given luminaire.

Musco Lights   A popular aerial platform that adds supplemental television lighting to sports arenas. These truck-mounted cranes are used to surround a stadium and to place an array of around a dozen luminaires (one array per truck) high enough above the stadium to shoot over the walls onto the playing field.

Museum Lighting   An area of lighting that involves lighting artifacts and artwork associated with museum collections.

National Association of Broadcast Employees and Technicians (NABET)   A union in the broadcasting industry that represents directors of photography and lighting directors along with other engineers and technicians like camera men.

National Council for Qualifications for the Lighting Profession (NCQLP)   A professional certification agency used primarily for architectural lighting designers who must pass a comprehensive exam. If successful, the individual is "Lighting Certified" and may use the LC behind their name.

National Electrical Code (NEC)   A construction code that provides a set of standards for guiding the specification and installation of electrical equipment like lighting packages.

Naturalism   A school of style that represents an extreme form of realism.

Near-Side Key   A form of lighting in film and video setups in which the key light is placed on the side of the performer's face nearest the camera.

Neon   A lighting effect in which neon gas is placed in a glass tube that is bent into designer-determined shapes. The gas is energized by a transformer, causing the entire tube to give off light. Neon gives off an intense red light while other gases produce other colors like yellow, blue, and white.

Nets   See Butterflies.

Neutral   The wire that provides the return path for electricity in a circuit.

Neutral Density Filter (ND or NDF)   A media that is similar to gel but is instead used to drop the overall intensity of a lamp. More importantly, it drops the intensity without having an impact on the color temperature of the source.

Nodes   Termination points in a lighting control network that become the points

where an ethernet signal is converted to DMX ports

Non-Motivated Lighting   Lighting that is not tied to an apparent light source, with which the designer creates an image based on emotional responses, mood, or symbolic elements for a production or project.

Non-Tracking Console   A lighting console in which cue edits or changes can only be made a single cue at a time and where a modification cannot be incorporated into future cues.

Notation   1. A portion of the light plot that indicates the meaning of any data such as color, unit number, and channel assignment that is attached to the luminaires. 2. A way of recording blocking and performer movements through a series of sketches.

Notes   When it is not possible to make a change or to edit a cue immediately (on the fly), a designer makes a list of any problems that need to be fixed by the next rehearsal or performance. Technical notes require a crew and physical action (gel/focus changes, inoperable lamps, etc,), while board notes relate to console programming.

Obie   See Camera-Lights

Objective Lens   An assembly of high-quality optical lenses that are placed in front of a slide in a traditional projector. They are used to focus the image precisely onto a projection surface.

Occupancy Sensors   See Motion Detectors

Occupants   The people that will occupy or use an architectural space or environment.

Office Lighting   Architectural lighting that relates to lighting offices and business centers.

Off-line Editors   A simulator provided by most console manufacturers that replicates their console for a personal computer or laptop. They allow a designer to pre-program or edit a show without using the actual console.

Ohm's Law   Relates resistance to the voltage and amperage of a circuit. $I = E/R$.

Omnidirectional Light   A virtual light that creates light in all directions—away from the light source.

One-Night Stand   A form of touring in which a production is loaded-in, performed, and struck in a single day.

One-to-One Patching   A condition where all dimmers and channels share the same number assignments.

Online Catalogues   Product catalogues of cut sheets and other product literature that are created and distributed in electronic formats. The most popular forms are CDs or company Web sites.

On Location   Shooting a film or video in a natural setting—the actual setting or a place similar to where the action is to be set.

Onstage   1. Anything that is located in audience view. 2. A reference to come toward centerline. 3. Luminaires or hanging positions that are located on or above a stage.

On The Fly   Making and recording cue changes live or as the performance or rehearsal is in progress. In many live events, such as in concert lighting, a number of the cue sequences and much of the designing are completed on the fly.

Open-Backed Window   A display window that has no back and is open to the store behind the window.

Open Fixture   A landscaping luminaire in which no attempt is made to shield the lamp and its related components from the elements.

Optical Density   An expression of the relative ability of light to move through a material and the effect that it has on the speed of the light transmitted through it.

Opto-Isolator   A device placed on the control line to protect a console and other components from a power surge. The device forms a junction where the electrical impulses of the control signal are converted to a light source (usually an LED) and then back again to an electrical impulse.

Organisation des Scenographes, Techniciens et Arcitects de Theatre (OISTAT)   An international organization of theatrical designers and technicians that is affiliated with USITT.

Out-of-town Tryout   In many Broadway-destined productions, the production might be tried out in a smaller, lower-cost, out-of-town theatre. If successful, the show transfers to Broadway.

Overheads   A term used to reference the lighting units that are hung above the stage.

Overhire   Hiring theatrical crew members on a temporary or per-show basis.

Pack (Stack)   A reference to loading and storing theatrical equipment and scenery. Equipment can be stacked or packed in the trucks, wings, or almost anywhere as needed.

Page   A utility device on computer consoles that allows controllers to be assigned to different functions. This allows them to be reassigned throughout a production.

Painting With Light   The design aesthetic of creating the lighting images or looks/cues for a production. The process produces an image through a combination of individual lights and their colors, angles, intensities, and overall mixing.

Palettes   A series of functions that are assigned to a lighting console's encoders, submaster/channel controllers, and group displays that provide an operator with a means of organizing the data required for programming a show. Common palettes are nothing more than a selection of presets that are stored and organized by categories like focus points, color, gobo patterns, etc.

Pan   A pivoting adjustment of the side-to-side focus of a luminaire's orientation.

Pantograph   A studio accessory with scissor-like telescoping arms that is used to mount luminaires from a studio grid. It allows luminaires to be quickly pulled down to a lower height.

Paper Tech   A meeting completed prior to the first tech, during which cues and their placement are discussed by the director, designers, stage manager, and other personnel.

Paperwork   See Design Paperwork

PAR-Bar   An assemblage of PAR fixtures (usually six) that are rigged along with their circuiting into a module along a single pipe or section of unistrut (A U-shaped channel fabricated from steel). These modules are then mounted into trussing or lighting towers for a production.

PAR Can (PAR Fixture)   A luminaire using a PAR lamp as the basis of its design. They are durable and easily hung and focused but have no beam-shaping qualities other than through the selection of a specific lamp. The light produced by PAR Cans is harsh and crisp with relatively soft edges that allow adjoining units to easily blend with one another.

PAR Lamp (Parabolic Aluminized Reflector)   A lamp that contains a pre-defined lens, reflector, and filament. It is unique in that it is a complete fixture within a lamp.

PARnel   A relatively new fixture design by ETC that combines the light quality of a PAR with the spot/flood capabilities of a Fresnel. It is designed around the 575-watt HPL lamp and by turning a knob an electrician can vary the fixture's beam from a spot to flood setting.

Parabolic Reflector   A reflector that is very similar to a spherical reflector, with the exception that it is flattened to some degree. Due to its shape, light that strikes it after leaving the focal point is reflected in a way that creates parallel rays of light.

Parallel Circuit   A circuit that differs from a series circuit in that each device is wired directly to the power source. This results in components like lamps having access to the full amount of power despite any other lamps that might be wired into the circuit. Any

breaks in the circuit will only have an effect on those units that are directly wired to that part of a circuit.

Pastel Tints   Lightly colored gels or light that have a fair amount of most of the individual wavelengths and produce essentially white light that is tinted slightly in favor of a particular hue.

Patch   To assign a specific circuit to a dimmer or a dimmer to a channel.

Patchbay (Patch Panel, Interconnection Panel, or Interconnection Patchbay)   A piece of electrical hardware that allows circuit and dimmer assignments to be made in a theatre or studio where there are a limited number of dimmers. Plugs representing circuits are plugged into outlets that are associated with the assigned dimmers.

Pathway Lights   Landscape luminaires that are used to line sidewalks and driveways.

Pattern   See Gobo or Template

Payback   Determining the point in time where a lighting system saves enough money in maintenance and power savings costs to pay for itself.

Peaked Field   A beam pattern in which a concentrated hot spot is formed near the center of a spotlight beam.

Pendant   A classification of architectural luminaire where the unit is suspended from below a ceiling by a cord, chain, or other similar device.

Penetration   In daylighting, the depth to which light extends into a room from its exterior walls and windows.

Penumbra Effect   A problem associated with lensless projectors in which the filament size or surfaces are too large or numerous to produce a single image. It causes fuzzing or blurred edges in any images created by the projector.

Pepper's Ghost   A famous projection effect that uses mirrors and transparent materials like glass or plexiglass to reflect images of an object or "ghost" to new locations.

Performer Specials   Luminaires that are designated specifically to light a performer at a given movment(s) within a performance.

Perishables   See Expendables

Perimeter Lighting   Lighting that is designed to light the top wall surfaces that extend around the perimeter of a store or public building.

Personality   A series of settings for an automated luminaire or other device that allow specific parameters of the unit to be set for an individual application or preference. Sample settings might include placing the unit in an audio sensory mode, reversing the pan and tilt settings, or putting the unit in a power saving mode.

Perspective Lighting   Landscape lighting that creates an illusion of distance either by placing the light sources in a set of skewed lines that follow a perspective projection or by using lower-wattage sources at distances further from the viewer.

Phase   See Leg

Photo-Electric Sensor (Photosensor)   An electrical control device that switches circuits on and off by sensing light intensity levels.

Photometrics   The study of the quality and quantities of light.

Photopic Vision   That portion of vision attributed to the cone receptors that are responsible for both our color and detail vision within typical interior and exterior lighting illuminance ranges.

Piano Board   A dimming package that contains a framework with a collection of individual dimmer plates (six, twelve, or more dimmers) along with their associated handles and mastering levers.

Pick Point (Pick)   Any location along a truss or other structure where a cable is supported from overhead by some form of rigging such as a chain motor.

Pickup   1. A followspot coming on and lighting a specific target. 2. Location where an object is supported by an overhead cable, rope, etc.

Pigtail   A 12–24-inch cable that terminates in a female plug from a circuit along a raceway or distribution box. It can also refer to the lead wires and male plug coming from a luminaire.

Pile-On   A cueing function where additional lights or effects are added or layered on top of whatever lighting already exists on the stage.

Pin Matrix   A pinned plugging system on "rock and roll" preset consoles that was laid out as a grid to electronically assign control channels to submasters, which in turn featured bump/flash buttons.

Pinspots   A nickname that many designers have given to ERS spotlights, which are based on a 3½-inch diameter lens. The name doesn't match the optical characteristics of these fixtures. Club owners also use pinspots, but these are small spotlights that produce an intense shaft of light through the smaller filaments of DC lamps.

Pitch   A screen property that relates to the size or spacing of the smallest elements of a display (i.e., the spacing between the clusters of LEDs that define a pixel for the screen). Pitch is important because it determines a screen's resolution and optimal viewing distance or range.

Pitting   A form of corrosion in landscape luminaires that causes the metal finish to become rough and pitted.

Pixel   The smallest degree of resolution in a digital image. If an image or projection is enlarged beyond this point, the squares representing this resolution simply get larger with no further development in details.

Pixelation   An effect in digital imaging where if an image is enlarged beyond a given point where the individual pixels become separated and form a distortion of the image.

Plane (Zone)   A distribution pattern associated with dance lighting based on movement patterns along pathways across the width of the stage (between each set of legs).

Plano Lens   A lens with essentially two flat sides.

Plano-Convex Lens   The most popular lens used in the lighting industry. It has one flat side, while the other is convex.

Plano-Convex Spotlight (P-C spotlight)   See Box-Spot

Plasterline   A reference line for measuring distances in the upstage/downstage directions that is based on an imaginary line across the width of the proscenium located between the furthest upstage edges of the proscenium wall.

Plate   See Dimmer Plate

Plenum   See Ceiling Cavity

Plot and Light   A method of film and video lighting where a lighting director actually selects and plots the lighting for a studio or shoot in the same way that theatrical designers design a light plot.

Plotter   A large-format printer used in printing large-scaled drawings like light plots.

Plotting Service   A company that owns a large-format plotter that prints CAD files or draftings for a fee.

Point Illuminance Method   An architectural lighting calculation that determines illuminance at a specific point through an examination of light as both a direct component and various indirect components from a given source(s).

Point Light Source   The principle by which luminaire and lamp manufacturers strive to create the smallest light source possible by concentrating the majority of the light at a focal point, which makes any associated lens or reflector all the more efficient.

Point of Purchase   A base for sales personnel. It is where sales are conducted and typically contains cash registers and counters for completing the paperwork and packaging of a transaction.

Point of View   See Image of Light, Lighting Scheme, or Lighting Concept

Port   A hanging position above an audience that provides the same function as a beam, with the exception that these are openings in the ceiling that only house four to six lighting instruments each.

Portable Generator   See Generator

Portrait Lamp   A fixture usually placed directly above or below a frame that uses a tubular incandescent lamp and shade on an adjustable arm.

Post Lights   A luminaire mounted on a post or pole (e.g., a streetlight, bollard, or lamp post).

Post-Occupancy Evaluation   A process that takes place after a client has taken occupancy of a space that checks client satisfaction, fixes or modifies any issues that may have developed, and helps the client understand how to maintain and operate an installation.

Power (P)   The rate of doing work. In the case of lighting, it is usually expressed in wattage, which relates to how much power it takes over time to produce a given amount of light.

Power Density   A determination of how much energy is consumed per unit area of a building (watts per square foot). Many municipalities limit a building's power density based on factors like the type of tasks required and its location.

Power Formula   Relates Power (P) or wattage to the voltage (E) and amperage (A). $P = I \times E$

Power Grid   The networked system of wiring that delivers power from a generating plant to a customer.

Practical   A working fixture on a set like a table lamp, chandelier, or wall sconce.

Preset control   An electronic dimming method in which duplicate sets of controllers (presets) are provided for each channel/dimmer. Operators shift between presets for different cues, alternating live presets with those used for upcoming cues.

Preview Mode   See Blind and Blind Mode

Prismatic Glass (Variegated Glass Filters)   A form of plastic or glass that contains a textured surface that refracts and diffuses any light that passes through it. These accessories are placed in the gate of a luminaire in much the same way as a gobo is used.

Primary Coil   One of several coils found in a transformer. This coil is associated with the source voltage and will induce a current in a secondary coil(s).

Primary Colors Basic elements of light (red, blue, and green) that are used in various combinations to produce every other color of light.

Primary Focus The area or subject with the strongest focus in a room or on a stage.

Primary Focal Point A point associated with a reflector or lens that relates to where light is focused to or from.

Primary Lighting See Ambient Lighting

Production Meeting A meeting between the designers, director, and department heads which is used to check progress between departments and to discover and resolve any issues that might develop between departments.

Production Number A large-scale song and dance piece that typically involves most, if not all, of the company of performers in a highly spectacle musical number. They are often found as opening and finale numbers for the different acts of a musical.

Product Unveiling A specific type of corporate production where a "show" is about introducing a new product for the very first time.

Profile Spotlight A variation of the ellipsoidal reflector spotlight (ERS) that is in popular use throughout Europe. European designers tend to call all ERS spotlights profile spots.

Programming (Programming Phase) 1. Placing the lighting commands (intensity levels, cues, moving light instructions) into a console. 2. First phase of architectural projects, in which fact finding is used to determine the client's needs.

Programmer (Moving Light Operator) The person responsible for the programming and operation of a console that controls moving lights. The title has evolved to include anyone who programs a lighting console (both conventionals and movers).

Projection Booth (Spotlight Booth) A room located near the back of an auditorium that houses projection and control equipment, followspots, and their crews.

Project Manager The individual on architectural projects who is assigned to a project and becomes the liaison between the designer and construction crews.

Projector A piece of equipment that is used to project an image to another location or surface/screen.

Projector Bay A cubby-hole set into the upstage wall of a stage that gives projectors an increased throw distance.

Proportional Patch Provides a method for channels or dimmers to be locked into a maximum intensity setting that is lower than 100%.

Prototype (Template) A master CADD drawing that contains all of the major elements of a space or facility. Prototypes eliminate redrawing features that are shared by many drawings (title blocks, facility outlines, reference lines, keys, etc.).

Punchlist A list of items that are damaged, forgotton, or incorrectly installed on an architectural or permanent installation. It ensures that a contractor is aware of and fixes problems.

Quantity of light See Quantity versus Quality

Quantity versus Quality A lighting philosophy where architectural designers now strive to create quality-driven rather than simply quantity-driven lighting designs (footcandle requirements). While intensity is still factored into lighting a particular situation, there are now other elements like color, angle, and glare that are also factored into the overall quality of the design.

Quartz Lamp See Tungsten-Halogen Lamp or TH-lamp

Queue A waiting area in theme parks that gives the appearance of a shortened line by arranging the line in a series of rows that turn back on one another while also leading to additional staging areas or chambers with more queues and waiting times.

Rack A metal cabinet used to house electronic components. Sound components and dimmers are the most common racks found in the entertainment industry. Racks may be portable or permanently installed in a facility.

Radial ERS The earliest version of the ellipsoidal reflector spotlight (ERS), which made use of lamps that burned in a base up configuration with their lamp housings being located on the top back of an instrument.

Rain Curtain A theatrical drape of highly reflective metallic material like mylar that is slit into strips approximately 1/4" wide. When treated with light they sparkle and shimmer. The most popular ones are silver and take on the color of any light that strikes them.

R-Lamp (Reflector Lamp) A lamp that contains a reflector and diffuse lens that allows the light to be concentrated in a pool that spreads gently away in a single direction. It is similar to a PAR Lamp.

Rate A control that allows for modifying the timing of a cue. Rate settings allow operators to speed up or slow down cueing during a performance.

Ray-tracing A special feature of visualization programs that calculates the effect of a vast number of light rays from each light source in a project. The calculations are quite specific and time consuming but result in an image that often approaches photorealism in detail.

Rear Projection A form of projection where the projector(s) are placed behind a translucent screen or projection surface.

Rear-Projection Screen (RP screen) A screen made from special materials that are translucent and allow an image to be projected from behind the screen while remaining visible on its surface.

Recessed Luminaires A classification of architectural luminaires based on a mounting position that is mounted within a wall or ceiling.

Recommended Practice A set of design guidelines that represent common techniques and practices in special areas of architectural lighting design. These are not codes and aren't subject to regulation but represent what most designers would consider appropriate practices for a given application.

Red Shift (Amber Drift) The effect of a light changing color as the intensity of a lamp is dimmed (becoming more red/amber).

Reducing Screen See Dimming Screen

Reflected Ceiling Plan An architectural drafting that indicates the layout of a ceiling with peaks, trays, domes, etc. Lighting designers use this to locate their luminaires and often simply add the lighting information directly to the plate, converting it into a form of light plot or lighting layout.

Reflected Radiation Component (RRC) A component used in calculating horizontal illuminance that expands illuminance calculations to account for various reflected elements. The calculation is essentially the same as the Lumen Method with the coefficient of utilization being substituted with this additional factor.

Reflection A method in which light waves or an image are redirected off of a surface.

Reflective Light Meter An exposure light meter that is used by standing near a subject and measuring the light that reflects off of it. This forms an accurate means of measuring exposure since it measures the amount of light actually leaving the surface of the subject.

Reflector An optical device that uses reflection to gather and redirect light.

Reflector Lamp See R-Lamp

Reflector Unit, Panel or Board, Shiny Board Frames or panels used in video and film production that are covered with reflective materials to reflect light into a scene. The source can be a luminaire that is hung nearby or a distant source like the sun.

Refraction A physical property in which light is bent while passing through materials of different densities.

Remote Device Management (RDM) A relatively new control protocol that should provide plug-and-play features to lighting consoles and equipment. Once plugged into a network, the console locates and determines the type and number of fixture attributes for a unit while also assigning control channels to each attribute.

Rendering An image of a project that is created by a designer. These are often done by a computer in lighting applications and illustrate how the lighting will appear on an imaginary setting. In reality, it only offers an approximation of the final image but may approach photorealism if taken to an extreme.

Rental House A company specializing in the rental and sale of theatrical equipment.

Re-patch To reassign/re-plug circuits during a performance or rehearsal.

Repertory Light Plot A light plot that supports several different productions. While many of the general systems are shared, specials, recoloring, and refocusing are often used to address specific needs of each of the individual productions.

Request for Information (RFI) A formal request for information or a conflict resolution sent by the general or sub contractor to a designer through the architect. The lighting designer formally responds to the RFI to either resolve the conflict, clarify the information, or answer any other questions that may have developed.

Residential Lighting Lighting the interiors and exteriors of homes and private residences.

Residuals A weekly fee paid to designers on a long-running show that is based on a percentage of the box office receipts.

Resistance (R) An electrical property that relates to a material or object creating a barrier to electrical flow.

Resistance Dimmer A specific form of dimmer in which electrical resistance is introduced to a circuit to regulate the intensity of the lights. It is an especially wasteful form of dimming and requires dimmers to be loaded to full capacity.

Resolution The degree of detail that is displayed in a projected or digital image.

Restore Cue A cue that is repeated from an earlier time in a production.

Retail Lighting Lighting associated with sales displays and retail stores.

Retrofit A variation of lamp that is a TH-lamp replacement for an earlier lamp design. They have a smaller bulb but maintain the same base and LCL of the lamp that they are replacing.

Revealing Form A function of lighting that relates to enhancing dimensionality or revealing the sculptural or 3-dimensional elements of a subject.

RGB (Red, Green, and Blue) A digital signal format used on screens, monitors, and projectors which is a composite signal that combines separate inputs of each of the primary colors for video or digital images.

Rider See Contract Rider

Rhythm A function of light that relates to lighting movement and transitions. As tensions mount and resolve, the lighting should underscore the dramatic action and may appear to be very subtle or dramatic to an audience.

Ride Vehicle The cars or motorized vehicles that carry guests in a theme ride or attraction.

Riding the Plot When an electrician or lighting assistant makes constant reference to the light plot and guides the progress of a focus through calling out the channels of the luminaires as they are needed.

Rim Lighting Light or a lighting systems that etches or rings(rims) a subject from the side and back, particularly the backlight system.

Rim Light A variation of backlight used in film and video lighting that is offset to the side of a subject and tends to have a higher elevation than kickers. It produces a wrapping effect that models or edges (rims) a subject and helps to separate them from the background.

Ring Top A piece of hardware consisting of a metal loop that is screwed to the top of a boom pipe and provides the connection for a tie-off rope.

RMS Voltage (VRMS) A measurement of the overall average voltage across legs of a multi-phase power system. It may also be called the Root Mean Square Voltage.

Road Case A special shipping case used for transporting sensitive lighting and sound gear that is made of durable materials and lined with specially fitted foams to protect the case's contents.

Road House A theater that typically presents touring productions.

Road-tap See Company Switch

Roadway Lighting Lighting that provides illumination to highways and streets.

Rods 1. The pencil-sized electrodes that are used in arc light sources like followspots. They are made out of carbon and have a copper sheathing over them. 2. Optical sensors in the eye that respond to a wide range of light sensitivities and are responsible for our scotopic vision.

Rolling Dimmer Rack A portable dimmer rack that is fashioned like a road case with wheels and is used for touring.

Room Cavity Ratio (RCR) A volume associated with the Lumen Method calculation that relates the volume (height and area) of an entire room to the portion of the room with which we are concerned regarding illumination levels. It is also used as one of the variables that determine the efficiency of a luminaire and design solution.

Rooster Mount A method of mounting a luminaire in which the unit is spun up so that it is mounted directly above the pipe.

Root Mean Square Voltage See RMS Voltage (VRMS).

Ropelight A decorative effect that places miniature lamps (often of several different circuits or colors) in a flexible plastic tube. The tube is then used to outline structures.

Rotary Dimmer A dimmer (usually an autotransformer) that is often self-contained and operated from a knob or handle attached to a rotary shaft that extends through the center of the dimmer.

Roundels Circular glass filters that are installed in many striplight fixtures.

Rover A portable boom that is relatively short (usually less than 4 feet), contains very few luminaires (often only one or two), and is equipped with dollies so that it can be easily moved around as needed.

Run A circuit or cable that leads from one location to another. It can also be related to the cable distance that lies between two electrical devices.

Run the Barrel A focus command in which the lens barrel of a lighting instrument is set in the all the way forward position which is usually associated with producing the softest beam edges.

Run-through A type of rehearsal in which a segment of a play, musical, etc. is run or rehearsed without interruption. This may be as small as a few pages or a scene to as much as the entire play.

Rushes See Dailies

Safety Cable A segment of 1/8" aircraft cable (about 2' long) equipped with a loop and special snap fitting that allows lighting instruments to be further attached to a hanging position and prevents a unit from falling due to failure of a yoke or C-clamp.

Safety Lighting Landscape or street lighting that is used primarily for visibility. It directs people to different parts of a property while also helping them to avoid hazards and navigate through a space safely.

Saturation See Chroma

Saturation Rig A special type of lighting rig or grid used in film and video studios in which the grid is pre-hung and cabled heavily with a variety of luminaires and accessories. The LD simply chooses the gear from what they see is available, patches and focuses the units, and makes them work for the particular setup. They are popular in studios that are rented on a daily basis (e.g., taping commercials).

Save 1. To record a show and all of its cue information into the console or backup system. 2. To turn off a unit that is no longer needed (when the focus of the unit is complete or it is no longer desired in a cue).

Scanner (Moving Mirror) 1. A type of automated luminaire in which a moving mirror is placed at the front of the unit to direct the light to different locations. 2. A form of laser projection in which a laser beam is rapidly moved along a path. We cannot distinguish this movement, and through perception, connect the points and see the image as a series of lines that lie along the path of the laser. We use scanning to trace or draw basic images.

Scene Machine An effects projector by GAM that combines superior optics and a more intense light source with a series of modular motion effects that can be used to produce a desired image and motion.

Scenic Breakdown A listing of the specific scenes, locations, and time frames that occur in a script or performance event.

Scenic Floorplan A variation of floorplan that in addition to providing information about a facility also provides specific information about the scenic design for a production.

Scenic Specials A lighting instrument that is focused specifically to a scenic element of a production (e.g. a light focused to a sculpture or picture frame, a wall decoration, a tree, or scenic surface).

Schedules See Design Paperwork

Schematic Development The second phase of architectural design development, in which the initial concepts are refined and developed into the foundations that will set the tone for the rest of the project. It sets the major parameters and starts to lock the team into some basic ideas.

Sconce A decorative luminaire that is mounted to a wall surface.

Scoop See Ellipsoidal Reflector Floodlight or ERF

Score The sheet music or orchestration of an opera, musical, or other music related event.

Scotopic Vision That portion of vision attributed to the rods photoreceptors that are sensitive to light across a wide range of wavelengths and luminous levels. It is responsible for our sight at levels of low illumination and our peripheral vision.

SCR (Silicon Controlled Rectifier) An electronic component used in electronic dimming that is turned on and off (fired) through a low-voltage signal current to selectively sample or control the high-voltage output of a dimmer.

Screen A specially treated surface that is used as a projection surface. Screens come in a variety of sizes, colors, and shapes and perform with varied degrees of success. They may be used for both front or rear projection.

Scrim 1. A special type of scenic fabric with a loose weave that when treated with front light appears opaque but becomes transparent when lit from behind. 2. In film and video lighting scrims are metal meshes that are placed in front of light sources to drop the intensity of a lamp—different densities drop the intensity by various increments. Scrims lower the intensity while having no effect on color temperature, which cannot be achieved in dimming (red shift).

Scrim-Through A combined lighting/scenic effect in which a scrim that is front lighted and appears opaque is made transparent to reveal a scene behind it through lighting the objects behind the scrim. The reverse process is known as a scrim-back.

Script Analysis A careful study of a script. It gives the first indication of themes, plot, characters, settings, mood, style and specific lighting requirements of a play.

Scrollers (Automated Color Changers) An automated color changer that uses individual filters taped together to form a scroll. The scroll is rolled back and forth to specific positions that correspond to the different colors.

Sculpting/Modeling Systems A lighting system or collection of luminaires characterized by washes of back and side light that enhance depth perception.

Seasonal Affective Disorder (SAD) A form of seasonal depression which is due to the individual not being exposed to enough sunlight.

Secondary Coil A coil(s) in a transformer that has the induced voltage produced in it. This voltage is proportional to that of the primary coil and is dependent on the relative number of turnings in each coil.

Secondary Colors A combination of equal mixtures of any two primary colors. In light, these include: magenta, cyan, and amber.

Secondary Focus An area or object that has focus brought to it but which does not have the primary focus.

Secondary Lighting See Accent Lighting

Secondary Panels (Panel Boards) Circuit boxes fed through feeder cables from a building's primary distribution center that bring power to all of the branch circuits in a given area of a building.

Secondary Service Conductors Heavy duty cables that carry the main power supply into a building and to the main switchboard.

Second Team A group of stand-ins in television and video shoots that are used for lighting and camera rehearsals to replicate the blocking while the real actors (first team) are getting into costume and makeup.

Section (Sectional View) A drafting representing a room or performance venue from a side view. The section is typically drawn as if you were to cut through a facility along the centerline of the stage and is used to determine beam coverage, lighting angles, approximate throw distances, and masking sightlines.

Security Lighting Lighting systems that make a property more visible and less shadowed to discourage prowlers and other criminal activities.

Selective Visibility Revealing to an audience only what they need to see in order to gain an understanding of an event.

Semi-Direct Luminaire An IESNA classification of luminaire based on a distribution pattern in which a significant amount of light is directed upward (10–40%) but the majority is still directed downward (60–90%).

Semi-Indirect Luminaire An IESNA classification of luminaire based on a distribution pattern in which a significant amount of light is directed downward (10–40%) but the majority is directed upward (60–90%).

Semi-Recessed Luminaire A classification of architectural luminaires based on a mounting position being partially contained within a wall or ceiling.

Series Circuit A circuit in which the leads of each device are sequentially connected together in a daisy chain with the first and last devices being connected to the power supply.

Service The actual power configuration or number and capacity of wires brought into a building from a power utility.

Service Entrance The point where the electrical service enters a building.

Set Levels See Cue-In

Set List (Play List) A listing of the order of the songs that will be performed for music related performances like concerts.

Set Mount A lighting instrument or practical that is mounted directly to the scenery.

Setup (Shot) An element of television and film production based on the filming of a scene and individual camera placement. Each camera angle along with its adjustments for lighting and other production elements forms an individual shot.

Set Wireman The individual on a film or video crew who is in charge of wiring and maintaining all of the practicals that are mounted on a set.

Shadow Box (Moon Box) 1. A lighting effect in which lamps are enclosed in a light-tight box having a designed pattern or image cut out of its front panel. Gel is used to color the cutout, while scrim may be put across its front to mask the design when not in use. Moon boxes and simulated neon signs are often created in this manner. 2. A small window display (often as small as a foot square) that is placed at eye level.

Shadowing A method of casting shadows in landscape lighting in which a luminaire is placed in front of the plants and trees where it will not only light the subject but also cast its shadow onto the background as an element of the design.

Shadows Shadows are represented by either the area of an object that is not lit or the pattern of darkness that is cast by an illuminated object (cast shadow).

Shakedown The initial period of a tour (often a week or so) during which the production is tested out and tweaked. This can relate to design items (the cues, staging, and lighting itself), the load-in and strike process, arrival order and stacking of trucks, size of crews (touring and local), etc.

Shielding A method of constructing roadway luminaires so that their light is forced downward and not to the sides or upward. It protects drivers from glare.

Shins (Shin Buster/Shin Kicker) A luminaire that creates low-angled sidelight that is mounted at floor level at the base of a boom.

Shiny Board See Reflector Unit or Reflector Panel/Board

Shoe A part of a mechanical dimmer that contains an electrical contact that is moved across the dimmer to sample voltage at different points over a dimmer's coils.

Shoebox Design An ellipsoidal reflector spotlight (ERS) design in which the housing or body is based on a rectangular (shoebox) shape rather than the traditional cylinder of most ERS designs.

Shop Order An inventory of all the materials and equipment that will be required to complete a lighting design.

Short-arc Lamp Modern arc sources commonly used in followspots, projectors, and other high-intensity units like moving lights. The lamp makes use of a heavy glass bulb with electrodes permanently built into the lamp. On operation, an arc forms between the electrodes with no need for trimming or adjustment.

Short Circuit Creating an accidental flow of electricity. When two hots come into direct contact with one another, the neutral, or ground, causing a short circuit, this commonly results in shocks, sparks, and a possible fire.

Short-Throw Followspots Followspots designed with a range of beamspreads that are appropriate for a small venue. These throw distances are optimally between 25 to 50 feet.

Shot See Setup

Showcase Lamp A special version of incandescent tube lamp that is long and thin and has been designed specifically for shelf lighting. It is also popular in cabinet lighting and frequently used in both retail and museum applications.

Show Control A manner of linking several different control systems together so that all events/cues can be triggered by a single console. Lights, pyro, and other effects are often triggered by the sound track of a performance.

Showroom Special theatres often associated with cruise lines and casino or nightclubs that have well-equipped fly houses, lighting equipment, and stages but where the audience areas are more like ballrooms. The houses often include tables and bars in addition to traditional theatrical seating. The ceilings are usually relatively low which can result in overall flat lighting from the front of house. Vegas singer and comedy acts frequently perform in these facilities.

Shutters The most important controls in an ellipsoidal reflector spotlight (ERS). They

are four metal plates that are inserted into the field of light to flatten or shape a spotlight's beam.

Shutter Speed A camera setting that indicates how long film is exposed to light.

Sidearm An iron or hardware item that provides a method of mounting lighting fixtures to the side of a batten or boom while keeping the pan and tilt adjustments in their standard orientations.

Sidelight A lighting distribution angle that comes from the side and helps to model and give three-dimensional form to a subject.

Silhouette Lighting Lighting the background behind an object rather than the object itself.

Silicon Controlled Rectifier See SCR

Silks See Butterflies.

Sine Wave Dimmers A recent innovation in dimming technology that makes use of IGBT dimming to produce a more effective, less noisy (electronically) dimmer by using a much higher sampling rate of the AC current than traditional SCR dimmers.

Single-Source Lighting (Single-Source System) A form of general illumination in which either an actual single light source is used to illuminate the stage or a series of individual instruments are used in such a way as to give the illusion that light is coming from a single source.

Site Plan A drafting that contains all the buildings, walkways, and landscape features of a property. A landscape lighting designer uses this to plot their design.

Site Survey A visit to the location where a lighting installation or design will actually take place. It is an opportunity to observe the facility, take measurements, and to seek out any unique concerns that may not be readily observed in the plans.

Skydrop Essentially the same scenic background as a cyc, with the exception that it is colored a light tint of blue.

Skylight 1. An important component of daylighting. It relates to the more consistent overall diffuse glow of the sky as a lighting element (a result of scattering and general diffusion in the atmosphere). 2. A window-like architectural feature that is mounted in a roof or ceiling and allows daylight to enter a building.

Slide A source of original artwork for a projection. In most cases slides are made of translucent or transparent materials that allow light to pass through them.

Slide Patch A special type of patch panel where all of the circuits are arranged in rows along one axis (horizontal or vertical) while all of the dimmers are arranged along the opposing axis. A sliding contact is assigned to each of the circuits or dimmers along one of these axes and is moved along the axis and snapped into position over the corresponding circuit or dimmer to which the assignment is going to be made.

Slot See Cove

Slow Blow A fuse or circuit breaker failing due to excessive heat in a circuit. The breaker often appears to trip for no reason. Slow blows are most often due to conditions like excessive resistance being created in a circuit by extra-long or under-sized jumpers, loose connections, or a slight overload of a circuit.

Smart Preset Boards The first memory boards. They were special variations of a preset board that had features that could store cues in a temporary memory.

SMPTE (Society of Motion Picture and Television Engineers) A professional organization associated with technicians of the film and television industries. The organization set the standard for synchronizing various production elements (sound, lights, pyro, machinery, etc.) through its SMPTE show control.

Snell's Law See Law of Refraction

Snoot (Top Hat) An accessory that blocks spill by preventing light from opening up or spreading too quickly once leaving a luminaire. It is also used to control glare from backlights. Video and film professionals prefer to call it a snoot, while theatrical professionals use "top hat."

Socopex (Socapex) Cables A popular form of multi-cables used in entertainment applications. These multi-cables have special electrical fittings on each end for adapters (break-ins and break-outs) to be connected to their ends, which separates the cable into individual male and female connectors for each circuit.

Soft Light A type of light associated with the film and video industry characterized by diffuse illumination that does not display any prominent shadows. It is often associated with fill light and is used to soften any shadows created by a key light.

Soft-Lights A classification of luminaires in the film and video industry that produce a nice shadowless light over a large area. The fixtures lack a lens system and are often outfitted with diffusion media to ensure a soft, shadowless source of illumination.

Soft Patch Assigning dimmers and other control attributes to specific channels or controllers on a lighting console. Since the assignments are done electronically, the actual

load of the dimmers does not factor into the assignments.

Softscape The growing elements or plants, foliage, and trees of a landscape design.

Solid Core Conductor A type of wire in which the conductor is a single piece of solid copper or metal.

Sound Stage A large, warehouse-like facility that is used for large scale film and video productions. It is a larger version of a studio and contains lots of open space and a flexible lighting system that is easily modified to the many scenes and productions that may share the floor at any given time.

Sound Wing A stack of speaker cabinets stacked on either side of a concert stage. The sound wings supply the general PA or sound for the audience.

Space Light See Chicken Coop

Space Manipulation Using architectural lighting to alter an occupant's perception of a space.

Spacing Criteria A set of conditions such as illuminance levels and mounting heights that are used to determine how far apart architectural luminaires may be spaced from one another.

Sparkle See Glitter

Special A luminaire that is used for a specific need or function.

Specialty Areas A variation in area lighting that creates additional lighting areas that mimic the actual lighting areas but are based on special needs like a variation in height or hanging restrictions. They are lit to give the appearance of being part of the same lighting environment.

Specialty Lighting (Themed Lighting) Lighting that is associated with themed design. It is a combination of traditional and entertainment based lighting design. Now more often called specialty lighting rather than themed lighting.

Special Visibility Lighting in which luminaires or lighting are assigned to a particular need of visibility that cannot be achieved by the general illumination or area lighting.

Specify A manner of identifying and providing documentation (on paper) of the exact performance and installation requirements of an architectural or other lighting installation or design.

Specular Reflection A type of reflection created from materials that have a shiny or mirrored surface that follows the Law of Reflection quite specifically.

Spherical Reflector A reflector based on the shape of a sphere that reflects light back through the focal point of the reflector.

Spidering See Home Runs

Spike (Surge) A very sudden increase in voltage that can create a safety hazard or may damage equipment. A surge will typically last for less than a second.

Spill Stray or unwanted light. Spill is due to scattered reflections or the continuation of light beyond a target onto objects that a designer does not want to light.

Spill Rings A video and film lighting accessory that functions the same way as an egg crate, with the exception that they are used on circular-faced luminaires.

Spin the Bottle To rotate a PAR lamp to orient the axis of the lamp's filament.

Splitfader A variation of crossfader that includes a second fader (wired in opposition to the first) to allow a board to fade between different presets with different up and down rates and proportions.

Spot Focus The position in a Fresnel spotlight where the lamp or reflector assembly is moved toward the back of the unit that causes the light to converge over a central point.

Spotlight A luminaire that has well-defined edges and a fairly narrow distribution pattern, which is often used for creating accents. As a rule, spotlights contain lenses.

Spotlight Booth See Projection Booth

Spotlighting A form of lighting where specific objects or performers are pointed up or given focus through creating an accent on them. This may be achieved by adding intensity, sharpness, different colors, or other contrasting features to the light.

Spot Luminaire An automated fixture that is used as a spotlight and has beam edges that can be focused to a sharp edge. These luminaires often contain effect devices, several manners of producing color, and one or two gobo wheels that can hold up to five or more gobos, as well as moving attributes like pan and tilt.

Spot Meter A reflective light meter that measures light through a very narrow portion of a camera's field. Spot meters are good for measuring contrast ratios between areas of high and low illumination within a camera frame.

Spot Relamping A manner of relamping that requires maintenance workers to replace lamps as burnouts occur.

Spotting Light (Spotting Lamp) A low-wattage lamp (usually red) that is placed at the rear of an auditorium to aid dancers in keeping their orientation (facing front) while making pivoting movements.

Spread Reflection A type of reflection in which most light from a source is reflected off a surface as predicted by the Law of

Reflection, but due to an uneven surface this is not as specific or directional as a specular reflection.

Spud A pin-like fitting that slips into a receiving piece of hardware and allows a film or video luminaire to be quickly mounted to a stand or other support device.

Stack See Pack

Stage Mode A console mode that displays the channels and their associated intensity levels that are actually live and on stage.

Staging the Story A function of lighting where we consider the techniques of producing a production by finding theatrical mechanisms for presenting the story or event to an audience.

Stair Light A special architectural luminaire that is designed to be mounted or recessed directly into the structure of stairs and directs light downward onto the treads.

Starting Address The first channel of any DMX-controlled device. It represents the first attribute and is the one that a fixture's addressing switches will be set to.

Step Lens A less popular version of the plano-convex lens that removes elements of the plano surface, leaving the convex surface intact. This lens produces a series of concentric rings in the beam of many spotlights and has been discarded as an effective lens in the lighting industry.

Step-down Transformer A transformer that is used to lower an AC voltage. The primary coil will be larger or contain more windings than the secondary coil.

Step-up Transformer A transformer that is used to raise an AC voltage. The secondary coil will be larger or contain more windings than the primary coil.

Stepper Motors Small motors used in the movement of automated lighting attributes that create motion by rotating through a series of steps that relate to an attribute's position. This motion can appear jerky, especially at slow speeds.

Stepping Effect The effect by which a laser emits energy, in which the corresponding wavelengths of each waveform are in sync with all other waveforms, with the effect producing a higher amplitude and energy level.

Stiffener An accessory that is mounted to a batten and taped to its associated lift cables to prevent a pipe from spinning. It is very similar to a sidearm, which may be used in its place.

Storyboards 1. Simple drawings that give an indication of each camera shot for film or video production along with the visual composition of each shot. 2. In theatrical applications, the storyboard is used as an informational sketch that indicates the lighting composition and qualities for a given moment.

Straight Run See Daisy Chain

Stranded Conductor A type of wire in which a number of individual strands of copper or other conductive wire are woven together to form a larger conductor.

Street Lighting A variation of roadway lighting that not only lights the street but also the sidewalks and surrounding buildings, adding security and safety to an area.

Strike 1. Take down and remove all of the equipment used in a production. 2. Turning on or "striking" an arc light source.

Striplight A luminaire that uses multiple lamps arranged in a side-by-side fashion that form a "strip" of light. A typical unit contains three or four circuits in which every third or fourth lamp is wired and colored separately as a common circuit.

Strobe Light (Strobe) A special xenon lamp that can be set for especially rapid on-off sequences and can produce stop-action motion.

Structure See Dramatic Form

Studio A production facility for film and video production that is similar to a black box theatre and contains a large open area and lighting grid.

Style A function of lighting that relates to creating visual qualities that produce a characteristic overall quality for a production. Degree of realism may be used as a means of comparing styles. Style is specifically determined through the collaboration and discussions of the production team.

Stylization See Abstraction

Subject The object or individual that is being lit.

Submaster A dimming control that provides for an assignment of several individual dimmers or control channels that function together as a unit.

Subtractive Color Mixing A method of color mixing that occurs when various wavelengths of light are removed. All materials selectively absorb (or reflect) different wavelengths, which defines an object's natural color.

Subtransmission Lines Relatively high-voltage lines from substations that first reduce the voltage from transmission lines which in turn run to other substations that reduce the voltage even further so that it is safer to run into neighborhoods.

Sun-gun A battery operated hand-held lamp that is used on location shoots for film and video. It is similar to a spotting lamp.

Surface-Mounted Luminaires A classification of architectural luminaires based on a mounting position that is mounted directly to a wall or ceiling.

Surge See Spike

Suspended Luminaires A classification of architectural luminaires based on a mounting position below a ceiling, from a pendant or other device.

Suspension Grid (Tension Grid) A lighting grid found in many black box theatres that consists of a mesh of woven aircraft cable that permits electricians to walk directly above the theatre on the grid.

Swatch Book A booklet that provides a sample of the actual color filter, transmission charts, and other information for each filter in a manufacturer's specific series or product line of filters or gels. Samples of color correction, diffusion, and reflective materials are also frequently contained in swatch books.

Switch A device used to control the flow of power in a circuit. Open switches prevent the flow of electricity, while closed switches allow the current to flow.

Swivel Socket An accessory inserted into a standard socket that permits a lamp to be swiveled and focused in many directions.

Symbol Libraries A collection of CADD symbols or blocks that are created or purchased by the designer and stored for future use.

System (Lighting System) The combined use of multiple luminaires and washes that have similar if not identical functions to provide a unified appearance throughout an entire lit environment.

Tabbing-in Moving the torms of a larger stage in towards centerline. The practice is common for touring productions, which can then always play within a standard-sized proscenium opening.

Tag A label or identifier placed on a lighting layout along with a luminaire symbol that provides a reference to additional information relating to the fixture with which the tag is associated. This information might include: luminaire model number and manufacturer, finish, control information, lamp specification, etc.

Tail Down The practice of hanging a pipe below an existing batten or grid so that the luminaires can be hung from a lower trim height.

Take A shooting segment in film and video production. It involves a given setup, set of actions, and camera shot.

Talent The subject or performer that is to be lit in a video or film setting.

Tap A device that breaks either one or two phases of service off of a 3-phase service.

Task A visual requirement or job that must be performed successfully within a given set of lighting conditions in architectural applications.

Task Light A somewhat portable light that can be moved into position to provide specific illumination to a limited area for completing a given task.

Task Lighting Specification calculations and recommendations that are used to calculate minimum illumination levels for architectural applications representing a given visual task (function) or application requirement.

Technical Rehearsal See Dry Tech Rehearsal

Tech with Actors (Wet Tech) A rehearsal that focuses on the technical elements of a production but also includes the performers so that the performers and cues can be integrated with one another.

Template 1. A sheet of rigid plastic that is stamped with a variety of symbols that provide scaled silhouettes of lighting instruments and other architectural details that are traced onto a drafting or light plot. 2. A master CAD file that is used as a base drawing for more specific draftings like floorplans or light plots (also known as a prototype). 3. See gobo or pattern.

Tension Grid See Suspension Grid

Tentative Hookup A preliminary hookup that allows a lighting designer to work out the dimmer or channel assignments of a lighting design.

Tenting Placing a surround of diffusion material most of the way around a subject or setup to produce an evenly diffused lighting environment around the subject.

Terminator A hardware device or accessory that is plugged into the last unit of a DMX control line or run that helps prevent erroneous data from confusing the equipment along the data run.

Tertiary Colors See Intermediate Colors

Theatrical Lighting In themed attractions, the part of the lighting installation that is supplied by theatrical luminaires, control, and related lighting equipment.

Themed Design A form of design in which an environment is created along a specific theme and some form of entertainment is also achieved. A visitor or viewer is immersed in an interactive environment that has some form of story associated with it. Popular themed projects include: restaurants, stores, and theme parks.

Themed Lighting (Specialty Lighting) Lighting that is associated with themed design. It is a combination of traditional and entertainment based lighting design. Now more often called specialty lighting.

Theme An area of analysis where the playwright and director try to convey a message to an audience. Themes often relate to the social message(s) or meanings of a play.

Thinking Green A philosophy of designing buildings and lighting that are efficient and conserve natural resources while limiting byproducts that harm the environment.

Three-fer An adapter with three female plugs wired to a single male connector that allows lighting instruments to be combined together onto a common circuit.

Three-phase Power A form of power distribution in which three separate legs or hot wires are provided to a facility or piece of equipment.

Three-Point Lighting (Three-Point System) A common method of illumination for video and film that involves three light sources that create a variety of contrast ratios around a subject, which in turn emphasizes the modeling or sculpted qualities of a subject. It's also a common formula approach to lighting thrust and arena productions.

Three-way Switch A special type of switch that allows a circuit to be controlled through using one of several switches that are placed in different locations.

Three-wire System An electrical service that provides two hot wires (legs) and a common neutral.

Threshold Exposure The lowest exposure or light level setting at which a camera or film can record an image.

Throw Distance The line-of-sight distance measured from the luminaire to a target.

Tight Specifications Writing design specifications that are so specific that only the equipment desired by the designer can fulfill the requirements of a project.

Tilt An adjustment of a luminaire's beam in an upward or downward direction.

Timecode A series of signals that are placed at specific points in a soundtrack to automatically trigger light cues or other effects or events at a specific time. In effect, the timecode simply tells the console to execute a given cue number much like an operator would tell a console to execute a cue by hitting the "go" button.

Timer A switching device that makes use of an internal clock that turns electrical devices on and off at pre-determined times. An *astronomical clock* or timer is often used in architectural applications and is based on a 24-hour clock, which automatically adjusts for seasonal fluctuations and other factors like daylight savings time.

Tint A color that is combined with either white light or a mixture of other wavelengths that produce a softer, less saturated version of the original hue.

Title Block A segment of a drafting plate that provides essential information regarding the drafting. Information often found in the title block includes: production or project title, the producing organization or firm, theatre or building name, identification of the designer, scale, and date of the drafting.

Titles A line-by-line translation of an opera text that is projected onto a screen located either directly above or below the proscenium opening of a stage.

Toning Accents A wash of luminaires or lighting system that modifyies or tones the color of a space or object over a broad area.

Top Hat See Snoot

Topper A special form of flag used in the film and video industry that is used specifically to block the upper portion of a luminaire's beam.

Torm A name given to the first vertical sidelighting position that is just upstage of the curtain line on a proscenium stage. Some designers name torms in the same manner as booms.

Tracking A safeguard of making a hard copy of all the channel levels associated with each cue of a production.

Tracking Mode A console mode where changes made in one cue are copied or "tracked" through future cues. A lighting console that provides for tracking is often called a tracking console.

Track Luminaires A classification of architectural luminaires based on a mounting position being an electric path/rail or raceway.

Track Sheets A record of the individual channel levels for every cue contained in a production. Each cue's count information is also fully documented along with any effects or other information related to the control of the show.

Transfer Circuits/Transfer Panels Permanent circuits that are run to a location where they can be reassigned. Transfer circuits are common in road houses where the FOH circuits terminate at an interface where they can be assigned to either the house lighting system or a touring company's dimmers.

Transformer An electrical device that uses coils and magnetism to modify voltages. They can either *step-up* or *step-down* the voltage depending on the relative number of turnings in the primary and secondary coils.

Transformer Schedule A schedule used in landscape lighting that is similar to a conventional dimmer schedule. This schedule organizes the equipment by transformer assignments and their associated circuits/loads.

Transitions Relates to the process and visual changes that occur while advancing from one cue to another.

Transition Zone (Transition Area) An area or zone created in museum and gallery lighting where additional exhibits and transitional lighting are designed with the primary purpose of providing an area and time for a viewer's eyes to adjust to the lighting levels between adjoining areas.

Translucence A property that allows light to pass through a material and will allow a viewer to observe light and shadows but at the same time obscures the ability to see directly through the material.

Transmission Relates to the lighting wavelengths that pass through a gel, diffuser, or other material. Transmission relates to the percentage of radiant energy that continues beyond the filter and can be expressed as a total output across all wavelengths or as an output within specific wavelengths. *Transmission rate* relates to the percentage of light that actually passes through a material like a gel. More saturated gels have lower transmission rates.

Transmission Lines The heavy-duty power lines that are used to transfer power over long distances.

Transmission Rate See Transmission

Transmission Substation A network of heavy metal cables, insulators, mast-like structures, and transformers that are used to either boost or lower the voltage of electricity as it is transported from a power plant to a customer. Those near a power plant that boost the voltage are called transmission substations, while those in neighborhoods that lower the voltage are called distribution substations.

Traveler A drapery that parts at the center and opens and closes across the stage.

Trees See Booms

Triac An electronic component in electronic dimmers that functions in essentially the same way as SCRs.

Trim 1. The height of a hanging or mounting position, like a batten, measured from the stage floor to its working height. 2. The range settings of a dimmer from the point where the load goes out (*low trim*) to the point at which the load comes to full intensity (*high trim*).

Trimming 1. Adjusting the movements and relative positions of the rods in a carbon arc unit for optimal performance. 2. An adjustment of a dimmer's voltage so that full movement of the dimmer corresponds to both a smooth/even and complete range of intensities.

Triple-hang A manner of providing a third alternative in color or focus for a general lighting system or area.

Trombone A zoom/focus assembly found on followspots that allows the beam angle and focus range of the spotlight to be easily modified.

Troffer A popular architectural luminaire based on the use of fluorescent tubes and housings that fit as flat panels within standard drop-ceiling grids.

Trunions Hardware that is used to mount striplights as floor units (one per side).

Truss A framework of reinforced metal tubing that becomes the support mechanism for lighting, sound, and other theatrical elements. These modular structures are popular in the touring industry because they are simply bolted together and often have all the lighting equipment already pre-hung.

Tungsten-Halogen Lamp (TH-lamp or Quartz Lamp) A special version of incandescent lamp that uses a mixture of halogen gas and the tungsten-halogen process to create a more efficient and longer lasting light source.

Tungsten-Halogen Process The halogen in a TH-lamp results in tungsten particles being deposited on the hottest portion (filament) of the lamp rather than the cooler bulb, creating a recycling effect that increases lamp life while also preventing the cloudy buildup on the bulb that affects the performance of traditional lamps.

Tweak A process of making refinements in the lighting cues and design throughout the rehearsal process.

Two-fer An adapter with two female plugs wired to a single male connector that allows lighting instruments or cables to be combined together.

Two-Way Barndoor An accessory that is placed in the front of a luminaire (frequently Fresnels) which has two moveable panels that can be adjusted into the beam of light for controlling spill or glare.

Two-wire System An electrical service that provides a single hot wire and neutral.

Unified Production A production in which all of the design and performance elements reinforce one another to form a cohesive whole in which nothing appears to be out of sync or place with the other elements.

Unistrut A channel of steel that is essentially U-shaped with flanged edges used to hang stage equipment like luminaires with bolts or other specialized hardware. PAR-bars are often fashioned from unistrut.

United Scenic Artists (USA) The union that represents lighting, scenic, sound, and costume designers, along with scenic artists and most recently, projection designers. It is now affiliated with IATSE.

United States Institute for Theatre Technology (USITT) An organization that represents designers and technicians across all disciplines of stagecraft throughout the entertainment profession.

Universe A unit of control based on a single control cable and its associated 512 individual channels of control.

Uplighting An unnatural angle where objects are lit from below. It is a dramatic angle and is often used for drawing focus or creating a special effect.

Valence Lighting Lighting that is used to light vertical displays and walls in which the luminaires (often using fluorescent tubes) are hidden behind a linear panel while the light is distributed upward and downward.

Value A component of color used to describe a color's overall lightness or darkness based on a gray-scale.

Value Engineering Relates to using lower-quality equipment and installation practices than originally specified in order to increase a contractor's profit margin or to lower the overall costs of the installation for the client.

Variegated Glass Filters (Prismatic Glass) A form of plastic or glass with a textured surface that refracts and diffuses any light that passes through it. These accessories are placed in the gate of a luminaire in much the same way as a gobo is used.

Vectorscope An instrument that breaks a video signal down into its composite colors or wavelengths and plots the individual color signals in a radial format on an electronic screen. White is found at the center of the circle, while each of the primary and secondary colors are located at various points around the radius. The further from the center that a signal is plotted, the more saturated the color.

Verdigris (Verdi Green) An anodized finish that is used to retard the corrosion of metal landscape luminaires. It resembles a black and green marbleized effect.

Video Assist System An in-lens video camera used to capture a film camera's framing and to provide immediate feedback for what has been filmed.

Video Controller (VC) or Video Engineer   A control system (and person) that controls the video output for a production. The VC controls all elements of the image on the master monitor, which becomes the final signal that is broadcast or recorded.

Video Wall   A composite wall of tiled LCD panels or video monitors that together produce a large-scaled screen or video display. Each tiled panel may display either an independent image or a small portion of a larger image.

Virtual Design   Any design that is created by computer simulation.

Virtual Lighting   Lighting that is created for a virtual environment within a computer.

Visibility   The principle of using light to reveal or illuminate objects. It's the primary function of lighting.

Visible Spectrum   That portion of the electromagnetic spectrum to which the human eye is sensitive and where individual wavelengths of light are visible. It is found approximately in the range of 400 (violet) to 700 (red) nanometers.

Vista Lighting   A form of landscape lighting that provides supplemental lighting of an area that has a panoramic view of a distant landscape.

Visual Acuity   Being able to manipulate the visual stimulus and environment so that a visual task may be completed. It is a function of factors like the size of the subject, distance between subject and viewer, surface reflectivity, amount of illumination, and the sensitivity of the sensors.

Visual Comfort Probability (VCP)   A lighting calculation based on the angle between an observer and a light source and survey data that enables a designer to determine the degree of offensiveness of glare and other negative impacts that a luminaire and mounting position can have on an occupant.

Visual Fatigue   A process by which a viewer's eyes grow tired due to certain optical sensors being over stimulated by an unchanging visual environment.

Visual Task   A visual skill or job that requires an appropriate level of visibility in order to perform the job successfully.

Visualization   The use of a computer and specialized software to pre-program and simulate a production or architectural design. It produces images that approximate what the final design might look like under the actual lights.

Voltage (E)   A measurement of the electrical potential difference that exists between two points and is measured through a unit

known as the volt. We may also refer to voltage as electromotive force (EMF).

Voltage Drop   A measured drop in voltage that occurs as electricity is conducted through greater distances as the resistance in a circuit gets larger.

Vomitory (Vom)   An aisle found in thrust and arena theatres that is typically placed on the corners of adjoining audience sections.

Walkthrough   1. A film or video first rehearsal of a setup where the actors arrive for a blocking rehearsal and the director establishes their movement patterns. In this context, designers may also call this a *dry run*. 2. A tool in some visualization programs that permits a viewer to manipulate their view to complete a simulated exploration of a virtual space.

Wall Pack   A classification of wall-mounted luminaires in which a grazing light is cast away from the fixture along the wall while a decorative shade shields the viewer from the light source.

Wall Pocket   A theatrical distribution box containing three to six circuits that is located along the perimeter walls of a stage.

Wall Reflected Radiation Component (WRRC)   A component used as a factor in calculating vertical or wall illuminance that expands the illuminance calculations to account for various reflected elements. The calculation is essentially the same as the Lumen Method, with the coefficient of utilization being substituted with this additional factor that represents vertical illuminations.

Wall Sconce   A decorative luminaire that is mounted to the surface of a wall.

Wall-Washer   An architectural luminaire that is typically mounted as a surface or recessed ceiling mount whose light grazes or washes a vertical surface like a wall.

Warm Colors   Light that has an abundance of red, yellow, and orange wavelengths. They produce responses of tension or action and appear to advance towards us.

Warming Current   A small current used to pre-heat lamp filaments so that a sudden surge like bringing a dimmer to full won't over stress a lamp.

Wash   Using several luminaires to cover a significant portion of scenery, stage, or other area designated by a designer. The individual fixtures are blended from one unit to another to give the appearance of being lit by a single light source.

Wash Light   See Linear Light

Washed Stage   A lighting formula for general illumination that dates back to wash

variety luminaires and light sources that were typically candle or lantern flames. Horizontal strips of luminaires were typically hung above and across the stage, while additional luminaires were placed on stands to the sides of the stage. This lighting was often characterized by a strong use of footlights to help soften the shadows that were cast on the performers by the overhead lights.

Wash Luminaire   Automated fixtures that have soft edges so that a series of them can be blended together to produce a wash. Another significant difference between wash luminaires and spot luminaires is their lack of features like patterns/gobos and other features like shutters that make more controllable forms of light.

Wash System   A group of luminaires that share common characteristics (e.g. angle and color) and operate together to produce an even coverage over an area that is larger than what a single spotlight can cover. The individual units work together (each covering a portion of the area) to produce a uniform coverage over the entire area.

Watt (P)   A measurement of the rate of doing work and can be thought of in terms of how much power that a task might be using or consuming.

Wavelength   A manner of measuring and describing waves that correlates to the distance between the points in which a wave undergoes a complete cycle (often measured peak to peak).

Well Lights   Landscape luminaires that are nothing more than a cylinder containing a lamp and its electrical components, buried so that the face of the lamps are about even with the surface of the ground.

West Virginia Formula   Based off the Power Formula, it relates the wattage of a circuit to the voltage and amperage. $W = V \times A$

Wet Tech   See Tech with Actors

Wheel   A mechanical control device that allows a board operator to manually adjust any channel levels or rates that are placed under its control.

White Balance   A process where video cameras are adjusted for overall color temperature sensitivity through registering what the camera sees as white light. This process ensures faithful overall color reproduction.

Wiggle Lights   See Intelligent Lights, Moving Lights, Automated Lights, and Luminaires.

Window Well   An architectural feature that sets a building's windows deeper into a wall surface, providing additional protection from the effects of direct sunlight.

Wing Panel An accessory that provides a set of manual faders to a control console or personal computer running software that converts the computer into a lighting control system.

Wire A component for conducting electricity that contains a metal conductor covered by insulation that shields it from other conductors. A wire by definition only contains one conductor.

Wireless Dimming A relatively new form of control in which information such as a DMX signal is transmitted through dedicated radio frequencies. Similar to the manner in which wireless mics are controlled, a receiver is addressed and then assigned channel information just as any other soft-patching is done. Some of these systems may also include a power supply so that there are actually no control or power wires leading to the circuit at all.

Wish List A worksheet that lists all of the functions that a lighting designer intends to create throughout a design. It is then used to determine the number and type of luminaires, number of control channels or dimmers required, etc., but more importantly is used to prioritize this list and to determine ways in which the uses and associated lights can be consolidated, re-patched, or cut in order to make the design practical.

Working Trim The trim or height at which a hanging position is flown to and from where the lights are actually used for a production and focused from.

Worklight (After Hours or Cleaning/Maintenance) Lighting A lighting system that is used after hours by maintenance and cleaning staff in restaurants, nightclubs, or other facilities that operate under low illumination levels during normal business hours. In the theatre, worklights are used for general illumination for load-ins and load-outs, rehearsals, and work calls where the stage lighting is not required.

Work Notes Notes that relate to technical or mechanical issues that require a crew and need to be fixed by the next rehearsal or performance (e.g., burned out gel or lamps, adding a unit, or dropped focuses are common examples of work notes).

Workplane In lighting calculations, the plane in which a visual task is completed. In most cases it represents a horizontal plane that extends across an entire room. For instance, a plane representing the height of all the desks in a classroom or office.

Writing a Show Blind Preprogramming a show in a remote location without the benefit of being able to see the stage and the effects of light on it.

Wye See Four-wire System

Xenon Lamp A special form of short-arc lamp that is used in followspots and other luminaires.

Yoke A U-shaped bracket that supports the actual body of a theatrical luminaire that is then attached to a hanging position by a C-clamp. Tilt adjustments are made by setting the bolts or handles that attach the yoke to the luminaire while pan adjustments are made by setting the bolt that attaches the yoke to the C-clamp.

Yoking Out Spinning the C-clamp around a pipe so that a luminaire is mounted somewhere between straight-down and 90° upward. This variation in hanging is used to help shoot around obstructions like adjoining luminaires.

Zonal Cavity Method See Lumen Method

Zone See Plane

Zone Lighting A lighting formula for general illumination that forms a variation of the washed stage and is often used where a layered effect (wing and drop setting) might be created through the scenery. It is especially popular in dance productions. Zone lighting makes use of wash luminaires that are used primarily to light the scenery from above but is then supplemented by high-angled sidelight (the most dominant lighting angle), backlight, and a limited amount of front fill.

Bibliography

Ball, David, *Backwards and Forwards: A Technical Manual for Reading Plays* (Carbondale and Edwardsville, IL: Southern Illinois Press, 1983).

Barbizon Lighting Company, *Electricians Pocket Book (Version 4.0)* (New York: Barbizon Lighting Company, 2007).

Bartlett, Brandon, Jesse K. Miguel, Phillip Miller, Adam Nobel, Todd Peterson, and Martha Rowlett, *3D Studio Architectural Rendering*, (Indianapolis, IN: New Riders Publishing, 1996).

Beard, Richard R., *Walt Disney's Epcot: Creating the New World of Tomorrow* (New York: Harry N. Abrams, Inc. Publishers, 1982).

Bellman, Willard F., *Lighting the Stage: Art and Practice*, 3rd ed. (Louisville, KY: Broadway Press, 2001).

Birn, Jeremy, *[Digital] Lighting and Rendering* (Indianapolis, IN: New Riders Publishing, 2000).

Bowers, Brian, *Lengthening the Day: A History of Lighting Technology* (Oxford: Oxford University Press, 1998).

Box, Harry C., *Set Lighting Technician's Handbook: Film Lighting Equipment, Practice, and Electrical Distribution*, 3rd ed. (Burlington, MA: Focal Press, 2003).

Boylan, Bernard R., *The Lighting Primer* (Ames, IA: Iowa State University Press, 1987).

Brandston, Howard M., *Learning to See: A Matter of Light* (New York: Illuminating Engineering Society of North America, 2008).

Brady, Susan and Nena Couch, eds., *Documenting: Lighting Design*, (New York: Theatre Library Association, 2007).

Briggs, Jody, *Encyclopedia of Stage Lighting*, (Jefferson, NC: McFarland and Company, Inc., Publishers, 2003).

Bright, Randy, *Disneyland: Inside Story*. (New York: Harry N. Abrams, Inc. Publishers, 1987).

Brown, Blain, *Motion Picture and Video Lighting*, 2nd ed. (Burlington, MA: Elsevier, Inc., 2008).

Brown, Karen M. and Curtis B. Charles, *Computers in the Professional Practice of Design* (New York: McGraw-Hill, Inc., 1995).

Cadena, Richard, *Automated Lighting: The Art and Science of Moving Light in Theatre, Live Performance, Broadcast, and Entertainment*, 2nd ed. (Burlington, MA: Focal Press, 2010).

Cadena, Richard, *Electricity for the Entertainment Electrician and Technician* (Boston: Focal Press, 2009).

Cadena, Richard, *Lighting Design for Modern Houses of Worship* (Las Vegas, NV: Timeless Communications, 2008).

Carson, Verne and Sylvia E. Carson, *Professional Lighting Handbook*, 2nd ed. (Stoneham, MA: Butterworth-Heinemann, 1991).

Caruso, James R. and Mavis E. Arther, *Video Lighting and Special Effects* (Englewood Cliffs, NJ: Prentice-Hall, Inc., 1991).

Carver, Gavin and Christine White, *Computer Visualization for the Theatre: 3D Modeling for Designers* (Burlington: MA: Focal Press, 2003).

Dillon, Maureen, *Artificial Sunshine: A Social History of Domestic Lighting* (London, UK: National Trust Enterprises, Ltd., 2002).

Dong, Wei and Kathleen Gibson, *Computer Visualization: An Integrated Approach for Interior Design and Architecture*, (New York: McGraw-Hill, 1998).

Dunlop, Beth, *Building a Dream: The Art of Disney Architecture* (New York: Harry N. Abrams, Inc. Publishers, 1996).

Elenbaas, W., *Light Sources* (New York: Crane, Russak and Company, Inc., 1972).

Essig, Linda, *Lighting and the Design Idea* (Fort Worth, TX: Harcourt Brace College Publishers, 1997).

Essig, Linda, *The Speed of Light* (Portsmouth, NH: Heinemann Press, 2002).

Ferncase, Richard K., *Film and Video Lighting Terms and Concepts* (Newton, MA: Focal Press, 1995).

Fielder, William J. and Frederick H. Jones, *The Lit Interior* (Oxford: Architectural Press, 2001).

Fitt, Brian and Joe Thornley, *Lighting by Design: A Technical Guide* (Oxford: Focal Press, 1992).

Fitt, Brian and Joe Thornley, *Lighting Technology: A Guide to the Entertainment Industry*, 2nd ed. (Oxford: Focal Press, 2002).

Friedel, Robert and Paul Israel, *Edison's Electric Light: Biography of an Invention*. (New Brunswick, NJ: Rutgers University Press, 1986).

Gillette, J. Michael, *Designing With Light*, 5th ed. (New York: McGraw Hill Companies, Inc., 2008).

Gloman, Chuck B. and Tom Letourneau, *Placing Shadows: Lighting Techniques for Video Production*, 2nd ed. (Woburn, MA: Butterworth-Heinemann, 2000).

Gordon, Gary, *Interior Lighting for Designers*, 4th ed. (Hoboken, NJ: John Wiley and Sons, Inc., 2003).

GTE Products Corporation, *Sylvania/GTE Lighting Handbook for Television, Theatre and Professional Photography* (Danvers, MA: GTE Products Corporation, 1984).

Hart, John, *Lighting for Action* (New York: Amphoto, 1992).

Hays, David, *Light on the Subject* (New York: Limelight Editions, 1989).

Holshevnikoff, Bill, *ARRI Lighting Handbook: How to Get the Most from Your New ARRI Kit* (Blauvelt, NY: ARRI, Inc., 2000).

Huntington, John, *Control Systems for Live Entertainment*, 3rd ed. (Burlington, MA: Focal Press/Elsevier, 2007).

Illuminating Engineering Society of North America, *An Introduction to Light and Lighting (ED 50)* (New York: Illuminating Engineering Society of North America, 1991).

Illuminating Engineering Society of North America, *IESNA Lighting Education 100 (Fundamental Level)* (New York: Illuminating Engineering Society of North America, 1993).

Illuminating Engineering Society of North America, *IESNA Lighting Education 150 (Intermediate Level)* (New York: Illuminating Engineering Society of North America, 1993).

Illuminating Engineering Society of North America, *IESNA Lighting Handbook*, 9th ed., ed. Mark Rae (New York: Illuminating Engineering Society of North America, 2000).

Illuminating Engineering Society of North America, *IESNA Lighting Ready Reference*, 3rd ed. (New York: Illuminating Engineering Society of North America, 1996).

Illuminating Engineering Society of North America, *IESNA Lighting Ready Reference*, 4th ed. (New York: Illuminating Engineering Society of North America, 2003).

Illuminating Engineering Society of North America, *Museum and Art Gallery Lighting (RP-30-96)* (New York: Illuminating Engineering Society of North America, 1996).

Illuminating Engineering Society of North America, *Recommended Practice for Lighting Merchandising Areas (RP-2-01)* (New York: Illuminating Engineering Society of North America, 2001).

Ingham, Rosemary, *From Page to Stage* (Portsmouth, NH: Heinemann, 1998).

Johnson, David, ed., *Universal Studios Islands of Adventure (Special Supplement to Entertainment Design)* (New York: Intertec Publishing, 1999).

Johnson, Glenn M., *The Art of Illumination: Residential Lighting Design* (New York, NY: McGraw-Hill, 1999).

Kalay, Yehuda E., *Architecture's New Media: Principles, Theories, and Methods of Computer-Aided Design* (Cambridge, MA: The MIT Press, 2004).

Karlen, Mark and James Benya, *Lighting Design Basics* (Hoboken, NJ: John Wiley and Sons, Inc., 2004).

Keller, Max, *Light Fantastic: The Art and Design of Stage Lighting*, (New York: Prestel Verlag, 1999).

Kook, Edward F., *Images in Light for the Living Theatre* (New York: Edward F. Kook, 1963).

Kramer, Wayne, *The Mind's Eye: Theatre and Media Design from the Inside Out* (Portsmouth, NH: Heinemann, 2004).

Kundert-Gibbs, John, Mick Larkins, Dariush Derakhshani, and Eric Kunzendorf, *Mastering Maya 8.5* (Indianapolis, IN: Wiley Publishing Company, Inc., 2007).

Kundert-Gibbs, John, ed., *Maya: Secrets of the Pros* (Alameda, CA: Sybex, Inc., 2002).

Kundert-Gibbs, John and Dariush Derakhshani, eds., *Maya: Secrets of the Pros*, 2nd ed. (Alameda, CA: Sybex, Inc., 2005).

Kurtti, Jeff. *Since the World Began: Walt Disney World, the First 25 Years* (New York: Hyperion, 1996).

Laseau, Paul, *Architectural Representation Handbook: Traditional and Digital Techniques for Graphic Communication* (New York: McGraw-Hill, 2000).

Lindsey, Jack L., *Applied Illumination Engineering*, 2nd ed. (Liburn, GA: The Fairmont Press, Inc., 1997).

Lowell, Ross, *Matters of Light and Depth* (New York: Lowell-Light Manufacturing, Inc., 2000).

Lyver, Des and Graham Swainson, *Basics of Video Lighting* (Oxford: Focal Press, 1995).

Marling, Karal Ann, ed., *Designing Disney's Theme Parks: The Architecture of Reassurance* (New York: Flammarion, 1997).

McCandless, Stanley, *A Syllabus of Stage Lighting*, 5th ed. (New Haven, CT: Yale University, 1941).

McCandless, Stanley, *A Method for Lighting the Stage*, 4th ed. (New York: Theatre Arts Books, 1958).

McCarthy, David, Ste Curran, and Simon Byron, *The Art of Producing Games* (Cambridge, England: The Ilex Press Limited, 2005).

Millerson, Gerald, *Lighting for Television and Film*, 3rd ed. (Woburn, MA: Focal Press, 2000).

Mills, Kenneth H., Judith E. Paul, and Kay B. Moormann, *Applied Visual Merchandising*, 3rd ed. (Englewood Cliffs, NJ: Prentice-Hall, Inc., 1995).

Mobsby, Nick, *Practical Dimming*, (Cambridge, UK: Entertainment Technology Press, 2006).

Mobsby, Nick, *Practical DMX* (Cambridge, UK: Entertainment Technology Press, 2006).

Moody, James L., *The Business of Theatrical Design* (New York: Allworth Press, 2002).

Moody, James L., *Concert Lighting: Techniques, Art, and Business*, 3rd ed. (Newton, MA: Focal Press, 2009).

Morris, Dave and Leo Hartas, *Game Art: The Graphic Art of Computer Games* (New York: Watson-Guptill Publications, 2003).

Moyer, Janet Lennox, *The Landscape Lighting Book* (New York: John Wiley and Sons, Inc., 1992).

Mumm, Robert C., *Photometrics Handbook*, 2nd ed. (Lousiville, KY: Broadway Press, 1997).

Narboni, Roger. *Lighting the Landscape* (Basel, Switzerland: Birkhauser, 2004).

NFPA (National Fire Protection Association), *NFPA 70: National Electrical Code (NEC) 2008* (Quincy, MA: National Fire Protection Association, 2007).

Novitski, B. J., *Rendering Real and Imagined Buildings: The Art of Computer Modeling from the Palace of Kublai Khan to Le Corbusier's Villas*, (Gloucester, MA: Rockport Publishers, Inc., 1998).

Palmer, Richard H., *The Lighting Art: The Aesthetics of Stage Lighting Design*, 2nd ed. (Englewood Cliffs, NJ: Prentice Hall, 1994).

Parker. W. Oren, R. Craig Wolf, and Dick Block, *Scene Design and Stage Lighting*, 9th ed. (Boston: Wadsworth, 2009).

Penzel, Frederick, *Theatre Lighting Before Electricity* (Middletown, CT: Wesleyan University Press, 1978).

Pilbrow, Richard, *Stage Lighting Design: The Art, The Craft, The Life* (New York: Design Press/Quite Specific Media Group, Ldt., 1997).

Pegler, Martin M., *Visual Merchandising and Display*, 4th ed. (New York: Fairchild Publications, 1998).

Portas, Mary, *Windows: The Art of Retail Display* (New York: Thames and Hudson, Inc., 1999).

Rafferty, Kevin, *Imagineering: A Behind the Dreams Look at Making the Magic Real* (New York: Hyperion, 1996).

Reid, Francis, *Lighting the Stage: A Lighting Designer's Experiences* (Boston: Focal Press, 1995).

Rhiner, James L., *A Complete Guide to the Language of Lighting* (Elk Grove Village, IL: Halo Lighting Division, McGraw-Edison Company, 1983).

Robbins, Claude L., *Daylighting: Design and Analysis* (New York: Van Nostrand Reinhold Company, 1986).

Rosenthal, Jean and Lael Wertenbaker, *The Magic of Light* (New York: Theatre Arts Books/Little, Brown and Company, 1974).

Russell, Sage, *The Architecture of Light* (La Jolla, CA: Conceptnine, 2008).

Sandström, Ulf, *Stage Lighting Controls* (Oxford: Focal Press, 1997).

Sapsis, Bill, *Heads Up and Tales* (Lansdowne, PA: Sapsis Publications, 2007).

Saxby, Graham, *Manual of Practical Holography* (Oxford: Focal Press, 1991).

Schiller, Brad, *The Automated Lighting Programmer's Handbook* (Burlington, MA: Elsevier, Inc./Focal Press, 2004).

Smith, Fran Kellogg and Fred J. Bertolone, *Bringing Interiors to Light: The Principles and Practices of Lighting Design* (New York: Whitney Library of Design, 1986).

Shelley, Steven Louis, *A Practical Guide to Stage Lighting*, 2nd ed. (Boston: Focal Press, 2009).

Simpson, Robert S., *Lighting Control: Technology and Applications* (Burlington, MA: Focal Press, 2003).

Steffy, Gary, *Architectural Lighting Design*, 2nd ed. (New York: John Wiley and Sons, Inc. 2002).

Steffy, Gary R., *Lighting the Electronic Office* (New York: Van Nostrand Reinhold, 1995).

Szenasy, Susan S., *Light: The Complete Handbook of Lighting Design* (Philadelphia, PA: Running Press Book Publishers, 1986).

Tharp, Twyla, *The Creative Habit: Learn It and Use It for Life* (New York: Simon & Schuster, 2003).

Thomas, James, *Script Analysis for Actors, Directors, and Designers*, 4th ed. (Boston: Focal Press, 2009).

Turner, Janet, *Designing with Light: Public Spaces* (New York: Watson-Guptill Publications, 1998).

Turner, Janet, *Designing with Light: Retail Spaces* (New York: Watson-Guptill Publications, 1998).

Vasey, John, *Concert Sound and Lighting Systems*, 3rd ed. (Woburn, MA: Butterworth- Heinemann Press, 1999).

Viera, Dave, *Lighting for Film and Electronic Cinematography* (Belmont, CA: Wadsworth Publishing Company, 1993).

Walne, Graham, *Projection for the Performing Arts* (London: Focal Press, 1995).

Warfel, William B., *The New Handbook of Stage Lighting Graphics* (New York: Drama Book Publishers, 1990).

Warfel, William B. and Walter R. Klappert, *Color Science for Lighting the Stage* (New Haven, CT: Yale University Press, 1981).

Watson, Lee, *Lighting Design Handbook* (New York: McGraw-Hill, Inc., 1990).

Weishar, Peter, *Digital Space: Designing Virtual Environments* (New York: McGraw-Hill, 1998).

Whittaker, Ron, *Video Field Production*, 2nd ed. (Mountain View, CA: Mayfield Publishing, Company, 1996).

Wojtowicz, Jerzy, *Virtual Design Studio* (Hong Kong: Hong Kong University Press, 1995).

Index